REGISONAL SILVICULTURE

OF THE
UNITED STATES

REGIONAL SILVICULTURE
OF THE
UNITED STATES

SECOND EDITION

Edited by

JOHN W. BARRETT
The Institute of Agriculture
THE UNIVERSITY OF TENNESSEE

A WILEY-INTERSCIENCE PUBLICATION

JOHN WILEY & SONS   New York • Chichester • Brisbane • Toronto

Library of Congress Cataloging in Publication Data

Barrett, John W   ed.
   Regional silviculture of the United States.
   "A Wiley-Intersience publication."
   Includes index.
   1.   Forests and forestry—United States.
I.   Title
SD143.B33   1980   634.9'0973   80-17129
ISBN 0-471-05645-6

Printed in the United States of America

10 9 8 7 6 5 4 3 2 1

Contributors

Dr. David L. Adams

Head of Department of Forest Resources
University of Idaho

Dr. John W. Barrett

Professor of Forestry Emeritus
The University of Tennessee

Dr. T. W. Daniel

Professor Emeritus, Silviculture
Utah State University

Dr. Henry L. Hansen

Professor of Forestry
University of Minnesota

Dr. John A. Helms

Associate Professor
The University of California

Dr. Norwin E. Linnartz

Professor of Forestry
Louisiana State University

Dr. Clair Merritt

Professor of Forestry
Purdue University

Dr. David R. M. Scott

Professor of Silviculture and Ecology
The University of Washington

Dr. David M. Smith

Professor of Silviculture
Yale University

Dr. David Wm. Smith

Associate Professor of Forest Soils and Silviculture
Virginia Polytechnic Institute and State University

Dr. L. C. Walker

Hunt Professor of Forestry
Stephen F. Austin State University

Preface

The silviculturist of today is operating in a vastly different situation than in the early 1960s when the first edition of this text was published. The rising concern over environmental quality, public involvement in decision-making regarding public lands, increasing demands for a variety of forest benefits, and a flood of legislation, litigation, and agency directives have made a significant impact on silvicultural thought and practice. Recognition is given to this new social and political dimension of silviculture particularly in Chapter 1.

The heart of silviculture is, as it has been for centuries, the production of wood for man's use. Within the past decade, however, we are seeing the beginning of the use of silvicultural practices to improve wildlife habitat, enhance recreational sites, protect watersheds and regulate stream flow regimen, and provide innumerable environmental amenities. As these new applications of silviculture are in their infancy, their treatment in this edition is simply introduced.

There has been a substantial increment in silvicultural knowledge since the first edition was published. This was another reason for a revised up-to-date treatment of regional silviculture.

Several basic ideas were retained from the first edition. These include the assessment of the significant biological, physical, and economic qualities of forest regions and their effect upon silvicultural practices. Each chapter was prepared by a silviculturist familiar with the respective region. Except for the introductory chapter, the others follow a consistent outline. The revision is more successful in this respect than the first edition. Finally, stress has been put on fundamental information about edaphic, physiographic, and climatic site factors, along with ecological relationships, silvical characteristics of predominant species, and silvicultural practices.

No introductory statement about silvicultural practices would be complete without recognition of the importance of implementation. The wisest of silvicultural prescriptions is of little value unless it is implemented effectively. Frequently the practitioner does not have the opportunity to supervise the operation or observe the results. This underscores the need for silvicultural decisions to be properly documented with adequate instructions for the conduct of the operation.

It is a pleasure, as editor, to thank my colleagues for their efforts. As was true in 1962, the list of acknowledgments to those who have assisted us evidences our efforts to produce a useful, authoritative, and readable reference. The valuable secretarial help given by Virginia Atkins and Lavonda Phelps is also recognized.

JOHN W. BARRETT

Knoxville, Tennessee
July 1980

Acknowledgments

This revision like the first edition, has benefited from the help of many people to whom the authors express their sincere appreciation. Barton M. Blum, Stanley M. Filip (retired), Robert M. Frank, William B. Leak, and Dale S. Solomon, USDA Forest Service; David M. Smith, Yale University; and Ralph D. Nyland, State University of New York, College of Environmental Science and Forestry, reviewed Chapter 2. The Forest Inventory Section, North Central Forest Experiment Station provided statistical information for Chapter 3. B. C. Fischer and W. R. Byrnes, Purdue University, reviewed Chapter 4 and Patty Karnehm prepared the manuscript. Terry L. Sharik reviewed portions of Chapter 5. M. Victor Bilan, Gerald Lowry, and Kenneth Watterston, Stephen F. Austin State University; Ted W. Daniel, Utah State University; Thomas Croker (retired), Lowell K. Halls, and John J. Stransky, USDA Forest Service, reviewed Chapter 6. Norbert V. DeByle and G. H. Schubert, USDA Forest Service, helped with Chapter 7. Donald Hanley, Federic Johnson, Roland Mahoney, James Moore, and Karel Stoszek, University of Idaho and Raymond Boyd and Charles Wellner (retired) USDA Forest Service assisted with Chapter 8. Philip M. McDonald and John C. Tappeiner, USDA Forest Service, gave considerable assistance with Chapter 9. David L. Reukema, USDA Forest Service, Robert Zasoski, University of Washington, and Carolyn Scott assisted with Chapter 10. David Johnson, USDA Forest Service, Mark Ralston, University of Washington, and Carolyn Scott helped with Chapter 11.

A special note of appreciation is due the USDA Forest Service for making available many of the book's illustrations and resource data. Mrs. Erwin Raisz gave permission for the use of the map "Landforms of the United States," portions of which are used throughout the book.

My wife Vivian has contributed significantly to both the 1962 publication and the 2nd edition. She has helped proofread all manuscripts, galleys, and page proofs. During the lengthy process of revising the book she provided support and understanding.

J.W.B.

Contents

REGIONAL SILVICULTURE
OF THE
UNITED STATES

1

The Forests of
the United States

David M. Smith

The United States and the lands under its jurisdiction have representatives of almost every kind of vegetation that occurs on earth. It is as if the forests of all Eurasia were compressed into a single country. Puerto Rico, southern Florida, Hawaii, and the Pacific Islands have tropical forests. Much of Alaska is treeless tundra; typical steppes or grasslands cover the Great Plains, and deserts of nearly all degrees of aridity are found in the Southwest. However, American foresters deal mainly with closed forests of conifers and broadleaved deciduous trees that typify the humid parts of the Temperate Zone. Even these are more diverse than the foresters of most nations are called upon to manage. Comprehension of all these kinds of forest vegetation depends on building some idea of both the pattern and the causes of the wide variation that exists.

GEOLOGY AND EVOLUTION OF THE AMERICAN FORESTS

The forest pattern is governed in part by the shape, structure, and latitudinal position of the continent as well as the history of changes in these characteristics. Most of North America is a single plate of the earth's crust which was once pushed against Europe and Africa but then started a northwestward drift that still continues (Calder, 1972; Flint and Skinner, 1977). Although it has since gone through subsequent cycles of erosion and lifting, the long Appalachian Mountain chain of the eastern edge was first squeezed upward by the continental collisions.

In its westward drift, the North American Plate has for a long time impinged upon the plate that lies mainly under the Pacific Ocean. One of the earliest collisions raised the Rocky Mountains. A later one tilted upward the huge slab called the Sierra Nevada and also set off the volcanic activity and other forms of uplift that built the Cascade Range. The current interaction causes the uplift of the very steep and unstable Coast Ranges.

As these various north-south mountain ranges have undergone cycles of uplift and erosion, they have sometimes existed as long islands with shallow seas between or adjacent to them. Most of the lower-lying parts of the continent are formed from sedimentary materials eroded from the mountains. Igneous and metamorphic rocks abound only in areas that are or were formerly mountainous. Sedimentary deposits predominate; even the present mountains consist partly of sandstones, limestones, and other uplifted sedimentary rocks.

The species composition of vegetation at any particular place and time is the product of all that has gone on before, even many millions of years before (Daubenmire, 1978). One thing that helps maintain some order in all the confusion is the attempt to keep the various scales of time and space sorted out in proper relationship to each other. The fact that the Northern Hemisphere vegetation differs very strikingly as to families and genera of plants from that of the Southern Hemisphere is the result of a dimly understood separation of habitats that took place during the time when all the continents were pushed together into a single huge "world island." This was about 250 million years ago.

North America drifted away from close contact with Eurasia in Cretaceous time, approximately 100 million years ago. It was then covered mainly with tropical vegetation since it was drifting through low latitudes. It did, however, maintain sporadic contact with Europe by way of Greenland and Scandinavia, and more recently with Siberia through Alaska. These contacts help explain many close similarities of North American and Eurasian species. Plants evolve more slowly than animals. Most modern plant genera were in existence in Miocene time, 13 to 26 million years ago, and most modern species were in existence in the Pliocene Epoch, which started 13 million years ago.

During most of the vast stretch of geological time in which North America drifted northwestward from its collision with Africa and Europe, it was at low latitude. Its continually evolving freight of vegetation was originally adapted to warm, humid, tropical climates and was predominantly composed of trees. Plants developed the arborescent habit, with its efficiencies of foliar display and competition with other plants, in a comparatively short period of evolutionary time after they moved onto dry land. In the Eocene Epoch, 40 to 60 million years ago, North America was a low continent clothed with a rich forest of many genera even as far north as northern Canada.

Since that time the climate, aside from important fluctuations, has become colder and has exhibited more pronounced regional variations in temperature and precipitation. This climatic change took place partly because of the continuing drift of the continent to higher latitudes and partly because of the sequential uplift of north-south mountain ranges in the west. These mountain ranges sealed off increasingly large areas of the continent from the Pacific Ocean winds that bring precipitation and also reduce extremes of temperature.

Many genera of trees simply retreated to the tropics, but others evolved the various kinds of dormancy that enable them to survive winters of cold or dryness. Herbaceous species, which are basically characterized by long periods of dormancy and comparatively short ones of growth, became much more prominent. The climatic barriers formed by mountains and the development of larger treeless areas increasingly subdivided the forest flora so that regional differences in genera and species became accentuated.

In the Pliocene Epoch, about 10 million years ago, the climate of the western part of the continent had become too cool in the wet coastal regions and too dry in the warmer parts for very many of the broadleaved angiosperm trees to persist. The conifers, which had earlier thrived mainly on the cool mountain tops, came to predominate because of their adaptation to the shortages of available water which are, among trees, fully as much the result of low temperature as they are of deficiencies of precipitation. The eastern part of the continent remained more hospitable to the angiosperms because of the warm, rain-bearing winds from the Caribbean Sea and adjacent Atlantic Ocean that periodically bathe the region.

When the continents had drifted far enough poleward about 2.5 million years ago, the stage was set for the onset of the Pleistocene Epoch, the geologic age of ice and man. Slight and regular cyclical changes in the earth's orbit around the sun and the degree of tilting of its axis in relation to the sun set off periodic episodes of warming and cooling. When it gets cool enough, the winter snows cease to melt completely over such places as Quebec and Laborador as well as in the higher mountain ranges. Mountains of ice accumulate and the ice begins to flow outward under the pressure of its own weight. The broader the permanent snow cover, the greater is the heat loss from reflection of sunlight; the higher the ice mountains build, the more is the annual accumulation of snow and ice. The slightly earlier uplift of the Coast Ranges may have helped set the stage for this by shutting off the northern part of the continent from the warming winds off the Pacific Ocean. During at least three interglacial stages, virtually all of the ice melted. The present time is neither the warmest nor the coldest. Except for a relatively few mountain glaciers, all the ice had melted from the North American mainland about 12,000 years ago, but essentially continental glaciers still cover Greenland and Antarctica.

At their maximum extent the continental glaciers covered most of the area north of a line from Long Island to the present courses of the Ohio and Missouri rivers and thence to Puget Sound. Large but isolated mountain glaciers extended southward along the mountain ranges of the West. Except for southwestern Wisconsin and the lowlands of northern and central Alaska, the northern half of the continent was covered by ice.

As the ice advanced, the North American vegetation had plenty of avenues of retreat. No east-west chains of mountains blocked southward migration. So much water was locked in the glaciers that the level of the seas dropped and exposed broad areas of the continental shelves, thus providing new dry-land refuges as well as a bridge from Alaska to Siberia. There is evidence that spruce grew in Texas during the glacial stages. The mountains of Central America still have a temperate forest that includes many species that are the same as, or very similar to, those now found in the southern Appalachians, so it is possible that this region provided another refuge.

As the ice retreated the forests moved northward again. About 5,000 years ago the climate was warm enough that some species grew slightly farther north than now. Since then the climate has cooled; in a few thousand years the ice may start to return.

Contemporary vegetation is the product of the developments and changes that have taken place in the long span of time just described. Most of the differences now recognized among species have arisen from adaptation to different sets of site factors. Major differences evolved when the natural range of single ancestral species has been subdivided by the formation of such barriers as seas, high mountains, glaciers, deserts, or other areas where the species could not grow.

Severe climatic conditions have undoubtedly eliminated many species, and the modern forests of any locality are simpler because of such losses. On the other hand, the climatic contrasts between various regions are greater than in most geologic ages, and more forested regions are isolated from one another. If there were an east-west mountain range from the Carolinas to California, like the Alps of Europe, most of the forest species of preglacial North America would have been herded to extinction against an insurmountable barrier as they were in most of Europe. The forest was pushed into several separate north-south avenues of retreat, however, and a number of combinations of species appear to have relatively recent common ancestry. It takes no stretch of imagination to believe that eastern and western white pine, eastern and western hemlock, jack and lodgepole pine, white and Engelmann spruce, and some other combinations within genera were once the same and have become different by separation into regions with dissimilar environment. Perhaps we now see the various geographical races of Douglas-fir and ponderosa pine differentiating into species before us.

These more recent separations give an inkling as to the nature of those of an earlier time that caused such differences as those between loblolly and shortleaf pine, red and sugar maple, ponderosa and Jeffrey pine, red and black oak, all of these being species which have now come back together and may even grow in the same stands. In another frame of reference, a consideration of the kind of events that took place in the ancient past makes it easier to understand the substantial difference between the forests of the Sierra Nevada and those of the Coast and Cascade ranges, or between the Boreal Forest and those that lie to the south of it. Although these forests are now contiguous and, given enough time, could intermingle completely, they tend to remain different because they were once isolated from one another.

Some differences in forest composition cannot be explained without reference to the remarkable events of the geological past, but most of them are the result of site factors that are still influential.

CLIMATE

The composition and vigor of forests depend largely upon the characteristics of the climate, especially those which govern temperature and soil moisture. Forests normally exist only where precipitation, at least in some seasons, exceeds evaporation by a margin sufficient to leave a dependable surplus of soil moisture for growth of trees. This means that forests tend to occur only where the precipitation is above the average for the world's land surface. However, at high latitudes where evaporation is low, forests can persist with very low precipitation, provided that summer temperatures are sufficiently favorable. Low temperatures can also prevent the development of forests at high elevations.

The more favorable the regime of moisture and temperature, the greater is the number of species. However, economic forestry usually proceeds most successfully where environmental conditions are just sufficiently limiting to reduce the number of species to manageable proportions, especially if the limitations discourage hardwoods and favor conifers. This is why the biologically favorable site conditions of the southern Appalachians, for example, are less welcome to the forester than the somewhat drier soils of the nearby Coastal Plain or the summer-dry climate of the coastal Pacific Northwest. The ability of the forester to take advantage of highly favorable conditions for growth depends on the degree to which the luxuriant vegetation can be controlled.

Precipitation

Forests are so dependent upon moisture that they can be thought of as creatures spawned by the oceans; normally it is only over the oceans that air masses are moistened sufficiently to yield significant amounts of rain and snow in subsequent passage over land. Furthermore, the essential moistening can take place only when the water surface is warmer than the air mass passing over it; vertical convective movement of the water vapor occurs only when the atmosphere cools rather rapidly with increasing height. Therefore, the main sources of precipitation are warm tropical seas, although secondary sources exist where very cold Arctic air passes over merely cool water surfaces at high latitudes. Evaporation and transpiration from land surfaces are rarely sufficient to moisten the air enough for it to yield precipitation later.

Rain or snow falls only when deep layers of moist air are cooled to the saturation point by lifting. Such lifting either can be bodily lifting over mountains (orographic precipitation) or masses of cold air (frontal precipitation) or can result from showers induced within the moist air mass by the heating of land surfaces (convective precipitation). Forests exist only in areas where air currents from the right kind of water surfaces can penetrate and be lifted enough to yield the requisite amount of precipitation.

The patterns of precipitation over North America can be thought of most simply in terms of atmospheric circulation around the great subtropical anticyclones that lie over the oceans between latitudes 20° and 40° N. These great mountains of warm air form high-pressure areas that induce continual clockwise movement of air around themselves. The Azores—Bermuda High over the North Atlantic, for example, carries cool air southward in the vicinity of western Europe and northwestern Africa, and this air is strongly moistened in its passage through the belt of easterly trade winds that ultimately leads across the Caribbean Sea and the Gulf of Mexico. Virtually all the precipitation that falls over the United States east of the Rocky Mountains and over eastern Canada is derived from the northward flow of this moist air. It is significant that the western boundary of the eastern forest runs north from the western extremity of the Gulf of Mexico. After leaving North America, the moist tropical maritime air moves toward Europe in the belt of prevailing westerly winds, and, after being cooled with substantial loss of moisture, much of it again moves southward over Europe and the eastern North Atlantic to complete the circuit around the great anticyclone.

A comparable kind of circulation exists over the Pacific. However, the situation with respect to precipitation in the western United States is complicated by the presence of a series of high mountain barriers and, even more, by the meteorological characteristics of the eastern ends of subtropical anticyclones. The region lies many thousands of miles from the original source of the moisture; little precipitable moisture is derived from the very cold waters immediately offshore. Furthermore, the oceanic anticyclones are not symmetrical mounds of warm air but are actually great lobes that tilt eastward so that they overhang the western shores of the continents at high elevations. This creates a condition in which warm air overlies cooler air. This circumstance, together with the tendency for the air in the anticyclones to sink, causes great resistance to the upward movement of air that must take place if it is to cool and release snow or rain. This condition prevails throughout the year near the Tropics of Cancer and Capricorn along the western shores of the continents. It produces most of the great deserts of the world such as the Sahara, the Kalahari of Southwest Africa, and the desert of western Australia. The North American counterpart of these is the Sonoran Desert, of which the Mojave Desert is a northern outlier.

The subtropical anticyclones shift poleward in summer and toward the Equator in winter. Therefore, the rainless summers which they cause on the western shores of the continents vary in length according to latitude. The dry summers of southern California are very long; those of Washington are comparatively short, and the effect is ordinarily absent north of southern British Columbia. In fact, along the southern coast of Alaska the precipitation is very heavy and quite evenly distributed throughout the year.

Precipitation Regimes. The shifting patterns of atmospheric precipitation cause differences in seasonal distribution as well as in total amount. Kincer (1922) distinguished six main types of distribution within the main portion of the United States (Fig. 1-1).

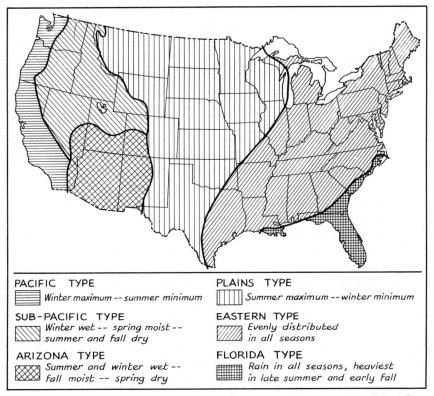

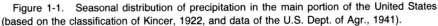

PACIFIC TYPE
    Winter maximum -- summer minimum

SUB-PACIFIC TYPE
    Winter wet -- spring moist -- summer and fall dry

ARIZONA TYPE
    Summer and winter wet -- fall moist -- spring dry

PLAINS TYPE
    Summer maximum -- winter minimum

EASTERN TYPE
    Evenly distributed in all seasons

FLORIDA TYPE
    Rain in all seasons, heaviest in late summer and early fall

Figure 1-1. Seasonal distribution of precipitation in the main portion of the United States (based on the classification of Kincer, 1922, and data of the U.S. Dept. of Agr., 1941).

The *Eastern type* prevails over most of the forested portion of the East. The predominantly deciduous forests of the region are induced by average annual precipitation that exceeds 35 inches over most of the area and is almost evenly distributed throughout the year. Virtually all of this comes from the northward movement of warm, moist air from the warm seas to the south. The Great Lakes contribute some additional precipitation during late fall and early winter, when very cold air from the north moves over their relatively warm, unfrozen surfaces. This results in spectacularly heavy snowfall within a few dozen miles of the lake shores, but the effect is otherwise negligible.

The *Florida type* is limited to coastal areas from Louisiana to North Carolina. It is like the Eastern type but has additional amounts of rain from heavy showers in late summer and tropical storms in early fall.

The *Plains type* is characterized by a pronounced summer maximum of rainfall, induced mainly by showers in the moist air flowing northward from the Gulf of Mexico and the Caribbean. It prevails from the crest of the Rocky Mountains eastward to Lake Michigan and the Ozarks. This regime typifies the interior grasslands of continents. Forests exist only in the mountainous areas and those parts of the Central States where the annual precipitation exceeds 20 to 25 inches; elsewhere they are confined to stream bottoms.

The *Pacific type* prevails in the coastal region west of the crests of the Cascade Range and the Sierra Nevada. Virtually all the precipitation comes in the cyclonic storms of the cold half of the year. In general, it varies in amount from very light to extremely heavy with increase in both latitude and altitude. The vegetation varies correspondingly from sparse desert scrub to the most luxuriant conifer forests of the world.

The *Sub-Pacific type* differs in that the winter maximum of precipitation is prolonged into the spring because of convective showers during that period. At that time, enough moist air still comes in from the Pacific to cause precipitation when the land surfaces are heated. This type prevails over all of the Intermountain Region north of the southern parts of Utah and Nevada. The amounts of precipitation derived from winter snows are sufficient to support forests only on the mountains. Most of the moisture from the Pacific Ocean is precipitated from the air as it is lifted over the high mountains to the west of this region.

The *Arizona type* involves a very peculiar regime found in Arizona and New Mexico. During the winter a very limited amount of precipitation is derived from cyclonic storms moving in from the northern Pacific Ocean. Pronounced drought is normal in spring. Midsummer brings a burst of showers and thunderstorms in streams of moist air from ocean waters west and east of Mexico. The subtropical anticyclones have then moved far enough north to allow the northern fringe of the moist trade winds to penetrate the Southwest. Rains from this source diminish in the fall. The annual precipitation is sufficient to support forests only at high elevations.

Temperature

Virtually all the forests of North America are subject to a winter dormant period induced by low temperature. Only in the xeric woodlands at low elevations in California is there a tendency toward a complicated pattern of seasonal dormancy resulting from summer drought. Provided there is an adequate supply of soil moisture, the vigor and complexity of forests are strongly influenced by the temperature regime and the length of the frost-free growing season. The continental temperature pattern is governed by three factors which , in order of importance are (1) latitude, (2) location with respect to oceans, and (3) altitude. On the Atlantic Coastal Plain from New Jersey southward and at low elevations along the Pacific Coast, the average growing season exceeds 200 days each year. At the higher latitudinal and altitudinal limits of the forest, the average frost-free period is roughly 30 days each year. Along most of the southern boundary of Canada, except close to large bodies of water and in the high western mountains, the average growing season is roughly 100 to 120 days.

The temperature climate of the interior of the continent is typically *continental*, with very cold winters and correspondingly hot summers. Along the western coast of the continent a distinctly *maritime* climate prevails; the moderating influence of the Pacific Ocean tends to prevent extremes of temperature. A relatively mild climate prevails from southern Alaska down to central California; but for the mountain barriers it would extend much farther into the continent. Because of the strong influence of the prevailing westerly winds, the climate of the Atlantic Coast is more nearly continental than maritime, so the difference in temperature between winter and summer is much more pronounced than on the Pacific Coast. The moderating influence of the oceans extends considerably farther north of the western shores of continents than on the eastern shores. It is for this reason that the growing season in southern New England is of about the same length as that of the Panhandle of southeastern Alaska while that of the flatwoods of southern Georgia is equal to that of the fog belt along the coast of Washington.

FOREST REGIONS

The numerous kinds of forests found in North America have been classified in many different ways. Since they change over time as well as in space, it is necessary to distinguish between the forest that was, that is, and several different kinds that might be. The various classifications also differ because of varying opinions about the interpretation of facts. Vegetation maps are both useful and misleading because on paper they have to show boundary lines whereas the real boundaries in the vegetation are often blurred transition zones.

A valuable frame of reference is the classic map (Fig. 1-2) of Shantz and Zon (1924) which was an attempt to show the original forest found by European settlers, apparently in terms of the species that dominated the crown canopy. This interpretation neatly evades the problem of describing the ever-changing variations that human treatment continually superimposes on forests. Likewise it avoids the debatable interpretations involved in deducing the nature of theoretically disturbance-free climax forests, which are among the important kinds that might come to exist. The most thoroughgoing attempt in that direction is the map of Küchler (1964) of the "potential" natural vegetation. Figure 1-3 is a representation of the nature of present forests based on the national timber surveys and, therefore, somewhat weighted by the important contribution that conifers make to timber volume. A more detailed representation, Küchler's interpretation of potential vegetation, and many useful geological and climatic maps can be found in the National Atlas (U.S. Geol. Surv., 1970).

Among the comprehensive works on plant geography are Shelford (1963), which integrates plant and animal geography, and Daubenmire (1978), which includes a synopsis of the evolutionary development of vegetation.

The classification represented by the headings of subsequent chapters of this book is not intended to be a purely natural one because it serves also as a framework for the consideration of the human uses to which forests are put in

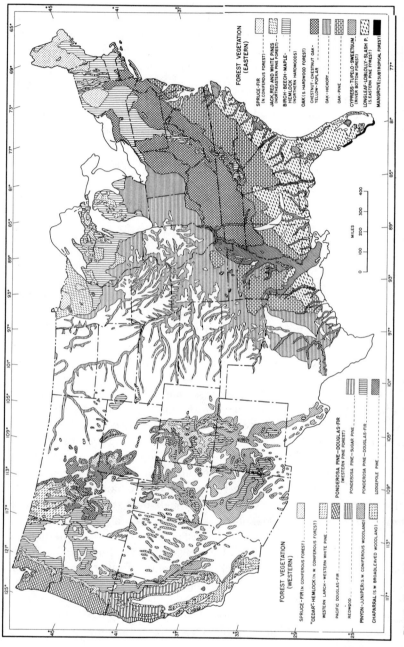

Figure 1-2. Distribution of the major types of natural forest vegetation in the main portion of the United States. This map, originally prepared by Shantz and Zon (1924), depicts the forest as it was before the time of settlement, but not necessarily the climax vegetation (U.S. For. Serv.).

10

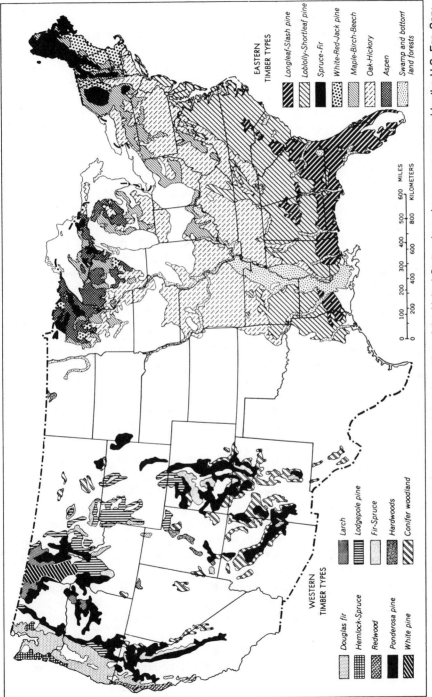

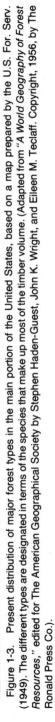

EASTERN TIMBER TYPES

Longleaf-Slash pine
Loblolly-Shortleaf pine
Spruce-Fir
White-Red-Jack pine
Maple-Birch-Beech
Oak-Hickory
Aspen
Swamp and bottom land forests

WESTERN TIMBER TYPES

Douglas fir
Hemlock-Spruce
Redwood
Ponderosa pine
White pine
Larch
Lodgepole pine
Fir-Spruce
Hardwoods
Conifer woodland

Figure 1-3. Present distribution of major forest types in the main portion of the United States, based on a map prepared by the U.S. For. Serv. (1949). The different types are designated in terms of the species that make up most of the timber volume. (Adapted from "*A World Geography of Forest Resources*," edited for The American Geographical Society by Stephen Haden-Guest, John K. Wright, and Eileen M. Teclaff. Copyright, 1956, by The Ronald Press Co.).

different regions. It is also partly based on political boundaries, which seldom coincide with natural ones.

Forest composition also varies with time as well as human treatment. Large areas have been cleared for farms and then allowed to revert to unnaturally pure stands of conifers. Heavy cutting or repeated fires have sometimes caused displacement of conifers by hardwoods, especially where aspen replaced millions of acres of pine and spruce around the Great Lakes. Such effects often took place over large areas rather suddenly. Subsequent developments in the vegetation proceed fast enough so that a forester may see forests in a given decade and locality that have not been seen before and will not be seen again. It is also the role of foresters to make the constructive kinds of changes in species composition that meet the requirements of society.

The purpose of this chapter is to convey some understanding of the present distribution of natural groups into which North American forests may be divided. The very broad classification chosen for the purpose is depicted in Fig. 1-4 and based on the debatable hypothesis that each major kind of forest came into being on some kind of large "island" created when the continent was subdivided by seas, mountain ranges, deserts, grasslands, or glaciers.

The Eastern Deciduous Forest

The relatively favorable climate of the eastern third of the United States supports one of the most complicated and variable aggregations of vegetation in the temperate regions of the world. It has literally hundreds of species of trees, most of them hardwoods. Deciduous trees cover most of the area and, from the standpoint of the naturalist, largely determine the general characteristics of the forest. On the other hand, the comparatively small number of coniferous species cover substantial areas and in many localities are more important to the forester than the hardwoods.

The seemingly chaotic mingling of species and multiplicity of forest-cover types observed in the Eastern Deciduous Forest easily become bewildering. Consequently, an otherwise inordinate amount of attention must be devoted to describing the indistinct but systematic pattern in which the myriad combinations of species are arranged. All is not chaos; this forest is, like every other, ruled by the environment; there simply are so many species that changes in the environment, in either time or space, affect the rearrangement of an unusually large supply of the raw material that goes to make up stand composition.

Basically, there is a central zone just west of the Appalachian Mountains, in which the environment favors maximum complexity. The majority of the most important hardwood species of the deciduous forest occur in this center of distribution, sometimes growing together in the same stands. Arranged around this center are other zones in which the environment is, in varying degrees and for different reasons, less favorable. The less favorable the environment, the simpler is the composition of the forests.

As one progresses from the center of distribution, some tree species drop out

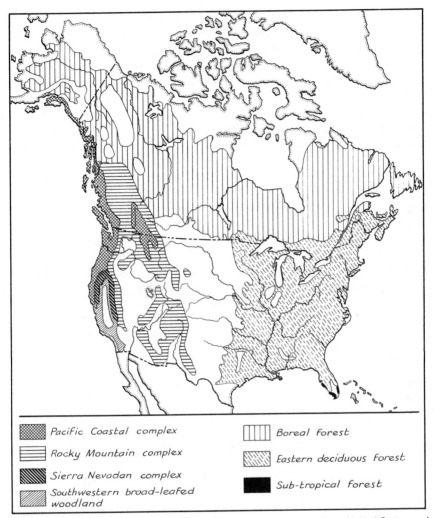

Figure 1-4. The major formations of the original forest vegetation of the United States and Canada (adapted from maps of the U.S. For. Serv. and *Forest Regions of Canada,* Canada, Forestry Branch, 1959).

and the total number that might be found in single stands on the best sites gradually drops from twenty or more down to two or three. On the other hand, some species, including many important commercial conifers, do not occur at the center of distribution. Such species are especially common at places remote from the center of distribution and, whether hardwoods or softwoods, usually represent biological adaptations to restrictive site conditions. Among the hardwoods, however, the most important effects encountered are changes in the proportions of species drawn from the population of the central zone. Those that are well adapted increase; those that are not dwindle or disappear.

A few species, such as white and black oak, mockernut hickory, and red maple, are sufficiently adaptable to appear in almost all parts of the deciduous forest, although their vigor and appearance may vary considerably. A handful of species, such as yellow buckeye and cucumbertree, are limited to the center of distribution and, although not common, are among the indicator species of this zone. Many others, including yellow-poplar, black walnut, sweetgum, black locust, and white ash, tend to be restricted to good sites within a central zone that, though broad, falls far short of the limits of the Eastern Deciduous Forest.

Perhaps of greatest significance are those species that occur in the center of distribution but become of greater importance in regions farther away. The best examples of such species are: sugar maple, which abounds farther north; chestnut, which was formerly common to the east; and the hickories, which become more important to the west. In fact, such obvious differences as exist among various parts of the Eastern Deciduous Forest arise chiefly from the proportions in which such species spread out from the center of distribution.

The oaks represent the most important genus of the Eastern Deciduous Forest, being by all odds the most common hardwoods of all but the colder regions. While some of the oaks occur far and wide, most of the dozens of species represent adaptations to extremely wet or dry sites.

The number of species of oaks and pines generally increases southward. This is a manifestation of the fact that Mexico is the center of concentration of these two genera with hundreds of oaks and dozens of pines.

There are a number of species that are best adapted to the less favorable environments found around the edges of the Eastern Deciduous Forest and do not occur in the center of distribution. The most important of these, especially from the commercial standpoint, are practically all of the Eastern conifers. These are called part of the Eastern Deciduous Forest only by virtue of the rather tortured logic involved in the fact that they maintain a foothold in it. Only shortleaf pine, eastern hemlock, and eastern redcedar occur in the center of distribution. However, as one goes southward, northward, and eastward from the center of distribution, the various well-known conifers generally become increasingly prominent. Examples of specially adapted "peripheral" species, hardwood and softwood, include Nuttall oak of the southern bottomlands, red pine of dry sites in the north, bur oak of the prairie fringe, Atlantic white-cedar of the coastal bogs, longleaf pine and turkey oak of dry southern uplands, black ash of northern swamps, and baldcypress of the deepest southern swamps, to mention but a few.

Any attempt to name and map the various regional variants of the Eastern Deciduous Forest should be viewed with indulgent skepticism. Attempts to name the variants in terms of the component species prove satisfactory only where poor site conditions allow only several species to predominate. For example, the classification of forest-cover types of the Society of American Foresters (1954) works well only for the simpler types. The most satisfactory solution to the problem of terminology is to refer to the very complicated formations in terms of the geographic regions with which they are most closely associated.

This compromise is followed in the map of the Eastern Deciduous Forest shown in Fig. 1-5. The boundaries are the same as those shown in the classic vegetation map of Shantz and Zon (1924) and in Fig. 1-3, except that the spruce-fir and pine types of the northeastern fringe of the country are combined. However, the names chosen for the different formations are a combination of both new and old terms which appear to carry a minimum of misleading connotations.

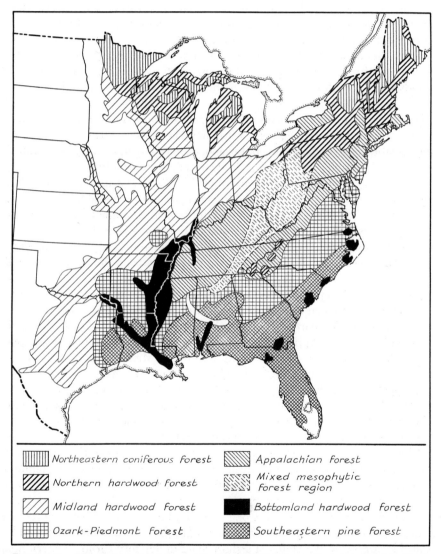

▥ Northeastern coniferous forest	▨ Appalachian forest
▰ Northern hardwood forest	▨ Mixed mesophytic forest region
▱ Midland hardwood forest	■ Bottomland hardwood forest
▦ Ozark-Piedmont forest	▩ Southeastern pine forest

Figure 1-5. The major subdivisions of the Eastern Deciduous Forest as it existed in the original vegetation of the eastern United States. The Mixed Mesophytic Forest Region is shown as part of the Appalachian Forest. Only the broadest belts of the Bottomland Hardwood Forest are shown (adapted from Shantz and Zon, 1924; Braun, 1950).

The Appalachian Forest. The richest mixture of species is found in the area identified by Braun (1950) as the Mixed Mesophytic Forest Region. This region lies mainly on the Appalachian Plateau, west of the mountains of the same name. It is shown in Fig. 1-5 as a subdivision of the Appalachian Forest.

Braun demonstrated that many of the major species of the Eastern Deciduous Forest grow in mixed stands in the climax forests of the Appalachian Plateau. For example, one virgin stand in the Cumberland Mountains of Kentucky had 21 species represented in a 259-tree sample of the canopy: yellow-poplar, sugar maple, the white-leaved form of basswood, beech, chestnut, yellow buckeye, white ash, cucumber-tree, blackgum, northern red oak, chestnut oak, shagbark hickory, butternut, sassafras, mulberry, mockernut hickory, yellowwood, pignut hickory, American elm, black locust, and black walnut. White oak, red maple, and yellow birch were also common in nearby stands. Very complex mixed stands of the sort described are limited to the very mesic "cove" or ravine sites.

The great diversity of species in the Mixed Mesophytic Forest results from a nearly optimum combination of environmental conditions. The average annual precipitation is 40 to 55 inches, but evaporation is only moderate; temperatures are not unfavorable; the soils are derived mainly from sedimentary rocks and tend to be deep and more fertile than most forest soils. Other regions may have warmer temperatures, more rainfall, less evaporation, or more fertile soils, but none in the East offers such a favorably integrated combination. The fact that this region is not now regarded as one of the best places in the country to practice forestry results partly from existing limitations on ability to control stand composition by silvicultural means and partly from the paucity of native conifers.

The Mixed Mesophytic Forest Region has been considered apart from the rest of the Appalachian Forest only because of its special significance as a center of distribution. The parts of the Appalachian Forest (Fig. 1-5) that lie to the west and east of the Appalachian Plateau are only slightly simpler in composition. The section that extends westward to the Mississippi River is characterized by lower precipitation and higher temperatures. As in all other parts of the Appalachian Forest, the oaks predominate. Chestnut never was very important, but certain species, such as black walnut and the hickories, are more abundant than in the Mixed Mesophytic Forest Region. Shortleaf pine and eastern redcedar are the only significant conifers.

The eastern portion, which covers the lower elevations of the Appalachian Mountains and extends northeastward to southern New England, is definitely simpler. However, on deep, fertile soils that are moist but well drained, there are stands with compositions approaching the complexity of the Mixed Mesophytic Forest. There is a strong tendency for the various oaks to predominate; and chestnut was equally prominent until the chestnut blight reduced this valuable species to the status of a short-lived understory shrub. Eastern hemlock and eastern white pine are the most important conifers. The simpler composition of this part of the Appalachian Forest probably results from the fact that the soils are generally poorer than those west of the mountains; higher elevations and latitudes also induce lower temperatures, but the precipitation is the same or heavier.

The Northern Hardwood Forest. The transition from the Mixed Mesophytic Forest to an adjacent, simpler formation is most strikingly illustrated by the status of the Northern Hardwood Forest. This forest is characterized by mixtures of sugar maple, American beech, and yellow birch, although it may include other species as well. The Northern Hardwood Forest is almost universally recognized, yet it is too often thought of as unrelated to the rest of the Eastern Deciduous Forest. It is, instead, best regarded as the variant resulting from the migration of a few of the species of the Mixed Mesophytic Forest to localities which are, because of higher latitude or elevation, colder but not otherwise substantially less favorable. The species that were hardy enough to make the transition increased in abundance at the expense of those that could not migrate to a colder climate, leading to the development of a much simpler and quite different mixture of species.

The Northern Hardwood Forest exists in close association with the Northeastern Coniferous Forest and often has an important coniferous component of hemlock, white pine, and spruce. However, there are large areas where site conditions are sufficiently favorable for conifers to be almost totally absent because of their limited ability to compete with hardwoods on good sites.

At its upper altitudinal and latitudinal limits, the Northern Hardwood Forest intermingles with the true firs, the spruces, paper birch, aspen, and other species characteristic of the Boreal Forest, to such a great extent that clear boundaries are hard to define. The northern limit of the Eastern Deciduous Forest and the Northern Hardwood Forest is usually taken as where sugar maple and most hardwood species other than birches or aspens cease to occur.

The Midland Hardwood Forest. This belt, sometimes designated as the "oak-hickory forest," separates the grasslands from the rest of the Eastern Deciduous Forest. It projects eastward to western Ohio and southern Michigan into an area that covers most of the Corn Belt; the portion of this projection that extends to Indiana is often referred to as the Prairie Peninsula, because its natural vegetation included extensive areas of interspersed patches of closed forest and open grassland. The oak-hickory forest is a variant of the Eastern Deciduous Forest, induced by low precipitation and high evaporation. The precipitation increases south of the projection; however, the northern limit of this projection is controlled not by an increase in precipitation but by a gradual decrease in evaporation resulting from lower temperatures.

The forest consists primarily of various species of oak; the hickories are generally no more important than a modest variety of species from other genera. As elsewhere, the greatest variety of species is found where conditions of soil moisture are most favorable. Most of the species are drawn from those of the Mixed Mesophytic Forest. However, there are a few exceptions such as bur oak, and jack or northern pin oak. There are very few conifers. Except for the unglaciated portion south of the Missouri River, the soils are so good that more than three-quarters of the forest has been cleared for agriculture.

The Ozark-Piedmont Forest. This forest, often called the "oak-pine forest," extends in a broad belt from New Jersey to Texas, being most characteristic of the Piedmont Plateau. Many of the hardwood species of the Mixed Mesophytic Forest are well represented, but it is most distinctly characterized by the presence of various hard pines. Shortleaf pine is most common in the interior portion of the belt and loblolly along the southern portion; pitch and Virginia pine abound in the northeastern extremity. The oaks predominate over the other hardwoods; southern red oak, which is almost absent from the Mixed Mesophytic Forest, also appears. These changes in composition are associated with warm temperatures and, to a lesser degree, with poor soils. these two factors, singly or in combination, tend to reduce the amount of available soil moisture; increased evaporation is particularly important in this respect and almost entirely counteracts any effect of increased precipitation. The prevalence of fire favored the maintenance of an admixture of pine in the forest before settlement and to a greater extent thereafter.

The Southeastern Pine Forest. Most of the lower Atlantic Coastal Plain is covered with sand laid down in the beach deposits of retreating seas. The sites tend to be dry in spite of the heavy rainfall, and they have always been subject to very frequent fires. Consequently, very extensive natural stands of longleaf pine developed on most of the area and it was not often that hardwoods were able to develop to any important extent. In the original forest, fire caused slash pine to be confined to a rather limited place in small swampy depressions. The hardwoods that do exist on most of the upland sites of this region are rather feeble relatives of the main family of the eastern hardwoods. In addition to the more common species, they include several xerophytic oaks such as turkey, blackjack, and bluejack oak. The Southeastern Pine Forest is part of the Eastern Deciduous Forest only by the doubtful virtue of the fact that it might very gradually be replaced by the hardwoods if fire were excluded. The site factors which restrict the hardwoods allow the remarkably rapid growth of hard pines for which this region is famous.

The Bottomland Hardwood Forest. The broad flood plains of the South and most of the Mississippi Basin support forests that are sometimes almost as rich in species as is the Mixed Mesophytic Forest. The soils are of alluvial origin, derived from the deposits left by the shifting courses of the meandering rivers. The portions of these valley bottoms sufficiently elevated to be free of annual flooding sustain excellent growth and stands of roughly the same species as those of the Appalachian Forest. The extensive portions that are flooded annually have many species especially adapted to the conditions. However, most of these are recognizable relatives of upland species. Because of its unusual site conditions and sharply bounded topography, the Bottomland Hardwood Forest is the one component of the Eastern Deciduous Forest that stands out as a well-defined entity.

The Northeastern Coniferous Forest. In the original forest various conifers tended to predominate on those sites in the Lake States, New York, New England, and the higher Appalachian Mountains that were either too moist or too dry for vigorous growth of hardwoods. Spruce and fir are most prevalent on sites that are excessively wet and poorly aerated because of poor drainage or an excess of precipitation over evaporation. The various pines of the region may exist as physiographic climaxes on dry sites, especially the sandy soils. The moist, well-drained sites within this forest are occupied by the northern hardwoods, which also intermingle with the conifers in varying degrees on the less favorable sites. The portions dominated by spruce and fir could be regarded as outliers of the Boreal Forest, but most ecologists regard the Eastern Deciduous Forest as extending to the northern limits of the ranges of any species found on the Appalachian Plateau.

The Boreal Forest

The simplest of the North American forest formations is the Boreal Forest, which extends continuously from the Atlantic shores of Canada to the interior of Alaska (Fig. 1-4). The predominant and typical species are white and black spruce, trembling aspen, balsam poplar, and paper birch. Other species found in limited parts of the eastern portion of the belt are balsam fir, red spruce, tamarack, northern white-cedar, jack and red pine, and bigtooth aspen. Lodgepole pine and subalpine fir enter the belt in Alaska and the Yukon. The greatest diversity of species is found in the southeastern portions where the Boreal Forest intergrades with the Eastern Deciduous Forest and where the regime of temperature and precipitation is more favorable than in regions lying to the northwest. The Boreal Forest may be thought of as the product of short growing seasons, low temperatures, and cold soils which may fluctuate from excessively moist in the spring to excessively dry in the rooting stratum late in the summer. It appears to have originated as a distinct formation on unglaciated portions of Siberia and Alaska at times when the rest of the North American vegetation was forced to migrate southward.

The Western Conifer Forest

The forests of the western half of the continent are dominated by conifers. Hardwood species occur, but the areas covered are minor and of very little commercial importance. Some deciduous species akin to a few of those of the Eastern Deciduous Forest maintain a feeble foothold in the stream bottoms where a stable supply of moisture exists through the dry summers. The ubiquitous trembling aspen forms sizable stands on some of the higher mountains. Red alder grows on a variety of sites in the humid fog belt along the coast. In the foothills of the Southwest there are extensive woodlands of various oaks and other species, many of them evergreens and all of them adapted to extremely dry conditions. Elsewhere the conifers hold sway over the region, because of their adaptation to dryness, low temperature, or both.

In general, the localities that are moist because of high altitude or latitude also tend to be cold and the warm localities tend to be subject to dry seasons of varying length.

Almost all the commercially important conifer forests of the West are in mountainous country, and the changes in elevation are so great that the various forest types are usually segregated into fairly distinct altitudinal belts. Furthermore, most of the forest types (Soc. Am. Foresters, 1954) contain no more than several species. On the other hand, there are about 50 species of softwoods alone in the whole Western Conifer Forest, and there is a substantial diversity of combinations of site conditions. However, there are so many sharp dividing lines induced by great changes in site factors, and so much topographic compartmentation, that the variations are not especially difficult to comprehend. In other words, the Western Conifer Forest lacks the bewilderingly kaleidoscopic variations of the Eastern Deciduous Forest. It looks like a random patchwork when shown in the horizontal in maps like those of Figs. 1-2 and 1-3, but there is some degree of real uniformity within most of the patches shown. Simplicity emerges if the forests of any region of the West are viewed in their vertical projection so that the altitudinal zonation becomes apparent. The altitudinal zonations of particular regions are described in Chapters 7−11. The three main parts of the Western Conifer Forest are shown in Fig. 1-4.

Both the Pacific Coastal Complex and the Sierra Nevadan Complex have their localities of optimum site conditions in which the diversity of species reaches a maximum. The forests of these localities bear the same relationship to the less complicated forests seemingly derived from them that the Appalachian Forest bears to the Eastern Deciduous Forest. The distribution center of the Pacific Coastal Complex is found on the Olympic Peninsula of northwestern Washington; that of the Sierra Nevadan Complex forms a belt along the middle elevations of the western slopes of the Sierra Nevada. The Rocky Mountain Complex appears to be a simplified derivative of the other two, but it has an affinity to the Boreal Forest as well.

The Pacific Coastal Complex.   This formation is largely confined to the belt that lies west of the crests of the Cascade Range and the Canadian Rockies. Its northern end lies south of the Alaska Range, and the portion of it termed the Coast Redwood Belt extends southward along the California coast to the vicinity of San Francisco. It also appears in modified form in a kind of island surrounded by the Rocky Mountain Complex on the western slopes of the Rockies in northern Idaho, eastern Washington, western Montana, and southeastern British Columbia. The so-called western white pine type of this locality is actually a variable mixture of species that are also prominent in other forest types west of the Cascades.

The two species that are most typical of the Pacific Coastal Complex are western hemlock and western redcedar; others, such as coast redwood, Sitka spruce, and coastal silver fir, are confined to relatively restricted parts of this formation. The most abundant and important species, Douglas-fir, is a very adaptable tree found far and wide throughout the West.

The Pacific Coastal Complex occupies the most humid region of western North America, and, at least along the coast itself, the temperatures are mild and the growing season far longer than might be inferred from the high latitudes. In the Alaskan and Canadian portions rainfall is well distributed throughout the year. South of the international boundary, soil moisture stored from winter precipitation blunts much of the effect of the rainless summers. In a very narrow belt along the coast there is also a significant amount of summer precipitation derived from "fog drip," that is, from the very small particles of water that make up fog or clouds and coalesce to form large drops on the needles of trees.

The Sierra Nevadan Complex.   This group of conifers is almost entirely confined to the western slopes of the Sierra Nevada and the Cascades of southern Oregon. The region is characterized, at the forested elevations, by very heavy winter precipitation and long, dry summers. This forest formation intermingles at its northern end with the Pacific Coastal Complex. The difference between the two formations is probably fully as much the result of some very ancient geological separation as of present climate. The characteristic species confined to this area are sugar pine, Jeffrey pine, incense-cedar, and California red fir. The most important commercial species, ponderosa pine, is found throughout the West.

The Rocky Mountain Complex.   The portion of this complex that lies within the United States occupies the forested elevations from the eastern foothills of the Cascades and Sierras to the Great Plains, except for the part of the Inland Empire dominated by the western white pine type. It also extends along the mountains from the Yukon Territory to central Mexico. All of the important species, such as ponderosa pine, Douglas-fir, Engelmann spruce, subalpine fir, and lodgepole pine, appear to be derived from the flora of regions closer to the Pacific Coast. The only species confined to the area are those such as the rare Colorado blue spruce and various small pines adapted to very high or low elevations. The forests of the region occur only at high elevations, where the growing seasons are short. They must also endure the rigors of annual periods of low precipitation, although the time and duration of these seasonal droughts vary widely. In the large area north of Arizona and west of the Rockies, virtually all the precipitation is from the winter snows, and the lower the latitude the longer the summer drought. In Arizona and New Mexico this pattern is interrupted by showery precipitation in midsummer, and the driest periods come in spring and fall. East of the Rocky Mountains most of the precipitation comes in the summer. These differences in distribution of precipitation and other environmental factors have induced distinct geographical strains within the species of the region. As in other parts of the West, there is tremendous variation in species with altitude but surprisingly little with great changes in latitude.

THE SOCIAL DIMENSION OF SILVICULTURE

Most of this book is intended to convey an understanding of the almost changeless natural factors that govern the geography of silviculture on a large, variable landmass. Because forestry serves the needs of people, silviculture has both social and natural dimensions.

It is no accident that the subsequent chapters involve a categorization of the forest that follows socially ordained political boundaries as well as natural ones. It should be noted that an effort is made to treat each natural grouping only once, so that an important forest type that occurs in two or more regions is intensively treated in one chapter only.

The human demands placed on forests are so variable that it is fortunate that forest vegetation usually is flexible and resilient. Because of this, silviculture can be quite variable. Natural factors set limits on what is possible, but after these natural limitations are taken into account, the next considerations are the management objectives that society and ownership, public or private, have set for a given tract of forest land. The objectives are usually plural rather than singular. Even though a private owner may regard economic timber production as the primary objective, society exercises an increasing degree of control over the wild animals that live on the land and the water that flows from it. The kind of silviculture practiced by different owners also varies in intensity because not all are equally able to make long-term investments.

Regeneration by planting and similarly intensive silvicultural practices are increasingly common but far from universal on industrial and some public holdings. Multiple-use silviculture approaches full manifestations only on public forests. It is important to remember that most American forests are in small private holdings; the owners of these are seldom able to apply intensive silviculture or achieve full development of the principles of sustained yield or multiple use.

Mounting social concern about forests increases the number of laws and regulations that directly or indirectly control silvicultural practice. Under the U.S. Constitution most of the power to regulate forestry rests with the states, so one must anticipate the development of 50 different sets of laws. The most common of these have to do with sources of danger such as fire, pesticides, and erosive soil disturbance on watersheds. Under American law, wild animals are the property of the people of each state, so there have long been state laws about wildlife. Aesthetic concerns have also become the subject of laws in some states. Perhaps it is not entirely facetious to note that certain parts of this book are void where prohibited by law. However, not all of the growing body of law restricts the latitude of silvicultural practice. More and more of it, coupled with important incentives, simply requires the intelligent practice of silviculture.

Because of all these sources of variation, there is no one best mode of silviculture for any given tree species or forest type. Even if social factors remained the same, no one species can be depended upon to have the same ecological adaptations throughout its range. There is really no substitute for formulating silvicultural systems and prescribing treatment on the basis of rather narrowly specific kinds of stands within single ownerships and small localities. This book is not intended to tell any forester what to do, but only to stimulate analytical thought about and understanding of a vast and diverse stretch of forest geography.

BIBLIOGRAPHY

Braun, E. L. 1950. *Deciduous forests of eastern North America.* Blakiston Co., Philadelphia. 596 pp.

Calder, N. 1972. *The restless earth, a report on the new geology.* Viking Press, New York. 152 pp.

Daubenmire, R. 1978. *Plant geography, with special reference to North America.* Academic Press, New York. 338 pp.

Flint, R. F., and B. J. Skinner. 1977. *Physical geology.* 2nd ed. John Wiley, New York. 594 pp.

Kincer, J. B. 1922. Precipitation and humidity. In *Atlas of American agriculture.* Sup. of Docs., U.S. Govt. Print. Off., Washington, D.C.

Küchler, A. W. 1964. The potential natural vegetation of the conterminous United States. *Am. Geog. Soc., Special Res. Publ. 36.* 116 pp.

Rowe, J. S. 1959. Forest regions of Canada. *Can For. Br. Bull. 123.* 71 pp.

Shantz, H. L., and R. Zon. 1924. Natural vegetation. In *Atlas of American agriculture.* Sup. of Docs., U.S. Govt. Print. Off., Washington, D. C.

U.S. Dept. Agr. 1941. *Climate and man, yearbook of agriculture, 1941.* Sup. of Docs., U.S. Govt. Print. Off., Washington, D. C. 1,248 pp.

Soc. Am. Foresters. 1954. *Forest cover types of North America.* 4th ed. Washington, D. C. 67 pp.

Shelford, V. E. 1963. *The ecology of North America.* Univ. of Ill. Press, Urbana. 610 pp.

U.S. For. Serv. 1949. Areas characterized by major forest types in the United States. Map from Natl. Surv. of For. Resour. Washington, D. C.

U.S. Geol. Surv. 1970. *The national atlas of the United States of America.* U.S. Dept. Int., Washington, D.C. 417 pp.

2

The Northeastern Region

J.W. Barrett

LOCATION

The Northeastern Region includes the six New England states and New York. Prominence of the Northern Hardwood and Northeastern Coniferous forests gives this unit a distinct ecological character. Other qualities that are somewhat unique to the area are climate, geology, and topography. Because of ecological similarities the seven states are often grouped in silvicultural discussions. Further, the large local population and attractiveness of the region to tourists subject many forest lands to heavy use for a variety of purposes. The region extends from the New York–Boston megalopolis to the wilds of the unorganized territory of northern Maine (Fig. 2-1).

FOREST STATISTICS

Area

The forests of the seven Northeastern states comprise about 49.5 million acres, which is about 70 percent of the total land area.[1] Maine is the most heavily wooded state with about 90 percent of the land area classified as forest, followed by New Hampshire (86 percent); Vermont (76 percent); Connecticut, Massachusetts, and Rhode Island (59 percent); and New York (56 percent). Thus, in the populous and highly industrialized Northeast the forests and their multiple benefits are important to the way of life and economy of many areas.

Almost all of the forest land has the inherent capacity to grow usable crops of timber and thus would be classified as commercial. So the region has a large potential for timber production.

Most of the noncommercial forest land is so classified because it has been

[1]Unless otherwise noted forest statistics have been compiled from Ferguson and Mayer (1970), Ferguson and Kingsley (1972), and Kingsley (1974, 1976a, and 1977).

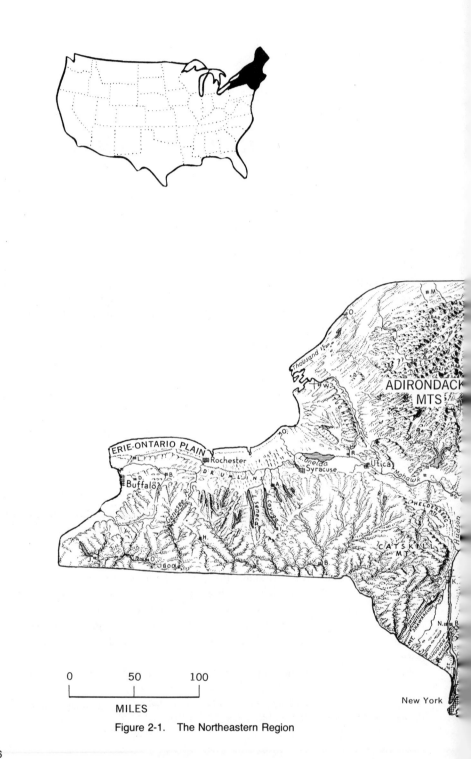

Figure 2-1.   The Northeastern Region

designated for uses other than wood growth. This category includes almost 2.5 million acres of New York woodland, located in forest preserves where an amendment to the State Constitution precludes commercial logging of state ownerships.

Character of Forest Land Ownership

About 94 percent of the commercial forest land in this region is privately owned. Over 50 percent is owned by individuals, corporations, churches, and other organizations. Individual ownerships are by far the most numerous. Purchase of forest land for second or vacation home sites has resulted in considerable fragmentation of ownerships. In Vermont the average timberland owner has held the land for only about 7 years (Armstrong, 1975). Forest industries hold 24 percent of the private forest land. Farm ownerships total 14 percent, which is appreciably less than 10 years ago. Several studies have indicated the reluctance of individual owners to sell timber because of the effect of logging on aesthetics or the environment (Canham, 1971; Hamilton, 1971; Hamilton et al., 1973). Thus the amount of forest land actually available for timber production is probably less than the total classified as commercial. A survey of the objectives of individuals owning forest land in southern New England notes that most owners do not seem unalterably opposed to harvesting. Kingsley (1976b) concluded that "the productive potential of the regions' private forest land might be increased if owners could be made aware that judicious and limited timber harvesting could serve to protect and enhance the very values they derive from their forest land while at the same time helping to defray the cost of forest land ownership." However, it is estimated that at the present time in this area about 44 percent of the privately owned commercial forest land is withdrawn from the timber producing base.

Average size of individual holdings is small. In Massachusetts it is less than 25 acres (Peters and Bowers, 1977), in Vermont 51.6 acres (Kingsley, 1977), and in New Hampshire 46.7 acres (Kingsley, 1976a).

The pattern of forest-land ownership in Maine differs from the general conditions in the region. Maine's forest industries, mainly pulp and paper, hold nearly 50 percent of the forest land. These ownerships, several over a million acres, are concentrated in the large northern counties. Northern New York also contains several large forest industry holdings.

The White Mountain National Forest centered in New Hampshire with a portion in Maine, the Green Mountain National Forest in Vermont, and the Acadia National Park in Maine are important federal properties. However, forest land in state ownership is about twice the area of the federal holdings.

Forest Inventory

Hardwoods constitute about 52 percent of the volume of growing stock on commercial forest land. The three species, American beech, yellow birch, and sugar maple, that characterize the northern hardwood forest comprise about one-third of the hardwood cubic foot volume. This is a reduction from previous surveys and reflects logging practices that have selected these species in preference to others. The spruces, balsam fir, and eastern white pine are the most important softwoods (see Table 2-1).

THE PHYSICAL ENVIRONMENT

Physiography

The major portion of the region consists of upland plateaus ranging between 500 and 1,500 feet in elevation. This peneplain matrix is frequently interrupted by mountain peaks and valley lowlands. The leveled, rolling surface is a northern extension of the Appalachian Highlands.

The mountains are usually monadnocks, remnants of summit peneplains resulting from earlier cycles of uplift and erosion or the remains of volcanic intrusions. Most prominent of the mountain schemes are the Adirondacks of northern New York (Fig. 2-2), the Green Mountains of Vermont and western Massachusetts, and the White Mountains of New Hampshire. The Adirondacks are a southern segment of the Laurentian Upland while the other two are parts of the Appalachian system. The White Mountains, containing the Presidential Range with Mount Washington about 6,290 feet above sea level and four other peaks above 5,300 feet, are the highest in the Northeast. Mount Katahdin in Maine reaches above 5,300 feet. The timberline occurs at about 4,000 feet throughout the region.

The lowlands include a number of areas below 500 feet in elevation. These include all or parts of the Seaboard Lowlands of New England, the Connecticut River Valley, the valleys of the Mohawk, Hudson, and St. Lawrence rivers, and the Erie-Ontario Plains in New York. Settlement and industry throughout the Northeast have tended to locate in lowland areas because of greater accessibility and opportunities for farming (Fig. 2-3). Consequently, woodland ownership is greatly fragmented in these areas.

Rivers of the Northeast offered the first means of moving logs from the forest to the mill and certain of the more important rivers once were declared public waterways. One reason floatable softwoods were preferred by the early forest industries was the ease of water transportation. A multitude of lakes large and small embellish the northeastern countryside. To illustrate, the Adirondacks of New York have over 2,000 lakes and ponds (Lull, 1968). The many lakes and streams contribute to the recreational attractiveness of the region.

Geology and Soils

Geologically this is a very old region. Some of the most ancient metamorphic rock formations in the world are found quite generally in New England and the Adirondacks. Throughout the ages, sediments have been buried, metamorph-

TABLE 2-1

Net Volume of Growing Stock on Commercial Forest Land in the Northeastern Region (in Million Cubic Feet—Minimum d.b.h. 5.0 Inches)

Species	Connecticut, Massachusetts, and Rhode Island	New York	Vermont	New Hampshire	Maine	Total
Softwoods						
Spruces and balsam fir	68.4	650.2	870.0	1,088.9	10,756.3	13,433.8
White and red pine	1,134.3	1,277.9	387.1	1,456.3	1,516.6	5,772.2
Hemlock	378.9	1,082.0	378.6	563.9	1,151.0	3,554.4
Other	117.9	170.6	82.3	30.8	1,339.3	1,740.9
Total softwoods	1,699.5	3,180.7	1,718.0	3,139.9	14,763.2	24,501.3
Hardwoods						
Sugar maple	270.8	1,997.2	1,083.2	450.5	1,230.0	5,031.7
Yellow birch	96.4	396.6	331.7	416.5	744.2	1,985.4
Beech	115.3	780.4	236.3	271.1	658.2	2,061.3
Soft maples	987.8	1,614.6	450.3	854.8	1,614.9	5,522.4
Oaks	1,950.6	1,431.3	113.1	623.2	306.0	4,424.2
Paper birch	99.9	175.8	282.1	399.9	740.4	1,698.1
Ashes	197.5	600.3	181.3	132.2	293.4	1,404.7
Aspens	61.7	414.5	135.2	153.2	665.3	1,429.9
Other	612.4	1,608.4	199.0	137.3	237.8	2,794.9
Total hardwoods	4,392.4	9,019.1	3,012.2	3,438.7	6,490.2	26,352.6
Total all species	6,091.9	12,199.8	4,730.2	6,578.6	21,253.4	50,853.9

Figure 2-2. A view of the Adirondack Mountains of New York State (U.S. For. Serv.).

Figure 2-3. A vista of forested hillsides and valley farmlands in the Northeast (U.S. For. Serv.).

osed, and subsequently intruded with magnas before being thrust upward by convolutions in the earth's crust.

Present-day elevation differences are mainly due to the resistance of bedrock to erosion. The mountains and plateaus, comprised as they are of the hardest materials, have most successfully resisted the leveling process while the relatively soft, loosely consolidated rocks of the valleys have been readily broken down and worn away.

The mountain sections and upland plateaus are formed principally of granitic igneous and metamorphic bedrock. This material, containing a high percentage of quartz, reduces to coarse-textured or moderately coarse-textured acid soils of relatively low fertility. In contrast, valley soils mainly derived from finer-textured sometimes-calcareous parent material are moderately textured with greater fertility. In some places throughout the region limestone outcrops or shale and slate parent material results in finer-textured productive forest soils.

If soil genesis had been in place, it would be easy to generalize about forest soils in the Northeast. Mountain and high-plateau soils would be relatively low in fertility, grading into more productive lowlands and valleys. This simple pattern has been modified greatly by glaciation.

During the Pleistocene Epoch, ice masses moved down from the north to cover practically all of the Northeastern Region. Ice sheets several thousand feet thick probably covered even the tallest peaks. The typical results of glacial action, namely, U-shaped valleys, smooth-sided mountains, scooped-out and kettle lakes, peat bogs, and a heterogeneous mantle of glacial deposits, are evident.

The manner in which transported glacial drift was deposited has in large measure determined present site quality. Unsorted drift or till generally produced the best forest sites. These deposits are comprised of heterogeneous materials ranging in size from large glacial erratics to clay. They are usually found on mid-slopes of hills and higher mountains and on tops of lower mountains. At the other end of the scale, the coarser water-transported, sorted, and often stratified drift found in kames, eskers, outwash plains, and glacial lake shores and bottoms usually produced poorer sites (Donahue, 1940). Soil depth, texture, and drainage are also important factors in determining site productivity. More recently Leak (1976) has related habitat types, site productivity, and silvicultural implications to substratum, drainage conditions, certain features of elevation, and aspect.

A compact stratum or fragipan located from a few inches to several feet below the surface is characteristic of many till soils in this region. Perched water tables, water seeps, and soggy ground well upslope or even on hilltops are typical spring phenomena associated with the presence of this impervious zone. Where the hardpan is close to the surface site productivity decreases.

Finally, disrupted drainage patterns, scouring-out of glacial basins, kettles, and the blocking of waterways with glacial material has created numerous ponds and lakes. Swamps and bogs have frequently developed in the shallow depressions.

Thus, although the Northeast is old geologically, the glaciation has created young soils and conditions are quite variable. Often there are striking differences in site quality among areas only short distances from each other. This feature is important. Silviculturists must be aware of these soil and site differences if they are to make sound decisions.

Soils of this region are classified as podzols or brown or gray-brown podzolic. These would be of the order Spodosols and Alfisols, respectively, according to the new comprehensive soil classification system. The true acid podzols are usually found in the higher elevations. They are associated with coarse soils, abundant precipitation, cool climate, and conifer cover. Where these conditions occur, mor may accumulate to a depth of several inches and the leached A_2 horizon is well defined. Even under hardwood cover, if the other conditions hold, there is a tendancy for an appreciable A_2 to develop.

The brown or gray-brown podzolic soils are generally related to the features of fine-textured soils, warmer temperatures, and hardwood cover found at lower elevations and in the southern part of the region. Mull humus can be expected with these conditions although mor may occur on the drier sites. In mountainous country, mull will rarely be found except in the most favorable spots.

Climate and Weather

The Northeast is a cool humid region. The prevailing west-to-east air-mass movement results in a typically continental climate except for areas along the Atlantic Coast. As noted by Lull (1968), "Most of the major storm tracks of the United States funnel eastward over the northeast." Differences in climate within the region are occasioned by the north-to-south span and wide ranges in elevation.

Precipitation is abundant and evenly distributed over the year. Average annual precipitation ranges from about 32 inches to over 52 inches with most of the area having 40 inches or more. Soil moisture deficiencies seldom occur. Mean annual snowfall for southern New England is about 32 inches. The mountains of the north may have four times this amount (Lull, 1968).

The number of frost-free days varies from as few as 90 on the mountains to twice that number in the southern part of the region. Also, the severity of winter increases dramatically from south to north. Northern stations have recorded more than 60 days of subzero readings while such temperatures occur only rarely in localities near the southern coast (U.S. Dept. Agr., 1941).

The fire season occurs in two rather brief parts. In the spring a period of high fire danger is usually experienced just before the flush of foliage. At this time forest fuels are in a cured condition, there are brief periods without rain, during the daytime temperatures rise into the 80's or 90's, relative humidity is low, and winds are frequently brisk. Greening of the vegetation brings an end to this period. The fall season generally follows killing frosts during the dry pleasant respite of "Indian summer."

The varied assortment of northeastern weather includes occasional hurricanes that have caused severe damage in certain places. In general the most severe losses to these winds have been on the southerly and easterly slopes, and conifers tend to suffer more than do the hardwoods. On occasion in some localities ice storms may cause considerable crown breakage.

MAJOR FOREST TYPE GROUPS

About 40 different cover types are found in this region. It is possible, however, to combine a number of types into type groups for the purpose of discussing silvicultural treatments. Four type groups, namely, spruce-fir-hardwood, northern hardwood, white pine-hemlock-hardwood, and oak have been designated for the region. These type groups tend to be arranged spatially in both geographically and altitudinal patterns.

The spruce-fir-hardwood type group dominates the highest elevations and the northern interior portions of the region. These areas are characterized by cold temperatures and relatively coarse, sometimes poorly drained, acid soils. The northern hardwood type group mainly includes the beech-birch-maple association shown in Figure 2-4. The northern hardwoods blends into the oak type group on some of the warmer drier sites throughout the region. The oak type group is predominant in southern New York, Connecticut, Rhode Island, and southeastern Massachusetts. White pine-hemlock-hardwood is associated with the coarser-textured, well-drained soils of the Seaboard Lowlands, the Connecticut River Valley and the eastern slopes of the Adirondack Mountains.

It should be recognized, however, that the situation is far from homogeneous within any one of the geographic areas. For example all of the type groups mentioned above occur in the Adirondack and White Mountains areas that are delimited as spruce-fir-hardwood.

Figure 2-5 presents a simplified diagrammatic illustration of the altitudinal arrangement of certain type groups in the mountain or northern areas. Typical soil-site relationships are shown. Tamarack and black spruce are likely to be the first tree species to invade bog soils adjacent to glacial ponds. Black spruce only 2 or 3 inches in diameter growing on these harsh sites may exceed 150 years of age. Northern white-cedar sometimes occurs near the edge of bogs or swamps where limestone is present. Occasionally, eastern white pine or red spruce are found on high spots or hummocks. Crown closure ranges from very open on the poorest sites to dense on the better ones.

The presence of more site-demanding species in the forest community is related to an increase in elevation and improved drainage, that is, deeper soils. Associated with better growing conditions, balsam fir, eastern hemlock, red maple, red spruce, and yellow birch become more prominent with an occasional white pine, beech, sugar maple, or ash. Stands on the better sites close tightly and competition is an important ecological factor. Along with vegetation soils will be different. The peat is replaced usually with some form of glacial

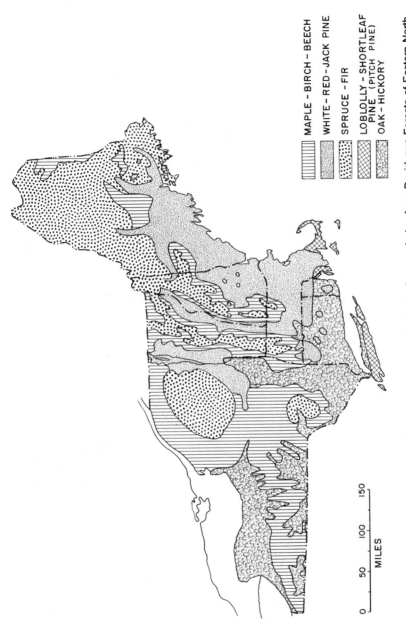

Figure 2-4. A classification of forest type groups in the Northeast (by permission from Deciduous Forests of Eastern North America by E. Lucy Braun, Copyright, 1959, The Blakiston Co., Philadelphia).

MAPLE – BIRCH – BEECH

WHITE – RED – JACK PINE

SPRUCE – FIR

LOBLOLLY – SHORTLEAF
PINE (PITCH PINE)

OAK – HICKORY

0   50   100   150
MILES

35

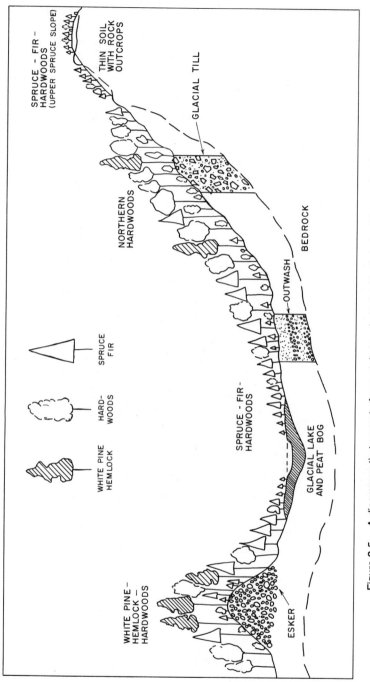

Figure 2-5. A diagrammatic transect of mountain terrain in the Northeast, with associated type groups.

36

outwash. The profile will show a well-defined A_2 horizon overtopped by a mor humus. With increased soil depth and improved fertility and drainage the more demanding sugar maple and American beech will force their way into the stand. The spruce-fir-hardwood type group that was predominantly softwoods on the poorer sites finally gives way to the typical northern hardwoods, namely, American beech, yellow birch, and sugar maple with an admixture of red spruce, hemlock, red maple, white pine, white ash, black cherry, and other species. Thus the occurrence of the spruce-fir-hardwood type will range from the poorest sites to the ecotone where the spruce and fir yield to more aggressive but more demanding hardwoods. Typical of the best northern hardwood sites are deep, well-drained soils comprised usually of unsorted glacial till perhaps with a mull humus layer.

Upslope site again becomes restrictive for the hardwoods. Red spruce and balsam fir tend to dominate on the thin-soiled higher elevations. Thus the spruce-fir-hardwood type is most prevalent on the poorer extremes of the topographic transect, namely, on the thin-soiled cold mountain tops, on outwash plains where the effective soil depth is limited by high water tables, and finally on bogs and poorly drained soils adjacent to ponds and lakes. Stands comprised predominantly of spruce-fir are typically associated with high soil moisture.

In southern New England the spruces, fir, tamarack, and northern white-cedar occur rarely. Poor aeration is a limiting site factor only in swamps where red maple is prominent. The variety of hardwood species, especially of the oaks, becomes much greater and deep mesic soils of the lower slopes may contain as many as 20 different species.

Throughout the region the occurrence of the white pine-hemlock-hardwood type group is typically associated with coarse drier soils. In Fig. 2-4 this would most likely be on the esker.

HISTORY OF FOREST USE

Agriculture

A vast, almost unbroken forest covering from 90 to 95 percent of the land area confronted the first settlers in New England (Kellogg, 1909). In many respects the colonists must have regarded the forest as an obstacle that harbored their enemies and had to be destroyed to make room for cultivation. It should be noted, however, that early writers described the open parklike nature of many forest areas created by wildfires or intentional burning by the Indians.

The period from 1790 to 1830 saw a surge of hopeful farmers into the area. Land clearing and farming reached their peak between 1820 and 1880 when it was estimated that forests covered only 27 percent of Connecticut, 74 percent of Maine, 40 percent of Massachusetts, 50 percent of New Hampshire, 34 percent of Rhode Island, and 35 percent of Vermont (Harper, 1918). Several developments making farming in this region less attractive started the tide of land abandonment that is only now drawing to a close.

Utilization

Initially, white pine comprised the bulk of the timber harvested in the Northeast. However, about mid-1800s in the northern areas spruce sawlogs also found favor in the lumber industry. Extensive areas were cut over for these two species. Ordinarily only a few trees per acre were taken and this light form of logging made little change in the composition of the forest.

Lumber manufacture rose to a maximum of 3,170 million board feet in New England about 1907 (Wood, 1935), but production of certain states had culminated long before that time. The peak was reached in New York before 1870 and in Vermont by 1887.

In early times the old-growth hardwoods were not attractive to the lumber industry. Many trees were malformed and defective and logs were difficult to move by stream driving. Except for the most accessible areas and special use needs the early cutting bypassed the hardwoods to skim off floatable high-value softwoods.

However, in the more heavily populated southern portion of the region, hardwoods played a more important role. Here quantities of hardwoods were once cut as domestic and industrial fuel, for charcoal to operate smelting furnaces, for use in lime kilns, and for the important export trade in potash. Heavy timber removals at short intervals and the replacement of chestnut by other species has resulted in the domination of these forests by aging coppice stands of oak.

Hardwoods have come into their own as sawtimber only in recent years. Prices for high-quality sugar maple, yellow birch, and paper birch have increased greatly. This reflects changes in logging and hauling techniques, greater use of the hardwood species, and the decreasing supply of high-quality material.

The pulp and paper industry has contributed greatly to the Northeastern economy. At the outset, long-fibered spruce and aspen provided the bulk of the raw material. Subsequently, balsam fir became acceptable and more recently, with the developments of new pulping techniques, dense hardwoods are being utilized. Although still limited in extent whole tree chipping has now moved into the woods of the Northeast.

Protection

Shortly after the turn of the century fires swept over large areas in northern Maine, New Hampshire, Vermont, and the Adirondacks. These fires were the consequence of large accumulations of softwood slash, periods of unseasonably dry weather, and carelessness.

Now all the forest land in the Northeast is under organized fire protection.

Generally this region can be considered one of the most fireproof in the country. However, on rare occasions abnormally dry weather sets the stage for large fires. Conditions can become critical in remote or wilderness areas where there has been considerable timber mortality. So the potential for large serious fires cannot be overlooked.

Grave losses have resulted from insect and disease depredations. The chestnut blight was a serious blow to the productivity and value of forests in southern New England and New York. Birch dieback and the bronze birch borer have killed large quantities of highly valuable paper and yellow birch. Mortality of beech caused by the beech scale-bark disease syndrome has had a significant effect on forest composition. The gypsy moth is an important pest with oaks. Although a minor forest problem, death of American elms from the Dutch elm disease is distressing because the beauty of so many picturesque New England towns was greatly enhanced by the presence of large stately elms. Periodic outbreaks of the spruce budworm has caused catastrophic losses in the spruce-fir forest.

The Forests Today

The forests of the region have suffered greatly from mistreatment. Heavy cutting in predominantly spruce-fir stands lacking advance regeneration has created an environment that delays or even precludes the establishment of desirable regrowth. In mixed stands the less desirable lightly cut hardwoods often increased at the expense of more closely utilized conifers.

Repeated high grading, partial cutting based upon economic selection, has caused the greatest degradation in the northern hardwoods. Accessible areas have been logged repeatedly, the best trees being taken first so that the quality of the growing stock has steadily declined.

The preceding statements, made in 1962, are still appropriate for large areas. The most recent forest surveys generally report an appreciable increase in growing stock but they also show a decrease in quality. Overcutting of the commercially desirable species has resulted in an expansion of the elm-ash-red maple type at the expense of the more valuable beech-birch-sugar maple. Northeastern forests are, in general, given low-intensity management with high acreage harvested. Average growth of wood is less than one-half of the potential of fully stocked natural stands (Herrick, 1977). Adoption of more intensive silviculture for timber production in the region has not as yet made significant gains.

On the other hand, interest in the noncommodity benefits provided by the forests of the region has grown tremendously. Opportunities exist for the application of silvicultural skills to improve wildlife habitats, create desirable environments for forest recreation, manage watersheds, and furnish other amenities. In many instances these objectives can be blended into silvicultural prescriptions that make timber production more attractive.

SILVICULTURE OF THE MAJOR TYPE GROUPS

Spruce-Fir-Hardwood Type Group

Place in Ecological Succession.   On the better sites in the region softwoods are at a distinct ecological disadvantage when compared with hardwoods. The hardwoods are in general endowed with a capacity for establishment and rapid early growth that enables them to surpass their softwood associates. Beech and sugar maple are considered very tolerant to tolerant and yellow birch and red maple intermediate in tolerance. Each of these hardwoods produce abundant seed crops at frequent intervals, and once established may start rapid juvenile height growth (Fowells, 1965). Sugar maple with adequate light can reach 5 feet in height within 5 years (Godman, 1957). Open-grown yellow birch are vigorous and they may reach 30 inches in 2 years (Jarvis, 1957). Red maple has the growth capacity to overtop other species that originate about the same time.

Conversely, seeds of the conifers are relatively small and the young seedlings grow slowly. Two-year-old red spruce seedlings are likely to be less than 1 inch tall with root penetrations of from only 2 to 3 inches (Place, 1955; Heinselman, 1957). White spruce growth is also slow but root penetration is somewhat greater than for red and black spruce (Nienstaedt, 1957). Balsam fir shoot development is about the same as the spruces for the first several years; but root penetration is significantly deeper, reaching 3 to 5 inches after the first year (Place, 1955; Hart, 1959b).

Hardwoods generally sprout when cut or broken, which gives them an additional competitive advantage over softwoods, which do not have this capacity. Red maple is a prolific sprouter often developing multistem clumps when coppiced. Also, beech sometimes produces numerous root suckers, which may be stimulated by injury to the roots.

Beech and sugar maple are long-lived trees, old growth exceeding 300 years in age. They have the ability to persist under suppression for some time and still respond well to release. Thus on good sites it can be expected that beech and sugar maple will ultimately reach into the upper canopy and then dominate the stand.

Red spruce has certain silvical characteristics that enable it to hold a place in the northern forest even on the best hardwood sites. These are great tolerance of shade, long life, ability to respond to release even after prolonged suppression, persistence of a single growing tip, and relative freedom from insect, disease, and animal damage. Examination of the life history of a red spruce found in the upper canopy with hardwoods may reveal numerous periods of suppression followed by release. It may have taken over a century for the spruce finally to become a codominant. Also, eastern hemlock, a long-lived tolerant species, maintains itself with mixed hardwoods on some sites.

Tubbs (1976) showed that allelopathy may be an important factor in the survival of certain species on sites where sugar maple is abundant. Newly germinated seedlings of black spruce, tamarack, jack pine, white spruce, northern white-cedar, and yellow birch were repressed when grown in sugar maple root exudate.

With the competitive advantages in favor of the hardwoods only the restrictive nature of the sites to the more demanding hardwood species enables the spruce-fir-hardwood type to occupy large areas. In the ecotone where spruce-fir-hardwood type group species blend with the northern hardwoods silvicultural practices must favor the softwood components if a high proportion of them is desired in the stand. This is an especially important consideration because it is contrary to usual cutting practices which take only the larger-diameter hardwoods for sawlogs but reach into the smaller-diameter conifers for pulpwood.

Growth Rates.   The wide variation in the quality of spruce-fir-hardwood sites is matched by a similar range in growth rates. Trees growing on bogs or at high elevations may never reach merchantable size. On sites classified as commercial, average annual net growth may reach 50 to about 70 cubic feet per acre per year (Hart, 1964; Frank, 1977a). Higher growth rates are associated with stands in which conifers predominate.

Growth predictions in the spruce-fir-hardwood stands that often are uneven aged are difficult. Since spruce may persist for long periods of time and then respond to release, traditional measures of site index associated with height and age are of little value. Red spruce in the open may reach breast high in less than 15 years, whereas in the forest it may take from 40 to 45 years (Murphy, 1917). Bowen (1964) has described certain correlations that may be used as guides of expected growth. He concludes that length of live crown, initial d.b.h., and tree growth in basal area for a 5-year period before partial cutting are predictors of growth following the harvest.

Rotation Age or Size.   Frank and Bjorkbom (1973) recommended that balsam fir and black spruce can be grown to a maximum size of 10 to 12 inches d.b.h. and red and white spruces to 14 to 16 inches for pulpwood and 18 to 20 inches for sawlogs. Several investigations indicate the time that might be required to achieve these sizes. McLintock (1952) found that although the average age of a number of 11-inch red spruce was about 148 years, the trees ranged in age from 89 to 235 years. Also, some trees in the 14- to 16-inch-diameter classes were only 90 to 100 years old. Robertson (1942) observed the average age of a sample of red spruce in the 8-inch class was 124 years with a range from 63 to 160 while those in the 12-inch class averaged 165 years with a range from 88 to 206. This information indicates that with intensive management pulpwood could be grown in 80 to 90 years and rotations for sawlogs would be in excess of 100 years.

Balsam fir is host to a wide variety of fungi and rots are so extensive that by the time trees of this species are only 60 to 70 years old they are highly susceptible to windthrow and wind breakage. Thus the pathological rotation for balsam fir is generally no more than 70 to 90 years in the interior and northern areas and 50 to 60 years along coastal Maine and in southern areas regardless of tree size (Frank and Bjorkbom, 1973).

Cultural Practices. Depending upon stand structure and conditions and objectives of management a variety of silvicultural harvest and regeneration systems may be successful. Individual-tree selection, group selection, shelter-wood, and clearcutting all have their place. The seed-tree system is not applicable because the spruces and balsam fir are shallow rooted and subject to severe windthrow.

Soil moisture is a critical factor in the regeneration of spruce and balsam fir. The influence of this factor is, of course, conditioned by other elements of the habitat. Generally the soil moisture regime is much more favorable for regeneration under a canopy than in the open where insolation and wind dry out the soil beyond the depths of the tiny roots of young seedlings. This is particularly important when the forest floor, covered by mosses and humus, is relatively undisturbed by logging. These substances tend to dry out more rapidly than mineral soil when the stand is opened. There is also evidence that high soil temperatures may cause mortality of young seedlings. These considerations point up the need for either well-established regeneration prior to final harvest or provisions for shelter of the site.

In the absence of natural disturbance and harvest by man, the spruce-fir-hardwood type usually develops as an uneven-aged stand. When this is the case, the individual tree-selection or the group-selection methods may be the most desirable. Frank and Bjorkbom (1973) listed the advantages as: providing a continuous forest cover and periodic harvest; more fully utilizing the growing space on a vertical plane; maintaining more stable environmental conditions; producing a more stable plant and animal population; reducing fire hazard from slash accumulation; reducing the chance of losing the whole stand at once through insect attacks, disease, or other natural catastrophe; and making the stand more attractive to the aesthetic-conscious public. They noted disadvantages as: more complicated management; more difficult and expensive harvesting operations; need to cover a larger area to obtain a given volume; and finally the difficulty of preventing logging damage to and death of reserved trees.

The selection system implies tree marking. Control gained by marking avoids the danger of removing too many trees in portions of the forest and not removing enough in others; this occurs all too frequently with the use of diameter-limit cutting. However, the prevailing mode of cutting in spruce-fir stands involves the use of diameter limits of varying sizes and degrees of sophistication.

Marking enables the forest manager to discriminate among species and individuals to favor the more desirable elements and to make desired adjustments in stand structure and composition. The fir can be harvested at younger ages and smaller sizes before substantial losses to insects and disease take place. A common practice is to cut all merchantable fir. Spruce can be grown for longer rotations. Frank (1977a) reported that the selection system with a 5-year cutting cycle in which fir is heavily cut is the only one that does not show an increase in the number of balsam fir seedlings when compared with shelterwood, commercial clearcutting, and two other less intensive selection system treatments.

Final harvest, timber-stand improvement , thinnings, and, if need be, weeding or cleaning are conducted simultaneously in the selection system. Short cutting cycles of 10 years or less are more efficient than 20 years in eliminating cull trees or poor-risk trees that are likely to become cull (Frank, 1977a). Marking priority for cutting according to Frank and Bjorkbom (1973) should be the following:

1. Poor-risk trees.
2. Poor-quality trees.
3. Slow-growing trees.
4. Less-desirable species.
5. Improvement of spacing.
6. Mature trees of good quality.

It has been recommended that 40 to 50 percent of young, vigorous stands might be harvested safely but it would be risky to remove a similar amount from older ones (Frank and Bjorkbom, 1973). Residual trees in these stands usually respond to release, doubling or perhaps even tripling their growth rate. However, basal area should not be reduced below 75 to 100 square feet per acre. Lower density than this invites excessive losses to windthrow. An increase in the percentage of balsam fir in the stand will probably result in greater losses to wind. Also, residual trees, either spruce or fir, are likely to be blown down if they extend above the general level of the canopy. When all these factors are observed in marking and cutting, losses will be minimized (McLintock, 1954; Westveld, 1953). In fact, losses by windthrow and breakage may be almost as great on uncut areas as in lightly cut stands where 15 to 35 percent of the volume was removed (Grisez, 1954). Site characteristics such as soil depth, moisture regimes, exposure, and wind flow patterns must also be considered in potential windthrow evaluations.

Although this discussion of the relationships among factors influencing windthrow losses in spruce-fir-hardwood has been included with the selection system, the points mentioned are appropriate for any type of partial cutting.

Clearcutting may be desirable when advance reproduction is present and the overstory is comprised mainly of trees above the minimum-commercial-diameter limit. When this is done the advance softwood reproduction should be sufficiently large to withstand competition from less desirable species. Frank (1977b) advised that advance regeneration should average 6 inches in height when competition following harvest is not expected to be severe. Otherwise the advance regeneration should be at least 1 to 2 feet high. Westveld (1953) recommended that spruce and fir reproduction should be 5 feet to assure ultimate dominance on the better sites while 6 to 12 inches is adequate on poor sites.

Defective, low-vigor, mature, and overmature stands may have to be clear-cut to avoid large losses by windthrow that could follow even light partial cutting. Also heavy infestations of insects or disease or severe mortality may make clearcutting desirable.

It is important to note that clearcutting in northern forests lacking well-established advance regeneration may deliver the site to *Rubus* spp. This is true with the northern hardwood as well as the spruce-fir-hardwood type. Once the overstory is reduced below 50 percent of the original basal area of well-stocked old-growth stands, numbers of *Rubus* increase dramatically (Barrett *et al.*, 1962). Often the dense stands of *Rubus*, bracken fern, and less desirable species may hold the site for 10 to 25 years. Ultimately commercially valuable species will force their way through the cover but the rotation will have been prolonged by the time it takes for this to occur. The problem is more severe on some sites than others but to-date the reasons for this are not clear.

The shelterwood system may be used in relatively even-aged or even-sized stands to obtain reproduction prior to final harvest. Timing of the final removal of the shelterwood overstory will depend upon the development of adequate numbers of well-established regeneration. Scarification of the soil during logging should enhance the germination and early growth of spruce and fir. Characteristics of well-established regeneration have been discussed earlier in connection with clearcutting.

Strip clearcutting with mechanized felling, delimbing, and bunching equipment is now being used in the Northeast. This type of logging will likely increase. Frank and Bjorkbom (1973) suggested that when the strips are no wider than one-half the heights of the trees being harvested the method can be considered a variant of the shelterwood method. The wider the strip the more this technique approaches clearcutting. Advantages of mechanized strip cutting are larger volumes yielded per acre covered and less dependence upon a large labor force. A major disadvantage is the inability to adjust the harvesting procedures to secure regeneration in those portions of the strip where reproduction is lacking. Studies in Maine report that seedfall is heaviest in the south and east directions from standing timber. So clearcut strips could be oriented either north-south or east-west, and timber removal should progress to either the west or the north. Numbers of seed appear to be more than adequate for restocking areas up to five chains from the source in a good seed year and may be adequate in a typical year. However, numbers of seed diminished rapidly at more than one chain from the uncut edge (Randall, 1974).

There is some evidence that survival of small advance spruce-fir regeneration is not greatly disturbed by mechanized winter logging. Also the length of the strip is not a factor in stocking if it does not exceed about one-quarter of a mile (Frank and Putnam, 1972). Skidroads longer than one-quarter of a mile increases traffic approaching and at the landing resulting in significant site damage. One study shows that strip clearcutting did not degrade a spruce-fir site in central Maine (Czapowskyj *et al.*, 1977).

Intermediate treatments are important in the management of relatively productive spruce-fir-hardwood stands. Spruce and fir offer a valuable crop, while except for yellow and paper birch, hardwoods that occur in this type are generally inferior in quality and of low value. The two birches often are of higher quality in association with spruce-fir than when they are found with beech and maple.

The desirability of cleaning depends upon the intensity of competition from less valuable species and the benefit to be derived. On the better sites two or even three cleanings at 4- to 5-year intervals may be required to assure dominance of the conifers. On the poorer sites it may not be necessary to clean at all if advance softwood regeneration is at least a foot tall. Generally, when spruce and fir are growing at least 6 inches in height per year, there is little need for cleaning (Westveld, 1953). Frank (1977b) suggested cleaning, when needed, in even-aged stands with an average height about 12 feet and again when competition becomes apparent.

Liberation cutting may result in impressive increases in growth of spruce-fir. Intolerant pioneer species such as aspen and paper birch will not inhibit growth of a softwood understory to the same degree as the very tolerant, long-lived sugar maple and beech. The intolerant species are short-lived and their relatively sparse foliage permits sufficient light to pass through the canopy to maintain vigor in the softwood regeneration. On the other hand full canopies of maple and beech provide intense competition to subordinate conifers. When this situation exists, release of the conifers may increase height growth up to 15 times.

Although seldom used at present, thinnings have a place in spruce-fir-hardwood silviculture. In keeping with the general growth characteristics of tolerant species, basal area may be reduced to about one-half that of fully stocked spruce-fir-hardwood stands without suffering a significant reduction in net growth. Frank (1973) observed that 70- to 75-year-old white spruce released on three or four sides doubled their growth rate. Thinning is also recommended for mixed spruce-fir. The precautions noted previously in regard to windthrow must be observed. Thus, depending upon stand and site conditions, thinnings may remove from as little as 10 percent of the basal area to as much as 50 percent. One of the most common problems in young even-aged stands of spruce and fir is overstocking. When this occurs precommercial thinning or thinning small-sized material is necessary to avoid prolonging the rotation. Early removal of balsam fir would make stands less susceptible to spruce budworm attack. Growing stock guides have been developed for use in stand-density control of even-aged stands (Fig. 2-6).

Except for research there has been little interest to date in fertilization, forest tree improvement, and artificial regeneration in the management of spruce-fir-hardwoods. The use of strip clearcutting, however, and the need to obtain reproduction where it is lacking is now resulting in some planting including the production of containerized seedlings.

The spruce-fir-hardwood type is valuable for wood production, watershed protection, wildlife habitat, recreation, and aesthetics. So far, silvicultural prac-

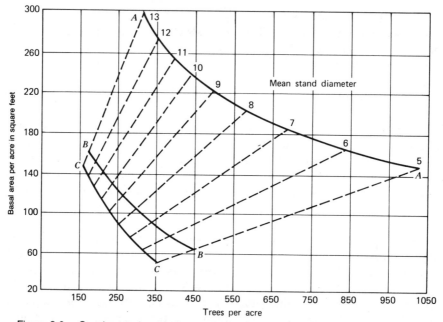

Figure 2-6. Growing stock guide for even-aged spruce-fir, based on the number of trees in the main canopy, average diameter, and basal area per acre. Above the A level is overstocked. Stands between the A and B levels are adequately stocked. Stands between the B and C levels should be adequately stocked in 10 years or less. Stands below the C level are understocked (Frank and Bjorkbom, 1973).

tices have been directed primarily at wood production with minor modifications to accommodate the other benefits. Only in rare instances has the wildlife manager or recreation planner turned to the silviculturists for assistance in the modification or creation of forest environments to suit their purposes. Strong (1977) evaluated deer-yard management in spruce-fir forests of New Hampshire and Maine. He concluded that, although neither even-aged or uneven-aged management systems are exclusively appropriate for both timber and deer, most silvilcultural guidelines are written for timber production and not multiple use.

Susceptibility to Damage.   The spruce budworm is the most damaging insect pest of spruce and fir. This defoliator feeds principally on balsam fir, white spruce, and red spruce, but despite its name prefers fir to spruce. Mature fir of low vitality and stands with a high proportion of fir are particularly susceptible to attack. Periodic outbreaks of budworm defoliate and eventually kill large numbers of trees. The balsam wooly aphid is causing increased damage and mortality throughout the range of the eastern balsam firs.

As noted previously, balsam fir is host to a wide variety of wood-rotting fungi. However, red heart, *Stereum sanguinolentum*, causes most of the trunk rot in live balsam fir trees. Overmature or old-growth red spruce are often infected with red ring rot and red-brown butt rot.

Red spruce and balsam fir are thin barked and highly susceptible to fire damage. Fires of only moderate intensity usually eliminate the existing spruce and fir, so fire prevention is a must in the management of many-aged stands or during the rotation of even-aged ones. There is some evidence that prescribed burning may be useful in regenerating over-aged forests.

The softwoods found in the spruce-fir-hardwood type are relatively free of deer damage. Red spruce is a starvation diet and, although balsam is sometimes browsed, other species are normally preferred. Except for damage to the birches, deer browse in this type does more good than harm, serving as a natural means of hardwood control.

Insects, diseases, and animals in addition to the above-mentioned cause damage to species found in the spruce-fir-hardwood type. However, those listed are considered to be the most important.

Northern Hardwood Type Group

Place in Ecological Succession. American beech, yellow birch, and sugar maple (Fig. 2-7) provide the base of the northern hardwood type group that is variously supplemented with an admixture of other species in harmony with environmental conditions. One or more of the primary constituents of this type may yield to other species in certain localities. Yet, except for the southern part of the region, beech, birch, and sugar maple give general character to the hardwood forest of the Northeast.

Red spruce is a natural associate of this type throughout the northern part of the region. White pine may be prominent on xerophytic sites. Hemlock and red maple are common associates. On mesophytic sites, especially in the southern localities, yellow-poplar, red and white oak, basswood, black cherry, and white ash may become important components of the stand. In the drier southeastern part of the region, pitch pine, hickories, and oaks, especially chestnut and scarlet, are important associates. As a consequence of forest destruction or heavy cutting, aggressive pioneer species such as aspen, paper birch, or pin cherry, may occupy the site or be found in mixtures with the other species.

Because of environmental conditions mainly related to amount and distribution of precipitation and soils, the northern hardwood type of the Northeastern Region differs somewhat from its counterpart in the Lake States. This is an important consideration in comparing hardwood silvicultural practices in the two regions. The range of red spruce does not extend into the Lake States. Beech is found only as far west as eastern Wisconsin. Sugar maple, yellow birch, and hemlock are found throughout the Lake States Region, but in western Minnesota they are of decreasing commercial importance and may be absent or regarded as botanic oddities. Conversely, in that area basswood becomes more important. The effects of the east-west climatic gradient on the forest associations are illustrated in Table 3-2. Further, as a result of severe

Figure 2-7.   A stand of sugar maple on the Bartlett Experimental Forest (U.S. For. Serv.).

forest fires in the late 1800s, aspen and other pioneer species occupied large areas in the Lake States. Some of these stands are still in early stages of succession.

Significant aspects of northern hardwood ecology have already been discussed in connection with spruce-fir-hardwood (p. 40). This integrated treatment is desirable because it reflects the natural interweaving of these two type groups in many forested areas.

Growth Rates. Several studies have reported growth rates of well-stocked northern hardwood stands. These predictions range from a maximum of about 400 board feet per acre per year on the best sites to about 200 board feet on good sites. Growth of uneven-aged stands is estimated as 200 board feet per acre per year of sawtimber and veneer logs plus 15 cubic feet of pulpwood (Leak et al., 1969). According to this report peak gross basal-area growth occurs with 80 to 100 square feet of basal area per acre in trees 5.0 inches d.b.h. and over. Solomon (1977a) noted that production (net increase) in even-aged stands of sawtimber is greatest with 80 square feet of basal area per acre, 30 percent of which is sawtimber size. In uneven-aged stands he recommended 60 square feet of basal area per acre with 45 to 60 percent in sawtimber for intensively managed stands, and 80 square feet with 45 percent in sawtimber for less intensively managed stands. Average annual diameter growth under these conditions would be about 0.10 to 0.13 inch for sawtimber and 0.09 to 0.12 for poletimber in uneven-aged stands (Solomon, 1977b).

Forty-five- to 60-year-old northern hardwood stands on good sites in the Lake States produced 300 board feet (Scribner) per acre per year. Diameter growth rate on sawlog sized trees may average 0.2 inch per year with stand densities below 75 square feet of basal area per acre. Individual-tree selection seemed well suited to satisfy owners' objectives for high-quality sugar maple (Erdmann and Oberg, 1973).

Solomon (1977c) has developed a growth model of natural and silviculturally treated even-aged northern hardwood stands beginning at the sapling stage and continuing through the final harvest cut. The model employs several thinning strategies and incorporates growth projections, thinning operations, paper birch-aspen mortality, and harvesting.

Site index curves have been prepared by stem analysis for 13 hardwood species growing in northern Wisconsin and Upper Michigan. They permit comparisons among species and demonstrate that height growth curves for these species are polymorphic and differ, over time, from the typical site indices based upon harmonized curves (Carmean, 1978).

It needs to be emphasized that the figures mentioned above are the results of management and are rarely realized in existing untended depleted hardwood forests. Average annual production at present is likely well below 100 board feet or 40 cubic feet per acre per year.

Rotation Age or Size. The determination of rotation age may be based upon optimizing returns from the forest investment, culmination of mean-annual increment, or other means. When financial considerations are the guide, recognition must be given to the tremendous diversity in the economic worth of individual trees. This diversity is caused first by the wide variation in grade yield from tree to tree and among species; and second, by the range of values among the several lumber grades and among the same grade of different species. Lumber grade recovery in hardwoods is related to species, size of bole, and pattern of defects in the tree. These several factors have been incorporated into a quality index for selected eastern hardwood species (Mendel and Peirsol, 1977). To illustrate, the range of values among species in the Northeast using a log grade 1 and a scaling diameter inside bark of 18 inches, the quality index for sugar maple is 1.06, beech, 0.89, birch 1.18, and soft maple 1.05. Thus for the same log size and grade birch is about one-third more valuable than beech. For the same species a 24-inch sugar maple log grade 1 has a quality index of 1.16 while that for a log grade 3 drops to 0.76.

A study in the Lake States shows the greatest proportion of value increase may come from grade improvement. Over a 10-year period with a diameter growth of 1.8 inches, a ½-log height increase, and a 1 grade improvement in a 16-inch, 2-log, butt log grade 2 tree, 44 percent of the $12.35 value increase would be contributed by grade improvement, 35 percent from diameter growth, 12 percent by height, and 9 percent from combined effect of diameter growth and grade change (Godman and Mendel, 1978).

Thus both species and quality play a significant role in the manipulation of hardwood stands to maximize economic returns. Individual stems must be evaluated. It requires skilled judgment to decide when a relatively good stem of a less commercially valuable species should be retained rather than a defective tree of a more valuable species. Because of this, marking in hardwoods is likely to continue to be an art rather than an exact science for some time to come.

Notwithstanding the complications raised by the wide range in value, product, and growth rates, attempts have been made to establish rotation ages or sizes for northern hardwoods. One of the more recent guides is provided by Leak et al. (1969). Based upon financial maturity they recommend the following d.b.h. tree-size objectives: yellow birch one log 16 to 19 inches, two logs 18 to 22 inches; sugar and soft maple one log 16 to 17 inches, two logs 18 to 20 inches; beech one log 15 to 16 inches, two logs 18 to 19 inches; paper birch one log 11 to 15 inches, two logs 12 to 15 inches; and white ash one log 15 inches, two logs 15 to 18 inches. Tubbs (1977a) noted that most northern hardwoods are economically mature when they reach 20 to 24 inches d.b.h. Interest rates used in these computations are important in determining the length of rotation. Although a highly valuable tree, paper birch is relatively short-lived, reaching maturity in 60 to 75 years; beyond this age the species generally deteriorates rapidly.

A study by Blum (1961) revealed the difficulty of fixing rotation age in uneven-aged forests. He reports a difference of 115 years between the oldest and youngest tree of 14 inches d.b.h. in one stand.

Cultural Practices.   Northern hardwood stands range from even-aged to all-aged in structure. Consequently they lend themselves to either even-aged or uneven-aged management. The decision about which one to use depends upon existing stand structure and objectives of ownership.

Often old-growth stands are multistoried rather than many-aged with a large number of size classes. In multistoried stands the forest floor may be covered with sugar maple reproduction less than 1 foot tall but more than 10 years old. It is not unusual to find 50,000 to 100,000 maple seedlings per acre and practi-

cally no beech or birch. In the sapling sizes the beech may be the most prominent (Barrett *et al.*, 1962). The lack of the relatively high-value yellow birch and
sugar maple in the intermediate size classes and the presence of low-value
beech ready to take advantage of any openings that might occur presents the
silviculturist with a difficult problem. This is compounded when the advance
regeneration of sugar maple is relatively old and of poor vigor. There is considerable evidence that the storied condition is the result of deer browse (Tierson
et al., 1966). Deer prefer the sugar maple and birch and rarely eat the beech.

With less pressure from deer (densities of fewer than 1 deer per 40 acres)
old-growth stands may develop a wide range of size classes with a better representation of sugar maple in the pole and sapling size material. However, the
less tolerant but more valuable yellow birch will be found mainly in the overstory.

Even-aged stands may occur on old fields and elsewhere as a consequence of
forest destruction or clearing. A full assortment of types ranging from valuable
white pine or northern hardwoods to worthless aspen (off site), gray birch, or
pin cherry may occupy those areas. Where the sites have not been depleted
and a seed source is available, excellent stands of high-value species are growing vigorously. In fact some of the best hardwood stands found in the Northeast
are on old fields where only limited farming took place following clearing.
These particular stands evidence some advantages of even-aged management of
northern hardwoods for sawtimber production. Also large openings have permitted the high-value paper birch to become established. Conversely site depletion resulting from severe fires or exploitive agriculture has usually given
rise to slow-growing and/or poorly stocked stands. Large areas of misshapen
and widely spaced short aspen with an understory of bracken fern can be found
on Adirondack lands that burned more than half a century ago.

The wide range in stand conditions found in the hardwoods of the Northeast
results in a variety of appropriate cultural practices. The practice selected
should be ecologically sound and meet the objectives of ownership.

The appropriate use of clearcutting in the management of northern
hardwoods has been reported by a number of investigators during the past
decade. Clearcutting requires the complete removal of all trees more than 2
inches d.b.h. or even less. This is in contrast to commercial clearcutting, that
is, the removal of only those trees with a market value (Fig. 2-8).

Clearcutting may be desirable if well-established advance reproduction is
present in sufficient quantity to assure regeneration of the new stand. When
advance regeneration is used it must be sufficiently tall and vigorous to outgrow
invading pioneer species and shrubs. The term well-established is important.
Experience shows that regeneration that is not well-established usually cannot
endure the shock of heavy opening and either dies or is overcome by competition from shrubs. Sugar maple regeneration should be examined to see if it is
only superficially rooted in the humus rather than mineral soil or if repeated
browsing or competition has resulted in low vitality. These conditions could
lead to heavy mortality in the advance regeneration following clearcutting.

Also clearcutting might be desirable if the overstory is long overmature,

Figure 2-8. The result of a commercial clearcutting in a high-value old-growth northern hardwood stand. The amount of worthless overburden that would occupy a large proportion of the area unless remedial action is taken is evident. Merchantability limits were set fairly low for this cut, so conditions are better than those usually expected.

comprised largely of stems above the merchantable size limit, and defective. In this case it is a question of saving what is present, before additional losses are caused by fungi, insects, and weather. Measures to regenerate the stand should precede or accompany the harvest if advance reproduction is inadequate. This could involve elimination of undesirable advance reproduction, site preparation, provision for seed source, and/or planting.

Clearcutting favors the less tolerant species as compared to light partial cutting. With site preparation and a seed source, regeneration will be composed roughly of ²/₅ intolerants, ¹/₅ intermediates, and ²/₅ tolerants (Leak *et al.*, 1969). Thus clearcutting will encourage reproduction of more valuable species such as yellow and paper birch and white ash.

An influx of *Rubus* spp. and other herbaceous material invariably follows clearcutting on most hardwood sites in the region. Also cutting small stems results in considerable sprout growth. In time, regeneration of desirable tree species pushes its way through this cover. Marquis (1967) reported that 30 years after clearcutting an old-growth stand in New Hampshire, aspen, paper birch, and white ash, had become established as dominant species with red maple, yellow birch, sugar maple, and beech as codominants or in the lower crown classes. Heights ranged from 32 to 43 feet. Nyland and Irish (1971) noted that three years following clearcutting adequate regeneration of desirable species was growing up through berry bushes that were waist high. In contrast to these studies, some practioners contend that severe competition from the berries, hobble bush, and other woody plants will prolong rotations by 10 years or more. Clearcutting of immature stands may lead to a high proportion of weed species, especially *Rubus* spp. and pin cherry. Although these weed species do not prevent regeneration of commercially desirable species, they do retard the growth (Leak *et al.*, 1969). Red maple is a prolific sprouter with multistem clumps often providing severe competition to more desirable regeneration (Solomon and Blum, 1967).

Germination and early growth of some northern hardwood seedlings is enhanced by site preparation. This is especially true for both yellow and paper birch. A mixing of mineral soil with organic material provides a more productive site than where the humus layer is stripped off the surface.

The shelterwood method is becoming recognized as one of the most reliable systems for establishing even-aged stands of northern hardwoods. This technique opens the stand sufficiently to encourage regeneration of less tolerant species. The cut is heavy enough so that site preparation can be undertaken to stimulate the germination and establishment of certain valuable species such as yellow and paper birch, white ash, and white pine. The residual trees following the first cut provide some protection from damaging late-spring frosts and high summer temperatures as well as discourage the encroachment of weed species into the area. The importance of this early protection for a number of species is well recognized. If the shelterwood is selected of high-quality stems, valuable increment should be added before time of final harvest and the reserving of these kinds of trees for seed pays heed to proper genetical principles.

The shelterwood method is particularly suitable when the advance reproduction is absent or to be eliminated and replaced with a more desirable type. To illustrate, if beech is strongly represented in the subordinate crown classes it might be killed, concurrent with the regeneration cut and site preparation. The same action should be taken with regard to advance regeneration of low vigor or poor quality.

Godman and Tubbs (1973) provided guides for the use of the shelterwood in Lake States forests. They advised that the stand should be more than 40 years old for seed production, the first cut should admit 40 percent of sunlight, marking of trees to be cut should be from below, residual trees should be vigorous with a full crown, and yellow birch should not be left because of its susceptibility to environmental changes and the high incidence of sapsucker attack on open grown birch. The overstory should be harvested as soon as the new seedlings are well established. Well established means deep root systems, ability to respond to full sunlight, and advantage over competing vegetation. These characteristics will be found when the regeneration is about 3 feet in height.

Patch and strip clearcutting are also used in the harvest and regeneration of northern hardwoods. The present emphasis on strip clearcutting is due to the increasing use of mechanized fellers and bunchers. Whole trees are chipped at the landing. With current practices the strips are relatively narrow, one or two chains wide, and about one-third of the stand is cut. Patch clearcutting approaches the characteristics and results associated with clearcutting, discussed previously, as the size of the area harvested grows larger.

Individual-tree and group selection has long been used with the northern hardwoods. The cutting of individual trees or small groups of two or three trees favors the tolerant species, namely, beech, sugar maple, hemlock, and spruce (Leak and Filip, 1975). Peak gross basal-area growth occurs with 80 to 100 square feet of basal area growing stock in trees over 5 inches d.b.h. (Leak et al., 1969). Filip (1973) recommended a 10- to 20-year cutting cycle. The optimum stocking in the Lake States of northern hardwoods for maximum board foot growth of high-quality sawlogs is recommended as 70 square feet of basal area per acre in trees 10 inches d.b.h. and over when the cutting cycle does not exceed 15 years (Tubbs, 1977a). Tubbs (1977b) reported that selective cutting in an old-growth forest reduced the average age of 20- to 24-inch trees by 100 years and that of 4-inch trees from 100 to 48 years.

One of the major advantages of partial cutting is aesthetics. A residual stand continuously covers the area and disturbance from logging is not so apparent. Also this type of harvest provides repeated yields for small ownerships. Production of high-quality and veneer logs is often the goal with individual-tree selection. There is one serious potential problem with this method. During past times, "high grading" has been done under the guise of individual-tree selection resulting in serious forest degradation.

Group selection in which small areas, 0.1 to 0.6 acre in size, are cut has sometimes given excellent results. Such cuts have encouraged the establishment of the more valuable but less tolerant species such as yellow birch and white ash.

Group selection with groups averaging ½ acre in size, practiced in a 114-acre tract in New England, has resulted in a stand with $1/3$ to $1/4$ of trees in d.b.h. classes from 4 to 12 inches comprised of yellow birch and other species intermediate in tolerance. Diameter distribution closely follows an inverse J-shaped curve with the average q between numbers of trees in successive 2-inch-diameter classes of 1.6 (Leak and Filip, 1977). However, difficulty in relocating patches makes it impractical to use this method with area control.

Thus it is obvious that landowners have a variety of options for harvesting northern hardwoods and obtaining regeneration. Each method has its advantages and disadvantages. Reproduction almost invariably occurs following harvest. The time of establishment and the composition of the reproduction will vary according to the method used.

Financial returns have been calculated for harvest in one mature beech-birch-maple stand in New England. A diameter-limit cut yielded the highest conversion surplus $22.89 per cubit of products, followed by clearcut with $13.37, then selection down to 5-inch diameter with improvement cut $9.14, and lastly patch cutting of $1/10$ to $2/3$ acre with improvement cut $8.50 (Filip, 1967). Although the dollar values are out of date they still provide a comparison among the several methods.

Timber-stand improvement is indispensable in the directed rehabilitation of the forests of the Northeast. The wide extent of poor hardwood growing stock makes this no little problem. The land is burdened with culls, defective trees, and low-value species. Elimination of poor material is a major hardwood silvicultural problem. Improvement cuts can be heavy, removing up to 50 percent of the volume without significantly disturbing the forest environment to the detriment of the residual-tree growth rate and advance regeneration (Farnsworth and Barrett, 1970). Guidelines have been prepared for selection marking in hardwoods that combines stand improvement with financial maturity (Trimble, et al., 1974). Martin amd Rudolph (1975) pointed out that timber stand improvement may be more rewarding financially than thinning.

There is ample evidence of the stimulation of individual-tree growth rate in northern hardwoods by thinning. Filip (1977) reported thinning in a 25-year-old stand of paper birch increased basal-area growth of crop trees in a 3-year period by 100 percent. A Lakes States study in a 40-year-old stand showed yellow birch diameter growth was more than doubled through crown thinning. Dominants showed the greatest response. Thinning apparently had no significant effect on epicormic sprouting of sugar maple (Books and Tubbs, 1970). Crop-tree thinning in even-aged stands of yellow birch saplings increased basal area growth over controls by 100 percent (Hannah, 1978). Hannah (1974a) has shown that partially or fully released trees have more water available at lower tension than stems that are not released. These results join the many previous reports of appreciable increasing in growth rate following thinning. A stocking guide based upon number of trees per acre in the main canopy, average d.b.h., and basal area per acre has been developed to assist the silviculturist (Fig. 2-9).

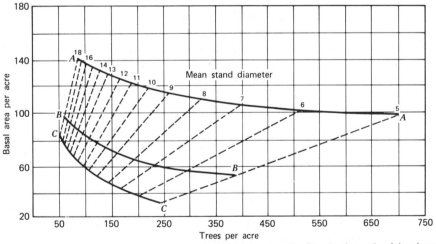

Figure 2-9. Stocking chart for even-aged northern hardwoods. Stands above the A level are overstocked, between the A and B levels adequately stocked, between the B and C levels should be adequately stocked in 10 years, below the C level understocked. Thinnings should be considered when stocking is at least midway between the B and A levels (Filip, 1973).

Precommercial thinning is now being given serious consideration in silviculture of northern hardwoods. The returns from the treatment should be sufficient to pay the cost. When this prerequisite appears to be likely, precommercial thinning should be made as early as possible after stand establishment, probably when mean stand diameter is between 1 and 2 inches (Hocker, 1977). There is some evidence that thinning yellow birch 7 to 11 feet tall results in a significant increase in height growth (Hannah, 1974b). Weeding in a 7-year-old paper birch–quaking aspen stand of fire origin resulted in a paper birch stand in contrast with the untreated control that was essentially pure aspen with a few overtopped birch 24 years following treatment (LaBonte and Nash, 1978).

Pruning has gained little popularity to date in the silviculture of northern hardwoods. However, it has been noted that less growing stock would be required if crop trees were pruned. Also with yellow birch, pruning may increase log value and reduce decay (Solomon and Blum, 1977).

There has been little planting of hardwoods in the Northeast and when this has been done it usually failed. The use of fertilizers has been limited. Although there is some concern about site depletion resulting from whole-tree logging and chipping there is little definite information about nutrient cycling and possible nutrient deficiencies.

Susceptibility to Damage. Hardwoods generally and northern hardwoods in particular are very susceptible to changes in the environment following heavy cutting. The primary cause of death of residual trees is the exposure to which they are suddenly subjected, although they may have appeared vigorous prior to cutting (Boyce, 1948).

Beech is damaged by low temperatures and frost kill. Frost crack is the cause for considerable defect. Beech bark disease, caused principally by the fungus *Nectria coccinea* var. *faginata* that infects minute feeding wounds in the bark made by the beech scale is the most lethal disease of beech throughout the region. Damage is especially great in dominant and codominant crown classes.

Birch dieback and post-logging decadence, maladies of yellow birch associated with changes in the environment, have been especially damaging. Trees weakened by birch dieback are susceptible to attack of the bronze birch borer, and this secondary assault often ensures the death of the tree.

Nectria canker causes considerable damage to hardwoods, particularly yellow birch. *Hypoxylon* canker is severe on aspen.

Significant heart rot fungi include *Fomes igniarius,* the most common cause of cull in aspen, maple, beech, and other hardwoods; *Fomes connatus,* found primarily on sugar and red maples; *Ustilina vulgaris,* a frequent cause of butt rot in sugar maple, beech, and other hardwoods; and *Polyporus glomoratus* and *Poria obliqua,* which cause serious losses in beech, sugar and red maple, and yellow and white birch (Silverborg, 1954).

The sugar maple borer permits entry of discoloration and decay organisms. Any form of partial cutting results in some damage to residual trees inviting decay. The gypsy moth has caused considerable losses to oaks in the southern part of the region. Mention has been made earlier of the Dutch elm disease. Other insect pests, defoliators and wood borers, and fungi cause losses from time to time.

Deer, mice, voles, and rabbits cause some damage to northern hardwoods. Deer browse may be severe on yellow birch, sugar maple, and white ash; moderate on aspen, black cherry, hemlock, and white pine; and low on beech.

White Pine-Hemlock-Hardwood Type Group

Place in Ecological Succession.   White pine was the preeminent species most eagerly sought by the loggers in the original forests of the Northeast. Generally it occurred with other softwoods, notably hemlock, in a mixed forest that was predominantly hardwood. Majestic individual pine stems often towered by as much as 50 feet above surrounding mature hardwoods.

In the virgin forest, white pine became dominant only on soils inclined to be droughty such as eskers (Fig. 2-10), kames, outwash plains, and the shores and terraces of old glacial lakes. Elsewhere the development of stands heavy with white pine was the consequence of forest catastrophes.

People were, to a great extent, responsible for the creation of the eastern white pine region. The farm clearings they carved out of the wilderness and subsequently abandoned were often reclaimed by white pine forests on the coarser soils. This generation of old-field stands became the backbone of the eastern white pine industry in the late 1800s. White pine is still the most abundant species in New Hampshire (Kingsley, 1976a).

For the most part the forest communities largely comprised of white pine are transient, occupying a subclimax ecological niche. On relatively coarse, droughty soils the white and red pines might comprise major portions of the climax forest. The ultimate forest on mesophytic sites would consist of the more tolerant hardwoods and hemlock.

Cultural Practices.   Cultural practices relating to white pine-hemlock-hardwoods are discussed in detail in Chapter 3.

Oak Type Group

Place in Ecological Succession.   The oak type considered in this chapter is prominent in southern New York and parts of Connecticut, Massachusetts, and Rhode Island. Located close to early settlements, those forests have been among the most intensively used and widely abused in this country. Repeated cuttings have eliminated much of the softwood components and converted the high hardwood forest to coppice. As a consequence today there are large areas of sprout forest dating from the cessation of fuelwood cutting early in this century.

The prevailing forests are secondary communities, usually even-aged, in which as many as 30 species may be present. The most important oaks are

Figure 2-10.   A natural unmanaged white pine stand about 150 years old, containing 40,000 board feet per acre growing on the crest of an esker.

white, red, black, scarlet, and chestnut. Other important hardwoods are: beech; sugar and red maple; hickory species; white, red, and black ash; yellow and black birch; yellow-poplar; basswood; and butternut. Hemlock is the most abundant softwood at present. Pitch and white pine, and redcedar and Atlantic white-cedar were other important conifers found in the original forest.

The statement has been made that not a single species finds its optimum habitat in this locality (Hawley and Hawes, 1912). This implies that a wide range of "climax" associations may be encountered. The intermediate to very intolerant pitch pines and oaks that grow on xerophytic sites lay claim to the thin-soiled, dry, poor sites for considerable time. On the better soils of the lower slopes, coves, and valley bottoms, hemlock, sugar maple, beech, yellow-poplar, and red oak may be prominent. Lutz (1928) suggested that the hemlock-hardwood association might be the climatic climax on a wide range of sites in this area.

Cultural Practices.   Cultural practices relating to oak-hickory are discussed in detail in Chapter 4. However, a unique feature of the oak type listed in this chapter is the role played by hemlock. The very tolerant eastern hemlock, although once drastically reduced by cutting and fire, seems to be recuperating and very well may hold the key to increased forest productivity in the area. Smith (1955) believed that hemlock attains its optimum development in a zone that includes southern New England. He advocated a form of silviculture in this area that utilizes the ability of hemlock to become established beneath cover, persist for long periods of time even under suppression, and then respond to release.

FOREST BENEFITS

Forests in this region contribute significantly to the economy and well being of society in a variety of ways. Forests provide multibenefits principally because of their proximity to large populations. Although the original intention in this chapter revision was to show how various silvicultural practices related to the spruce-fir-hardwood and northern hardwood type groups would contribute to these benefits, examples were too limited to make this possible.

Silviculture in this region is directed toward timber production with other benefits largely incidental to this activity. However, increasing public use of the forests, public involvment in forest management decisions, and changes in forest ownership patterns will likely rearrange future priorities. The silvicul-turist must become more concerned with the manipulation of the forest to create environments that will satisfy a variety of objectives. Even though wa-tershed protection, wildlife habitat development, or creation of forest recrea-tion environments may in some places in the future become the primary objec-tive of the silviculturist, this by no means rules out timber production. Thus, the term "multiple use" takes on real meaning in this region. The brief discus-sion that follows provides some idea of the importance of various forest benefits and their relation to silviculture.

Recognition of the changing role of forests in the Northeast was made by Blum (1977) at the symposium on intensive culture of northern forest types. He wrote: "There is no doubt that we face a new era in the management of north-ern forests. The production of wood products is no longer the primary objective of many owners, and increased pressure for social values of our forests is being felt by all landowners." However, during the same symposium Baskerville (1977) noted that although many benefits flow from the forest, 95 percent of the discussion of intensive culture of northern forest types was concerned with the production of wood. He attributed the fact that the profession had been largely ineffectual in the promotion of intensive forest management in northern forests to failure to answer questions in people's minds about why various silvicultural manipulations were desirable. These comments give some perspective to the following discussion of the benefits provided by forests in the Northeast.

Aesthetics and Recreation

Noyes (1969) advised that an objective of silviculture along highways should be to develop and maintain the attractive aspects of a vigorous, productive, well-managed forest, which provides aesthetic as well as other traditional multiuse values. Further, bringing good forest practices down to the roadside is an excellent educational tool to use with the public. Light and frequent harvest cuttings, weeding, thinnings, and pruning operations should be tempered with a concern for aesthetics. Richards (1975) emphasized the role of the silviculturist in green-space forestry. Here the forester's expertise is clearly needed in the development of complex self-monitoring, vegetation systems that meet a variety of urban-related needs.

Recreation is big business in the Northeast. In 1970 it was estimated to be a 450-million-dollar industry in Maine (Ferguson and Kingsley, 1972). Kingsley (1974) wrote that in southern New England the abundance of forested land, coupled with adequate rainfall, provides the area with a favorable summer climate attractive to vacationers. In Vermont there were 2.8 million skier days at the state's 70 developed ski areas during the 1974–1975 winter. The same winter there were 34,715 snowmobiles registered (Kingsley, 1977). As in other northern states, the use of snowmobiles has been the source of much controversy and concern. In New Hampshire there were 275 camping areas in 1974, 244 of which were privately owned. During that year almost 4 million people visited facilities operated by the Division of Parks. There were 2.4 million skier days in the winter of 1974–1975 (Kingsley, 1976a). An analysis by Foster and Dahlfred (1973) has ranked recreation as the fifth most important industry in New Hampshire. Recreation uses of forest land are also prominent in New York State and southern New England.

Water

Forested watersheds in the Northeast offer protection against downstream flooding and high sediment loads in the streams. In this highly industrialized region with its large population quality of water is important.

Although a number of persons have investigated the relationship between silvicultural practices and water quality in the Northeast, one of the most recent reports is by Hornbeck and Federer (1975). Among their conclusions are : progressive strip cutting with one-third of the watershed harvested at 2-year intervals increased streamflow appreciably especially during summer; regrowth would limit increased water yield to 3 to 4 years; cutting 25 1-acre patches is not likely to produce as much water as a 25-acre clearcut; single-tree selection is less effective than heavier cuts in increasing water yield; there is little likelihood of flooding if no more than 25 percent of an area is clearcut; none of the stream water from timber-harvested areas had nutrient concentrations higher than drinking water standards, but some localized eutrophication of small streams may occur after clearcutting; New England may be more susceptible than other areas to the nutrient leaching problem, due largely to coarse-textured soils and their low ability to hold nutrients, particularly when plant cover is lacking; and stream flow from a hardwood-forested watershed may be 2 to 3 inches greater than from one with conifer cover, the increase occurring in the dormant season. Patric (1977) described practices that will minimize soil erosion in harvesting operations. He concluded that little erosion results from most logging activities but that the most serious problem comes from logging roads.

Wildlife

Forests provide habitat for both nongame and game species. There is considerable evidence that populations of big game, especially deer, have increased since the turn of the century. Shaw (1977) suggested that intensive timber management can be made compatible with suitable habitat for wildlife if silvicultural operations provide diversity in plant communities (i.e., timber types) and interspersion of these diverse communities occurs in place and time. Intensive cultural operations can be made to provide the right.mixture of diversity and interspersion to serve the priority needs of the landowner. Morton (1976) and Shaw (1969) described techniques for improving wildlife habitat. The concern for deer wintering yards mainly in the spruce-fir-hardwood type influences silvicultural practices on both public and private forest lands. This appears to be the one instance where wildlife habitat may take priority over timber production.

Wood

During the past 10 years the harvest of saw timber has increased by 3 billion board feet and the harvest of cordwood by 5 million cords (Simmons, 1976). In 1958 New York State led all others in the nation in the absolute amount of employment and value added generated by timber. In 1967 employment based upon timber in New York provided the equivalent of 224,240 full-time jobs (Burghart, 1974). Irland (1975) reported that forest products in New England are a 3.2-billion-dollar industry. In 1971 New England produced 2 percent of the nation's lumber, 6 percent of the pulpwood, 14.2 percent of the paper, and 2.7 percent of the paperboard. One out of every 15 persons employed in manufacturing was in a forest industry. In Maine this figure was about one out of every four.

Thus, it must be recognized that the forest products industries are a vital part of the economy of the Northeast. This provides the silviculturist a real challenge—how to produce the raw material for an industry that is highly important to the region and at the same time enhance the yield of a variety of nontimber benefits.

BIBLIOGRAPHY

Armstrong, F. H. 1975. The valuation of Vermont forest land 1968 to 1974. *Univ. Vt. Dept. For.*, Burlington. 8 pp.

Barrett, J. W., C. E. Farnsworth, and W. Rutherford, Jr. 1962. Logging effects on regeneration and certain aspects of microclimate in northern hardwoods. *J. For.* 60:630–639.

Baskerville, G. 1977. Let's call the whole thing off! In Proc. Symp. Intensive Culture of Northern Forest Types. *USDA For. Serv. Gen. Tech. Rep. NE-29.* 356 pp.

Blum, B. M. 1961. Age-size relationships in all-aged northern hardwoods. *USDA For. Serv. Res. Note NE-125.* 3 pp.

Blum, B. M. 1977. Foreword. In Proc. Symp. Intensive Culture of Northern Forest Types. *USDA For. Serv. Gen. Tech. Rep. NE-29.* 356 pp.

Books, D. J., and C. H. Tubbs. 1970. Relation of light to epicormic sprouting in sugar maple. *USDA For. Serv. Res. Note NC-93.* 2 pp.

Bowen, A. T., Jr. 1964. The relation of tree and stand characteristics to basal area growth of red spruce trees in partially cut stands in eastern Maine. *Univ. Maine Agr. Exp. Stn. Bull. 627.* Orono. 34 pp.

Boyce, J. S. 1948. *Forest pathology.* 2nd ed. McGraw-Hill Book Co., Inc., New York. 550 pp.

Braun, E. L. 1950. *Deciduous forests of eastern North America.* The Blakiston Co., Philadelphia, 596 pp.

Burghart, H. E. 1974. The role of timber in New York's economy. *North. Logger Timber Process.* 22(10):33, 66–69.

Burghart, H. E. 1974. The role of timber in New York's economy. *North. Logger Timber Process.* 22(10):33, 66–69.

Canham, O. 1971. Timber ownership and supply in New York. Ph.D. dissertation. State Univ. Coll. For., Syracuse, 301 pp.

Carmean, W. H. 1978. Site index curves for northern hardwoods in northern Wisconsin and upper Michigan. *USDA For. Serv. Res. Pap. NC-160.* 16 pp

Czapowskyj, M. M., R. V. Rourke, and R. M. Frank. 1977. Strip clearcutting did not degrade the site in a spruce-fir forest in central Maine. *USDA For. Serv. Res. Pap. NE-367.* 8 pp.

Donahue, R. L. 1940. *Tree growth as related to soil morphology.* N.Y. (Cornell) Agr. Exp. Stn., Ithaca. 44 pp.

Erdmann, G. G., and R. R. Oberg. 1973. Fifteen-year results from six cutting methods in second-growth northern hardwoods. *USDA For. Serv. Res. Pap. NC-100.* 12 pp.

Farnsworth, C. E., and J. W. Barrett. 1970. Responses to silvicultural treatment of the northern hardwoods type five years after logging. In *Proc. Sixth World For. Cong., Madrid.* 3:2338–2343.

Ferguson, H., and E. Mayer. 1970. The timber resources of New York. *USDA For. Serv. Resour. Bull. NE-20.* 193 pp.

Ferguson, H., and P. Kingsley. 1972. The timber resources of Maine. *USDA For. Serv. Resour. Bull. NE-26.* 129 pp.

Filip, S. M. 1967. Harvesting costs and returns under 4 cutting methods in mature beech-birch-maple stands in New England. *USDA For. Serv. Res. Pap. NE-87.* 14 pp.

Filip, S. M. 1973. Cutting and cultural methods for managing northern hardwoods in the Northeastern United States. *USDA For. Serv. Gen. Tech. Rep. NE-5.* 5 pp.

Filip, S. M. 1977. High yield silviculture for northern hardwoods. In *High-Yield Forestry. 1975 Ann. Mtg. Soc. Prot. N.H. For.* Concord. 16 pp.

Foster, B. B., and V. R. Dahlfred. 1973. New Hampshire's outdoor recreation activities and their role in the state's economy. *N. H. Agr. Exp. Stn. Res. Rep. 29.* Durham. 29 pp.

Fowells, H. A. 1965. Silvics of forest trees of the United States. *USDA For. Serv. Agr. Hdb. 271.* 762 pp.

Frank, R. M. 1973. The course of growth response in released white spruce—10-year results. *USDA For. Serv. Res. Pap. NE-258.* 6 pp.

Frank, R. M. 1977a. Indications of silvicultural potential from long-term experiments in spruce-fir types. In Proc. Symp. Intensive Culture of Northern Forest Types. *USDA For. Serv. Gen. Tech. Rep. NE-29.* 356 pp.

Frank, R. M. 1977b. Silvicultural options for obtaining high yields in spruce-fir. In *High-Yield Forestry. 1975 Ann. Mtg. Soc. Prot. N. H. For.* Concord. 16 pp.

Frank, R. M., and E. L. Putnam. 1972. Seedling survival in spruce-fir after mechanized tree harvesting in strips. *USDA For. Serv. Res. Pap. NE-224.* 16 pp.

Frank, R. M., and J. C. Bjorkbom. 1973. A silvicultural guide for spruce-fir in the Northeast. *USDA For. Serv. Gen. Tech. Rep. NE-6.* 29 pp.

Godman, R. M. 1957. Silvical characteristics of sugar maple. *USDA For. Serv. Lake States For. Exp. Stn. Pap. 50.* 24 pp.

Godman, R. M., and J. Brooks. 1971. Influence of stand density on stem quality in pole-size northern hardwoods. *USDA For. Serv. Res. Pap. NC-54.* 7 pp.

Godman, R. M., and C. H. Tubbs. 1973. Establishing even-aged northern hardwood regeneration by the shelterwood method—a preliminary guide. *USDA For. Serv. Res. Pap. NC-99.* 9 pp.

Godman, R. M., and J. J. Mendel. 1978. Economic values for growth and grade changes of sugar maple in the Lake States. *USDA For. Serv. Res. Pap. NC-155.* 16 pp.

Grisez, T. J. 1954. Hurricane damage on Penobscot Experimental Forest Experiment Station. *USDA For. Serv. Northeast. For. Exp. Stn. Res. Note 39.* 1 p.

Hamilton, L. S. 1971. Aesthetic forestry? Yes! Say a Cornell professor's new findings. *North. Logger Timber Process.* 19(7):38.

Hamilton, L., J. Rader, and D. Smith. 1973. Aesthetics and owner attitudes toward suburban forest practices. *North. Logger Timber Process.* 22(3):18−19, 38−39.

Hannah, P. R. 1974a. Crop tree thinning increases availability of soil water to small yellow birch poles. In *Proc. Soil Sci. Soc. Am.* 38(4):672−675.

Hannah, P. R. 1974b. Thinning yellow birch saplings to increase main leader growth. *Univ. Vt. Agr. Exp. Stn. Res. Rep.* Burlington. 9 pp.

Hannah, P. R. 1978. Growth of large yellow birch saplings following crop tree thinning. *J. For.* 76:222−223.

Harper, R. M. 1918. Changes in the forest area of New England in three centuries. *J. For.* 16:442−452.

Hart, A. C. 1959a. Silvical characteristics of red spruce. *USDA For. Serv. Northeast. For. Exp. Stn. Pap. 124.* 18 pp.

Hart, A. C. 1959b. Silvical characteristics of balsam fir. *USDA For. Serv. Northeast. For. Exp. Stn. Pap. 122.* 22 pp.

Hart, A. C. 1964. The Penobscot management-intensity demonstration plots. *USDA For. Serv. Res. Pap. NE-25.* 24 pp.

Hawley, R. C., and A. F. Hawes. 1912. *Forestry in New England.* John Wiley, New York. 479 pp.

Heinselman, M. L. 1957. Silvical characteristics of black spruce. *USDA For. Serv. Lake States For. Exp. Stn. Pap. 45.* 30 pp.

Herrick, O. W. 1977. Impact of alternative timber management policies on availability of forest land in the Northeast. *USDA For. Serv. Res. Pap. NE-390.* 14 pp.

Hocker, H. W., Jr. 1977. Silvicultural potential for pre-commercial treatment in northern hardwood types. In Proc. Symp. Intensive Culture of Northern Forest Types. *USDA For. Serv. Gen. Tech. Rep. NE-29.* 356 pp.

Hornbeck, J. W., and C. A. Federer. 1975. Effects of management practices on water quality and quantity: Hubbard Brook Experimental Forest, New Hampshire. In Proc. Symp. Municipal Watershed Management. *USDA For. Serv. Gen. Tech. Rep. NE-13.* 196 pp.

Irland, L. C. 1975. Importance of forest industries to New England's economy. *North. Logger Timber Process.* 23(4):16−17, 38−39.

Jarvis, J. M. 1957. Cutting and seedbed preparation to regenerate yellow birch. *Can. Dept. North. Affairs and Natl. Resour., For. Br. Tech. Note 53.* 17 pp.

Kellogg, R. S. 1909. The timber supply of the United States. *USDA For. Serv. Cir. 166.* 24 pp.

Kingsley, N. P. 1974. The timber resources of Southern New England. *USDA For. Serv. Resour. Bull. NE-36.* 50 pp.

Kingsley, N. P. 1976a. The forest resources of New Hampshire. *USDA For. Serv. Resour. Bull. NE-43.* 71 pp.

Kingsley, N. P. 1976b. The forest-land owners of Southern New England. *USDA For. Serv. Resour. Bull. NE-41.* 27 pp.

Kingsley, N. P. 1977. The forest resources of Vermont. *USDA For. Serv. Resour. Bull. NE-46.* 58 pp.

LaBonte, G. A., and R. W. Nash. 1978. Cleaning and weeding paper birch a 24-year case history. *J. For.* 76:223–225.

Leak. W. B. 1976. Relation of tolerant species to habitat in the White Mountains of New Hampshire. *USDA For. Serv. Res. Pap. NE-351.* 9 pp.

Leak. W. B., D. S. Solomon, and S. M. Filip. 1969. A silvicultural guide for northern hardwoods in the Northeast. *USDA For. Serv. Res. Pap. NE-143.* 34 pp.

Leak, W. B., and S. M. Filip. 1975. Uneven-aged management of northern hardwoods in New England. *USDA For. Serv. Res. Pap. NE-332.* 15 pp.

Leak, W. B., and S. M. Filip. 1977. Thirty-eight years of group selection in New England northern hardwoods. *J. For.* 75:641–643.

Lull, H. W. 1968. A forest atlas of the Northeast. *USDA For. Serv. Northeast. For. Exp. Stn.* 46 pp.

Lutz, H. J. 1928. Trends and silvicultural significance of upland forest successions in southern New England. *Yale Univ. School For. Bull. 22.* New Haven. 68 pp.

Marquis, D. A. 1967. Clearcutting in northern hardwoods results after 30 years. *USDA For. Serv. Res. Pap. NE-85.* 13 pp.

Martin, A. J., and V. J. Rudolph. 1975. Evaluating northern hardwood timber stand improvement opportunities in northern Lower Michigan. *Mich. State Agr. Exp. Stn. Res. Rep. 267.* East Lansing. 10 pp.

McLintock, T. F. 1952. Practical management of spruce and fir—some observations: *N. Y. Forester* 11(2):1–3.

McLintock, T. F. 1954. Factors affecting wind damage in selectively cut stands of spruce and fir in Maine and northern New Hampshire. *USDA For. Serv. Northeast. For. Exp. Stn. Pap. 70.* 17 pp.

Mendel, J. J., and M. K. Peirsol. 1977. Quality index tables for some eastern hardwoods species. *USDA For. Serv. Res. Pap. NE-370.* 10 pp.

Morton, W. B. 1976. Managing deer on private lands in the Central Adirondacks. *North. Logger Timber Process.* 25(4):6–7, 35–37.

Murphy, L. 1917. The red spruce: its growth and management. *USDA Agr. Bull. 544.* 100 pp.

Nienstaedt, H. 1957. Silvical characteristics of white spruce. *USDA For. Serv. Lake States For. Exp. Stn. Pap. 55.* 24 pp.

Noyes, J. H. 1969. Woodlands, highways, and people. *Univ. Mass. Coop. Ext. Serv. Publ. 33.* Amherst. 21 pp.

Nyland, R. D., and H. J. Irish. 1971. Early response to clearcutting in northern hardwoods. *State Univ. Coll. For. Appl. For. Res. Inst. Res. Note 2.* Syracuse. 1 p.

Patric, J. H. 1977. Soil erosion and its control in Eastern woodlands. *North. Logger Timber Process.* 25(11):4, 5, 22, 23, 31, 51.

Peters, J. R., and T. M. Bowers. 1977. Forest statistics for Massachusetts. *USDA For. Serv. Resour. Bull. NE-48.* 43 pp.

Place. I. C. M. 1955. The influence of seed-bed conditions on the regeneration of spruce and balsam fir. *Can. Dept. North. Affairs and Natl. Resour. For. Br. Bull. 177.* 87 pp.

Randall, A. G. 1974. Seed dispersal into two spruce-fir clearcuts in eastern Maine. *Univ. Maine Life Sci. Agr. Exp. Stn.* Orono. 21(8):1–15.

Richards, N. A. 1975. Forestry in an urbanizing society. *J. For.* 72:458–461.

Robertson, W. M. 1942. Some growth characteristics of red spruce. *Can. Dept. Mines and Resour. Can. For. Serv., Silvic. Res. Note 70.* 11 pp.

Safford, L. G. 1968. Ten-year average growth rates in the spruce-fir region of northern New England. *USDA For. Serv. Res. Pap. NE-93.* 20 pp.

Shaw, S. P. 1969. Management of birch for wildlife habitat. In Proc. Birch Symp. *USDA For. Ser. Northeast. For. Exp. Stn.* 183 pp.

Shaw, S. P. 1977. Compatibility of intensive culture with recreation, water and wildlife management. In Proc. Symp. Intensive Culture of Northern Forest Types. *USDA For. Serv. Gen. Tech. Rep. NE-29.* 356 pp.

Silverborg, S. B. 1954. Northern hardwoods cull manual. *State Univ. Coll. For. Bull. 31.* Syracuse. 45 pp.

Simmons, F. C. 1976. Forest industry opportunities and problems in the Northeast. *North. Logger Timber Process.* 24(7):8–9, 26–27, 29.

Smith, D. M. 1955. Management of hardwoods in southern New England. Mimeo. 4 pp.

Solomon, D. S. 1977a. The influence of stand density and structure on growth of northern hardwoods in New England. *USDA For. Serv. Res. Pap. NE-362.* 13 pp.

Solomon, D. S., 1977b. Growth rates of northern hardwoods under uneven-aged management. *North. Logger Timber Process.* 25(8):18, 38.

Solomon, D. S. 1977c. A growth model of natural and silviculturally treated stands of even-aged northern hardwoods. *USDA For. Serv. Gen. Tech. Rep. NE-36.* 30 pp.

Solomon, D. S., and B. M. Blum. 1967. Stump sprouting of four northern hardwoods. *USDA For. Serv. Res. Pap. NE-59.* 13 pp.

Solomon, D. S., and B. M. Blum. 1977. Closure rates of yellow birch pruning wounds. *Can. J. For. Res.* 7:120–124.

Strong, K. F. 1977. Evaluation review of deer yard management work in New Hampshire and Maine. *N. H. Fish Game Dept.* Concord. 117 pp.

Tierson, W. C., E. F. Patric, and D. Behrend. 1966. Influence of white-tailed deer on the logged northern hardwood forest. *J. For.* 64:801–803.

Trimble, G. R., J. J. Mendel, and R. A. Kennell. 1974. A procedure for selection marking in hardwoods. *USDA For. Serv. Res. Pap. NE-292.* 13 pp.

Tubbs. C. H. 1976. Effect of sugar maple root exudate on seedlings of northern conifer species. *USDA For. Serv. Res. Note NC-213.* 2 pp.

Tubbs. C. H. 1977a. Managers handbook for northern hardwoods in the North Central states. *USDA For. Serv. Tech. Rep. NC-39.* 29 pp.

Tubbs, C. H. 1977b. Age and structure of a northern hardwood selection forest 1929–1976. *J. For.* 75:22–24.

U.S. Dept. Agr. 1941. *Climate and man, yearbook of agriculture 1941.* U.S. Govt. Print. Off., Washington, D.C. 1,248 pp.

Westveld, M. 1953. Ecology and silviculture of the spruce fir forests of eastern North America. *J. For.* 51:422–430.

Wood, R. G. 1935. *A history of lumbering in Maine 1820–1861.* Univ. Maine Studies, Ser. 2. No. 33. Orono. 267 pp.

3

The Lake States Region

Henry L. Hansen

LOCATION

The Lake States Region includes those portions of Minnesota, Wisconsin, and Michigan where the Northeastern Coniferous Forest, the Northern Hardwood Forest, and part of the Midland Hardwood Forest occur (see Figs. 1-5 and 3-1). This classification recognizes both the climax aspects of the forests as presented by Braun (1950) and the reconstruction of the original vegetation by Schantz and Zon (1924). In western Minnesota the rather abrupt transition from forest to grassland furnishes a convenient and biotically meaningful boundary. In southern Michigan, east-central Wisconsin, and central Minnesota, however, the forest intermixes as a continuum with the Oak-Hickory Forest as shown in Fig. 3-2.

FOREST STATISTICS[1]

Area

Approximately 52 million acres, or 43 percent of the total area of Michigan, Minnesota, and Wisconsin, is forested. The ratio of forest to nonforest area decreases from east to west and from north to south reflecting the increasing dominance of agriculture. About 49 million acres of the total area are classed as commercial. Three million acres are noncommercial including stands with a growth capacity of less than 20 cubic feet per year, and park areas, or wilderness excluded from timber utilization. As shown in Table 3-1, the area of commercial forest diminished almost 2.5 million acres in the 25-year period from 1952 to 1977.

---

[1]Unless otherwise indicated, statistical information as to areas, ownership, utilization and inventory is from unpublished data from the U. S. Forest Service, 1979 National Timber Assessment Document provided by the North Central Forest Experiment Station, St. Paul, Minnesota.

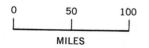

Figure 3-1.   The Lake States Region.

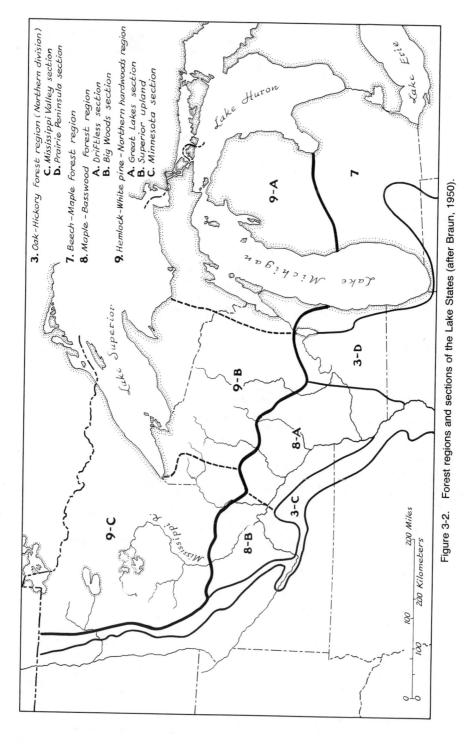

3. Oak–Hickory forest region (Northern division)
   C. Mississippi Valley section
   D. Prairie Peninsula section

7. Beech–Maple forest region
8. Maple–Basswood forest region
   A. Driftless section
   B. Big Woods section
9. Hemlock–White pine–Northern hardwoods region
   A. Great Lakes section
   B. Superior upland
   C. Minnesota section

Figure 3-2.   Forest regions and sections of the Lake States (after Braun, 1950).

The Lake States forest is predominantly hardwoods, an area ratio of about 3 to 1 (Table 3-1). The aspen-birch type complex is by far the largest with almost 15 million acres. Spruce-fir is the major conifer type.

Character of Forest Land Ownership

The public owns almost 40 percent of the total commercial forest area in the Lake States, and in Minnesota public ownership exceeds 52 percent. County ownership is more important in Wisconsin and Minnesota than in Michigan, which has the largest acreage in state ownership.

Small ownerships are characteristic of the region. In Minnesota and Wisconsin over one-half of the private forest land is in parcels of less than 100 acres. Farmers own almost 30 percent of the total forest area. Industrial ownership is less than 10 percent, and over one-fourth of the total forest area is owned by miscellaneous nonfarm, nonindustrial owners.

Forest Inventory

The Lake States have a total growing stock volume of almost 45 billion cubic feet. This is nearly double the volume estimated 25 years ago. However, approximately 5 percent of the potential productive forest area is still nonstocked. This acreage, together with the poorly stocked acreage, poses a problem and silvicultural challenge. A hypothetical average acre has a growing stock volume of about 1,000 cubic feet. The softwood stands are somewhat better stocked than are the hardwoods.

Forest Industries

The number of primary wood-using industries had decreased sharply from over 5,000 in the 1950s to 1,101 in 1973. However, the total volume processed

TABLE 3-1

Area of Commercial Forest Land by Forest Type, 1977 (Thousand Acres)

Forest Type	Michigan	Minnesota	Wisconsin	Total
White-red-jack pine	1,856.6	1,136.1	1,208.0	4,200.7
Spruce-fir	3,006.6	3,713.0	1,347.2	8,066.8
Oak-hickory	2,039.5	970.4	2,681.4	5,691.3
Elm-ash-cottonwood	1,669.8	1,778.7	1,163.1	4,611.6
Maple-beech-birch	5,153.9	937.4	3,551.0	9,642.3
Aspen-birch	4,479.6	5,958.0	4,201.6	14,639.2
Nonstocked	572.2	1,606.4	325.7	2,504.3
Total	18,778.2	16,100.0	14,478.0	49,356.2

Source: Prepared from unpublished data from the U.S. Forest Service, 1979 National Timber Assessment Document provided by the North Central Forest Experiment Station, St. Paul, Minnesota.

has steadily increased. This has been a common pattern in each of the three states. A great variety of industries is represented including those producing lumber, veneer, pulp and paper, chemical wood, charcoal, furniture, cooperage, woodenware, lath, shingles, excelsior, and other minor products.

The region is an important paper-making center utilizing 4.69 million cords in 1975 (Blyth and Hahn, 1977). Wisconsin's 24 pulp mills makes it a leading state in the country's pulp and paper industry.

A strong trend toward an increased ratio of hardwood to softwood utilization has taken place for several decades. Similarly, the amount of residues such as slabs, edgings, and veneer cores utilized for fiber products, fuel, and miscellaneous minor products has increased in recent years. In Wisconsin, it was estimated that 87 percent of coarse residues generated at primary mills was utilized (Blyth et al., 1976) Utilization of fine residues and bark is less complete.

Aspen continues to be the leading pulpwood species comprising over 50 percent of the total utilized in Minnesota. In Michigan and Wisconsin there is some indication that its use may be at a plateau being replaced in part by other hardwoods.

Other Forest Benefits

Proximity to population concentrations in lower Michigan, Illinois, and Ohio has resulted in increasing recreational use of the Lake States Region forests. The mosaic of forests and lakes characteristic of much of the region attracts millions of tourists annually. The forests are the major habitat for much of the nation's population of white-tailed deer, grouse, and other game and fur-bearing species. Income from tourism, fishing and hunting licenses and related expenditures, canoeing, and other forms of recreational use rival returns from forest products on some of the public forests. This raises serious questions related to the multiple-use policies on public lands in parts of the region.

The aspen type illustrates the great potential for integrating management for pulpwood, deer, and grouse production. This type is the major pulpwood source for the region. In addition, it provides prime habitat for white-tailed deer and ruffed grouse. Byelich et al. (1972) point to inadequate commercial harvesting of aspen as a factor in the declining deer herd in Michigan. In Minnesota, Gullion's (1972) long term studies of ruffed grouse emphasize the critical role of aspen leaves and staminate flower buds as the major year-long food resource. The potentials as well as the problems of integrating such multiple uses on other forest types needs to be given serious consideration in silvicultural planning.

THE PHYSICAL ENVIRONMENT

Physiography

Except for the unglaciated driftless area in southwestern Wisconsin and southeastern Minnesota, the region's landscape is a product of glacial activities. In northeastern Minnesota the typical Laurentian Upland features of exposed ledges of crystalline rocks, thin soil mantles and rock basin lakes prevail with elevational variations of up to 2,000 feet. Numerous lakes, rock outcrops, and morainic deposits give a generally young geologic appearance to the regional landscape.

The Lake States lie in the drainage areas of three major systems: Michigan drains entirely into the Great Lakes—St. Lawrence system; Wisconsin waters flow into the Great Lakes and into the Mississippi; Minnesota rivers flow into three systems, namely, the Mississippi, the Great Lakes, and Hudson Bay. All three states are relatively well supplied with water adequate for the support of a large pulp and paper industry.

Numerous swamps and bogs dot the entire area, with the Upper Red Lake Bog in Minnesota being the largest northern bog in the country. These cool, moist locations furnish a retreat for the southward extension of black spruce and tamarack, typically boreal species, well into the general oak-hickory area.

Geology and Soils

The glacial history of the Lake States Region, together with its position straddling a climatic transition from the humid East to the subhumid plains, has given rise to a great complexity of soils and landforms.

Major soil groups are podzols and gray-brown podzolics. These soils are of the order Spodosols and Alfisols, respectively, in the present soil orders and approximate equivalents. The podzols are somewhat atypical in Minnesota under conditions of lower precipitation. In the "snow belt" of Upper Michigan they have deeper, leached A_2 horizons even under hardwood cover.

The geologic features include predominantly those formations resulting from glaciation such as outwash plains and fans, morainic deposits, till plains, eskers, kames, glacial lake deposits and beaches, and rock outcrops exposed and scoured by glacial action. Some differences in forest composition have been related to glacial drifts from different origin centers. The maple-basswood forest of the "big woods" area of south-central Minnesota, described in detail by Daubenmire (1936), has been related to the calcareous gray drift soils which were carried by glacial action from the Keewatin ice center.

In addition, there are other physiographic features, not necessarily glacial in origin, including sand dunes, aeolian deposits, alluvial flats and terraces associated with the major rivers, and the eroded loessal plateau of the driftless area in southwestern Wisconsin and southeastern Minnesota.

Because individual tree species have different patterns of ecological requirements that can be met best on certain soils, it is obvious that some degree of relationship exists between the kinds of soils and the tree species growing on them. However, these relationships may be changed by overriding influences of climatic differences, may be modified by local conditions of physiography, or may be masked by past practices of logging, grazing, or other activities.

The critical importance of the moisture regime has been recognized and incorporated into the system for classifying and evaluating forest sites in Ontario (Hills, 1952). If Lake States Region soils are grouped under three broad moisture classes, xeric, mesic, and hydric, some of the affinities of tree species are more easily considered.

The driest soils are predominantly sands. Throughout the region these sands are largely occupied by jack pine, red pine, and scrub oaks. Fire and logging have tended to favor jack pine over red pine, and the sprouting oaks have frequently completely taken over the most badly abused areas. Sandy areas with less drastic fire history and somewhat better moisture conditions may have some white pine.

The thin soil mantles overlying rock outcrops are droughty. Soils overlying sandstones, quartzites, and siliceous shales are probably most droughty and commonly support pines and scrub oaks. However, the mantle soils of the Porcupine Mountains of Upper Michigan support fine stands of northern hardwoods, with sugar maple as the predominant species. Any effect of the petrographic origin of soils on rock outcrops and thus on the species of trees the soils support is usually overwhelmed by the effects of local climate, slope, exposure, soil depth, and elevation.

Hydric soils may be organic, consisting of peats and mucks, or may be gley loams or clays. On poorly drained areas peat accumulates to various depths. The type of forest found on such soils varies with depth to mineral soil, origin of the peat, and degree of drainage.

Studies of the nature of bog genesis and peatland development emphasize the significance of water movement in determining the nutrient levels and consequent site productivity of these systems (Heinselman, 1970).

Woody peats have been formed under conditions providing for some degree of water movement. They are capable of supporting a range of species from the acid-tolerant black spruce and tamarack to northern white-cedar and such swamp hardwoods as black ash, elm, and red maple.

Moss peats originate largely from sphagnum in shallow lakes and ponds as well as in the large "upland bogs" of northern Minnesota, and support only black spruce or tamarack. The pH of such soils may be as low as 3.5 to 4.5.

Poorly drained mineral soils occur in portions of northeastern Minnesota and as lacustrine clays along the south shore of Lake Superior in northwestern Wisconsin. These soil support stands of black spruce, balsam fir, and northern white-cedar, in contrast to the pines and northern hardwoods of the better-drained adjacent areas. They have been recognized as "ground water podzols" or "gley podzols," and, because of the boreal character of the forest supported by them have contributed to the mistaken idea that the entire Lake States coniferous area is boreal.

On mesic soils, the soil-forest relationships are more complicated and affinities of individual species for certain soil conditions are less obvious. Texturally, these better soils are usually loams. The nutrient levels, as well as the moisture relations, affect forest productivity and species affinities. Sugar maple, beech, yellow birch, and basswood along with hemlock in the east tend to occupy the best soils, with white pine as an occasional tree. On lighter soils, white pine frequently predominates.

Such seral species as quaking aspen and paper birch have a wide range of soil adaptability. Kittredge (1938) found quaking aspen to occur on eight different soil-texture classes from sand to clay loam, and peat, and on 54 different soil types. These soil types were poorly correlated with aspen site productivitiy. Only when a broader grouping along lines of soil-profile patterns was developed did the soils show strong predictive values in terms of aspen productivity.

Climate and Weather

The region has a strongly continental climate with great temperature extremes and fluctuations. An ameliorating influence from the Great Lakes is felt in those areas lying close to the east and south of them. Parts of the Upper Peninsula of Michigan have a modified marine climate. Much of the east shore of Lake Michigan, extending inland a considerable distance, enjoys a climate mild enough to support a fruit-growing industry impossible at similar latitudes in Wisconsin and Minnesota. During the winter, when prevailing winds are from the west and northwest, the temperatures on the Wisconsin side are often dramatically lower than they are to the east of Lake Michigan.

Two other major sources of climatic variation exist. The region straddles a general moisture gradient from the more humid conditions in the east to drier conditions in the Great Plains. This has produced major changes in vegetation from continuous forest, to forest with prairie interspersion, to prairie with forest on the less rigorous sites, and finally to the prairie vegetation of western Minnesota. The effects of this climatic variation on tree species has been mentioned in Chapter 2. The other intraregional variation is a product of the usual temperature gradient going from south to north.

Average annual precipitation varies from about 24 to 32 inches, with a rather sharp decrease in Minnesota, correlated with the transition from forest to prairie. Most of this precipitation is a product of the general cyclonic storm movements which travel from west to east along the Canadian border, some of which move northeast after entering the Mississippi Valley from the west. Thunderstorms are a frequent source of summer rains.

In the area under the greatest influence of the Great Lakes, rains are usually frequent and of a light-drizzle nature. Marquette, Michigan, with a moderate annual rainfall of about 32 inches, has 165 days a year during which a measurable amount falls, each day receiving on the average only 0.20 inch.

Seasonal distribution of precipitation varies from east to west. In Michigan, there is only slightly more precipitation in the warm half than in the cold half of the year. In Minnesota, over 55 percent of the annual precipitation falls in four months from May through August. This concentration of the total precipitation during the growing season somewhat offsets the reduced total amount compared with farther east.

There is probably little precipitation over the general area as a result of orographic air uplift. Except for the north shore of Lake Superior and the south-shore area in Upper Michigan, there is relatively little physiographic relief, and any such effects are of a local rather than regional nature. The abundance of inland lakes probably has some effect on local microclimate. This is especially true in the area near some of the larger lakes in Minnesota, where changes in vegetation are an obvious response to the modified microclimate and give rise to interesting tree distribution abberations.

The relative frequency of drought years probably has greater significance than the average annual precipitation in accounting for the replacement of forest by prairie vegetation in the western limits of this region. The number of years during a 40-year period when the annual precipitation was less than 20 inches increased from only four in Michigan and Wisconsin to more than 16 in the prairie-forest transition in western Minnesota; that is, there were only four dry years in Michigan and Wisconsin during this period as compared with over 16 in western Minnesota (U.S. Dept. Agr., 1941).

Snowfall is heaviest in the "snow belt" of the Upper Peninsula of Michigan, where 115 to 130 inches fall annually. A snow blanket usually covers the region for 120 to 140 days from December to April.

Except for those areas in which the climate is moderated by the Great Lakes, this region is characterized by some of the greatest temperature extremes in the United States, with lows below −50 ° F. and highs up to 110 ° F. Winters are typically long and cold and summers short and relatively cool except for occasional extremes. The average number of days without killing frost varies from a low of 80 to 90 days in the Upper Michigan snow belt to as high as 150 days south in the region. Frost penetrates to depths of 30 to 48 inches over most of the region, and the extreme cold and light snow cover of parts of Minnesota permit freezing to from 72 to 84 inches (U.S. Dept. Agr., 1941).

Weather is commonly sunny both winter and summer in Wisconsin and Minnesota. During the growing season, sunshine prevails during about 70 percent of the daytime hours except in Michigan where it drops to 60 percent. The relatively high ratio of sunshine, combined with the long summer days at these northern latitudes, tends to reduce the significance of temperature as a limiting factor to forest growth, in spite of the short growing season.

Winter winds are commonly west or northwest. In the summer, there is less constancy of direction, with winds from all southerly points generally prevailing. Tornadoes are largely restricted to the southern portions of the three Lake States.

Climatic Injury to Forest Stands

Drought is a climatic phenomenon of considerable importance in this region, especially in Minnesota. Here it is a major factor limiting westward tree distribution. During a 40-year period at the Cloquet Experimental Forest (Schantz-Hansen and Jensen, 1956) precipitation remained below normal as long as five consecutive years.

Injury resulting from excessively high temperatures is difficult to distinguish from drought injury, because the same weather patterns frequently produce both. It is known that surface soil temperatures in the Lake States can exceed the lethal high temperatures for plant tissues by 10 ° C. or more and, if prolonged, can undoubtedly injure tender young seedlings, especially in the ground-line area. This type of injury has been recognized in tree nurseries as "white spot." It has also been noted rather frequently on balsam fir and eastern white pine when the thin, dark bark is exposed to the full effects of solar radiation.

Low-temperature injuries due to late spring freezes or early fall frost are often seen but, except for frost pockets, are not general enough to affect silvicultural treatments. Frost heaving of young seedlings is to be expected throughout the region, especially on fine-textured soils.

A type of injury presumably occurring in the winter period and commonly referred to as "winter injury" is fairly common in conifers. It first shows up as reddish discoloration of the needles as winter gives way to spring, and it subsequently kills the affected foliage and sometimes the tree. Exotics of questionable hardiness are especially subject to this injury. Whatever weather factors cause winter injury are most frequent in the western part of the Lake States. Perhaps the most severe of such weather combinations occurred in 1947, when widespread damage took place on cultivated ornamentals and in field plantations of Scotch pine, Austrian pine, Norway spruce, ponderosa pine, and other exotics. The occurrence of these extreme weather conditions precludes forest plantings of exotics except from climatic analog sources.

THE MAJOR FOREST TYPE GROUPS

It is necessary to develop a classification of types which can serve as a framework within which to organize the information basic to the consideration of silvicultural procedures and techniques.

Practical considerations dictate that the forester must begin with the vegetation presently on the area. The Society of American Foresters (1954) cover-type classification that rates types on a scale of moisture affinity is useful in this connection. Most of the three Lake States is included within the Northern Forest Region. The "big woods" area of Minnesota, as well as the southern portions of Wisconsin and Michigan, is considered to be in the Central Hardwood Region. It is recognized that chaos would result from any attempt to classify all species combinations. Thus only those which occur over a wide range and in the aggregate occupy considerable acreage are included. Even with this simplification, 27 different cover types are listed which are well represented in the Lake States Region. Of these, eight are primarily Boreal Forest Region types, 15 are primarily of the Northern Forest Region, and four are from the Central Hardwood Region.

Because of their current wide usage and inter-regional scope, two other forest classifications are given special consideration. These are the classification of the deciduous forests of eastern North America by Braun (1950) and the forest-regional classification of Canada by Rowe (1959).

Most of the Lake States is included in Braun's hemlock—white pine—northern hardwood regions, which is the largest one in her "Deciduous Forest Formation" and extends through the northern Lake States and the Northeast (see Fig. 3-2). Braun considers this zone to be one where climax types from both north and south interpenetrate and where "physiographic climaxes" of jack pine, red pine, and white pine occur on the dry sites. While this is conceptually understandable, the silvicultural problems of the pines and the hardwoods are so different that they must be described separately. The northern hardwood mixtures of sugar maple, yellow birch, hemlock, basswood, and minor hardwoods will be considered as varients of the northern hardwood type group.

Rowe, in his revision of Halliday's (1937) earlier classification, recognizes broad geographic belts or zones as forest regions equated with stable, climatically controlled forest formations characterized by the presence of certain climax dominants. This is essentially the climax concept of Clements. With minor exceptions the Lake States are bordered, according to the Canadian classification, by sections of the Great Lakes—St. Lawrence Forest Region.

The Boreal Forest Region has direct contact with the Lake States only in extreme northwestern Minnesota, through the Manitoba lowlands and the aspen-oak sections in Canada. This association of aspen and oak continues in Minnesota as a narrow belt between the prairie and the pine and northern hardwood associations (Bakuzis and Hansen, 1965).

On the basis of these considerations, and recognizing several instances of ecological inappropriateness, the following major groups of types will be used as the framework within which to discuss the Lake States Region forest and its silviculture: pine (jack, red, eastern white), aspen, swamp conifers, northern hardwoods, and spruce—balsam fir—paper birch.

HISTORY OF FOREST USE

The significant history of man's activities which seriously affected the forests of the Lake States started with the great agricultural expansion of the mid-1800s. Lumber for the farms of the Ohio River Valley and the interior prairie country of Illinois came largely from Michigan and Wisconsin pineries. In the 10 to 20 years following the Civil War, considerable logging activity was already going on in Michigan. Following the period of tremendous growth when the prairies of the Midwest were settled, the logging of the Lake States forests increased at fever pitch, moving to Minnesota as the best of the timber to the east was logged. In 1902, the region led the rest of the country in timber production. This grand era came to an end about 1910, when the bulk of the good white and red pine was gone.

Overexpansion of farming in later years induced the clearing of vast acreages of submarginal soil types and the destruction of the forest regeneration that might have followed the logging. Land-clearing fires, and wildfires that were considered good because they got rid of slash that was a hinderance to farming, were widespread. Some of the most devastating fires in the history of the country burned in this region. The Peshtigo and Michigan fires of 1871 burned over 3 million acres of Wisconsin and Michigan. In Minnesota, the Hinckley fire of 1894, the Baudette fire of 1910, and the Cloquet fire of 1918 burned over ½ million acres, causing appalling loss of human life and destruction of the forest. A factor which contributed both to this picture of destruction by fire and to the subsequent economic plight was the large-scale swamp-drainage activity in northern Minnesota. These economically unsound ventures not only dried out vast areas of swamps and contributed to their destruction by fire but also bankrupted some forest countries and laid the foundation for the vexing forest taxation problems which still prevail.

During the period from about 1920 on through the depression years of the 1930s, land abandonment in the poorer farming countries went on at a great rate. Millions of acres of farms were abandoned and reverted to public ownership. Many of these farms constituted the first land to be planted to trees in the upsurge of tree planting in later years.

The Forests Today

The Lake States Region forests are far from ideal as to species composition, timber quality, and other considerations. Several major results of mistreatment are obvious. A vast increase in fire types, especially jack pine and aspen, followed the fires of the agricultural expansion and forest exploitation years. Jack pine occupies more land than any other conifer in the Lake States. Aspen, covering over 15 million acres, is by far the most widespread type in the region.

The large acreage of non-stocked or poorly stocked forest land and the acreage classed as brush create serious problems.

Because much of the forest area of the region was logged 60 to 80 years ago, there has not been sufficient time to produce sawlog-sized trees on any appreciable acreage. However, a large area has now reached pulp and pole-timber sizes, and these stands are the source of supply for the present pulp and paper industry.

Along with the reduction in quantity of large-size timber available currently is an accompanying decrease in log quality. This is due not only to the absence of large logs, but also to the high-grading type of logging operation that prevailed in earlier years. This is especially true in the valuable northern hardwood types.

Several technological developments since World War II have significantly affected forest practices and utilization potentials. The synthesis of 2.4-D as a safe and effective selective herbicide made it possible to release conifers from hardwood and brush competition cheaply. The development of the machine tree planter stimulated a planting boom on both public and private land; and in the ensuing years most available, open idle land has been reforested. In the paper industry technological developments now enable the utilization of most tree species including aspen and others formerly considered weed species.

Mechanization of logging has resulted in tree length skidding and transport, in chipping in the wood or at the mill, and in other processing changes. These raise new questions of ecological impact and regeneration problems while greatly increasing utilization efficiency.

SILVICULTURE OF THE MAJOR TYPE GROUPS

Pine Type Group: Jack Pine

Included in this group are the boreal and northern forest cover types in which jack, red, or eastern white pine play a dominant role. A major study of the phenotypic variations in morphological characteristics of jack pine over its range from the Atlantic seaboard to the Northwest Territories was made by Schoenike (1976).

Place in Ecological Succession.   Jack pine normally occurs on the drier sandy soils to which it is well adapted and on which it escapes the competition of more tolerant species. Over one-half of the volume of growing stock is found in Minnesota, and the species reaches its best development there and in the Boreal Forest Region in Canada where the species is at its optimum. While jack pine is present on extreme xeric sites, it can also be found on sandy loams capable of supporting white pine, paper birch, quaking aspen, and the native oaks. Extensive stands occur on sandy plains of glacial, fluvial, or lacustrine origin. On such sites it is often the predominant or only tree species present. In northeastern Minnesota and adjacent Ontario, jack pine associates with black spruce on the gravelly loams and rocky soils of the Laurentian Shield.

On the driest sites in the northern part of the Lake States, the jack pine's only competitor is red pine. Because logging and repeated fires have tended to eliminate red pine from most of these sites, jack pine has the appearance of an edaphic climax type. However, where red pine seed sources are available, that species will probably tend to replace the smaller, shorter-lived jack pine. On these poor sites brush is almost absent, and pine regeneration is often aggressive or at least adequate. On similar dry sites farther south, the oaks are strong competitors and jack pine has difficulty maintaining its dominance.

Where jack pine occurs on the better sandy loams it is always transitional in nature and is succeeded by mixtures of white pine, aspen, oak, and minor hardwoods of moderate tolerance. Its presence on such sites is a result of fires and logging which have tended to expand the extent of occurrence of the species so that this tree is dominant on sites where, in the absence of these disturbances, it would be only a minor species.

On the present jack pine-black spruce sites in Minnesota jack pine will probably lose ground to the more tolerant spruce unless aided by fire, wind, or management. Observations over a 14- to 16-year period on overmature stands of this mixture indicate probable replacement by black spruce, white spruce, balsam fir, and paper birch (Eyre and LeBarron, 1944).

Growth Rates.   Until it is about 20 years of age, jack pine outgrows any of its competitors except aspen suckers (Cheyney, 1942). During the first 50 years, height growth of over a foot a year is maintained on average sites. However, this species is short-lived compared to red and white pines. While extreme ages of over 150 years have been reported, most trees are overmature in from 60 to 100 years. Trees on the better sites in Minnesota have somewhat greater longevity.

Because natural stands are seldom well stocked over large areas, yields are usually low, often less than one-quarter cord per acre per year. However, data for well-stocked, unmanaged stands (Gevorkiantz, 1947) indicate annual yields of from one-quarter to one-half cord per acre. Management efforts aimed at salvaging mortality and concentrating growth through thinnings can double yields of such stands. Maximum size attained by the species varies with site, and ranges from about 10 to 25 inches d.b.h. and from 60 to 100 feet in height.

Rotation Age or Size.   On the better sites, jack pine stands begin to produce harvestable quantities of pulpwood in about 30 to 35 years and sawlogs in 50 years. However, recommended rotation ages exceed these figures in order to take advantage of accelerated average annual growth rates. For pulpwood, rotations of 50 to 55 years are recommended (Eyre and LeBarron, 1944). For poles, piling, and sawlogs, rotations of 60 to 80 years are advised. The maximum rotations for larger products are possible only on the better sites, where sustained growth of the species can be expected before rots reduce sound tree volumes.

One of the considerations in deciding when to cut jack pine stands relates to the development of brush understories. On the lighter sands, brush seldom is a problem in reasonably well-stocked stands. Such stands can be harvested for pulp before brush invasion can occur. On medium to good sites, if the stands are brush free at early ages, it is sometimes possible to harvest for pulp before brush understory develops. On such sites brush invasion is almost inevitable if longer rotations are practiced. In this event, the owner must decide whether the greater returns from the larger products on a longer rotation are offset by the added costs of obtaining reproduction after brush has become a serious problem.

Some effort has been made to determine site productivity by vegetational and soil indicators. In Minnesota, using site index as a standard indicator of productivity, rather weak correlations with soil-texture classes were noted, while vegetational indication was found to have greater significance (Hansen, 1946, 1952). Wilde *et al.* (1949) reports yields of well-stocked jack pine stands at 60 years of age from about 14 cords per acre on windblown sands to over 35 cords on the better Plainfield and Vilas sandy soil types in central Wisconsin.

Cultural Practices.   In deciding which type of silvicultural treatment to apply to jack pine stands, special consideration should be given to the following characteristics of the species and variations in its occurrence:

1. Cones may be serotinous or open, and the nature of the seed-distribution process is sharply different for each.

2. Serotinous cones must be scattered close to the ground for satisfactory seed release.

3. The species is highly intolerant; it does not recover from suppression, and seedlings do not establish under shade.

4. Where brush is absent, as on poor sites and under dense stands, reproduction is usually easy to obtain.

5. Seed germination is best on mineral soil.

6. Mixtures with other species introduce difficulties in silvicultural treatment.

On poor sites, jack pine almost always occurs in pure brush-free stands, and management is relatively simple. In Lower Michigan and Central Wisconsin there is some association with oak even on the poor sites. Because of the extreme density of stocking of some of these poor-site stands, it may be desirable to make an early thinning in the small saplings. This would be a noncommercial operation aimed at enlarging the crowns of the remaining trees and concentrating growth on 2,000 or fewer stems per acre. Costs should be kept to a minimum by thinning on a mechanical spacing basis before the stand is 20 years old.

Because of the slow growth and low returns to be expected on poor sites, it may not be economically feasible to make early thinnings. However, it is normally possible to make one later commercial thinning before the final harvest. Such thinning must be from the lower crown classes at about 40 years. If this cut is heavy enough, it may also serve as a seeding cut where cones of a nonserotinous nature prevail. The brush-free character of the stand and lack of heavy ground-cover competition makes pine seedling establishment fairly certain. The stand should be clearcut at about age 50 with lopping and scattering of slash.

On medium and good sites jack pine may occur either in pure or in mixed condition. Unless a high stand density has been maintained brush is usually a problem, at least after the trees have reached pulpwood size. As a result, silvicultural management is more complicated than on the poor sites. Because of competition regeneration is often difficult, and planting may be necessary.

Well-stocked stands on these better sites should be thinned as soon as it is economically possible. This will normally be between the ages of 20 and 40 years. Such thinnings should be made from below, and special attention should be paid to the removal of porcupine-girdled, gall and stem-canker infected, misshapen, and otherwise diseased or injured trees. If red pine or spruce occur in the stand, they should be favored on these better sites. Over much of the Lake States Region, per-acre volumes as low as 3 to 4 cords can be cut economically.

The only economically feasible way of dealing with the brush competition problem is by using selective herbicides. Sprays of 2,4-D have been applied effectively to control hazel, aspen, birch, and oak for many years. Aerial applications using helicopters provide the best control over placement of the herbicide and access to small loading areas. The control of brush by spot spraying in early stages of its invasion or expansion in jack pine stands has been proposed but not yet tested on a significant scale (Tappeiner and Dahlman, 1971).

Response to thinning of stands located on the Chippewa National Forest has been excellent. Ten years after cutting, plots from which 44 percent of the basal area had been removed had regained or even exceeded the original basal area (Eyre and LeBarron, 1944).

Stands managed on a pulpwood rotation should be harvested at 50 to 55 years. A decision as to harvest method will be affected by the relative abundance of serotinous and open cones present on the trees. If open cones predominate, a seeding cut may be made about five years in advance of the final harvest cut. This should remove over one-half of the total volume, leaving the larger-crowned trees with good cone crops. The final harvest should be made as a clearcutting as soon as regeneration is established. If regeneration is inadequate, the forest floor should be scarified using heavy equipment such as the Athens-type disk plow. If the remaining cone-bearing trees fail to seed in these exposed soil areas, planting after final stand removal will be necessary.

If the cones are predominantly serotinous, there is no reason for making a preharvest seeding cut. Such stands should be clearcut, preferably in connection with seedbed scarification. Cone-bearing slash should be lopped and scattered over the scarified area. Scarification following rather than preceding logging may often be necessary because of the difficulty of getting tractor equipment between the trees in well-stocked stands. The lopped and scattered cone-bearing slash would then be worked into the disked soil. Several Canadian reports (Larsson et al., 1949; Sonley, 1950) conclude that mechanical logging including cable-yarding adequately prepares the ground and distributes the slash.

Tests using fire to regenerate jack pine from cones in slash have generally failed. Early tests in Minnesota, in which logged areas with lopped slash were burned broadcast, were failures (Eyre, 1938). Other tests in Ontario (Farrar et al., 1954) were also failures. In all cases the fire either burned too hot and destroyed the seed or else it failed to run through the slash uniformly enough to open the cones. The critical importance of getting the cones close to the ground surface is emphasized by studies showing that cones lying on the ground open in about a week of hot weather while those 6 inches above the ground open only after one or two months (Eyre and LeBarron, 1944).

Stands managed for larger products than pulpwood should be thinned at about 10-year intervals to profitably salvage mortality and to increase the growth rate of the trees selected for the final crop. Methods for making the harvest cut will be similar to those previously described for pulpwood harvests.

Presence of mixtures of other species may modify silvicultural procedures. If red pine is present in adequate stocking, the stand should be converted to this higher-value species by the gradual removal of the jack pine in a series of thinnings.

Relatively little is known about the silviculture of jack pine-black spruce mixtures. The susceptibility to windthrow of the black spruce makes it hazardous to leave by a removal of the protecting jack pine overstory. Gradual removal of the jack pine, with the object of favoring the conversion to black spruce, and exposing trees of the latter species by a series of partial cuts is a possible procedure. Clearcutting of both species, together with scarification, may reestablish the original combination, but the method has not been tried sufficiently to make possible an evaluation of the technique.

In the southern limits of its range jack pine frequently mixes with oak. In these mixtures the oaks are usually of low value and suppress the pine. Aerial spraying with 2,4-D is effective as a release operation. Such treatment can also improve deer habitat. The out-of-reach oak, which the deer prefer as browse and for the acorns, is knocked back while at the same time stimulated to sprout from the root collar (Krefting and Hansen, 1969). Jack pine stands in a matrix of aspen types provide winter cover for white-tailed deer (Fedkenheuer and Hansen, 1971). Consideration should be given to plan cuttings so as not to clear an entire winter yarding area.

Susceptibility to Damage.   Jack pine is not usually subject to loss from wind until the tree becomes overmature. This species is well rooted except where growing on shallow soils over rock, as is the case in some of the jack pine−black spruce stands. In overmature stands, wind damage is usually a result of breakage of trees where rot is well advanced.

The jack pine budworm has caused considerable damage to jack pine stands. This defoliator is especially numerous in poorly stocked stands with orchard-type trees having an abundance of staminate flowers on which the insect feeds. Mortality is especially heavy among understory saplings and reproduction. Losses as high as 33 percent in sapling-size material were reported from Michigan in a 1949 to 1952 outbreak (Benjamin, 1953). Several kinds of sawflies defoliate jack pine, subsequently reducing growth rates. The pine sawyer beetle and the pine engraver attack trees weakened by injury or old age.

Rots are caused by *Polyporus schweinitzii*, *Fomes pini*, and *Fomes pinicola*. Studies have shown fire-damaged trees to be especially subject to this type of injury (Kaufert, 1933). Several stems rusts attack trees of all ages. The more common include the gall rust and the sweetfern rust. These kill few trees but reduce growth and quality of wood. Some needle rusts exist, but the extent of their damage is uncertain.

Porcupines, deer, snowshoe hares, and squirrels do some damage that may, in some localities, be serious. Where porcupines become abundant they may girdle and kill or badly deform 10 percent or more of the trees in areas affected. Deer seem to prefer jack pine to most other conifers except white-cedar and hemlock. Hare damage to young seedlings may be a serious problem in peak abundance years, such as occurred in the mid-1930s. Damage by squirrels consists of the girdling and killing of twigs incidental to the cutting of cones.

Because many jack pine stands have originated following fire, the seriousness of wildfire as a source of mortality and tree injury is not always understood. Fires in seedling jack pine stands can cause almost complete mortality. As the trees get larger, damage is less from ordinary surface fires. However, the high incidence of decay in fire-scarred jack pines has previously been noted. The retention of low branches and frequent association with oaks, which often retain their leaves into the spring fire season, greatly contribute to the possibility of fires crowning in these types.

Pine Type Group: Red Pine

Place in Ecological Succession. The site affinities of red pine are similar to those of jack pine (Rudolf, 1957). The former is somewhat less adaptable to the very driest sites and of somewhat wider occurrence on the sites having slightly better moisture and fertility relationships.

There is considerable difference of opinion as to the successional role of red pine. On the driest sites, where it is a common associate of jack pine, it is probably a permanent type or edaphic climax. Its longer life, greater size, and slightly greater tolerance enable red pine to succeed jack pine. A portion of this transitional chronology has been recorded over a 30-year period of record for several stands (Spurr and Allison, 1952).

While some observers account for the presence of red pine almost entirely in terms of postfire origin, the species is probably capable of perpetuating itself in the absence of fire on the lightest soils. On better sites and with the elimination of fire, red pine will be replaced by white pine, aspen, birch, and minor hardwoods. In these situations it will survive only as scattered single trees.

On somewhat moister sites, an understory of spruce and balsam fir may be present under the red pine. On these sites, the spruce and fir is often of low quality and has a very short life span. If sufficiently dense, this spruce-fir cover serves to suppress the development of brush, which otherwise would prevail.

Fire has undoubtedly played an important role in the ecology of the species. In young stands of jack and red pines, fire tends to kill the red pine and increase the abundance of the jack pine with its serotinous cones and ability to seed and regenerate on a postfire seedbed. However, older and larger red pines are able to stand burning which often kills white pines. Similarly, aspen and birch may be killed back to produce an overstory of red pine trees and an understory of aspen sucker growth and birch sprouts. These two-storied stands are common.

Like fire, brush plays a critical role in red pine ecology. On all but the lightest soils, brush is capable of invading red pine stands unless crown-canopy densities are well maintained. Red pine is incapable of establishing regeneration under even moderate densities of brush cover. Many stands, following logging and in the absence of other more tolerant tree species, have reverted to brush types and constitute much of the problem acreage in Lake States forest areas.

Growth Rates. In Wisconsin, yields at 100 years of well-stocked stands are reported as from 7,000 board feet per acre on sandy, hardpan podzols to over

15,000 board feet on the better podzolic sands (Wilde *et al.*, 1949). Yields of from about 9,000 board feet to over 27,000 board feet per acre from unmanaged stands at 100 years are cited from Lake States data (Eyre and Zehngraff, 1948). Volumes of virgin growth averaging 30,000 board feet per acre and running to over 40,000 board feet have been reported in northern Minnesota for individual stands of 40 acres and larger. Site-index tables for red pine cover a height range of from 40 to 70 feet at 50 years (Gevorkiantz, 1957).

The pattern of height growth for the species is intermediate between those for jack pine and white pine. While individual red pines over 300-years old have been reported in Minnesota, the average age at which they were destroyed by wind was found to be between 200 and 225 years (Hansen and Duncan, 1954).

Mean-annual increment in board feet was found to culminate between 120 and 140 years in red pine stands (Eyre and Zehngraff, 1948) and at 93 years in a mixed red pine-jack pine stand (Schantz-Hansen, 1931). Growth of well-stocked wild stands on a 50-year pulpwood rotation varies from about one-half to 1 cord per acre per year, depending on site quality. Yields from plantations have been reported to vary from 1 to 1 and one-half cords per acre per year (Allison, 1943; Zasada and Buckman, 1957).

Rotation Age or Size. Red pine can be utilized for a great variety of products including fence posts, pulp, poles, piling, sawlogs, and other minor uses. Rotations will, of course, vary with the product. While pulpwood-sized material can be grown in about 25 to 35 years, rotations that short do not begin to utilize the growth potential of the species. Since the species is so well adapted to multiple-product management, it is seldom desirable to harvest on a short-rotation pulpwood basis. General recommendations for sawlog rotations vary from 80 to 140 years (Eyre and Zehngraff, 1948; Ricker and Zasada, 1958a).

Cultural Practices. The excellent technical properties of red pine lumber, its good growth rate, and its relative freedom from serious insect and disease enemies make it a highly preferred management species in much of the Lake States Region. Because of these traits, it is well suited to intensive management geared to removal of a variety of products by a series of intermediate and harvest cuttings over a fairly long rotation of 120 to 140 years.

Pruning to improve wood quality is an accepted practice with this high-value species. While this species prunes naturally better than most other conifers, little clear lumber will be produced in less than 80 to 100 years, and pruning at an early age is considered profitable. For poles and piling, only natural pruning is required. These products will normally be removed from the stand before the sawlog harvest. Pruning not over 100 trees for the final crop is all that is considered necessary. Since it is desirable to clear a 16-foot butt log, this will require two operations, the first at about 15 years and the second at about 25 years. With this arrangement there is no danger that the branch removal will retard the tree growth rate. Information from young plantations in Lower

Michigan (Slabaugh, 1957) indicates that dominants and codominants about 16 feet in height can have up to 50 percent of their live crown removed by pruning without reducing their chances of retaining dominance over their neighbors. This agrees with studies of the effect of pruning on growth of 18-year-old red pines in plantations (Bickerstaff, 1946).

Some young sapling stands have as many as 10,000 to 20,000 stems per acre (Schantz-Hansen, 1945). It is doubtful if stands with 5,000 or more young trees per acre can maintain even reasonably satisfactory growth or differentiate into crown classes to hasten the natural thinning process. Such stands should be thinned before they reach 20 years to a spacing of about 6 × 6 feet.

Commercial thinning can be done at 25 to 30 years in well-stocked plantations and in 30 to 40 years in wild stands. At this age on average to good sites red pine will yield over a cord per acre per year. Thinnings for pulp can profitably be made at 5 to 10 year intervals until larger-sized products become available. Jack pine, aspen, and other species should be removed concentrating growth on the more valuable red pine.

Cutting to leave a basal area of from 90 to 110 square feet per acre gives an approximate guide to stocking levels which will encourage rapid tree growth. Most of the early cutting should be done in the lower crown classes. As the larger trees become big enough for small poles and piling, identification of the final crop trees should be made. These are best selected from the codominants with their smaller crowns and branches. Removal of the largest dominants will concentrate growth on the better-formed codominants.

In managing red pine for poles (Guilkey, 1958), it is emphasized that the best-formed trees with no sweep, crook, or other defects and with small limbs must be favored. As an aid to developing such trees, early stand density should be maintained at a high level to prevent the growth of large branches. Stands with basal areas of at least 120 square feet per acre have the highest proportion of trees meeting pole requirements.

Experience on the Chippewa National Forest (Eyre and Zehngraff, 1948) supports the shelterwood system as the basis for harvesting and regenerating red pine. Sometime after about 120 years the stand should be heavily cut by a series of operations, rather than a single removal cut, to reduce the volume by about one-half leaving about 50 final crop trees. During these cuttings regeneration should establish unless brush has become a problem. If brush is a problem, it should be controlled as described for jack pine stands. A basal area of 80 square feet or less per acre may be retained to obtain the added growth of high-quality wood on the residual overstory, as long as no harm is done to the seedlings.

Red pine is the most widely planted species in the Lake States Region. An extensive review of the history of forest planting in the Lake States (Rudolf, 1950) furnishes some guides as a basis for planting on soils having over 50 percent silt plus clay. On the better sandy loams with 30 to 50 percent silt plus clay, red pine should be planted only where there is no overstory and over 80 percent of full sunlight is available.

The species is best suited to planting on loamy sands and light sandy loams having from 15 to 30 percent silt plus clay. On the lightest sands jack pine is preferred to red pine under conditions of full exposure to sun. On these soils red pine can be planted under partial shade.

Transplant stock three to four years old is recommended for most sites. Where conditions are most favorable, such as with a minimum of competition or a favorable soil-moisture regime, 2-0 seedling stock may be used. During recent years there has been a strong tendency to plant containerized stock. Regardless of the nature of the planting stock, competition from overstory trees and brush must be reduced. Aerial applications of 2,4-D and 2,4,5-T have been useful in this connection. However the use of 2,4,5-T has now been suspended.

Susceptibility to Damage.   The species is very windfirm, and little loss occurs until overmature trees infected with stem rots suffer trunk breakage. In young stands, icing of the crowns accompanied by wind sometimes results in top breakage especially in dense stands.

Red pine has been considered remarkably free of serious insect enemies. In recent years, possibly as a result of extensive planting of the species, several insects have caused damage increase. In Wisconsin and Michigan, the Saratoga spittle bug has been causing serious trouble in young plantations where it damages and often kills trees of small sapling size. The jack pine budworm also kills red pine reproduction under infected overstory jack pine. Pine sawyer beetles and bark beetles do some damage to low-vigor trees injured by storm or drought.

Red pine is also free of serious disease. While rots are present in some overmature trees, they seldom cause damage in managed stands.

The snowshoe hare may cause seedling mortality of some significance in peak abundance years, and the white-tailed deer browses on twig tips in winter. However, both these animals usually seem to prefer jack pine or white pine if it is available. Porcupine damage may be a serious problem locally.

Pine Type Group: Eastern White Pine

Place in Ecological Succession.   The ecological affinities of eastern white pine may be expressed in terms of two general relationships. First, the species occupies sites having a wider range of moisture and nutrient levels than is the case with either red or jack pine. Second, it demands better site quality for optimum development than the other native pines do.

In Wisconsin, Curtis (1959) reports white pine occurring as poorly developed trees on the driest sands and being present on over one-third of the black spruce and tamarack bogs at the other extreme of the moisture range. It grows best, however, on deep loams and sandy loams having high nutrient levels.

Because of the wide range of soil conditions on which it occurs, white pine has a great variety of associates. On the drier sands, it mixes with jack and red pines and is the most tolerant, longest-lived, and largest of these native pines.

Aspen, paper birch, and red maple are also common associates on the sandy soils, especially those soils with somewhat better moisture conditions.

On moister and cooler sites, white pine associates with balsam fir and white spruce. In this mixture it is the least tolerant of the conifers and maintains an overstory position by virtue of large size and great age. Soils on which this type occurs are more strongly podzolized than those which support the mixed-pine types.

On the very best sites the white pine occurs with the more tolerant northern hardwoods. On these sites the species attained its greatest age and largest size growing as isolated dominants among such hardwoods as sugar maple, yellow birch, elm, and basswood. Mature white pine on these sites may tower well above the hardwood associates.

There is much disagreement as to the successional role of this species. Certainly, considering the wide range of site conditions on which white pine grows, it is to be expected that its successional relationships will also vary.

Some observers (Graham, 1941; Maissurow, 1935) stress the role of fire in the distribution of eastern white pine, accounting for the presence of the tree entirely in relation to this factor. Others (Bergman, 1924) include white pine as a component of the climatic climax in parts of this region. On the lighter soils it should be considered a permanent type, or a "physiographic pseudoclimax," in the terminology of the monoclimax concept. On the heavier, more mesic soils this pine occurs in mixtures with tolerant hardwoods, where its competitive advantages are large size and longevity. It is futile to speculate as to whether the species would or would not be present in such stands if there had been no fires in times past. Fires do not introduce a species into an area or stand but merely increase its abundance if it is a "fire type" species. Probably other normal events such as wind damage would also make openings in which a few eastern white pines could maintain a foothold in the hardwood stands.

Growth Rates. The most detailed information on the growth rate of eastern white pine in the Lake States comes from a study in Wisconsin (Gevorkiantz and Zon, 1930). The results of this study are said to apply to Minnesota conditions also. Using an age of 100 years for purposes of comparison, board-foot yields per acre of even-aged fully stocked stands were found to be 32,000 on poor sites, 55,000 on medium sites, and 74,000 on good sites, using the Scribner Dec. C. rule. Mean-annual board-foot growth was found to culminate at 120 years on poor sites, 100 to 110 years on medium sites, and 90 to 100 years on good sites. Cubic-foot growth culminated at about 70 years on all sites. Plantation growth has been found to exceed these rates on similar sites.

Rotation Age or Size. Unlike red pine, eastern white pine is seldom used for wood in the round such as posts, poles, and piling. Further, white pine is not a high-yielding pulp species nor is it used as a source of other fiber products. The species is unexcelled for finishing lumber and for millwork and other related purposes because of the excellent technical properties of the wood.

However, all these uses require the conversion of logs into lumber, which in turn puts a premium on larger trees which can be grown only on long rotations.

White pine in fully stocked, unmanaged stands is shown to vary from 10.5 to 14.2 inches d.b.h. on poor and good sites, respectively, at age 100 (Gevorkiantz and Zon, 1930). Trees of this size yield only small sawlogs and have very little clear lumber. Knots and rot are the main sources of degrade. Knot reduction is attained only by pruning and growing large logs.

Since mean-annual board-foot growth culminates at 90 to 120 years, the greatest economic returns, which are based largely on the production of clear, knot-free lumber, can be expected sometime later. Rotations of 120 to 160 years seem desirable, with the shorter periods on the best sites. These coincide with rotation ages recommended for the National Forest white pine stands (Ricker and Zasada, 1958b), but are shorter than those recommended for Lower Michigan (Soc. Am. Foresters, Cutting Practices Committee, Lower Mich. Chapter, 1959).

Cultural Practices.   Because eastern white pine grows under such a variety of conditions, the development of uniform silvicultural recommendations is impossible. Silvicultural practices must be guided largely by two important considerations:

1.   What other species are associated with the white pine, and what are their relative values and ecological relations to the white pine?
2.   What is the market situation, especially with respect to the outlets for small material from intermediate cuts?

In the mixed pine types the preference usually will be for red pine first, the white pine next, and last for jack pine, unless the site is very dry, in which case white pine may be entirely "off site." This order of preference should serve as a partial guide for intermediate cuttings.

In associations with white spruce and balsam fir, the white spruce is a desirable associate by virtue of its pulpwood and sawlog value. On favorable sites the spruce reaches a size intermediate between balsam and white pine. Furthermore, this species has a tolerance advantage over the white pine which helps maintain it in this mixture. The balsam can be removed in intermediate cuttings for pulpwood and usually regenerates aggressively enough to form a perpetuating second-story canopy.

Maintaining white pine in mixture with northern hardwoods is more difficult. The hardwoods are usually more tolerant, and some species sprout well from stumps. Maintaining the pine requires more intensive management than frequently is possible. Where practicable, however, early weeding and release cuttings or herbicidal treatments should be undertaken to kill back the hardwoods and free the white pine. If this is not feasible, the stand should be managed for hardwoods while maintaining the pine as fully as possible.

Some suggested guiding principles for the silvicultural management of white pine are the following:

1. It is generally agreed that white pine stands should be managed on an essentially even-aged basis.

2. A shelterwood form of regeneration cutting is best suited to the ecology of this species (Ricker and Zasada, 1958b; Soc. Am. Foresters, Cutting Practices Committee, Lower Mich. Chapter, 1959).

3. Since the species has limited market possibilities for small and low-quality material but is unexcelled for uses requiring large, high-quality logs, emphasis must be given as early as possible to the improvement of quality, particularly through the reduction of degrade due to knots and crook. This implies pruning and the maintenance of full stocking.

4. The incidence of white pine weevil can be reduced by maintaining a protective overstory over the white pine during seedling and sapling stages. Since the pine can stand a moderate amount of suppression, this can be done with reasonable safety but with some sacrifice of growth rate. After it becomes necessary to release the pine, maintenance of relatively dense stands will help to reduce the amount of crook in weevil-damaged trees.

5. High overhead shade should be maintained at about 40 percent for the first 20 years (Ricker and Zasada, 1958b), because the species sunscalds when young and early partial shade seems to suit it.

6. White pine regeneration should not be released by cutting sprouting hardwoods until the pine is large enough to complete successfully with the sprouts. In Lower Michigan, where oaks and aspen were the species removed, it was found that release should not be effected until the pines were 6 to 8 feet tall (Engel, 1951).

7. Mortality from blister rust can be minimized by concentrating management efforts on existing stands and planting only in areas where rust hazard is low.

Susceptibility to Damage. Eastern white pine is normally windfirm and not subject to uprooting except in swampy areas or on thin soils over rock or hardpan. Overmature trees are badly rotted and subject to trunk breakage.

The white pine weevil is a serious source of damage. This insect kills the terminals, and when a lateral assumes this position the resultant crook often badly damages tree form and log quality. Injury is largely confined to seedling and sapling trees and is worst in fully exposed stands.

The pales weevil kills young seedlings on recently cutover pine lands. The adults lay their eggs in the inner bark of fresh pine stumps, and the new crop of insects attacks nearby white pine seedlings (Brown, 1959). Freshly cutover areas should not be planted to white pine until the second season after logging.

The seriousness of white pine blister rust is well known. Control efforts have been directed toward eradication of the various species of Ribes, research along genetic lines toward the selection or development of resistant strains of white pine, and in more recent years such intensive measures as canker pruning and the application of chemicals to infected trees.

Porcupines, snowshoe hares, and deer kill eastern white pines as they do red and jack pines. Deer strongly prefer it to the other pines, as probably does the snowshoe hare. The extent of this damage is difficult to evaluate and fluctuates widely with local conditions.

Eastern white pine is the least tolerant of fire of any of the native pines. While young, its thin bark is readily damaged even by light fires (Cheyney, 1942). Stands with only a few white pines associated with red pines will regenerate predominantly to white, thus suggesting that the high ratio of red in the virgin overstory will probably have been a result of early fire history.

Aspen Type Groups

Place in Ecological Succession. Aspen grows on a great variety of sites within the Lake States Region. Kittredge (1938) found aspen on 54 different soil types in Minnesota and Wisconsin. Its site affinities in the Lake States have probably been more widely studied than those of any other species (Westveld, 1933; Kittredge, 1938; Wilde and Zicker, 1948; Stoeckeler, 1948 and 1960; Graham *et al.*, 1963).

Aspen is well represented in several climatic areas within the Lake States, as is indicated by the several forest associations in which it takes part. This tree is a common associate of such boreal species as jack pine, black spruce, white spruce, balsam fir, and paper birch. It also occurs in mixture with red pine, white pine, several oaks, northern hardwoods, and minor species of the northern coniferous and deciduous forests. In addition, aspen is the major element in the prairie-savanna woodland to the west.

In general, the dry, sandy soils are the poorest sites for the species. The best sites are those with mesic moisture relationships and average nutrient levels. Kittredge (1938) found an improvement of aspen site coincidental with the lines of forest successional development, both xeric and hydric, to the hydromesic subclimax (elm-ash) and the mesic climax species (sugar maple, white pine).

Several authors (Wilde and Zicker, 1948; Stoeckeler, 1960) stress the influence of ground water on aspen site quality. Permanent water levels no shallower than about 2 feet and no deeper than about 7 feet appear to be optimum.

The degrading effect of repeated burnings on site, has been noted by Stoeckeler (1960), who estimated possible site-index reductions of 10 to 15, especially on sandy soils.

In the Lake States the highly intolerant aspen is a purely successional type.

Tremendous capacity to produce root suckers, combined with vigorous early growth makes aspen a very successful and aggressive invading species in cutover and burned stands of other species. Disking, light burning, and logging all increase the number of suckers produced.

Aspen has changed from weed status to where by 1970 it provided 50 percent of the roundwood pulpwood harvested in the Lake States Region. Its future and successional status has been a matter of increasing concern. Inventory projections assuming continuation of historic trends of cut, growth and utilization indicate that except for Minnesota "positive practices" are needed to ensure a flow of aspen sufficient to meet needs during the next 15 to 25 years (Leuschner, 1972). Earlier forecasts have been made of the extent to which the existing aspen acreage in the Lake States is being naturally converted to other species (Heinselman, 1954). These estimates indicate that by 1990 about one-third, or nearly 6 million acres will convert to other species mostly to northern hardwoods and spruce-balsam fir types. Less than 100,000 acres were expected to convert to pine.

Growth Rates. On the best aspen sites in the Lake States large trees 2 feet d.b.h. and 100 feet tall occur. However, on most areas the species is a small- to medium-sized tree which grows rapidly for about 50 years and then quickly becomes overmature.

A range of site index up to 90 has been reported by Schlaegel (1972) and from 39 to 79 by Zehngraff (1947). The latter reports gross yields of 50 to 60 cords per acre on well-stocked stands on better sites. On the poorest sites much of the aspen never attains merchantable size.

Rotation Age or Size. Rotations recommended for national forest management purposes vary from 35 on poor sites to 65 on very good sites (Jacobs *et al.*, 1958). On the poor sites only small pulp can be grown, while the rotations specified will grow sawlogs and veneer bolts on the best sites.

Cultural Practices. Because of the intolerance of the species and the even-aged character of pure aspen stands, clearcutting should be practiced at rotation ages. Leaving 15 percent of the crown cover or 30 square feet of basal area per acre reduces root suckering (Sandberg and Schneider, 1953).

The question of thinning aspen stands in the Lake States has been given much attention (Zasada, 1952; Day, 1958; Sorenson, 1968; Schaegel and Ringold, 1971; and Hubbard, 1972). In general, the desirability of precommercial thinnings are questionable and stands past about 40 years of age do not respond profitably from the release. However, most studies document the advantages of thinnings at intermediate ages from about 20 to 40 years. These, except on poor sites, salvage mortality, add significantly to total yield, and reduce the rotation needed to produce merchantable tree sizes. Unmerchantable residual trees should be killed by girdling, herbicidal treatment, or some other method. Dormant-season cutting is favored for maximum suckering. Regeneration by suckers is usually adequate and often superabundant.

In mixed stands with pine, spruce, or fir, conversion to the more valuable species is usually of economic advantage. Because of the intolerance of aspen, conversion to these other species simply by cutting the aspen first and leaving the other species as an overstory to repress the aspen suckers is usually possible. Some aspen will always persist in the openings, and this may be desirable as a reserve in the event reproductions of the other species do not become well established. White pine, spruce, and balsam fir benefit by a protective aspen overstory during their early years. Where these species are present as well-stocked understories to the aspen, it may be advantageous to harvest the aspen in several steps, thus extending the shelter period as long as desired.

Susceptibility to Damage. Defoliators including the forest tent catepillar and the large aspen tortrix are probably the most significant insect enemies of aspen (Batzer, 1972). Repeated defoliations are required to induce tree mortality, but some loss in radial growth and consequent yield reduction has been reported (Duncan and Hodson, 1958).

Wood rots and cankers are responsible for most of the disease problems with aspen (Christensen *et al.*, 1951; Anderson, 1972). By far the most common of the fungi causing heart rot of aspen is *Fomes igniarius*. Presence of the typical "horses' hoof" conks has been a traditional sign to foresters of stand overmaturity. *Hypoxylon mammatum* causes cankers on the branches or trunk, which eventually kill the tree by girdling. Open stands have a higher incidence of this disease than do well-stocked stands but there does not seem to be a correlation with site index or tree vigor.

Northern Hardwoods Type Group

This type is basically similar to the northern hardwoods described in Chapter 2. Emphasis will be made here only on those features wherein this type is unlike its northeastern counterpart.

An aspect of the occurrence of the northern hardwoods in the Lake States Region is that, in addition to the north-south transition of species, there is an equally pronounced east-west transition from Michigan to Minnesota. This feature has been mentioned earlier (Table 3-2). The ecological place held by spruce in the Northeast is probably assumed by balsam fir in the Lake States.

In Lower Michigan the type grades into the beech-sugar maple type, with beech playing an important role and with yellow-poplar, red oak, white oak, and black walnut entering as minor species.

To the south and west in Wisconsin and Minnesota the type transition is to sugar maple—basswood, with the basswood ecologically codominant and larger than the sugar maple, and the sugar maple decreasing in both size and abundance westward.

It should be emphasized not only that there is an east-west transition in which a number of species disappear going west, but also that the range of sites on which the type occurs changes drastically. In Upper Michigan, northern hardwoods are present under a wide range of site conditions. In Minnesota, the type as identified by dominance of sugar maple is found only on the most fertile soils and in proximity to large lakes, where the local climate is moderated. Table 3-2 summarizes the broader aspects of regional variation of this type.

The type is definitely climax and aggressively recaptures the site after logging under most conditions. Aspen, paper birch, balsam poplar, and black cherry are everywhere pioneer species which tend to occupy disturbed stands until succeeded by the more tolerant hardwoods.

Growth Rates and Rotation Age or Size.   Growth of the main species in this type may be considered to be about the same for the eastern part of the Lake States Region as has been described for the Northeastern Region in Chapter 2. However, the growth rate rapidly declines in going west. In western Minnesota sugar maple only rarely reaches merchantable size and quality. In eastern Wisconsin and Upper Michigan, both sugar maple and yellow birch attain large size and excellent quality as they do farther east.

On the basis of lumber-grade-recovery studies and tree-growth data, Eyre and Zillgitt (1953) recommend growing northern hardwoods to a size limit of about 24 inches d.b.h. However, they cite other studies supporting rotation diameters of 19 or 20 inches as the maximum beyond which it is not economic to retain the trees.

Cultural Practices.   With some minor differences, this type as found in the eastern part of the Lake States Region is essentially similar to its counterpart in the northeast. A full discussion of the silviculture and destructive agents of this type group was presented in Chapter 2.

TABLE 3-2

Regional Variations in Composition of Old-Growth Northern Hardwood Forests
(Percent of total number of trees 2 inches and larger)

Species	Western upper Michigan	Northeastern Wisconsin	Northern lower Michigan	North-central Minnesota
Sugar maple	33.9	25.9	34.8	29.8
Hemlock	23.8	28.6	8.3	—
Yellow birch	12.3	10.6	1.4	[a]
Basswood	2.1	7.4	8.3	37.6
Beech	0.3	5.4	18.3	—
Elm[b]	0.9	5.9	13.4	3.1
Miscellaneous conifers[c]	16.4	4.8	0.4	11.7
Miscellaneous hardwoods[d]	10.3	11.4	15.1	17.8
All species	100.0	100.0	100.0	100.0

Source: From 1936 forest-survey data compiled by Eyre and Zillgitt, 1953.

[a] Less than 0.5 percent.

[b] Mostly American elm.

[c] White spruce, balsam fir, and eastern white pine.

[d] White ash, paper birch, red maple, hophornbeam, black cherry, white oak, red oak, and aspen.

Swamp Conifer Type Group: Black Spruce

Place in Ecological Succession.   Black spruce occurs as a major species in three cover types in the Lake States Region. Two of these are listed by the Society of American Foresters (1954) as major types. In Michigan, the species' associates on muck soils are balsam fir, tamarack, northern white-cedar, balsam poplar, elm, black ash, and red maple. This type occupies relatively small acreage, and space does not permit treatment of it separately from the pure black spruce swamp type.

Black spruce also associates with jack pine and sometimes aspen and paper birch, usually as a fairly even-aged understory in an upland rather than a swamp type. This type, boreal in occurrence, is limited to portions of the Superior National Forest in Minnesota on the Laurentian Shield formation. Reference to silviculture of this type has been made in the jack pine section.

The major type in which the species occurs is the swamp black spruce type. This is of special importance in Minnesota, where, with tamarack, it covers more than 1.5 million acres. Soils there are organic, with peat accumulations varying in depth from 1 or 2 to over 30 feet. Tamarack, which also occurs as a pure type, is a common associate of black spruce.

The nature of black spruce and related northern swamp types is best understood within the general framework of northern peatland systems. Such systems are identified in three major physiognomic groups: bogs, fens, and swamps which can be defined by parameters of water chemistry and plant association patterns (Heinselman, 1970).

Vegetation on these major peatland systems is distinctive and has been described in classification systems by various authors including Jeglum *et al.* (1974) Fox *et al.* (1977) as well as in earlier studies. Bogs are characterized by a relatively simple flora dominated by sphagnum mosses and ericaceous shrubs. They are strongly acid and deficient in minerals and oxygen.

The richest swamps are dominated by northern white-cedar, black ash, black spruce and tamarack. The vast acreage of peatlands in Minnesota has been described as a black spruce—feathermoss forest by Heinselman (1970). This is the source of most of the valuable spruce pulpwood.

The ecological processes involved in wetlands are very complicated depending on such variables as climate changes over long periods of time, slope, and drainage. Two distinctly different processes exist. One, the hydrarch succession, is the classic lake filling process in which the spruce forest is a late stage sometimes being replaced by white-cedar or swamp hardwoods.

A different process, paludification, is a result of an excess of water because of climate or poor drainage making an area increasingly wet and encouraging invasion by sedges, sphaghnums and bog forest onto formerly upland areas and creating "raised bogs." Black spruce and tamarack may play a role in this succession, but because of the very acid and low nutrient conditions such bogs are less productive.

On the acid swamps, black spruce has all the appearances of a climax type. This species tends toward uneven-aged or storied structure unless disturbed by fire or logging, and it regenerates reasonably well under its own shade both by layering and as seedlings. Fire-origin stands are common and are even-aged.

Black spruce cones are semiserotinous and fire in a stand of seed-bearing age frequently regenerates a good stand of black spruce. A second fire before the trees attain cone-bearing age converts the area to brush, sedge meadow, or grass. Millions of acres of such cover in the Lake States Region, which upon examination are found to have charred wood buried in the muck, are evidence of this destructive postfire successional pattern.

Growth Rates. In general, shallow peat swamps are more productive than deep peats; swamps where there is enough physical relief to provide for water movement are better than stagnant swamps; and well-decomposed, successionally advanced swamps are probably more productive than raw, undecomposed sphagnum accumulations. However it is difficult to relate black spruce swamp-site quality to one or two single factors.

Slow growth is inevitable on such adverse sites as characterize this type. Over large areas the volume actually being logged will probably average about 10 cords per acre. This, of course, reflects great variations in stocking density and site quality. Yield tables (Fox and Kruse, 1939) show that well-stocked, unmanaged stands on good sites grow at the rate of less than one-half cord per acre per year. On poor sites the rate is about one-tenth cord per acre per year. Some of the better stands yield from 30 to 50 cords per acre of this excellent-quality pulpwood.

Rotation Age or Size. While black spruce in swamps may attain an ultimate age of 200 or more years, mean-annual increment culminates at about 100 years on good sites and 152 years on poor sites. At that time, dominants average about 55 to 60 feet tall, with an average d.b.h. of about 7 inches on better sites. However, these are average values and there is actually a wide range of sizes. Thin foliage, dead twigs, and dying tops evidence overmaturity and general decadence of trees 100 to 150 years old. Ultimate size of swamp-grown spruce ranges up to 14 inches d.b.h. and 80 feet high.

Upland black spruce trees are much shorter lived than those in swamps. Trees from 60- to 80-years old exhibit considerable butt rot, and they are usually blown down before reaching 100 years.

Cultural Practices. Possible heavy mortality by blow-down is one of the major considerations involved in silvicultural recommendations for this type. Upland stands and those growing on shallow swamps are particularly susceptible. Partial cutting in these stands is very hazardous, and clearcutting in strips or patches is prescribed. Intermediate cuttings in such stands are too hazardous to attempt.

In partial cuttings the initial cut should concentrate on the removal of stag-headed trees, those with thin crowns and an abundance of dead branch tips, mistletoe-infected trees, and trees with short crowns indicative of poor vigor. When stands are to be clearcut, the rotation age will approximate the age of growth culmination. However, since even the fire-origin stands are not strictly even-aged, and because selection of trees to be cut in partial cuttings is so dependent on tree vigor, the designation of fixed rotation ages or sizes is almost pointless.

On the deeper swamps, where wind throw is not so serious, either partial cuts geared to all-aged management or clearcuts aimed at even-aged stands may be possible. Thinning may be started in immature stands as soon as enough volume for an economic operation can be obtained. The poorer trees should be removed in these cuttings, especially those with short or injured crowns or with mistletoe infections. LeBarron (1948) found in a survey of a great variety of cuttings in Minnesota that, where no more than 50 percent of the volume or 40 percent of the basal area was removed, total mortality including wind damage during the five years following logging was minor. Other authorities (Kee *et al.,* 1958) recommended leaving 80 to 100 square feet of basal area per acre to maintain a wind-firm stand. Some regeneration will follow even such light thinnings.

Most recent evidence favors harvesting these stands on a clearcut basis, using strips or patches. Heinselman (1959) found that some form of clearcutting or shelterwood stimulated greater regeneration than did either single-tree or group selection. In addition, the ratio of desirable seedlings to the less desirable layers was considerably higher following the heavy cuttings. Strips not over 150 feet wide and patches of one-quarter to one-half acre are recommended as small enough to regenerate well and not large enough to encourage excessive wind damage. When regeneration is established on the cut areas, new strips or patches should be started so that the entire stand is removed in a series of two to four cuttings. The shelterwood system was also found to create excellent conditions for regeneration in most stands.

Unfortunately, there are no known techniques for successful planting of Lake State swamp areas. Until methods which are both practical and successful are developed, the several million acres in the Lake States which have reverted to alder brush, sedge meadows, and other worthless types will depend upon extremely slow natural successional processes to convert them to forest types.

Susceptibility to Damage.   While a number of insects attack black spruce, few cause serious economic loss. The spruce budworm defoliates some spruce where balsam fir or white spruce are associated species. Among diseases, the dwarf mistletoe causes the most damage; it produces "witches-broom," which stunts tree growth and eventually causes death. Because infection spreads rather slowly in a spot pattern, it can be controlled by clearcutting infected areas, together with an isolation strip in adjacent healthy timber. All infected reproduction should also be destroyed.

Spruce mortality may be severe in areas flooded because of beaver dams or road-building activities which disrupt normal drainage patterns.

Spruce-Fir-Hardwood Type Group

Place in Ecological Succession.   Of all the types in the region, this is perhaps the most heterogenous and consequently the most poorly defined. Balsam fir is usually considered the key species characterizing this type. The spruces, especially white spruce, are commonly associated, but in fewer numbers. The major cover types with these core species are balsam fir and white spruce—balsam fir—paper birch (Soc. Am. Foresters, 1954).

The balsam fir is a boreal type with black spruce, white spruce, and paper birch. However, in the Lake States this type often contains aspen plus northern hardwoods on the mesic sites, and swamp hardwoods on the wetter sites. The occurrence of this boreal type in the Lake States is limited largely to northern Minnesota and Upper Michigan on the cooler, wetter sites of swamp borders or on poorly drained clay sites on upland positions. In many cases it is not a natural type but is the product of logging which removed a dominant overstory of pine or hardwoods.

The spruce—balsam fir—paper birch type, together with associated aspen, pine, northern white-cedar, sugar maple, black ash, and yellow birch, is more widespread and occurs on better sites. The greater age and larger size of white spruce offset to some extent its lesser tolerance, compared with balsam fir, and thus enables it to persist. This type is usually uneven-aged or at least irregular in size distribution. The balsam occupies a subdominant position but may be well represented numerically.

Balsam fir may be considered to have the status of a climax dominant species on wet sites associated with poorly drained clay soils onto which pine and the northern hardwoods are unable to enter. On the better sites it gives way to a more mixed association. Balsam's typical position in most of the Lake States is that of a subordinate species under an overstory of northern hardwoods, white pine, aspen, and birch in various mixtures. Frequently, this arrangement of stand composition is mistakenly viewed as a stage in succession leading to the development of a spruce-balsam climax as is present in the Boreal Forest.

The different role played by balsam fir in the Lake States (Great Lakes—St. Lawrence Region) as compared with the Boreal Region is evidenced in the comparative ecographs (Fig. 3-3). First, balsam fir in the Lake States grows on a much more restricted range of site conditions and is consequently not as widespread within the region. Second, it loses out to white pine on the medium nutrient level sites of a somewhat xeric nature, and to the swamp hardwoods on the better wet sites. On the very best sites, balsam cannot stand the competition of the tolerant hardwoods such as sugar maple and basswood.

Growth Rates.   Because of the mixed character of most of the stands of this type group, and because the history of suppression which balsam fir and spruce have experienced in different stands has varied, it is difficult to generalize about growth rates. Gevorkiantz and Olsen (1950) have attempted to facilitate growth studies and predictions which recognize the influences of degree of competition and variations in stand composition as well as the customary variables of age and site quality. Data indicate that well-stocked stands on the better sites may be expected to grow more than one-half cord per acre per year. Mature stands of various densities on medium to good sites contain from 20 to 50 cords of rough wood per acre.

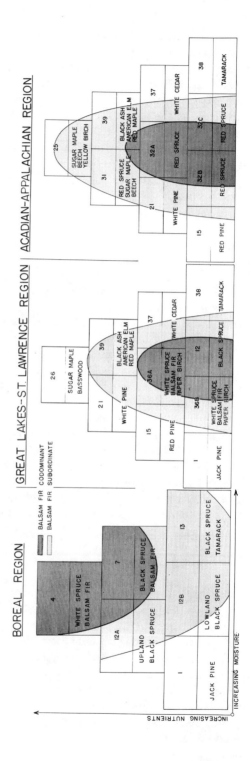

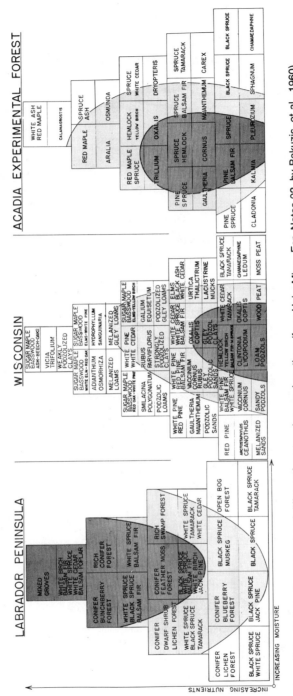

Figure 3-3. Balsam fir ecographs of different forest regions and sections (from Univ. Minn. For. Notes 92, by Bakuzis, et al., 1960).

Rotation Age or Size. Pathological condition is the controlling factor in setting rotation age for balsam fir, because of the early incidence of butt and trunk rots in this species. In the Lake States, 80 percent of the trees 80 to 90 years old have butt rot (Kaufert, 1935). It is generally agreed that rotations past 70 years are hazardous.

Because white spruce is adapted to most sites which grow balsam fir, and because the spruce is preferred in balsam fir, little planting has been done using the latter species. Stoeckeler and Skilling (1959) suggest planting the species in 1 to 3 row strips at 100 foot intervals under aspen or aspen-birch stands to provide a seed source to encourage conversion of these types to more valuable softwoods. Direct seeding attempts in Wisconsin have, in general, had little success except under ideal conditions and with ground preparation such as disking.

BIBLIOGRAPHY

Allison, J. H. 1943. Forty years' growth of planted pines in north central Minnesota. *J. For.* 41:449–450.

Anderson, G. W. 1972. Diseases. *In* Aspen pp. 74–82. *USDA For. Serv. Gen. Tech. Rep. NC-1* 154 pp.

Bakuzis, E. V., and H. L. Hansen. 1965. *Balsam fir—a monographic review.* Univ. Minn. Press., Minneapolis, 445 pp.

Batzer, H. O. 1972. Insects. *In* Aspen pp. 83–87. *USDA For. Serv. Gen. Tech. Rep. NC-1* 154 pp.

Benjamin, D. M. 1953. The jack-pine budworm—a menace to Michigan jack pine. *U.S. For. Serv., Lake States For. Exp. Stn. Tech. Note 376.* 1 p.

Bergman, H. F. 1924. The composition of climax plant formations in Minnesota. *Pap. Mich. Acad. Sci.* 3:51–60.

Bickerstaff, A. 1946. Effect of thinning and pruning upon the form of red pine. *Can. Dominion For. Serv. Silvic. Res. Note 81.* 26 pp.

Blyth, J. E., A. H. Boelter, and C. W. Danielson. 1975. Primary forest products industry and timber use, Michigan, 1972. *USDA For. Serv. Resour. Bull. NC-24, 45 pp.*

Blyth, J. E., and J. T. Hahn. 1977. Pulpwood production in the Lake States by county, 1976. *USDA For. Serv. Res. Note NC-223.* 4 pp.

Blyth, J. E., E. F. Landt, J. W. Whipple, and J. T. Hahn. 1976. Primary forest products industry and timber use. Wisconsin, 1973. *USDA For. Serv. Resour. Bull. NC-31.* 61 pp.

Braun, E. L. 1950. *Deciduous forests of eastern United States.* The Blakiston Co. Philadelphia. 596 pp.

Brown, R. C. 1959. Eastern white pine insect damage and control. *In* What's known about managing eastern white pine. *U.S. For. Serv., Northeast. For. Exp. Stn. Pap. 121.* 69 pp.

Byelich, J. D., J. L. Cook, and R. I. Blouch. 1972. Management for deer. *In* Aspen. pp. 120–125. *USDA For. Serv. Gen. Tech. Rep NC-1.* 154 pp.

Cheyney, E. G. 1942. *American silvics and silviculture.* Univ. Minn. Press, Minneapolis. 472 pp.

Christensen, C. M., R. L. Anderson, A. C. Hodson, and P. O. Rudolf. 1951. Enemies of aspen. *U.S. For. Serv. Lake States For. Exp. Stn. Aspen Rep. 22.* 16 pp.

Curtis, J. T. 1959. *The vegetation of Wisconsin.* Univ. Wisc. Press, Madison, 657 pp.

Daubenmire, R. F. 1936. The "Big Woods" of Minnesota. Its structure, and relation to climate, fire, and soils. *Ecol. Monog.* 6:223–268.

Day, M. C. 1958. Thinning aspen in Upper Michigan. *Mich. Agr. Exp. Stn. O. Bull. 41.* 9 pp.

Duncan, D. P., and A. C. Hodson, 1958. Influence of the forest tent caterpillar upon the aspen forests of Minnesota. *For. Sci.* 4:71—93.

Engel. L. G. 1951. Releasing white pine from oak and aspen. *U.S. For. Serv. Lake States For. Exp. Stn. Tech. Notes 346.* 2 pp.

Eyre, F. H. 1938. Can jack pine be regenerated without fire? *J. For.* 36:1067—1072.

Eyre, F. H., and R. K. LeBarron. 1944. Management of jack pine stands in the Lake States. *USDA Tech. Bull. 863.* 66 pp.

Eyre, F. H. and P. Zehngraff. 1948. Red pine management in Minnesota. *USDA Cir. 778.* 70 pp.

Eyre, F. H., and W. M. Zillgitt. 1953. Partial cuttings in northern hardwoods of the Lake States. *USDA Tech. Bull. 1076.* 124 pp.

Farrar, J. L., D. W. Gray, and D. Avery. 1954. Jack pine reproduction. *Pulp and Paper Mag. of Can.* 55:136—146.

Fedkenheuer, A. W., and H. L. Hansen. 1971. Winter cover use by white-tailed deer (*Odocoileus virginianus*) in St. Croix State Park, Minnesota. *Minn. For. Res. Notes 223.* 4 pp.

Fox, G. D., and G. W. Kruse, 1939. A yield table for well-stocked stands of black spruce in northeastern Minnesota. *J. For.* 37:565—567.

Fox, R., T. Malterer, and R. Zarth. 1977. Inventory of peat resources in Minnesota. Unpubl. progress report, *Minn. Dept. Nat. Resour. Div. of Minerals.* 36 pp.

Gevorkiantz, S. R. 1947. Growth and yield of jack pine in the Lake States. *U.S. For. Serv. Lake States For. Exp. Stn. Paper 7.* 11 pp.

Gevorkiantz, S. R. 1957. Site index curves for red pine in the Lake States. *U.S. For. Serv. Lake States For. Exp. Stn. Tech. Note 484* 2 pp.

Gevorkiantz, S. R., and L. P. Olsen. 1950. Growth and yield of upland balsam fir in the Lake States. *U.S. For. Serv. Lake States For. Exp. Stn. Pap. 22* 24 pp.

Gevorkiantz, S. R., and R. Zon. 1930. Second-growth white pine in Wisconsin. *Univ. Wis. Agr. Exp. Stn. Res. Bull. 98.* 40 pp.

Graham, S. A. 1941. Climax forests of the Upper Peninsula of Michigan. *Ecology* 22:355—362.

Graham, S. A., R. P. Harrison, Jr., and C. E. Westell, Jr. 1963. *Aspens: Phoenix trees of the Great Lake Region.* Univ. Mich. Press. Ann Arbor. 272 pp.

Guilkey, P. C. 1958. Managing red pine for poles in lower Michigan. *U.S. For. Serv. Lake States For. Exp. Stn. Pap. 57.* 21 pp.

Gullion, G. W. 1972. *In* Aspen, pp. 113—119. The basic habitat resource for ruffed grouse. *USDA For. Serv. Gen Tech Rep. NC-1.* 154 pp.

Halliday, W. E. D. 1937. A forest classification for Canada. *Can. Dept. Resour. and Devlpmt. For. Res. Div. For. Serv. Bull. 89.* 50 pp.

Hansen, H. L. 1946. An analysis of jack pine sites in Minnesota. Ph. D. dissertation. Univ. Minn. 115 pp.

Hansen, H. L. 1952. Indicator value of plants in jack pine sites. *In Proc. Minn. Acad. Sci.* pp. 19—22.

Hansen, H.L., and D. P. Duncan 1954. The management of Itasca State Park to meet recreational objectives. *Proc. Soc. Am. For.* 210 pp.

Heinselman, M. L. 1954. The extent of natural conversion to other species in the Lake States aspen-birch type. *J. For.* 52:737—738.

Heinselman, M. L. 1959. Natural regeneration of swamp black spruce in Minnesota under various cutting systems. *USDA Prod. Res. Rep. 32.* 22 pp.

Heinselman, M. L. 1970. Landscape evolution, peatland types and the environment in the Lake Agassiz Peatlands Natural Area, Minnesota. *Ecol. Monogr.* 40:235—261.

Hills, G. A. 1952. The classification and evaluation of site for foresty. *Ont. Dept. Lands and For. Div. Res. Rep. 24.* 41 pp.

Hubbard, J. W. 1972. Effects of thinning on growth and yield. *In* Aspen pp. 126–130. *USDA For. Serv. Gen. Tech. Rep. NC-1* 154 pp.

Jacobs, H. C., Z. A., Zasada, and J. L. Arend. 1958. Timber management guide for the national forests of the North Central States: aspen-paper birch type. *U.S. For. Serv.* Washington D.C. 16 pp.

Jeglum, J. K., A. N. Boissenneau, and V. F. Haavisto. 1974. Toward a wetland classification for Ontario. *Can. For. Serv. Great Lakes For. Res. Centre, Inf. Rep 0-X-215.* 54 pp.

Kaufert, F. H. 1933. Fire and decay injury in the southern bottomland hardwoods. *J. For.* 31:64–67.

Kaufert, F. H. 1935. Heart rot of balsam fir in the Lake States. with special reference to forest management. *Univ. Minn. Agr. Exp. Stn. Tech. Bull.* 110. 27 pp.

Kee, D. N., S. J. Dolegaard, and Z. A. Zasada. 1958. Timber management guide for the national forests of the North Central States: black spruce type. *U.S. For. Serv.* Washington D.C. 14 pp.

Kittredge, J., Jr. 1938. The interrelations of habitat, growth rate and associated vegetation in the aspen community of Minnesota and Wisconsin. *Ecol. Monog.* 8:153–246.

Krefting, L. W., and H. L. Hansen. 1969. Increasing deer browse by aerial applications of 2,4-D. *J. Wildl. Mgmt.* 33:784–790.

Larsson, H. C., N. F. Lyon, and G. W. Cameron. 1949. Regeneration studies on spruce-fir, spruce, pine and poplar lands in the mid-western and western regions, 1948. *Ont. Dept. Lands and For. Div. Res. Rep. 19.* 66 pp.

LeBarron, R. K. 1948. Silvicultural management of black spruce in Minnesota. *USDA Circ. 791.* 60 pp.

Leuschner, W. A. 1972. Projections of inventories in the Lake States. *In* Aspen pp. 10–15. *USDA For. Serv. Gen. Tech. Rep. NC-1.* 154 pp.

Maissurow, D. K. 1935. Fire as a necessary factor in the perpetuation of white pine. *J. For.* 33:373–378.

Ricker, D. R., and Z. A. Zasada. 1958a. Timber management guide for the national forests of the North Central States: red pine type. *U.S. For. Serv.* Washington, D.C. 13 pp.

Ricker, D. R., and Z. A. Zasada. 1958b. Timber management guide for the national forests of the North Central States: white pine type. *U.S. For. Serv.* Washington, D.C. 12 pp.

Rowe, J. S. 1959. Forest regions of Canada. *Can. Dept. Northern Affairs and National Resour. For. Br. Bull. 123.* 71 pp.

Rudolf, P. O. 1950. Forest plantations in the Lake States. *USDA Tech. Bull. 1010.* 171 pp.

Rudolf, P. O. 1957. Silvical characteristics of red pine. *U.S. For. Serv. Lake States For. Exp. Stn. Pap. 44.* 32 pp.

Sandberg, D., and A. E. Schneider. 1953. The regeneration of aspen by suckering. *Univ. Minn. For. Notes 24,* 2 pp.

Schantz-Hansen, T. 1931. Current growth in Norway pine. *J. For.* 29: 802–806.

Schantz-Hansen, T. 1945. Some results of thinning fifteen-year-old red pine. *J. For.* 43:673–674.

Schantz-Hansen, T., and R. A. Jensen. 1956. Forty years of weather at the Cloquet Experimental Forest. *Univ. Minn. Agr. Exp. Stn. Bull. 436.* 20 pp.

Schantz, H. L., and R. Zon. 1924. *Natural vegetation. In* Atlas of American Agriculture. *U.S. Gov. Print. Off.* Washington, D.C. 29 pp.

Schoenike, R. E. 1976. Geographical variations in jack pine. *Univ. Minn. Agr. Exp. Stn. Bull.* 304.47 pp.

Slabaugh, P. E. 1957. Do pruned red pine trees remain dormant? *US For. Serv. Lake States For. Exp. Stn. Tech. Note 476.* 2 pp.

Schlaegel, B. E. 1972. Growth and yield of managed stands. *In* Aspen pp. 109−112. *USDA For. Serv. Gen. Tech. Rep. NC-1* 154 pp.

Schlaegel, B. E., and S. B. Ringold. 1971. Thinning pole-size aspen has no effect on number of veneer trees or total yield. *USDA For. Serv. Res Note. NC-121.* 2 pp.

Soc. Am. Foresters. 1954. *Forest cover types of North America.* 4th ed. Washington, D.C. 67 pp.

Soc. Am. Foresters, Cutting Practices Committee, Lower Mich. Chapter. 1959. Recommended forest cutting practices for Lower Michigan. 37 pp.

Sonley, C. R. 1950. Cable yarding in relation to forest management. *Pulp and Paper Mag. of Can.* 51:274−276.

Sorenson, R. W. 1968. Size of aspen crop trees little affected by initial sucker density. *USDA For. Serv. Res. Note NC-51.* 4 pp.

Spurr, S. H., and J. H. Allison. 1952. Growth of mature red pine. *Minn. For. Notes 9.* 2 pp.

Stoeckeler, J. H. 1948. The growth of quaking aspen as affected by soil properties and fire. *J. For.* 46: 727−737.

Stoeckeler, J. H. 1960. Soil factors affecting the growth of quaking aspen forests in the Lake States. *Univ. Minn. Agr. Exp. Stn. Tech. Bull. 233.* 46 pp.

Stoeckeler, J. H., and D. D. Skilling. 1959. Direct seeding and planting of balsam fir in northern Wisconsin. *U.S. For. Serv., Lake States For. Exp. Stn. 72.* 22 pp.

Tappeiner, J. C. II, and R. A. Dahlman, 1971. Control of young hazel undergrowth by light application of 2,4-D. *Univ. Minn. For. Res. Notes 231.* 4 pp.

U.S. Dept. Agr. 1941. *Climate and man, yearbook of agriculture, 1941.* Gov. Print. Off. Washington, D.C. 1248 pp.

Westveld, R. H. 1933. The relation of certain soil characteristics to forest growth and composition in the northern hardwood forest of northern Michigan. *Mich. State Univ. Coll. Agr. Exp. Stn. Tech. Bull. 135.* 52 pp.

Wilde, S. A., and E. L. Zicker, 1948. Influence of the ground water table upon the distribution and growth of aspen and jack pine in Central Wisconsin. *Univ. Wisc. Coll. of Agr. and Wis. Conserv. Dept. Tech. Note 30.* 12 pp.

Wilde, S. A., F. G. Wilson, and D. P. White. 1949. Soils of Wisconsin in relation to silviculture. *Wisc. Conserv. Dept. Publ. 525.* 171 pp.

Zasada, Z. A. 1952. Reproduction on cut-over swamplands in the Upper Peninsula of Michigan. *U.S. For. Serv. Lake States For. Exp. Stn. Pap. 27.* 15 pp.

Zasada, Z. A., and R. E. Buckman. 1957. Growth and yield of a young red pine plantation in northern Minnesota. *U.S. For. Serv. Lake States For. Exp. Stn. Tech. Note 491.* 2 pp.

Zehngraff, P. 1947. Possibilities of managing aspen. *U.S. For. Serv. Lake States For. Exp. Stn., Lake States Aspen Rep. 21.* 23 pp.

4

The Central Region

Clair Merritt

LOCATION

The Central Region extends from the prairie borders west of the Mississippi River to the Alleghany and Cumberland plateaus of eastern Ohio and Kentucky, and from the northern limit of the driftless area in Wisconsin and Minnesota to the Boston Mountains in northwestern Arkansas (Fig. 4-1). All or portions of 14 states are included in this region (Table 4-1). Most of the Midland Hardwood Forest (Fig. 1-5) lies within its borders as well as portions of the Appalachian Forest, the Ozark-Piedmont Forest and the Mixed Mesophytic Forest Region.

Boundaries for the Central Region were drawn rather arbitrarily and do not coincide with political subdivisions. Though forest types through this portion of eastern United States are not sharply delimited, prominence of the oak-hickory type group was used as a general guide in defining this region. Nevertheless, considerable areas of this major Eastern hardwood-type occurs outside the Central Region.

FOREST STATISTICS[1]

Area

Forests of the Central Region occupy about 50 million acres, or approximately 15 percent of the total land area. Actual percentages of forested land range from less than 1 percent in South Dakota to 57 percent in northwestern Arkansas (Table 4-1). Total forest area has declined slightly over the last 25

[1]Statistical data not otherwise referenced have been compiled from Barnard and Bowers, 1977; Chase and Strickler, 1968; Chase, Pfeifer, and Spencer, 1970; Choate and Spencer, 1968; Earles, 1976; Hedlund and Earles, 1970; Kingsley and Mayer, 1970; Merz, 1978; Murphy, 1977; Ostrom, 1976; Spencer, 1969; Spencer and Thorne, 1972; Stone, 1966; Troutman and Porterfield, 1974; U.S. Bureau Census, 1973; U.S. For. Serv. 1971; U.S. For. Serv. 1973.

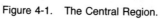

MILES

Figure 4-1.   The Central Region.

TABLE 4-1

Distribution of Population, Land, and Forest Area by States in the Central Region

State	Population (millions)	Land Area (million acres)	Commercial Forest Area (million acres)	Percent Forest
Ohio	10.652	26.251	6.329	24.1
Indiana	5.194	23.161	3.837	16.6
Illinois	11.114	35.795	3.680	10.3
Iowa	2.825	35.868	1.459	4.1
Missouri	4.677	44.189	12.365	28.0
Southern Michigan[a]	6.009	9.238	2.757	29.8
Southwestern Wisconsin[a]	1.412	11.024	2.545	23.1
Southern Minnesota[a]	3.007	20.741	1.604	7.7
Southeastern South Dakota[a]	0.228	5.579	0.050	0.9
Eastern Nebraska[a]	1.361	47.000	0.805	1.7
Eastern Kansas[a]	2.077	47.576	1.321	2.8
Northeastern Oklahoma[a]	0.133	2.571	1.077	41.9
Northwestern Arkansas[a]	0.456	11.000	6.268	57.0
Central Kentucky[a]	2.500	16.625	6.178	37.2
Total region	51.645	336.618	50.275	14.9

[a] Statistics compiled from counties included within region as defined herein.

years and further declines are expected in the future. However, commercial forest area has increased in some states. Ohio has experienced a 17 percent increase, principally in the southeastern hill country, forest land in Kansas has increased 8 percent, and in Kentucky 3 percent.

Significant to forest management is the large population concentrated in this region. In 1970 almost 52 million people resided within its boundaries; a ratio of about one person for each forested acre. Thirteen of the 50 largest metropolitan areas of the US are either within the region or close thereto. Transportation facilities are extensive rendering all portions of the area easily accessible to population centers.

The region contains some of the most productive agricultural and hardwood forest land in the country, especially in the glaciated area commonly known as the Corn Belt. However, the quality of sites for timber production on shallow-soil ridges and upper south slopes in unglaciated portions of the region, especially in the Ozarks, is often low to poor, as is the 8.5-million-acre Claypan Region of south central Illinois (Holland, 1962). Nevertheless, the majority of the unglaciated hilly land is highly productive. None of the forest land in the southeast hill country of Ohio, for example, is considered to be unproductive because of adverse site conditions (DeBald and McCay, 1969).

Character of Forest Land Ownership

Approximately 90 percent of the commercial forest land in the region is privately owned. Farmers, the largest single class of forest land owners, have approximately 52 percent of the total. However, this figure is subject to considerable variation. In Iowa farmers own about 68 percent of the commercial timberland, whereas in eastern Ohio they own 38 percent. Industry holds less than 2 percent of the total.

Average woodland ownership size is also variable ranging from approximately 20 acres in the glaciated farm belt to about 100 acres in the hilly lands to the south. In Iowa where much woodland occurs in narrow strips, average woodland size is less than 15 acres. Nevertheless, these small areas are locally significant through their effect on the use of adjacent land in providing protection from wind, game cover, and forest products (Hartong and Moessner, 1956).

A significant trend in recent years is the shift of forest ownership to the nonfarm private sector (Doolittle, 1978). These individuals hold land for a variety of reasons including speculation, recreation, and second homes. Timber production is often of minor concern. On the other hand, some of these owners, many of whom are professional people, are intensely interested in proper management techniques and are more likely to follow recommended treatments than is the farm owner.[2]

Even though a sizable number of forest owners do not wish to harvest timber for aesthetic reasons, average tenure of ownership is short (about 15 years in Indiana) and sooner or later much of the available timber comes on the market as lands are sold and exchanged.

Forest Inventory

At least 73 tree species are native to the Central Region (Merz, 1978; Crankshaw et al., 1965). Of these, hardwoods comprise the vast majority making up 95 percent of the total growing-stock volume.

The most extensive forest type group, oak-hickory, occupies 72 percent of the forest acreage. In the five states which are included in their entirety within this region, oak species alone comprise 48 percent of the total cubic-foot volume of growing stock. Softwoods make up three percent of the total.

The next largest type group, elm-ash-cottonwood, a lowland type occurring throughout the region, occupies about 17 percent of the acreage.

Softwoods occur both naturally and in plantation throughout the region. Most of the naturally occurring softwood species are located in southeastern Kentucky and Ohio and in the Ozark Plateau Province of Missouri and northwestern Arkansas. Shortleaf pine is the major species but eastern redcedar is also locally important. In Missouri, for example, redcedar occurs in either pure stands or mixed with hardwoods on about 248,000 acres (Spencer and Essex,

[2]Personal correspondence with Robert Koenig, Indiana Division of Forestry.

1976). In Kentucky the type is estimated to cover 470,000 acres (Gansner, 1968). Elsewhere in the region it occupies smaller acreages.

For most part softwoods grow in stands in which hardwoods, principally oak, make up 50 percent or more of the trees. This mixed type occupies about 4 percent of the total forest land in the region.

Timber volume is increasing throughout the Central Region as annual growth consistently exceeds removals by 1 to 2 percent. However, average timber quality continues to decline as cut is concentrated in trees expected to yield high-quality veneer and sawtimber. A significant potential exists for future improvements in quality since increasing volumes are concentrated in small-diameter trees which are graded low simply on the basis of size (DeBald and McCay, 1969).

THE PHYSICAL ENVIRONMENT

Geology and Physiography

Almost ⅔ of the Central Region has been glaciated. Much of the land area north of the Ohio River westward to its confluence with the Mississippi River, then northwestward to and along the Missouri River was covered by one or more advances of the ice sheet during the Pleistocene Epoch. Most of the glaciated area was covered by the Wisconsin ice sheet, the last of the great advances. With the notable exception of the unglaciated Driftless Area in southwestern Wisconsin and adjoining areas, the topography is level and gently rolling with low relief and composed of till and outwash plains, old lake beds, beaches, moraines, and other glacial features. Loessal deposits of varying thicknesses cover portions of the region, particularly on lands east and northeast of the major river systems.

All the parent materials south of the glaciated boundary are sedimentary. This area is divided into three provinces, the Ozark Plateaus, the Interior Low Plateau, and the Appalachian Plateaus (Fenneman, 1938).

The Ozark Plateaus Province of southern Missouri, northern Arkansas, and northeastern Oklahoma is subdivided into the Ozark Highland and the Boston Mountains (U.S. For. Serv., 1969). It consists of uplifted Paleozoic sedimentary rock which has been highly dissected by stream erosion into steep-sided mountains with narrow, rolling ridgetops and deep narrow valleys (U.S. For. Serv., 1977c; Braun, 1950). Limestone is prominent in the Ozark Highland and sandstone and shale in the Boston Mountains. Elevations range from about 400 to 2,750 feet.

The Appalachian Plateaus Province is represented in this region by a narrow belt of land along the eastern edge of Ohio. It is an area of steep hills and narrow valleys with few well-organized ridges (Kingsley and Mayer, 1970).

The Interior Low Plateau Province lies between the two previously described provinces in Kentucky, southern Indiana, and Illinois. Its topography is dependent on the nature of the underlying rock structure, but in general is much less precipitous. This province includes the highly fertile Bluegrass country of Kentucky, underlain by Ordovician limestones; the Knobs area of Indiana and Kentucky, a region of more rugged topography typified by rounded hills, limestone caverns, and sinkholes; and the Shawnee physiographic section which is a hilly area of variable topography containing both limestones and sandstones. The vegetation is complex and variable.

Considerable coal mining, primarily open pit, takes place in the Central Region. Deposits of Pennsylvanian-age coal lie close to the surface in portions of Ohio, Indiana, Illinois, Kentucky, Iowa, and Missouri. Early state legislation requiring revegetation of disturbed land generated considerable interest in tree-planting techniques. More stringent legislation of recent years is encouraging development of mined lands for grass and grain crops rather than trees. In 1968, for example, 38 percent of the strip-mined land in Indiana on which reclamation plans had been approved by the state were planted to trees. Another 60 percent was approved for noncultivated range land, most of which is now in pioneer stages of forest succession—excellent wildlife habitat. In 1977 comparative figures were 7 percent for forests and 11 percent for range.[3]

Soils

Soils of the glaciated areas are relatively young. However, ages may vary from 1 million to possibly only 10,000 years depending on which glacial stage was the last to cover the area. Soils are predominantly Alfisols or Mollisols (Fig. 4-2). Both Alfisols and Mollisols also occur in unglaciated Kentucky (USDA Soil Survey Staff, 1975).

Alfisols are characterized by an argillic horizon and moderate to high base saturation. A fragipan may be present. Alfisols in the Central Region were originally covered by deciduous hardwood forest but are now largely under cultivation. Severely eroded soils may have only an argillic horizon below an Ap horizon and reestablishment of forests of valuable hardwood species is extremely difficult.

Alfisols in southwestern Wisconsin, southeastern Minnesota, eastern Iowa, southern and western Illinois, eastern Missouri, southern Indiana and Ohio, northeastern Arkansas, and western Kentucky were developed in loess of variable thickness deposited on soils of varying age and composition. Many contain fragipans. Quality of sites for tree growth is consequently variable and often difficult to estimate.

Mollisols are base-rich, very dark colored soils typical of grasslands. They have considerable organic matter incorporation in the upper horizon. Though primarily formed under grass, many were formed under forest which has largely been removed.

The Mollisols, suborder Aquolls, of western Kentucky are wetter soils with

[3]Data provided by Richard McNabb, Indiana State Reclamation Forester

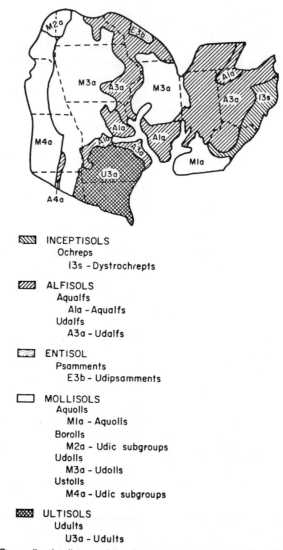

INCEPTISOLS
  Ochreps
    I3s - Dystrochrepts

ALFISOLS
  Aqualfs
    Ala - Aqualfs
  Udalfs
    A3a - Udalfs

ENTISOL
  Psamments
    E3b - Udipsamments

MOLLISOLS
  Aquolls
    Mla - Aquolls
  Borolls
    M2a - Udic subgroups
  Udolls
    M3a - Udolls
  Ustolls
    M4a - Udic subgroups

ULTISOLS
  Udults
    U3a - Udults

Figure 4-2. Generalized soil map of the Central Region (Adapted from USDA, Soil Survey Staff, 1975).

high water tables and some mottling. They occur on broad flats, seepy hillsides, or on calcareous drift or loess.

The Ozark Plateaus are primarily Ultisols, suborder Udults. These soils originally supported both conifers and hardwoods. They are freely drained, acid, humus-poor soils containing an argillic horizon. Bases released by weathering are largely concentrated in the vegetation and in the upper few centimeters of the soil. Cultivation of these soils requires soil amendments and many originally cleared for farms have reverted to forest cover.

The soils of the Appalachian Plateau of eastern Ohio are mostly Inceptisols, suborder Ochrepts. They were formed from generally acid parent materials. They are udic and contain no fragipan. Hardwood forests were the principal original cover.

Climate and Weather

The Central Region is characterized by a continental humid to subhumid climate. Summers are hot and winters cold. However, due to the broad extent of this region, considerable variation occurs in local patterns of temperature and precipitation.

In central Arkansas, for example, mean annual precipitation is 42 inches, mean total snowfall is 5 inches, and the mean annual temperature is 61 °F. In contrast, mean values for Minneapolis, Minnesota, are about 26 inches for precipitation, 46 inches for snowfall, and temperature 44 °F. Respective average growing season lengths are 100 days in Minnesota and 180 days in northern Arkansas.

Climatic averages in other parts of the region generally range between these extremes, although individual locations and years show considerable departure from mean values. Areas east and southeast of the Great Lakes, for example, experience much heavier than average snowfall. In Youngstown, Ohio, 21 inches of snow has been recorded in one 24-hour period.

For the region as a whole, about 53 percent of the annual precipitation falls in the five months of April through August, providing excellent conditions for tree growth. Mean annual precipitation is about 38 inches.

Destructive winds, often in the form of tornadoes, occur in all parts of the region, though they tend to be more frequent to the southwest. Oklahoma recorded an average of 56 tornadoes each year for the period 1956–1975. Thirty-five occurred annually during the same period in Nebraska, 32 in Missouri, 17 in Minnesota, 15 in Ohio, and 9 in Kentucky (U.S. Dept. of Commerce, 1976). Though tornado paths are relatively narrow, cumulatively they can cause considerable damage to the forest.

The range in climatic values has pronounced effect on species distribution. The ranges of several northern species, for example, terminate in southern Illinois while those of a number of southern species reach their northern limit in the same area (Merz, 1978). Similarly Friesner (1937) called Indiana a "critical botanical area" where northern and southern species meet.

HISTORY OF FOREST USE

The present occurrence, condition, and management of central hardwoods types must be understood in the context of local land-use history which in turn is closely tied to its geography. Early access to this region was provided by the major waterways and their tributaries. By 1820 lands along and adjacent to the Ohio River, the lower reaches of the Wabash River, and Lake Erie were rapidly being settled. Expansion was stimulated as the railroads began pushing into the region in the 1850s, and by 1890 the entire region was under development (U.S. Dept. Int., 1970).

Early land clearing for agriculture was largely confined to hilly well-drained soils since settlers did not recognize the basic fertility of the level, often wetter, lands of the glaciated areas (Melhorn, 1956). Consequently, most of the uplands south of the glacial boundary were cleared of forest. The poor farming practices of the day soon led to severe soil erosion and loss of fertility. As farmers learned to drain and till the flatter areas of the glaciated regions to the north, land abandonment in the southern hills became widespread. Today these uplands are largely occupied by even-aged stands of low-quality hardwoods, usually oak-hickory, and some pine and mixed pine-hardwoods. Resident agriculture occupies the interspersed more productive gentle slopes, terraces, and bottomlands. In areas of southern Ohio, Indiana, and Illinois the summits of flat-topped hills are covered with deep loessal deposits and many have been converted to grassland agriculture.

Woodlands that were not originally cleared were invariably heavily cut to provide the timber needs of an expanding population. The highest quality trees were in greatest demand, but markets for firewood, ties, and mine props opened the way for even greater destructive cutting.

High-grading, grazing, and burning of the woodlands continued into the depression years of the 1930s when forest products sometimes constituted the medium of exchange in rural communities. Management practices have improved considerably since that time but the woodlands of today represent the culled-over remains of once magnificent forests and will continue to bear the scars of mismanagement well into the future.

Compounding the problem of current management is the lack of markets for the variety of primary forest products which could be produced. While excellent markets exist for veneer-quality hardwood sawlogs, small- and low-quality logs are difficult to sell. Intermediate cuttings are therefore largely precommercial and pressure is great to high-grade stands.

Due to the nature of the topography, the southern hilly portions of the Central Region contain relatively large contiguous woodlands. In glaciated areas, woodlands occupy primarily the portions of the land which cannot be easily worked for row crops. They are therefore limited in size and widely dispersed. Along the prairie fringes of the Central Region, these wooded areas tend to be located on steep bluffs and ravines and in stringers along poorly drained bottomlands. Elsewhere, especially through the central and northern portions of Ohio, Indiana, Illinois, and eastern Iowa, they are found on rough or rocky land, poorly drained uplands, along stream banks and on bottomlands subject to overflow. Small woodlands of just a few acres may contain a range of sites from good to poor and the forester must adjust management practices to accommodate these variations.

Recent land-use developments in the Central Region give considerable cause for concern. Urban expansion is continuing so rapidly that serious consideration is being given in some communities to land-use zoning (Huemoeller et al.,

1976). An agrarian society still dominates in the western portions of the region, but the east is rapidly becoming industrialized. Less than 10 percent of the population in Ohio is estimated to be employed in agriculture, fisheries or forestry, while in Iowa this figure exceeds 25 percent. Recreation and second homes are also exerting considerable impact on the rural landscape. Land prices reflect this pressure and timber management for pure economic return is becoming impractical in many areas.

Sizeable conversion of forest to nonforest land is also taking place in the Missouri-Arkansas area. In Missouri, 1,746,000 acres of forest were converted between 1959 and 1972 to other uses, principally pasture (Spencer and Essex, 1976). This change of forest to grassland exerts a major impact on wildlife, aesthetics, and timber production.

The history of silvicultural practices in the Central Region has been marked by vociferous conflict, particularly as regards the role of clearcutting in regeneration. Largely in reaction to past indiscriminate high grading and commercial clearcutting, state forestry organizations of the region almost unanimously began to promulgate partial cutting, usually selection, as the appropriate management technique. The opposing camp, led by U.S. Forest Service researchers, recommended clearcutting, particularly in oak-hickory types. They argued that silvical requirements of the more valuable species, efficiency in logging, simplicity of regulation, and requirements for stem-quality development were best satisfied by this method. Nevertheless, the states continue to advise and practice selection cutting even though the composition of many oak-hickory timber stands subject to this treatment is trending to less valuable tolerant species. A principal argument is that the periodic monetary returns of partial cutting tend to maintain owners' interest in management. An even more compelling argument is that many owners simply do not wish to clearcut. Amenity values are of equal or greater importance to them and partial cutting is therefore the indicated procedure, regardless of stand composition consequences.

MAJOR FOREST TYPE GROUPS

The Central Region forest is one of great complexity. Though generally classified as oak-hickory, it includes such diverse cover types as elm-ash-cottonwood on the lowlands, beech-sweetgum-pin oak flats, mixed pine-hardwood on the dry soils of the southern portion of the region, eastern red-cedar primarily on thin, limy soils but universally present as a pioneer, northern hardwood intergrades in the north, and scattered prairie grasslands and savannas from Iowa through north central Illinois, Indiana, and Ohio. Interspersed among these types are various mixtures of the oaks, with hickory, elm, sugar maple, ash, yellow-poplar, black walnut, and a host of others. It is not uncommon to find woodlands as small as 10 acres containing 15 to 20 commercial tree species. Silvical characteristics and management possibilities for some of these species are found in Tables 5-4 (page 164) and 5-6 (page 196).

Presettlement forest types probably conformed closely to soil and drainage variations. Today this correspondence is often difficult to discern. Land drainage for agriculture and a history of severe high-grading coupled with indiscriminate grazing and burning has distorted original patterns, even completely eliminating some species from localized areas.

Oak-hickory is said to be the most extensive timber type in the United States (Watt *et al.*, 1973). The type group is usually defined as including all stands in which oaks or hickories, singly or in combination, comprise 50 percent or more of the trees. White oak-red oak-hickory (Soc. Am. For., 1967) is the principal cover type. However, post oak-black oak, scarlet oak, bur oak, chestnut oak, white oak, and northern red oak cover types are also included in the oak-hickory type group.

Oak-hickory types are found on sites ranging from deep, loamy productive soils to dry, shallow-soil ridgetops. However, under current management practices the oak-hickory type is rapidly being replaced on many of the better sites by other species. It is commonly believed that the widespread occurrence of oak-hickory throughout eastern United States is primarily due to a history of recurrent wildfire and heavy cutting. With modern, efficient wildfire control and a trend to partial cutting, oaks and hickories are declining in importance on many sites.

The best timber growing sites in the region are those with deep, mesic soils. Many such areas are still occupied by oak-hickory cover types, or by mixed-oak stands (Ill. Techn. For. Assoc., 1965), but these types are largely temporary.

Better sites are usually occupied by a diverse mixture of hardwood species. In southern Michigan and in much of central and northern Indiana and Ohio, beech and maple are important components of the forest. This intergrade with the northern hardwood forest has been classified by many as beech-maple (Braun, 1950; Bailey, 1976; Lindsey and Schmeltz, 1970). In eastern Ohio the species mixture becomes even richer and merges with the Mixed Mesophytic Forest Region of Braun (1950). For the purposes of this discussion both of the above intergrades will be lumped into a mixedwoods type group. However, it is instructive to consider the ecoregional classifications of Bailey (1976) in Fig. 4-3.

The second largest type group in the region, elm-ash-cottonwood, is found principally in bottomlands and floodplains bordering the many rivers and streams. The principal components of the type are American elm, green ash, eastern cottonwood, and silver maple, occurring singly or in combination (Shifley and Brown, 1978). Major associates include hackberry, American sycamore, black willow, and boxelder. Typical sites are extremely productive.

Eastern redcedar, the most widely distributed conifer of tree size in eastern United States, is found in every state east of the 100th meridian and in Canada (Fowells, 1965). It occurs either in pure stands or in association with shortleaf pine, Virginia pine, or hardwoods of the oak-hickory type, particularly blackjack oak, post oak, and winged elm. It grows on a wide variety of sites, but it does best on deep, moist, well-drained alluvial soils (Arend and Collins, 1949). Redcedar is very intolerant and cannot withstand hardwood competition

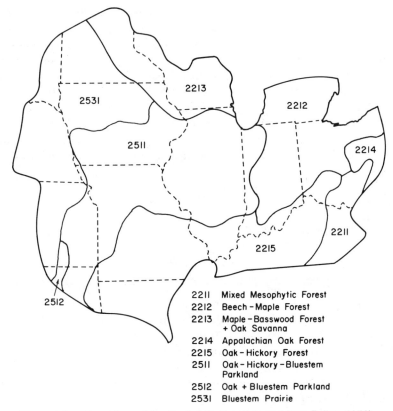

2211	Mixed Mesophytic Forest
2212	Beech – Maple Forest
2213	Maple – Basswood Forest + Oak Savanna
2214	Appalachian Oak Forest
2215	Oak – Hickory Forest
2511	Oak – Hickory – Bluestem Parkland
2512	Oak + Bluestem Parkland
2531	Bluestem Prairie

Figure 4-3.   Ecoregions of the Central Region (Adapted from Bailey, 1976).

on the better sites (Williamson, 1965). It is usually found, therefore, as a pioneer on old fields, pastures, or "glades," which are areas of thin, dry, rocky soil with intermittent rock outcrops (Ferguson *et al.*, 1968; Arend, 1950). Redcedar is also common to fence rows where seed is dropped by birds and rabbits.

Often considered to be a type associated primarily with alkaline soils, Arend and Collins (1949) found that redcedar tolerates high soil acidity reasonably well. They pointed out that redcedar accumulates large amounts of calcium in its foliage and subsequent litter-fall rapidly decreases acidity in the A_1 horizon. Alkalinity in the soil is therefore a consequence of redcedar occupancy. This trait led Broadfoot (1951) to recommend eastern redcedar for soil rehabiliation and flood control purposes.

Eastern redcedar has been highly prized for its rich color, aroma, and durability. Old-growth forests were quickly cut over and the type is greatly reduced today in volume, quality, and extent.

Pine and pine-hardwoods types, scattered across the southern portions of the Central Region, are limited in extent but locally important. The northern limits of both shortleaf and Virginia pine touch this region. A major source of the pine-hardwood type, however, derives from reforestation efforts on old fields which are essentially hardwood-climax sites. Plantations of shortleaf, Virginia, loblolly, eastern white, and red pine have been established. Seldom has planting been followed up with release operations as hardwoods began to invade. Much of the pine-hardwood type has also originated from conversion operations on poor-quality hardwood sites. Stands of hardwoods, usually oak-hickory, have been clearcut and replaced with the higher yielding conifers, principally shortleaf pine. In the Boston Mountains of Arkansas, for example, site indices of 60 and less for oak are considered to be pine sites. In the absence of continued cultural care, hardwoods have reinvaded and pine-hardwood mixtures have resulted.

SILVICULTURE OF THE MAJOR TYPE GROUPS

Oak-Hickory

With few exceptions one or more of the oak and hickory species dominate at least some portion of the forest of every state east of the 100th meridian (U.S. For. Serv., 1965). Cumulatively, almost 50 percent of the commercial forest land in eastern U.S. is occupied by this type group.

In the Central Region white, northern red, and black oak are the principal species. Others of lesser importance are bur oak, one of the most drought-resistant oaks and a major component in prairie-fringe forests; scarlet, post, and blackjack oaks on the drier sites in the southern portion of the region; and chestnut oak in the south central and east. Others such as pin, swamp white, and southern red oak are also present. One or more of the several species of hickory are almost always associated with the oaks. Locally the hickories may dominate the stand, but usually they are minor components.

Oaks and hickories are associated to some degree with almost every other species in the Central Region. Since recommended silvicultural practices vary with the site and species association, discussion of the oak-hickory type group will be subdivided into two categories; successionally stable (climax or near climax) and subclimax stands.

Successionally Stable Stands.

PLACE IN ECOLOGICAL SUCCESSION. Successionally stable oak-hickory types are widely represented throughout the region. In the glaciated area these sites are characterized by steep south-facing slopes and well-drained coarse-textured soils (Lindsey and Schmelz, 1970), such as sandy-outwash plains and old beaches and dunes. In the unglaciated hilly portions of the region, oak-hickory sites are typically ridgetops, upper north and east slopes, and upper and middle south and west slopes (Roach and Gingrich, 1968). The frequency of oak-hickory also increases towards the western edge of the region where precipitation/evaporation ratios become more limiting to tree growth.

GROWTH RATES.   Site indices for climax stands probably maximize between 60 and 70 for oak, though this is variable across the region. Oak-hickory can be maintained on better sites but with increasing difficulty as site quality improves.

Information on growth and yield is scarce. Available data indicate, however, that in unmanaged stands mean-annual growth culminates between age 50 and 70 years for all units of measurement (Gingrich, 1971). Yields on site 55 will approximate 2,900 cubic feet per acre at 80 years. On site 75 yields will be about 5,000 cubic feet. In southwestern Wisconsin Gevorkiantz and Scholz (1948) reported yields for unmanaged stands at age 80 on very poor sites to be 2,000 cubic feet per acre. On very good sites yields reached 4,600 cubic feet.

Yields in managed stands which include periodic thinning are significantly greater. Gingrich (1971) reports yields on site 55 at 60 years of age to be 3,900 cubic feet per acre. On site 75 at the same age estimated yields exceed 6,300 cubic feet.

Growth rates of individual trees vary widely with species, diameter, site, and vigor. In Illinois, relative diameter growth rates for selected species on good sites are as follows: yellow-poplar is an excellent grower; northern red oak, black oak, and scarlet oak are good growers; white oak and southern red oak are medium growers; and the hickories are slow growers (Ill. Tech. For. Assoc., 1965). Average annual gross growth observed over a 5-year period in 13 Indiana woodlands was 204 board feet per acre, Doyle scale.[4] The lowest rate observed was 104 and the highest was 295 board feet per acre.

ROTATION AGE OR SIZE.   Rotation lengths for 20- to 24-inch sawtimber on site classes 55 to 74 (Fig. 4-4) assuming regular thinning are estimated to be 75 to 90 years (Roach and Gingrich, 1968). These values represent relative growth potential for the site and may not indicate rotations and diameters for maximum economic return in any given situation. Landowners who sell stumpage and require rates of return on invested capital of 6 percent or greater, are more likely to find that diameters of sawtimber-quality trees should not exceed 16 to 18 inches if return to capital is to be maximized.[5] Veneer-quality trees may be grown to larger diameter, generally 3 to 6 inches more, for equivalent rates of return. These values assume that average conditions prevail, however, and no previous thinnings have taken place. With a regular program of thinning, growth rates can be expected to increase and the indicated diameter limits may be raised.

Pulpwood rotations, recommended for poorer sites where such markets exist, average 50 years. Site indices for such areas are 40 to 50 for black oak (Fig. 4-5). Even with timely thinning 90 to 120 years are required to grow 16- to 18-inch sawtimber on these sites and interest rates of return will be extremely low. With no thinning Gingrich (1971) estimates that dominant trees will average about 12 inches in diameter at 80 years. On site 75 for oak, and also without thinning, dominants should average about 18 inches at the same age.

[4]Unpublished study. Dept. For. and Nat. Resour., Purdue University.
[5]Unpublished study by W. L. Mills and J. C. Callahan, Purdue University.

Figure 4-4.   An average site for oak-hickory in Ohio representing the probable upper limit of site quality for climax oak-hickory (U.S. For. Serv.).

CULTURAL PRACTICES.   Shade tolerant species are usually of low vigor on climax oak-hickory sites. Consequently they constitute a minor component in most stands and do not offer significant competition to the more valuable species.

The indicated silvicultural practice under such conditions is some form of even-aged management, or at the very least, group selection in which the groups equal or exceed 1 acre in size. However, the success of any reproduction method in the oak-hickory type is largely dependent on advanced regeneration. Stump sprouts may also form a significant proportion of the new stand. Regeneration surveys are recommended before scheduling reproduction cutting (Sander *et al.*, 1976) and the number of potential stump sprouts should be included in this estimate.

Most species of oak prefer partial shade for establishment, but none tolerate dense overstories. Kramer and Decker (1944) found that photosynthesis in seedling oaks maximized at about one-third full sunlight with slight decreases at higher intensities. Red oak seedlings were observed by Phares (1971) to be taller at 30 percent full sunlight than at either 10 percent or 100 percent, though total dry-weight accumulation was somewhat higher in full sunlight. Oak reproduction in Missouri could not survive overstory densities of 100

Figure 4-5.   A poor ridge-top site for oak in Missouri. Oak-hickory regeneration is easy to obtain in these open stands where understory competition is slight. Principal species are black oak, post oak, blackjack oak and hickory (U.S. For. Serv.).

square feet of basal area per acre, but at 80 square feet the number of surviving seedlings gradually increased (Clark and Watt, 1971). In West Virginia Carvell and Tryon (1961) found the ability of oak regeneration to persist in the understory to be positively correlated with percent sunlight reaching the forest floor.

After establishment, height growth of oaks and hickories is maximized at full sunlight (Sander and Clark, 1971). Minckler and Woerheide (1965) found heights of oaks 10 years after release to be maximized in openings as small as one tree height except on south, east, and west edges. However, one tree-height openings would not likely exceed 0.18 acre in size, even on the best sites. Thus the affected portions may constitute a significant proportion of the total.

In order to develop sufficient size and vigor to survive competition following release, seedlings should be greater than 0.6 inches in diameter at the ground line and 4.0 feet in height (Sander et al., 1976). This may require 10 to 20 years or longer. During this early developmental period, tops usually die back periodically and then resprout giving the seedling sprout a deceptively young appearance (Fig. 4-6). Root systems continue to expand, however, so that upon

Figure. 4-6.   The oak seedling on the left is one year old and one half foot tall. On the right is
the same seedling six years later, still one half foot tall (U.S. For. Serv.).

full release the seedling sprout enters a period of rapid, vigorous height growth
(Clark and Watt, 1971). Bey (1964) found differences in ages between roots and
tops of seedling sprouts as great as 37 years.

A major problem during the establishment phase is maintenance of sufficient
light to assure oak survival, but not enough to encourage the regeneration of
competitors. Since minimal light requirements for oak overlap that of potential
tolerant competitors, it is primarily on the poorer sites for the tolerant species
that oak survives well unaided.

Theoretically, shelterwood is the ideal regeneration method for the oak-
hickory type. In fact, it may be argued that all currently recommended
methods of oak regeneration, from clearcutting to group selection, are in reality
but variants of shelterwood since advance regeneration must be present for
successful stand establishment. When adequate advance regeneration is not
present in mature stands for example, the recommendation is to reduce the
overstory density to stimulate seed production (Sander, 1977). These cuts
would be the preparatory and seeding cuts in the shelterwood method.

Sander and Clark (1971) suggest that when applying shelterwood, several
light cuttings are preferable to one heavy cut. This practice would maintain a
relatively closed canopy and thus suppress understory development of competing species. In this operation the poorer trees and lower crown classes should
be removed. Logging damage will occur at each entry, but most damaged
seedlings will resprout.

Deliberate use of shelterwood is rare in the Central Region. Optimal cutting sequences and densities have not been determined. Compounding the problem of controlling understory competition is the fact that oaks are not good seeders. In a 28-year study of seed production in Indiana stands Den Uyl (1961) did not observe a single year in which the seed crop of white, red or black oak was judged as heavy. Most seed crops were rated light. The acorns were consumed by weevils, mice, and rodents, and few survived the first winter.

Seed production in the hickories was somewhat better, but weevils and rodents eliminated most of the crop. Few seedlings of either oak or hickory were observed during the study. What were thought to be seedlings, often were found on close examination to be root sprouts.

Clearcutting has been strongly advocated by some people for reproduction of the oak-hickory type when advanced reproduction is present. In practice, however, the application of this method has usually been limited to large ownerships, principally national forests.

The great majority of smaller ownerships are managed by some form of selection cutting. Selection management in oak-hickory has its pitfalls. Single-tree selection favors tolerant species and when desirable tolerant species are absent from the mixture, the method becomes more or less a sophisticated variant of high-grading. Continued cutting results in a dwindling population of large trees over a static understory of various tree and shrub species. Eventually the overstory density is reduced to the point where light reaching the understory is sufficient to permit the accumulated reproduction to begin height growth (Watt et al., 1973; Brinkman and Liming, 1961). A new even-aged stand then results and a long time period elapses before trees again reach merchantable size.

Many oak-hickory stands will initially exhibit a range of diameter classes, from large to small, resembling the classical uneven-aged structure. Careful analysis, however, will usually reveal these stands to be in fact even-aged. The smaller trees are simply slower growing individuals of the same population which have been overtopped and suppressed by their faster growing neighbors.

In this situation application of single-tree selection has mixed results. Smaller trees which have somehow maintained deep, well-developed crowns may respond to release and reach larger size. Smaller-crowned trees of low vigor will likely not respond and simply stagnate (Fox, 1973; Minckler, 1957).

Group-selection cutting in successionally stable oak-hickory stands may be aesthetically desirable but has little to recommend it as a means of securing regeneration. As previously noted, unless oak seedlings are present before cutting, few will appear in the new stand. The amount of reproduction, therefore, is not related to the size of the opening.

Though opening size is not critical in obtaining oak regeneration, it does have other important effects. These relate to the geometric relationship of circumferential length to area of opening (Sander and Clark, 1971). Circumference increases directly with the length of the radius. Area increases with its square. Thus one 4-acre opening has only one-half the total perimeter of four 1-acre openings.

Small openings have a high percentage of their total area immediately adjacent to the large trees surrounding them. Consequently, the majority of the seedling reproduction is subject to the shade and root competition of the older trees. Furthermore as the crowns of the larger trees expand into the openings, direct overhead skylight is blocked off from the developing reproduction beneath. Height growth is reduced and mortality increased. Visually this competition is evidenced by a mounding effect in the reproduction. Seedlings are much shorter around the edges of an opening than at the center. For best growth of the reproduction, circular openings should not be less than one-half acre in size (Sander and Clark, 1971). In 70-foot timber, a one-half acre opening would approximate 2 and one-half tree heights in width, and at the B level of density for the Upland Central Hardwood Stocking Guide (Gingrich, 1967) would require the removal of approximately 19 trees about 20-inch d.b.h. (Fischer, 1979). In openings of this size about 60 per cent of the total available direct solar radiation would impinge on the opening floor (Fischer and Merritt, 1978).

To maximize light entering small openings and minimize edge effect, circular shapes should be created. Periodic enlargement will also help alleviate problems of stem quality, root competition, and overhead shading. To be maximally effective with subsequent cuttings, east-west axes should be increased more than north-south. Once an opening is sufficiently large to admit light from the sun at noon, further lengthening of its north-south dimension will have little effect on the total amount of light admitted.

The higher number of peripheral trees around a given area of small openings as compared to larger openings can have a major effect on wood-quality production since exposed stems of many species develop epicormic sprouts. Either the stands should be marked so as to leave low-quality trees around the opening edges, or the largest dominants should be left. Vigorous trees tend to produce fewer epicormics than do less vigorous (Smith, 1965). However, species plays a major role in epicormic branching and, unfortunately, the oaks are especially susceptible to this phenomenon. It has been recommended, therefore, that where quality is a major consideration, a low border- to cut-acreage ratio (i.e., large openings) be maintained.

For wildlife objectives many small openings may be more desirable than a few large openings due to the higher proportion of "edge." Wildlife managers may actually prefer to use larger openings, however, in order to satisfy home range and territorial requirements of bird and animal species, but the geometric principal remains the same.

When the selection system is practiced in oak-hickory stands, a critical question of stand structure must be addressed. Data regarding understory light levels for optimal establishment of advanced reproduction are lacking. A common practice is to create scattered small openings in portions of the stand where such cutting would be most advantageous, in groups of mature trees, for example, and to cut the remaining stand on a "selective" basis. There are few if any good silvicultural guides for this latter practice. The cut is most frequently dictated by economics. Ecological effects are largely ignored. However, on xeric sites stands tend to be more open and competition from tolerants is minimal. Advanced oak regeneration will more likely be adequate in these areas.

The group-selection method has been criticized by some as being impractical for sustained-yield management of uneven-aged stands because no realistic procedure for regulating harvests in small groups has yet been devised. However, Alexander and Edminster (1977) feel that it can be done by treating the stand as a whole rather than as a series of little stands. Volume yields on broad areas can be regulated by periodic inventories and specific cutting areas can be defined by careful compartment examination. These procedures are expensive to conduct and maintain, and the consequent regulation will not be very precise.

For most forest ownerships in the Central Region, however, there seems little reason to regulate for strict sustained even-flow yields. Both the forest and the marketplace are dynamic entities and regulation must be sufficiently flexible to meet unforeseen changes. Also it is ecologically foolish, if not practically impossible, to attempt uniform yields on forest areas as small as the average-sized ownership in the region. Periodic harvests are, however, desirable for the reasons explained previously. These can be accommodated by group selection so long as uniform volume yields are not required.

There is still much to learn before interplanting oaks on a commercial scale can be recommended (McElwee, 1970). The problem is not with the planting method since initial survival is usually high. The major limitation is the initial slow growth and competition from other species (Russell, 1971). Competition must be controlled, either through maintaining overstory stand density or by cleaning. Prescribed burning is a possibility for competition control, although only a few studies have been made as to its feasibility (Little, 1973; Johnson, 1974). Interest in the use of controlled fire as a tool in hardwood silviculture is increasing in the region.

The use of herbicides to eliminate competition before cutting and to suppress resprouting of competitors after cutting has been suggested (Johnson, 1976; Sander, 1977). Mechanical means of controlling competition may also be used.

In one study of interplanting hardwoods in oak clearcuts, Johnson (1976) found that size and root-shoot ratio were better criteria for judging planting-stock quality than age. Sander (1977) recommended that any oak seedling, natural or planted, be allowed to reach the recommended minimum size before release (p. 123).

Despite the considerable effort expended in recent years by state forestry organizations to upgrade management in forests of the Central Region, many stands, if not most, contain high volumes of undesirable species, low-quality stems, and culls. Spencer and Essex (1976) estimate that 61 percent of the live trees in Missouri, 1 inch and larger in diameter, are rough or rotten. Many states also report sizeable areas of understocked timberland, but Gingrich (1970) has pointed out that the usual reference to understocking in hardwood stands generally refers to quality stems and desirable species rather than total stocking *per se*. Therefore, a widespread and immediate need for improvement cutting and thinning is indicated.

It is economically difficult to justify any intermediate cutting on poor sites. Thinning response is often slow, rotations are long, and the lower-quality material removed in early thinnings is difficult to market. When applied, improvement in stand quality should be a principal objective since premium prices are paid for high-quality hardwood timber.

On better sites greater opportunity exists for significant return on intermediate investments. Gingrich (1970) suggests that attention should be concentrated on individual trees of high crown class, vigor, and potential quality rather than on whole stands. Timber stand improvement designed merely to remove poor trees in a stand without regard to the effect of such removal on better trees is seldom good policy.

In an intensive study of density effects on growth in oak-hickory stands, Gingrich (1967) developed stocking and density criteria which are independent of site quality, stand age, and stand structure (Fig. 4-7). Between A and B levels on the chart, total growth is about equal, though individual tree growth will vary widely. Stands are not considered worth managing if stocking falls below C level. Thinning guides recommend reducing density to B level except where stocking exceeds 90 percent in previously uncut stands. In this situation stands must be opened gradually since more space will be provided than crowns can quickly occupy and epicormic branching may lead to loss of stem quality (Roach and Gingrich, 1968). Since stem quality is the key to economic management of hardwoods, maintenance of sufficient densities at young ages to promote

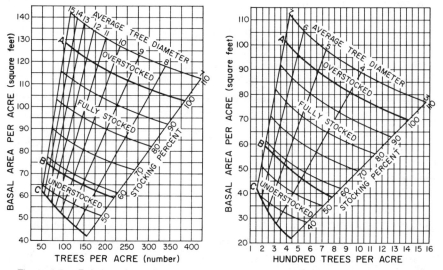

Figure 4-7. Relation of basal area, number of trees, and average tree diameter to stocking percent for upland hardwoods in the Central Region. Tree diameter range: 7 to 15 inches (left), 3 to 7 inches (right) (U.S. For. Serv.).

natural pruning and produce long, clear stems is also critical. Artificial pruning offers possibilities for improving quality of some hardwoods, but except for black walnut (Callahan and Smith, 1974), it has not been shown to be economically feasible.

SUSCEPTIBILITY TO DAMAGE.   Protection from unregulated grazing is essential in the management of central hardwood woodlands for the growth of high-quality material (Den Uyl, 1958). Four stages of woodland deterioration resulting from grazing have been recognized; early, transition, open park and final (Den Uyl et al., 1938). As grazing continues and stands open up through mortality or cutting, the inability of tree reproduction to become established leads eventually to the development of a sod cover. Up to this point, removal of the grazing animals will lead to prompt restoration of forest floor conditions and subsequent natural regeneration. This has been termed by Den Uyl as constituting "light" grazing. It includes both the early and transition stages of deterioration. After a sod has become established, 20 years or more will generally be required before desirable tree species can reinvade the area. The condition results from "heavy" grazing, which term combines both the open-park and final stages. The latter is nothing more than shaded pasture.

Carefully controlled grazing might be a possible management technique in the preparation of sites for oak seeding. Carvell and Tryon (1961) found, for example, that a history of stand disturbance, including grazing, was closely correlated with the amount of oak regeneration. Grazing may also be the indicated optimal land use for extremely poor sites for hardwoods such as is illustrated in Fig. 4-5. However, problems associated with grazing generally outweigh advantages. Soil compaction and root injury result in reduction of vigor leading in turn to high mortality, especially among the oaks, during periodic droughts which occur in the region. Also, wounds produced on both roots and basal portions of stems by animal hooves provide entrance for wood rotting fungi. Resultant volume losses from growth reduction and cull are considerable. The general consensus is that grazing of woodlands in the Central Region is not compatible with production of high-quality hardwood timber.

Protection from wildfire is likewise indispensable to good management. Berry and Beaton (1972) found that almost 25 percent of decay infections and over 40 percent of total decay volume in oak-hickory forests were attributable to wildfire. Hardwoods above 4 inches are not often killed by fire but the basal wounds which result are ideal entrance points for disease.

Basal wounds are also commonly found on residuals following logging. Particular care must be exercised to prevent such damage, especially along skid trails and near landings. Careless felling of the typically large-crowned hardwoods also causes stem abrasions along upper portions of stems.

Reduction in decay volume can be obtained by early thinning in clumps of oak sprouts. Sprouts with the least likelihood of heartwood union with companion sprouts and with the parent stump should be favored. These include stems originating near or below ground level and those separated from others by a low

U-shaped crotch. Sprout stems joined by a high union or a V-shaped crotch should be either left alone or the entire clump cut (Sander, 1977).

Maintenance of adequate density in young stands to shade out side branches before they develop heartwood also helps reduce incidence of decay.

Of the many insect and disease enemies of oak-hickory forests, probably the most threatening is oak wilt. No species of oak is known to be immune to the disease (Jones and Phelps, 1972). It is spread both through root grafts and by at least two groups of insects. At the present time, it is not of great economic consequence, except in localized areas, but it does contain tremendous potential for damage. Control is generally effected through some form of killing or harvesting infected trees to prevent the formation of fungus mats. Interruption of root grafts by killing all oaks within 50 feet of an infected tree or injecting toxic gases into the soil is also essential.

The gypsy moth is spreading westward into the Central Region but is currently limited to localized infestations. Entomologists do not expect this insect to create serious economic problems over most of the region because of the scattered and diverse nature of the woodlands. Defoliation caused by the gypsy moth is presently of concern primarily in areas of human habitation where aesthetic values are important, such as in shade trees and areas of high-recreational use. In this sense the moth is more of a nuisance insect in the Central Region than one possessing major potential economic impact. More severe problems may develop in the future when the moth becomes established in those portions of the region with larger continuous areas of the oak-hickory type.

Other damaging insects in the region include the Columbian timber beetle, carpenterworm, red oak borer, white oak borer, variable oak leaf caterpillar, forest tent caterpillar, oak leaf roller, and the northern walkingstick. Several insects feed on acorns such as the nut weevils, moth larvae, and gallforming cynipids (Fowells, 1965). Control of these several insects is best accomplished by removal of low-vigor and defective trees during intermediate cutting operations (Sander, 1977). Chemical control is seldom economically justified.

OTHER FOREST BENEFITS.   Management practices for watershed objectives in oak-hickory stands are similar to those applied in other hardwood types. Likewise, problems associated with aesthetic objectives are similar. Volumes of logging slash, for example, increase from single-tree selection to clearcutting, occasionally creating problems in the latter instance in high-use recreation areas. In general, slash disposal is not practiced in this region. Demand for wood as a fuel may change this practice in the near future.

A wide variety of wildlife species inhabit oak-hickory woodlands including white-tailed deer, red and fox squirrels, fox, raccoon, wild turkey, and ruffed grouse. On the Hoosier National Forest in Indiana, different species identified include 48 mammalian, 32 reptilian, 27 amphibian, 272 avian, and 100 fish (U.S. For. Serv. 1977b).

Diversity in habitat is the key for management of these many wildlife species as previously discussed. Group selection would seem the best technique for this single purpose. However, in apparent compromise with timber production objectives, national forests in the region utilize clearcutting with restrictions as to size of opening. On the Wayne-Hoosier National Forest, openings are restricted to 30 acres or less and area control is used to create diversity in age classes (U.S. For. Serv. 1977a). Since the production of mast is essential for many species of wildlife, 40 percent of each 400-acre block of timber is required to be maintained in mast producing trees 40 years of age and older. Other requirements for maintenance of habitat diversity include 10 percent of each 400-acre block in timber at least 85 years of age, 5 to 10 percent in scattered coniferous stands, 15 percent in brushland, and 3 percent in permanent openings. Den trees for squirrels and raccoon should be available at the rate of about 1 tree per 2 and one-half acres.[6] A few dead snags and other defective trees are left standing to provide sites for the many cavity-nesting bird species in the area.

Subclimax Stands.   Subclimax oak-hickory stands occur on the better sites, approximately oak site-index 70 and greater (Fig. 4-8). Ecologically, they would be better classified as beech-maple, mixed mesophytic, western mesophytic, or mixedwoods, depending on location and terminology preferred.

Due to the richness of the flora on those good sites, any given species, or species group such as oak-hickory, may temporarily predominate in a given stand. Den Uyl (1961) described the cyclic nature of regeneration, pointing out that the future composition of the main stand will largely depend on whatever species mixture happens to be dominant in the regeneration layer when the overhead canopy is removed. Periodic fire favors species in the regeneration able to sprout vigorously and repeatedly. Similarly, grazing favors the less palatable species. Since oaks and hickories are both fire resistant and unpalatable, they tend to dominate the reproduction under such conditions. If sufficient light is available in the understory, they will persist over long periods until released by some chance or planned event. This ability may explain the present widespread occurrence of oak-hickory on the better sites.

Current management practices which include fire control, grazing exclusion, periodic partial harvesting, and little or no thinning, combine to favor species other than oak-hickory. Consequently many present oak-hickory stands are rapidly reverting to types dominated by more tolerant species. In a recent tally of the regeneration on 1,000 milacre plots taken in 10 partially cut woodlands on good sites in southern Indiana, only 1.2 percent of the plots contained red oak seedlings and 1.1 percent contained white oak seedlings.[7] In all cases oaks were prominent in the overstory. Dominant species in the regeneration layer were sugar maple, elm, ironwood, dogwood, beech, sassafras, and paw paw. According to Graney,[8] oak-hickory stands on good sites in the Ozarks, long

[6]Personal communication from R. E. Mumford, Purdue University.
[7]Unpublished data from a study by B. C. Fischer, Purdue University.
[8]Personal communication with D. L. Graney, Fayetteville, Arkansas.

Figure 4-8. Mixed woods stand on an excellent site in Indiana. Trees in foreground are yellow-poplar and black walnut. These stands usually contain a minor component of oak in the mixture, but oak-hickory types on such sites are subclimax. (U.S. For. Serv.).

considered the "heartland" of the type, are regenerating strongly to red maple and associated species when fire is excluded.

No regime of silvicultural treatments yet devised has been consistently effective in regenerating oak on the better sites. Elimination of the abundant competition characteristic of these sites is essential for both establishment of oak and its maintenance in the new stand following release. A small component of oak may prove adequate in the long run, however. It has been observed by Oliver (1975) that a very small proportion of red oak in a developing mixed stand may eventually dominate the stand as the growth rate of associates declines.

Since oak regeneration is difficult to obtain on good sites, the silviculture of such areas should follow that discussed in the mixedwoods type group until better techniques have been developed.

Mixedwoods Type Group

Place in Ecological Succession.   Mixed hardwood stands in the Central Region not classified as climax oak-hickory or elm-ash-cottonwood, are grouped for discussion in mixedwoods. As described in the previous section, subclimax oak-hickory types are ecologically part of this group. Species composition in stands of the mixedwoods type group may vary from nearly pure stands of intolerant species such as yellow-poplar, to complicated mixtures of species of all shade-tolerance categories. The trend to the shade tolerants is strong, but a great variety of species is usually represented in the reproduction.

Typical sites include deep, well-drained fertile soils in the glaciated portion of the region and, lower slopes and coves in unglaciated hilly land.

Growth Rates.   Due to the variability and complexity of stands of the mixedwoods type group, statements of average annual growth are of little value. However, in one unpublished study in Indiana, four woodlands measured over a period of 12 years grew at an average annual gross rate of 360 board feet per acre Doyle scale. Yearly fluctuations in the weather caused large differences in growth. In one woodland annual growth varied from 227 board feet per acre in a dry year to 486 board feet per acre in a wet year. The highest gross growth rate observed was 538 board feet per acre per year over a four-year period.

Rotation Age or Size.   Site quality is variable but is generally high. Minimum site indices are about 70 for oak and 80 for yellow-poplar. With a regular program of thinning 24- to 28-inch sawtimber can be grown in 60 to 75 years on the best sites (Roach and Gingrich, 1968). Reference should be made to the discussion in the oak-hickory type group relative to the effect of high interest rates on rotation diameters.

Cultural Practices.   The presence of valuable shade tolerant as well as intermediate and intolerant species in mixedwoods stands permits use of any reproduction method. Both even-aged and uneven-aged stand structures are common and either structure is relatively easy to develop. Thus, the choice of a silvicultural system or regime is largely dictated by the objectives of management.

Despite the fact that the selection system is the one most commonly applied in the Central Region, guidelines are not well established. Silvicultural recommendations for management of uneven-aged stands in cove hardwoods (Chapter 5) and the northern hardwoods type group (Chapter 2) are useful for reference.

Proper application of the selection system requires decisions as to appropriate stand structures (refer to Ill. Tech. For. Assoc., 1965, for guides), but few stands are actually managed on this basis. Most cutting tends to emphasize harvesting of quality stems with unmerchantable trees being removed at other times in timber stand improvement operations.

A major argument supporting current practice is the utter disarray of most stands. Few are in condition for institution of formal management and rehabilitation cutting is a necessary first approach.

If single-tree selection is to be applied, rehabilitation cutting should follow sound improvement principles. Cull trees should be killed, overstocked patches should be thinned, and high-risk and low-quality merchantable trees should be cut. The lack of good markets and the poor quality of material removed in such cuts usually limits the application of ideal rehabilitation cutting. More often the poorer trees must be combined in a sale with better-quality timber. Gradual improvement of the woodland is accomplished over a period of time.

Similar procedures should be followed with group selection except that only cull trees competing with crop trees need be killed until that particular place is to be regenerated (Ill. Tech. For. Assoc., 1965). Group openings should be created where patches of overmature, high-risk, or low-quality trees occur.

Following application of rehabilitation cutting, goals should be set for species composition, structure, and tree quality. These goals must harmonize the owners objectives with stand conditions and site. Suggested guidelines have been provided by the Illinois Technical Forestry Association (1965).

Clearcutting is the usual method applied in the even-aged management of the mixedwoods type group. Patches vary in size, but in general are related to the size of the ownership. Larger ownerships usually require sizeable minimum stand areas to render mapping, record keeping, road building, and use of large equipment economical (Roach and Gingrich, 1968). These limitations must also be considered when applying clearcutting to other species type groups in the Central Region.

Whether applying even- or uneven-aged silviculture, an important key to the species composition of the future stand is the present composition of the understory. Whatever species are left to occupy openings can be expected to dominate that portion of the future stand, regardless of the species in the overstory.

Among the several tolerants commonly found in the understory of mixedwoods stands are sugar maple, beech, dogwood, eastern hophornbeam, and American hornbeam. White ash, which is tolerant in the seedling stage, may also be present. Both white ash and sugar maple are capable of producing high-quality veneer logs, though good-quality sugar maple is found primarily in northern parts of the region.

When less tolerant species such as yellow-poplar, black walnut, black cherry, or white ash are to be reproduced, openings in the stand should be at least as wide as the height of the surrounding timber (Minckler and Woerheide, 1965). All undesirable advanced reproduction above 2 inches in diameter must be removed. Mechanical site preparation is an advantage for light-seeded species, but the expense of such treatment makes it seldom practical for the average woodland owner. Scheduling of logging just prior to seedfall or in late winter or early spring must usually suffice to provide this disturbance. On the other hand, logging when soils are wet may cause severe soil damage through deep rutting and compaction.

Due to the wide variety of species, both tree and shrub, which tend to invade openings on the better sites, cleanings are usually needed at an earlier age than on less productive areas. Planted seedlings in particular may need weeding within two years. Openings should also be periodically enlarged to overcome crown encroachment from adjacent older trees.

When the advanced regeneration is composed of satisfactory intermediate to intolerant species, immediate full release is indicated. Cleaning may also be necessary.

Thinning recommendations for even-aged mixedwoods stands follow those given by Gingrich (1971), or the Illinois Technical Forestry Association (1965). Reference is made to discussions about thinning in hardwoods in Chapters 2 and 5.

Susceptibility to Damage. Stands of the mixedwoods are intermingled with those of the oak-hickory type group. Other than a possibly lower fire danger on the more mesic sites of the mixedwoods, little difference exists in damage susceptibility between the two groups.

Elm-Ash-Cottonwood Type Group

Place in Ecological Succession. This type group might better be termed Lowland-Depressional Hardwoods after Lindsey and Schmelz (1970). It encompasses the entire successional sequence of stands from pioneer to climax. Sites occupied include bottomlands, flood plains, upland depressional areas including swamps, and some lake margins (Soc. Am. For., 1967; Petty and Jackson, 1966). It most commonly occurs as long narrow strips of timberland along the many streams throughout the Central Region.

Typical site conditions favoring the type-group are neutral soils with high clay content, high available water, and for many species a high percent of nitrogen in the soil (Lindsey and Schmeltz, 1970).

Differences in physiography, soils, climate, flooding, pollution, damming, drainage, and species adaptations are important factors affecting natural and artificial variants in this type-group. Some species such as cottonwood, sycamore, and green ash, for example, are able to survive long periods of flooding by producing adventitious roots (Hosner, 1959). Swamp white oak, a shallow rooted tree, is found principally in upland depressional areas with poor soil aeration (Fowells, 1965). Pin oak is a common associate. When such sites become elevated 10 to 12 inches above the water table, beech and other mesic site hardwoods often enter the mixture. Some upland depressional areas underlain with hardpans have standing water for lengthy periods in the spring and during the summer are quite xeric. Black oak may associate in such situations with the wetter site species.

The successional sequence in Central Region lowland forests is similar to that of the southern hardwoods on bottomlands as discussed in Chapter 5 in that the evolution of physiographic sites exerts a profound effect on the seral communities which occur (Lindsey et al., 1961). These communities in turn exert their continuing altering influence on the site.

However, few floodplain climax stands are to be found today due primarily to heavy cutting and clearing of land for agriculture. Once magnificent forests in which dominants reached 200 feet in height and 7 feet or more in diameter are no longer present, though scattered individuals of large size may still be found. Most extant stands represent early successional stages.

Cultural Practices.   Most stands of the elm-ash-cottonwood type group in the Central Region have been exploited rather than managed. Silvicultural research has been very limited. Minckler (1958) suggested initiating management with a heavy improvement cut and harvest cutting to remove trees not suitable for growing stock. He found reproduction in large gaps to be composed chiefly of desired species which responded rapidly to the increased light. In a later study, Hosner and Minckler (1960) described the complexity of bottomland forests, comparing them with the types found along the lower Mississippi River. They found adequate advance regeneration occurring under closed canopies, but noted that openings in the canopy were required to maintain individual tree vigor. Undesirable species such as American elm, boxelder, dogwood, privet, and deciduous holly were predominant in the understory but more desirable species tended to persist and eventually take over the stand.

Due to the similarity of this type group to the southern bottomlands hardwoods, reference should be made to Chapter 5 for further details on management.

Susceptibility to Damage.   Two diseases, Dutch elm disease and phloem necrosis, caused by a virus, have all but eliminated elm as an important species in the Central Region. As in other parts of the country, the greatest economic loss from these diseases is in shade and ornamental trees (Hepting and Fowler, 1962).

Dutch elm disease develops slowly and trees usually reach seed-bearing age before succumbing. Dense elm reproduction often follows disturbance and the vigorous seedlings offer strong competition for other species in the regeneration which have greater likelihood of survival.

Eastern Redcedar Type Group

Place in Ecological Succession.   Eastern redcedar is classed as a slow-growing, short- to medium-lived tree. However, trees 300 years of age, 120 feet tall and 4 feet in diameter have been reported (Ferguson *et al.*, 1968; U.S. For. Serv., 1965). The type is temporary except possibly on the driest sites where replacement is very slow (Fowells, 1965).

Growth Rates.   Site indices range from 60 feet at 50 years on the best sites to 25 feet on the poorest. Depth of soil was found to be the principal factor affecting site quality, but height growth is also positively correlated with stocking density (Arend and Collins, 1949).

Rotation Age or Size.   Rotations for products are usually short since utilization standards for redcedar are low, both for size and allowable defects. Posts can be produced in 20 to 30 years, sawtimber in 40 to 60 years.

Cultural Practices.   Redcedar is reported to be the most desirable conifer for windbreaks (Van Haverbeke, 1977), and ranks high among the desired species for Christmas trees (Sowder, 1966). It is an excellent species for management on small farms due to its ability to grow on sites too rough or dry for agricultural crops, its desirability for fence posts, and its salability in small sizes permitting short rotations and handling with ordinary farm equipment (Ferguson *et al.*, 1968). Cedar glades in the Ozarks are also highly important for wildlife habitat and forage for livestock (Spencer and Essex, 1976). Notwithstanding these advantages, redcedar is seldom managed as a crop in the Central Region.

The silvical and economic characteristics of redcedar combine to favor even-aged management. New stands may be established naturally or artificially through direct seeding or planting. Seedlings survive better under open canopies than closed, and establishment is improved if seedbeds are cleared of litter (Parker, 1952). First year seedlings prefer light shading over open sunlight (U.S. For. Serv. 1974).

Seeds should be treated for dormancy before direct seeding. Cold stratification in sand at 41 ° F for 30 to 120 days is recommended (U.S. For. Serv., 1974).

In addition to proper site selection, success in establishing redcedar is heavily dependent on control of vegetative competition. Both mechanical and chemical methods have proven feasible.

Stand density must be maintained both for maximum height growth and volume yield. Competing hardwoods must be strictly controlled, however, for maximum redcedar growth. Use of herbicides is recommended to minimize resprouting of the hardwoods. Redcedar is resistant to 2,4,5-T (the continued use of this herbicide is questionable) and 2,4-D and aerial applications may be made to release the redcedar from undesirable broadleaf vegetation.

Ferguson *et al.* (1968) recommended maintaining dense stands for maximum post production. One or two thinnings for posts are suggested for the longer sawlog rotations. Thinnings should be light to maximize formation of the more valuable heartwood. However, redcedar does not differentiate well into crown classes and overly dense stands tend to stagnate.

Susceptibility to Damage.   Eastern redcedar is resistant to most insect pests. It is susceptible to *Fomes annosus*, however, and to cubical rot fungi which attack the heartwood. These latter diseases gain entrance primarily through dead branch stubs. Limbs should not be pruned because wounds will not heal (Jelley, 1937).

Eastern redcedar is an alternate host for the cedar-apple rust, a disease which does little harm to the redcedar but which seriously damages malaceous hosts. Some states require elimination of all cedars and junipers within 1 mile of apple orchards (Boyce, 1938).

Grazing must be carefully regulated in redcedar stands, especially during the early years, and fire cannot be tolerated at any time. The thin barked redcedar is usually killed in the heat of single surface fires (Ferguson, *et al.*, 1968).

Pine-Hardwoods Type Group

Recommended silvicultural practices for pine-hardwood types in the Central Region are essentially the same as those described for the type in other regions. The preponderance of small ownerships and the lack of markets make it more difficult, however, to utilize intensive modern technology.

In portions of the Central Region north of the natural range of shortleaf pine, many plantations of this species have been damaged in recent years by unusually cold winters. Consequent mortality and loss of vigor is hastening transition from pure pine to pine-hardwood types. On some of the better old-field sites, eastern white pine is being successfully substituted for shortleaf pine. The trend to climax hardwoods is particularly strong on these areas and current management is usually not sufficiently intensive to prevent development of pine-hardwood mixtures at early ages. Hardwood species in natural mixtures usually represent nearby seed sources of pioneer types. Introduction of selected, more valuable hardwood species at planting time is being tested on a limited basis.

HARDWOOD PLANTING

Planting of hardwoods on forested sites in the Central Region has met with mixed success. Excellent results have been obtained with large-caliper yellow-poplar, $^{10}/_{32}$ or larger (Funk, 1964; Russell, 1977), and black walnut on good sites (Krajicek, 1975). Sugar maple, red maple, and white ash were successfully established in southern Wisconsin clearcuts, while red oak and basswood did less well (Johnson, 1976). Hilt (1977) also found red oak to be difficult to establish regardless of site quality or cultural treatment. Avoidance of poor sites, use of large, well-balanced planting stock, and control of competition are important keys, but no guarantee, to success (Hilt, 1977; Funk, 1964; Williams, 1966; Byrnes, 1966).

Planting of black walnut on open sites is an established practice in the Central Region. Accelerating demand for the species, particularly in export markets, has created a shortage of large walnut trees and dramatic price increases for quality logs.

Investors can expect modest rates of return on plantation culture with intensive management (Callahan and Smith, 1974). Fertile soil, wide spacing, weed control, pruning, and timely thinning are essential to a successful enterprise. Unfortunately many landowners have attempted to capitalize on the expanding market with incomplete information and many plantation efforts have failed as a result of planting on poor sites and lack of weed control (Clark, 1962). Recommendations on site evaluation, fertilization, genetics, pruning, thinning, and related topics are discussed by Schlesinger and Funk (1977) in their "Manager's Handbook for Black Walnut."

Direct seeding of hardwoods in the Central Region has not been generally successful. Major problems are the heavy destruction of seed by rodents, and the need for well prepared sites followed by a consistent program of weed control. Few small woodland owners are prepared to make the necessary investments in money and time to successfully direct seed hardwoods, especially when effective rodent control measures have yet to be developed. However, chances for success can be increased by delaying seeding in the spring until alternative natural food materials appear in the woods (Crozier and Merritt, 1964).

BIBLIOGRAPHY

Alexander, R. R., and C. B. Edminster. 1977. Regulation and control of cut under uneven-aged management. *USDA For. Serv. Res. Pap.* RM-182. 7 pp.

Arend, J. L. 1950. Influence of fire and soil on distribution of eastern redcedar in the Ozarks. *J. For.* 48:129–130.

Arend, J. L., and R. F. Collins. 1949. A site classification for eastern redcedar in the Ozarks. *Soil Sci. Soc. Am. Proc.* 13:510–511.

Bailey, Robert G. 1976. Ecoregions of the United States. *USDA For. Serv.*, Ogden, Utah.

Barnard, J. E. and T. M. Bowers. 1977. A preview of Kentucky's forest resource. *USDA For. Serv. Res. Note* NE-234. 11 pp.

Berry, F. H. and J. A. Beaton. 1972. Decay in oak in the Central Hardwood Region. *USDA For. Serv. Res. Pap.* NE-242. 11 pp.

Bey, C. F. 1964. Advance oak reproduction grows fast after clearcutting. *J. For.* 62:339–340.

Boyce, J. S. 1938. *Forest pathology.* McGraw-Hill Book Co., Inc., New York. 600 pp.

Braun, E. L. 1950. *Deciduous forests of eastern North America.* The Blakiston Co., Philadelphia. 596 pp.

Brinkman, K. A., and F. G. Liming. 1961. Oak and pine reproduction responds to overhead release. *J. For.* 59:341–346.

Broadfoot, W. M. 1951. Soil rehabilitation under eastern redcedar and loblolly pine. *J. For.* 49:780–781.

Byrnes, W. R. 1966. Site preparation and weed control. *In Black walnut culture, Walnut Workshop Proc.*, Carbondale, Ill. p. 20–27.

Callahan, J. C., and R. P. Smith. 1974. An economic analysis of black walnut plantation enterprises. *Purdue Univ. Agr. Exp. Stn. Res. Bull. 912.* 20 pp.

Carvell, K. L., and E. H. Tryon. 1961. The effect of environmental factors on the abundance of oak regeneration beneath mature oak stands. *For. Sci.* 7(2):98–105.

Chase, C. D., R. E. Pfeifer, and J. S. Spencer, Jr. 1970. The growing timber resource of Michigan. *USDA For. Serv. Resour. Bull. NC-9.* 62 pp.

Chase, C. D., and J. K. Strickler, 1968. Kansas woodlands. *USDA For. Serv. Resour. Bull. NC-4.* 50 pp.

Choate, G. A., and J. S. Spencer, Jr. 1968. Forests in South Dakota. *USDA For. Serv. Resour. Bull. INT-8.* 40 pp.

Clark, F. B. 1962. A survey of black walnut plantings in Indiana. Unpubl. paper given at Ind. Hdwd, Lbrman's Assoc. meeting, Indianapolis. (quoted in Callahan and Smith, 1974).

Clark, F. B., and R. F. Watt. 1971. Silvicultural methods for regenerating oaks. *In* Proc. Oak Symp. pp. 37–43. *USDA For. Serv. Northeast For. Exp. Stn.*

Crankshaw, W. B., S. A. Qadir, and A. A. Lindsey. 1965. Edaphic controls of tree species in presettlement Indiana. *Ecology* 46(5):688–698.

Crozier, R., and C. Merritt. 1964. Rodent pilferage of northern red oak acorns. *Purdue Univ. Agr. Exp. Stn. Res. Progress Rep. 116.* 2 pp.

Dale, M. E. 1972. Growth and yield predictions for upland oak stands 10 years after initial thinning. *USDA For. Serv. Res. Pap. NE-241.* 21 pp.

DeBald, P. S., and R. E. McCay. 1969. The timber resources of the Ohio hill country. *USDA For. Serv. Res. Bull. NE-14.* 75 pp.

Den Uyl, D. 1958. A twenty year record of the growth and development of Indiana woodlands. *Purdue Univ. Agr. Exp. Stn. Res. Bull. 661.* 52 pp.

Den Uyl, D. 1961. Natural tree reproduction in mixed hardwood stands. *Purdue Univ. Agr. Exp. Stn. Res. Bull. 728.* 19 pp.

Den Uyl, D., O. D. Diller, and R. K. Kay, 1938. The development of natural reproduction in previously grazed farmwoods. *Purdue Univ. Agr. Exp. Stn. Bull. 431.* 28 pp.

Doolittle, W. T. 1978. Constraints on forest management in the eastern hardwood region. *In* Proc. Uneven-aged Silviculture and Management in the United States, pp. 63–66. *USDA For. Serv. Tbr. Mgmt. Res. Washington, D.C.*

Earles, J. M. 1976. Forest statistics for east Oklahoma counties. *USDA For. Serv. Resour. Bull. SO-62.* 40 pp.

Fenneman, N. M. 1938. *Physiography of Eastern United States.* McGraw-Hill Book Co., New York 714 pp.

Ferguson, E. R., E. R. Lawson, W. R. Maple, and C. Mesavage. 1968. Managing eastern redcedar. *USDA For. Serv. Res. Pap. SO-37.* 14 pp.

Fischer, B. C. 1979. Managing light in the selection method. In Regenerating oaks in upland hardwood forests. Proc. 1979 John S. Wright Forest. Conf. *Purdue Univ., Dept. For. and Natural Resour.*

Fischer, B. C. and C. Merritt. 1978. SHADOS: A computer model to simulate light energy distribution in small forest openings. *In Proc. Second Central Hdwd. For. Conf.* pp. 302–319. Purdue Univ. Lafayette.

Fowells, H. A. 1965. Silvics of forest trees of the United States. *USDA For. Serv. Agr. Hdbk. 271.* 762 pp.

Fox, H. W. 1973. Response of white oak to overstory release. *U. Ill. Agr. Exp. Stn. For. Res. Rpt.* 73-2. 2 pp.

Friesner, R. C. 1937. Indiana as a critical botanical area. *Indiana Acad. Sci. Proc.* 46:28-45.

Funk, D. T. 1964. Premium yellow poplar seedlings—8 years after planting. *USDA For. Serv. Res. Note* CS-20. 4 pp.

Gansner, D. A. 1968. The timber resources of Kentucky. *USDA For. Serv. Res. Bull.* NE-9. 97 pp.

Gevorkiantz, S. R. and H. F. Scholz. 1948. Timber yields and possible returns from the mixed-oak farmwoods of southwstern Wisconsin. *USDA For. Serv. Lake States For. Exp. Stn. Pub. No.* 521. 72 pp.

Gingrich, S. F. 1967. Measuring and evaluating stocking and stand density in upland hardwood forests in the Central States. *For. Sci.* 13(1):38-53.

Gingrich, S. F. 1970. Effects of density, thinning and species composition on the growth and yield of eastern hardwoods. In *The silviculture of oaks and associated species*, 26-35. USDA For. Serv. Res. Pap. NE-144. pp. 26-35.

Gingrich, S. F. 1971. Management of young and intermediate stands of upland hardwoods. *USDA For. Serv. Res. Pap.* NE-195. 26 pp.

Hartong, A. L. and K. E. Moessner. 1956. Wooded strips in Iowa. *USDA For. Serv. Cent. St. For. Exp. Stn. For. Serv. Rel.* 21. 15 pp.

Hedlund, A. and J. M. Earles. 1970. Forest statistics for Arkansas counties. *USDA For. Serv. Resour. Bull.* SO-22. 52 pp.

Hepting, G. H. and M. E. Fowler. 1962. Tree diseases of eastern forests and farm woodlands. *USDA For. Serv. Ag. Info. Bull. No.* 254. 48 pp.

Hilt, D. E. 1977. Introduction of black walnut and northern red oak seedlings in an upland hardwood forest in southeastern Ohio. *USDA For. Serv. Res. Note* NE-241. 5 pp.

Holland, I. I. 1962. Timber marketing in the Claypan Region of Illinois. *Ill. Agr. Exp. Stn. Bull. No.* 689. 40 pp.

Hosner, J. F. 1959. Survival, root and shoot growth of six bottomland tree species following flooding. *J. For.* 57(12):927-928.

Hosner, J. F. and L. S. Minckler. 1960. Hardwood reproduction in the river bottoms of southern Illinois. *For. Sci.* 6(1):67-77.

Huemoeller, W. A., K. J. Nicol, E. O. Heady, and B. W. Spaulding. 1976. Land use: Ongoing developments in the North Central Region. *Center Agr. Rural Develop. Iowa St. Univ.* 294 pp.

Hutchison, O. K., and O. D. McCauley. 1961. The small-woodland owner in Ohio. *USDA For. Serv. Cent. St. For. Exp. Stn. Tech. Pap. 183.* 12 pp.

Ill. Techn. For. Assoc. 1965. Recommended silviculture and management practices for Illinois hardwood forest types. 46 pp.

Jelley, M. E. 1937. Eastern red cedar. *J. For.* 35:865−867.

Johnson, P. S. 1974. Survival and growth of northern red oak seedlings following a prescribed burning. *USDA For. Serv. Res. Note NC-177.* 3 pp.

Johnson, P. S. 1976. Eight-year performance of interplanted hardwoods in southern Wisconsin oak clearcuts. *USDA For. Serv. Res. Pap. NC-126.* 9 pp.

Jones, T. W., and W. R. Phelps. 1972. Oak wilt. *USDA For. Serv. Forest Pest Leaflet* 29. 7 pp.

Kingsley, N. P., and C. E. Mayer, 1970. The timber resources of Ohio. *USDA For. Serv. Res. Bull.* NE-19. 137 pp.

Krejicek, J. E. 1975. Planted black walnut does well on cleared forest sites—if competition is controlled. *USDA For. Serv. No. Cent. For. Exp. Stn. Res. Note NC-192.* 4 pp.

Kramer, P. J., and P. J. Decker, 1944. Relation between light intensity and rate of photosynthesis of loblolly pine and certain hardwoods. *Plant Physiol.* 19:350−358.

Lindsey, A. A., R. O. Petty, D. K. Sterling, and W. VanAsdall. 1961. Vegetation and environment along the Wabash and Tippecanoe Rivers. *Ecol. Monolog* 31:105−156.

Lindsey, A. A., and D. V. Schmelz. 1970. The forest types of Indiana and a new method of classifying midwestern hardwood forests. *In Proc. Ind. Acad. Sci.* 79:198–204.

Little, S., 1973. Use of fire—comments from the Northeast. *J. For.* 71:633–634.

McElwee, R. L. 1970. Artificial regeneration of hardwoods. *In* The Silviculture of Oaks and Associated Species, 17–25. *USDA For Serv. Res. Pap. NE-144.*

Melhorn, W. N. 1956. Geology of Indiana—effects of glaciation on plants and soils. *Ind. Nursery News* 17(12):2–6.

Merz, R. W. 1978. A forest atlas of the midwest. *USDA For. Serv. No. Cent. For. Exp. Stn.*

Minckler, L. S. 1957. Response of pole-sized white oak trees to release. *J. For.* 55:814–815.

Minckler, L. S. 1958. Bottomland hardwoods respond to cutting. *USDA For. Serv. Central St. For. Exp. Stn. Tech. Pap. 154.* 10 pp.

Minckler, L. S., and J. D. Woerheide, 1965. Reproduction of hardwoods 10 years after cutting as affected by site and opening size. *J. For.* 63:103–107.

Murphy, P. A. 1977. East Oklahoma forests: Trends and outlook.*USDA For. Serv. Resour. Bull. SO-63.* 20 pp.

Oliver, C. D. 1975. Development of red oak (*Quercus rubra* L.) in mixed species, even-aged stands in central New England. Ph.D. dissertation, Yale Univ. New Haven, 223 pp.

Ostrom, A. J. 1976. Forest statistics for Iowa, 1974. *USDA For. Serv. Resour. Bull. NC-33.* 25 pp.

Parker, J. 1952. Establishment of eastern redcedar by direct seeding. *J. For.* 50:914–917.

Petty, R. O. and M. T. Jackson. 1966. Plant communities. In *Natural features of Indiana.* Edited by A. A. Lindsey, Ind. Acad. Sci. 600 pp.

Phares, R. E. 1971. Growth of red oak (*Quercus rubra* L.) seedlings in relation to light and nutrients. *Ecology* 52(4):669–672.

Roach, B. A., and S. F. Gingrich. 1968. Even-aged silviculture for upland central hardwoods. *USDA For. Serv. Agr. Hdbk. 355.* 39 pp.

Russell, T. E. 1971. Seeding and planting upland oaks. *In* Oak Symposium Proc. pp. 49–54. *USDA For. Serv. Northeast For. Exp. Stn.*

Russell, T. E. 1977. Planting yellow poplar—where we stand today. *USDA For. Serv. So. For. Exp. Stn. Gen. Tech. Rep. SO-17.* 8 pp.

Sander, I. L. 1977. Manager's handbook for oaks in the north central states. *USDA For. Serv. Gen. Tech. Rep. NC-37.* 35 pp.

Sander, I. L., and F. B. Clark. 1971. Reproduction of upland hardwood forests in the Central States. *USDA For. Serv. Agr. Hdbk. No. 405.* 25 pp.

Sander, I. L., P. S. Johnson, and R. F. Watt. 1976. A guide for evaluating the adequacy of oak advanced reproduction. *USDA For. Serv. Gen. Tech. Rep. NC-23.* 7 pp.

Schlesinger, R. C., and D. T. Funk. 1977. Manager's handbook for black walnut. *USDA For. Serv. Gen. Tech. Rep. NC-38.* 22 pp.

Shifley, S. R., and K. M. Brown, 1978. Elm-ash-cottonwood forest type bibliography. *USDA For. Serv. Gen. Tech. Rep. NC-42.* 56 pp.

Smith, H. C. 1965. Effects of clearcut openings on quality of hardwood border trees. *J. For.* 63:933–937.

Soc. Am. For. 1967. *Forest cover types of North America (exclusive of Mexico).* Washington, D.C. 67 pp.

Sowder, A. M. 1966. Christmas trees, the tradition and the trade. *USDA Agr. Inform. Bull. 94.* 31 pp.

Spencer, J. S., Jr., 1969. Indiana's timber. *USDA For. Serv. Resour. Bull. NC-7.* 61 pp.

Spencer, J. S., Jr., and B. L. Essex, 1976. Timber in Missouri, 1972. *USDA For. Serv. Resour. Bull. NC-30.* 108 pp.

Spencer, J. S., Jr., and H. W. Thorne, 1972. Wisconsin's 1968 timber resource—A perspective. *USDA For. Serv. Resour. Bull. NC-15.* 80 pp.

Stone, R. N. 1966. A third look at Minnesota's timber. *USDA For. Serv. Resour. Bull. NC-1.* 64 pp.

Troutman, F. H. and R. L. Porterfield. 1974. The role of Arkansas forests in the state's economy. *Univ. Ark. Coll. Bus. Admin. Publ. D-16.* 68 pp.

U.S. Bureau Census. 1973. *Census of population: 1970.* Vol. 1. Characteristics of the population. Part 1. U.S. Summary. Government Printing Off., Washington, D.C.

U.S. Dept. Agr. Soil Survey Staff. 1975. Soil taxonomy. *USDA Soil Cons. Serv. Agr. Hdbk.* 436. 754 pp.

U.S. Dept. Commerce. 1976. *Climatological data, Annual Summary.* National Climatic Center, Asheville, N.C.

U.S. Dept. Interior, Geological Survey. 1970. *The national atlas of the United States of America.* U.S. Government Printing Off., Washington, D.C. 417 pp.

U.S. For. Serv. 1965. Timber trends in the United States. *USDA For. Serv. For. Resour. Rep.* 17. 235 pp.

U.S. For. Serv. 1969. A forest atlas of the south. *So. For. Exp. Stn. and S.E. For. Exp. Stn.* 27 pp.

U.S. For. Serv. 1971. Design for the future. *USDA Northeastern Area State and Private Forestry.* 40 pp.

U.S. For. Serv. 1973. The outlook for timber in the United States. *USDA For. Serv. Rpt.* No. 20. 367 pp.

U.S. For. Serv. 1974. Seeds of woody plants in the United States. *USDA For. Serv. Agr. Hdbk.* 450. 883 pp.

U.S. For. Serv. 1977a. Draft midlands area guide/hoosier forest plan. *Wayne-Hoosier National Forest.* Bedford, Ind. 125 pp.

U.S. For. Serv. 1977b. Fish and wildlife management plan, Hoosier National Forest, Indiana. *Wayne-Hoosier National Forest.* Bedford, Ind.

U.S. For. Serv. 1977c. Timber management plan, Ozark National Forest: Draft environmental statement. *Ozark St.-Francis Nat. For.,* Ark. 60 pp.

Van Haverbeke, D. F. 1977. Conifers for single-row field windbreaks. *USDA For. Serv. Res. Pap.* RM-196. 10 pp.

Watt, R. F., K. A. Brinkman and B. A. Roach. 1973. Oak-Hickory. In *Silvicultural Systems for the Major Forest Types of the United States,* USDA For. Serv. Ag. Hdbk. No. 445. p. 66-69.

Williams, R. D. 1966. Planting stock grades. In *Black walnut culture, Walnut Workshop Proc.,* Carbondale, Ill. p. 16-17.

Williamson, M. J. 1965. Eastern redcedar (*Juniperus virginiana* L.). In *Silvics of forest trees of the United States.* USDA Agr. Hdbk. 271. pp. 212-216.

5

The Southern Hardwood Region

David Wm. Smith

Norwin E. Linnartz

LOCATION

The Southern Hardwood Region as discussed herein includes (1) the bottomland hardwoods along the major river courses throughout the Atlantic and Gulf Coastal Plains and in the Coastal Plain wetlands, (2) the Brown Loam Bluffs of mixed upland hardwoods along the eastern edge of the Mississippi River Valley, and (3) the upland hardwoods of the Appalachians. Geographically, the region extends from Pennsylvania southwest along the Ohio River to southern Illinois to eastern Oklahoma, southward to the Gulf of Mexico and Florida and, northward along the Atlantic coast to the northern extremities of Chesapeake Bay (Fig. 5-1).

Of major importance in this region are the upland hardwoods of the Appalachians and large contiguous areas of bottomland hardwoods located on the original floodplain of the Mississippi River and its major tributaries. The latter despite the heavy encroachment of land clearing during the past two decades. The numerous swamps, bays, and pond margins throughout the South Atlantic and Gulf Coast states also contain millions of acres of bottomland forest types, although this acreage too has been reduced in recent years by drainage and other encroachments.

Bottomland hardwoods occur to some extent along all the major and minor streams in all states east of the Great Plains. Likewise, there are many other areas of uplands in the South, such as the Interior Highlands discussed in Chapters 4 and 6, which contain a significant acreage and volume of commercial hardwood species.

The extensive encroachment of agriculture into the bottomlands and the

THE SOUTHERN HARDWOOD FOREST REGION

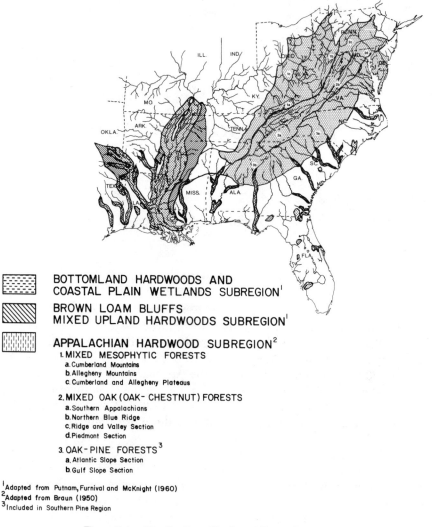

BOTTOMLAND HARDWOODS AND
COASTAL PLAIN WETLANDS SUBREGION[1]

BROWN LOAM BLUFFS
MIXED UPLAND HARDWOODS SUBREGION[1]

APPALACHIAN HARDWOOD SUBREGION[2]
1. MIXED MESOPHYTIC FORESTS
   a. Cumberland Mountains
   b. Allegheny Mountains
   c. Cumberland and Allegheny Plateaus

2. MIXED OAK (OAK- CHESTNUT) FORESTS
   a. Southern Appalachians
   b. Northern Blue Ridge
   c. Ridge and Valley Section
   d. Piedmont Section

3. OAK- PINE FORESTS[3]
   a. Atlantic Slope Section
   b. Gulf Slope Section

[1] Adapted from Putnam, Furnival and McKnight (1960)
[2] Adapted from Braun (1950)
[3] Included in Southern Pine Region

Figure 5-1.   The Southern Hardwood Forest Region.

widely dispersed nature of the hardwood areas throughout the South make an assessment of the total southern hardwoods resource extremely difficult. Therefore, our discussion will be confined to the three general areas enumerated above.

FOREST STATISTICS

Area

The area in commercial hardwood forest types in the South has been estimated to be about 143 million acres (Sternitzke, 1975) out of a total of 229 acres of commercial forest land (USDA For. Serv., 1978). However, extensive clearing of prime bottomland hardwood forests for agriculture and conversion of oak-pine uplands to pine plantations make hardwood forest area statistics only approximations at best.

The loss of millions of acres of high-quality hardwood forests on the bottomlands of the Mississippi River and its tributaries is an accomplished, and perhaps irreversible, fact. The economic advantages of growing soybeans and raising beef cattle have encouraged private landowners to convert prime hardwood sites to cropland and pastures. According to USDA Forest Service data (1974), the South as a region lost 7.36 million acres of commercial forestland between 1962 and 1970. Much of this occurred in the Mississippi River Valley where bottomland hardwood forests were reduced about 20 percent. Though the pace may have slowed, this conversion from forests to cropland has continued into the 1970s.

In the mid-1930s, 11.8 million acres of the lower Mississippi River Valley were classified as forest; by 1969 some 3.7 million acres had been converted to other uses (Sternitzke and Christopher, 1970). Between 1959 and 1969, almost 1.3 million acres, or 39 percent, of the Mississippi Delta in Arkansas were cleared (Hedlund, 1971); forest area in the North Delta of Louisiana decreased by 38 percent—over 716 thousand acres—between 1964 and 1974 (Murphy, 1975), with individual parishes (counties) losing from 30 percent to as high as 71 percent (Earles, 1975). Frey and Dill (1971) studied land-use changes between 1950 and 1969 in the Mississippi Valley extending into Tennessee, Kentucky, and Missouri and found that only 31 percent—7.5 million acres—of this area was still in forests in 1969 in contrast to the 11.5 million acres, or 48 percent, in 1950; conversely, cropland had increased from 10 million acres in 1950 to 13.7 million acres in 1969.

What then remains in the Mississippi River Valley? Probably about 7.5 million acres of bottomland hardwood types growing on sites which are too difficult or too costly to clear, drain, and cultivate. Of this acreage, about 1.2 million lie inside the levees where they are subject to annual flooding (Frey and Dill, 1971) and will likely remain in forests. In aggregate, however, there are still over 33 million acres of bottomland or other wetlands hardwood forest types in the South (Table 5-1).

TABLE 5-1

Summary of Southern Hardwood Forest Resource Data

State	Total Commercial Forest[a]		Bottomland and Wetland Hardwoods[b]		Upland Hardwoods	
	Area (thousand acres)	Net Volume, Hardwood Growing Stock (million cubic feet)	Area (thousand acres)	Net Volume, Growing Stock (million cubic feet)	Area (thousand acres)	Net Volume,[g] Growing Stock (million cubic feet)
Alabama	21,333	9,900	3,099	3,046	6,706[d]	6,854
Arkansas	18,207	10,086	3,129	3,033	7,592[d]	7,053
Florida	15,330	4,208	3,732	4,208	n.s.[e]	n.s.[e]
Georgia	24,812	11,521	3,154	4,617	5,711[d]	6,904
Kentucky	11,902	11,052	1,038[c]	781[c]	9,363[f]	10,271
Louisiana	14,527	8,152	5,635	5,217	3,159[d]	2,935
Mississippi	16,892	7,571	4,219	3,751	3,664[d]	3,820
North Carolina	19,562	15,389	2,706	3,797	9,934[f]	11,592

Oklahoma	4,323	1,051	426	268	843[d]	783
Pennsylvania	17,478	22,577	209[c]	130[c]	17,269[f]	22,447
South Carolina	12,176	7,121	2,090	3,635	2,979[d]	3,486
Tennessee	12,820	10,217	720	863	8,915[f]	9,354
Texas	12,512	4,916	1,774	1,409	3,775[d]	3,507
Virginia	15,939	14,144	425	536	12,535[f]	13,608
West Virginia	11,484	13,061	814	765	9,740[f]	12,296
Total	229,297	150,966	33,170	36,056	102,185	114,910

[a] From USDA For. Serv., 1978.

[b] Data for Florida, Georgia, North Carolina, and South Carolina derived from Boyce and Cost (1974); for Virginia, from Cost (1976); for the other states furnished by Renewable Resources Unit, South. For. Exp. Stn., USDA For. Serv. except where noted.

[c] Estimated from most recent state survey and USDA For. Serv. (1978).

[d] Does not include oak-pine type.

[e] n.s. = not a significant area/volume.

[f] Includes a portion oak-pine type.

[g] Net volume hardwood growing stock minus Bottomland and Wetland net volume growing stock.

Included in Table 5-1 are some 4 million acres of hardwood forests growing in the Brown Loam Bluffs, a strip of loess-covered and deeply dissected uplands lying along the eastern side of the Mississippi River Valley from just north of Baton Rouge, Louisiana, to the Ohio River (Fig. 5-1). Also included in Table 5-1 are the upland hardwood forests of the Interior Highlands described in Chapters 4 and 6.

The Appalachian Hardwood Forest delineated by Braun (1950) as the Mixed Mesophytic Forest, Oak-Pine Forest, and the unglaciated Oak-Chestnut Forest is found on about 131.7 million acres of the east-central United States which is 5.8 percent of the total U.S. land area. This includes the Piedmont Plateau discussed in Chapter 6. Highly variable physiographic features, coupled with diverse local and regional climatic conditions, have resulted in complex and heterogeneous forest systems. The effect of Atlantic and Gulf Coast weather patterns, large elevation and aspect differences characteristic of the Appalachian Mountains, and the presence of large river basins have directly and indirectly influenced the high ecological amplitude and diversity prevalent in the Appalachian Hardwood Forest. These conditions tend to make it the transitional region between the Northeastern and Central hardwoods to the north and west and the Coastal Plain Southern Pine and Southern Bottomland Hardwoods to the east, south and west. The states where Appalachian hardwoods are found include all, or parts of, Pennsylvania, Maryland, West Virginia, Virginia, North and South Carolina, Kentucky, Tennessee, Georgia, and Alabama.

Character of Forest Land Ownership

As is characteristic throughout the South, probably less than 10 percent of the hardwood forests are publicly owned. About 20 percent are owned by forest industries, with farmers and other individuals owning the remaining 70 percent.

It is in the farmer ownership category where most of the decreases in bottomland hardwoods have occurred. However, even some forest industry owners have succumbed to economic pressures and have converted a portion of their holding to agriculture. One such company in the North Louisiana Delta, for example, plans to convert about one-third of its total ownership to agricultural purposes; most of the clearing being done by this company is in the wetter, less productive hardwood sites where overcup oak-water hickory and sugarberry-American elm-green ash types (Soc. Am. For., 1954) predominate.

Almost all of the hardwood forests in the Brown Loam Bluffs are privately owned.

Approximately 62 percent of the land within the Appalachian Hardwood Subregion is classed as commercial forest land. Of the commercial forest land, 12 percent is public, 8 percent is owned by forest industry, 31 percent is farmer owned, and 50 percent is classed as miscellaneous private ownership.

Forest Inventory

More than 70 commercially important tree species make up the complex and varied hardwood forest of the South. Some are characteristically bottomland species, others occur only on uplands, but some are found on both bottomland and upland sites. Furthermore, extending into the South at higher elevations in the Appalachians are hardwood and softwood species more characteristic of the Northeast. Softwoods such as Atlantic white-cedar and loblolly, slash, pond, and spruce pines may occur on bottomland and other wetland sites in association with the hardwoods and baldcypress. In the uplands, loblolly, shortleaf, Virginia, pitch, Table-Mountain, and white pines are often found in association with upland hardwoods. Altogether, the tree species that constitute the Southern Hardwood Forest are as varied as are the sites found in this heterogeneous region.

In 1977, the Southern Hardwood Region contained an estimated 151 billion cubic feet of growing stock (USDA For. Serv., 1978), comprised of about 36 billion cubic feet of hardwoods growing in bottomlands and wetlands, and 115 billion feet in upland hardwood (Tables 5-1 and 5-2). Total hardwood growing stock in the Appalachian forest[1] is 66 billion cubic feet with 70 percent of the volume in hard hardwoods[2] and 30 percent in soft hardwoods.[3] Sawtimber volume is 147 billion board feet with 72 percent in hard hardwoods and 28 percent in soft hardwoods.

About 90 percent of the hardwood inventory is in private ownership. South-wide, the ratio of annual growth to removals in 1970 was 1.3 for growing stock and 1.0 for sawtimber. Net annual growth in 1970 amounted to only 16.7 cubic feet per acre, far below the South's average potential site productivity of 50 to 85 cubic feet.

In critical supply are high-quality trees of large diameters in species suitable for face veneer for furniture and panelling. Under present inventory and management levels, more and more of the hardwood lumber and veneer in the future must come from smaller trees of lower quality or inferior species.

The Forest Today

The hardwood forests of today, on both bottomlands and uplands, reflect not only the varying tolerances and growth rates of the species that comprise them, but also their history of high-grading, past agricultural use, the abuses of

[1]Acreage and volume figures for the Appalachian Forest are less than those in Table 5-1 and 5-2 because several of the states contain no Appalachian Forest types and other states are only partially covered.

[2]Hard hardwoods: sugar maple, all commercial oaks, birch (sp), hickory (sp), American beech, black locust, black walnut, mulberry (sp), honey locust, dogwood, persimmon (forest grown), American holly.

[3]Soft hardwoods: red maple, buckeye (sp), butternut, hackberry, yellow-poplar, cucumbertree, sweetgum, magnolia, sweetbay, water tupelo, sycamore, cottonwood, black cherry, basswood (sp), elm (sp), box elder, and willow.

TABLE 5-2

Net Volume of Hardwood Growing Stock on Commercial Timberland in the Southern Hardwood Forest Region by Species/Species Group and State[a]

State	White Oaks	Red Oaks	Hickory	Maple	Beech, Ash, Basswood	Sweet-gum	Tupelo, Black-gum	Yellow-Poplar	Cotton-wood, Aspen	Walnut, Cherry	Other Hardwood	Total
Alabama	1,585	2,412	1,104	216	380	1,626	998	622	33	32	892	9,900
Arkansas	2,793	2,926	1,166	98	327	1,296	354	3	91	59	973	10,086
Florida	352	823	118	305	310	405	1,213	35	2	4	641	4,208
Georgia	1,579	2,854	738	574	316	1,820	1,887	995	8	46	704	11,521
Kentucky	2,716	2,507	1,561	888	972	136	231	1,053	33	171	784	11,052
Louisiana	893	1,835	604	172	591	1,494	1,248	30	112	14	1,159	8,152
Mississippi	1,241	1,983	643	111	279	1,184	706	276	109	36	1,003	7,571
North Carolina	2,867	2,962	875	1,354	664	1,631	1,697	2,143	23	80	1,093	15,389
Oklahoma	355	307	141	10	40	29	19	0	24	4	122	1,051
Pennsylvania	4,619	4,870	651	5,284	2,083	0	107	694	661	2,071	1,537	22,577
South Carolina	750	1,666	330	407	286	1,346	1,440	405	64	10	417	7,121
Tennessee	2,759	2,432	1,417	550	537	400	233	864	66	150	809	10,217
Texas	968	1,645	336	47	204	892	250	0	49	6	519	4,916
Virginia	3,983	3,316	1,090	942	642	740	336	2,164	5	109	817	14,144
West Virginia	2,792	2,830	1,229	1,663	1,148	0	138	1,472	14	584	1,191	13,061
Total	30,252	35,368	12,003	12,621	8,779	12,999	10,857	10,756	1,294	3,376	12,661	150,966

Source: USDA For. Serv., 1978.
[a] All measurements in units of million cubic feet.

livestock grazing and uncontrolled fires. The end result has been a general lowering in quality if not in total quantity. Recent Forest Service statistics reveal that 22 percent of the total hardwood timber volume in the South is in rough and rotten trees (USDA For. Serv., 1974). The same statistics also indicate that more of the hardwood growing stock now is in small-sized trees (less than 17 inches in diameter) and less in the larger, high-quality sawtimber and veneer sizes than in 1952.

Yet another important factor is in the changes in species composition that have occurred. In the early history of hardwood logging—and even in the recent past—stands of mixed hardwood were commonly "creamed" of the largest and highest quality trees of only those species in demand at the time. The hardwood forests of today, therefore, contain a much higher proportion of inferior and less desirable species than was present in the original forests. For example, only about 15 percent of the growing stock and sawtimber volumes are composed of select white and red oaks. Only one-fifth of the hardwood land supports desirable trees; that is, trees of good form and vigor and of preferred species. An estimated 90 percent of the South's hardwood forests require cultural treatments, such as improvement cuttings, cull-tree removal, or thinnings, in order to achieve a high level of output which will approach the potential site productivity (USDA For. Serv., 1974). Just as present hardwood forests reflect past harvesting so will the future stands be influenced by the management practiced today. A shift in product use from predominately sawtimber to pulpwood or a combination of sawtimber and pulpwood has substantially changed the alternative regeneration methods and the composition of stands that result from natural regeneration. In stands where pulpwood is the primary product the rotation age is substantially less than for sawtimber. Pulpwood rotations of from 25 to 45 years encompass the threshold period when many hardwood species are maturing and becoming reliable seed producers. Thus, stands resulting from natural regeneration after pulpwood harvests are often substantially different than those following sawtimber rotations. Similarly, changes in the degree of crop removal greatly alter site conditions after harvest. In the past, sawtimber harvests were characterized by the removal of select sawlogs with a large amount of wood and slash being left on the site. Today, the complete removal of the above ground portion of trees down to stems 4 inches in d.b.h. is not an uncommon practice. The resulting moisture, temperature, light, and potential regeneration sources are greatly altered. Natural regeneration under these conditions, in terms of stem origin, species composition, spatial distribution, density, and diversity, is not known nor fully understood.

Without question, the potential for increased production of high-quality hardwoods for sawtimber and veneer is there; and many examples of good hardwood management can be found throughout the region. But much more sound silviculture needs to be applied if prime hardwoods are to continue as an important segment of Southern forestry.

The use of wood as an alternative energy source has shown a marked increase since 1977. The impact on the timber resource is yet unknown and the ultimate use of wood for home heating and other energy uses is only speculative at this time. Perhaps this new demand will provide an economically attractive market for previously unmerchantable products of much needed intermediate silvicultural manipulation in Southern hardwood stands.

The composition of the hardwoods forests of the South can best be described as heterogeneous. Most hardwood forests are so variable in species composition and the changes so subtle that the recognition of specific forest cover types is often quite difficult. A large number of the forest cover types of eastern North America listed by the Society of American Foresters (1954)[4] can be found in the Southern Hardwood Region. However, many of these forest types merely reflect changes in the proportion or different combinations of species. Some species are only ephemeral components and will be forced out of a stand by the greater persistence of their competitors. In the bottomlands, species composition often changes with only minor topographic variation. In the uplands, moisture gradients as determined by percent slope, slope position, and aspect significantly affect site quality and therefore influence species composition.

In view of the often extreme variability of sites and the heterogeneous nature of the Southern Hardwood Forest, discussion of each forest cover type (Soc. Am. For., 1954) would not be very meaningful. Therefore, several general type groups in each of the three general physiographic subregions described in the opening paragraph of this chapter are discussed.

BOTTOMLAND HARDWOODS SUBREGION

Physiography

The topography of bottomlands is characteristically flat, but even slight variations in elevation are associated with considerable differences in soils, drainage conditions, and forest species composition. A generalized view of the physiographic features along major streams similar to the Mississippi River is shown in Fig. 5-2. Two main physiographic features, the first bottoms and the terraces, were first recognized by Putnam (1951). The first bottoms have been formed by the present drainage system and are subject to frequent flooding (less so if protected by man-made levees). Terraces were formed by older drainage systems and represent former floodplains. The transition from first bottom to terrace may be quite distinct or rather gradual. Sometimes there may even be rather abrupt rises to adjacent uplands. Where unprotected, low terraces may flood occasionally, but upper terraces flood only during extremely high floods.

Variation in elevations within the bottoms and terraces results in (1) ridges, (2) flats, (3) sloughs, and (4) swamps. In addition, new land areas, or fronts, are

---

[4]The Society of American Foresters was in the process of revising the Forest Cover Types at the same time that this textbook was being revised. Thus, the reader should refer to the revised version of the Forest Cover Types.

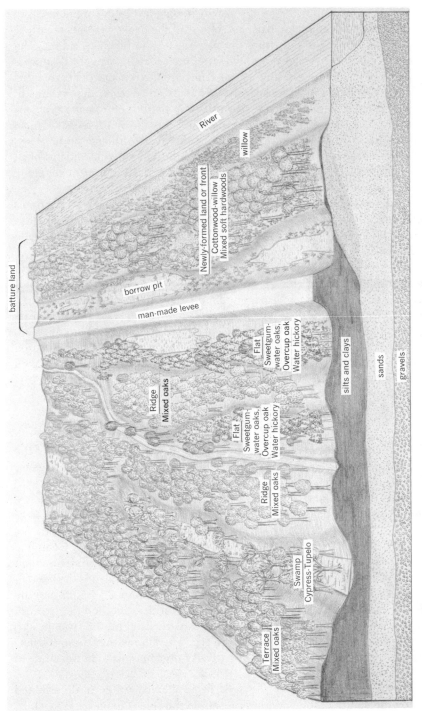

Figure 5-2. A generalized view of a flood plain on a large river, showing differences in physiography and associated species.

common along river banks. Ridges are usually the highest land, commonly from 1 to 10 feet above the adjoining flats, and often are the banks or fronts of former stream courses. The flats constitute the general terrain between ridges. The sloughs are shallow depressions in which water collects but normally disappears during the first half of the growing season. They are the remains of nearly filled stream courses or present drainageways. Swamps are distinct depressions in which water stands throughout the year except in periods of extreme drought. The new lands or fronts (bars, towheads, etc.) are the most recent stream depositions, many being formed constantly by the river. Although perhaps less extensive and distinct, similar topography is exhibited by the floodplains of all major streams. Specific forest type groups or species associations can generally be recognized on each of the topographic features described above.

Interspersed throughout the Coastal Plain pine lands are numerous bottoms containing small intermittent and free-flowing creeks, which may vary in width from a few hundred feet to a mile or more. These creek bottoms are subject to considerable local changes in water level during the growing season. Other reasonably productive hardwood sites within the Coastal Plain are the inland muck swamps, coastal and estuarial swamps, bays, and hammocks. The swamps are usually flooded yearlong from impoundment of rainwater and seepage, whereas the bays are peaty swamps where the permanent water table appears to be at or near the soil surface. Hammocks (called bay-galls in Louisiana) are localized areas on Coastal Plain flatwoods sites. These areas may be depressed or raised above the surrounding terrain and, though not generally associated with a stream, are usually well drained but with ample moisture for growth of hardwoods.

Geology and Soils

The character of the present landscape of the major bottomland areas of the South was formed during the Quaternary Period of geologic time (Fenneman, 1938). A sequence of marine deposition of sands, silts, and clays associated with intermittent rises in the sea level and subsequent uplifting of the land surface resulted in development of a series of terraces making up the Coastal Plain of the southeastern United States. As the land surface was raised, an undulating topography was formed as the seaward drainage patterns developed. Continual erosion of the uplands and deposition of eroded materials along the streams and at the sea outlets has resulted in the pattern of alluvial bottomlands depicted in Fig. 5-2. Large inland swamps, such as the Dismal Swamp of Virginia and the Okefenokee of Georgia, were formed when later terraces blocked the seaward drainage of low-lying land areas. Broad tidal estuaries and coastal swamps also formed as the streams discharged into the sea. The land within these swamps varies from permanently inundated low areas of organic soils to better-drained ridges or hammocks of mineral soil.

The nature, or character, of the soils in an alluvial valley is determined largely by the nature of the materials present in the river's drainage area which serves as the erosional source of the deposits of mineral soil. Alluvial soils derived from the sandy materials of the Coastal Plain will be coarse textured, but many alluvial soils derived from erosion of the less-weathered, grassland prairie soils will be high in expanding clays. The Lower Mississippi River Valley and such tributaries as the Red River are examples of the latter. Thus, bottomland soils may be clayey, silty, or sandy depending on the origin of the deposits and their location in relation to the river.

The normal pattern along major rivers is deposition of coarse materials (i.e., sands) along the banks with progressively finer sediments deposited in sequence away from the river. A series of alternating sandbars and silty clay sloughs are formed as a result of constantly shifting river channels. The sandbars are soon covered by cottonwoods and the sloughs by willows. As the young trees trap the load of sediments carried by flood waters, layers of silty clay may cover the previous sandbars, while the sloughs act as settling basins to accumulate very fine clays and silts. When subject to frequent flooding and deposition, as is the case of the batture land, soils often show stratification of different-sized soil particles. Soils of the natural ridges along stream channels usually consist of silt loams, very fine sandy loams, and silty clay loams. The depressed and flat backswamp soils are generaly poorly drained clays (Lytle, 1960).

A feature common to all bottomland soils is the indistinct profile development, even though the soils are very complex and differ markedly in age and in physical and chemical properties. Variations in texture range from newly deposited sands to older deposits of clay. Soil structure may vary from the single grains of sands to the compact blocky structure of clays. Soil reaction generally ranges from slightly acid (pH 6) to alkaline (above pH 7), although soils along minor streams in the lower Coastal Plain may be more acid. The soils also generally contain moderate amounts of organic matter and are well supplied with the required mineral nutrients for tree growth (Lytle, 1960); however, nutrient status varies a great deal with differences in soil colloids. Soil aeration and drainage also vary considerably, and variations in species associations are most often reflections of aeration and drainage conditions in bottomland soils.

Climate and Weather

The climate of the southern bottomland hardwoods may be classed as humid to subhumid. Annual precipitation, chiefly rainfall, is between 42 and 64 inches and is generally well distributed throughout the year. Warm-season precipitation (April to September, inclusive) ranges between 22 and 34 inches (USDA For. Serv., 1969). Late summer to early fall is customarily the driest part of the year. Moderate droughts occur irregularly every few years, while severe prolonged droughts may occur once every two or three decades.

The Bottomland Hardwoods Subregion is characterized by a relatively long frost-free season, ranging from about 210 days at the northern limit to over 300 days in the coastal areas (USDA For. Serv., 1969). In general the average temperatures increase from north to south in the bottomlands. Mean January temperatures range from about 40 °F in the northern sections to about 55 °F along the Gulf Coast. Mean July temperatures average about 81 °F throughout the region, but maximum summer temperatures often exceed 100 °F. Unseasonably early autumn frosts and late spring freezes sometimes occur and profoundly affect the growth of trees and seedling mortality. Also, abrupt temperature changes especially during the winter months are characteristic of much of the region.

Prolonged droughts, ice storms, hurricane winds in coastal areas, and tornadoes inland are infrequent but characteristic climatic phenomena of the region. Such infrequent climatic occurences, however, may significantly affect the conditions or local composition of the forests. For example, the blight or dieback and eventual mortality of sweetgum growing on tight clay soils have been attributed to drought conditions extending over several consecutive years (Toole and Broadfoot, 1959).

History of Forest Use

Much of the early cutting of bottomland forests throughout the South was to clear land for agriculture. Extensive areas were cleared and the land planted in cotton, and later in other crops. Logs and lumber for local construction and fuelwood were the chief outlets for the timber, both from the land-clearing operations and from high-grading of stands left in timber. Extensive commercial clearcutting did not get underway until about 1900. The earliest loggers in the bottomlands took only the largest trees of the best species, gradually lowering their quality and species requirements each successive time the area was cut. These practices generally have continued to the present time.

As discussed earlier, in the Mississippi River bottomlands, especially in the Delta areas of Arkansas, North Louisiana, and Mississippi, extensive land clearing for agriculture has significantly reduced the acreage of bottomland hardwood forests. Although the pace has slowed somewhat, conversion of forests to agriculture is continuing, with the ultimate acreage to remain in forests being highly conjectural. It is clear, however, that the lower Mississippi River Valley is rapidly losing its importance as a producer of prime bottomland hardwoods.

The other major river bottoms throughout the South have been subjected to a similar pattern of land use and timber harvest. However, these bottomlands have not come under the recent heavy pressure of extensive land clearing, although farming is an important enterprise along many sections of these rivers.

Major Forest Type Groups

Except for the cottonwood and willow types on newly formed land and the cypress-tupelo of the swamps, the bottomland hardwood forests of the South present an extremely heterogeneous mixture of species. These mixtures are often strongly influenced by past cutting practices, and species composition often changes with only minor topographic changes. The resultant forest stands are so variable in species composition and the changes so subtle that the recognition of specific cover types is often quite difficult. The Society of American Foresters (1954) listed 23 types that fit the bottomland hardwoods. Putnam (1951) grouped these 23 types into eight broad types, whereas the USDA Forest Service (1974) usually groups all bottomland species into only two type groups: oak-gum-cypress and elm-ash-cottonwood.

A type-group classification for the southern bottomland hardwoods is shown in Table 5-3, although this classification is somewhat arbitrary and species composition may vary considerably within each type.

Silviculture of the Major Type Groups

In addition to the characteristics shown in Table 5-3, the ecological relationships, growth rates, rotation ages or sizes, and cultural practices pertinent to each major type group are discussed below. The relative value and tolerance of the major tree species are listed in Table 5-4. Value ratings of hardwoods, however, vary considerably from tree to tree, depending upon a number of factors such as size, form, and defects. Sometimes a tree of a relatively low-value species may be more desirable than a defective specimen of a high-value species. Value ratings may also vary with product use and from one area to another.

Cottonwood and Willow Type Group.   Eastern cottonwood and black willow are the pioneer species on recent alluvial deposits along the major waterways, most extensively along the Mississippi River and its tributaries. Both species are extremely intolerant, rapid growers, but short lived. They can not tolerate competition from weeds and vines and require moist, bare mineral soil to become established. Because they are so intolerant of shade, they will not succeed themselves. New stands are always even-aged, very dense, and most often either pure cottonwood or pure willow (Fig. 5-3).

PLACE IN ECOLOGICAL SUCCESSION.   Cottonwood establishes itself on the higher, better-drained, and coarser-textured sediments. Black willow, on the other hand, usually becomes established on the low-lying, wet, fine-textured alluvium. Cottonwood is succeeded by the riverfront hardwoods—silver maple, American elm, sugarberry, American sycamore, pecan, green ash, and boxelder. In later stages of succession, sweetgum and the red oaks comprise the major species on these pioneer cottonwood sites. On low areas with fine-textured soils, black willow is replaced by baldcypress, green ash, American elm, red maple, and sugarberry, frequently with an understory of swamp-privet. These species are followed much later in succession by overcup oak, water hickory, and persimmon; with continued sedimentation these sites may eventually become low flats and support Nuttall oak (or laurel oak in the Southeast) and even water oak. Willow is also the pioneer when sloughs, swamps, and oxbow lakes begin to fill with sediment. The willow is succeeded by

TABLE 5-3

Description of the Major Type Groups of Southern Bottomland Hardwoods

| Type Group | Importance | | Sites Occupied | Major Species | Associated Species | Comments |
	Extent	Commercial Value				
Cottonwood and willow	Minor	Cottonwood, high; willow, low to medium value	Newly formed land along rivers; cottonwood predominates on ridges and better-drained flats; willow predominates on the wetter low flats, sloughs, and depressions	Eastern, cottonwood Black willow	Pecan American sycamore Sugarberry Hackberry Green ash American elm Red maple Silver maple Boxelder Baldcypress Waterlocust Honeylocust	Pioneer species, succeeded by the associated, more tolerant species; cottonwood has very rapid growth rate, excellent quality, and is a prized species for veneer and hardwood pulp; willow also grows rapidly but is less valuable; both are extremely intolerant and require bare, moist, mineral seedbed for natural regeneration
Cypress-tupelo	Minor, except in lower Mississippi River Valley and coastal areas.	High value when baldcypress predominates; otherwise low to medium value	Chiefly in low poorly drained flats, deep sloughs, and swamps in first bottoms and terraces; common in swamps of coastal plains and river estuaries	Baldcypress Water tupelo Swamp tupelo	Pondcypress Swamp cottonwood Red maple Water hickory Black willow American elm Overcup oak Nuttall oak Laurel oak Waterlocust	A permanent type; commonly in mixture but each species may be found in pure, even-aged stands; water tupelo is the component in swamps of alluvial flood-plains and estuaries; swamp tupelo predominates in nonalluvial and coastal swamps

Type	Importance and occurrence	Value	Site and major species				Remarks
Mixed bottomland hardwoods	Major; found on all major and minor stream bottoms and associated terraces	Depends on major species; mostly medium to high value, except overcup oak-water hickory on poorly drained slack-water sites	All sites; major species vary according to site: sweetgum and water oaks prevalent on heavy-textured soils of flats and low ridges; sweetgum and mixed oaks on ridges and better drained flats; overcup oak and water hickory on heavy clays of low, poorly drained flats and shallow sloughs	Sweetgum Water oak Willow oak Nuttall oak Swamp chestnut oak (Cow oak) Cherrybark oak Green ash Sugarberry Hackberry American elm Overcup oak Water hickory	Laurel oak Pin oak Shumard oak White oak Pecan American sycamore Boxelder Hickory spp. Red maple Silver maple Cedar elm Winged elm Persimmon Honeylocust Waterlocust Pumpkin ash White ash River birch Baldcypress Black tupelo Swamp tupelo American beech Southern magnolia	Persimmon Sweetbay Green ash	Species associations depend on sites and successional stage; some species associations are transitional between pioneer cottonwood-willow type and more permanent associations; past high-grading has increased proportion of poorer species, such as the elms, sugarberry, boxelder, and maple; minor stream bottoms in Coastal Plain usually contain fewer species overall, with smaller proportion of wet-site species

Source: Adapted from Putnam, 1951 and Putnam et al., 1960.

TABLE 5-4

Relative Value, Growth Rate, Tolerance, and Management Possibilities of Common Bottomland Hardwoods

Relative Value of Species	Growth Rate	Tolerance to Competition	Tolerance to Periodic Flooding	Management Possibilities
Highest Value				
Green ash	Medium	Intolerant	Tolerant	Favor in management; seedlings need early release; sprouts well; good for planting
Pumpkin ash	Medium	Intolerant	Tolerant	Favor on good sites
Eastern cottonwood	Very rapid	Very intolerant	Tolerant	Grow and manage in pure plantations; thin natural stands
Baldcypress	Slow to medium	Moderately tolerant	Very tolerant	Favor; pure even-aged stands should be thinned to prevent stagnation; sites make regeneration difficult
Sweetgum	Medium to good	Intolerant	Intermediate	Favor on good sites; an efficient sprouter from both roots and stumps; often planted for pulpwood
Cherrybark oak	Good to excellent	Intolerant	Very intolerant	Best red oak; favor in management
Delta post oak	Medium	Moderately intolerant	Very intolerant	Favor on well-drained sites in lower Mississippi Valley
Shumard oak	Good to excellent	Intolerant	Very intolerant	Favor on good ridge soils and well-drained bottoms; occurs most often as scattered individuals
Swamp chestnut oak (cow oak)	Medium to good	Moderately intolerant	Intolerant	One of best white oaks; favor in management; good mast tree

162

Species				Remarks
American sycamore	Good to excellent	Very intolerant	Tolerant	Favor in management; sprouts well from stumps; can be planted from cuttings or seedlings
Intermediate Value Hackberry	Poor to medium	Very tolerant	Intermediate	Needs release from shading for best form and growth; favor on flats in northern part of region
Sugarberry	Poor to medium	Very tolerant	Intermediate	Best form and growth when released from shading early; favor on flats if better species are not present
Southern magnolia	Medium	Tolerant	Intolerant	Found mainly in minor or secondary stream bottoms within 100 to 200 miles of coast; manage and favor if sound and not too limby
Silver maple	Excellent	Intolerant	Tolerant	Favor along major streams; best in southern Ohio River Valley
Nuttall oak	Good to excellent	Intolerant	Intermediate	Favor on wet sites in recent alluvium
Water oak	Good to excellent	Intolerant	Intermediate	Favor on best sites; subject to epicormic branching when released
Willow oak	Good to excellent	Intolerant	Tolerant	Favor on ridges and high flats; growth poor on flats underlain by hardpan
Pecan	Medium to good	Moderately intolerant	Intermediate	Favor on recent loamy riverfronts of Mississippi River system; nuts heavily used by wildlife; seedlings subject to grazing damage
Swamp tupelo	Medium	Moderately intolerant	Very tolerant	Thin dense stands to prevent stagnation; difficult to regenerate because of site conditions

TABLE 5-4, continued

Relative Value of Species	Growth Rate	Tolerance to Competition	Tolerance to Periodic Flooding	Management Possibilities
Water tupelo	Medium	Intolerant	Very tolerant	Can be managed along with its chief associate, baldcypress; difficult to regenerate on its usual sites
Black willow	Excellent	Very intolerant	Tolerant	Manage on riverfront lands in Mississippi River system; sprouts vigorously; pure stands stagnate early, so frequent thinnings are essential; natural reproduction requires bare, wet mineral soil
Low Value				
River birch	Good	Intolerant	Intermediate	Short-lived; prolific reproduction on bare, moist, mineral soil
Swamp cottonwood	Good to excellent	Moderately intolerant	Very tolerant	Commonly associated with baldcypress and tupelos; favor the better species
American elm	Medium	Tolerant	Intermediate	Generally of poor form; manage only if better species are absent
Cedar elm	Poor	Tolerant	Intermediate	Very hard wood used only for pallets and local-use lumber
Winged elm	Poor to medium	Tolerant	Intolerant	Normally small tree; not as good as American elm
Black tupelo	Poor to medium	Moderately intolerant	Intolerant	Low value because of tendency to warp; commonly grows with white oaks, winged elm, and hickory in creek bottoms

Species				Remarks
Hickory spp.	Poor to good	Very tolerant	Intolerant	Probably should be managed on best sites for tool handles and other specialty products
Honeylocust	Medium	Intolerant	Intermediate	Best growth on better ridges of new alluvium; seed pods are excellent mast, so favor if needed for wildlife purposes
Waterlocust	Good	Intolerant	Tolerant	Widely scattered; poor form and small size; only fair mast producer
Red maple	Medium to good	Tolerant	Tolerant	Manage only if of good form; dependable reproduction on wet sites
Red mulberry	Poor to medium	Very tolerant	Intolerant	A small understory tree highly prized for fence posts; seeds readily and sprouts well
Laurel oak	Good to excellent	Intolerant	Tolerant	Poorest of red oaks; should not be managed unless the only species present on site
Overcup oak	Poor to medium	Moderately intolerant	Tolerant	Poorest of white oaks; eliminate whenever better species are available on site
Pin oak	Good to excellent	Intolerant	Intermediate	Excessive limbiness precludes management for factory lumber
Water hickory	Poor	Moderately tolerant	Tolerant	Accepted with sweet pecan for factory lumber if free of ring shake; only best quality trees on poorly drained flats warrant management

TABLE 5-4, continued

Relative Value of Species	Growth Rate	Tolerance to Competition	Tolerance to Periodic Flooding	Management Possibilities
Common persimmon	Poor	Very tolerant	Intermediate	Very high value for specialty products if market is available; scattered occurrence may preclude such uses; probably should be retained for wildlife food source
Weed Species Boxelder	Excellent	Moderately tolerant	Moderately tolerant	Rarely of commercial size; practically only value is for wildlife food source; invader under cottonwood and river-front stands
American hornbeam and Eastern hophornbeam	Poor	Very tolerant	Intolerant	Sometimes used for pulpwood; must be eliminated for natural regeneration of desirable species; also common in upland hardwood stands

Planertree	Poor	Moderately intolerant	Very tolerant	Will take over wet sites unless eliminated when desirable species are removed
Roughleaf dogwood	Poor	Tolerant	Intermediate	Usually sparse but can preempt open areas on low ridges and better drained flats
Swamp-privet	Poor	Tolerant	Tolerant	Dense stands preclude desirable reproduction on wet flats and shallow sloughs
Common buttonbush	Poor	Moderately intolerant	Very tolerant	Shrub that will take over deep sloughs and swamps after heavy cutting
Hawthorn spp.	Poor	Very tolerant	Intolerant	Scattered understory tree on ridges and well drained flats but may become thicket in openings
Possumhaw	Poor	Tolerant	Tolerant	Grows on heavy soils of flats or low ridges and will prevent desirable reproduction in openings

Source: Adapted from Putnam, 1951; Putnam et al., 1960; and USDA For. Serv., 1965.

Figure 5-3. Cottonwood-willow stands. Upper photo shows young stand started on newly formed bottom area. Lower photo shows mature stand with understory of invading species, such as boxelder, green ash, and silver maple (U.S. For. Serv.)

baldcypress and the tupelos in areas where water stands most of the year. In the shallow sloughs, willow is usually followed by overcup oak and water hickory along with green ash, persimmon, and Nuttall oak in some situations (Putnam et al., 1960).

GROWTH RATES.   Eastern cottonwood is the fastest growing tree in North America. Height growth is extremely rapid in youth but culminates at an early age. Height growth of seedlings on good sites is 12 feet or more per year (McKnight, 1969). Diameter growth is also quite rapid, often averaging 1½ inches per year, and 6 to 8 inches of diameter growth in 10 years is quite ordinary. Black willow also grows rapidly but not as fast as cottonwood. Dense stands of willow tend to stagnate at an early age, and then growth rates decline to almost nothing.

ROTATION AGE OR SIZE.   Rotation ages of both species for pulpwood is from 12 to 20 years and for sawlogs from 30 to 35 years, depending on site quality. In managed plantations on good sites, cottonwood is often grown on a 12-year rotation for pulpwood and 20-year rotation for sawlogs. On good sites cottonwood can be economically grown to 26 to 28 inches d.b.h.

CULTURAL PRACTICES.   The growth of natural, even-aged stands of cottonwood and willow (as well as sweetgum, baldcypress, and the tupelos) can be enhanced greatly by thinnings, especially if sawtimber is the desired final crop. In very dense natural stands of cottonwood, a precommercial thinning may be desirable. However, such stands may not require precommercial thinning because the rapid growth of the species soon results in expression of dominance and concomitant heavy mortality of the less vigorous young trees. The first commercial thinning should be applied as soon as possible after a stand reaches merchantable pulpwood size. Maximum volume production is attained by thinning early and often. In each thinning, the smaller trees of poorer quality should be removed and the vigorous dominant trees should be provided room to grow. In other words, thinning should be from below (McKnight and Johnson, 1975; Shropshire, 1971).

Unlike cottonwood, black willow does not assert dominance and dense pure stands stagnate early in life. As soon as economically feasible, willow stands should be thinned from below and thereafter at 5-year intervals, to prevent excessive mortality and maintain adequate diameter growth on vigorous trees (Putnam, 1951; Obye, 1958).

Cottonwood and willow, because of their extreme intolerance and exacting seedbed requirements, are difficult to regenerate naturally. In most cases, the final harvest cut of these two species will free a good stand of mixed riverfront hardwoods which have become established under the cottonwood or willow overstory (Putnam, 1951). Elimination of the very tolerant weed species, namely boxelder and swamp-privet, is essential if the new stand of desirable species is to have a chance to grow and develop.

Black willow can be regenerated naturally by the seed-tree method, provided the site is flooded long enough in the spring to kill most of the competing vegetation before the willow seeds are disseminated in May and June. If flooding does not provide the required bare seedbed, then mechanical site preparation is required. However, willow is not generally valuable enough to warrant site preparation costs.

Cottonwood can also be regenerated by the seed-tree method with site preparation. But virtually all cottonwood regeneration today is established by planting cuttings of genetically improved stock at wide spacings. Such a plantation is shown in Fig. 5-4.

The following steps are critical for successful cottonwood plantations (McKnight, 1970):

1. Choice of proper planting site—fertile, moist but well drained, loamy bottomland soils are the best.

2. Intensive site preparation—all potential competing vegetation must be eliminated and deep plowing improves soil structure and aeration; site preparation must be done during the dry part of the year preceding planting.

3. Use of good planting stock—genetically improved planting stock is available from forest nurseries; cuttings should be 20 inches long and one-half to 1 inch in diameter.

4. Proper planting techniques—cuttings should be planted 18 inches deep with 2 inches above ground; uniform spacing within and between rows is required for subsequent cultivation; spacing of 12 x 12 feet has been found to be best.

5. Frequent cultivation after planting—thorough first-year cultivation is critical; a first cultivation in the direction of planting and the second-across planting rows is recommended; cultivation to a depth of 6 inches is very beneficial; the need for cultivation during the second year depends on the weed problems and the growth rate of the cottonwood trees.

6. Protection against animals, fire, insects, and disease—deer must be excluded the first year and domestic livestock for a somewhat longer period; insect and disease problems are reduced when careful site selection and clean cultivation produce healthy, vigorous trees; fire protection is essential in cottonwood plantations after the first year.

Pruning of planted cottonwood is desirable if high-quality saw and veneer logs are the intended final product. The timing and frequency of thinnings are related to initial spacing and management goals. For maximum growth, regular and heavy thinning at 3- to 5-year intervals will be necessary to maintain stand density at 80 to 90 square feet of basal area per acre. On good sites, the first thinning is usually needed at age 6 to 8 years and a final harvest of 28-inch saw and veneer timber is possible at age 28 (McKnight, 1970).

Although many variables determine the costs of establishment and returns

Figure 5-4.   A five-year-old cottonwood plantation on the Mississippi River floodplain in Arkansas (USDA For. Serv.).

from cottonwood plantations, rates of return can range from 7 to over 15 percent (Dutrow et al., 1970).

For more detailed information about cottonwood culture, the reader should refer to Maisenhelder (1960), McKnight and Biesterfeldt (1968), Hansbrough (1970), Mohn et al. (1970), and Kaszkurewicz (1973).

SUSCEPTIBILITY TO DAMAGE.   Natural stands of both cottonwood and willow are tolerant of flooding and siltation under normal conditions. However, seedling stands, especially newly established plantings, suffer significant mortality when inundated for several weeks after foliation (Kennedy and Krinard, 1974; Baker, 1977). Mortality and growth losses are much less severe when flooding occurs during the dormant season or if the tops of foliated seedlings remain above flood levels during the growing season.

Young cottonwood plantations and nurseries are susceptible to damage by a number of insects and diseases (Morris et al., 1975). The more important insects are the cottonwood twig borer, the cottonwood leaf beetle, and the clearwing borers. Registered chemicals are available for the control of these insects in cottonwood nurseries and plantations.

No important disease has been epidemic in southern cottonwood plantations, according to McKnight (1970). However, several canker diseases are responsible for losses of up to 20 percent during the first season in plantations established with unrooted cuttings (Morris et al., 1975). Melampsora rust sometimes defoliates cottonwood of all ages and thereby reduces growth.

Newly established cottonwood plantations are quite susceptible to browsing damage by deer and domestic livestock, which must be excluded for a year or two. Cottonwood of all ages can be killed or severely damaged by wildfires and fire protection is a must.

Willow suffers little from insects and diseases, although the cottonwood leaf beetle and Melampsora rust may sometimes partially defoliate trees. Willow also is susceptible to mortality or serious wounding by wildfires. Severe droughts that lower the water table can result in serious mortality on certain sites.

Cypress-Tupelo Type Group.   Characteristics of this type are shown in Table 5-3, and information about the species normally associated with the type is presented in Table 5-4.

Baldcypress and water tupelo are the chief species in the deep sloughs and swamps of the first bottoms and terraces, especially in the lower Mississippi River Valley. Such sites usually hold water for most of the year. In non-alluvial swamps of the Coastal Plain and along coastal estuaries, swamp tupelo is the chief associate of baldcypress, but both tupelos may be present in some situations. All three species may grow in more-or-less pure stands. Other common associates are pondcypress, sweetbay, and redbay (Putnam, 1951; Putnam et al., 1960).

PLACE IN ECOLOGICAL SUCCESSION.   Baldcypress and the tupelos normally succeed black willow on sites where water stands most of the year, and the type is permanent on such sites. Either artificial drainage or continuing sedimentation over a long period of time may alter these sites so that other species, such as green ash, American elm, red maple, sugarberry, water hickory, overcup oak, Nuttall or laurel oak, and persimmon, may become established and ultimately replace the cypress and tupelos.

GROWTH RATES.   Although baldcypress has been considered to be a slow-growing tree, increases in diameter and height of second-growth stands compare favorably with those of many bottomland hardwoods. Baldcypress averages 2 inches or more in diameter growth every 10 years and about 1 foot per year of height growth during the first 100 years (USDA For. Serv., 1965). The tupelos do not normally attain the large size or the age of baldcypress growing on similar sites, but the tupelos are faster growers than cypress. Water tupelo will reach 6 inches d.b.h. and 40 feet in height at age 25 and 20 to 26 inches of diameter growth in 50 to 70 years. Swamp tupelo also averages from 3 to 4 inches of diameter growth in 10 years (USDA For. Serv., 1965).

ROTATION AGE OR SIZE.   Optimum rotation age for baldcypress is probably 150 years or longer, but the desired maximum diameter rather than age should determine the rotation period. Proper management of even-aged baldcypress stands should produce a mean annual growth of 225 to 250 board feet per acre over a 100-year rotation. Even-aged tupelo stands on average sites can be managed on a 75-year rotation (USDA For. Serv., 1965).

CULTURAL PRACTICES.   Baldcypress and the tupelos should be managed in even-aged stands; their silvical characteristics, the nature of existing stands, and the swamp sites on which they prevail make even-aged management almost mandatory (Putnam *et al.*, 1960; Stubbs, 1973).

Most stands are overcrowded and all three species assert dominance poorly, so growth slows early in life and the stands stagnate. Such a situation will certainly lead to longer sawtimber rotations unless these stands are thinned. McKnight and Johnson (1975) recommend a commercial thinning of even-aged stands when dominant trees average 8 to 10 inches d.b.h., a second thinning when dominants average 14 to 16 inches d.b.h., and a third when they average 20 to 22 inches. In each thinning, the smaller trees of poorer quality should be removed to favor the more vigorous dominant trees. Cypress-tupelo stands often carry more than 150 square feet of basal area per acre, and residual density after thinning may still be rather high but a basal area of 110 square feet or less should be the goal of thinnings.

Clearcutting is probably the most practical harvest cutting method for baldcypress-tupelo stands (McKnight and Johnson, 1975; Stubbs, 1973). Logging of swamp sites can only be done under dry conditions which are also an essential requirement for seed germination of these species. Tupelo and cypress seeds will not germinate under water, but the seeds may remain viable for two years and will germinate when water recedes. Seedlings generally grow rapidly in height and soon are tall enough to avoid submergence during the growing season. Advance regeneration of swamp tupelo is often present and seedlings sprout vigorously so that a clearcut harvest is possible. In any case, understory weed species such as buttonbush, swamp-privet, and planertree must be controlled (if present) for a new stand of cypress-tupelo to become established successfully.

SUSCEPTIBILITY TO DAMAGE.   Flooding is generally not harmful to this type. In fact, the type exists because normal flooding eliminates competing vegetation prior to seed germination and foliation of cypress and tupelo. Nonetheless, a major change in normal water levels, either deeper flooding or severe drainage, will sharply decrease growth and may cause·mortality, especially of the tupelos (USDA For. Serv., 1965).

Fire is a major enemy of all bottomland hardwoods, and cypress-tupelo stands are no exception. Fortunately, these swamp sites are not often dry enough to burn, but the evidence of past wildfires in the form of butt rot can be seen in many stands.

Relatively few diseases or insects cause widespread damage to cypress and tupelo. The only serious disease of baldcypress is the wood-destroying *Stereum* heartrot fungus which causes "peckiness" in old trees. This fungus enters rotted branch stubs in the crown and slowly works down in the heartwood to the base of the tree, producing a pitted or chambered effect (Davidson et al., 1960). A defoliating insect, the cypress looper has been reported as a problem in parts of Arkansas and Louisiana (Morris, 1955).

The tupelos are sometimes defoliated by the forest tent caterpillar. In localized areas, this defoliation can be serious enough on occasion to slow down growth and even kill smaller trees.

Mixed Bottomland Hardwoods Type Group.   As indicated in Table 5-3, this type group occurs on all major and minor stream bottoms and terraces throughout the South. Even though a number of Society of American Foresters Forest Cover Types can be identified in bottomlands, the types are so intermingled and species composition on many sites is so complex that it is more meaningful to discuss this broad species association rather than specific cover types. Table 5-4 provides specific information about the 12 major and over 20 associated species which are included in this type group.

PLACE IN ECOLOGICAL SUCCESSION.   Several successional stages may be evident in bottomlands, especially along major rivers, and often they are associated with distinct topographic features which reflect the pattern of alluvium deposition. The species composition of each successional stage is generally determined by the frequency of flooding and/or the degree of wetness of the site.

In the first bottoms which are subject to periodic or frequent overflow, the riverfront species—silver maple, American elm, American sycamore, sugarberry (or hackberry), boxelder, pecan, and green ash—succeed cottonwood on the higher, better drained fronts. In later succession, these species are joined or replaced by sweetgum and the water oaks. The pioneer black willow on lower riverfronts with fine-textured soils is succeeded by baldcypress, green ash, and their associates if the site remains somewhat of a shallow swamp. These species are followed much later by overcup oak, water hickory, and persimmon. Continued sedimentation may change such sites to low flats which also support Nuttall oak, willow oak, and water oak. The best and highest sites in first bottoms may support cherrybark oak, sweetgum, and other species more characteristic of advanced stages of succession (Putnam *et al.*, 1960).

In the second bottoms (or terraces), low ridges commonly support swamp chestnut oak, cherrybark oak, Shumard oak, water oak, and winged elm. Flats are usually occupied by sweetgum, willow oak, Nuttall oak (or laurel oak in the Southeast), green ash, red maple, and persimmon. In the lowest, poorest drained flats and sloughs in the terraces, overcup oak and water hickory are dominant (Putnam *et al.*, 1960).

The smaller river and creek bottoms in the Coastal Plain do not usually exhibit distinct successional stages. Here species composition often includes beech, yellow-poplar, magnolia, and pines along with the better white oaks, the hickories, and most of the species characteristic of older alluvial ridges in the big bottoms (Fig. 5-5).

Figure 5-5.   One-hundred-year-old cherrybark oak and sweetgum on the Tombigbee River bottom, Alabama. (USDA For. Serv.)

GROWTH RATES.   Growth rates vary considerably among the species and even within the same species growing on different sites or under different stand densities. Growth rate is also influenced by tree size; the best 10-year diameter growth occurs on trees in the 20- to 28-inch-diameter class and the least in the 6- to 12-inch class (Putnam *et al.*, 1960). Although subject to much variation, the highest-value species (Table 5-4) are generally considered to be average or better in relative growth rates when compared to all bottomland species. Low-value and weed species generally exhibit relatively poor growth rates. There are, of course, always exceptions; for example, boxelder among the weed species is considered to be a fast grower. Under good management on good sites, mixed bottomland hardwood stands should average 4 inches of diameter growth per decade.

ROTATION AGE OR SIZE.   Mixed bottomland hardwood forests usually contain several age classes and a variety of species with different growth rates, so there is no fixed rotation age for harvesting stands or trees. Instead, the prospective growth rate, site adaptability, and potential product value of the individual trees determine their maturity. Better adaptation to the site or higher quality and vigor of the individual stem may justify leaving a less desirable species in preference to one of generally higher value. For example, a good-quality water hickory may be preferred as growing stock over a low-quality swamp chestnut oak, generally considered to be a more valuable tree, on poorly drained flats. Thus, the rotation of individual trees or stands will depend to a large extent upon the site, potential quality, and tree vigor in relation to adjacent trees.

Maturity guides have been developed for sweetgum and for Nuttall, willow, and cherrybark oaks (Guttenberg and Putnam, 1951). According to these guides, merchantable trees of low vigor are mature regardless of diameter, and large trees of high vigor need not be harvested merely because of their large diameters. The same standards also generally apply to other species of similar value and growth rates. However, the slower-growing or less valuable species are best harvested at smaller diameters.

CULTURAL PRACTICES—NATURAL STANDS.   Almost always, the first cultural practice required in a previously unmanaged or mismanaged mixed bottomland hardwood forest is a general improvement cutting. The goal of this improvement cutting should be to remove the overmature, damaged, and low-quality trees to release the more desirable growing stock. In general, the following kinds of trees should be cut:

1. All overmature trees.
2. Most fully mature trees that are not likely to continue an acceptable annual value growth until the next cutting; some mature trees which are not likely to be lost, to deteriorate, or to damage surrounding growing stock may be "stored" until the next cut.
3. Trees likely to suffer mortality, damage, decay, or degrade.

4. Trees seriously competing with better individuals.
5. Trees of inferior species if their growing space can be better utilized by more valuable species.

Proper selection of trees for removal, considering the merits of each individual tree in relation to others in the stand, will create the essential openings for reproduction and the release to stimulate growth of the growing stock ("leave") trees (Putnam *et al.*, 1960).

After an improvement cutting, cull and weed trees should be killed to further enlarge openings for reproduction or release growing stock. Thus, some of the income derived from the improvement cutting should be reinvested in cull-tree removal. Thereby much good can be accomplished at small cost. Injection of cull and weed trees with herbicides is most economical. Several herbicides, especially 2,4,5-T ester in diesel fuel or 2,4,5-T amine in water have been used successfully for deadening cull and weed trees. However, a recent EPA regulation prohibited the use of 2,4,5-T for forestry purposes. As an alternative, undiluted 2,4-D amine applied with a metering injector gives equally good results. The injector should be set to delivery from one-half to 1 milliliter of 2,4-D per injection with injections spaced about 3 inches apart (McKnight and Johnson, 1975).

Improvement cuttings will maintain or even increase the uneven-aged or many-aged nature of most mixed hardwood stands. Such a condition is not only good hardwood management, it is also good habitat management for wildlife. The diversity of species and age classes, interspersed with openings, produce a good supply of browse and other food. A managed healthy forest is also aesthetically pleasing.

Thinning of even-aged stands of bottomland hardwoods is desirable where pulpwood or other markets for smaller trees are available. Trees in the lower-crown classes—ones of low vigor—tend to develop more epicormic branches than do dominant, vigorous trees (Hedlund, 1964). Therefore, thinning should be from below. Thinnings can easily be included with the improvement cutting or a harvest cutting.

Pruning is not generally practiced in bottomland hardwoods. Most of the valuable species are rather intolerant and, if grown in closed to moderately closed stands, natural pruning produces clean-boled trees. Most of the more tolerant species which tend to be limby even when grown in dense stands are usually not valuable enough to warrant the cost of pruning.

Several methods of harvest cutting can be used for natural regeneration of mixed bottomland hardwoods. The choice of methods depends on the composition and density of the advanced regeneration, on the sprouting characteristics of the trees to be cut, and on whether the stand is even-aged or uneven-aged (Johnson, 1973).

Among the methods adapted to even-aged management, clearcutting is suitable for regeneration of most species, if (1) advanced regeneration is already present, (2) good sprouting species are to be cut, or (3) an adequate number of light-seeded intolerant species are available to seed in large areas and a good seedbed is also available. Complete removal of all undesirable components, especially the very tolerant weed species, is critical in *all* hardwood regeneration systems.

The seed-tree method is not very useful in bottomland hardwoods. Johnson and Krinard (1976) concluded that seed trees of sweetgum and red oaks did not significantly influence the establishment or development of reproduction on two sites in southeastern Arkansas. Most reproduction was of sprout origin or from seedlings present in the understory at the time of cutting.

The shelterwood method can be used quite successfully with heavy-seeded species, particularly the oaks (McKnight and Johnson, 1975). The method provides enough seed for reproduction and has some suppressing effect on unwanted understory vegetation. Seedlings of green ash, water hickory, sugarberry, and most oaks can be stored in the understory for 5 to 15 years and will grow rapidly upon release (Johnson, 1975). Establishment of reproduction before the overstory is removed will diminish the effects of vines and rank herbaceous growth which are common in openings on bottomland sites.

The group-selection method is perhaps the most suitable one for regenerating stands of mixed composition and age classes (McKnight, 1966). This method best maintains or improves the uneven-aged character of many mixed bottomland hardwood stands. Openings created by group selection should be at least one-half acre and may range up to several acres in size. Tolerance of the species being regenerated, sprouting ability of the trees to be cut, and reproduction already present for release determine the size of the group to be harvested.

In the final analysis, the type of reproduction obtained by any harvest method depends on the suitability of the seedbed in relation to the available seed source, the amount and nature of advanced reproduction on the ground, and the sprouting ability of the species removed (McKnight and Johnson, 1975). Quite often, natural regeneration of mixed bottomland hardwoods is a simple matter of complete removal of the overstory, including all weed trees, because reproduction of desirable species (such as green ash and the oaks) is already present and other reproduction will develop rapidly from sprouts (e.g., sweetgum). On the very wet sites, the existing species usually will be perpetuated regardless of the regeneration system employed because those species (e.g., water hickory and overcup oak) are virtually the only ones that can be regenerated naturally on such sites.

Without question, a good knowledge of the site and seedbed requirements of the species is required for successful silvicultural treatment of this heterogeneous type.

CULTURAL PRACTICES—ARTIFICIAL REGENERATION. Direct seeding has not proven feasible for artificial regeneration of bottomland hardwoods, but most of the important species in this type group can be planted successfully. American sycamore, yellow-poplar, sweetgum, green ash, and several of the oaks are planted on a commercial scale. Pecan, water tupelo, and baldcypress also have been planted experimentally.

The following principles are basic to the establishment of hardwood plantations (McKnight and Johnson, 1975):

1. *Plant species suited to the site.* An excellent guide is available for estimating the suitability of sites for planting cottonwood, sweetgum, sycamore, green ash, Nuttall oak, water and willow oak, and cherrybark oak (Baker and Broadfoot, 1977).
2. *Prepare the site.* Complete site preparation to eliminate all weeds, vines, and shrubs is essential.
3. *Use good stock.* Vigorous seedlings with a minimum root-collar diameter of three-eighths of an inch should be used.
4. *Plant properly.* Planting stock must be handled properly and planted at root-collar depth. Spacing should be 10 to 12 feet apart to permit cultivation.
5. *Care for the plantation.* Cultivating to control weeds is not only desirable but virtually essential, especially during the first year. The degree of cultivation depends on the site conditions and growth rate of the plantation. Plantings should also be protected from browsing by deer and cattle and from fire.

Planting of hardwoods will never be as extensive as pine plantings, but the acreage of hardwood plantations has increased rapidly in the past decade. Most hardwood plantings are established for pulpwood production, but it is quite likely that such valuable species as sweet pecan and cherrybark oak will be planted for sawtimber production.

CULTURAL PRACTICES—WILDLIFE HABITAT.   Many wildlife biologists consider the mixed bottomland hardwoods of the Coastal Plain to represent one of the most productive wildlife habitats on the North American continent. White-tailed deer, wild turkey, squirrels, rabbits, water fowl, and many nongame species of birds and mammals abound in bottomland hardwood forests. Fertile alluvial soils, abundant water, high-quality food of great variety, relative freedom from fire, usually accessible agricultural fields, and good escape cover all contribute to provide this favorable habitat (Glasgow and Noble, 1971).

It is generally recognized that group selection and clearcutting in small patches are most conducive to improvement of habitat for deer and turkey. Mature stands of mixed species, with a high proportion of oaks, are most favorable for squirrels and also turkey. Hardwood plantations offer good habitat for deer, wild turkey, rabbits, and quail for several years between the end of cultivation and complete crown closure. The ideal is diversity of tree species and age classes with no excessively large plantations of pure species.

Mixed bottomland hardwood forests can, and often do, provide an economic return from the wildlife resource (Haygood, 1970; Glasgow and Noble, 1971).

Hunting leases for $1 per acre per year are quite common, and some leases are up to $5 per acre per year. Not only can hunting leases provide an economic return from the systematic harvest of game species, they can also contribute significantly to hardwood management in the way of fire protection and upkeep of access roads.

SPECIAL PROBLEMS IN MANAGEMENT.   Two special problems must be considered in the management of mixed bottomland hardwoods: i.e. epicormic sprouting and better utilization. With the exception of green ash, all species in this type have a tendency to develop epicormic branches. The problem is most severe in young trees and in older trees of low vigor. Thus, young stands should not be thinned too heavily and only healthy, vigorous trees in the dominant and codominant crown classes should be left in exposed positions after cutting in older stands.

Proper utilization continues to be a major obstacle to intensive management of mixed bottomland hardwoods. The large number of species and the wide range in quality among and within the different species present a very real challenge to proper utilization. It is not unusual to find 10 to 15 different species within a few acres because sites are so intimately intermixed. Not only do the inherent qualities of each species differ, there is a wide variation in quality and form of logs and trees within a species. The lack of integrated markets makes it economically impossible to cut most stands properly. As a result, much low-grade material cannot be harvested, and the cost of eliminating this poor material to make way for more desirable growing stock then becomes an additional stand investment which few owners are willing to expend. The energy shortage may open new markets so that elimination of low-quality hardwoods can be done at a profit, or at least at much lower cost.

SUSCEPTIBILITY TO DAMAGE.   Wildfires are the scourge of hardwood forests. Although the bottoms are often too wet to burn, dry periods frequently occur in fall and early winter and pose a serious danger of wildfires, especially during the hunting season. Fires kill almost all seedlings and small saplings and severly damage poles and many sawtimber trees. Sprouting, however, is usually vigorous from the stumps of the small fire-killed trees, so in most cases the forest is not permanently destroyed.

The greatest losses from fire are the results of rot, stain, and insects that enter fire wounds. None of the bottomland species are resistant to fire damage and the resultant rot. About 90 percent of heartrots, the chief cause of cull in southern hardwood stands, enter the base of the trees through wounds caused by fire (Toole, 1959). Such rots are especially serious because the most valuable part of the stem, the butt log, is degraded or destroyed.

Concentrated grazing by cattle can cause severe damage to bottomland hardwoods by eliminating reproduction of many species, deforming small trees that are not killed, and reducing growth caused by soil compaction and restricted water movement. Browsing of young seedlings and saplings by deer can also be a serious problem at times.

No serious insect or disease epidemics occur in mixed bottomland hardwoods, and insects and disease seldom kill southern hardwood trees in managed stands. However, they do cause major economic losses by lowering wood quality and reducing tree growth (Abrahamson and McCracken, 1971). Decay, especially butt rot, causes more volume loss in hardwoods than all other diseases combined. Trunk borers are the most serious insect pests and cause enormous losses in value each year. Defoliating insects, such as the forest tent caterpillar, cause reduced growth in localized areas but seldom kill trees.

Periodic flooding is characteristic of much of the mixed bottomland hardwoods type. The effects of flooding may be either beneficial or detrimental, depending upon the time and duration. Flooding during the dormant season causes little harm to any of the species and may, in fact, improve subsequent growth of dominant trees. Even seedlings of most species can survive extended flooding during the dormant season, and some species even tolerate saturated soil conditions in the summer, but few can withstand complete inundation after foliation (Broadfoot and Williston, 1973). Large trees of most of the species in the mixed bottomland hardwoods type can tolerate short periods of flooding during the growth season, but few species can survive continuous flooding for the entire growing season.

BROWN LOAM BLUFFS SUBREGION

Physiography and Soils

The Brown Loam Bluffs, in sharp contrast to the flat topography of the adjacent Mississippi River Valley, are much higher in elevation and sharply dissected with numerous ravines. This zone of wind-deposited loess is from 5 to 25 miles wide and 100 to 600 feet above sea level. The loess deposit is as much as 100 feet thick along its western margin, becoming thinner eastward and northward, and the topography likewise becomes less severe.

The Brown Loam Bluffs are made up of soils which have developed from wind-deposited silts of late Pleistocene geologic age. These sediments form a mantle ranging in thickness from 2 feet to more than 100 feet over unconsolidated sands, sandy clays, and gravels of earlier Pleistocene age. The soils are well-drained and moderately permeable but highly erosive and in parts of the area occur on steeply sloping and hilly topography. The surface soils are brown silt loams with brown to yellowish-red silty clay loam subsoils, with good moisture-holding capacity. Soil reaction is medium to strongly acid, and organic matter and mineral nutrients are generally low (Lytle, 1960).

History of Forest Use

In the Brown Loam Bluffs, the ridges and bottoms were cleared for farming in pre-Civil War days. Only slopes too steep for cultivation remained in timber. But farming was largely abandoned during the Civil War and the old fields soon reverted to trees (Johnson, 1958). The deeply dissected topography with steep slopes and highly erosive soils is a fortuitous circumstance for the hardwood industry, for it virtually assures that this area, potentially one of the most productive hardwood sites in the nation, will remain in hardwood timber.

Forest Composition

Differentiation of species associations are not nearly so pronounced in these uplands as on the bottomlands. Nonetheless, variations in slope position do influence forest composition and site quality. Sites range from the somewhat drier narrow ridgetops to steep slopes with definite moisture gradients to the very moist ravine bottoms.

More than 50 tree species are found in the Bluff forests, including some loblolly and shortleaf pine in the southern portions. Outstanding specimens of cottonwood, sassafras, cherrybark oak (Fig. 5-6), basswood, black cherry, and yellow-poplar grow here, and even black walnut in the northern portion. Other common species are southern red oak, Shumard oak, white oak, swamp chestnut oak, chinkapin oak, sycamore, sweetgum, white ash, winged elm, several hickories, and American beech. Flowering dogwood is quite common in the understory as are the weed species, blue beech and ironwood (American hornbeam and eastern hophornbeam). According to Johnson (1958), hardwood timber grows at the rate of 400 to 500 board feet per acre per year, and it is generally free of insect damage.

Cultural Practices

In general quality, Bluff forests are no different than most other hardwood forests. Improvement cuttings, cull-tree removal, and group-selection harvest are essential if the Brown Loam Bluffs Subregion is to reach its potential productivity. Cherrybark oak and Shumard oak should be among the favored species on all sites. In addition, yellow-poplar, white ash, cottonwood, and black walnut do well in coves and bottoms. Ash, yellow-poplar, and sweetgum should be encouraged on lower and middle slopes, while white and southern red oaks should be managed on upper slopes. Pine excells on eroded ridge tops. Among the other species listed previously, only the hickories and beech do not warrant encouragement in management (Johnson, 1958).

A great deal of care is required in logging Bluff forests. Logging roads and skid trails must be located properly to avoid excessive erosion. Skidding from the slopes, coves, and bottoms is best done with a power winch situated along the ridges.

Natural regeneration of preferred species is generally no problem if cuttings create suitable openings and proper seedbed conditions. These openings and newly regenerated areas will also improve the habitat for deer and turkey which, along with squirrels, abound in the Bluffs.

Figure 5-6.   Cherrybark oak on colluvium at the base of the slope in the silty uplands (Brown Loam Bluffs) of Mississippi. (USDA For. Serv.)

APPALACHIAN HARDWOOD SUBREGION

It is important that a full understanding and an appreciation of the complexity and diversity of the Appalachian Hardwood Forest be achieved before attempting to discuss silvicultural alternatives. To do this, the general distribution pattern and a description of three hardwood forest classifications, based on the work of Braun (1950), are discussed before going into the silviculture of the four selected major type groups. A summary of land ownership and timber volumes of the Appalachian Hardwood Forest is presented in Table 5-5. The type groups selected for discussion are associations in this forest that develop along a moisture/productivity gradient and are found throughout the Appalachian Hardwood Subregion. These type groups, in order of increasing productivity potential, are (1) chestnut oak−scarlet oak found in the least productive sites characterized by shallow soil, steep slopes, southerly exposure, or low rainfall, (2) white oak−black oak, (3) sugar maple−red oak, and (4) yellow-poplar−mixed hardwood found on sites with deep well-drained soil, moderate slopes, northerly exposure, cove position or abundant rainfall.

Physiography

The Appalachian Hardwood Subregion, as described in this section, is located within the unglaciated part of the east-central United States. It encompasses most of four major physiographic provinces: (1) Appalachian Plateau, (2) Ridge and Valley, (3) Blue Ridge, and (4) Piedmont Plateau (Fenneman, 1938). Since the Piedmont Plateau is included in Chapter 6, it will be given minor treatment in this chapter.

The westernmost physiographic province of the Appalachian Hardwood Subregion is the Appalachian Plateau which consists of four sections: (1) the Allegheny Mountains located in north-central West Virginia and central Pennsylvania; (2) the unglaciated Allegheny Plateau which includes the remainder of West Virginia, southwestern Ohio and northeastern Kentucky; (3) the Cumberland Mountains located in the southwestern tip of Virginia, southeastern Kentucky and a small portion of northeastern Tennessee; and (4) the Cumberland Plateau located in south-central Kentucky, central Tennessee and northern Georgia. In general, the Appalachian Plateau is characterized by essentially flat-lying rock strata which gives way to irregularly shaped hills and valleys. The Allegheny Mountain section is plateau-like and separated by deeply eroded valleys and gorges. The mountains tend to be well-defined longitudinal ridges and more or less longitudinal valleys in West Virginia. Furthermore in western Maryland and south-central Pennsylvania the valleys are high, broad and plateau-like with elevation difference between ridges and valleys being less than in West Virginia. The elevations range from nearly 3,000 feet in Pennsylvania to nearly 5,000 feet in West Virginia. The adjoining unglaciated Allegheny Plateau to the west is more dissected than the Allegheny Mountains, and loses elevation as it tends toward the Ohio River. To the west of the Ohio River in Ohio and Kentucky the elevations on the western edge of the Al-

TABLE 5-5

Summary of Total Land Area, Commercial Forest Area, Ownership Patterns, and Net Growing Stock and Sawtimber Volume by Forest Regions[a] in the Appalachian Hardwood Subregion[b]

	Mixed Mesophytic Forests	Mixed Oak (Oak-Chestnut) Forests	Oak-Pine Forests	Appalachian Hardwood Forests—Total
Land Area *(millions of acres)*				
Total land area	48.9	38.4	44.4	131.7
Commercial forest land	33.0	21.0	28.5	82.5
Ownership Class *(commercial forest land)* *(millions of acres)*				
National Forest	2.1	2.8	1.4	6.3
Other public	2.2	1.8	0.7	4.7
Total public	4.3	4.6	2.1	11.0
Forest industry	2.4	0.6	3.5	6.5
Farmer owned	7.5	6.2	10.9	24.6
Miscellaneous private	18.8	9.6	12.0	40.4
Total private	28.7	16.4	26.4	71.5
Net Growing Stock *(billions of cubic feet)*				
Hard hardwoods[c]	21.8	14.8	9.8	46.4
Soft hardwoods [c]	8.0	5.0	6.4	19.4
Total	29.8	19.8	16.2	65.8
Sawtimber *(billions of board feet)*				
Hard hardwoods [c]	46.0	34.0	25.2	105.2
Soft hardwoods [c]	14.6	11.1	16.3	42.0
Total	60.6	45.1	41.5	147.2

[a] Forest regions are delineated by Braun, 1950.

[b] Estimated from most recent USDA For. Serv. state forest survey reports.

[c] See page 151 for species list of hard and soft hardwoods.

legheny Plateau are 1,200 to 1,400 feet and gradually decrease toward the Ohio River. The Cumberland Mountains are generally much lower in elevation than the Alleghenies, ranging from 2,500 to 3,000 feet in elevation. The Cumberland Plateau shares a similar position to the Cumberland Mountains as the Allegheny Plateau does to the Allegheny Mountains.

The Ridge and Valley physiographic province is a group of well-defined long narrow ridges and intervening valleys that lie between the Blue Ridge and Appalachian Plateau provinces. The ridges and valleys form a near-continuous band tending northeast to southwest from east-central, central, and south-central Pennsylvania through western Maryland, the eastern panhandle of West Virginia, western Virginia, and Tennessee, northwest Georgia through northwestern Alabama to the Gulf Coastal Plain of central Alabama. Few streams cut across the rock trends and rectilinear or trellis drainage patterns are characteristic. Rock outcrops are common with rock strata heavily folded and often ranging from strongly inclined to almost vertical. The province includes the "Great Appalachian Valley," which traverses almost the entire length of the province. The Ridge and Valley ranges from 25 to 80 miles wide with highly variable ridge elevations ranging from less than 2,000 to more than 4,500 feet. Valleys range from 1,000 to 2,000 feet lower than adjacent ridges.

Immediately to the east of the Ridge and Valley lies the Blue Ridge province. It stretches from south-central Pennsylvania through Maryland, central Virginia, western North Carolina to western South Carolina and the northeastern corner of Georgia. North of Roanoke, Virginia, it is characterized by a high, rugged and narrow mountain chain averaging about 10 miles wide. South of Roanoke the Blue Ridge widens and develops into a high upland, characteristic of a dissected mature erosion surface. It broadens to about 70 miles wide in North Carolina. The elevations vary from only 1,200 feet near Washington, D.C., to peaks over 6,000 feet in North Carolina and averages from 3,000 to 4,000 feet.

The Appalachians are drained by a network of river systems flowing into either the Atlantic Ocean or the Gulf of Mexico. Major rivers include the Ohio, Susquehanna, Potomac, James, Roanoke, Broad, Yarkin, Clinch, New, and Tennessee. Natural lakes are virtually absent; however, water storage reservoirs are common, some very large such as Norris Lake in eastern Tennessee which covers about 34,000 acres.

Geology and Soils

Geologically the Appalachian Hardwood Subregion can be separated into two major areas of differing rock formations (Bowman, 1914). The southeastern or crystalline area is often referred to as the Older Appalachians and includes the present day Piedmont and Blue Ridge physiographic provinces. The northwestern area consists primarily of sedimentary material and includes the Ridge and Valley, and the Appalachian Plateau provinces.

In the mid-Paleozic geologic era the Older Appalachians were a land mass at the eastern edge of a great inland sea that stretched across the central Midwest. The deepest part of this sea was near the eastern edge where the Appalachian Mountains are today. During the Paleozoic Era this part of the sea collected thousands of feet of sediment from the adjacent land masses. Near the end of the Paleozoic Era during the Permian Period (which began about 275 million years ago) tremendous earth pressures from beneath caused a buckling and uplifting which formed the Appalachian Mountains from the bottom of the inland sea. Erosional forces for the next 85 million years, during the Mesozoic Era, reduced the mountains to a near level peneplain. At the end of the Mesozoic Era, during the Cretaceous Period (which began about 135 million years ago), the Appalachians were uplifted and reelevated with the eastern part being raised the highest. The eastern end of this slanting plateau is the present day Blue Ridge and Smoky Mountains (Janssen, 1973).

The southeastern area consists of very old, much deformed and resistant igneous and metamorphic rocks. In the northwestern area soils are derived largely from sandstone, shale, limestone, and dolomite parent materials.

The wide variation in the physiography, parent material, vegetation, and climate under which soils have developed has resulted in extreme variability within a small area. When texture of the subsoil, depth of the subsoil and other physical changes resulting from previous management activities are taken into account, the number of soil types and soil series is often increased several times.

The texture of the soil ranges from coarse sand, through friable sandy, silt and clay loams to plastic clay, depending on the nature of the parent material and the influence of other soil-forming factors. Forested areas that have not been seriously eroded usually have coarse-textured surface soils varying from sandy loams to sandy clay loams, although silt loams and clay loams are commonly associated with fine-textured parent materials that are low in quartz.

Appalachian Plateau.   The rocks of the Cumberland Mountains are mainly massive and resistant sandstone and conglomerate. While the Allegheny Mountains have a great deal of sandstone material, shale also is important and influences soil development (Fenneman, 1938). The soils are generally very strongly acid (pH 4.5 to 5.0) and extremely acid (pH below 4.5) where derived from sandstone and shale, and strongly acid (pH 5.1 to 5.5) where there is a limestone influence. They are usually well-drained to moderately well-drained and the soil solum ranges from 24 to 36 inches on upland, gently sloping sites. Sandstone and shale parent materials are the most common; however, there are some forest soils developed from limestone. These more fertile limestone soils are found mostly in valleys and on gentle slopes; however, they are usually in pasture or used for cultivated crops. If slopes are excessive or rock outcrops prevalent, precluding agriculture, limestone derived soils usually support highly productive stands of the more site demanding tree species.

The geologic material of the Cumberland Plateau is characterized as being interbedded sandstone and shale with the sandstone being the dominant rock type. They are considered to be stronger and more resistant than most rocks of the Allegheny Plateau (Fenneman, 1938). The broad uplands are composed of a relatively flat sandstone cap that has not been as severely dissected as the Allegheny Plateau.

The Allegheny Plateau is a mature, severely dissected surface characterized by steep slopes and narrow valleys. The slopes are often broken by several benches formed from interbedded sandstone and shale material that exhibits vastly different weathering rates. The relief of the Allegheny Plateau is much less than in the adjacent mountains and normally ranges from 400 to 700 feet. Near the Ohio river the range in relief decreases to only 200 to 300 feet, hills are rounded and the slopes are more gentle.

The soils of the plateaus tend to be deeper, less acid (pH 5.1 to 5.5), usually more developed and moderately drained. Soils developed from shale or having a strong shale influence tend to have restricted internal drainage and on flatter areas are considered poorly drained.

In the steeper areas of West Virginia and Kentucky localized landslides and soil slumps are common in clay soils derived from shale. These slides generally are less than an acre in size and occur in the lower slope positions. Identifying these soil conditions is critical when planning and constructing access and haul roads for forest management operations.

The soil orders (Soil Survey Staff, 1975) represented in the Appalachian Plateau are primarily Ultisols, and Inceptisols, with Alfisols and Spodosols being found to a very limited extent.

Ridge and Valley. The dominant forest soils of the steep slopes and ridges of the Ridge and Valley are derived from sandstone and shale while soils in the lower slope position and valleys are often derived from limestone or have a limestone influence. Most of the sandstone- and shale- derived soils are considered somewhat excessively or excessively drained, low in natural fertility, and very strongly acid (pH 4.5 to 5.0) to strongly acid (pH 5.1 to 5.5). The soils with limestone influence (most of which are in agricultural uses) are well drained to moderately well drained, of medium fertility, and medium to strongly acid (pH 5.1 to 6.0).

The Ultisols and Inceptisols are the most prevalent soil Orders (Soil Survey Staff, 1975) with Alfisols being present to a very limited extent. When compared to the other physiographic provinces the soils in the Ridge and Valley are probably the least developed and show less variability than any others in the Appalachian Hardwood Forest.

Blue Ridge. The soil parent material on the northwestern, mid to lower slopes of the Blue Ridge physiographic province are composed of highly metamorphosed sedimentary rocks (Robinson et al., 1961) which, when weathered, form soils with characteristics similar to those of the adjacent Ridge and Valley. However, the greater part of the Blue Ridge is underlain by crystalline rocks with includes granite, geneiss, schist, mica schist and greenstone of Precambrian materials (Robinson et al., 1961).

As in the Ridge and Valley, forested soils of the Blue Ridge are prevalent on the steep slopes and ridges. In the northern part of the Blue Ridge soils are similar to those of the Ridge and Valley while in the southern portion, including the Great Smoky Mountains, the soils are often similar to those found in the higher elevations of the Appalachian Plateau. Drainage, soil reaction, and fertility are similar to that found in soils of the Ridge and Valley.

Climate and Weather[5]

Appalachian Plateau. The climatic and weather conditions in the Cumberland Mountains are nearly excellent for tree growth. The frost-free period is about 160 days per year with a mean annual precipitation of 48 to 52 inches with the higher elevations receiving somewhat more. Rainfall is well distributed throughout the growing season with droughty conditions seldom occurring. The normal daily average temperature in January is about 36 °F, and in July 71 °F. The growth potential of the Allegheny Mountains is somewhat less than in the Cumberlands primarily because of the shorter growing season and cooler temperatures of the more northern latitude and higher elevations. The frost-free period averages 150 days per year with some areas at higher elevations being as low as 120 days. The annual precipitation is about the same, however, annual snowfall ranges from 48 to 64 inches with snow cover occurring for about 80 days per year. The temperatures are cooler with the normal daily value in January about 30 °F and in July is 65 °F.

Throughout the Cumberland and Allegheny plateaus the climatic and weather conditions are good to excellent for tree growth. In the Cumberland Plateau the average annual frost-free period is 180 days while in the Allegheny it is only 150 days. The precipitation is well distributed over the year with a mean annual of 44 to 48 inches. Snowfall in the Cumberland Plateau is low and usually only remains for a few days; however, in the Allegheny Plateau there is about 35 inches of snowfall and snow cover averages 60 days per year. In the Cumberland the normal daily January temperature is about 37 °F and in the Alleghenys about 33 °F while the July temperature is about 75 °F in both plateaus.

At the higher elevations strong winds during the winter and spring months causes damage to forest vegetation especially on exposed upper slope positions and ridge lines.

Ridge and Valley. The general conditions for tree growth are not as good in the Ridge and Valley because of the somewhat lower rainfall and aspect effect of the northeast to southwest tending ridges. In the northern part of the Ridge and Valley the frost-free period is 150 days, annual precipitation is 38 to 42 inches, of which there is 24 to 32 inches of snow. Snow cover usually occurs for 40 to 60 days per year. Low rainfall during the later summer months causing localized drought conditions is common in the northern part of the province, especially on the south and southwest aspects. In the southern part of the province the frost-free period increases slightly to 160 days, the annual precipitation increases substantially to 48 to 52 inches and snowfall is usually less than

[5]Climatic information from U.S. Dept. of Commerce, 1968; Lull, 1968; USDA For. Serv., 1969.

24 inches while snow cover is from 20 to 40 days per year. In the north, mean daily January temperature is about 33 °F and 36 °F in the south. In July the mean daily average temperature is about 71 °F in the north, with the southern region being about two degrees warmer.

Ice storms with accompanying high wind can cause severe damage to forest cover in Ridge and Valley and Blue Ridge physiographic provinces. These storms are most likely to occur during the months of January through March. Such a storm in Virginia occurred in the late winter of 1979. Damage included broken tops and limbs in virtually all trees over large acreages, as well as complete up-rooting of trees, especially pine, on the steeper slopes.

Blue Ridge. The climatic conditions of the Blue Ridge do not differ significantly from those in the adjacent Ridge and Valley except for slightly greater precipitation at the higher elevations of some areas. Lower snowfall and fewer days with snow cover are due to the effects of southeasterly winds from the Atlantic Coast area.

History of Forest Use

Prior to the landing of the early settlers in what is now the eastern United States, the Indians often maintained open forests, especially in the plateau country and near the streams, by partial clearing and annual burning of the grass (Marsh, 1882). When this part of the country was settled, the pioneers not only drew upon the forests for food for themselves and their livestock but they also used the wood for fuel, shelter, and many other purposes. Forests had to be cleared away before habitations could be built and fields planted.

In the Cumberland and Allegheny plateaus of West Virginia, Kentucky and Tennessee, land clearing followed by abandonment often occurred. In many of these areas the relatively steep slopes were cleared for pasture and submarginal agriculture. The advent of tractors and other mechanized farm equipment precluded farming on many of the steeper slopes. In addition, the industrialization of the Ohio, Kanawha, and similar river valleys provided high-paying work for many people who previously had been conducting marginal farming operations. These two events have resulted in the conversion of a great deal of once pastured and farmed land back to forest cover. Much of this land is now in low-quality mixed hardwood-pine stands of small-sawtimber size. Often pure stands of pines resulted after abandonment. After the pines were harvested, on all but the poorer sites, hardwoods usually seeded in under the pines and again became dominant in the succeeding stand.

The forests of the northern part of the subregion have been subjected to almost continuous cutting since the first sawmills were erected near the middle of the 17th century (Dana, 1930). Extensive logging began in the southern Appalachian Mountains later than in other eastern regions. It developed in response to the increasing demand for the great variety and high quality of hardwood products that could be obtained from the virgin forests. As an example, the logging of virgin hardwoods in the West Virginia highlands occurred between 1870 and 1920. This era was marked by boom towns which sprang up around lumber mills and the building of logging railroads that used the famous Shay gear-driven locomotives which could negotiate grades of ten percent or more. It is estimated that band sawmills operated at 200 locations in West Virginia during the lumber boom. As many as 25 mills, in as many boom towns, were operating between 1900 and 1920, in Pocahontas County, West Virginia (Clarkson, 1964). Today only 10 of these towns are still on the map. Those that are left have only a small fraction of the population that they had during the lumber hayday.

The kind and quality of products have undergone a great change since mountain lumbering began. Seventy-five years ago only black walnut, black cherry, and the largest and choicest yellow-poplar, white pine, basswood, cucumber-tree, and white oak were worth taking from the woods (Frothingham, 1931). By 1930 black, scarlet, and chestnut oaks, and chestnut, which earlier had been passed by, were being logged extensively. In addition, sugar maple, birch, beech, spruce, hemlock, silverbell, blackgum, red maple, and many other species also had sufficient value to warrant cutting for one or more uses. With the increased use of hardwoods for pulp and other forms of modified wood nearly all species occurring in the area can now be utilized.

Historically wildfire has been one of the most destructive agents in Appalachian hardwood forests. Fires have not only killed young stands but successive burns have so damaged the trunks of larger hardwoods that decay has greatly reduced wood quality and caused early decline of many stands. Surface fires in hardwood stands cause a heavy loss in soil fertility by destroying the leaf litter—the main source of organic matter and protective cover from erosion. Severe burns in the plateau hardwood stands has often caused a retrogression to a pine subclimax. Today as a result of a major effort in fire prevention and fire suppression, the loss of forest resources from wildfire are at a minimum.

Hardwood Forests[6]

The three hardwood forest systems that comprise the Appalachian Hardwood Subregion are (1) mixed mesophytic forests, (2) mixed oak (oak-chestnut) forests, and (3) oak-pine forests (Fig. 5-1, Table 5-5).

Mixed Mesophytic Forests.   Mixed mesophytic forests are located primarily in the Appalachian Plateau Province and the three components of these forests correspond in name and occurrence to the Cumberland Mountains, the Allegheny Mountains, and the Cumberland and Allegheny Plateau physiographic sections. From an ecological standpoint, these forests are probably more complex and diverse than any other in the Eastern Deciduous Forest of North America.

Mixed mesophytic forests are located near the center of the eastern

[6]The summary descriptions of the three forests as discussed in this section are based on Braun's (1950) work and field observations of the author.

hardwood forests and develop best on moist, well-drained upland sites. They probably reach their best development in the Cumberland Mountains and grade toward oak-hickory forests to the west, hemlock-white pine-northern hardwood to the north, mixed oak (oak-chestnut) to the east, and oak-pine to the south. The mixed mesophytic forests extend into Ohio; but that portion is included in the Central Hardwood Region (Chapter 4).

Dominant tree species include sugar maple, American beech, yellow-poplar, white basswood, yellow buckeye, northern red oak, white oak, eastern hemlock, and to a lesser extent, yellow birch, sweet birch, black cherry, white ash, red maple, blackgum, black walnut, cucumbertree, bitternut hickory, and shagbark hickory. White basswood and yellow buckeye are probably the most characteristic overstory species in the region; however, they are of minor importance in terms of stand density and volume. Common understory woody species include flowering dogwood, serviceberry, striped maple, redbud, sourwood, blue beech, hophornbeam, and great rhododendron. A number of species are found in the climax forest.

The Mixed Mesophytic Forest contains 37 percent of the total land area of the Appalachian Hardwood Subregion and 40 percent of the commercial forest land. Public forest land makes up 13 percent of the commercial forest land within the region. Forest industry owns 7 percent, 23 percent is in farm ownership, and 57 percent is in miscellaneous private ownership. The growing stock accounts for 45 percent and the sawtimber 41 percent of the total hardwood volume within the Appalachian Hardwood Subregion (Table 5-5).

The forests of the Allegheny Mountains are a transition zone between Mixed Mesophytic Forest and the Northern Hardwood Forest. The growth potential of the Allegheny Mountains is somewhat less than in the Cumberland Mountains primarily because of the more severe climatic conditions associated with more northern latitudes and generally higher elevations. Above elevations of about 4,000 feet stands with varying amounts of sugar maple, red maple, cucumbertree, beech, and yellow birch give way to pure stands of red spruce.

The Cumberland and Allegheny Plateau area in the highlands between the Cumberland and Allegheny Mountains is very rugged and the species composition does not vary significantly from that found in the mountains. As the plateaus tend toward the Ohio River they lose elevation, relief lessens, and the slopes become more gentle. This terrain is typical of southwestern Pennsylvania, western and southern West Virginia, and eastern Kentucky. Forests of this area have an increased component of oak and hickory species. On the more adverse and exposed sites chestnut, scarlet, and black oaks and the hickories are the major species present. Depending on the stage of succession, pitch, Virginia, and shortleaf pines may be present in varying amounts. In addition to seedlings of overstory species the understory also includes blueberry, huckleberry, Viburnums, mountain laurel, and great rhododendron. In poorly-drained lower-slope and flat positions, beech, red maple, pin oak, and sweetgum (except in the very northern section) are major species. In southern Kentucky, Tennessee, and northern Alabama the topography is less dissected and is more of a rolling upland plateau that reflects the sandstone geologic material that predominates. The species are similar to those described above with the addition of southern red oak and post oak.

Mixed Oak (Oak-Chestnut) Forests. Within the Appalachian Hardwood Subregion mixed oak forests occupy all of the Blue Ridge and the Ridge and Valley provinces as well as a portion of the Piedmont Plateau in northern Virginia and southeastern Pennsylvania. For the most part, the entire area is mountainous and is noted for extremes in slope, aspect, elevation, and climate, resulting in a wide range of forest cover types and species mixtures. It is also the area where majestic stands of American chestnut and oak once were a major part of the landscape. Today the American chestnut is no longer a part of the forest canopy; however, the total impact of the rapid loss of this species is still not fully known. The stands are still in a transition state with a species composition that approaches a climax stage of succession being several generations in the future. Probably one of the most characteristic features of the mixed oak forests is the almost ubiquitous presence of ericaceous species in the understory. This heath layer includes azalea, blueberry, huckleberry, and laurel. The geographic sections described below include the (1) Southern Appalachians, (2) Northern Blue Ridge, (3) Ridge and Valley, and (4) part of the Piedmont.

The climax forest varies considerably because of the extreme variability in site conditions. The most common climax species include white, northern red, and chestnut oaks, shagbark hickory and American beech. On the more fertile sites (coves, eastern aspects and areas of higher rainfall) the climax species are those expected in mixed mesophytic forests and include sugar maple, white basswood, yellow-poplar, white ash, and eastern hemlock.

The mixed oak forest comprises 29 percent of the total land area of the Appalachian Hardwood Subregion and 26 percent of the commercial forest land. Public land accounts for 21 percent of the commercial forest land within the region. Forest industry owns 3 percent, farms occupy 30 percent, and 46 percent is in miscellaneous private ownership. The growing stock accounts for 30 percent and the sawtimber 31 percent of the total hardwood volume within the Appalachian Hardwood Subregion (Table 5-5).

The Blue Ridge physiographic province from Roanoke, Virginia southwest to and including the Great Smoky Mountains is extremely variable with elevations ranging from about 1,300 feet to over 6,000 feet. Three principal forest groups provide the best description of the range of species found within the section (Soc. Am. For., 1926). The first is the northern forest, which is found at the higher elevations and includes red spruce, Fraser fir, yellow birch, and red maple with fir and spruce often occurring in pure stands at the highest elevations. The second group is the moist slope and cove forests which include sugar maple, beech, sweet birch, white ash, northern red oak, yellow-poplar, white oak, shagbark hickory, and white pine. In general, the species composition resembles that found in the Mixed Mesophytic Forest. The third and largest group is the dry slope and ridge forest which includes chestnut, scarlet, black, and white oaks, pignut hickory, and shortleaf, pitch, Table-mountain, and Virginia pines. Valleys and coves in the higher rainfall areas in the southern part of this section contain highly productive stands of yellow-poplar, beech, yellow buckeye, sweetgum, Fraser magnolia, sugar maple, and eastern hemlock.

The northern portion of the Blue Ridge Province extends from Roanoke northeast through Maryland and terminates in southeastern Pennsylvania. In general, the species composition of this section is much more consistent and more typical of the mixed oak region. The most common species include northern red, white, and chestnut oaks, sugar maple, and eastern hemlock. On the better sites sugar maple, white basswood, northern red oak, and yellow-poplar become dominant, while on the poorer, more exposed sites chestnut, scarlet, and white oaks are most abundant.

The most typical mixed oak forests are found in the Ridge and Valley Province. On most medium slopes white oak is the most common species. Associated species are similar to those in the northern Blue Ridge.

Oak-Pine Forests.   The oak-pine forests are located primarily in the Piedmont Plateau Province as far west as central Alabama and thus do not include western Alabama, Mississippi, and any area west of the Mississippi River. Since primary coverage of the Piedmont is in Chapter 6, this discussion is centered on the hardwoods.

The oak-pine forests include 34 percent of the total land area of the Appalachian Hardwood Subregion and 35 percent of the commercial forest land. Only 7 percent of the commercial forest land within the region is in public ownership. Forest industry owns 12 percent, farmer-owned land is 38 percent, and 43 percent is in miscellaneous private ownership. The growing stock includes 25 percent and the sawtimber 28 percent of the total hardwood volume within the Appalachian hardwood forest (Table 5-5).

White oak is probably the most common overstory species. Other major component species include red maple, and black, scarlet, southern red, post, and blackjack oaks, and pignut and mockernut hickories. Intermixed with these hardwood species are varying amounts of loblolly, shortleaf, Virginia, and longleaf (southern portion only) pines depending on the past land-use patterns. Post oak, blackjack oak, and Virginia pine are more prevalent on the drier aspects and sites containing eroded and/or heavy clay soils. Other species include sourwood, flowering dogwood, blackgum, winged elm, and chestnut oak. Sassafras is a common early successional species. The understory usually contains abundant ericaceous species. In the lower lying areas above streams and rivers beech, willow oak, sweetgum, red maple, water oak, American holly, sweet bay, flowering dogwood, and loblolly pine are common associates.

Silviculture of the Major Type Groups

Available moisture for plant growth is probably the most important single factor that directly and indirectly influences site productivity within the subregion. The major type groups discussed in this section span this moisture gradient.

It is the exception rather than the rule to find pure stands in Appalachian hardwood forests. There are more than 30 major hardwood species that comprise the majority of stands. Each of these species has a range of environmental conditions under which it is capable of competing. In any one stand it is common to have 10 to 15 overstory species, as well as numerous understory species, present within a few acres.

The primary objective of any silvicultural system is to insure the regeneration of a stand following harvest. Barring severe site disturbance, which could be caused by a natural disaster or by man during or after the harvest, natural regeneration virtually always occurs in Appalachian hardwood forests. Whether the natural regeneration that occurs will meet the product objectives established by the forest manager is a separate question. The silvicultural systems discussed in the following sections will assume that natural regeneration occurs, knowing that if it fails an appropriate artificial regeneration plan will be implemented.

A summary of some important silvical and management information for major tree species of the Appalachian Hardwood Subregion is contained in Table 5-6.

Chestnut Oak-Scarlet Oak Type Group. This type group represents species found on the poorest sites in the Appalachian Hardwood Subregion and includes oak site indices of 50 (base age 50) and less. The most common sites inhabited by this group are those with shallow, sandy or gravelly, dry soils that are usually associated with steep slopes, ridge tops, and south or southwest aspects. In general, these low-quality sites are not as common in the Piedmont Plateau and when they do occur, they are often associated with severely eroded and abandoned forest land. Species commonly associated with the chestnut oak-scarlet oak type group are sassafras, bear oak, blackgum, pitch pine, Table-mountain pine, and Virginia pine (Fig 5-7). In the Piedmont Plateau post oak and blackjack oak are also major constituents of the poor sites. The understory of these stands usually have an abundance of eracaceous species.

PLACE IN ECOLOGICAL SUCCESSION.   In general, the presence of pine is temporary and suggests that wildfire or other major disturbance has occurred in the past. If left undisturbed, the relatively short-lived pine species will be over-topped and succeeded by the much longer-lived and more shade-tolerant oaks. On sites that have been subjected to repeated fire the species composition may be almost pure pine. Pitch, Table-mountain, and Virginia pines are all very shade intolerant pioneer species with Table-mountain pine being the most intolerant. Chestnut oak on the other hand is intermediate in tolerance being more tolerant than any of the associated species except perhaps blackgum which is also intermediate. Blackgum is susceptible to fire damage and only rarely will it be dominant within its age group (USDA For. Serv., 1965). Scarlet oak is one of the least tolerant of the oaks; however, it is more tolerant than the associated pines.

Stands composed of pine and hardwood in the main canopy are subclimax. In the absence of disturbance the pines will give way to hardwoods, until an oak

TABLE 5-6

Relative Value, Growth Rate, Tolerance to Competition, Longevity, Importance for Wildlife, and Management Possibilities of Common Appalachian Hardwoods

Relative Value of Species	Growth Rate	Tolerance to Competition	Longevity	Importance for wildlife	Management Possibilities
Highest Value Sugar maple	Medium	Very tolerant	Long	Low-Moderate	Favor on better sites; develops well in understory; most desirable of very tolerant species
Black cherry	Medium-fast	Intolerant	Medium	High	Favor on good and excellent sites; vigorous seedlings, and prolific sprouter
Yellow-poplar	Fast	Intolerant	Medium	Moderate-low	Favor on good and excellent sites; excellent form; best under even-aged management
Cucumbertree	Medium-fast	Intermediate-intolerant	Medium	Low	Favor on good sites; usually not abundant
Basswood	Medium-fast	Intermediate	Medium	Low	Favor on good and excellent sites; high quality clumps of sprout origin are characteristic
Black walnut	Medium-fast	Intolerant	Medium	High	Favor on moist, well drained, fertile sites; does best on soils with limestone influence; very valuable
White oak	Medium-slow	Intermediate	Very long	High	Favor on all sites; good quality even on poor sites; susceptible to epicormic branching

Species					Remarks
Northern red oak	Fast	Intermediate	Medium-long	High	Favor on fair sites and better; noted for clear bole and good quality; susceptible to epicormic branching
Sweetgum (Table 5-4)					
Yellow birch	Medium	Intermediate	Medium	Moderate	Favor at higher elevations on moist sites; limited in extent; easily damaged by fire
White ash	Medium-fast	Intermediate	Medium-long	Low	Favor on good sites; seedlings are shade tolerant; responds well when released
Intermediate Value Red maple	Medium-fast	Tolerant-intermediate	Medium	Moderate	Favor on poor sites for pulpwood; found on wide range of sites; prolific sprouter; sawtimber products valuable if quality is good
American beech	Slow	Very tolerant	Long	High	Generally not favored; found on wide range of sites; acceptable for pulpwood; often low quality; susceptible to fire damage
Pignut hickory	Slow-medium	Intermediate	Medium-long	High	Favor on better sites; usually not abundant; prolific sprouter; susceptible to fire damage
Shagbark hickory	Slow	Intermediate	Medium-long	High	Favor on better sites; prolific sprouter; susceptible to fire damage
Mockernut hickory	Slow	Intolerant-intermediate	Long	High	Favor on fair to good sites; good sprouter; susceptible to fire damage

TABLE 5-6, continued

Relative Value of Species	Growth Rate	Tolerance to Competition	Longevity	Importance for wildlife	Management Possibilities
Bitternut hickory	Slow	Intolerant	Long	High	Favor on fair to good sites; prolific sprouter; susceptible to fire damage; not as abundant as other hickories
Chestnut oak	Slow-medium	Intermediate	Long	High	The most desirable species on very low site indices; prolific sprouter; occurs on wide range of sites
Sweet birch	Medium	Intermediate-intolerant	Medium	Moderate	Usually an abundant reproducer on clearcuts of fair to good sites; susceptible to fire damage
Southern red oak	Medium	Intolerant-intermediate	Medium	High	A component in the southern part of the region; good quality in well stocked stands; favor in management
Black oak	Medium-fast	Intermediate	Medium	High	Favor on fair and poor sites; produces seed early in life; well adapted to drought conditions
Black locust	Fast	Very intolerant	Short-medium	Low-moderate	Favor on disturbed areas; seeds remain viable for many years; good for specialty products
Low Value Blackgum	Medium	Intermediate	Medium-long	Moderate	Usually not abundant; prolific sprouter; quality low; susceptible to fire damage
Yellow buckeye	Medium-fast	Tolerant	Medium	Low	Usually not abundant; found on moist fertile sites

Species					
Fraser magnolia	Medium	Intermediate	Medium	Low	Not a species to be favored; not abundant; restricted to higher elevations on cool moist sites
Scarlet oak	Medium-fast	Intolerant	Medium-short	High	Not usualy favored for management due to generally poor quality; good pulpwood species on fair to poor sites; prolific sprouter
Sassafras	Medium	Very intolerant	Short	Moderate	Pioneer species that is usually not of commercial size
Post oak	Slow	Intolerant	Short-medium	Moderate-high	Managed as a primary species on very poor sites; sprouts prolifically after fire; very drought resistant
Sourwood	Medium	Intermediate	Short	Low	Abundant in clearcut areas; prolific sprouter; commonly found with upland oaks; commercially not important
American holly	Very slow	Tolerant	Short-medium	Low	Common to the Piedmont in the understory of hardwood stands; wood used for novelty items; aesthetically important
Flowering dogwood	Very slow	Very tolerant	Short-medium	Moderate-high	A common understory species across a wide range of hardwood sites aesthetically important

Source: USDA For. Serv., 1965; Halls, 1977; Harlow et al., 1979; Trimble et al., 1974; Trimble, 1975.

Figure 5-7.   Low-quality chestnut oak on a steep marginal site in the Ridge and Valley Physiographic Province of Virginia. Pitch pine can be seen in the background.

climax is attained. Chestnut oak with a small component of scarlet oak and blackgum will probably be the primary climax species except in the Piedmont Plateau where post oak and blackjack oak are also climax species. Since pitch pine occurs only in the extreme western part of the Piedmont and Table-mountain pine is absent, Virginia pine is the subclimax pine found on marginal sites in the Piedmont Plateau. This discussion of forest ecology, as it relates to the Piedmont Plateau, supplements the information provided in Chapter 6.

GROWTH RATES.   Growth rates under the harsh conditions described are extremely slow and rotation ages very long. Based on an average growth rate of 25 rings per inch of radial growth, chestnut oak requires 100 years to reach a mean d.b.h. of 11 inches for small sawtimber. The expected volume growth is less than one-third of a cord per acre per year and about 82 board feet.

ROTATION AGE OR SIZE.   Using the site-index-40 curve for chestnut oak (Carmean, 1971) the height at a rotation age of 100 years would be 60 feet and at 135 years is estimated to be 70 feet. Using Schnur's (1937) yield table for fully stocked, even-aged stands, the 100-year-old stand would produce 2,590 cubic feet and the 135-year-old stand would produce an estimated 11,000 board feet (Int. one-quarter rule) per acre. Based on Carmean's (1971) site-index curves, the expected yield for scarlet oak would be slightly less.

The 135-year rotation age for chestnut oak is possible; however, the longevity of scarlet oak is much less and it is very doubtful whether it will attain this age without a substantial decline in vigor or even death (Core, 1971).

CULTURAL PRACTICES.   The product alternatives for these marginal sites are restricted by the physical conditions of the steep mountains that dominated the type group. Slightly more flexibility is possible on Piedmont Plateau sites where slopes are not as steep, nor as extensive, therefore making access easier. Probably the most important use of the type group is nonconsumptive in that it provides vegetative cover for watershed protection. Any silvicultural manipulations will have an *a priori* objective of maintaining watershed integrity, therefore, site condition may preclude the harvesting of any wood products. Where harvesting is acceptable, pulpwood and sawtimber production are viable product alternatives, and both are compatible with wildlife habitat and cover requirements.

Stands of the chestnut oak-scarlet oak type group have been subjected to severe high-grading, wildfire, and the loss of American chestnut from the main canopy. Because the original quality was low, there was a substantial portion of the stand left in the form of undesirable species and poor-quality trees after the initial harvest. This along with the loss of the chestnut, usually resulted in two-storied stands composed of culls in the dominant and codominant crown classes, and poor-quality intolerant and intermediate species in the intermediate and suppressed classes. In addition, wildfire has been prevalent and has further reduced stand quality resulting from butt rot, especially in scarlet oak and blackgum (Korstian, 1927).

In hardwood stands the preferred species are chestnut oak followed by scarlet oak, and in mixed hardwood-pine or pure pine stands, pitch pine is the preferred pine species followed by Virginia pine. The primary product is pulpwood when one considers the probable low quality of sawtimber that could be obtained in a 135-year rotation, even under the best management conditions. However, the availability of suitable markets must be considered. The eventual market for firewood products is not known; however, it is a viable alternative. Should the firewood market develop it would provide an outlet for the products of intermediate cuts which would enhance the sawtimber alternative.

The combination of access, high logging costs, the intermediate shade tolerance of the primary species, and low volume production greatly restricts the development or perpetuation of uneven-aged stands and therefore the use of the selection method of regeneration. Under certain circumstances the group-selection method may be an alternative; however, it would probably be more realistic to use 1- to 5-acre cuts and refer to it as an even-aged forest using the patch clearcutting method.

The heavy-seeded nature of the primary species, the generally shallow soil, and exposed nature of the stands preclude the seed-tree method. A two-cut shelterwood method may be an alternative; however, there is virtually no scientific base for its application. The primary disadvantage is that it requires access into the area at least twice for harvesting a relatively low volume. If the method is used, probably at least 20 years between the seed cutting and the final harvest is required in order to ensure that the advance regeneration is well established and will be competitive with the stump sprouts of final-harvest trees. Depending on site conditions, up to 60 percent of crown canopy could be removed in the seed cuttings. The advantage of the shelterwood system is that it would tend to select against regeneration of the more intolerant pines. Also it should increase the percentage of seedling origin regeneration in that the sprouting ability of cut stumps is substantially reduced in partial light. The only source of sprouting would be from the stumps of the final harvest trees.

The clearcutting method is probably the most reliable alternative; however, it has certain constraints. The clearcuts should normally be small and not exceed 25 to 30 acres. The cutting units should be carefully laid out to protect drainage ways and facilitate the harvesting system. As a result of the steep slopes, and generally rocky terrain the use of wheeled skidders is restricted. In order to reduce the high cost of road construction, and erosion problems resulting from road construction and the use of wheeled skidders, the use of a skyline harvesting system should be considered (Kochenderfer and Wendel, 1978). It reduces road requirements and is environmentally far superior because there is virtually no site disturbance. Such systems are presently being used by industry on steep Appalachian slopes.

The harvesting objective is to remove all stems down to 1 inch d.b.h. and rely on natural regeneration. The natural regeneration would be a combination of seedling sprouts and stump sprouts. With stump sprouts being a primary source of regeneration, it is imperative that the stump height be as low as possible (4 inches or less) so that the probability of subsequent butt rot is minimized (Roth and Sleeth, 1939). Assuming the exclusion of fire, under the clearcutting method the probability of significant pine regeneration is low even if some pine was present in the stand prior to harvest.

When considering the good natural hardwood regeneration that occurs following clearcutting, the adverse site conditions, and increased cost, the conversion of this type group to artificially regenerated pine stands is not recommended.

The use of intermediate cutting practices is usually not required with a pulpwood product objective and cannot be justified for a sawtimber objective unless there is a market, such as firewood, for harvested material.

White Oak–Black Oak Type Group. The white oak–black oak type group is the most widespread group in the Appalachian Hardwood Subregion. It represents those stands that are on fair sites having oak site indices of 51 to 65 (base age 50). In the mountains, components of this group are most often found on the mid and lower slopes of southern and western aspects, and upper slopes and ridge tops on northern and eastern aspects. They are also found on the broad valleys in the Ridge and Valley, and Blue Ridge provinces, and on many of the gently sloping uplands of the Piedmont Plateau. Generally, these mixed oak stands occur at elevations below 3,000 feet (Core, 1966).

PLACE IN ECOLOGICAL SUCCESSION. In the mountainous regions the species composition is dominated by combinations of white, black, scarlet and chestnut oaks, pignut hickory, shagbark hickory, red maple, and to a lesser extent by mockernut hickory, blackgum, American beech, sweet birch and black locust (Fig. 5-8). In the Piedmont Plateau and the southern extremities of the mountainous provinces, sweet birch is absent, shagbark hickory and northern red oak occurrence is greatly reduced, while southern red oak and post oak become common associates. In mixed stands eastern white pine is an important species in the mountainous regions, while Virginia pine is found on most sites. Shortleaf pine is found in all areas except the very northern part of West Virginia and most of Pennsylvania. Within its range, loblolly pine is found scattered throughout the mixed stands. Numerous eracaceous species, sourwood, blackgum, serviceberry, and flowering dogwood are commonly found in the understory.

On the sites described above white oak will become dominant in the stand. It is the most shade tolerant of the oaks and equal or only slightly less tolerant than the associated hickories. It has the ability to live vigorously for long periods as an overtopped tree, it responds quickly to release, has a moderately fast growth rate in full sunlight, and has great longevity (USDA For. Serv., 1965). Black oak exhibits similar characteristics; however, it grows slightly faster but does not demonstrate the longevity of white oak. Both pignut hickory and shagbark hickory are intermediate in shade tolerance, probably being slightly more tolerant than the oaks; however, they have a slower growth rate. All of the above species are climax species and would be common associates in climax stands. In addition, most of the other upland oaks, blackgum, red maple, and American beech, depending on location and conditions, may be part of the climax stand. Blacks locust is a common secondary succession pioneer species that is usually associated with abandoned farm or pasture land.

The presence of a major pine component in a mixed stand suggests a major disturbance in the past. Activities or events such as harvesting followed by fire, field or pasture abandonment, and wildfire would result in a secondary succession. Eastern white pine is a possible exception to the above. White pine, the most shade tolerant of the eastern pines, ranks very close to the oaks in tolerance. It is a long-time occupant and is very slow to yield its position in a stand to invasion and ultimate replacement by the slightly more tolerant oaks and hickories. White pine does not possess the extreme longevity of white oak and some of the hickories, and in the absense of any disturbance, it is ultimately succeeded by these species. Thus, stands containing white pine would be consid-

Figure 5-8.   A typical stand of white oak, black oak and scarlet oak with a site index of 60. The stand is 60 years old located on a gently sloping south aspect in southwestern Virginia.

ered to be subclimax. Seedlings of white pine definitely benefit from the protection of a hardwood canopy. Although it rarely seeds into exposed open areas such as abandoned fields, white pine becomes established under moderately open hardwood stands. It usually survives and readily responds to openings in the stand made either naturally or by partial cuttings. When this occurs, the relatively greater growth rate of white pine as compared to the oaks, eventually results in it becoming a dominant part of the stand overstory.

GROWTH RATES.   Using a white oak site index of 60 as a base, site-index comparisons for several common species in the southern Appalachians (Doolittle, 1958; Fig. 5-9) are somewhat higher than for the same species in the Piedmont Plateau (Olson and Della-Bianca, 1959; Fig. 5-10). In the mountains, Doolittle (1958) showed that for a white oak site index 60, shortleaf and pitch

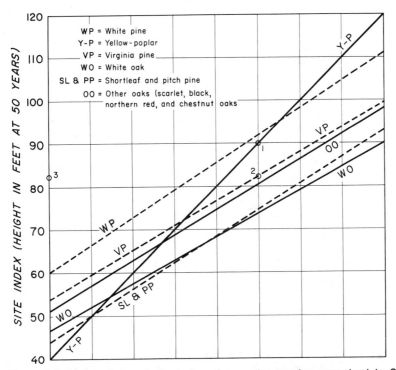

Figure 5-9. Comparisons of site indices for species on the same land in Southern Appalachians. For example, on land that is site index 90 (1) for yellow-poplar read down (2) and across (3) to find that this land averages about 82 for Virginia pine (Doolittle, 1958).

pine site indices would be almost the same as white oak (one foot lower) while the other oaks, yellow-poplar and Virginia pine are between 66 and 68 feet, and white pine is 76 feet. On the Piedmont, Olson and Della-Bianca (1959) found that for a white oak site index 60, the yellow-poplar site index was only 50 feet, the shortleaf pine about 54 feet, while the black oak site index was higher at about 64 feet, and the scarlet and northern red oak index was the highest at 69 feet. The data suggest that oaks are probably the best species alternative for fair sites of the white oak—black oak type group, except for white pine in the mountains, which shows a significant height growth advantage.

Characteristic growth increments for oak and hickory on these fair sites are between 16 and 20 rings per radial inch of growth. This would require rotation ages of between 65 and 80 years for pulpwood and 90 to 110 years for small sawtimber. An average annual growth rate of slightly less than one-half cord for pulpwood and 185 board feet per acre is expected under managed conditions.

ROTATION AGE OR SIZE.   Using a site index 60 and a 70-year pulpwood rotation, the estimated yield on a fully stocked, even-aged upland oak stand would be about 3,300 cubic feet per acre, and using a 95-year small-sawtimber rotation the yield would be about 17,500 board feet (Int. one-quarter rule) per acre (Schnur, 1937).

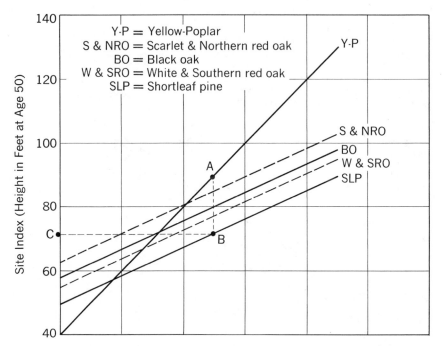

Figure 5-10.   Comparisons of site indices for species in the Virginia-Carolina Piedmont. For example, on land that is site index 90 (A9 for yellow-poplar), read down (B) and across (C) to find that this same land averages about 72 for shortleaf pine (Olsen and Della-Bianca, 1959).

CULTURAL PRACTICES.   Reference is made to the discussion of the oak-hickory type group in Chapter 4. Sawtimber, pulpwood, and specialty products such as railroad ties and mine props are viable product alternatives depending on the present condition of the stand in question. As has already been stated most of the hardwood stands have been subjected to abusive cutting practices in the past. For existing stands, an evaluation of the present stand is a necessary first step when considering the viable product objectives and the silvicultural techniques necessary to achieve these objectives. Historically, this evaluation has been based on the experience and ability of the individual forest manager. To improve this situation a study was recently initiated by Sonderman and Brisbin (1978) that establishes the base-line data necessary to develop a quality classification system for young hardwoods using empirical measurements of individual tree characteristics that can be related to the future product potential of a stand. Some of the characteristics initially considered are d.b.h., crown class, crown ratio, total height, height to first fork, sweep and crook, rot and seams, and limb count and limb-related defects. The classification system is based on a biological description of the tree that can be quantified (indexed) and evaluated in numerous product combinations at any point in time.

Where integrated uses such as wildlife, aesthetics, and other nontimber values are important, and where site conditions are particularly fragile, the development and perpetuation of uneven-aged forests are appropriate. This is best accomplished by a combination of group selection and patch cutting accompanied by improvement cutting as needed to maintain stand quality. In these situations selection cutting will return more long-term values and total timber volume; however, short-term financial returns will be less than for even-aged systems (Minckler, 1974; 1978). Individual-tree selection will not reproduce a new stand in which oak will dominate (Minckler et al., 1961). The more tolerant and less desirable species such as red maple and beech will be favored (Trimble et al., 1974) by this method.

The shelterwood method seems to be the most appropriate one for reproducing oaks if advance oak reproduction is poorly distributed or not present at the time of cutting (Trimble et al., 1974). Research results are not available to define the timing or intensity of shelterwood cutting; however, a two-cut shelterwood system with at least 15 years between seed cutting and the final harvest will be required. Other conditions will be similar to those discussed in the chestnut oak—scarlet oak section.

The seed-tree method is a possible alternative in that it may allow the forest manager some control of species composition by providing a larger percent of reproduction of seed origin. The amount of this control is yet unknown; however, it is probable that it would not change the species composition more than 15 percent over that attained by the clearcutting on a comparable site. In the central Appalachian 55- to 60-year-old mixed oak stands (site index 60) the seed-tree method has been used on an experimental basis. All trees 5 inches in d.b.h. and larger, except for 30 well-spaced seed trees per acre, were harvested (Wendel and Trimble, 1968). The seed trees were removed three years after the initial harvest. Reproduction after three growing seasons averaged about 13,500 stems per acre with 42 percent being of sprout origin. The distribution of stems was excellent. Twelve years after the initial harvest there were 1,900 stems per acre remaining of which 700 were commercial species and 50 percent of the total reproduction was of sprout origin. Sassafras and red maple were most abundant; however, chestnut oak, red oak, and sweet birch were also present. The number of desirable species was judged adequate for future stand management (Smith et al., 1976).

When ample advance regeneration of oak species is present the clearcutting method can be used very effectively. In determining the size and design of the harvesting units all physical-site constraints such as percent slope, drainage, and soil characteristics must be considered as well as potential problems with visual impacts and the impact on wildlife. The size of the clearcut could vary from an acre to as much as 25 to 30 acres. With the much longer rotations for sawtimber and the acorn production of mature oaks, the amount of advance regeneration of seed origin is expected to be high. Stump sprouting will be much reduced because the stumps are fewer and older. The regeneration following a pulpwood harvest will undoubtedly be dominanted by stump sprouts from the more abundant and smaller stumps, and the greatly reduced seed source from which to obtain advance regeneration of seed origin.

When using conventional harvesting systems for pulpwood production, all stems down to 5 inches in d.b.h. are normally cut. However, there are usually a substantial number of living stems 1 to 5 inches in d.b.h. remaining on the site. Commonly the numbers range between 300 and 600 stems per acre of which about two-thirds have been broken or bent during the harvesting operation (Trimble and Rosier, 1972). Generally, there are not enough of these residual stems, and they are scattered and of too low quality to form a desirable stand. If left, they are inherent wolf trees capable of adversely affecting the quality of the new stand. The use of power saws has proven to be the most efficient and cheapest method to eliminate the small undesirable residual stems (Trimble and Rosier, 1972). The need to remove the small stems is greatly increased when the species composition is undesirable and includes such species as red maple and beech. Sites should be identified where there are sufficient stems of desirable species of good quality remaining to establish the new stand because they will develop faster than stands where the small stems have been removed (Fig. 5-11).

As a result of the steep terrain in the mountainous regions, harvesting on the fair and good sites (site indices to 65 to 80) has been greatly hampered by the high cost of extensive road systems and in many cases slopes that are too

Figure 5-11.   A small clearcut in mixed hardwoods in north central West Virginia. The stand was about 65 years old, has a site index of 65 to 70 and was dominated by northern red oak and sugar maple. The site located on a northwest aspect, shows little disturbance and virtually no residual stems.

steep to log safely, and without site damage. Kochenderfer (1977) estimated that for the normal skidder-type logging operation road spacing seldom exceeded 150 feet, with 1 mile of road required to log about 20 acres. Even with this road system many of the slopes are too steep to log effectively with a wheeled skidder or even crawler tractors. With the use of a skyline harvesting system it is possible to log about 80 acres from 1 mile of road (Kochenderfer and Wendel, 1978) and slopes of up to 60 percent. The distances between roads may be as much as 1,100 feet or more depending on the type of skyline equipment employed. In West Virginia and Virginia commercial operations are utilizing skyline yarding systems for whole-tree harvesting of pulpwood material. These systems are designed for on-site whole-tree chipping and if well laid out can efficiently clearcut up to 20 acres on steep terrain with a single set and cause virtually no site disturbance. Using whole-tree harvesting and skyline yarding the utilization of harvested material is at a maximum and the residual stems left following a conventional harvest are conspicuously absent.

On the sites represented by the white oak—black oak type group white pine is a viable species alternative depending on the product and use objectives of the forest manager (Lancaster and Leak, 1978). The basis of this decision is substantiated by the site-index comparison of Doolittle (1958) which showed white pine to have a significant height-growth advantage over the associated oaks. The most realistic objective would be to develop a mixed stand where white pine composed at least 50 percent of the main canopy. A method to accomplish this, as proposed by Wendel (1971), is to underplant white pine seedlings at an appropriate spacing, perhaps 10 × 10 feet, prior to the hardwood harvest cut. Allow the white pine to become established for a period of about five years before proceeding with the harvest cut. The time between underplanting and overstory harvest is based on the time required for the white pine to be of sufficient size to be competitive with hardwood sprouts and not so large that they will be severely damaged by the harvesting operation. This practice is probably best suited for use on oak site indices of 55 to 65 (Wendel, 1971).

The objectives for applying intermediate cutting practices to existing stands should be to bring them to a stocking level that will result in good volume growth and to increase the quality of the desired species. In many cases the present stand condition is so poor that the product alternative cannot be met and the only viable alternative is to regenerate the stand at the earliest opportunity. The concepts and procedures of the silvicultural guide written by Roach and Gingrich (1968) for the upland hardwoods of the Central states, discussed in Chapter 4, are generally applicable to the mixed-oak stands of the Appalachian hardwood forest. The silvicultural techniques they recommend may have to be modified to enhance the benefits from other forest resources such as water, wildlife, and recreation.

Diameter-limit cutting, as practiced in this subregion, is best characterized as an intermediate silvicultural operation in that the objective is not to obtain regeneration. It is a technique that is questioned by many foresters; however, it

is being used on many Appalachian hardwood stands and with certain modification may be a valid intermediate cutting practice.

The objective of diameter-limit cutting is to establish a minimum diameter
that will result in harvesting only trees that are more-or-less financially mature.
The intent is to leave sufficient growing stock to occupy the site and develop
into the future stand (Trimble, 1971). Under this system only the larger trees
are harvested therefore constituting a high-grading, while trees below the
diameter limit are left to grow; thus, the residual stand contains both good- and
poor-quality stems of desirable and undesirable species. Hutnik (1958) recommended that the diamter-limit cut be used as an initial cut in order to get the
stand in condition for future management. Smith and Lamson (1977) have
recommended the practice be modified to include a flexible diameter limit so
that cultural treatments such as an improvement cut could be accomplished
below the diameter limit. This modification would approach a free thinning.
One of the assumptions that is made when applying the diameter-limit cut is
that the residual stems will respond to the release by the partial cutting. There
is ample evidence that hardwoods, especially the oaks, do respond to release
over a wide range of ages (Scholz, 1948; Minckler, 1957; Carvell, 1969; Smith
and Lamson, 1977).

The diameter-limit cutting method is easily applied and requires very little
skill in its execution, therefore, the opportunity for misuse and mistakes is
substantial. The stand evaluation procedure used to establish the diameter
limit, on the other hand, is critical and requires a skilled professional forester to
accomplish. The diameter-limit cut, if modified to include a flexible diameter
limit for stand improvement, is a viable silvicultural tool, especially on previously unmanaged or mismanaged Appalachian hardwood stands. It is probably
most appropriately used as a one-time operation in a given stand with other
intermediate practices being implemented as appropriate in the future.

Sugar Maple–Red Oak Type Group.   The sugar maple–red oak type group
consists of a relatively large number of diverse species having a wide range of
silvical characteristics. The stands are variable in composition, being productive mixtures of northern, southern, and central hardwood species which cover
a site-index range of 66 to 80 (base age 50).

The sites dominated by this type group are those that are generally cool with
good moisture conditions throughout the growing season. The type group may
occur to some degree on the gently sloping, lower slope positions, of southern
and western aspects. On northern and eastern aspects it occurs extensively on
moderate to steep slopes, of mid- and upper-slope positions and in the coves.
The type group is most abundant in the Appalachian Plateau, and at the mid
elevations and above in the Ridge and Valley and Blue Ridge provinces. In the
Piedmont Plateau the type group is least abundant and usually only found on
moderately sloping northern and eastern aspects, and in the adjacent coves.

PLACE IN ECOLOGICAL SUCCESSION.   The species composition falls within
the Mixed Mesophytic Forest described by Braun (1950). Among the most

important tree species are northern red oak, yellow-poplar, sugar maple, black cherry, white ash, basswood, American beech, white oak, and cucumbertree (Fig. 5-12). Of lesser importance are red maple, Fraser magnolia, sweet birch, yellow buckeye, American elm, black walnut and the hickories. Eastern white pine and eastern hemlock are commonly associated conifers. Sugar maple, the birches, cucumbertree, Fraser magnolia, yellow buckeye, basswood, black walnut, white pine, and hemlock are not found on Piedmont Plateau sites. Sweetgum and southern red oak are Piedmont Plateau and southern mountain components of the sugar maple−red oak type group.

The understory of this type group is quite diverse with some of the more common species being flowering dogwood, spicebush, sassafras, hawthorns, eastern hophornbeam, American hornbeam, redbud, serviceberry, sumacs,

Figure 5-12. Good quality, small-sawtimber stand composed of yellow-poplar, cucumbertree, yellow birch and beech. It is 65 to 70 years old and located on a lower slope (site index 75 for oak) in the Allegheny Mountains of West Virginia.

great rhododendron, and striped maple. The latter two species are not found on Piedmont sites.

Forest stands in this type group are represented by a wide range of successional stages. As a result of the high productive potential of these sites, and the most important species being classed as shade intolerant or intermediate, many stands will remain in a subclimax state as a result of management. The major climax species are sugar maple, beech, and hemlock. Sugar maple is the only high-value timber species and its growth rate is much slower than those of its more intolerant associates. The primary subclimax species are northern red oak, basswood, white oak, cucumbertree, white ash, black cherry, yellow-poplar, and white pine. Of lesser importance are the hickories, red maple, other oaks, sweet birch, and elm. Black walnut is extremely valuable and adapted to the productive sites; however, it is only an occasional component of this type group. Sweetgum is a valuable component within its natural range, while sassafras, bigtooth aspen, and black locust, when within their natural range, are pioneer species. As a result of the high reproductive capacity of the major species in this type group, site conditions seldom reach the degree of disturbance where these pioneer species could be competitive.

GROWTH RATES. The growth rates of this type group are such that the stands are very important commercially. Assuming an average growth increment of 14 rings per radial inch, it will require about 55 years to produce a pulpwood stand with a mean d.b.h. of 8 inches and 75 years for a small sawtimber stand with an average d.b.h. of 11 inches. The annual growth rates would be about 0.65 cord and 270 board feet per acre per year. These yields are comparable with those predicted by Gingrich (1971) for comparable managed upland oak stands thinned at 30 years.

ROTATION AGE OR SIZE. Based on a site index of 75 for upland oaks, the expected yield of a fully stocked, even-aged stand would be about 3,500 cubic feet per acre on a 55-year rotation and 20,000 board feet (Int. one-quarter rule) on a 75-year sawtimber rotation (Schnur, 1937). Normal rotation ages are such that veneer-sized trees are a usual component of the upper-diameter classes.

CULTURAL PRACTICES. A wider variety of products, product combinations, and uses are possible as site quality increases and the silvical characteristics exhibited by the predominant species become more diverse. As a result of better growth, the potential for increased quality, and higher product yields a better economic situation exists, thereby allowing more flexibility in the viable silvicultural alternatives that can be implemented. This condition exists, especially at site indices above 70 to 75, in stands of the sugar maple—red oak type group.

Sawtimber and veneer are probably the most important commercial products. Pulpwood is important and is sometimes a primary product; however, it is more important in conjunction with sawtimber where it is a product of intermediate harvest cuts. A pulpwood market allows for the utilization of lower-quality material, species that are less desirable for sawtimber and veneer, and for residues.

The regeneration potential of species found in stands of the sugar maple—red oak type group is very high. All of the hardwoods sprout vigorously and advance reproduction of sugar maple and beech develops prolifically even under closed canopies. Reproduction of species of intermediate tolerance usually occurs in small openings and on these good sites can persist for a number of years (Trimble, 1973a). Seed of species requiring moderate to full sunlight, such as white ash, yellow-poplar, and black cherry remain viable for several years in the forest floor (Clark, 1962; Leak, 1963; Wendel 1977). With the variety of species present and the effective reproductive mechanisms involved, there is abundant natural reproduction following any system of cutting. Different degrees of shade tolerance among the species, however, lead to changes in the proportions of the species present depending on the silvicultural system employed (Trimble, 1973a).

Uneven-aged management with single-tree selection or group selections are viable silvicultural regeneration methods that can be implemented; however, there are species constraints and economic implications that should be considered. Regardless of the present species composition, the implementation of the single-tree selection method will eventually result in a stand composed almost entirely of the very tolerant sugar maple, beech, and to a lesser extent hemlock. This method will result in the least amount of canopy and site disturbance, and has application where visual impacts may be great and canopy integrity is important. Attempts to make selection cuttings heavy enough to encourage regeneration and the development of less tolerant species are likely to result in reduced stand growth through understocking and impairing stand quality by high-grading (Trimble, 1973a). Trimble et al. (1974) have developed a method of applying single-tree selection to hardwood stands. The marking criteria includes the normal silvicultural factors such as quality, vigor, and species, however, it also incorporates economic guidelines for selecting trees to cut. The economic guidelines are in the form of rates of return for individual trees. Rate-of-return information is based on the financial-maturity concept. The system does not provide as strict regulations as the more classical method that tailors the residual stand to a predetermined diameter distribution; however, Trimble et al. (1974) believe that if the method is applied judiciously, the regulation potential is adequate and stricter control is not necessary.

Group-selection cutting of areas an acre or less in size offers a viable means for allowing the development of stands containing higher-value shade-intolerant and intermediate species such as black cherry, yellow-poplar, white ash, and northern red oak. There is often a great deal of confusion as to the difference between a group-selection cut and a small clearcut. As long as the opening is not recognized and recorded as a separate stand, and regulation is achieved through control of diameter distribution (uneven-aged regulation), then the opening is considered to be a group-selection cutting under even-aged management rather than a small clearcut under even-aged management (Marquis, 1978). Group-selection cutting, with larger-sized openings, creates a stand of many small even-aged groups of trees. For this reason it has been referred to as even-aged silviculture with uneven-aged management (regulation). It becomes very difficult to control diameter distribution when cutting must be restricted to fairly large openings and all trees in those openings must be cut (Marquis, 1978). In addition, it requires a great deal of skill and time on the part of the forester doing the evaluation and marking. Even-aged regulation of areas by age class becomes much more efficient and effective, and should receive prime consideration for openings larger than one acre.

When determining the size of openings needed to obtain the desired species composition, it is also necessary to consider the problem of epicormic branching on border trees. Epicormic branching can substantially degrade logs and greatly reduce the value of harvested trees. Trimble and Seegrist (1973) found that in circular openings of one-half acre and larger, the amount of branching did not change; however, it was significantly greater than in openings of one-fifth acre or less. Epicormic branching was greatest on white and red oak, followed by basswood, black cherry, and chestnut oak.

Even-aged management systems favor the fast-growing, high-value, less-tolerant species. Because both management costs and harvesting costs are lower when compared to an uneven-aged stand, even-aged management is preferable where wood production is the main objective (Trimble et al., 1974).

The shelterwood method theoretically should have an advantage in favoring species of intermediate shade tolerance and should provide some species control. This can be accomplished by carefully selecting the species to be removed in the seed cutting and in determining the intensity of the cut. As previously discussed, the extent of species control is probably limited and the procedures for applying the shelterwood method have not been verified in Appalachian hardwoods.

The seed-tree method has been applied to good (site index 70) and excellent (site index 80) sites in Appalachian hardwoods (Wendel and Trimble, 1968). Prior to harvest the good sites contained yellow-poplar, red oak, hickory, chestnut oak, and white oak, and the excellent sites contained sugar maple, red oak, white oak, black cherry, yellow-poplar, and hickory. Twenty well-distributed seed trees were left on the good sites and 10 were left on the excellent sites. All seed trees were harvested three years after the third growing season. After 12 years there was a wide variety of acceptable species present and most management objectives could easily be met. Sweet birch, sugar maple, yellow-poplar, and black cherry were the dominant species on excellent sites and sugar maple, sassafras, red oak, red maple, and yellow-poplar were most prevalent on the good sites (Smith et al., 1976). The development of grapevine on both sites was very abundant and is a serious threat to future sawtimber stands.

The clearcutting method probably offers the greatest potential for successful practice of intensive forest management where wood production is the primary objective (Trimble, 1973a). The shelterwood and seed-tree methods just described are valid alternatives; however, they cost more to implement and do not have any apparent advantage over the clearcut method on these sites where abundant natural regeneration of desirable species virtually always occurs. The clearcutting method provides for maximum reproduction of desirable shade intolerant species (McGee, 1975; McGee and Hooper, 1970; Trimble and Hart, 1961) and is easy to regulate for timber production. If the size of clearcut is kept between 25 and 30 acres, wildlife and watershed objectives are usually compatible. Where aesthetic considerations are paramount and the appearance of newly clearcut areas may be objectionable, clearcutting may be precluded or perhaps limited to small acreages.

On sites dominated by the sugar maple—red oak type group there is seldom a problem with the establishment of a natural stand of mixed hardwoods following any type of even-aged regeneration cut. Whether the species composition and quality are satisfactory will depend on the product objectives. If pulpwood is the primary objective it is doubtful whether any intermediate cultural practices can be justified or are needed. An exception to this is related to the control of wild grapevines. When sawtimber and veneer are the objectives, certain species are more desirable than others, and some form of release cutting, a thinning, and perhaps fertilization need to be considered.

The establishment and uncontrolled growth of wild grapevine following clearcutting is a serious problem on the better sites (site indices of 70 and above) in the central and southern Appalachians (Trimble and Tryon, 1974; McGee and Hooper, 1975). The damage greatly affects tree quality by breaking and twisting tops and limbs, by completely covering the crown causing reduced photosynthesis, and by augmenting ice, snow, and wind damage (Trimble and Tryon, 1974). Substantial damage has also been reported on sites of similar quality following regeneration by the seed-tree method (Smith *et al.*, 1976). The wild grapevines originate both from seeds and by sprouting; however, the damage from sprouts is more serious because they grow so much faster. Grapevines do provide valuable wildlife food and habitat (Shutts, 1974) and it is not recommended that they be eradicated; however, they should be controlled. Very few methods are available to control the vines once they become established following the clearcut. For control it is recommended they be cut near ground level several years before the harvest cutting. This technique should cause the stumps of the vines to die from the shading effects of the overstory (Smith and Smithson, 1975).

High-quality mixed hardwood stands will develop even without any type of precommercial silviculture being applied (Della-Bianca, 1975). However, an intensive cleaning consisting of cutting all woody stems other than selected crop trees, resulted in a significant increase in diameter of the crop trees when applied to an 11-year-old mixed hardwood stand that had been clearcut. The costs of an intensive cleaning are high and even when the increased wildlife benefits are included the costs may well exceed the benefits. Crop-tree release is a less intensive cleaning method where crop trees are selected and then competing vegetation within a radius of about 5 feet around the crop tree is cut.

Studies indicate that the practice should not be implemented until the crown canopy has closed, and the dominant and co-dominant trees are about 25 feet tall. At this stage the stands will be accessible, potential crop trees can be identified and the potential problem of grapevine competition will be greatly reduced (Trimble, 1971, 1973b; Lamson and Smith, 1978). The number of crop trees to be released should probably be between 100 and 140 trees per acre and the selection should be made from trees already in the dominant or co-dominant crown position.

Stump sprouts are a major source of reproduction on virtually all sites in the Appalachian Hardwood Subregion. When the major product objective is pulpwood with sawtimber being secondary, the emphasis is on fiber production rather than tree quality and the source of reproduction is not important. On good sites, tree quality is of primary importance because it is the value-determining factor for sawtimber and veneer. Therefore, stump sprouts are a potentially important source of sawtimber trees if the quality is good. In the past, the greatest problem with trees of sprout origin has been the high incidence of butt rot, which greatly reduced sawtimber quality. The primary causes have been attributed to repeated occurrence of wildfire and sprouts that originated high on the stump (Roth and Hepting, 1943). With present-day fire control, harvesting methods that result in low stumps, and an intensity of management that includes thinning sprout clumps to eliminate poorly formed and high origin stumps, the quality of stumps is greatly improved (Fig. 5-13A and 5-13B). Results of recent studies show that the abundance and quality of stump sprouts is such that many can be considered as potential sawtimber crop-trees (Wendel, 1975; Lamson, 1976), thus reducing the importance of obtaining seed origin reproduction.

Many of the stands encountered in the Appalachian Hardwood Subregion are second-growth, unmanaged and from 40 to 60 or more years of age. When bringing these stands under management it is often necessary to conduct some type of conditioning cut. In accomplishing this, it is necessary to have a knowledge of the response of different species to partial cuttings. In stands of this age group, Trimble (1967) found that diameter increase was greatest with northern red oak followed closely by yellow-poplar, then sugar maple, basswood, black cherry, white ash, and chestnut oak, in descending order. This type of information is also helpful in making decisions concerning the species to favor in thinning similar mixed hardwoods in the future.

Thinning stands of the sugar maple—red oak type group is usually necessary if the stand is to yield the primary product in a minimum of time. Thinnings should favor trees from the larger size classes of the desired species that are of sufficient number and quality to provide a full yield. In general, a large percentage of the mixed hardwood stands on good sites are in need of thinning and a tremendous volume is lost annually because of mortality resulting from over-stocking (Craft and Baumgras, 1978). Basal areas of 150 square feet per acre are probably not uncommon while the basal area under managed conditions should be about half or between 70 and 80 square feet per acre. To aid in regulating

Figure 5-13-A. Typical 15-year-old yellow-poplar sprout clump on a good—excellent site (site index 80 for oak) that had been clearcut.

Figure 5-13B. An adjacent 15-year-old yellow-poplar sprout clump that has been thinned to release the two highest quality, dominant stems.

and implementing intermediate cuttings, Roach (1977) has developed a stocking guide for stands of Allegheny hardwoods that is applicable to the sugar maple—red oak type group. The guide includes procedures for evaluating stocking and stand conditions, thinning even-aged stands, determining minimum residual stocking, distributing the basal-area cut in a stand, and using the guide for selection cutting.

Pruning is generally not required in stands of this type group because the density is sufficiently high that natural pruning is effective and the most important species such as yellow-poplar, red oak, basswood, and black cherry exhibit good natural pruning. Under conditions of poor stocking, pruning of potential veneer quality stems of high-quality species such as black cherry and black walnut may be justified (Grisez, 1978).

Fertilization of mixed hardwoods in the Appalachians shows promise as a means of increasing growth under specific conditions (Lamson, 1978). However, before any large-scale fertilization is undertaken, additional information is needed in order to characterize the nutrient status of the soils involved, the types of deficiencies that exist, the species requirements, and reliable methods of testing and evaluating a given soil-site-species condition. In addition, the effects on water quality must be known as well as the impacts on other potential forest uses.

SPECIAL PROBLEMS IN MANAGEMENT.   The sites dominated by this type group are located on cooler aspects with relatively deep and often fine-textured soils, and having abundant moisture. These conditions are important from a watershed standpoint and therefore may indirectly affect silvicultural alternatives. Springs and seeps are prevalent, and streams often emerge in the small drainages. Considerable erosion hazard must be expected from logging roads if they are not constructed and maintained properly. The high timber production associated with these sites may indirectly contribute to the erosion potential by tempting loggers to return periodically for fast-growing, high-quality trees (Trimble *et al.*, 1974). Damage to the watershed is best avoided by critically analyzing proposed silvicultural alternatives, and then carefully designing access and hard roads to minimize travel in drainageways and moist lower slopes. The use of a skyline cable yarding system should certainly be considered.

Yellow-Poplar–Mixed Hardwood Type Group   The yellow-poplar–mixed hardwood type group is a highly productive combination of hardwood species, dominated by yellow-poplar, and found on land with site indices of 81 and above (base age 50). The yellow-poplar–mixed hardwood and the sugar maple–red oak type groups, if combined, would be nearly equivalent to the Appalachian Mixed Hardwood type described by Trimble (1973a). The separation of the two type groups is deemed appropriate because of the pronounced characteristic of yellow-poplar to respond so vigorously to increasing site quality. At site indices near 80, yellow-poplar is about equal in its competitiveness to associated species. As site quality decreases, so does the competitive ability of yellow-poplar (Doolittle, 1958; Olson and Della-Bianca, 1959). However, when comparing the site indices of several associated species on the same land, yellow-poplar exhibits a marked and continued increase in height growth as the site index increases above 80. As an example, with a site index of 110 for yellow-poplar, the associated hardwood species fall far behind in height growth with the most competitive species having a site index of about 93 (Fig. 5-9 and 5-10). The margin of difference continues to increase as site quality increases. In the Appalachians, white pine is competitive up to a site index of 95, but then even it falls behind the more responsive yellow-poplar (Fig. 5-9). The common species in the yellow-poplar–mixed hardwood type group are similar to those found in the sugar maple–red oak group except that the yellow-poplar component increases as site quality increases.

PLACE IN ECOLOGICAL SUCCESSION.   The type group is restricted to the very best sites; those characterized by deep, well-drained soils of gently sloping eastern and northern aspects and associated coves. Abundant rainfall, well distributed over a long growing season, is also prerequisite. For the most part, these conditions are restricted to the mountains and plateaus of West Virginia, North Carolina, Tennessee, and Kentucky. There is potential for a wide range of successional stages in the yellow-poplar—mixed hardwood type group; however, because of the high commercial value of the less tolerant species, the stands will generally be kept in a subclimax stage by design.

GROWTH RATES.   The very rapid growth rates provide strong incentives for careful and intensive management of timber stands on these excellent sites. As an example, a natural unthinned stand of even-aged yellow-poplar with a site index of 110 at age 70, would yield an estimated 44,760 board feet (Int. one-quarter rule) or 7,760 cubic feet per acre (Beck and Della-Bianca, 1970). This assumes 150 trees and 184 square feet of basal area per acre. The d.b.h. of the mean tree would be 15 inches and the stand would include trees with diameters as high as 24 inches. The growth rate under the above conditions averages 640 board feet per acre per year.

ROTATION AGE OR SIZE.   Rotation ages of less than 50 years for sawtimber are not uncommon with stands with veneer-quality stems being produced in from 50 to 75 years on the better sites.

CULTURAL PRACTICES.   The rapid growth rate and generally excellent timber quality produced on these sites dictate that the primary products will be a combination of high-quality sawtimber and veneer. Pulpwood would be a secondary objective and provide an outlet for products of early intermediate cuts and residues from sawtimber and veneer cuttings.

The combination of topography, soil, and climatic conditions that produce the excellent site quality reflected by the presence of the yellow-poplar—mixed hardwood type group is unique and certainly not widespread. The sites are generally small, perhaps as large as 10 acres, and exhibit a much elongated shape that conforms to the coves and lower-slope positions that prevail. In many cases, it may not be possible to treat these sites as separate stands; however, their potential should be recognized and considered in the management planning process.

The regeneration methods considered for the sugar maple—red oak type group are also appropriate for this type group. The clearcut method would maximize the competitive advantage demonstrated by yellow-poplar and therefore result in it being the favored and most abundant species. If the proportion of other species such as northern red oak, basswood, white ash, and black cherry is to be increased, regeneration methods which increase the amount of shade during the period of reproduction establishment will be required. The shelterwood method should be considered as well as the group-selection method with the opening size kept small enough to restrict the occurrence of intolerant species.

Any attempts to change the species composition of stands dominated by yellow-poplar by implementing a crop-tree release would very likely fail because of the growth rate advantage of yellow-poplar when compared to the associated species.

Thinning is strongly recommended on all excellent sites where yellow-poplar is a dominant species. The majority of unthinned natural yellow-poplar stands are overstocked for maximum board-foot and diameter growth (Beck and Della-Bianca, 1975). They found that board-foot growth increases with increasing basal area up to a maximum and then decreases. The level of residual stocking at which board-foot growth is maximized increases with site quality. As a general rule, between the ages of 30 and 70 years, maximum rates of board-foot growth are reached at basal areas approximately equal to site index. For example, maximum board-foot growth is reached at 90 square feet of basal area per acre on site 90, and 100 square feet on site 110. The estimated 5-year annual growth rate following thinning of a 40-year-old yellow-poplar stand on a site 110 cut to a residual basal area of 110 square feet, is 800 board feet (Int. one-quarter rule) per acre (Beck and Della-Bianca, 1975). Similar growth rates could be expected following future thinnings conducted at intervals of perhaps 10 years.

As a result of the probable intensive management, the species composition, high vigor, and relatively isolated stands, it is doubtful that disease and insect problems will be of concern.

Wildlife and water-quality concerns are similar to those in the sugar maple—red oak type group. Visual impacts will be relatively minor when the generally small size and the protected, less visible, locations of the stands are considered.

Susceptibility to Damage Most of the important hardwood species of the Appalachian Hardwood Subregion are relatively free of severe insect and disease problems. Undoubtedly the very diverse nature of the typical mixed hardwood stands helps to avoid major losses at any given time. One of the most important deterrents to insect and disease problems is to maintain vigorous and healthy stands.

There are numerous butt rot organisms that will cause reduced quality and in some cases even death. Usually they are a result of some form of damage such as logging or fire. Reasonable care in general forest operations will generally minimize this type of damage. Oak wilt is still active; however, it appears to be endemic within the Appalachian hardwoods (Hanson, 1977). The gypsy moth is the major potential insect problem within the Appalachian Hardwood Subregion. The pest is more serious in this area than in the Central Region. At the present time the major problem is occurring in Pennsylvania; however, the moths have been found in West Virginia and northern Virginia. In 1974, 318,000 acres were defoliated in Pennsylvania and in 1976 this area increased to 732,000 acres (Hanson, 1977). The total loss (not including 1976) has been 236 million board feet of sawtimber and 234 million cubic feet of pulpwood, with a combined value of $8.4 million. Ninety-four percent of the trees killed were oak (Hanson, 1977).

Other damaging agents or problems resulting in reduced growth or mortality have been discussed elsewhere.

Wildlife Habitat[7]. Silvicultural manipulations play a key role in providing food and cover for wildlife. Timber harvest and stand-improvement practices will create successional variety and produce good-quality wildlife habitat.

In the Appalachian Hardwood Subregion the more popular game species include white tailed deer, grey squirrel, ruffed grouse, and wild turkey. Other game animals that attract sportsmen are cottontail rabbits, bobwhite quail, raccoon, opossum, muskrat, and some waterfowl. Nongame species that contribute to aesthetic and recreational attractiveness are flying squirrels, chipmunks, groundhogs, and a wide variety of seasonal bird populations.

When considering wildlife as a component of the forest management objectives, the density and type of overstory cover is not as important for most small game species habitats as is the edge effect produced by stand removal. The raccoon and cottontail rabbit, for example, are more dependent on cultivated and crop-production areas for survival and often move across farms, orchards, and forest edges in pursuit of their food and cover requirements (Trippensee, 1948). As long as there is a mixture of wooded and agricultural or recently harvested forest land, local populations of small game should persist.

The white-tailed deer is probably one of the most widespread and sought after game species in the Appalachian Hardwood Subregion. It is also the species whose food requirements most necessitate manipulation of forest vegetation. If cover and food requirements of the white-tailed deer are satisfied, then the forest will probably be sufficiently diverse to provide most of the forest needs of other wildlife species.

Of all environmental factors influencing populations, food is the only one currently feasible to manipulate significantly (Giles and Snyder, 1970). In addition, browse is particularly essential to the maintenance of healthy wildlife populations because it remains available during the food-scarce winter period when annuals and green foliage disappear (Shaw and Ripley, 1965).

The most general statement that can be made about browse production and forest management is that most timber harvesting practices increase the yield of woody browse plants (Jordan, 1970). Any removal of the overstory will stimulate browse production and understory regeneration. When designing a harvesting operation it is important to consider cutting intensity, stand age, species present, and harvest-area size in order to optimize increases in browse production.

Thinned stands of mixed oak produce more sprout browse while thinned cove hardwoods produce more seedling browse (Knierim *et al.*, 1971). In general, sprouts are preferred (Moore and Johnson, 1967). Three years after a heavy thinning in a stand of southern Appalachian hardwoods, seedling browse was four times more numerous than sprout browse yet the sprouts received over half of the total utilization. According to Shaw and Ripley (1965) browse and twig production is inversely related to both crown closure and basal area. Browse density is more significantly related to crown closure and exhibits a

[7]Compiled with the assistance of S. A. Nottingham, III.

straight-line relationship while its association with basal area shows a J-shaped curve.

Knierim *et al.* (1971) found that in 35-year-old even-aged stands in the southern Appalachians, the mixed oak type on good sites produced more seedling origin browse when thinned to and maintained at 100 square feet of basal area per acre than when thinned to 73 square feet of basal area. In similar cove hardwood stands, preferred palatable browse is maximized at about 90 square feet of basal area per acre. Lower basal areas (68 to 76 on good sites) will stimulate even more sprout browse in the mixed oak type if they are compatible with other objectives.

Percentage of basal area removed has also been used as a criterion for determining optimal cutting intensity (Patton and McGinnes, 1964). An improvement cut in a mixed oak-pine type in southwestern Virginia having an average basal area of 70 square feet per acre removed up to 78 percent of the basal area. Before the improvement cut, the area averaged 290 stems per acre of trees 4 inches in d.b.h. and above. Ninety percent of the trees were in the 4- to 8-inch-diameter class and 40 to 60 years old. The lightest cut felled 30 percent of the basal area and increased palatable browse production from 10 to 31 pounds per acre. When 80 percent of the basal area was removed, browse production reached 154 pounds per acre in the first year after the cut, a 15-fold increase.

Improvement cuts have been used to stimulate browse production. Della-Bianca and Johnson (1965) found that an intensive improvement cut that removed all woody stems except crop trees from an 11-year-old southern Appalachian hardwood stand that had been previously clearcut resulted in a significant increase in browse production over control stands. Treated lower slope stands contained 10 times more browse (805 pounds) per acre than treated upper-slope stands.

Clearcut and selection-cut methods favorably affect browse production with both size and intensity of cut affecting utilization by wildlife (Harlow and Downing, 1969). Clearcutting produces a substantial number of stems for spring browsing and supplies more winter forage than uncut areas. However, clearcuts greater than 50 acres produce such an abundance of growth that the regeneration soon becomes too dense and is relatively inaccessible to deer. Desirable browse in small clearcuts (1 acre) quickly declines due to intense deer utilization and overstory competition. This suggests that medium-sized clearcuts (15 to 20 acres) are more appropriate since they produce ample browse that remains available for a longer period of time. In uneven-aged stands, heavy selection cuts that reduce basal area to 60 square feet per acre produce less total browse but have an advantage over clearcuts in that they remain accessible to deer. Another advantage of selection cuts is that some mast producing oaks may be left in the stand.

Even-aged silvicultural systems are effective producers of good wildlife habitat if careful consideration is given to the arrangement of the different aged stands. Hypothetically, if one considers an 80-year rotation and four age-class groups then approximately 50 percent of the planned management units should be composed of an even distribution of 40- to 80-year-old stands. These older stands are the mast producers, a food that is important to many wildlife species, especially deer, turkey, and squirrel. Also of importance in this scheme is the proximity of pole and sapling stands to sawtimber stand. Each newly regenerated stand should be surrounded by sawtimber and at least two 20-acre patches of sawtimber should adjoin each pole and sapling stand. This age distribution would provide a steady supply of both browse and mast. However, it must be remembered that at least half the management unit should be of mast-producing age and that it may be necessary to delay regeneration of some stands past maturity so that this balance may be achieved and maintained. Once such a distribution is achieved, no animal would ever be far from a mast source or succulent new growth. This is particularly important to species with a short cruising radius. In addition, wide-ranging species would tend to be distributed more evenly.

Increasing browse production necessitates opening the forest canopy. However, the effects of opening the canopy are temporary. Murphy and Ehrenreich (1965) found that browse and forage production was greatest 3 to 6 years after cutting in pine stands and 6 to 10 years following cutting in white oak stands. In mixed hardwood types, desirable browse production begins to decline 5 years after cutting (Patton and McGinnes, 1964). After forage has declined, consideration must be given to the quality of regeneration in the openings. The sites should remain productive and continue to produce quality timber so the land retains its value and scenic beauty.

Site and opening size largely determined the quality and quantity of production in a forest opening. Growth and species differences in the 10-year reproduction on different sites and in different sized openings are attributable to differences in light and soil moisture (Minckler and Woerheide, 1965). Openings with a diameter equal to the height of the adjacent trees (1-sized opening) in eastern mixed oak types receive 45 to 75 percent full sunlight depending on aspect, and 2-sized openings (diameter equal to 2 times the height of adjacent trees) receive 65 to 90 percent. Opening size strongly affects the species composition of saplings 10 feet and taller. On northerly slopes and coves one-quarter- and one-half-sized openings have significantly fewer desirable yellow-poplar saplings than three-quarters- to 2-sized openings. On southerly slopes there is a greater number of desirable oak saplings in the larger openings. Reproduction of yellow-poplar and other desirable species is more abundant in coves and on northerly slopes than on drier sites. Oaks are more abundant on southerly slopes and ridges. Openings with diameters larger than twice the height of surrounding trees apparently will not greatly increase growth of reproduction because light and soil moisture differ little between these openings and larger ones.

Discussion up to this point has been concerned with various methods of cutting that are designed to increase browse and forage production. Prescribed burning is a technique used primarily in pine stands of the south to stimulate growth of browse. It may be used when and where cutting is not compatible with overall management objectives. Prescribed burning has an immediate effect on the quality and yield of forage in pine forests (Halls *et al.*, 1964), and is a very inexpensive means of habitat improvement (Dills, 1970). Prescribed burning is being used very effectively on the Piedmont as a silvicultural technique primarily for hardwood control on upland sites being converted to pine production. Its use, however, is not recommended for mountain hardwoods since they are very susceptible to damage and death from even light burns, and fire on steep slopes is difficult to control, even under ideal conditions, and the potential for soil/site damage outweighs any benefits that may be derived (Wells *et al.*, 1979).

Overpopulation of wildlife can have an adverse effect on regeneration of forest stands when excessive browsing destroys new regeneration. This has occured in the Allegheny Plateau of Pennsylvania where regeneration has failed following clearcutting as a result of excessive deer browsing (Marquis, 1975a; Jordan, 1967; Grisez, 1957). When the initial regeneration fails, it becomes very difficult to reestablish the regeneration. The seed sources become limiting over time (Marquis, 1975b) and herbaceous vegetation often becomes established. Certain of these species have been shown to interfere with the growth and development of any seedlings present (Horsley, 1977a, 1977b). Deer browsing also continues to restrict seedling growth, and artificial hardwood regeneration is not successful unless the seedlings are protected (Marquis, 1977). In general, these factors can be greatly reduced by limiting cutting to stands that contain abundant advance reproduction, or by using the shelterwood method where the final harvest is not accomplished until the regeneration has grown out of the reach of the browsing deer (Marquis *et al.*, 1975).

LITERATURE CITED

Abrahamson, L. P., and F. I. McCracken. 1971. Insect and disease pests of southern hardwoods. In Proc. Symp. on southeastern hardwoods. *SE Area, S&PF, USDA For. Serv.*, Atlanta, GA. pp. 80–89.

Baker, J. B. 1977. Tolerance of planted hardwoods to spring flooding. *South. J. Appl. For.*. 1(3):23–25.

Baker, J. B., and W. M. Broadfoot. 1977. A practical field method of site evaluation for eight important southern hardwoods. *USDA For. Serv. Gen. Tech. Rep. SO-14.* 31 pp.

Beck, D. E., and L. Della-Bianca. 1970. Yield of unthinned yellow-poplar. *USDA For. Serv. Res. Pap. SE-58.* 20 pp.

Beck, D. E., and L. Della-Bianca. 1975. Boardfoot and diameter growth of yellow-poplar after thinning. *USDA For. Serv. Res. Pap. SE-123.* 20 pp.

Bowman, I. 1914. *Forest physiography.* John Wiley & Sons, Inc., New York. 759 pp.

Boyce, S. G., and N. D. Cost. 1974. Timber potentials in the wetland hardwoods. In M. C. Blount (ed.) *Water resources, utilization, and conservation in the environment.* Taylor Printing Co., Reynolds, GA. pp. 130–151.

Braun, E. L. 1950. *Deciduous forests of Eastern North America.* The Blakiston Co., Philadelphia. 596 pp.

Broadfoot, W. M., and H. L. Williston. 1973. Flooding effects on southern forests. *J. For.* 71:584–587.

Carmean, W. H. 1971. Site index curves for black, white, scarlet, and chestnut oaks in the Central States. *USDA For. Serv. Res. Pap. NC-62.* 8 pp.

Carvell, K. 1969. The growth response of northern red oak following partial cutting. *W. VA Univ. Agr. Exp. Stn. Bull. 577,* Morgantown. 11 pp.

Clark, F. B. 1962. White ash, hackberry, and yellow-poplar seed remain viable when stored in forest litter. *Ind. Acad. Sci. Proc.* 72:112–114.

Clarkson, R. B. 1964. *Tumult on the mountains.* McClain Printing Co., Parsons, W. VA. 410 pp.

Core, E. L. 1966. *Vegetation of West Virginia.* McClain Printing Co., Parsons, W. VA. 217 pp.

Core, E. L. 1971. Silvical characteristics of five upland oaks. In Oak Symp. Proc. *USDA For. Serv. NE. Forest Exp. Stn.,* Upper Darby, PA. pp. 19–29.

Cost, N.D. 1976. Forest statistics for the Coastal Plain of Virginia, 1976. *USDA For. Serv. Resour. Bull. SE-34.* 33 pp.

Craft, P.E., and J. E. Baumgras. 1978. Products derived from thinning two hardwood timber stands in the Appalachians. *USDA For. Serv. Res. Pap. NE-422.* 8 pp.

Dana, S. T. 1930. Timber growing and logging practices in the Northeast. *USDA Tech. Bull. 166.* 112 pp.

Davidson, R. W., P. L. Lentz, and H. M. McKay. 1960. The fungus causing pecky cypress. *Mycologia* 52:260–279.

Della-Bianca, L. 1975. An intensive cleaning of mixed hardwood saplings—10 year results from the southern Appalachians. *J. For.* 73:25–28.

Della-Bianca, L., and F. M. Johnson. 1965. Effects of an intensive cleaning on deer browse production in the southern Appalachians. *J. Wildl. Mgmt.* 29:729–730.

Dills, G. G. 1970. Effects of prescribed burning on deer browse. *J. Wildl. Mgmt.* 34:540–545.

Doolittle, W. T. 1958. Site index comparisons for several forest species in the southern Appalachians. *Soil Sci. Soc. Am. Proc.* 22:455–458.

Dutrow, G. F., J. S. McKnight, and S. Guttenberg. 1970. Investment guide for cottonwood planters. *USDA For. Serv. Res. Pap. SO-59.* 15 pp.

Earles, J. M. 1975. Forest statistics for Louisiana parishes. *USDA For. Serv. Resour. Bull. SO-52.* 85 pp.

Fenneman, N. M. 1938. *Physiography of eastern United States.* McGraw-Hill Book Co., Inc., New York. 714 pp.

Frey, H. T., and H. W. Dill, Jr. 1971. Land use change in the southern Mississippi Alluvial Valley, 1959-69—an analysis based on remote sensing. *USDA Econ. Res. Serv., Agric. Econ. Rep. No. 215.* 26 pp.

Frothingham, E. H. 1931. Timber growing and logging practice in the southern Appalachian region. *USDA Tech. Bull. 250.* 92 pp.

Giles, R. H., Jr., and N. Snyder. 1970. Simulation techniques in wildlife habitat management. In *Readings in Wildlife Conservation.* J. A. Bailey, W. Elder, and T. D. McKinney (eds.) The Wildl. Soc., Wash., D.C., 1974. pp. 637–654.

Gingrich, S. F. 1971. Management of young and intermediate stands of upland hardwoods. *USDA For. Serv. Res. Pap. NE-195.* 26 pp.

Glasgow, L. L., and R. E. Noble. 1971. The importance of bottomland hardwoods to wildlife. In Proc. Symp. on southeastern hardwoods. *SE. Area, S&PF, USDA For. Serv.,* Atlanta, GA. pp. 30–43.

Grisez, T. J. 1957. Deer browsing in the Poconos. *PA. Game News* 28:7–10.

Grisez, T. J. 1978. Pruning black cherry in understocked stands. *USDA For. Serv. Res. Pap. NE-395.* 9 pp.

Guttenberg, S., and J. A. Putnam. 1951. Financial maturity of bottomland red oaks and sweetgum. *USDA For. Serv. Occas. Pap. 117. So. For. Exp. Stn.*, New Orleans. 24 pp.

Halls, L. K. (ed.) 1977. Southern fruit-producing woody plants used by wildlife. *USDA For. Serv. Gen. Tech. Rep. SO-16.* 235 pp.

Halls, L. K., R. H. Hughes, R. S. Rummell, and B. L. Southwell. 1964. Forage and cattle management in longleaf-slash pine forests. *USDA Farmers Bull. 2199.* 25 pp.

Hansbrough, T. (ed.). 1970. Silviculture and management of southern hardwoods. In Proc. 19th Ann. For. Symp., LA. State Univ. Press, Baton Rouge, LA. 145 pp.

Hanson, J. B. 1977. Forest pest conditions in the northeast '76. *USDA For. Serv. NE. Area S&PF, USDA For. Serv.*, Upper Darby, PA. 17 pp.

Harlow, R. F., and R. L. Downing. 1969. The effects of size and intensity of cut on production of some deer foods in the southern Appalachians. *Trans. N. E. Fish and Wildl. Conf.* 26:45−55.

Harlow, W. M., E. S. Harrar, and F. M. White. 1979. *Textbook of dendrology.* 6th ed. McGraw-Hill Book Co., New York. 510 pp.

Haygood, J. L. 1970. Wildlife recreation management in bottonland hardwoods. In Thomas Hansbrough (ed.), *Silviculture and management of southern hardwoods.* Proc. 19th Ann. For. Symp. LA. State Univ. Press, Baton Rouge, LA. pp. 122−134.

Hedlund, A. 1964. Epicormic branching in North Louisiana Delta. *USDA For. Serv. Res. Note SO-8.* 3 pp.

Hedlund, A. 1971. Arkansas Delta forest: a vanishing resource. *For. Farmer* 30 (4):13−14, 17.

Horsley, S. B. 1977a. Allelopathic inhibition of black cherry by fern, grass, goldenrod, and aster. *Can. J. For. Res.* 7:205−216.

Horsley, S. B. 1977b. Allelopathic inhibition of black cherry II. Inhibition by woodland grass, ferns, and club moss. *Can. J. For. Res.* 7:515−519.

Hutnik, R. J. 1958. Three diameter limit cuttings in West Virginia hardwoods—a 5-year report. *USDA For. Serv. Res. Pap. 106.* 13 pp.

Janssen, R. E. 1973. *Earth Science . . . a handbook on the geology of West Virginia.* Educational Marketers, Inc. Clarksburg, W. VA. 349 pp.

Johnson, R. L. 1958. Bluff Hills—ideal for hardwood timber production. *South. Lumberman* 197(2465):126−128.

Johnson, R. L. 1973. Oak-gum-cypress in the midsouth. In Silvicultural systems for the major forest types of the United States. *USDA Agric. Hdb. 445.* pp. 98−102.

Johnson, R. L. 1975. Natural regeneration and development of Nuttall oak and associated species. *USDA For. Serv. Res. Pap. SO-104.* 12 pp.

Johnson, R. L., and R. M. Krinard. 1976. Hardwood regeneration after seed tree cutting. *USDA For. Serv. Res. Pap. SO-123.* 9 pp.

Jordan, J. S. 1967. Deer browsing in northern hardwoods after clearcutting. *USDA For. Serv. Res. Pap. NE-57.* 15 pp.

Jordan, J. S. 1970. Deer habitat management in eastern forests. *J. For.* 68:692−694.

Kaszkurewicz, A. 1973. Establishment and early growth of *Populus deltoides* Bartr. Ph. D. dissertation. LA. State Univ., Baton Rouge, LA. 312 pp.

Kennedy, H. E., Jr., and R. M. Krinard. 1974. 1973 Mississippi River flood's impact on natural hardwood forests and plantations. *USDA For. Serv. Res. Note SO-177.* 6 pp.

Knierim, P. G., K. L. Carvell, and J. D. Gill. 1971. Browse in thinned oak and cove hardwood stands. *J. Wildl. Mgmt.* 35:163−168.

Kochenderfer, J. N. 1977. Area in skidroads, truck roads and landing after logging in the central Appalachians. *J. For.* 75:507−508.

Kochenderfer, J. N., and G. W. Wendel. 1978. Skyline harvesting in Appalachia. *USDA For. Serv. Res. Pap. NE-400.* 9 pp.

Korstian, C. F. 1927. Factors controlling the germination and early survival in oaks. *Yale Univ. School For. Bull. 19.* New Haven. 115 pp.

Lamson, N. I. 1976. Appalachian hardwood stump sprouts are potential sawlog crop tree. *USDA For. Serv. Res. Note NE-229.* 4 pp.

Lamson, N. I. 1978. Fertilization increases growth of sawlog-size yellow-poplar and red oak in West Virginia. *USDA For. Serv. Res. Pap. NE-403.* 6 pp.

Lamson, N. I., and H. C. Smith. 1978. Response to crop-tree release: sugar maple, red oak, black cherry, and yellow-poplar saplings in a 9-year-old stand. *USDA For. Serv. Res. Pap. NE-394.* 8 pp.

Lancaster, K. F., and W. B. Leak. 1978. A silvicultural guide for white pine in the northeast. *USDA For. Serv. Gen. Tech. Rep. NE-41.* 13 pp.

Leak, W. B. 1963. Delayed germination of ash seeds under forest conditions. *J. For.* 61:768–772.

Lull, H. W. 1968. A forest atlas of the northeast. *USDA For. Serv., NE. Forest Exp. Stn.* 46 pp.

Lytle, S. A. 1960. Physiography and properties of southern forest soils. In Paul Y. Burns (ed.), *Southern forest soils.* Proc. 8th (1959) Ann. For. Symp. LA. State Univ. Press, Baton Rouge, LA. pp. 1–8.

Maisenhelder, L. C. 1960. Cottonwood plantations for southern bottomlands. *USDA For. Serv. Occas. Pap. 179.* 24 pp.

Marquis, D. A. 1975a. The impact of deer browsing on Allegheny hardwood regeneration. *USDA For. Serv. Res. Pap. NE-308.* 8 pp.

Marquis, D. A. 1975b. Seed germination and storage under northern hardwood forests. *Can. J. For. Res.* 5:478–484.

Marquis, D. A.,1977. Devices to protect seedlings from deer browsing. *USDA For. Serv. Res. Note NE-243.* 7 pp.

Marquis, D. A. 1978. Application of uneven-aged silviculture and management on public and private lands. In USDA Forest Serv. *Uneven-aged silviculture and management in the United States,* USDA For. Serv. Washington, D.C. pp. 25–61.

Marquis, D. A., T. J. Grisez, J. C. Bjorkbom, and B. A. Roach. 1975. Interim guide to regeneration of Allegheny hardwoods. *USDA For. Serv. Gen. Tech. Rep. NE-19.* 14 pp.

Marsh, G. P. 1882. *The earth as modified by human action.* Charles Scribner's Sons, New York. 675 pp.

McGee, C. E. 1975. Regeneration alternatives in mixed oak stands. *USDA For. Serv. Res. Pap. SE-125.* 8 pp.

McGee, C. E., and R. M. Hooper. 1970. Regeneration after clearcutting in the southern Appalachians. *USDA For. Serv. Res. Pap. SE-70.* 12 pp.

McGee, C. E., and R. M. Hooper. 1975. Regeneration trends 10 years after clearcutting of an Appalachian hardwood stand. *USDA For. Serv. Res. Note SE-227.* 4 pp.

McKnight, J. S. 1966. Application of uneven-aged silviculture to southern hardwoods. In *Proc. Symp. on hardwoods of Piedmont and Coastal Plain.* GA. For. Res. Council, Macon, GA. pp. 61–64.

McKnight, J. S. 1969. Ecology of four hardwood species. In N. E. Linnartz (ed.), *The ecology of southern forests.* Proc. 17th Ann. For. Symp. LA. State Univ. Press, Baton Rouge, LA. pp. 99–116.

McKnight, J. S. 1970. Planting cottonwood cuttings for timber production in the South. *USDA For. Serv. Res. Pap. SO-60.* 17 pp.

McKnight, J. S., and R. C. Biesterfeldt. 1968. Commercial cottonwood planting in the southern United States. *J. For.* 66:670–675.

McKnight, J. S., and R. L. Johnson. 1975. Growing hardwoods in southern lowlands. *For. Farmer* 34(5):38–47.

Minckler, L. S. 1957. Response of pole-size white oak trees to release. *J. For.* 55:814–815.

Minckler, L. S. 1974. Prescribing silvicultural systems. *J. For.* 72:269–273.

Minckler, L. S. 1978. Flexible silviculture: help for environmental forestry. *National Park and Conservation Magazine—The Environmental Journal* 52:21–25.

Minckler, L. S., W. T. Plass, and R. A. Ryker. 1961. Woodland management by single-tree selection: a case history. *J. For.* 59:257–261.

Minckler, L. S., and J. D. Woerheide. 1965. Reproduction of hardwoods 10 years after cutting as affected by site and opening size. *J. For.* 63:103–107.

Mohn, C. A., W. K. Randall, and J. S. McKnight. 1970. Fourteen cottonwood clones selected for midsouth timber production. *USDA For. Serv. Res. Pap. SO-62.* 17 pp.

Moore, W. H., and F. M. Johnson. 1967. Nature of deer browsing on hardwood seedlings and sprouts. *J. Wildl. Mgmt.* 31:351–353.

Morris, R. C. 1955. Insect problems in southern hardwood forests. *South. Lumberman* 191(2393):136–139.

Morris, R. C., T. H. Filer, J. D. Soloman, F. I. McCracken, N. A. Overgaard, and M. J. Weiss. 1975. Insects and diseases of cottonwood. *USDA For. Serv. Gen. Tech. Rep. SO-8.* 37 pp.

Murphy, D. A. 1975. Louisiana forests; status and outlook. *USDA For. Serv. Resour. Bull. SO-53.* 31 pp.

Murphy, D. A., and J. H. Ehrenreich. 1965. Effects of timber harvest and stand improvement on forage production. *J. Wildl. Mgmt.* 29:734–739.

Obye, K. D. 1958. Thinning cottonwood and willow. In *Management of bottomland forests.* Proc. 7th Ann. For. Symp., LA. State Univ. Baton Rouge, LA. pp. 35–41.

Olson, D. F., Jr., and L. Della-Bianca. 1959. Site index comparisons for several tree species in the Virginia-Carolina Piedmont. *USDA For. Serv. SE. For. Exp. Stn. Pap. 104*, Asheville, NC. 9 pp.

Patton, D. R., and B. S. McGinnes. 1964. Deer browse relative to age and intensity of timber harvest. *J. Wildl. Mgmt.* 28:458–463.

Putnam, J. A. 1951. Management of bottomland hardwoods. *USDA For. Serv. Occas. Pap. 116, So. Forest Exp. Stn.*, New Orleans, LA. 60 pp.

Putnam, J. A., G. M. Furnival, and J. S. McKnight. 1960. *Management and inventory of southern hardwoods.* USDA Agr. Hdb. No. 181. U.S. Gov. Print. Off., Washington, D.C. 102 pp.

Roach, B. A. 1977. A stocking guide for Allegheny hardwoods and its use in controlling intermediate cuttings. *USDA For. Serv. Res. Pap. NE-373, NE. For. Exp. Stn.*, Upper Darby, PA. 30 pp.

Roach, B. A., and S. F. Gingrich. 1968. *Even-aged silviculture for upland central hardwoods.* USDA For. Serv. Agr. Hdb. 355. U.S. Gov. Print. Off., Washington, D.C. 39 pp.

Robinson, G. H., R. E. Devereux, and S. S. Obenshain. 1961. Soils of Virginia. *Soil Sci.* 92:129–142.

Roth, E. R., and G. H. Hepting. 1943. Origin and development of oak stump sprouts as affecting their likelihood to decay. *J. For.* 41:27–36.

Roth, E. R., and B. Sleeth. 1939. Butt rot in unburned sprout oak stands. *USDA Tech. Bull. 684.* 43 pp.

Scholz, H. F. 1948. Diameter-growth studies of northern red oak and their possible silvicultural implications. *IA. State Coll. J. Sci.* 22:421–429.

Schnur, L. G. 1937. Yield, stand and volume tables for even-aged upland oak forests. *USDA Tech. Bull. 560.* 88 pp.

Shaw, S. P., and T. H. Ripley. 1965. Managing the forest for sustained yield of woody browse for deer. In *Proc. Soc. Am. For. pp. 229–233.*

Shropshire, F. W. 1971. Hardwood management techniques of natural stands. In *Proc. Symp. on southeastern hardwoods. SE Area—S&PF, U.S. For. Serv.*, Atlanta, GA. pp. 1–7.

Shutts, L. M. 1974. Summer grape. In Shrubs and vines for northeastern wildlife. *USDA For. Serv. Gen. Tech. Rep. NE-9.* pp. 52–53.

Smith, H. C., and N. I. Lamson. 1977. Stand development 25 years after a 9.0-inch diameter-limit first cutting in Appalachian hardwoods. *USDA For. Serv. Res. Pap. NE-379.* 4 pp.

Smith, H. C., R. L. Rosier, and K. P. Hammack. 1976. Reproduction 12 years after seed-tree harvest cutting in Appalachian hardwoods. *USDA For. Serv. Res. Pap. NE-350.* 11 pp.

Smith, H. C., and P. M. Smithson. 1975. Cost of cutting grapevines before logging. *USDA For. Serv. Res. Note NE-207.* 4 pp.

Soc. Am. Foresters. 1926. Committee of the Southern Appalachian Section: a forest classification for the Southern Appalachian Mountains and the plateau and coastal region. *J. For.* 24:673–684.

Soc. Am. Foresters. 1954. *Forest cover types of North America (exclusive of Mexico).* Washington, D.C. 67 pp.

Soil Survey Staff. 1975. Soil taxonomy: a basic system of soil classification for making and interpreting soil surveys. *USDA Hdbk. 436.* U.S. Gov. Print. Off., Washington, D.C. 754 pp.

Sonderman, D. L., and R. L. Brisbin. 1978. A quality classification system for young hardwood trees—the first step in predicting future products. *USDA For. Serv. Res. Pap. NE-419.* 7 pp.

Sternitzke, H.. S. 1975. Shifting hardwood trends in the South. *South. Lumberman* 231(2872):72–73.

Sternitzke, H. S., and J. F. Christopher. 1970. Land clearing in the lower Mississippi Valley. *Southeast. Geographer* 10(1):63–66.

Stubbs, J. 1973. Atlantic oak-gum-cypress. In Silvicultural systems for the major forest types of the United States. *USDA Agric. Hdb. 445.* pp. 89–93.

Toole, R. E. 1959. Decay after fire injury to southern bottomland hardwoods. *USDA Tech. Bull. 1189.* 25 pp.

Toole, R. E., and W. M. Broadfoot. 1959. Sweetgum blight as related to alluvial soils of the Mississippi River floodplain. *For. Sci.* 5:2–10.

Trimble, G. R., Jr. 1967. Diameter increase in second-growth Appalachian hardwood stands—a comparison of species. *USDA For. Serv. Res. Note NE-75.* 5 pp.

Trimble, G. R., Jr. 1971. Diameter-limit cutting in Appalachian hardwoods: boon or bane? *USDA For. Serv. Res. Pap. NE-208.* 14 pp.

Trimble, G. R., Jr. 1973a. Appalachian mixed hardwoods. In silviculture systems for the major forest types of the United States. *USDA Agr. Hdbk. 445.* pp. 80–82.

Trimble, G. R., Jr. 1973b. Response to crop-tree release by 7-year-old stems of yellow-poplar and black cherry. *USDA For. Serv. Res. Pap. NE-253.* 10 pp.

Trimble, G. R., Jr. 1975. Summaries of some silvical characteristics of several Appalachian hardwood trees. *USDA For. Serv. Gen. Tech. Rep. NE-16.* 5 pp.

Trimble, G. R. Jr., and G. Hart. 1961. An appraisal of early reproduction after clearcutting in northern Appalachian stands. *USDA For. Serv. Res. Pap. 162.* 22 pp.

Trimble, G. R., Jr., J. H. Patric, J. D. Gill, G. H. Moeller, and J. N. Kochenderfer. 1974. Some options for managing forest land in the central Appalachians. *USDA For. Serv. Gen. Tech. Rep. NE-12.* 42 pp.

Trimble, G. R., Jr., and R. L. Rosier. 1972. Elimination of scattered residual saplings left after clearcut harvesting of Appalachian hardwoods. *USDA For. Serv. Res. Note NE-146.* 4 pp.

Trimble, G. R., Jr., and D. W. Seegrist. 1973. Epicormic branching on hardwood trees bordering forest openings. *USDA For. Serv. Res. Pap. NE-261.* 6 pp.

Trimble, G. R., Jr., and E. H. Tryon. 1974. Grapevines a serious obstacle to timber production on good hardwood sites in Appalachia. *North. Logger Timber Process.* 23(5):22,23,44.

Trippensee, R. E. 1948. *Wildlife Management, Volume I.* McGraw-Hill Book Co., New York. 479 pp.

U.S. Dept. Comm. 1968. *Climatic atlas of the United States.* U.S. Gov. Print. Off., Washington, D.C.

USDA For. Serv. 1965. Silvics of forest trees of the United States. *USDA Agr. Hdbk. 271.* U.S. Gov. Print. Off., Washington, D.C. 762 pp.

USDA For. Serv. 1969. A forest atlas of the south. *USDA For. Serv. So. For. Exp. Stn. and SE. For. Exp. Stn.*, New Orleans, LA, and Asheville, NC. 27 pp.

USDA For. Serv. 1974. The outlook for timber in the United States. *For. Resour. Rep. No. 20.* 374 pp.

USDA For. Serv. 1978. *Forest Statistics of the U.S., 1977.* USDA For. Serv. U.S. Gov. Print. Off., Washington, D.C. 133 pp.

Wells, C. G., R. E. Campbell, L. F. DeBano, C. E. Lewis, R. L. Fredriksen, E. C. Franklin, R. C. Froelieh, and P. H. Dunn. 1979. Effects of fire on soil:a state-of-knowledge review. *USDA For. Serv. Gen. Tech. Rep. WO-7.* 34 pp.

Wendel, G. W. 1971. Converting hardwoods on poor sites to white pine by planting and direct seedling. *USDA For. Serv. Res. Pap. NE-188.* 19 pp.

Wendel, G. W. 1975. Stump sprout growth and quality of several Appalachian hardwood species after clearcutting. *USDA For. Serv. Res. Pap. NE-329.* 9 pp.

Wendel, G. W. 1977. Longevity of black cherry, wild grape, and sassafras seed in the forest floor. *USDA For. Serv. Res. Pap. NE-375.* 6 pp.

Wendel, G. W., and G. R. Trimble, Jr. 1968. Early reproduction after seed-tree harvest cuttings in Appalachian hardwoods. *USDA For. Serv. Res. Pap. NE-99.* 16 pp.

6

The Southern
Pine Region

Laurence C. Walker

LOCATION

The Southern Pine Region as here defined includes the southern Atlantic and Gulf Coastal Plains, the Piedmont Province, and the Fall-Line Sandhills that lie between the Atlantic Coastal Plain and the Piedmont. It also takes in the Ozark and Ouachita mountains, usually known as the Interior Highlands. Bottomlands of the river courses, the swamps, the Brown Loam Bluffs, and the Mississippi Delta, while interrupting these physiographic provinces, will only occasionally contain southern pines and are, hence, covered in Chapter 5. The 320,000 square mile Coastal Plain supports the most extensive and productive forests of the South.

The region lies generally to the east of the Texas and Oklahoma prairies and to the south of the Missouri, Ohio, and Potomac rivers. As the Southern Appalachian and associated mountains are predominantly covered with hardwood forests, these areas are included in the Southern Hardwood Region. The location of the Atlantic Fall-Line may be readily recognized from political maps because it lies just southeastward of an axis joining many of the major cities of the East: Trenton, Philadelphia, Wilmington, Baltimore, Washington, Richmond, Raleigh, Columbia, Augusta, Macon, and Columbus. Physiographically, the Fall-Line marks the transition from the crystalline geologic formations of the Piedmont to the sedimentary formations of the Coastal Plain. In Fig. 5-1 this region includes the area of oak-pine forests, the Coastal Plain, and a portion of the Interior Highlands located in middle and southern Arkansas.

FOREST STATISTICS

Area

The total land area of the Southern Pine Region comprises about 200 million acres in 12 states. About 60 percent of the land is forested, most of which is potential commercial forest land. Almost 100 million acres are in pine types.

For the whole East, about 53 million acres are in the loblolly pine—shortleaf pine type. Over 18 million acres are in the longleaf pine—slash pine type, and approximately 14 million acres of forest land are unstocked. Growing stock of southern pines is 75 billion cubic feet. Sawtimber inventory is 260 billion board feet. Annual softwood sawtimber growth exceeds harvest by almost 6 million board feet (USDA For. Serv., 1974, interpolated).

The loblolly pine—shortleaf pine types support 7 million animal-unit-months of domesticated livestock and the longleaf pine—slash pine type about 11 million. Almost all of the 13 million and 12 million acres grazed in the respective types is considered exploitive. Less than 200,000 acres of longleaf pine and slash pine forests are intensively managed for livestock. None is so managed for the loblolly and shortleaf pine types (USDA For. Serv., 1977a).

Some 20 species of hardwoods of potential commercial value occur on pine sites in the Coastal Plain. These make up almost 50 billion cubic feet in small, low-quality stems (USDA For. Serv., 1976).

Character of Forest Land Ownership

About 90 percent of the forest land is privately owned. Companies hold less than 20 percent, about 40 million acres. Farmers and other relatively small owners combined hold about 144 million acres, or 72 percent of the total.

National forests and other federal holdings in the region encompass about 15 million acres. Also, considerable acreage is owned (and much of it is managed) by the U.S. Department of Defense. There are about 3 million acres in national parks and national monuments—which are not available for commercial timber management. Probably less than 1 percent of the land in pine types is set aside for park and similar uses (USDA For. Serv., 1974). About 10 wilderness areas are located in the region's Coastal Plain (USDA For. Serv., 1977a).

Forest Industries

Pulp-producing industries are the greatest users of wood in this region. There are about 114 pulp mills within its bounds, utilizing some 47 million cords of round wood and residues per year, principally for kraft paper and newsprint. Softwoods provide about three-fourths of the raw material (Bertelson, 1977). Two-thirds of the nation's pulping capacity is in the South.

Sawtimber accounts for 42 percent of the annual harvests. This includes bolts for plywood, which was first made from southern pine in 1962. As of this writing, almost 16 percent of the softwood sawtimber cut is utilized for plywood. Other important forest industries produce naval stores (Fig. 6-1), poles, pilings, crossties, and pallets, the latter two manufactured largely from hardwoods.

Other Forest Benefits

Forests of this region are relatively free from the demands of water-resource management. Also, the gentle relief reduces the pressure for cautious watershed protection measures in silvicultural operations. However, as Best Man-

Figure 6-1. Slash pine plantation in south Georgia, planted and streaked for naval-stores production (Ga. Forestry Com.).

agement Practices prescribed by the Environmental Protection Agency are mandated, silvicultural systems even for this region will involve consideration for minimal nonpoint source pollution.

Because the forests of these provinces (apart from the Interior Highlands) lack the aesthetic value attributed to mountainous areas, relatively little use is made of the woods for organized recreation and camping. However, the forests are extensively used by individuals for hunting and fishing and for private sportsmen's camps. Clubs have been organized on holdings of large industries as gestures of good will and in the interest of reducing wildfires, timber theft, and vandalism.

Population Shifts

Because of agricultural decline, people have been moving out of the region and from rural into urban areas, though recent censuses indicate a reversal in this trend. Mechanized agriculture, federal crop production limitations, land purchases by industry for forest use, and the elimination of the inefficient farmer are among the factors responsible for this reduction. As a result, the labor force which has remained in rural areas is more dependent than previously upon forest industry for employment. The current shift back to the smaller towns by industries will have an effect upon the woods-labor supply.

THE PHYSICAL ENVIRONMENT

Climate

Most of the region has a humid subtropical climate, characterized by high temperatures and abundant precipitation. Growing seasons are 180 days or longer, increasing to more than 320 days in the southernmost part of Florida. High temperatures over these long growing seasons provide abundant energy for tree growth.

Precipitation averages 40 to 60 inches annually. Its even distribution throughout the year is important for tree growth. In the southwestern part of the region, more rain falls in winter than in summer but, even there, summer rain averages more than 40 percent of the annual total. To the east, and especially the southeast, summer rain accounts for 50 to 60 percent of the annual total. This proportion rises to slightly more than 60 percent in southern Florida.

Although annual and seasonal statistics for the region show that it is well watered, the silviculturist should be aware that droughts frequently occur. The dry spell during the growing season that may last for several weeks, causing trees to lose vigor and predisposing them to lethal insect attack, is particularly critical.

A related problem is the mode of occurrence of the precipitation. Warm-season rainfall in the region is mainly in the form of thundershowers of high intensity and brief duration. Thunderstorms may be experienced 50 or more days per year in all but the eastern and extreme southwestern parts of the region. Since thunderstorms occur while the forest is in full foliage, the canopy intercepts some of the rainfall. Much of this intercepted precipitation may evaporate before reaching the soil. Thus, the southwestern part of the region is drier than other climatic indicators suggest.

Coastal Plain

Physiography.   Along the Atlantic Ocean and the Eastern Gulf, the Coastal Plain is characterized by a series of terraces oriented almost parallel to the present coastline. Toward the coast these terraces are lower in elevation and relief (hence the common designation "lower" coastal plain), and tend to be flatter and more poorly drained. Except where drainage is so poor that permanent swamps develop, such low terraces are called "flatwoods."

Lying approximately parallel to the coastline, the Western Gulf Coastal Plain, composed of alternating low ridges and valleys, produces "belted" topography. The Florida peninsula and the great alluvial valley of the lower Mississippi River interrupt these patterns and, hence, require separate description, the latter in Chapter 5.

From central North Carolina northward, the Atlantic Coastal Plain is indented by bays and estuaries penetrating halfway or more to the Piedmont, thus dividing the land into a series of peninsula-like tracts. Zones of poor drainage also include extensive undissected areas like the Okefenokee Swamp in Georgia and Florida, elliptical bays found on sandy terrain, and the more extensive pocosins of the lower terraces. Bays are shallow depressions with well-defined sandy rims, often enclosing lakes and peat swamps. Pocosins are swamps of organic soils, covering a few to several thousand acres, that have developed where dunes along shorelines impeded drainage (Fig. 6-2).

Bays and estuaries indenting the Gulf coastline and offshore barrier islands provide a pattern much like that along the Atlantic, but individual features tend to be smaller. Adjacent to the coast is a series of low and often poorly drained deltaic plains and grassy marshes. Next inland is a narrow zone of depositional

Figure 6-2.   Remnants of a pond pine stand on a very poorly drained section frequently swept by severe wildfire. The trees are about 8 inches d.b.h. and exhibit the typically deformed bole resulting from recurring fire injuries (T. E. Maki).

terraces, called the "Pine Hills." These are similar to those of the Atlantic Coastal Plain, but fewer, narrower, and less distinct. The innermost and most extensive division is a zone of belted topography developed on more steeply dipping beds alternating between fine- and coarse-grained sediments.

Departing from the general pattern of the Gulf Coastal Plain is the loess-covered and deeply dissected Brown Bluff Hills along the eastern side of the Mississippi River alluvial lowland, discussed in Chapter 5. Pines are often planted on these loess soils for erosion control.

Southward from southern Georgia, an extensive flat-topped plateau rises abruptly from the sea floor. In the northern part of the exposed section of this plateau is a central upland reaching an elevation of nearly 300 feet and containing broad flat areas, hills, swamps, and numerous lakes. The surface is mainly sandy, but underneath is soluble calcareous material. On either side of the central upland are terraced marine lowlands normally less than 100 feet in elevation and containing old and new beach ridges with intervening swales.

Geology and Soils.   The soils (Fig. 6-3) of the Coastal Plain are underlain by a variety of rock materials. These rocks, however, are of little consequence to soil genesis as the entire region is built of water-laid deposits of sand, clay, and marl. Most soils are sandy, although along the Fall-Line a few ledges of limestone clay occur with the coarse sand deposits, and red clays are found in the upper Coastal Plain of the East and in eastern Texas. Some sands and clays are derived from disintegrated rocks transported from the Piedmont. The lowermost beds in the region contain vegetable remains and brackish-water shells.

Upland soils of the Coastal Plain tend to be acidic and so strongly leached that organic matter and nutrient levels are low. The upper one to three feet of soil is mainly yellowish or reddish with textures varying from sand to clay, although sandy loam and silty loam are common (Pearson and Ensminger, 1957).

B horizons, often mottled red and yellow, are more clayey. In some cases hardpans have developed, usually due to accumulation of clay, aggradation, compaction, or fossil horizons (Nikiforoff *et al.*, 1948).

Under poorly drained conditions at low elevations, ground-water podzols and similar soils are found. These tend to show an organic-rich layer at the surface, underlain by a thin organic- and iron-rich hardpan which is either mottled yellow and brown or dark brown. Such soils are common from New Jersey to North Carolina (Hanna and Obenshain, 1957).

Another zone called "flatwoods" extends from central Alabama into northeastern Mississippi, terminating near the Tennessee line. It is a 6- to 12-mile-wide soil and physiographic region. At an elevation of only 200 to 300 feet, a smooth surface has developed on an outcropping of a cold, gray, stiff, poorly drained clay. When wet, the soil is sticky; when dry, it is hard and cracked. The cracks in dry weather and the crayfish holes in wet are the principal conductors of oxygen to lower horizons. (A descriptive local name for this soil is "crawfish gumbo.") Flatwood soils elsewhere are usually clay loam, sandy loam, or sand.

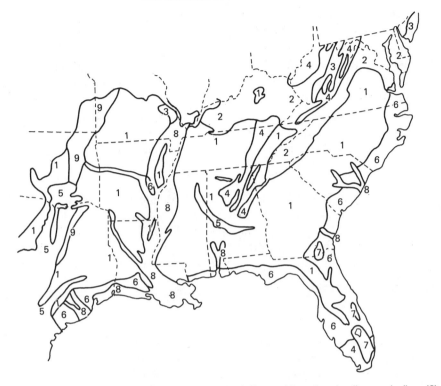

Figure 6-3. Soil regions of the southern United States. (1) red and yellow podzolics, (2) gray-brown podzolics, (3) podzols, (4) lithosols, (5) rendzina, (6) wiesenboden, ground-water podzol, and half-bog, (7) bog, (8) alluvium, (9) planosols (after U.S. Dept. of Agr., 1957). In the 7th Approximation World Classification, these are (1) Ultisols, (2) Alfisols, (3) Spodosols, (4) Entisols, (5) Mollisols, (6) Spodosols and Alfisols, (7) Histisols, (8) Vertisols, and (9) Alfisols and Ultisols.

Soils of the northernmost part of the Atlantic Coastal Plain are members of the Gray-Brown Podzolic group. Textures are about the same as for the Red-Yellow soils described earlier, although less acidic and higher in plant nutrients.

Soils of the coasts are characterized by beach and dune sand, peat and muck, or marsh deposits. As a rule profiles are poorly developed (Hanna and Obenshain, 1957; Henderson and Smith, 1957).

Other features of the Coastal Plain important in forestry are:

1. Savannas: These open, flat lands with poorly drained soils, often waterlogged, support poor growth of pine, dense hydrophytic shrubs, and grass. They are called "prairies" west of the Mississippi River.

2. Sand dunes and salt-spray sites: They are common on barrier islands and strips of the mainland up to one mile inland along the Atlantic and Gulf

coast. Deep, infertile sites—subject at frequent intervals to storm-blown salt or temporary flooding by seawater—favor xeric, salt-tolerant shrubs and trees such as waxmyrtle, yaupon, and live oak.

3. Western Florida sand hills: Areas of deep sands lie intermittently, at slightly higher elevations, with finer-textured soils. Originally longleaf pine, the new stands are generally slash pine.

4. New Jersey pine barrens: About half of the level, sandy Coastal Plain of this state is occupied by relatively open, pure, or nearly pure stands of pitch pine. Site quality in these areas is low, tree heights ranging from 25 to 55 feet at maturity. Within the barrens are "plains" supporting sprout pitch pine and scrub oak.

5. The Post Oak Belt of Texas: From 50 to 100 miles wide, this zone forms a transition between the pine and oak-pine types to the east and the tall-grass prairies (now mostly farmed) to the west. The soil, however, is a continuation of that of the pine-hardwood forest to the east. Stands are dominated by post and blackjack oaks. Except in the most favorable sites, tree growth is slow and form is poor.

Piedmont

Physiography. The Piedmont Province, extending from above the Potomac to Alabama, is the easternmost section of the Appalachian Highlands. It is narrow in the north—only 50 miles wide in Maryland, broadening to 125 miles in North Carolina and narrowing again further south. Elevations range from 300 to 1,200 feet above sea level. The province is covered in this chapter because of the similarity of the principal commercial forest species—loblolly and shortleaf pines and mixed hardwoods—to the Coastal Plain.

Geology and Soils. The rocks of this province are very old and most of them are metamorphic. Gneisses and schists, along with some marble and quartzite, cover about half of the surface area and tend to form uplands. About 20 percent of the surface consists of granite whose resistance to erosion also tends to produce uplands and some striking isolated features, the most notable being Stone Mountain in Georgia.

Piedmont soils are mainly either sandy loam or clay loam and slightly acid. Mineral nutrient content of virgin soil, except for nitrogen, is fairly high (Pearson and Ensminger, 1957). Soils developed on acidic rocks with high silica content (e.g., granite, including its metamorphosed forms) are usually coarser textured and lower in base elements than those formed on basic rocks. Soils derived from horizontal beds of schists are thin and dry, while vertical beds of schists produce deep, well-drained soils.

Widespread clearing and continuous cultivation of row crops on sloping land surfaces, porous surface layers over heavier subsoils, and intense rain storms have left the locality seriously eroded. Every part has lost 25 percent or more of its topsoil; from southern Virginia southward more than three-fourths of the

Piedmont has lost three-fourths or more of the loamy topsoil (U.S. Dept. of Agr., 1957).

Erosion has exposed the reddish subsoils, often plastic clay which cannot absorb more than an inch of water in 36 hours (USDA For. Serv., Southeast. For. Exp. Stn., 1951). Not only do these presently exposed surface soils absorb water poorly, they also have low organic matter content.

Interior Highlands

Physiography. Interior Highlands refers to two elevated physiographic provinces of unequal size and dissimilar character. The larger, lying north of the Arkansas River, is an area of broad plateaus and low mountains called the Ozark Plateaus of the Boston Mountains. The smaller Ouachita Province lies to the south. In both, the most important commercial species are shortleaf pine and upland hardwoods.

Geology and Soils. The Ozark Plateaus are formed on a broad, domed upwarp, consisting mostly of limestone and dolomite with large amounts of chert, and bounded by lowlands on all sides: Elevations rise to more than 2,200 feet. The valley of the Arkansas River occupies a structural and topographic trough 25 to 35 miles wide, most of which lies only 300 to 600 feet above sea level. Low ridges produced by minor folding are prominent features of the southern part of the valley.

The Ouachita Mountains, an area about 100 miles wide and 225 miles from east to west, consists of narrow, east-west folds and intervening valleys formed mainly on sandstones and shales. Elevations are as low as 500 to 600 feet in the east, but rise to about 2,600 feet near the Oklahoma-Arkansas boundary.

Steep slopes have lithosols high in concentrations of chert fragments. Soils derived from the cherty limestone are strongly acid and low in available nutrients. The best soils and the most luxuriant forests are developed on relatively pure limestone.

Sandstone of the ridges of the Ouachita Mountains produces shallow, stony soils of low fertility which are managed almost exclusively for forests. The shales of the valleys yield more productive, finer-textured soils, most of which have adequate internal drainage for good tree growth.

Because of the prevailing east-west orientation of the Interior Highlands, high insolation on south-facing slopes affects more of the forested land than in other moutainous regions in the East. This, combined with the erratic rainfall and high temperature, limits a large part of the mountain section to forest types adapted to poor soils and dry sites.

MAJOR FOREST TYPE GROUPS

Classification and description of the many forest types occurring over this diversified region have been handicapped by the relatively rapid changes in stand composition resulting from clearing, timber harvesting, and other activities of man. Information on original forest types is presented by Braun (1950), who recorded species composition data from observations on remaining undisturbed stands and from records surviving from pioneer days. Committees of the Society of American Foresters have described 63 recognizable forest types within the Southern Pine Region (Soc. Am. For., 1954). The periodic forest resource surveys made by the U.S. Forest Service afford the best available information on present-day forest-cover-type distribution.

The principal conifer forest cover types are loblolly pine, shortleaf pine, loblolly pine–shortleaf pine, slash pine, longleaf pine, slash pine–longleaf pine, and pine–hardwood. Lesser pines include Virginia, pond, spruce, and sand. Eastern redcedar occurs also with the complex mixture of hardwoods.

Coastal Plain

Major upland types include loblolly pine–shortleaf pine—23 percent of the total Coastal Plain forest; longleaf pine–slash pine—17 percent; oak–pine—14 percent; and oak–hickory—19 percent (Table 6-1). Pond pine, sand pine, Virginia pine, and redcedar make up less than 3 percent of the total. The proportion of hardwood in upland types and the relative area occupied by types in which hardwoods predominate are believed to have increased during the past century, although much abandoned farmland now grows pure pine.

The longleaf pine–slash pine type predominates on sandy flatwoods where hardpans underlie the surface soils. The type seldom regenerates naturally to the same two principal components; but, rather, converts to pure stands of either species. Slash pine is not found naturally west of the Mississippi, but planted stands have been established in Texas, Louisiana, and southern Arkansas.

TABLE 6-1

Approximate Area (in thousands of acres) of Pine and Pine-Related Forest, by Types, in the Physiographic Provinces of the Southern Pine Region

Major Forest Type	Coastal Plain	Piedmont	Interior Highlands
Longleaf–slash pine	21,095	593	—
Loblolly–shortleaf pine	28,980	11,462	3,799
Redcedar[a]	244	162	932
Pond pine	2,421	28	—
Virginia pine	139	1,723	—
Sand pine	422	—	—
Oak-pine	18,351	5,981	2,185
Total	71,652	19,949	6,916

Source: Compiled by author from recent published and unpublished forest survey data supplied by the U.S. Forest Service (USDA For. Serv., 1977a).
[a] Includes redcedar–hardwoods where separately estimated.

Loblolly pine, so called by the pioneers because it occurred in the "loblollies"—muddy holes—along the Atlantic coast, is found throughout the Coastal Plain except in lower peninsular Florida. It is often accompanied by shortleaf pine, sweetgum, oaks, and hickories. The latter two species, moderately tolerant of shade, reproduce under the canopy of the pines, whereas the pines seldom do so. Hence, in time, pure loblolly pine, shortleaf pine, or loblolly pine—shortleaf pine mixtures become pine—hardwood cover types and, upon elimination of the conifers by lightning (they are the tallest trees), bark beetles, fire, or harvest, ecological succession progresses to an oak—hickory climax type. Lesser broadleaf species will also invade the stand, making, under some conditions, a truly mixed hardwood, uneven-aged forest. On some sites, the climax forest may be magnolia—beech (Kurz, 1944). Openings in stands may result in the entrance here and there of a few pines while, under the canopies and in the openings, eastern redcedar may occur.

Although considered a moist-site species, loblolly pine has wide site tolerance and is often found on relatively dry areas. It is frequently associated with longleaf pine and when fire is excluded may replace the latter, especially after harvests. Shortleaf pine may invade with the loblolly pine in some areas.

Old-field stands of shortleaf and loblolly pines are common throughout the Coastal Plain. Where a seed source is available and the mineral soil is exposed, as by abandonment of cultivated land, dense old-field stands may occur. Where seed is scarce or where brush, forbs, or grass sod have captured the site, old-field stands are sparse, giving rise to "wolf" trees of poor form.

Spruce pine is rarely found in pure stands. It is associated with loblolly pine and hardwoods in the second bottoms and on the moist fringes surrounding longleaf pine forests. Pond pine is found in the pocosins and flatwoods of the Atlantic Coast, sand pine in the Florida peninsula and the West Florida sandhills, and Atlantic white-cedar, southern baldcypress, and pond-cypress in the swamps (Chapter 5).

Upland hardwood types, constituting nearly one-fifth of the Coastal Plain forests, are in part native and in part the result of past land use. Narrow bands of hardwoods occur along drainages and minor streams in areas otherwise dominated by pines.

Considerable land originally in pine, especially on sandhill sites, reverted after cutting to essentially pure scrub hardwoods. Perhaps even more extensive are the areas where removal of pine trees from pine-hardwood stands has left little but hardwoods, mostly red oak and sweetgum, as growing stock.

Piedmont Province

Before the intrusion of white settlers into the Piedmont, nearly one-half of that area was probably occupied by pine—mixed hardwood stands. Over one-third of the area supported only hardwoods, principally oaks and hickories on "red lands." The hardwoods have been discussed in some detail in Chapter 5. Pure pine stands were found on soils derived from sandstone or granitic rocks (Nelson, 1957). At present the forests of the Piedmont Province are classed as

35 percent loblolly pine—shortleaf pine, 19 percent oak—pine, 31 percent oak—hickory, 7 percent oak—gum—cypress, 5 percent Virginia pine, and 2 percent or less of longleaf pine—slash pine and elm—ash—cottonwood (Table 6-1). The loblolly pine—shortleaf pine type, while well distributed throughout the province, occupies more land in Georgia and South Carolina than in any other Piedmont state. Longleaf pine—slash pine and oak—gum—cypress types are found principally in Georgia, while the Virginia pine type is concentrated mainly in Virginia, North Carolina, and eastern Tennessee. Oak—pine and oak—hickory types occupy large areas throughout the province, accounting for one-half of the forested area.

Interior Highlands

Present forests of the Interior Highlands are classified as 68 percent oak—hickory, occurring on upland sites, and 5 percent other hardwood types, mostly in the bottoms. Loblolly pine—shortleaf pine types (here almost exclusively shortleaf) make up 15 percent of the forest area and pine—hardwoods another 7 percent. Greatest concentrations of shortleaf pine are on south- and west-facing slopes in the Ouachita Mountains of Arkansas and easternmost Oklahoma, where extensive pure pine stands have been maintained under public and industrial management.

Original hardwood forests of the Interior Highlands were rich in variety of species and value of timber products. Along streams and on lower slopes, white oak, black walnut, black cherry, elm, sycamore, sugar maple, and eastern redcedar attained large diameter and excellent form. On drier slopes and ridges, stands of red and black oaks, hickories, and other more xeric hardwoods prevailed, usually as poorly developed, marginally merchantable trees.

Eastern redcedar now occurs primarily on shallow soils, usually over relatively chert-free limestone. Although heavily cut for posts and lumber, there are indications that the type is maintaining itself and, perhaps, may be invading the overgrazed grasslands of the "glade" type in southwest Missouri. Maple (1957) reported growth rates for eastern redcedar on deeper soil high enough to indicate possibilities for economic culture in this region where post and lumber markets are available for material of small sizes.

HISTORY OF FOREST USE

Agriculture

Land clearing for agriculture on a grand scale began along the eastern seaboard as early as 1650 in the northern Coastal Plain and one-hundred years later in the South. Early settlers rapidly cleared land for cotton and tobacco—two crops with great soil-depleting potential. Though productive when first cleared, the soil lacked stability; the resulting erosion and infertility encouraged abandonment.

The hills of the Piedmont, among the most fertile areas of the South, were largely cleared for agriculture before 1860. By the 1930s, most topsoil had eroded away and gullies were so extensive that further cultivation was hopeless. Over 70 years ago one observer noted that both industrial communities and agrarian sites literally had washed down the hills (Hilgard, 1906). Many acres are still eroding, but much of the area has been stabilized by conversion to pasture or forest.

Logging

Somewhat independent of agriculture, the great migration of the lumber industry from the Lake States to the South occurred between 1890 and 1920. Much land, especially the flatwoods in the Southeast, has never been cultivated, but has been cut-over and naturally reforested several times. As recently as the late 1930s, virgin forests were cut in eastern Texas.

Next to agricultural abandonment, the most pronounced trend in land use is acquisition of sawmills and their holdings by large pulp and paper manufacturers. The end of World War II marked the beginning of this trend. Transfers of this nature continue to the present time.

Logging practices have run the course in the region: from ox teams and logging wheels to mule teams, ground skidders, tram railroads, and finally to rubber-tired tractor-skidding feller-bunchers and truck hauling (Fig. 6-4). Very

Figure 6-4.   Oxen teamed to haul logs from southern pineries of the virgin forest. Note the red-heart rot in the cross sections (Southern Pine Lumber Co. collection, Stephen F. Austin State Univ.).

few logs are moved by trains today; but pulp sticks are frequently concentrated in yards perhaps 50 miles from where they are cut, and then transported by rail as much as 150 miles to mills. Now, tree-length logging and integrated utilization are rapidly increasing in popularity. The whole bole is brought to the mill, and its destiny, or that of its parts, assigned to piling, poles, plywood, lumber, pulp, or posts. Trucks are rigged to load and haul isolated insect- or lightning-killed trees from the forests. Previously, these could not be removed economically, and insect infestations resulted.

The first paper mill in the South appeared in the 1930s; the first newsprint from southern pine was produced in 1939, and the first southern pine plywood was manufactured in 1962.

Silviculture

Cutting of the second-growth began in earnest during World War II. Shortly thereafter tree-planting and then direct seeding hastened the development of "The South's Third Forest." Hand-planting with dibbles on burned-over and cut-over lands was replaced largely by machines in the 1950s, though dibbles remain a useful tool on small tracts.

Silvicultural practices have progressed dramatically from the cut-out-and-get-out days, ending in the 1930s. Then regeneration was of little concern because wildfires precluded establishment of new stands. Yet, the second-growth forest did follow, many stands escaping fires or regenerating because of fire at the right time (to prepare seedbeds and control competition and disease). By this time, thinnings of pulpwood-size stems were marketed for the many new paper mills springing up throughout the area.

Thinning, often confused with selection regeneration harvests, resulted in sparse reproduction. Hence clearcutting and planting became common practices. This transition, most pronounced in the mid-sixties on government and industrial ownerships, was inevitable. Logging partially cut stands is costly, and getting natural regeneration following selection and shelterwood cutting is improbable. Thus, economics and ecology were teamed to encourage harvesting of large tracts, utilizing bulldozers to windrow the brush for burning and heavy disk plows to prepare the site.

As management intensified, the use of genetically superior planting stock—beginning in the 1950s—occurred. Seeds were obtained from superior trees in the forest, screened for quality throughout the region, and harvested from seed orchards of grafted control-pollinated stock where clones could be carefully monitored. Concurrently, nursery practices resulted in improved planting stock. Introduction of tube-grown seedlings for field planting occurred in the 1970s.

The discovery in the 1940s of synthetic hormones like 2,4-D and 2,4,5-T and ammate salts encouraged the use of these herbicides for controlling weed broadleaf trees in pine forests. In 1979 the use of 2,4,5-T was suspended by the Environmental Protection Agency. Loss of 2,4,5-T will make site preparation and hardwood control more difficult. Future use of the herbicide is in question.

THE FORESTS TODAY

A wide variety of conditions exist in the management of southern pine forests. Generally, those lands held by pulp and paper industries are as intensively managed as present-day knowledge and economics permit. Lumber companies, on the other hand, have not been as progressive. The national forests in this region are not usually intensively managed: Congressional appropriations preclude the U.S. Forest Service from keeping pace with private industry's silvicultural operations.

Small ownerships, including farm woodlands, are managed the least intensively. Although areas of less than 500 acres have profit-producing potential, the lack of capital for initiating silvicultural programs often makes the practice of forestry prohibitive. In recent years, establishment of tree farms, assistance from large-industry "public relations" foresters, enthusiasm imparted by industrially supported south-wide trade associations, financial assistance from the federal government, and educational aid by the agricultural extension service and state foresters have stimulated improved management on these small tracts.

Because of past fires, much of the land is now stocked with pines. Fires are still set promiscuously in many areas for snake eradication and tick control, to improve cattle browse, and to reduce brush. The effectiveness of burning for the first two reasons, frequently advanced by arsonists, has not been proved; but grass forage is enhanced for several months following a fire, and brush growth is checked.

Generally, the occurrence of the major southern pines relates to fire history. In the absence of fire, hardwoods encroach—from seeds and sprouts—and rapidly crowd out pine seedlings. Wildfires, of course, eliminate many pines, but on the whole have favored continuance of coniferous types. Today, prescribed burning is widely practiced for the following reasons:

1. Hazard reduction, as insurance against lethal wildfires.
2. "Rough"[1] reduction, to prepare seedbeds for natural reproduction.
3. Brownspot needle blight control in longleaf pine seedling stands.
4. Undesirable hardwood control in pine stands.
5. Grazing improvment.
6. Exposing seed in quail and turkey management.

The transition from sawlog to pulpwood production continues as logs of grade-3 quality are not uncommonly cut into 5-foot pulpwood bolts, perhaps partly because softwood growth exceeds harvest. Concomitant with increased pulpwood production is decreased use of the forest for naval stores, as tall oil, a by-product of pulping, supplies much of the demand. Chipping for gum, an

---

[1]The term "rough" designates the ground cover of longleaf and slash pine forests when unburned for one or more years.

industry which once stretched from the Atlantic Ocean to eastern Texas, is now almost limited to northern Florida and southern Georgia. However, improved chipping methods and stimulation of gum flow with sulfuric acid have encouraged production.

Among the many pressing problems in silviculture are (1) control of encroaching undesirable species on vast acreages of pine sites, (2) drainage of wet sites, (3) establishment of forests on dry, sandy sites, (4) economical management of low-quality sites, and (5) control of the southern pine beetle.

SILVICULTURE OF THE MAJOR TYPE GROUPS

Longleaf Pine–Slash Pine Type Group

Longleaf pine–slash pine forests are subject to conversion to pure stands of either species by use of certain regeneration practices. The natural occurrence together of the two species is difficult to maintain artificially. These, like all southern pines, require bare mineral soil for seed germination. But while longleaf pine seedlings in the grass stage benefit from prescribed burning for brownspot control, slash pine seedlings are readily killed even by low-intensity fires. Slash pines begin making height growth the first year; longleaf pines often delay 10 years, but, generally, under management they will begin height growth in the third to fifth growing season. After height growth begins, longleaf pine seedlings less than 10 feet tall are highly susceptible to fire injury. During the same period, slash pines, which may have already attained heights of over 15 feet, are rather resistant to fire injury and will endure prescribed burning for rough reduction and hardwood control. The lack of silvical harmony for the two species accounts for their exclusiveness in managed stands. Happenstance brought them together in nature.

Longleaf Pine.   Longleaf pine is most prevalent along the Gulf Coast from Louisiana to western Florida. Its demand upon the site is principally for adequate moisture without regard to soil texture or chemical composition. Where soil moisture is limiting, as is frequently the case due to vegetative competition, its growth is inhibited; yet its principal habitat is dry, upland sites where other pines do not endure the competition for soil water.

PLACE IN ECOLOGICAL SUCCESSION.   Longleaf pine, a fire subclimax type under natural conditions, continues to predominate only as long as periodic burning occurs. No doubt, grassy longleaf pine forests burned even in prehistoric times. Acreage in the type has been decreasing, giving way to slash pine along the coast and to loblolly pine in the western section of the region due to (1) fire exclusion, which favors competing species; (2) overcutting of longleaf pine followed by annual burning, which left vast expanses without even a seed tree; (3) hog grazing of seedlings rich in stored carbohydrate food; and (4) brownspot needle blight, which may effectively keep seedlings in the grass stage until they die.

GROWTH RATES. At 150 years, trees of old-growth stands often average 20 inches d.b.h. and yield four 16-foot logs. Structural materials cut from these stems are strong and durable. However, few old-growth stands remain. Second-growth managed forests are expected to grow considerably faster than the old natural stands, but wood density may be less, with a resulting decrease in the strength of the material.

In the early years—up to perhaps age 20—longleaf pine is often outgrown by slash pine due to the long periods the former may spend in the grass stage. In fully stocked, second-growth stands, longleaf pine on a site of average quality produces annually about 1 cord of pulpwood, or 200 to 400 board feet of sawtimber per acre. Trees large enough for sawlogs may be grown in 25 years. In 40 years, yields will range from 2,000 to 12,000 board feet per acre. Well-stocked stands contain about 750 stems per acre at age 15, and between 300 and 400 at age 30.

Predictions of site index based on soil features, developed by Coile and his students (Coile, 1952; McClurkin, 1953), are of particular importance for longleaf pine. Subsoil texture is the principal factor, site index increasing with an increase in fine particles. For southwestern Alabama, Hodgkins (1956) suggested that site indexing also be based upon topography. Coile noted an increase in site index with stocking density. This, however, is not always the case (Russell and Derr, 1956).

ROTATION AGE OR SIZE. The rotation age is principally dependent upon the product desired. For pulpwood, harvests may be at age 25; for sawtimber, 40-year rotations are feasible under intensive management.

CULTURAL PRACTICES—TIMBER PRODUCTION. Longleaf pine has a remarkable life history. Like other southern pines, almost two years are rquired from the time pollen is disseminated until cones are mature. Unlike the other species, longleaf pine seeds germinate shortly after dispersal in the fall. This provides for root growth during winter and, thereby, affords some degree of resistance against the hot, dry spells of the first summer. Also, a shorter period for seed consumption by birds and rodents is allowed. The 10-step calendar of events for natural regeneration in pure stands which follows is basically that of Croker and Boyer (1975).

1. Determine flower, cone, and seed production. Flowers may be counted with binoculars during the spring to ascertain probability of subsequent seed crops (month 0). Then, a year later, in the spring (month 12), cone-lets can be counted prior to cones maturing in the fall (month 18). Since abundant seed crops are sporadic and as much as 10 years apart, rotations cannot be rigidly established without supplemental seeding or planting or mechanically stimulating strobili production.

2. Harvest by seed-tree method. If sufficient seed is anticipated, the harvest of all but the seed trees should be made between late summer and early spring (months 5 to 11). About five uniformly spaced seed trees per acre are retained for subsequent stocking and insurance. In addition, cones on

trees felled in the harvest may mature, and their seed be disseminated. There is evidence that release of seed trees from competition 20 months before flowering (month -8) will appreciably improve seed crops by making available more soil moisture and light and increasing the chances of cross pollination. Complete nutrient fertilization also encourages cone production (McLemore, 1975). Seedfall is in the autumn (month 19) and germination soon thereafter (month 20).

An alternative is to make a shelterwood cut prior to seed fall (months 12 to 18), leaving about 40 trees per acre. Following seed germination, the stand is clearcut. Careful logging in final harvests will avoid serious damage to reproduction.

3. Round up hogs and cattle (month 18). Hogs are extremely detrimental to longleaf pine seedlings. Destruction by one animal occurred at the rate of over 800 trees per day (Wahlenberg, 1946). Cattle seldom browse longleaf pine seedlings, but trampling in heavily grazed areas may result in high seedling mortality.

4. Prescribed burn for seedbed preparation. Burning for rough reduction and to expose mineral soil should be done during the early winter, prior to seed fall (month 19) and germination, or in the previous winter (months 8 to 10). Contact of seed with mineral soil is necessary for germination. Other methods, though more expensive, of disturbing the rough and exposing the mineral soil are scalping, plowing, or raking.

5. Determine germination and stocking. Germination takes place within a few weeks after seed fall, conveniently enabling stocking counts during the dormant season when the rough does not camouflage the seedlings and before woody vegetation has had a chance to sprout following seedbed preparation. Milacre stocking should exceed 60 percent.

6. Survey for brownspot needle blight. Strip surveys should be run at the end of the first growing season to determine if blight is serious. If less than 300 milacres per acre are stocked with healthy seedlings, prescribed burning is suggested. Seedlings are considered unhealthy when more than 60 percent of the foliage is infected.

7. Second survey for brownspot control. If conditions warrant two or more years after the initial fire for blight control, another burn is prescribed. Again, a low-intensity winter fire, running fast with a steady wind out of the north, is preferred.

Fast-moving, low-intensity fires do not kill grass-stage seedlings because a ring of needle stubs remains unburned around the bud and thereby affords insulating protection. Once height growth starts, seedlings are easily fire-killed and remain vulnerable until about 10 feet tall. Height growth normally begins when seedlings reach an inch in diameter at the ground line.

8. Determine stocking and survival. Again, in the winter, milacre counts of survival should be made to determine if stocking is satisfactory. Sixty percent stocking is desirable.

9. Remove seed trees or shelterwood. If stocking is adequate, seed trees are removed. Timing of this harvest depends upon the conditions of the seedlings and thus the subjectively judged potential for successful stand establishment. Stagnation and loss of seedlings adjacent to the seed trees result when they are left (for insurance purposes) longer than necessary. This zone of interference was shown to extend to 50 feet (Walker and Davis, 1956). Needle casts also appreciably increase fuel supply, resulting in heavy seedling mortality close to seed trees from subsequent fires (Davis, 1955).

10. Remove hardwoods. As hardwoods compete with longleaf pine seedlings for soil moisture, light, and possibly nutrients, their removal is essential. The best time for the release of pines, for both survival and growth, appears to be during the first year after germination (Fig. 6-5). Early hardwood control is most effective on poor sites (Walker, 1954).

Group selection or clearcutting in patches is inadvisable because the "walls" or border trees of the residual forest retard seedlings in adjacent openings. This retarding effect exceeds the reach of tree crowns, extending as far as 55 feet. In addition to vigor, survival is also reduced near walls (Walker and Davis, 1954, 1956).

Intermediate management involves thinnings which reduce basal area to about 80 square feet per acre on average sites of well-stocked, evenly distributed stands that naturally attain a basal area of 120 square feet. Such thinnings may be necessary as frequently as every 10 years.

Precommercial thinning usually is not necessary. If needed, it should be done early, yet assuring a stand of 500 well-distributed crop seedlings per acre (Croker and Boyer, 1975).

Whether longleaf pines larger than sapling size respond to thinning seems to depend on the age and vigor of the trees, prethinning growth rate, and post-thinning rainfall. Heavy thinning of sapling stands increased diameter growth of the largest dominant trees but failed to increase total cubic-foot yields. The largest trees in unthinned stands may grow as rapidly in diameter as residual stems in heavily thinned areas, but because growth is usually stated in averages, stands with many trees per acre have less growth per tree than those with few stems.

Poor first-year survival has negatively influenced decisions regarding longleaf pine planting. Much early mortality is probably due to the drying out of seedlings from continued transpiration before the root system can become acclimated to the new site. Allen (1955) recommends clipping needles of planting stock to 5 inches (needles average 15 to 20 inches long) when lifted and minimizing the time between lifting and planting.

Plantations for gum naval stores generally are at about 12 × 12-foot spacing, which enables fast growth for early chipping and accessibility to faces. Elsewhere, planting is usually at 8 × 8-foot spacings.

Direct seeding is important in reforestation of longleaf pine (Fig. 6-6). It is

Figure 6-5. The 5-year-old seedling on the right was released from oak competition at age 1 and is now making height growth; the one shown on the left was never released (from Walker, 1954).

Figure 6-6.   Clearcut lands for which direct seeding is appropriate (U.S. For. Serv.).

most widely practiced in Louisiana, using seeds dipped in bird and rodent repellents.

CULTURAL PRACTICES—WILDLIFE HABITAT.   Perhaps no forests in eastern North America are managed for game production to the extent of longleaf pine. Perhaps, too, none affords more harmonious management practices for timber and game.

Wildlife enthusiasts are concerned about the effects of hardwood control on game, but chemicals and mechanical techniques now employed are inadequate for killing all of the shrubs and trees desirable for game. Of greater concern are the vast areas of unmerchantable dense pine and hardwood stands without understory plants that provide wildlife food and protection. Where intensive site preparation over extensive areas is practiced, one-fifth to one-third of the area should be left in untouched strips for wildlife food and cover. Ordinarily, however, game food is adequate, for these forests are interwoven with hardwood swamps, ponds, and drainages.

Bobwhite quail do well on cut-over and forested longleaf pine sites. This is especially so as mechanized large-scale agriculture, with reduced field borders and large improved pastures, has restricted quail and turkey habitat. On pine and pine-hardwood sites in the Southeast, one bird per 4 to 6 acres is good quail stocking. In the western part of the region, good stocking is one bird for 10 to 40 acres.

As longleaf pine is an infrequent seed producer and seeds from shrubs are insufficient in late winter, burning is prescribed to reduce the rough and thereby encourage perennial legumes. Quail require for roosting, nesting, and feeding a ground cover that is open below, but which furnishes some protection from winged enemies above. To obtain this habitat, fires are set in late winter, before Japan clover and other annual legumes germinate. Burning as early as January is detrimental to partridge peas, for fire-scarified seed may germinate prematurely near the warm surface of the blackened earth and be killed by later freezes. Burning after rains and at night when winds are still and the relative humidity high is recommended for initial fires in dense brush. Thinning overly dense stands, too, is advisable in order to encourage ground vegetation, although wood production may be sacrificed. Best quail habitat carries at least 30 percent less basal area than advocated for full stocking for timber production (Stransky, 1971a).

For turkey habitat, burning is prescribed every 3 to 4 years where fruits are dwarf varieties of blueberries or huckleberries. Such shrubs are not vigorous the year of a burn, even though occasional pruning by fire is beneficial.

Deer populations in longleaf pine forests are increasing rapidly due to law enforcement and the establishment on industrial forest lands of hunting clubs with exclusive rights. Production of deer is limited by the quality of the forest range; yet techniques, such as burning, that improve cattle forage may be beneficial to deer. While prescribed burning does not permanently affect forage quality, understory trees and shrubs are destroyed and, with them, their mast.

About 80 woody species of browse plants are available to deer in longleaf pine forests, half of which are starvation forage. Evergreen or semievergreen hardwoods and vines are preferred, while pines are browsed on severely overstocked range. Greenbrier is an especially good indicator plant: where plants are small, overbrowsing has been severe. The maximum average carrying capacity for longleaf pine lands is estimated at one deer per 26 acres by Goodrum and Reid (1958).

CULTURAL PRACTICES—RANGE MANAGEMENT.   Grazing on improved pasture is more economical than is the supplying of protein concentrates for supplementing forest range. Nevertheless, longleaf pine forests are grazed by beef cattle, often to their detriment. In much of the original forest, clearcutting and steam skidding took all large trees and knocked down small ones so that second-growth forests did not develop and a cover of bluestem grasses resulted. Because cattle ranged Coastal Plain forests for over 200 years, their migration to these cutover areas was natural.

Grazing animals trample seedlings, browse trees—mostly hardwoods, and with their hoofs expose soil to raindrop compaction and erosion. Stagheaded trees, caused by severe soil compaction, are easily killed by fire, insects, and disease. Grazing on silt-loam soils results in soil compaction sufficient to restrict water movement into and through the profile, particularly during intense rainstorms (Linnartz *et al.*, 1966).

Herbage production increases rapidly as basal area decreases below 40 square feet per acre. Yet, herbs and forbs also increase in stands above 120 square feet, probably because more light is penetrating the canopies, as such stands are generally older and have fewer trees. The grazing value of forests is negligible where 35 percent of the ground is shaded at noon (Shepherd, 1953), but this is not a very dense stand as shade in tight canopies is 60 percent or more at noon.

Prescribed burning improves quantity as well as nutritional quality of forage. However, most benefits from burning disappear long before repeat fires consistent with good silviculture are made. Grazing may be continued on a reduced capacity for fire-hazard reduction when stands close and prescribed burning is not harmonious with timber production (Fig. 6-7). Grazing capacity during spring and summer should be based entirely on burned acreages, one animal for 50 to 60 acres being typical for well-stocked stands.

Grazing capacity for an 8-month season is determined by the formula

$$\text{cow months} = \frac{\text{lbs. green grass}}{3,000}$$

This provides 3,000 pounds of green grass per month or 100 pounds per day, 40 percent of which is utilized (Campbell and Cassady, 1955).

Figure 6-7.   South Florida slash pine. Note tufted form in grazed and burned areas.

SUSCEPTIBILITY TO DAMAGE.   In addition to cone rust and needle blight, longleaf pine is subject to infection by red-heart rot and other pathogens which weaken trees to the degree that winds break limbs and stems.

Fusiform rust is, at present, not serious on longleaf pine. It is, however, reported that the encroachment of loblolly and slash pines, which are less rust resistant than longleaf pine, in sites previously supporting the latter species may increase the amount of inoculum available to infect longleaf pine (Wahlenberg, 1946).

Ips engraver bark beetles frequently attack longleaf pine stands following fires or during severe droughts, when trees are in a physiologically weakened condition. Control methods are not well established.

Pales weevil injures seedlings in freshly cutover lands. Prevention consists of waiting nine months before planting, or dipping the tops of planting stock in an insecticide (U.S. For. Serv., South. Forest Expt. Stn., 1958; Speers, 1958).

Especially in areas worked for naval stores, but recently on other sites as well, the southern pine beetle is troublesome, particularly during drought and unseasonably warm weather in winter. The black and red turpentine beetles usually breed in stumps and logs, but occasionally attack weak pines 6 feet up the trunk. The flow of resin from the pitch tubes in living trees usually drowns these beetles.

Rodents injuring longleaf pines include cotton rats and pocket gophers. Meanley and Blair (1957) reported a severe rat attack on 18- to 30-month-old seedlings in which stems were either nipped off at the ground line or girdled. Prescribed burning in fall or winter or poisoned baits in other seasons are recommended control measures.

Pocket gophers, soil-burrowing rodents, are particularly obnoxious in longleaf pine grass-stage seedling stands—both natural and planted—in sandy soils. Making extensive soil tunnels the size of an orange in their search for starch in roots, these animals can readily destroy 50 percent of the seedlings in a plantation.

Slash Pine

PLACE IN ECOLOGICAL SUCCESSION.   Slash pine is found naturally in drainages of Coastal Plain longleaf pine forests east of the Mississippi River; in moderately drained flatwoods of the southeast, particularly where protected from fire; and in sandy soils of the middle Coastal Plain. As a pioneer type, in the absence of fire, storm, or logging, it will likely be replaced with hardwoods. The presence or absence of certain mycorrhizae may also control in part the occurrence of this species.

GROWTH RATES.   Growth of slash pine on sites with an index of 90 may exceed 2 cords per acre per year at age 15, and may decline to about 1.3 cords at age 60. At 60 years, annual growth of trees 8 inches d.b.h. and larger is about 500 board feet per acre (Forbes, 1955).

For slash pine plantations 25 years of age, heights and, therefore, volumes are significantly influenced by soil drainage and by depth of the A horizon. In soils with less than 20 inches of A horizon, good drainage results in better growth. The influence of the depth of the A horizon when greater than 20 inches is not appreciable. Survival in plantations is also better on sites with high-quality ratings based on depth to fine-textured soil (Ralston, 1951; Ralston and Barnes, 1955).

ROTATION AGE OR SIZE.   While ages of slash pine stands may exceed a hundred years, economic maturity for second growth under management on most sites is at age 40 or less. Bennett's (1965) tables suggest that the maximum rotation age for plantations should be 20 to 25 years. At age 20, on site quality 70 land, d.b.h. will average almost 10 inches for trees spaced 12 × 12 feet.

CULTURAL PRACTICES—TIMBER PRODUCTION.   Thinnings in slash pine forests may begin as early as age 12. Live crowns should be maintained at least to one-third of the total tree length. Sapling- and pole-size stands frequently require thinning every 4 years, and sawtimber stands every 10 years. In the flatwoods, precommercial thinning to overcome stagnation is suggested for trees 15 to 25 feet in height, leaving a residual stand of about 600 trees per acre. On shallow soils underlain by hardpan, considerable windthrow results from partial cutting.

In naval-stores operations, thinning removes worked-out trees. Trees to be taken in intermediate cuttings are selectively marked five years before removal, and silvicultural treatments are thereby integrated with management for oleoresin production.

In addition to thinning, silviculture generally practiced for the pure slash pine type is relatively simple, consisting of prescribed burning for rough reduction, seed-tree cutting for natural regeneration, clearcutting and planting or seeding, and hardwood control.

Gallberry and titi accompany slash pine in wet areas and must be eradicated for satisfactory regeneration of the pine. Control is often with chemicals, using truck-mounted spray equipment and mist blowers.

In the sand hills of western Florida, slash pine is recommended for plantations, at a spacing of 8 × 8 feet. There, however, planting must be preceded by complete eradication of grass and hardwoods. Temperatures are, of course, higher when cover has been removed, but are not high enough to cause seedling mortality, even though rising to 125 °F (Woods, 1956). Soil moisture, on the other hand, is appreciably greater where herbaceous and scrub oak vegetation has been eliminated, resulting in more vigorous seedlings. Eradication of hardwoods and grass is by mechanical means, herbicides, and fire. On such sites, feeding roots of pine are mostly less than 3 inches deep in sandy soils, for frequent light summer rains that replenish surface soil moisture do not penetrate far into the profile. Surface soils are also richer in water-holding organic residue (Woods, 1957) (Fig. 6-8).

Slash pine is readily regenerated by direct-seeding if site preparation is employed. Growth as well as survival is improved by disking. Furrowing as an

Figure 6-8.   Slash pine planted in the sand hills following agricultural abandonment. Thinned at age 12, the stand is now 14 years old. Production has been 1.5 cords per acre per year (U.S. For. Serv.).

alternative is to be discouraged because seeds are washed away or submerged in trapped water, and soil erosion is apt to occur (Campbell and Mann, 1971).

Nitrogen and phosphorus fertilization is, under certain conditions, economically feasible in southeastern forests, especially for slash pine plantations. However, widespread fertilization in the West Gulf area is not anticipated. Costs, ecological considerations, and the inability to readily identify soils, sites, and species' races which can advantageously utilize the nutrient amendments hinder the practice (Shoulders and McKee, 1973).

CULTURAL PRACTICES—NAVAL STORES.   Rapidly receding markets now confine much of the crude oleoresin production to the northern Florida-southern Georgia area. Thus, slash pine is becoming the species principally worked. The naval stores program of the U. S. Forest Service advises the following practices:

1. Work only trees 9 inches d.b.h. or larger. The federal government's cost-share rates when funds are appropriated increase as the size of faced trees increases.

2. Work only selectively marked trees in order to obtain gum income before making improvement cuts or thinnings. Trees are marked three to eight

years in advance of cutting to ensure highest possible quality and volume of gum and/or other products.

3. Use double-headed nails for convenient removal of gutters and aprons prior to logging.

4. Maintain live bark-bars totaling 7 inches of the tree's circumference.

Sulfuric acid applied to fresh wounds causes disintegration of walls of epithelial cells surrounding ducts which contain oleoresin. Gum thus flows for a longer period, increasing the quantity while decreasing the labor cost of more frequen chipping. Bark chipping is done so that almost all wood is usable for subsequent sawlog and pulpwood harvests. While wood growth during gum extraction is reduced, this is more than offset by the value of the oleoresin.

The herbicide paraquat, when painted on a 1-square-inch wound, also stimulates resin production. Thus, gum and turpentine produced from chemically induced lightwood, or resin-soaked xylem, is expected to affect the naval stores industry (Roberts, 1973).

CULTURAL PRACTICES—RANGE MANAGEMENT. While slash pine forests are frequently grazed, little is known of proper techniques for integrating range and forest management. Although cattle rarely graze pine foliage where other green vegetation is available—which limits pine browsing to late winter and early spring, seedlings have a remarkable ability to recover from browse damage. Few trees are killed, but early growth may be retarded (Hughes, 1965). Trampling is to be expected in seedling stands, especially near watering holes, feeding grounds, and on overgrazed, burned, and disked areas. Injury caused by rubbing is severe on trees 2 to 6 feet tall. Growth may be reduced by as much as a third the first year after grazing begins, with three-fourths of the trees grazed displaying multiple leaders (Hopkins, 1950).

Cassady et al. (1955) recommend delaying grazing in young stands until after May 1, and then controlling the herd so that one-half of the green forage is left at the end of the season. This permits a grazing capacity of one cow per acre per month where stands are relatively open and grass is good. Grazing should be prohibited for at least the first year following seedfall to avoid trampling of seedlings.

Prescribed burning during the winter after slash pines are past the seedling stage is often necessary for maximum cattle weight gains. However, if employed more frequently than every 5 or 6 years, growth of trees is impaired. Once trees are above 10 to 15 feet tall, more frequent burning is not injurious to them. During the period that fire is excluded, grazing is desirable to reduce fuel accumulation. Cattle, however, must be controlled, for in migrating to areas most recently burned, they may browse 30 percent of the seedlings. Second-year height growth could then be reduced by 23 percent (Squires, 1947; Campbell, 1951; Halls et al., 1952). Seedlings may be dipped in commercial cattle repellents to discourage browsing.

High rates of nitrogen fertilizer (200 pounds per acre) may be recommended to improve grass production in fully stocked stands for up to two years following application. Appreciably increased yields of desirable forage species occurred in a 25-year-old old-field plantation on a deep, acid sandy soil when so treated (Hughes *et al.*, 1971).

CULTURAL PRACTICES—WILDLIFE HABITAT. Hunting is the principal recreational use of slash pine forests. Integrated management procedures for deer, turkey, and quail follow those outlined for longleaf pine.

SUSCEPTIBILITY TO DAMAGE. Ice storms are especially injurious to slash pine planted north of its natural range. Roberts and Clapp (1956) found severe pruning to be an effective method for straightening trees bent horizontally by a heavy ice load.

Insect pests include roundheaded borers, such as the southern pine sawyer, the turpentine borer, and the Texas leaf-cutting ant. The latter attacks young plantations when other green foliage is scarce. After trees become 2 or 3 feet high, fatal injury is seldom noted (Craighead, 1950).

Fusiform rust, resistance to which is possibly inherited, is the most serious problem of slash pine forests. Frequently 70 percent of the stems in a plantation will be cankered. No practical methods have been developed for its control because of the widespread occurrence of oaks, the alternate hosts. Certain fungicides, such as fermate, are used with success in nurseries. Any treatment which stimulates growth (cultivation, fertilization, bedding) may increase infection. *Fomes annosus* is also a serious threat to slash pine plantations. Because it is most prevalent after thinning and on sites previously row-cropped for agriculture, short rotations for planted stands may be necessary. Spread of the disease is reduced by applications of sulfur dust; but this, in turn, lowers soil pH (Froelich and Nicholson, 1973).

Loblolly Pine—Shortleaf Pine Type Group

Apart from the Interior Highlands and the northern reaches of the Piedmont Province, where shortleaf pine occurs in pure stands, loblolly and shortleaf pines are generally found together. The group, therefore, will be discussed here only as the mixed type. Suffice to note that loblolly pine becomes more important toward the southern extremity of the type range, while shortleaf pine often predominates where the two species are mixed to the north. Loblolly pine prefers wetter sites, attaining maximum growth on poorly drained, moisture-holding clays and clay loams, and often displays its best development on the edges of swampy areas.

Place in Ecological Succession. Moderately intolerant of shade as seedlings, the trees soon lose even that degree of tolerance. Hardwoods, especially oaks and hickories, encroach; eventually broadleaf trees take over the site (Fig. 6-9).

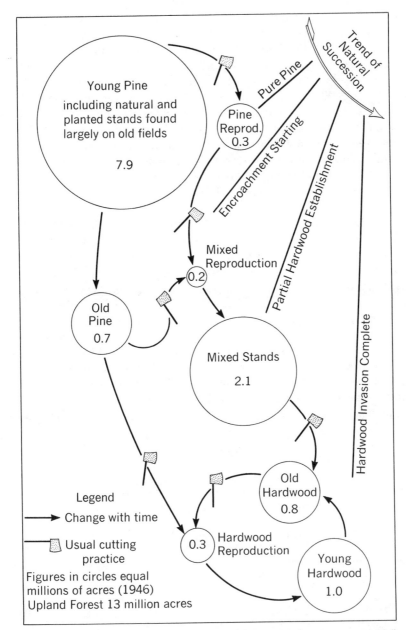

Figure 6-9. The result of man's and nature's combined influences upon loblolly pine-shortleaf pine forests. Nature tends toward climax hardwoods. Man cuts pines, in preference to hardwoods, and so hastens nature's swing toward hardwood types (W. G. Wahlenberg, U.S. For. Serv.).

Growth Rates. In young stands, 2 to 3 feet of height growth per year is common; and on land of average quality, growth of 75 to 85 feet in 50 years is not uncommon. On the best sites, heights of 110 feet for loblolly pine are attained in the same period (Grano, 1956).

Well-stocked loblolly pine—shortleaf pine pole and sawlog forests will have from 4,000 to 8,000 board feet per acre. Volumes occasionally exceed 12,000 board feet. On sites with index 70, 20-year-old stands with 780 trees per acre yield about 18 cords, with an annual growth of 0.9 cord. Sixty-year-old stands with 330 trees per acre produce almost 400 board feet per year, or 1.2 cords, and could yield over 20,000 board feet. Stands with a site index of 90, 60-years old, with 180 trees per acre, yield over 38,000 board feet and may grow about 640 board feet per year, or 1.6 cords (Forbes, 1955). Such stands, however, are rare.

Coile (1952) tabulated site indexes of loblolly pine stands in the Coastal Plain from Virginia to Alabama, based on soil texture, depth, consistence, and drainage characteristics. Quality of well-drained and imperfectly drained sites is not as high as it is for poorly drained soils with the same general profile characteristics as to depth and texture of subsoil (Table 6-2). This holds true for other areas as well. Soil-site data are especially useful if the land does not support stands of suitable age and stocking for direct determination of site index.

One example is cited where height growth of pines, 9 feet tall when control measures were applied to overstory hardwoods, was doubled, and diameter growth quadrupled in two seasons (Miller and Tissue, 1956). McClay (1955) reports, however, that elimination of understory hardwoods in an even-aged sawtimber-size stand of loblolly pine failed to produce increased growth of pines, perhaps because moisture and nutrient competition were not too severe.

TABLE 6-2

Excerpts of a Coile Soil-Site Table

Texture of Subsoil	Surface Drainage of Land	Site Index at Various Depths to Subsoil			
		6 Inches	18 Inches	30 Inches	42 Inches
Sand and loamy sand	Good	80	85	85	90
	Imperfect	90	90	90	95
	Poor	90	90	95	95
Loam, clay loam, sandy clay, and light clay	Good	85	90	100	105
	Imperfect	90	95	105	110
	Poor	90	100	105	115
Silty clay loam and silt loam	Good	90	95	105	115
	Imperfect	90	100	110	120
	Poor	95	105	115	125

Source: After Coile, 1952.

During a dry summer in Arkansas, soil water remained relatively high on sites where large cull hardwoods were removed, in contrast to severe depletion in a loblolly pine–shortleaf pine stand with understory hardwoods (Zahner, 1955). Even so, at the present time there is little reason to advocate elimination of any but overtopping hardwoods in established pine forests. In fact, Hopkins (1958) concluded that the production of pine of high quality for lumber was enhanced by maintaining 5 percent of the stand basal area in well-distributed subdominant hardwoods.

Pine seedlings not overtopped by hardwood sprouts in the third growing season have a good chance of remaining dominant. This can be attributed to the acceleration in successive years of pine annual height growth, while the growth of hardwood sprout clumps tends to decrease.

Rotation Age or Size.   Although pulpwood sizes are attained, on the average, in 20 years, commercial thinnings have been made as early as 7 years and frequently at 10 to 16 years on better sites. On the southeastern coast, small-size sawtimber can be produced on average sites in 40 years, and large-size in 65 years (Lotti, 1956). Rotation ages of 40 to 60 years for second-growth sawtimber and peeler logs are anticipated under reasonable management intensity. This should provide final-crop stems averaging about 15 inches d.b.h. at economic maturity.

Cultural Practices—Timber Production.   Various rules of thumb—mechanical and subjective—have been advanced for thinning. When a stand is so crowded that the live crowns of dominant and codominant trees are less than 30 to 40 percent of the total height, diameter growth is too slow, and thinning is therefore desirable. Once these relatively intolerant southern pines have had their live-crown ratio reduced below 20 to 25 percent by excessive competition, they may be unable to immediately respond to release. With severe stagnation, the period of recovery may be too long to make thinning economical. Even so, noncommercial thinning is rarely practiced.

Brender (1965) has cited the need for simple guides which would not sacrifice the "art" aspects of thinning, the reason for opposition to the "D+6" and other mechanical rules (Table 6-3). Thinning must reduce basal area below 100 square feet—perhaps to 70—in order to provide sufficient light in the upper crowns for good growth of shortleaf pine (Jackson and Harper, 1955).

Fertilization, with nitrogen and phosphorus, is an effective precommercial thinning technique for loblolly pine (Brender and McNab, 1978). A heavy application encourages growth of dominant stems which reduces the vigor of suppressed trees through competition. The expression of dominance, and thus subsequent natural thinning, occurs on nutrient-rich sites without fertilizer treatments.

Because single-tree selection results in an uneven-aged forest and perpetuates tolerant species, its use in harvesting in this type is limited. Group selection, on the other hand, creates adequate space for reproduction of even-

TABLE 6-3

Volume and Average Size of Trees Cut and Left Per Acre at Age 20 in First Thinnings of Loblolly Pine Plantations

Initial Spacing (Feet)	Trees (Number)	Basal area (Square Feet)	Volume (Cords)	Average d.b.h. (Inches)	Measure of Thinning (d/D)
4 × 4					
Cut	405	59	10.8	5.2	1.08
Leave	790	99	16.6	4.8	
Total	1195	158	27.4	4.9	
6 × 6					
Cut	256	55	11.9	6.3	1.11
Leave	479	86	18.0	5.7	
Total	735	141	29.9	5.8	
8 × 8					
Cut	180	47	10.7	6.9	1.01
Leave	352	88	20.3	6.8	
Total	532	135	31.0	6.8	
10 × 10					
Cut	105	40	8.3	8.4	0.98
Leave	218	87	18.7	8.6	
Total	323	127	27.0	8.5	

Source: Brender (1965), adapted from Muntz (1948).

aged units of these species on better sites. The work of Reynolds (1959) and others in southeast Arkansas, however, clearly indicates the usefulness of the selection system for this type in this zone.

Shelterwood regeneration has not been extensively used in loblolly pine stands. Meyer (1955) reported a heavy residual shelterwood restricted height growth of reproduction.

The seed-tree harvest method has been extensively employed. Chapman (1942) considered the retention of up to 10 seed trees per acre as economically desirable. Such a large number of seed trees serves as inducement for a later merchantable cut. Because of the rapid response to release inherent with this species, seed trees of high vigor and quality will assure the owner of no loss in stumpage value. These trees may be removed within two years after seedling establishment, with little damage to young growth, or they may be retained as fire insurance and harvested at the first thinning. Some will be killed by lightning. However, the stand density resulting from so many seed trees may necessitate precommercial thinning.

To stimulate seed production, seed trees may be released so as to free their tops on all sides. This should be done at least three years before the harvest cut. Lotti (1956) states 25,000 sound seeds per acre are required for adequate re-forestation on favorable locations in the Coastal Plain. This estimate is increased to 50,000 or more on areas of heavy brush or logging debris. Although heavy seed crops occur at three- to five-year intervals, by comparing the number of immature cones with old cones, crops can be estimated quite accurately six months to a year in advance. Some seeds of both species are produced every year.

Wenger (1957) reports that seed production of mature stands of loblolly pine in North Carolina varied inversely with the seed crop of the second preceding year and directly with May-to-July rainfall, thereby enabling prediction of seed yields three years in advance of seed germination. That study indicates that larger seed crops produced after crown release are a response to increased soil moisture rather than light.

Cones usually have about 60 percent of their seeds fertile. A few trees produce small amounts of good seed at 12 to 15 years of age, but the best yields are from trees over 35 years old (Lotti, 1956).

When severely damaged, as by fire, young shortleaf pines sprout, and it is the only important southern pine to do so. However, these sprouts result in poorly formed trees, often forked at the ground. Their removal in early thin-nings is recommended.

In Coastal Plain forests, loblolly pine growth is stimulated when phosphorus is applied to soils with less than 4 ppm of that element, provided nitrogen and moisture are favorable. Piedmont sites do not show similar response. Foliar analysis, as well as soil tests, are useful in the Coastal Plain for ascertaining nutrient deficiencies (Wells et al., 1973).

Water tables may rise considerably following clearcutting of the loblolly pine—shortleaf pine type in the flatwoods (Fig. 6-10). Thus, heavy spring rain-fall may result in standing water on poorly drained sites, making regeneration impossible. Growth of residual trees is reduced by these rising water tables, and logging becomes difficult. The total effect and economic desirability of drainage have not been adequately studied to enable recommendations for wet sites in which this type is found. It is reported, however, that ditching will lower the height of the water table as far as 1,000 feet from the ditch, and that height growth of trees is stimulated as far as 600 feet (Pruitt, 1947). Most of the lowered water table in areas of heavy clay soils will be due to leading away of surface water since, without a "head," lateral movement within the soil is not likely to exceed a foot.

Bedding is an alternative to draining when planting or seeding loblolly pine. Disking of convex-mounded beds to about 8 inches above the ground line about 8 feet apart in a poorly drained, fine-textured soil that is saturated in winter and dry in summer significantly improved height growth (Mann and Derr, 1970).

Loblolly pine is frequently planted, generally by machines at about 8 × 10-foot spacing, thus permitting trucks to pass between rows in subsequent thin-ning operations. The importance of proper depth of planting is stressed, deep-

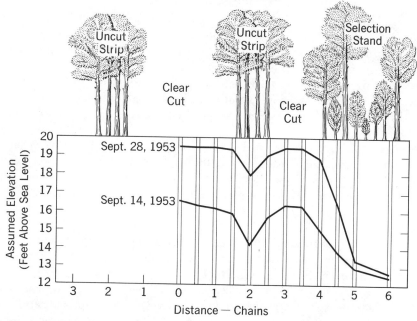

Figure 6-10. Typical water-table profiles from a series of temporary wells extending from a clearcut area into a selectively cut stand (U.S. For. Serv.).

planted seedlings displaying significantly better height growth than those inserted only to the root collar. Seedlings with one-fourth of the root exposed, however, suffer seriously in mortality and height growth.

Loblolly pine can be expected to be widely used in the next two decades for converting Coastal Plain hardwood sites to pine. It is becoming increasingly important for direct seeding. Shortleaf pine, thus far not used in direct seeding, is planted usually in that part of its range where loblolly pine does not grow naturally.

Where moisture may be a limiting factor, removal of vegetative competition is necessary. Seedlings on freshly prepared sites make better height growth than on those prepared a year before planting. Scalping the soil in open fields also enhances survival and growth (Bilan and Stransky, 1966).

Prompt regeneration is essential to avoid brush taking over a harvest site (Walker, 1963a) and because of financial interest accrual during the delay. Sunda and Lowry (1975) found delay to be economically costly.

A typical mechanical site preparation program consists of cutting all vegetation with a heavy-duty tractor-mounted horizontal knife, windrowing, and burning the windrows. Windrowing may be eliminated and the site only chopped and broadcast burned. Occasionally disking may follow the shearing operation. Other mechanical measures in use are bulldozing, crushing, root raking, and bedding. The latter practice mounds the soil to support seedlings at slightly elevated positions. Chemical herbicides are also employed—by injection, aerial spraying, and ground spraying—to control brush and weed trees. These chemicals are scrutinized by federal and state agencies to determine if transport to water supplies is deleterious.

The impact of site manipulation practices upon the soil becomes increasingly important as forests are managed more intensively. For Coastal Plain forests of all species, nonpoint source pollution is considered minimal because of the level terrain (thus slight runoff) and slow movement of nutrients and water through the soil, both laterally and downward. Maki (1976) noted that even where site preparation does not cause soil to wash to streams, sediment is shifted from one locale to another. Filter strips of vegetation are therefore recommended. In the rolling Piedmont, root raking that piles surface soil may significantly reduce site quality even two decades later. Shortly—perhaps by the time these words are in print—the use of residual fiber for fuel will be sufficiently economical to eliminate the waste of site preparation work on many sites.

Burning, as a tool for site preparation, adequately controls brush only when deciduous plants are in leaf and where the amount of such vegetation, due to sprouting, is dense (Trevison, 1977). Users of prescribed fire, however, should be aware that government may hold liable those responsible for poor visibility and failure to inform forestry agencies of anticipated ignition. Temperature inversions may also occur in populated areas downwind from burning forests, creating adverse public reaction (Mobley et al., 1977).

Cultural Practices—Wildlife Habitat. Little is known about integration of wildlife and timber management in loblolly pine–shortleaf pine forests. Sometimes, as in the Barrens of southern New Jersey, deer are too numerous and redistribution is necessary to avoid herd starvation and severe browsing of planted pines. Work conducted in East Texas forests indicated that considerable deer forage can be produced in well-stocked stands not encumbered with a dense midstory of hardwoods (Schuster and Halls, 1962).

Prescribed fire in small well-distributed units benefits deer. Usually such practices are carried out only if timber values are improved also. When the economic benefit (value of a harvested buck) of wildlife habitat improvement surpasses that of timber improvement, these practices will be done (Halls, 1975).

Thinnings have no noticeable adverse effect on deer habitat. In combination with prescribed fire, partial cutting may enhance the quantity of forage and browse in the stand. For high deer populations, openings are maintained in which patches of mast-bearing hardwoods are encouraged, enabling a carrying capacity of one deer to 20 acres. Supplemental food to further raise population densities include corn plots, pelleted feed in feeders, and salt blocks (Stransky, 1971b).

Quail and rabbits may be encouraged by placement of 25-foot cleared food lanes covering 12 to 15 percent of the area. The lanes should meander to provide the greatest perimeter of edge and to avoid cutting valuable trees.

Deciduous trees in the woods bordering the food lanes are thinned to increase interspersion of birds and, at the same time, to favor pines over oaks.

Concern for songbird habitat in forest management practices is important to the silviculturist. In a loblolly pine—shortleaf pine—hardwood forest, 28 of 35 species of plants important as food for these birds were more abundant 15 months after cutting on a clearcut area than in adjacent unharvested sites. Important among these pioneer species for bird food are grasses, sunflowers, and legumes (Stransky et al., 1976).

Cultural Practices—Water.   Shortleaf pine forests play a role in watershed management. In plantations of the South Carolina Piedmont, a 2-inch layer of undecomposed needle litter weighing over 4 tons per acre reduced raindrop impact appreciably. This litter layer, in the absence of humus, held from 0.01 to 0.09 inch of water after rain and, thereby, reduced erosion by providing time for infiltration to take place (Metz, 1958).

Destruction of humus exposes soil to the impact of raindrops. Thus, mor humus types should be prescribed burned with caution, for the exposure to the force of raindrops that then occurs is sufficient to seal pores and reduce infiltration to a negligible rate. Continual burning retards, at least theoretically, the formation of a desirable mull humus layer by eliminating litter that would in the course of time become incorporated with mineral soil. Also fire may reduce populations of organic-decomposing fauna and flora living in the unincorporated litter of the forest floor.

Cultural Practices—Range Management.   Forests of this type are grazed intensively only in the Ozark and Ouachita mountains. Total herbage production decreases as the shortleaf pine timber-stand density increases. Stands with 50 trees per acre 3 inches or larger support six times as much herbage as areas with about 400 trees. The noncommercial hardwood forests of post and blackjack oaks on southern and western exposures produce 50 percent more herbage than do the good white oak—black oak—hickory sites of northern and eastern slopes. In contrast to Coastal Plain forest ranges, there are more forbs than grasses in these uplands, and only one-fourth of the herbage is palatable to cattle.

Cultural Practices—Recreation.   Aesthetic harvests, a type of selection with subsequent slash disposal utilizing chipping machinery, are employed in recreation areas of this forest type. Managers should anticipate the eventual replacement of the pines with hardwoods as the former pass out of the stand at ages of usually no more than 130 years. Selectively reducing stand density in heavily used areas reduces the chance of tree mortality caused by soil compaction and poor aeration.

Susceptibility to Damage.   Various fungi are associated with the dying of needles of loblolly and shortleaf pines, but damage is usually not serious. While fusiform rust is most damaging in the seedling stage for loblolly pine, old trees often live for years with cankers on the main stem. Although the species should not be planted in high rust-incidence areas, losses in young plantations may be reduced by pruning infected branches before the mycelium reaches the main stems. Shortleaf pine is occasionally found with fusiform cankers and, more frequently, with cankers of eastern gall rust.

Old stands frequently suffer severe damage due to red-heart rot. Decay caused by this fungus and by butt rot results in more lumber degrading than all other coniferous fungi combined; yet it is seldom serious in stands less than 50 years old.

The red cockaded woodpecker, the only woodpecker to build nests in living trees, seeks out stems with red-heart rot for its home. As sanitation thinnings remove these infected trees, the bird has become endangered. To protect its habitat, diseased trees are retained even though this will encourage spread of the malady and loss of wood.

Little-leaf disease is generally a shortleaf pine problem in the Piedmont Province. However, there are cases of its occurrence in the Coastal Plain and on loblolly pine, usually—for both species—on eroded and abandoned farmland with dense clay subsoil. Ruehle and Campbell (1971) suggest the long-term solution to the problem depends on selection and propagation of disease-resistant strains. In the meantime, potentially susceptible sites are either used for growing tree species unlikely to be attacked or fertilized with nitrogen to stimulate pine root growth (Fig. 6-11).

Loblolly and shortleaf pines are attacked by the Nantucket pine tip moth. This insect is particularly injurious to trees less than about 7 feet tall, and damage is most severe on poor sites. Effects of the attacks are subsequently outgrown. Preventive measures include planting on favorable sites, mixing with resistant species, planting under an overstory, or planting at close spacing.

The southern pine beetle attacks middle and upper trunks of healthy pines of all ages during warm months. Foliage begins to fade from 10 days to 2 weeks after attack and rapid penetration of the sapwood by blue stain is characteristic. Death of the tree usually occurs quickly. Outbreaks generally begin in trees weakened by drought, lightning, fire, and windthrow; in overly dense stands; and on soil of poor internal drainage and low fertility. These serve as springboards for infestation of surrounding healthy stems. Susceptible areas should be kept under surveillance and infested trees immediately cut (without injuring residual stems), treated with insecticide, and—if possible—salvaged. The slabs then should be burned at the mill.

The black turpentine beetle attacks bases of weakened or injured trees. Fairly large areas of bark are often destroyed by the brood, although this insect normally breeds in stumps and cut logs, rarely killing trees. Damage is averted by avoiding excessive injury to trees in logging operations.

Other bark beetles of the genus *Ips* frequently attack weakened trees, particularly during drought. Since these secondary pests are found in freshly cut logs or blow-downs, logging slash should be disposed of when cutting ceases if infestation is likely.

Figure 6-11.   Little-leaf-diseased trees. At left, before being fertilized. At right, six years after application of nitrogenous fertilizers (Roth and Copeland, 1957; U.S. For. Serv.).

Thinning at frequent intervals to reduce competition aids in minimizing serious bark beetle outbreaks, even during drought. Controlling undesirable hardwoods and brush may result in increased availability of soil moisture, perhaps sufficient to be an effective deterrent to a severe attack.

Serious losses of young loblolly pine seedlings are caused by pales weevils. Pitch-eating weevils also damage seedlings and saplings on cutover areas.

Virginia Pine

Virginia Pine occurs throughout most of the Atlantic Coastal Plain from New Jersey to North Carolina, the Piedmont, and the Southern Appalachian Mountain region. However, its importance in forestry is relegated principally to the Piedmont from Maryland to North Carolina and the mountains of eastern Tennessee.

Place in Ecological Succession.   The species is an initial in old-field succession and following fire and other catastrophic land disturbance. It is generally replaced within two generations by loblolly pine–shortleaf pine or hardwood types. However, Virginia pine occurs with shortleaf pine in a virgin stand in northern Alabama (Walker, 1963b).

Two indicator types have been described delineating site potential for this species. The better sites—site index 50 to 70—are characterized by flowering dogwood and clubmoss, and bear oak and reindeer moss indicate average and poorer sites—site index 30 to 50 (Bramble, 1947).

Growth Rates.   In the Virginia mountains, growth of the species is expected to be about 0.3 cord per acre per year. An old-field stand on a fine sandy loam soil in the North Carolina mountains may produce 1 cord per acre per year.

Rotation Age or Size.   Rotation age and tree sizes for this species vary greatly by latitude and elevation. As the mean annual growth rate of merchantable stands in the north reaches a maximum as early as age 40 (Whitesell and Pickall, 1956), rotation ages of 30 to 40 years for pulpwood and 50 to 60 years for sawtimber are suggested.

Cultural Practices—Timber Production.   Clearcutting in strips or blocks and seed-tree harvests are recommended for Virginia pine. While natural regeneration occurs as far as one-quarter mile from seed sources, most seeds fall close to parent trees. With wide strips, few seeds fall in the center and on the windward side, as compared to the leeward side. Leaving more than 11 trees per acre in seed-tree cuttings does not improve seed dissemination, but windthrow of mature stems of this shallow-rooted species quickly reduces their number (Sucoff and Church, 1960).

Virginia pines sprout prolifically, but only shoots from saplings and seedlings develop into trees. Stumps of larger trees deteriorate before sprouts establish adequate root systems. Areas with small stems which are burned and killed are readily regenerated by coppice shoots. The sprouts, generally many per stump, subsequently produce short-lived trees of low quality.

Virginia pine is especially recommended for planting on eroded sites and old fields. Where once a weed tree, it is now planted commercially as a source of wood pulp on cut-over lands.

For direct seeding, site preparation and elimination of grass is necessary (Sowers, 1964). Provenance is important in survival and growth throughout the range (Genys, 1966). Stands beyond the sapling stage respond especially slowly or negligibly to thinning.

After stands are 10 years of age, there is no improvement of crop tree growth by removal of noncrop trees. Hence for stands having up to 9,000 stems per acre, thinning to about 5 × 5-foot spacing should be done by age 5. Canopies are expected to close in 3 years, allowing for rethinning to 7 × 7-foot spacing at age 10, and providing a growth response at age 19 of 1,550 cubic feet, inside bark, per acre (Miller, 1951). In addition to the limited growth response there are several other reasons for not thinning Virginia pine. Noncrop stems reduce sleet damage to crop trees, a serious problem in thinned stands; natural pruning is improved in crowded stands; and the gross cubic foot volume is increased.

Unpruned branches persist to the ground except, perhaps, on the best sites.

While pruning improves the quality of Virginia pine for sawlogs, eliminating live branches of 9-year-old trees to a height of 8 feet resulted in a slight decrease in diameter growth. Where sawlogs are anticipated, crop trees should be pruned to 8 feet at age 10 and released to allow 3 to 4 feet between crowns. Crown canopies will then close within 2 to 3 years (Williamson, 1953).

Cultural Practices—Other. Wildlife habitat is affected by silvicultural practices in much the same way as for other southern pines here described. Because Virginia pine is often near population centers—the cities of the Fall Line, aesthetic silviculture to provide for outdoor recreation may be of a higher priority than timber production. Little acreage of these forests is grazed. Virginia pine does cover vast watersheds, thus partial harvests with light-weight equipment and animal logging may be utilized to maximize the production of clear, clean water.

Susceptibility to Damage. Principal insect pests of Virginia pine are Nantucket pine tipmoths, southern pine beetles, and sawflies. Pitch canker is recognized by a copious flow of gum far in excess of that accompanying any other known disease. This and heartrot, the latter in older stands, are the principal disease problems.

Meadow mice may damage Virginia pines less than 10 feet tall in dense stands. Typically, the injury is a conspicuous wounding in winter when sap is the best available substitute for water which is then frozen and inaccessible (Church, 1954).

Lesser Southern Pines

Pond Pine Type. Although pond pine is of little economic importance, it does inhabit an appreciable area. Cones are retained for many years after seed dispersal, thus causing the casual observer to consider the species a more frequent seeder than it is. Following fire, sprouting is prolific. These sprouts are rather well formed, eventually proving suitable for pulpwood and sawlogs. Where seed trees are present, the species is adept at taking over open, abandoned fields. In regeneration practices, foresters often prefer slash pine to pond pine because of the former's better form. Pond pines do not grow to large sizes: 50-year-old stems will average about 10 inches d.b.h. (Koch, 1972).

Fire is the chief enemy of the type, yet pure pond pine stands occur in areas which are frequently burned. Viable seeds, which remain in sealed cones up to five years, may be released by the heat of prescribed burns during occasional prolonged dry periods. If less than 500 seedlings per acre occur, prescribed burning, which also prepares seedbeds by removing rough and litter, is suggested to encourage reproduction.

Pond pine is wind-firm, even on the wettest soils; but logging wet sites is so difficult that light cuts are not economical. On firmer soils, sawlog thinning at 10-year cycles is feasible. Final harvest methods include seed-tree and strip- or

group-clearcutting. On firm soil, seed trees may be harvested soon after reproduction is established, while on soft, pocosin land, seed trees can most economically be left until the next cut. Draining will increase productivity, but other
less desirable species, particularly hardwoods, will also be encouraged to invade heretofore pure stands (Fig. 6-12).

Grazing is often beneficial, particularly for seedling establishment in pond
pine forest types. Cattle trampling disturbs the surface litter and thus permits
seeds to readily reach a moist layer for germination. Decreased competition
from cane and other grazed forage results in increased pond pine growth.
While vigor of living trees is often improved, grazing may destroy seedlings and
denude trees to a height of 8 feet when forage is scarce. Occasionally taller trees
are "ridden down" and browsed. A capacity of one-third to one-half cow-month
per acre during the summer season is suggested (Shepherd *et al.*, 1951). The
species is notably resistant to insect and disease attack.

Sand Pine Type.   Sand pine, while locally harvested for pulpwood, is of
minor economic importance. In the dry sandhills of western Florida, however,
it has outgrown slash pine both on cleared sites and when planted without

Figure 6-12.   Canal for draining a pine stand in a North Carolina pocosin area. The terrain is
so level and the gradient so slight that flow is not noticeable (N. C. State Univ.).

release from competitive wiregrass and scrub oak. Nevertheless, release from vegetative competition results in stimulated growth.

As a serotinous species (except in West Florida), sand pine is dependent upon fire for its natural regeneration. When killing fire sweeps through a stand of cone-bearing trees, the cones usually open to release seed. Cones are produced early and may persist for many years, but seed viability appreciably decreases with age.

Silvicultural techniques call for prescribed burning for (1) hardwood control, (2) seedbed preparation, and (3) seed dissemination. The trees of this species are short-lived, stands breaking up soon after reaching 50 years of age (Koch, 1972).

Spruce Pine Type.   This wet-site type is highly desirable, but it is almost insignificant in the timber economy of the region. Silvicultural applications are closely allied to those for slash pine on similar sites.

Sonderegger Pine.   This hybrid of loblolly and longleaf pines, found throughout the longleaf pine region, is not a type but occurs as individual stems. The absence of nanism (longleaf pine's grass-stage) and the otherwise appearance of longleaf pine are its principal characteristics. Such trees are given no specific consideration in management practices.

Other Types

The baldcypress is discussed in Chapter 5. The limited importance of eastern redcedar causes its exclusion in this narrative. Upland hardwood silviculture is covered in Chapter 4. For this discussion one should realize that the oak-hickory (Chapter 4) and beech-birch-maple types (Chapter 2) comprise the climax forest for much of the Southern Pine Region. The pines occur and reoccur because fire, storm, insect infestation, and clearcutting have exposed the mineral soil and provided full sunlight when a seed source has been available.

LITERATURE CITED

Allen, R. M., 1955. Foliage treatments improve survival of longleaf pine planting. *J. For.* 53:724−727.

Bennett, F. A., 1955. The effect of pruning on the height and diameter growth of planted slash pine. *J. For.* 53:636−638.

Bennett, F. A., 1965. Growth and yield of planted slash pine. In A Guide to Loblolly and Slash Pine Plantation Management. pp. 221−241. *Ga. For. Res. Council Rep. 14.*

Bertelson, D. F., 1977. Southern pulpwood production, 1976. *USDA For. Serv. Res. Bull. SO-66.* 24 pp.

Bilan, M. V., and J. J. Stransky., 1966. Pine seedling survival and growth response to soils of the Texas Post-Oak Belt. *Stephen F. Austin State Univ. Sch. For.* Nacogdoches. *Bull. 12.* 21 pp.

Bramble, W. C., 1947. Indicator types for Virginia pine stands. *Penn. State Univ. For. Sch., Univ. Park Res. Pap. 8.* 8 pp.

Braun, E. L., 1950. *Deciduous forests of Eastern North America*. McGraw-Hill Book Co., Inc., New York. 596 pp.

Brender, E. V., 1965. Thinning loblolly pine. In A Guide to Loblolly and Slash Pine Plantation Management. *Ga. For. Res. Council Rep. 14*.

Brender, E. V., and W. H. McNab., 1978. Precommercial thinning of loblolly pine by fertilization. *Ga. For. Res. Council Pap. 90*. 8 pp.

Campbell, R. S., 1951. Extension of the range front to the South. *J. For.* 49:787−789.

Campbell, R. S., and J. T. Cassady., 1955. Forage weight inventories on southern forest ranges. *USDA For. Serv. So. For. Exp. Stn. Occ. Pap. 139*. 18 pp.

Campbell, T. E., and W. F. Mann, Jr., 1971. Site preparation boosts growth of direct-seeded slash-pine. *USDA For. Serv. Res. Note SO-115*. 4 pp.

Cassady, J. T., W. Hopkins, and L. B. Whitaker., 1955. Cattle grazing damage to pine seedlings. *USDA For. Serv. So. For. Exp. Stn. Occ. Pap. 141*. 14 pp.

Chapman, H. H., 1942. Management of loblolly pine in the pine-hardwood region in Arkansas and in Louisiana west of the Mississippi River. *Yale Univ. Sch. For. New Haven. Bull. 49*. 150 pp.

Church, T. W., 1954. Mice cause severe damage to Virginia pine reproduction. *USDA For. Serv. North. For. Exp. Stn. Res. Note 35*. 2 pp.

Coile, T. S., 1952. Soil and the growth of forests. *Adv. Agron.* 4:329−398.

Craighead, F. C., 1950. *Insect enemies of eastern forests*. U.S. Govt. Print. Off. Washington, D.C. 679 pp.

Croker, T. C., Jr., and W. D. Boyer., 1975. Regenerating longleaf pine naturally. *USDA For. Serv. Res. Pap. SO-105*. 21 pp.

Davis, V. B. 1955. Don't keep longleaf seed trees too long! South. For. Notes 98. *South For. Exp. Stn.*

Forbes, R. D., (ed.). 1955. *Forestry handbook*. The Ronald Press Co., New York. 1212 pp.

Froelich, R. C., and J. D. Nicholson, 1973. Spread of *Fomes annosus*. *For. Sci.* 19:7.

Genys, J. B., 1966. Geographic variation in Virginia pine. *Silvae Genetica* 15:72−76.

Goodrum, R., and V. H. Reid., 1958. Deer browsing in the longleaf pine belt. In *Proc. Soc. Am. For. Ann. Meeting*. pp. 139−143.

Grano, C. X., 1956. Growing loblolly and shortleaf pine in the Mid-South. *USDA Farmers' Bull. 2102*. 27 pp.

Halls, L. K., 1975. Economic feasibility of including game habitats in timber management. In *Trans. 40th N. Am. Wildlife and Nat. Resour. Conf.* pp. 168−176.

Halls, L. K., B. L. Southwell, and F. W. Knox., 1952. Burning and grazing in Coastal Plain forests. *Univ. Ga. Agr. Exp. Stn. Athens. Bull. 51*. 33 pp.

Hanna, W. J., and S. S. Obenshain., 1957. Middle Atlantic Coastal Plain. In *Yearbook of Agriculture USDA*. pp. 620−627.

Hedlund, A., and P. Jenson., 1963. Major forest types of the South. *Map. USDA For. Serv.*

Henderson, J. R., and F. B. Smith., 1957. Florida and flatwoods. In *Yearbook of Agriculture USDA*. pp. 595−598.

Hilgard, E. W., 1906. *Soils: their formation, properties, composition, and relations to climate and plant growth in the humid and arid regions*. Macmillan. New York. 593 pp.

Hodgkins, E. J., 1956. Testing soil-site index tables in southwestern Alabama. *J. For.* 54:261−266.

Hopkins, W. C., 1950. Grazing damages newly planted slash pine. *USDA For. Serv. South. For. Exp. Stn. So. For. Notes*. 65:2−3.

Hopkins, W. C., 1958. Relationship of stand characteristics to quality of loblolly pine. *La. State Univ. Agr. Exp. Stn. Baton Rouge. Bull. 517*. 57 pp.

Hughes, R. H., 1965. Animal damage. In A guide to loblolly and slash pine plantation management in southeastern USA. *Ga. For. Res. Council Rep. 14*. pp. 160−166.

Hughes, R. H., G. W. Bengtson, and T. A. Harrington., 1971. Forage response to nitrogen and phosphorus fertilization in a 25-year-old plantation of slash pine. *USDA For. Serv. Res. Pap. SE-82.* 7 pp.

Jackson, L. W. R., and R. S. Harper., 1955. Relation of light intensity to basal area of shortleaf pine in Georgia. *Ecology* 361:158–159.

Koch, P., 1972. Utilization of southern pines, Vol. I The Raw Material. *USDA For. Serv.* 734 pp.

Kurz, H., 1944. Secondary forest succession in the Tallahassee Red Hills. *Fla. Acad. Sci.* 7:59–100.

Linnartz, N. E., E. Hse, and V. L. Duvall., 1966. Grazing impairs physical properties of a forest soil in central Louisiana. *J. For.* 64:239–243.

Lotti, T., 1956. Growing loblolly pine in the South Atlantic states. *USDA Farmers' Bull. 2097.* 33 pp.

McClay, T. A., 1955. Loblolly pine growth as affected by removal of understory hardwoods and shrubs. *USDA For. Serv. Southeast. For. Exp. Stn. Res. Note 73.* 2 pp.

McClurkin, D. C., 1953. Soil and climatic factors related to the growth of longleaf pine. *USDA For. Serv. South. For. Exp. Stn. Pap. 132.* 12 pp.

McLemore, B. F., 1975. Cone and seed characteristics of fertilized and unfertilized longleaf pines. *USDA For. Serv. Res. Pap. SO-109.* 10 pp.

Maki, T. E., 1976. Impact of site manipulation on the Atlantic coastal plain. In *Proc. 6th So. For. Soils Workshop.* pp. 108–114.

Mann, W. F., Jr., and H. J. Derr., 1970. Response of planted loblolly and slash pine to disking on a poorly drained site. *USDA For. Serv. Res. Note SO-110.* 3 pp.

Maple, W. R., 1957. Redcedar growth in Arkansas Ozarks. *USDA For. Serv. South. For. Exp. Stn. South. For. Notes* 112:3.

Meanley, B., and R. M. Blair., 1957. Damage to longleaf pine seedlings by cotton rats. *J. For.* 55:35.

Metz, L. J., 1958. Moisture held in pine litter. *J. For.* 56:36.

Meyer, W. H., 1955. Some treatment effects on loblolly and shortleaf pine reproduction. *J. For.* 53:895–900.

Miller, W. D., 1951. Thinning in old-field Virginia pine. *J. For.* 49:884–887.

Miller, W. D., and O. C. Tissue., 1956. Results of several methods of release of understory loblolly pine in upland hardwood stands. *J. For.* 54:188–189.

Mobley, H. E., R. S. Jackson, W. E. Balmer, W. E. Ruziska, and W. A. Hough., 1977. A guide for prescribed fire in southern forests. *USDA For. Serv. South. Area State and Priv.* 40 pp.

Morriss, D. J., 1958. Basal area thinning guides for thinning in the South. *J. For.* 56:903–905.

Muntz, H. H. 1948. Profit from thinning variously spaced loblolly pine plantations. *South. Lumberman* 177 (2225):125–128.

Nelson, R. M., 1957. The original forests of the Georgia piedmont. *Ecology* 38:390–397.

Nelson, T. C., J. L. Clutter, and L. E. Chaiken., 1961. Yield of Virginia pine. *USDA For. Serv. Southeast. For. Exp. Stn. Pap. 124.* 11 pp.

Nikiforoff, C. C., R. P. Humbert, and J. C. Cady, 1948. The hardpan in certain soils of the Coastal Plain. *Soil Sci.* 65:135–153.

Pearson, R. W., and E. L. Ensminger., 1957. Southeastern uplands. In *Yearbook of Agriculture.* USDA. pp. 578–594.

Pruitt, A. A., 1947. Study of effects of soils, water tables and drainage on the height growth of slash and loblolly pine plantations on the Hoffman Forest. *J. For.* 45:836.

Ralston, C. W., 1951. Some factors related to the growth of longleaf pine in the Atlantic Coastal Plain. *J. For.* 49:408–412.

Ralston, C. W., and R. L. Barnes., 1955. Soil properties related to the growth and yield of slash pine plantations in Florida. *Soil Sci. Soc. Am. Proc.* 19:84–85.

Reeves, H. C., 1977. Use of prescribed fire in land management. *J. Soil and Water Conserv.* 32:102–104.

Reynolds, R. R., 1959. Eighteen years of selection timber management on the Crossett Experimental Forest. *USDA Tech. Bull. 1206.* 68 pp.

Roberts, D. R., 1973. Inducing lightwood in pine trees by paraquat treatment. *USDA For. Serv. Res. Notes SE-191.* 4 pp.

Roberts, E. G., and R. T. Clapp., 1956. Effect of pruning on the recovery of ice bent slash pines. *J. For.* 54:596–597.

Roth, E. R., and O. L. Copeland., 1957. Uptake of nitrogen and calcium by fertilized shortleaf pine. *J. For.* 55:281–284.

Ruehle, J. L., and W. A. Campbell., 1971. Adaptability of geographic selection of shortleaf pine to little leaf sites. *USDA For. Serv. Res. Pap. SE-87.* 8 pp.

Russell, T. E., and H. J. Derr., 1956. Longleaf height unaffected by stand density. *USDA For. Serv. South. For. Exp. Stn. South. For. Notes 101:2.*

Scheer, R. L., 1957. Sand pine—scrub or timber tree? *South. Lumberman* 195(2441):191–193.

Schuster, J. L., and L. K. Halls., 1962. Timber overstory determines deer forage in shortleaf-loblolly pine-hardwood forests. In *Proc. Soc. Amer. For. Ann. Meet.* pp. 165–167.

Shepherd, W. O., 1953. Effects of burning and grazing flatwoods forest ranges. *USDA Southeast. For. Exp. Stn. Res. Note 30.* 2 pp.

Shepherd, W. O., E. W. Dillard, and H. L. Lucas., 1951. Grazing and fire influences in pond pine forests. *N. C. Agr. Exp. Stn. Raleigh. Tech. Bull. 97.* 57 pp.

Shipman, R. D., 1958. Planting pine in the Carolina sandhills. *USDA For. Serv. Southeast. Exp. Stn. Pap. 96.* 43 pp.

Shoulders, E., and W. H. McKee, Jr., 1973. Pine nutrition in the west Gulf Coastal Plain: a status report. *USDA For. Serv. Gen. Tech. Rep. SO-2.* 26 pp.

Society of American Foresters. Committee on Forest Types. 1954. Forest cover types of North America (exclusive of Mexico). 67 pp.

Sowers, D. W., Jr., 1964. Suggested guidelines for direct seeding Virginia pine. *Northern Logger* 12(8):12 *et fol.*

Speers, C. F., 1958. Pales weevil rapidly becoming serious pest of pine reproduction in the South. *J. For.* 56:723–726.

Squires, J. W., 1947. Prescribed burning in Florida. *J. For.* 45:815–819.

Stransky, J. J., 1971a. Managing for quail and timber in longleaf pine forests. *Stephen F. Austin State Univ. Nacogdoches. Tex. For. Pap. 9.* 8 pp.

Stransky, J. J., 1971b. Integrated deer-habitat management and timber production in the South. *The Consultant* 16(4):89–90.

Stransky, J. J., L. K. Halls, and E. S. Nixon., 1976. Plants following timber harvest: importance to songbirds. *Stephen F. Austin State Univ. Nacogdoches. Tex. For. Pap. 28.* 13 pp.

Sucoff, E. I., and T. W. Church, Jr., 1960. Seed production and dissemination by Virginia pine. *J. For.* 58:885–888.

Sunda, H. J., and G. L. Lowry., 1975. Regeneration costs in loblolly pine management. *J. For.* 73:406–409.

Trevison, A., 1977. Site preparation using heavy equipment. In *Proc. Site Preparation Workshop.* pp. 16–17.

USDA For. Serv. Southeast. Forest Exp. Stn., 1951. Regenerating the "Big Scrub." *Res. News 14.* 2 pp.

USDA, 1957. *Yearbook of Agriculture.* 784 pp.

USDA For. Serv., 1958. *South. Forest Exp. Stn. Ann. Rep. 1957.*

USDA For. Serv., 1974. The outlook for timber in the United States. *FRR-20.* Washington, D.C. 367 pp.

USDA For. Serv., 1976. Hardwood distribution on pine sites in the South. *Res. Bull. SO-59.* 27 pp.

USDA For. Serv., 1977a. Basic timber resource statistics for the fifteen southern states. In *For. Farmer Man.* pp. 42–43.

USDA For. Serv., 1977b. The Nation's renewable resources—An assessment, 1975. *USDA For. Serv. FRR-21.* Washington, D.C. 243 pp.

Wahlenberg, W. G., 1946. Longleaf pine. *Chas. Lathrop Pack For. Found.* Washington, D.C. 429 pp.

Walker, L. C., 1954. Early scrub-oak control helps longleaf pine seedlings. *J. For.* 52:939–940.

Walker, L. C., 1963a. Hardwood control not always essential. *For. Farmer* 22(13):9.

Walker, L. C., 1963b. Natural Areas of the Southeast. *J. For.* 61:670–673.

Walker, L. C., and V. B. Davis., 1954. Forest walls retard longleaf. *So. For. Exp. Stn. So. For. Note 93.*

Walker, L. C., and V. B. Davis., 1956. Seed trees retard longleaf pine seedlings. *J. For.* 54:269.

Wells, C. G., D. M. Crutchfield, N. M. Berenyi, and C. B. Davey., 1973. Soil and foliar guidelines for phosphorus fertilization of loblolly pine. *USDA For. Serv. Res. Pap. SE-110.* 15 pp.

Wenger, K. F., 1957. Annual variation in the seed crops of loblolly pine. *J. For.* 55:567–569.

Whitesell, C. D., and A. J. Pickall., 1956. The present status of Virginia pine management. *Md. Dept. Res. and Ed. Release 56–58.*

Williamson, M. J., 1953. Young Virginia pine responds to thinning and pruning. *J. For.* 51:129.

Woods, F. W., 1956. Relation of soil moisture and temperature to weed control. *In Proc. South. Weed Conf.* pp. 161–165.

Woods, F. W., 1957. Factors limiting root penetration in deep sand of the southeastern Coastal Plain. *Ecology* 38:357–359.

Zahner, R., 1955. Soil water depletion by pine and hardwood stands during a dry season. *For. Sci.* 1:258–264.

Zahner, R., 1957. Mapping soils for pine site quality in south Arkansas and north Louisiana. *J. For.* 55:430–433.

Zoerb, M. H., Jr., 1977. A second look at operational plantations of improved slash pine. *Union Camp Corp. Woodlands Res. Note 33.* 3 pp.

7

The Middle and Southern Rocky Mountain Region

T. W. Daniel

LOCATION

The Middle and Southern Rocky Mountain Region, as covered in this chapter, includes the forested parts of the states of Arizona, Nevada, Utah, Wyoming, Colorado, New Mexico, and the western part of South Dakota. The Middle Rocky Mountains actually extend into southern Idaho and a part of Montana (Fig. 7-1) and, while the silvicultural practices for the various forest types in the region will hold for these areas, the statistics presented do not include them. The region is an area of high elevations, mostly above 4,000 feet, characterized by basins or valleys surrounded by mountains or plateaus which extend to elevations of 12,000 to 14,000 feet. As a whole, the region is semiarid, especially at elevations where the major population centers and the farms are located. Adequate rainfall to support forests occurs only at the higher elevations; 6,000 feet is an average lower limit for trees, except for those growing along the river banks.

FOREST STATISTICS

The casual traveler over the main highways of this region sees it as a vast treeless area. A few "scenic routes" for tourists, which follow the higher elevations, give a better impression of the true extent of the forests. The typical impression is due, first, to the normal location of highways along the usually treeless valley bottoms that take either the shortest route between valleys over intervening ranges or the cheaper, circuitous route, avoiding the necessity of climbing to the higher forested elevations; and, second, to the largely treeless nature of the region. Although the percentage of forest cover is low (23 percent excluding the forested area of the national parks), the total area of forest is large

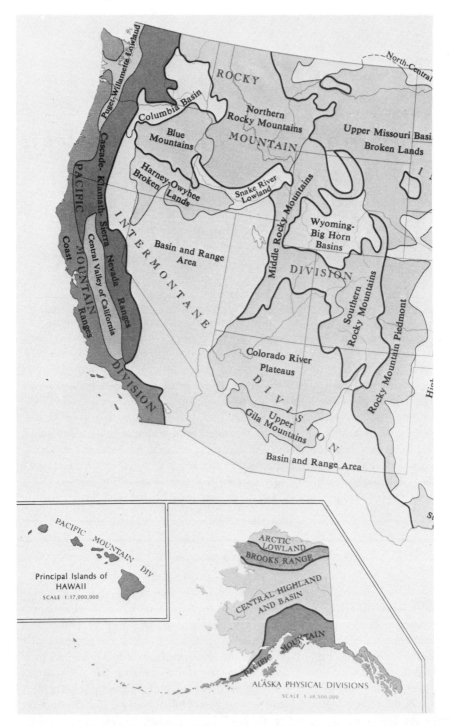

Figure 7-1.   Physical Subdivisions of Western United States, Alaska and Hawaiian Islands using Albers Equal Area Projection (U.S. Geol. Survey, 1966).

with 30 million acres of commercial timber, 8 million acres of commercial timber in various forms of reserves on the national forests, and 56 million acres of noncommercial forests.[1]

Areas

The total area of the region is 21 percent of the contiguous states and, while it is 23 percent forested, the division of forests among the states is uneven especially in terms of commercial area. Total forested area ranges from 11 percent in Nevada to 34 percent in Colorado (Arizona 25, New Mexico 23, Utah 30, Wyoming 16, and western South Dakota 20 percent). The proportion of commercial area varies between the Black Hills of western South Dakota with 91 percent to Nevada with 2 percent (Arizona 21, New Mexico 31, Utah 29, Wyoming 43, and Colorado 51 percent).

This region contrasts sharply with others in the distribution of major land uses. It has the lowest cropland percentage (5 percent) and the highest percentage of land used for pasture and range (66 percent).

Character of Forest Land Ownership

The unique feature of forest-land ownership in this region is the dominance of the federal government. Almost all of the noncommercial forest area is in public ownership. Commercial timber is 76.5 percent in public ownership and 23.5 percent in private ownership, mostly farmers. Of the commercial forests in public ownership, the national forests control 83 percent (without including the commercial areas in reserve categories), the Bureau of Land Management 4 percent (mostly in Wyoming, Colorado, and Utah), Bureau of Indian Affairs 9 percent (mostly Arizona and New Mexico), and states and other federal agencies 4 percent (mostly Utah, Colorado, New Mexico, and Wyoming). Wyoming has 43 percent of its commercial forests in various reserve categories, which does not include the areas in Yellowstone National Park, while the region as a whole has 21 percent.

The bulk of the private commercial forest area is in Colorado, New Mexico, and Wyoming. The average size of the private holdings ranges from 31 acres in the Black Hills to 850 acres in New Mexico.

Forest inventory

The distribution of commercial area and total inventory among the principal species is given in Table 7-1. The table indicates that the ponderosa pine is predominant in area, but the spruce-fir type surpasses it in cubic-feet and board-foot volumes. Economically the ponderosa pine is also the dominant species because of its excellent technical qualities and accessibility. The region has about 95 percent of its commercial volume in marketable species but the

[1]USDA For. Serv., 1978.

TABLE 7-1

Distribution of Area and Net Volume Among the Commercial Species, Exclusive of Reserved and National Park Volumes, of the Middle and Southern Rocky Mountain Region. (Board foot volume by International One-Quarter Inch Rule)

Species	Area (Thousand Acres)	Percent	Cubic Feet Billions	Percent	Board Feet Billions	Percent	Ratio (Board Feet/Cubic Feet)
Softwoods							
Douglas-fir	3,590	12.0	3.8	9.5	16.9	11.0	4.46
Ponderosa pine	11,848	39.7	10.9	27.2	45.3	29.6	4.16
Lodgepole pine	3,708	12.4	6.8	16.9	21.0	13.7	3.12
Engelmann spruce Subalpine fir	5,397	18.1	12.1	30.3	53.4	34.8	ES 4.79 SF 3.37
White fir	382	1.3	1.3	3.2	5.5	3.6	4.29
Other softwoods	324	1.1	0.8	1.9	3.0	2.0	3.98
Hardwoods							
Aspen	4,492	15.0	4.2	10.6	7.7	5.0	1.81
Cottonwood and others	124	0.4	0.1	0.4	0.4	0.3	3.22
	29,865	100	40.0	100	153.2	100	

Source: USDA For. Serv., 1978.

low board-foot to cubic-foot ratio indicates the prevalence of small-sized trees. This is particularly true of aspen, lodgepole pine, and subalpine fir. The small-sized trees reflects the average site quality of the region as well as the growth habits of the species. Site quality is adversely affected by the high elevations and short growing season as well as rainfall deficiencies during the growing season that is so characteristic of much of the region. If site 1 is the best and site 5 the poorest site capable of producing commercial timber, then the commercial forest area is apportioned as follows: site 2 is less than 1 percent; site 3 is 3 percent; site 4 is 25 percent; and site 5 is 72 percent.

Another characteristic of the region is the predominance of sawtimber which occupies 67 percent of the commercial forest area while poles cover 20 percent, saplings 7 percent, and nonstocked 6 percent. As a proportion of the cutover area, nonstocked and poorly stocked increases to 25 percent. The reasons for the high proportion of sawtimber are the inaccessibility of large areas of timber and the lack of interest until recently by industry because of the smallness of the trees and the lack of familiarity with the major species other than ponderosa pine.

Regional net growth exceeds the mortality losses with mortality about 42 percent of net growth in board feet and 47 percent in cubic feet. In Utah, the mortality exceeds net growth with mortality 111 percent of net growth in board feet and 107 percent in cubic feet. In the Black Hills of South Dakota where the forests have been under management the longest, the mortality has been reduced to 10 percent of the net growth. In the absence of a beetle epidemic, the Black Hills mortality is primarily the result of fire and suppression.

In terms of utilization, the regional average removal of commercial timber is 48 percent of net growth in cubic feet and 60 percent of net growth in board feet. However, in Arizona the volume removed exceeds net growth with 124 percent of cubic feet and 156 percent of board feet net growth cut. In New Mexico, there is 61 percent of cubic feet and 101 percent of board feet net growth cut. In conjunction with the difficulties of getting natural reproduction and the uncertainties of planting, the overcutting poses problems for the future.

The distribution of various forest cover types among the states is given in Table 7-2. Table 7-2 also lists the total area of forest land in the states exclusive of national parks. Reserved commercial forest land represents 8.5 percent (8,004,000 acres) of total forest area while the noncommerical area is 59.5 percent (55,592,000 acres) of the total. The noncommercial area is primarily the pinyon-juniper cover type.

Forest Industries

Lumber production is the principal use of timber accounting for about 76 percent of the cubic volume harvested and 84 percent of the board feet. Pulpwood and logging residues account for 15 percent of the cubic feet utilized and are supplied mostly from Arizona, Colorado, and South Dakota. Mine

TABLE 7-2

Nonreserved Commercial Area Distribution of the Various Forest Cover Types Among the States of the Region and Total Area of Forests Including Reserves and Noncommercial but Excluding National Parks.

Species	Distribution by States (Thousand Acres and Percent)							
	Arizona	Colorado	Nevada	New Mexico	Western South Dakota	Utah	Wyoming	Percent
Douglas-fir	186.0	1,294.7	2.9	995.6	—	552.3	558.4	
	5.2	36.1	0.1	27.7		15.4	15.5	100
Ponderosa pine	3,432.1	2,304.4	60.3	3,544.3	1,170.5	403.5	932.7	
	29.0	19.4	0.5	29.9	9.9	3.4	7.9	100
Lodgepole pine	—	1,736.7	8.3	—	—	495.7	1,466.7	
		46.8	0.2			13.4	39.6	100
Spruce-fir	145.2	2,964.4	13.6	471.5	24.3	777.5	1,000.5	
	2.7	54.9	0.3	8.7	0.5	14.4	18.5	100
Aspen	112.1	2,853.7	6.5	338.4	20.7	950.3	210.3	
	2.5	63.5	0.1	7.5	0.5	21.2	4.7	100
White fir	14.3	14.3	32.9	136.0	—	184.5	0.3	
	3.7	3.7	8.6	35.6		48.3	0.1	100
Other softwoods	5.9	68.1	9.1	51.7	—	40.8	148.8	
	1.8	21.0	2.8	15.9		12.6	45.9	100
Other hardwoods	—	78.5	0.7	—	28.6	—	16.5	
		63.2	0.5		23.0		13.3	100
Total	3,895.6	11,314.7	134.3	5,537.5	1,244.1	3,404.6	4,334.2	
	13.0	37.9	0.5	18.5	4.2	11.4	14.5	100
Total Forest Area	18,493.9	22,271.0	7,683.3	18,059.8	1,367.3	15,557.4	10,028.3	

Source: USDA For. Serv., 1978.

timbers, poles, posts, excelsior, charcoal, piling, and other products consume 4 percent of cubic volume harvested. Veneer in Colorado uses 2 percent of the regional output. Firewood and other uses account for 3 percent of cubic feet cut.

Two pulp mills in Arizona utilize the ponderosa pine thinnings and logging and mill wastes from the Coconino Plateau. The region has an abundance of the best pulping species with its huge area of spruce and fir, yet it is an undeveloped resource because of the lack of water. The water quality where available is poor.

Other Forest Benefits

Water.   A feature of the region, with an importance already suggested but which cannot be overemphasized, is the role that water plays in its thinking and economy. All but a minor portion of the total population lives in the arid and semiarid valleys within and around the mountains. Agriculture is wholly dependent upon irrigation, with the exception of limited areas suitable for dry farming. The only areas receiving enough precipitation to give usable runoff are the forest-covered slopes and the areas above the timber line. Dortignac's data (1960) from his detailed analysis of the Upper Rio Grande Basin provide a basis for calculating the water contribution of the various vegetative cover types. This calculation shows that 28 percent of the area (occupied by spruce-fir-aspen, ponderosa pine [mixed conifer], and mountain grassland cover types) yield 91 percent of the water. In Colorado, 97 percent of the runoff comes from the spruce-fir-aspen and mountain grassland areas, and in Utah most of the runoff comes from the forested slopes. Since grazing fees and timber production on most of the high elevation forested areas and mountain meadows do not compare with the values represented by their water production, it seems reasonable to assume that forest management or grazing practices which adversely affect water yield or its quality should be modified in favor of water. Water has become even more crucial with the need to develop the tremendous energy sources represented by the coal and oil shales in the region as water is the limiting factor in their availability.

The region is the source of many major rivers and their tributaries. Some of the more well-known rivers are the Snake, Colorado, Rio Grande, Pecos, Arkansas, Platte, and Yellowstone. In the lower reaches of these rivers, agriculture and industries have developed which depend on water originating in the mountains. Future development depends upon the region keeping control of a fair share of its water and maintaining the high-mountain watersheds in water-productive condition.

Grazing.   Grazing has occupied an important place since the settlement of the region because about two-thirds of the total area is only useful for this purpose. The grazing economy is dependent upon access to the summer forage on the forested parts to supplement winter use of the desert ranges. Investigations (Pearson, 1934) have shown that heavy, indiscriminate grazing and good silviculture do not mix; but controlled grazing with the right class of livestock may be compatible with good reproduction and growth.

Range use is divided according to season. Winter ranges are the semiarid or arid areas on which water is so scarce that the forage can only be utilized when winter snows are on the ground. Spring and fall ranges, located at intermediate elevations, provide fresh-green feed for spring lambing and sufficient water late in the fall. Summer ranges are at the high elevations, the forested zones. Balancing the use of these seasonal ranges is an acute problem because the capacity of the winter ranges exceeds all the others.

Reduction in livestock numbers to fit the needs of silviculture, watershed management, or even to maintain good range conditions is bitterly fought by the livestock industry. As the summer ranges are primarily on national forest lands, the interests of watershed management, good range practices, and silviculture have forced a series of livestock reductions on the livestock producer. Where a conflict of interest exists between grazing and watershed management, the balance is often in favor of watershed management on critical areas. This is illustrated by the actions taken on the flood-producing Davis County (Utah) watershed and on the Wellsville Range (Utah). After a series of severe floods and the drying up of local water supplies from springs were traced to conditions produced by overgrazing on private lands, local people purchased these areas and deeded them to the U.S. Forest Service, with the provision that grazing be excluded.

THE PHYSICAL ENVIRONMENT

Physiography

Two great barrier mountain ranges, the Rocky Mountains and the Sierra Nevada, help form the boundaries of the Middle and Southern Rocky Mountain Region. Because this area is too large and too varied in its physiographic elements to treat as a unit, it is best treated as several provinces, namely, Southern Rocky Mountains, Wyoming–Big Horn Basin, Middle Rocky Mountains, Colorado Plateaus, Basin and Range area of Nevada and western Utah, and southern Basin and Range area (Fig. 7-1). The Black Hills of South Dakota are included because they are of comparable structure to the Southern Rocky Mountains, only somewhat removed from the main mountain axis.

In terms of commercial timber some of these provinces are relatively unimportant, lacking almost any kind of forest cover. The Wyoming-Big Horn Basin, and the Basin and Range areas, and parts of the Colorado Plateaus are primarily deserts whose dryness and high altitude raise the elevation of the forest boundary of the ranges bordering them. The high evaporative power of west winds sweeping across these deserts during the growing season reduces the effectiveness of the annual rainfall and partially accounts for juniper in one place and ponderosa pine in another, both localities receiving about the same annual rainfall.

The Middle and Southern Rocky Mountains and the Colorado River Plateaus contain most of the commercial timber stands. The Southern Rocky Mountains rise abruptly from the Great Plains. Composed of two more or less parallel, deeply eroded anticlines, they are made up of several ranges whose crests are uniformly 12,000 to 14,000 feet high. Erosion has in most places exposed granite, except in the San Juan Mountains at the southern end of the inner ranges, which are of volcanic origin. The Colorado Front Range runs from the northern end of the Laramie Range to terminate abruptly at the south end of the Sangre de Cristo Range. Between the two main elements of the Southern Rocky Mountains are a series of large basins over 7,500 feet in elevation, which are kept relatively dry by the high ranges flanking them.

On the north and west of the Wyoming–Big Horn Basin are the Middle Rocky Mountains, separated from the Northern Rocky Mountains by two short ranges at the headwaters of the Yellowstone River. These mountains form individual ranges instead of continuous chains like the Southern Rocky Mountains.

The horizontal strata and the high elevation of the formations composing the Colorado River Plateaus are their most distinguishing features. The elevations of individual plateaus and the degree to which they have been dissected by erosion vary. They differ in forest cover with the high plateaus of Utah and the plateaus of central Arizona and New Mexico, possessing the best and most extensive commercial stands.

The plateau country is the area of the cliff dwellers, dinosaur bones, colorful and unusual rock formations, precipitous canyons, and sheer cliffs. It is a wild and desolate country, almost inaccessible until uranium and oil discoveries pushed roads into it. The Colorado River and its tributaries, the Green, San Juan, Yampa, and Virgin rivers, have cut spectacular canyons, some of which form the basis for national parks.

Geology and Soils

This region has been reduced to a low gradient (peneplane) probably twice since the Permian Period about 250 million years ago (Fenneman, 1931). This action twice wore down and buried the granite skeleton of mountains beneath great depositions of sediments until an accumulated depth of 25,000 feet has been measured. When the ocean covered large portions of the region during the first peneplaning, tremendous limestone depths accumulated. The second burial, in the Pliocene, some 30 million years ago, was terrestial; and because it was not quite as complete as the earlier one, many granite peaks and some segments of the first peneplane resisted erosion. The Middle and Southern Rocky Mountains have been raised since the last peneplaning, by slow uplifting, as linear anticlines or long waves with more or less low gradients on top and with steep sides without any faulting or block movement. Erosion accelerated as soon as the uplift began; and, since the uplift was slow, the streams followed the topography of that period and cut through the sedimentary rocks. When erosion exposed the granite beneath the sediments, the rise was so slow that instead of being deflected, the rivers cut through the granite. Erosion has exposed the granite base throughout the Middle and Southern Rocky Mountains, but the main rivers are still flowing in the same channels that fit an earlier topography. This development explains why, in this region, many of the main rivers, like the Green or the North Platte, cut through mountains instead of going around them.

In the Colorado River Plateaus the uplift formed such a broad, low-gradient anticline that the strata still retain their horizontal position. Variations in exposure to erosion, differences resulting from the effects of volcanic activity, and differences in the erosiveness of the strata have combined to account for the variations in elevation and degrees of dissection found among the plateaus.

The exceptions to these anticline formations are two ranges on the western boundary of the mountain provinces of the region; the Teton Range and the Wasatch Mountains are the result of block movements so executed as to create very complex geology. The Wasatch forms part of the east boundary of the northern Basin and Range area, within which the ranges are generally considered to be formed by block movements. On the west side of the northern Basin and Range area, the Sierra Nevada is also the product of block deformation.

Glaciation was restricted to the mountains and occurred on all the main ranges during the Pleistocene. The glaciation has been local, but it materially assisted in eroding the mantle of sediments.

The consequences of this geological history are reflected in the soils. The soils derived from the granites and volcanic outpourings tend to be coarser, with a high gravel content, and are characteristic of the mountains and steeper slopes. In contrast, the soils which have developed on limestones and sandstones or other sedimentary formations are heavier and are usually found on the plateaus or, as the result of erosion, in the basins. Generally, soil formation is a matter of chemical and mechanical breakdown of the parent material. In this region, mechanical action is dominant at the arid lower elevations and at the moist but cold high elevations. The warmth and moisture required for chemical action is lacking in these locations. At the middle altitudes, the two forces complement each other and develop the deepest soils on a given parent material. Erosion, aspect, slope, and cover may all modify the soil depth in any locality. Thus, soil depth depends upon many factors and in a given locality will depend upon which one or combination of these is dominant.

Climate and Weather

Generally, precipitation is greater with increasing elevation. The dispersion of arid basins and valleys among the ranges and plateaus throughout this region, however, complicates the relation of altitude and rainfall. Precipitation usually increases with altitude along a continuous slope, although some evidence indicates that the tops of mountain peaks receive less precipitation than the slopes immediately below.

Two plateaus of the same elevation and latitude may receive entirely different amounts of annual precipitation, depending upon the height each is above the adjacent basin. A plateau or range which is 2,000 feet above the adjacent basin has much less precipitation than one which is 4,000 feet above. As a result, the first plateau may be covered with sagebrush or juniper, and the second, ponderosa pine or Engelmann spruce. Equally important in the precipitation relationship to elevation is the location of higher ranges in the vicinity. A higher range across the path of the moist air mass reduces the rainfall at any lower elevation beyond the barrier, such as on the ranges in Nevada which are in the rain shadow of the Sierra Nevada. Whether the range is oriented parallel to the movement of moist air or at right angles also affects precipitation. A glance at the rainfall map (Fig. 7-2) shows that the areas with rainfall above 20 inches annually are scattered like islands throughout the region, at the tops of the higher ranges and plateaus.

The Pacific Ocean provides precipitation primarily in the winter and the Gulf of Mexico or the southwest Pacific are the sources of most of the summer moisture in the region. The principal patterns of rainfall distribution (U.S. Weather Bureau, 1957) are illustrated in Fig. 7-3. The information was obtained from weather stations whose precipitation was greater than 10 inches per year and less than 30 inches, in order to get the rainfall pattern of the forested parts and to eliminate the bias which the stations of very high rainfall would introduce. The Black Hills have little winter precipitation, from which level the precipitation rises rather uniformly to a peak in May and June and falls uniformly again to its winter values. Nevada has very little precipitation in summer, but precipitation peaks in December to March. Central Arizona and the Coconino Plateau have two peak periods: one in December and January of Pacific origin; and one in July and August of Gulf origin. A serious feature of the Arizona pattern is the droughty May and June and the tendency for a droughty autumn, a direct result of the failure of a tropical air mass to come in from the south in time to replace the Pacific air when it retreats to the north. The pattern in northwestern Colorado west of the Continental Divide lacks the extremes of the other precipitation regimes and is more or less uniform throughout the year. A feature which averages do not show is the sharp fluctuations in seasonal and annual rainfall; these fluctuations lead one to conclude that it is probably the unusual year rather than the average year which accounts for the presence or absence of a particular type on critical sites.

The rainfall patterns for the region generally show low winter precipitation east of the Continental Divide, with high precipitation during the growing season. Immediately west of the Divide, the rainfall is more evenly divided between winter and summer, but the contribution of the tropical air masses grows smaller toward the north, as shown by the significant decrease in August values. From central Arizona, the marked summer peak falls rapidly toward the north and west.

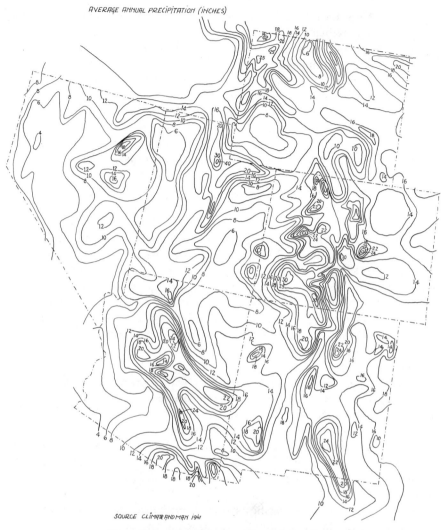

Figure 7-2.   Map of Regional Precipitation Pattern.

Patterns vary appreciably from year to year, but the variation is most obvious at the outer edges of the two kinds of air masses. Since moisture during the growing season is important for reproduction, the fluctuations in the amount of moisture contributed by the tropical air masses are often a major factor. Successful reproduction, in some localities like central Arizona and Utah, becomes a matter of how early in the spring the high pressure tropical air masses move into a position to favor the region with rain.

Snow is the usual form of precipitation throughout the region during the winter months, except in the lower elevations of Arizona and New Mexico. In

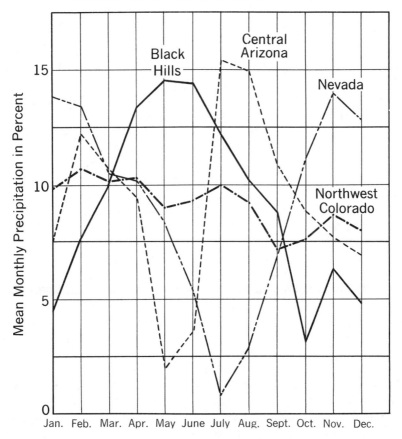

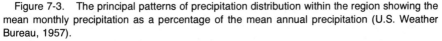

Figure 7-3.   The principal patterns of precipitation distribution within the region showing the mean monthly precipitation as a percentage of the mean annual precipitation (U.S. Weather Bureau, 1957).

the high rainfall zones it accumulates to considerable depths and mantles the soil from November to May, occasionally on north slopes even into July. East of the Continental Divide, snow does not accumulate at the intermediate elevations as it does west of the Divide, partly because winter precipitation is low and partly because the predominant west wind expands and warms as it drops down the east slope, melting the snow mantle.

Rainfall in the summer is either convective or orographic, with both processes occasionally operating together. Convective rains frequently reach very high intensities for relatively short periods at lower elevations. These cloudbursts account for the deep, intricate system of canyons in this typically arid region. At high elevations, convective rains do not commonly reach such intensities. Where summer rains constitute a major proportion of the precipitation, the most frequent rains are those that come in the afternoon, with only light to moderate intensity and last from a few minutes to an hour or two. It may rain almost every day at high elevations from Wyoming to southern New Mexico during some periods of the summer.

At elevations where commercial timber stands develop, freezing temperatures may occur in any month of the year. The length of the frost-free period as a measure of the growing season is not very accurate, but an average year may have a frost-free period of 90 to 110 days at 6,000 feet elevation and 30 to 50 days at 10,000 feet. Frost-free periods vary in length within the region, even for the same elevations. This variation is not necessarily associated with changes in latitude but occurs in local areas where topographic features warp trends (Baker, 1934). Frost, however, usually does little injury to the principal species within their natural zones other than delaying growth. The growing season is dependent upon total heat supply above the growth threshold rather than upon uninterrupted favorable temperatures. The duration, severity, and frequency of a freezing period once growth has started may well be a factor determining the upper altitudinal limits of a species. This idea suggests that Engelmann spruce and subalpine fir are more resistant to frost damage than ponderosa pine.

Generally, mean temperatures decrease with increased altitude. The mean monthly minimums show a temperature inversion at 9,400 feet elevation in Arizona with the minimum temperatures higher than at 8,540 feet. The range in temperature within the region is excessive, varying between 127 °F at Parker, Arizona (elevation 400 feet), to a −63 °F at Moran, Wyoming (elevation 6,740 feet). At Fort Valley, Arizona (elevation 7,397 feet), in the ponderosa pine type the range is from 94 °F to −33 °F; and in the lodgepole pine type at Moran, Wyoming, it is from 92 °F to −63 °F. These values are the extremes within the period of weather records, but approximately such values occur in any year. Mean annual temperature is lowest, with 32.3 °F at Yellowstone Lake, Wyoming (elevation 7,731 feet), in the lodgepole pine type and highest in the desert part of Arizona at Mohawk (elevation 538 feet), with 74.5 °F.

As a rule, winds do not build up to destructive velocities in the region at forested elevations. Occasionally, a severe blow-down in over-mature Engelmann spruce stands affects a large area, as on the White River Plateau in 1939 and on the San Juan National Forest in 1954. Blowdown occurs to an individual or a small group of trees rather than a mass windthrow, such as may be produced by hurricanes or tornadoes. Steady winds from the west are characteristic of high elevations, and the dessication produced is a common cause of the upper timber line. The occurrence of strong winds in the spring and fall requires careful cutting practices on exposed sites or in shallow-rooted stands.

THE MAJOR FOREST TYPE GROUPS

Over 60 species of trees, half of them conifers, without counting a greater number which reach only small-tree size, grow within the region. Many of these species will not be treated in detail because little is known of their silviculture, because some, such as the pinyon pines and the junipers, are best considered as a unit, or because some, as is the case with *Fraxinus, Juglans, Platanus, Robinia, Acer,* and *Quercus,* have only dendrologic interest rather than commercial value.

The seven primary forest cover types (Fig. 7-4) occurring over large areas of the region are: oak woodland, pinyon-juniper, ponderosa pine, Douglas-fir (mixed conifer type especially in Southwest), aspen, lodgepole pine, and spruce-fir. Transition zones between types are extensive and dominate some localities.

Characteristic of these types throughout the region is the persistence of a zonal pattern. A transect run from a low-elevation valley bottom to the crest of a high range would cross the forest cover types in a definite sequence anywhere in the region, except that all the types might not be present in any one transect. As the result of his experience in the Southwest, Merriam (1889) in defining his life zones, was the first to formally recognize that each species was associated with a particular climatic pattern and could be used as an indicator of that pattern.

Daubenmire (1943), after balancing the conflicts in the literature with his own experience, concludes that the factors causing this zonation of forest types are primarily moisture for the lower elevational limit of a species distribution and temperature for the upper limit. This explains the common inversion types as related to topography; the high-elevation types follow the cool, moist canyons to elevations below their usual altitudinal zone, or the lower-elevation types follow the warm ridges to elevations well above their usual zone. Daubenmire (1943) distinguished seven major vegetation zones as primarily characteristic of the Rocky Mountains. These are listed as follows, arrayed from alpine tundra that occurs at the highest to grassland desert that occurs at the lowest elevations:

1. Alpine tundra zone.
2. Engelmann spruce−subalpine fir zone.
3. Douglas-fir zone.
4. Ponderosa pine zone.
5. Juniper-pinyon zone.
6. Oak—mountain-mahogany zone.
7. Grassland and desert zone.

Each of the tree zones tend to occupy an altitudinal stratum of about 2,000 feet, when conditions are favorable for the reproduction of the key species. The spruce-fir type, however, is the only one reasonably consistent throughout the region, as the others are narrower or entirely missing in some areas. Their absence is due to climatic conditions that preclude establishment of reproduction (Baker and Korstian, 1931), or to a series of catastrophes that eliminated the more tolerant species over large areas and permitted pioneer species to replace themselves.

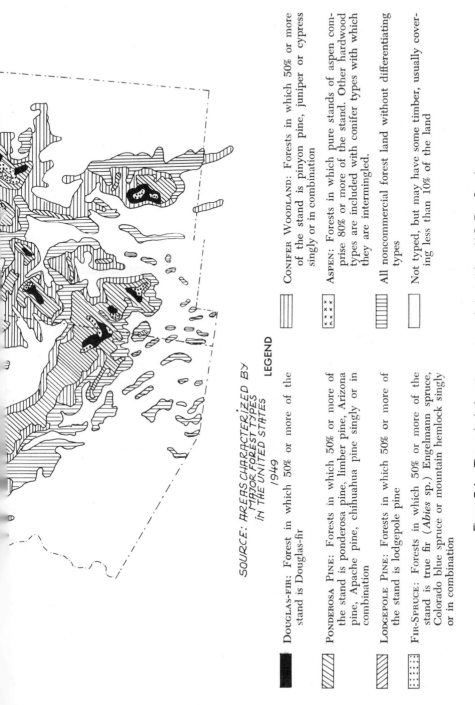

SOURCE: *AREAS CHARACTERIZED BY*
MAJOR FOREST TYPES
IN THE UNITED STATES
1949

LEGEND

DOUGLAS-FIR: Forest in which 50% or more of the stand is Douglas-fir

PONDEROSA PINE: Forests in which 50% or more of the stand is ponderosa pine, limber pine, Arizona pine, Apache pine, chihuahua pine singly or in combination

LODGEPOLE PINE: Forests in which 50% or more of the stand is lodgepole pine

FIR-SPRUCE: Forests in which 50% or more of the stand is true fir (*Abies* sp.) Engelmann spruce, Colorado blue spruce or mountain hemlock singly or in combination

CONIFER WOODLAND: Forests in which 50% or more of the stand is pinyon pine, juniper or cypress singly or in combination

ASPEN: Forests in which pure stands of aspen comprise 80% or more of the stand. Other hardwood types are included with conifer types with which they are intermingled.

All noncommercial forest land without differentiating types

Not typed, but may have some timber, usually covering less than 10% of the land

Figure 7-4. The region's forest cover types (adapted from U.S. For. Serv.).

293

The forest cover types, considered in relation to the precipitation pattern in Fig. 7-2, show a distinct zonation and regular pattern. Lodgepole pine and aspen cover extensive areas in the Douglas-fir zone and extend into the spruce-fir zone. Aspen has a wider distribution and elevational range than lodgepole pine but fails to appear on the type map, except in Utah and Wyoming, because it does not occur in extensive pure stands in other parts of the region. The ponderosa pine type is frequently shown in direct contact with the spruce-fir type, especially outside of the lodgepole pine distribution—as though the Douglas-fir zone were lacking. Actually, ponderosa pine predominates in the Douglas-fir zone in such places, but it is part of a mixed conifer type composed of ponderosa pine, Douglas-fir, white fir, other conifers, and aspen. Douglas-fir does dominate the cooler slopes within its zone and constitutes a prominent part of the understory on the warmer slopes.

HISTORY OF FOREST USE

Intensive exploitation of the timber developed when railroads opened up the region. The first mills in every section date from between 1870 to 1885. Before 1900, the mills of the region were sawing 250 million board feet per year, and the native lumber was supplemented by shipments from the east. In the mining districts, clearcutting and wildfires were prominent in the history of forest use. If the trees were not used for mining timbers, they were often converted to charcoal. Ensign (1888) reports the Leadville, Colorado, smelters alone as using 10,000 bushels of charcoal a day. This was the era of railroad building on a grand scale when ties, bridges, and construction material were taken from the nearest suitable stands. Trespass was common, and fires were the usual aftermath of logging.

In the Black Hills, ponderosa pine reproduced so readily or advanced reproduction was so plentiful where burns failed to destroy it that only areas repeatedly burned remained in the non-restocked category. In other parts of the region, clearcutting favored lodgepole pine and aspen because of aspen's capacity for prolific suckering and because of lodgepole pine's ability to reseed clearcut areas with the seed stored in its serotinous cones. Where everything merchantable was cut in stands of spruce-fir, Douglas-fir, and ponderosa pine, the uneven-aged character of the old-growth stands and the presence of low-value species (like aspen and subalpine and white firs) left them in productive condition. The lasting effects of fire depended upon the size of the burned area, the intensity of the fire, and how often the fires were repeated.

Fires in the Rocky Mountains occurred long before the advent of settlement. Clements (1910), in his detailed analysis of fires in lodgepole pine, found evidence of burns back in 1707, and it is likely that records of earlier burns have been lost for lack of surviving trees. The extensive areas of lodgepole probably owe their existence to periodic fires at the expense of Douglas-fir.

Fire and insects cause spectacular losses in the region, but the seriousness of diseases, root rots, and lightning cannot be underestimated. Two outbreaks of insects overshadow the constant attrition that is the yearly toll of these other destructive agents. In 1895, the Black Hills beetle began to reach epidemic numbers on the ridges in the northwestern part of the Black Hills, and the infestation spread until half the forested area was involved. By 1909, when the epidemic had passed its peak, it was estimated that 1.5 billion board feet had been killed.

Colorado experienced its biggest forest disaster following a widespread blow-down on the White River Plateau in 1939. Many factors contributed to the buildup of the Engelmann spruce beetle in the blowdown area. The most important was the lack of control measures resulting from the scarcity of manpower during the war period. Also, the protection of the overwintering insects from winter mortality by the heavy snows which buried the blowdowns favored their increase. The same snows prevented the woodpeckers and natural enemies from functioning as controls. There was an estimated loss of 4.5 billion board feet by 1953 when the epidemic was slowed down by control measures and lack of host species.

Sawtimber percentage for the various states (Table 7-3) does not reflect the actual conditions of the stands as sawtimber in some states may consist of a high percentage of partially cut areas with young growth like the Black Hills of South Dakota where very little area in old-growth stands remains. In Arizona and New Mexico, the sawtimber of the ponderosa pine type is predominantly young growth. The high percentage of poles in Colorado, Utah, and Wyoming is in large measure attributable to the presence of lodgepole pine and aspen on poor sites and poor sites are a large proportion of the areas.

The Black Hills, an island of timber in the midst of farming country, has experienced an early and steady demand for timber. The erection of the first sawmill in 1876 coincided with the first legislative authorization by Congress for a study of forest conservation. In 1899 the first sale of government timber under a contract calling for specific forestry practices was made in this area under the designation "Case No. 1."

SILVICULTURE OF THE MAJOR TYPE GROUPS

General

In every type of the Middle and Southern Rocky Mountain Region, forest management at this time is primarily concerned with the problems of harvesting old-growth timber. For a sound timber economy, the harvesting must meet the demands of sustained yield by assuring the restocking of cutover areas. This must be done in spite of the difficulties introduced by the general overmaturity of the timber and its susceptibility to windthrow, insects, and disease. When varied and frequently adverse climatic patterns, slow growth, relatively small tree size, long rotations, inaccessible stands, and the need to provide both

TABLE 7-3

Commercial Forest Land by States and Stand Size.

State	Area (Thousand Acres)	Percent			
		Sawtimber	Pole	Sapling	Nonstocked
Arizona	3,896	87.4	5.5	4.0	3.1
Colorado	11,315	51.3	30.4	7.5	10.8
Nevada	134	86.7	2.5	5.4	5.4
New Mexico	5,537	83.5	7.0	5.8	3.7
South Dakota (western)	1,244	67.9	24.5	6.9	0.7
Utah	3,405	67.8	22.6	7.7	1.9
Wyoming	4,334	64.7	22.6	8.0	4.7
Total	29,865				

Source: USDA For. Serv., 1978.

summer forage for grazing and recreational opportunities and facilities for increasing numbers of people are added as complicating factors, it is easy to realize why the region's silviculture provides a complex challenge. In addition, the limitation set by the finite water supply on the economic growth of the region has given high priority to managing the forests for maximum water yield, with minimum erosion from the steep slopes.

A second cutting cycle is underway in some areas. These cuts are for the most part in ponderosa pine stands that had previously been harvested under a modified shelterwood method in the Black Hills or under various forms of the selection method in other parts of the region. Intermediate cuts in young stands are being made or planned as outlets for the material developed and as the probable effects of precommercial thinnings on the allowable cut become policy.

With the exception of investigations on ponderosa pine in the Southwest and some on Engelmann spruce and lodgepole pine at Fraser Experimental Forest, the research devoted to management problems of the region's forests has been limited until recent years because range-management and watershed-management problems were the most pressing. As a result, silviculture recommendations are too heavily dependent upon observational data. The region has, however, a significant contribution to make to the nation's perpetual supply of forest products when management practices bring about the conversion of the under-stocked, overmature stands, which now have little or no net growth, to better-stocked and more productive stands.

Management practices are not a matter of special formulas to be applied to each type or stand but, rather, the result of an awareness of the ecological forces operating on each site combined with a knowledge of the silvics of the various species. The practices which are adequate within the zone of species optimum may well be inadequate in a zone of tension. In this region, because its predominantly semiarid climate makes forest growth possible only at the higher elevations on the many mountain ranges and plateaus, the tension zones between the cover types are conspicuous and extensive. Within the forested areas, because of the widely differing requirements of the tree species, numerous and complex zones of tension are created by the steep rainfall and temperature gradients as well as by the effects of aspect and by the complex soil patterns resulting from soils developing on parent material of varying geologic origins.

Silvicultural decision making has acquired a tremendous assist from the application of the habitat-typing technique (Daubenmire and Daubenmire, 1968) to the Northern Rocky Mountains and its spread into this region. Habitat types are discussed in Chapter 8. To illustrate, using habitat types in this region ponderosa pine stands are no longer looked upon as homogeneous populations that will respond well to a particular silvicultural prescription. Ponderosa pine may be the climax tree on any one of numerous habitat types for each of which the silvicultural prescription needs to be modified. However, it may be seral on many more habitat types and though mapped as a ponderosa pine cover type, the choices of what to do and how to do it have greatly expanded. Habitat typing has broken down the enormous areas covered by single forest cover types into components about which the responses of a species or combination of species to various silvicultural treatments can be reasonably well predicted. The habitat typing provides a base for improving the predictability of responses in the future.

A second major contribution to better silviculture in the region has been the development by the Forest Service of certified silviculturists who must approve any stand manipulation on national forest land. This has helped avoid serious errors in judgment like those that have been made in the past.

Rocky Mountain Ponderosa Pine Type Group

Ponderosa pine is native to every state in the region. Taxonomists recognize several varieties of the species, which can be distinguished by the morphology of the needles. Rocky Mountain ponderosa pine (*Pinus ponderosa* var. *scopulorum*) is the principal variety found in this region, although there is considerable argument over the varietal status, especially in the Southwest. Weidman's study (1939) indicates that racial physiological differences are more pronounced than the morphological, and they are inheritable adaptations to local environmental conditions. Thus, silvical characteristics like frost hardiness, rate of height and diameter growth, and longevity vary with locality within rather wide limits. Keen (1950) has gone so far as to suggest that, silvically, *P. ponderosa* var. *scopulorum* is a different tree than *P. ponderosa*, because their resistance or susceptibility to bark beetles is so markedly different, thereby permitting different silvicultural treatments.

Place in Ecological Succession. Ponderosa pine has the lowest elevational distribution of any commercial species in the region, with pinyon-juniper, woodland oak, or chaparral below it in the south, and sagebrush, grass, or sometimes juniper below it in the north. Ponderosa pine occurs at an elevation of 5,500 feet in Arizona and in Colorado, while in the Black Hills it drops to 3,300 feet. Ponderosa pine may reach elevations of over 9,000 feet but at the higher elevations it is limited to the warm south-facing slopes.

The lower elevations of the type are only indicative of the extreme at which adequate conditions for growth exist. There may be a greater difference in elevation of lower boundary because of aspect or variation in base level within a locality as among regional provinces. Rydberg (1913) describes Abajo Mountain (elevation 11,445 feet) in southeastern Utah as completely lacking in timber on the southern and western aspects at all elevations, while the northern and eastern slopes have a complete series of zones from pinyon-juniper to alpine. Irrespective of its actual elevation, the lower boundary is primarily determined by rainfall and evaporational stress, although the effectiveness of the rainfall may be modified by soil. Baker and Korstian (1931) give the mean annual precipitation for weather stations within the boundaries of the type as varying from 10 to 25 inches, yet extensive areas within the region with comparable annual rainfall fail to support stands of ponderosa pine. The annual rainfall total could be adequate; but, because of its unfavorable distributional pattern, high evaporational stresses, or unfavorable soil conditions, no ponderosa pine occurs.

At the lowest elevations, and where the type occurs in isolated stands, ponderosa pine is limited to sandy or gravelly soils because of their more favorable moisture supply. The light soils are more favorable to the establishment of ponderosa pine because they permit more rapid root penetration, allow a light rain to quickly reach a depth beyond evaporation loss, and because the low fertility of such soils places competing vegetation at a disadvantage. As moisture conditions become more favorable soil texture and depth become less restrictive. This type does well on soil of any origin and texture with a pH range of 4.5 to 7.5 provided it has good drainage and is not too calcareous. Meyer (1938) was unable to relate growth capacity of a stand to soil and concluded that "an intensive study of the correlation between site quality and the character of the soil would include much more than the soil's quality, texture, color, and depth." Heavier soils like a clay loam are associated with the better sites, provided they also have adequate moisture and drainage.

Ponderosa pine is a Transition Zone species (Merriam, 1898) and it forms a climax within its zone. However, its most productive sites are in the Douglas-fir zone where it is a seral species.

Ponderosa pine forms a climax in the Transition Zone because it is a drought-resistant species capable of surviving after the soil moisture has been reduced to the permanent wilting point (as measured by sunflowers). This is accomplished by the reduction of transpiration to a minute fraction of the losses with normal water supply (Fowells and Kirk, 1945). The characteristic resistance to drought does not mean that ponderosa pine is an economical user of water when water is readily available. Bates (1923) has shown that ponderosa pine transpires 4.98 grams per square centimeter of leaf surface in a season, while the mesophytic species, Douglas-fir and Engelmann spruce, lose 2.26 and 1.99 grams, respectively. Daniel (1942), using plants in water culture under controlled humidity and temperature, found ponderosa pine losing an average of 73 percent of sunflower losses at 90, 70, 50, and 30 percent relative humidities at 75 °F. The cooling effect of this high transpiration loss may increase the chances of the species to survive under the intense insolation common to the sites it dominates.

The ability of the ponderosa pine to resist drought is due in part to its root system. Berndt and Gibbons (1958) found ponderosa pine had a well-developed taproot and fairly uniform branching, unlike the finely branched root systems with masses of fine roots, of Douglas-fir, aspen, and lodgepole pine. They observed little difference in depth of root penetration among the species (about 5 feet), possibly because of inadequate moisture to wet the soil deeper. The form of the ponderosa pine's root system would permit free absorption of water at high soil-moisture levels, but the lack of intimate contact with the whole soil mass through a proliferation of fine rootlets, such as exists with the other species, would prevent the rapid pumping dry of the soil column in a droughty period.

Available moisture during the growing season is more limiting to the growth of ponderosa pine than is the size of the crown. Pearson's records (1943, 1950) indicate that a small-crowned tree can grow as fast after release as a large-crowned one. He places ground space after cutting (using it as a measure of access to moisture) on an equal footing with crown dominance and size as guides to silvicultural cutting when the crown of the dominant tree is at least one-third of the total height. Stuart and Roeser (1944) found in the Black Hills that crown development showed no particular influence on growth rate of thinned trees, as co-dominants often grew at a faster rate after release than dominants. They also attributed this to moisture being the most limiting factor for growth.

Ponderosa pine has a high heat requirement for best growth, which will be best met at lower elevations if sufficient moisture is available. On the west slope of the Sierra Nevada, ponderosa pine has a range in elevation of 6,000 feet, and the localities with the highest site quality are in the lower half of this elevational range. In the Middle and Southern Rocky Mountain Region, the usual range in elevation is about 2,000 feet but may reach 3,000 feet. This is the upper part of the altitudinal range of ponderosa pine and the heat available is below optimum for growth. Pearson's calculations (1931) of the physiological efficiency of the heat received in each zone indicates why ponderosa pine reaches its elevational limit in the Douglas-fir zone. Bates (1924) concludes that no surprising differences exist among various parts of the region in the temperature requirements of ponderosa pine, Douglas-fir, and spruce.

Ponderosa pine is an intolerant species, and its inability to compete under low-light or heavy-root competition is emphasized. The degree of its tolerance of low light was investigated by Pearson (1940) under no- or low-root competition. With more than 50 percent shade seedlings are too slender to resist snowbend, and with 67 percent or more shade the strikingly underdeveloped seedlings and transplants die within 10 years. In contrast, ponderosa pine can survive a high level of side shade if the tree gets direct overhead light, and this results in dense stands when conditions favor an even-aged wave of reproduction. Where the side shade comes from an adjacent overstory, the dividing line between where side shade is beneficial and where root competition becomes detrimental varies with the severity of the root competition. The lateral root development of conifers studied by Berndt and Gibbons (1958) averaged 70 percent of their height, while aspen's laterals extended 122 percent. Thus, the influence of tree-root competition must be added to the competition of ground vegetation. However, side shade is essential to a clean bole because too much light produces heavy branched and fast tapering stems.

Growth Rates.   Ponderosa pine in the region occurs in uneven-aged stands which are made up of a mosaic of small even-aged groups (Fig. 7-5). A group may cover several acres but usually is much smaller. An exception to the uneven-aged structure is the generally even-aged or two-storied structure of ponderosa pine in the Black Hills. In recent times the emphasis has been to convert the uneven-aged stands to an even-aged structure by clearcutting and planting. The practice has resulted in large nonstocked or poorly stocked areas. Growth is low in the unmanaged stands because they are characterized by deficient stocking or overstocking especially the 1919 age class of the Southwest. These stands have a predominance of older age classes with a generally poor age-class distribution, low-quality stems because of poor spacing and inadequate natural pruning, high mortality, slow growth of large trees, and inefficient use of available moisture (Pearson, 1950).

Growth potential in the region varies with the site quality and the diversity for ponderosa pine in the region is illustrated by the use of three different sets of site-index curves (Utah and Western Colorado, Meyer, 1961; Arizona and New Mexico, Minor, 1964; and Colorado Front Range, Mogren, 1956).

Site quality and density control the rate of growth of any species and the effect of density on ponderosa pine has been studied intensively at Flagstaff, Arizona (Schubert, 1974 and 1976). A series of growing stock level plots were established in 1962 in even-aged groups of 1919 reproduction (site index 88; Minor, 1964) at Taylor Woods. There were six levels of growing stock established from GSL-30 to GSL-150.[2]

Ponderosa pine remains physiologically young up to 200 years of age in its response to thinning. The 43-year-old groups at Taylor Woods had an average

[2]The growing stock levels (GSL's) are indices representing future basal areas when the average stand diameter is 10 inches or larger.

Figure 7-5.   Groupwise distribution of age classes, with a blackjack group in the foreground, in the uneven-aged ponderosa pine stands of the Southwest. Fort Valley Exp. For., Arizona with G.A. Pearson (U.S. For. Serv.).

density of 5,800 stems per acre with an average stand diameter of 2.6 inches (213.9 square feet of basal area per acre, Reineke SDI 648).[3] GSL-30 (19 square feet of basal area per acre after thinning) and GSL-150 (72 square feet of basal area per acre after thinning) had average periodic growths of 0.38 and 0.18 inches with an R^2 (correlation coefficient) of 0.96 between residual basal area and diameter increment. There were 515 trees left at GSL-30 and 1,953 trees at GSL-150 or SDI 62 and SDI 218. The specific gravity of the fast growth and slow growth remained the same.

[3]Reineke SDI is the number of trees per acre as if the average stand diameter were 10 inches.

Height growth increases with site quality but stand densities between GSL-30 and GSL-150 do not affect it. At SDI 648, the groups were badly stagnated but ponderosa pine height growth responded when the trees were released. Height growth decreases with age until there is very little added height growth beyond 160-years breast-height age. Height growth occurs primarily during the spring and early summer drought period and depends on the moisture stored in the soil from the winter precipitation.

Basal area increment increases with increase in stocking throughout the range of GSL-30 to GSL-150 in contrast to the effects of density on diameter growth. At the lower densities, there were insufficient trees to fully utilize the site potential for growth. When the number of trees increased to where they were adequate to completely utilize the site (about GSL-80), the basal area increment with further increases in number of trees (higher GSL's) tended to level off.

Volume growth parallels basal area increment within the limits where density has no influence on height growth except perhaps in very open stands where the form factor may change significantly. Mortality in old growth resulting from windthrow, fire, dwarf mistletoe, and insects is variable but ranges from 18 to over 50 percent of the annual gross growth in the Southwest. The losses occur generally in the largest trees which makes the proportion of value loss even greater. Under intensive management and shorter rotation ages mortality can be reduced to an insignificant level.

Rotation Age or Size.   Rotation age is a function of site, the intensity of management, and the desired average stand diameter. In unmanaged stands where stand densities are comparable to the 1919 age-class groups of the Taylor Woods or to the densities commonly found in the Black Hills, the rotation age depends on how soon some of the trees break out of the stagnated group. At 43 years with 2.6 inches diameter and no wild fire to reduce the density, the rotation age is in hundreds of years. Under intensive management which means one or two precommercial thinnings at GSL-70 level and a thinning cycle of 20 years in the even-aged groups, the rotation age (i.e., the rotation age in uneven-aged stands is the age at which the individual tree is considered mature) depends on site quality. In the Southwest for even-aged groups, if a 24-inch average stand diameter is desired, then the rotation age on site index 90 may be 120 years with a mean-annual increment (MAI) of 300 board feet per acre; on site index 75, 140 years with a MAI of 225 board feet per acre; and on site index 60, 160 years with MAI of 167 board feet per acre. In the Black Hills, the upper diameter limit is 16 to 18 inches and the rotation about 160 years because of the lower site quality. Yet the Black Hills has the highest average volume of sawtimber growing stock per acre in the region (if the small acreage of ponderosa pine on the east side of the Sierra Nevada in Nevada is neglected) because the forests are almost all well-stocked young growth.

Cultural Practices.   In the long history of uneven-aged stands in United States, economics acted as a guide to stand treatment. In the West, exploitation began in an era of railroads and railroad construction in mountainous terrain demanded heavy cutting to amortize its cost. In California and east of the Sierra Nevada and the Cascade Mountains, uneven-aged ponderosa pine stands were the initial objectives. When exploitation reached national forest timberlands, the constraint on the Forest Service to manage its land for sustained yield limited the cut to 80 percent of the merchantable volume. Dunning's tree classification (1928) for California met the need to differentiate among trees in terms of their growth potential so the 20 percent residual volume would provide the best base for future growth and stand regeneration.

The introduction of the logging truck and tractor skidding released management from the economic and silvicultural strait jacket imposed by an 80 percent cut. A 50 percent cut was initiated and the selection of trees to represent the residual 50 percent of the volume introduced serious problems. East of the Sierra Nevada and the Cascades in the pure stands of ponderosa pine, the western pine beetle was epidemic and the use of Dunning's tree classification left many susceptible trees. Keen's tree classification (1936) was developed and it improved greatly the cutover stand's resistance to beetle attack. A weakness of its use was the continuing heavy losses in the uncut parts of a forest because in cutting 50 percent of a stand the allowable cut was removed from a small area which meant slow progress in sanitizing the forest. Keen's classification failed to pick many susceptible trees when used with a lighter cut so Salman and Bongberg (1942) developed their method which sanitized an area more rapidly by cutting only 15 to 25 percent of the volume.

In this region, the mountain pine beetle is the most destructive insect in ponderosa pine stands but it does not behave like the western pine beetle. Keen's classification distinguishes high-vigor and low-vigor trees and in an epidemic of western pine beetle the high-vigor trees are quite resistant. In an epidemic of the mountain pine beetle, all trees are susceptible irrespective of vigor, so Keen's tree classification was modified by Thomson (1940) and Hornibrook (1939) to recognize the growth potential of different tree classes (a return to Dunning's purpose). Thomson recognized the earlier maturity of ponderosa pine in this region while Hornibrook did not.

In addition to the change in tree classification emphasis between regions, there developed two opposing ideas of how the 50 percent leave volume should be selected: Munger's maturity selection method (Munger et al., 1936) of the Northwest interior ponderosa pine and Pearson's improvement selection method (1942) for the Southwest. Munger's maturity selection emphasized the economics of tree harvesting and assumed that the silvicultural requirements for sustained yield would be taken care of by a cut which averaged 50 percent over the working cycle. In other words, it was not important what happened on any single acre so long as the average volume for the working circle was satisfactory. Under this practice, rough limby trees of low value, growing on land of low value, should be left though their competition creates unfavorable conditions for surrounding trees. It was the intent of the method to cut only those trees which would provide the maximum profit when 50 percent of the total volume was cut. The method has been reduced to a formula basis which allows the calculation of the actual cost of leaving a tree standing. In fact, Bruce (1942) was able to reduce the marking guides for ponderosa pine to an added scale on the Biltmore stick. One of the factors in establishing this cost was a 3 percent interest charge on the residual value of the tree (sale price of the lumber in the tree less the costs of producing the lumber). Pearson (1942) admits the validity of an interest charge by private operators who have a capital investment in their timber but disallows its validity when applied to government-owned timber. Munger (Pearson, 1942) repudiates Pearson's acre-by-acre silviculture as an investment that might pay off in greater yields per acre but would result in lower profits.

Pearson's improvement selection method tries to correct the typical failings of uneven-aged ponderosa pine stands and it has as its objective the building up of a balanced growing stock to capture each sites maximum production of quality logs. This is gained by sacrificing maximum profits in the first cutting cycle for increasing profits in succeeding cutting cycles. In practice, the marker necessarily considers each tree not only on its own merits (such as low or high value, fast or slow growth) but on whether the tree's presence is advantageous or detrimental to the total value increment of the community of trees in which it stands. Because of this concern for the community as well as for the individual, improvement selection markings are characterized by a percentage of cut in the blackjack groups (young ponderosa pines before the bark turns yellow), as high as 30 to 35 percent in marked contrast to maturity selection which removes none, where the removal of rough dominants releases the cleaner-boled trees. Figure 7-5 illustrates a blackjack group after the first cut. Group selection and maturity selection would call for almost clearcutting in marking mature groups, with possible provision for seed trees if the group were large enough. Improvement selection calls for leaving the high-quality smaller stems which can profit by release and cutting the large stems, even though the returns on removing some of the blackjacks are low. Frequently, the best interest of a stand demands removal of trees which have a negative value, in which case the cheapest effective means of removal is advocated. Poisoning is recommended when cutting might cause excessive injury to surrounding trees or might attract beetles.

Egan (1954) mentions that maturity selection was abandoned in 1946 in the Southwest in favor of improvement selection. However, the heavy cut of 50 percent of the volume would have prolonged the first cutting cycle, thus causing high mortality losses. The decision was made to apply improvement selection initially in two lighter cuts so that the area could be covered more rapidly. The initial cut was reduced to about 30 percent and a cutting priority set up for various types of trees found in the stands as follows: Priority 1, trees likely to die before the next cut, which are those severely damaged by lightning, heavily mistletoed, attacked by bark beetles, infected with limb rust, and otherwise in poor condition; Priority 2, undesirable trees that are not wanted in the stand because of active mistletoe, new limb-rust infection, high susceptibility to decay, advanced stages of decay, wolfish, and very large trees; and Priority 3, trees which need to be removed to improve spacing within the groups where cutting under the higher priorities has not been sufficient. In some decadent stands, first priority trees represent the whole harvest, while in vigorous stands considerable planned release may be possible. After the first cut reduces mortality losses, the second cut concentrates on release cuttings within the groups for rapid quality growth.

Reproduction. The requirements for natural regeneration in ponderosa pine (Schubert, 1974) are (1) a large supply of good seed, (2) a well-prepared seed bed, (3) a lack of competing vegetation, (4) a low population of seed-eating pests, (5) adequate moisture for early seed germination and seedling growth, and (6) protection from browsing animals and certain insect pests. The difficulty is to get these requirements to coincide because a deficiency,of any one of these "may either completely or partially negate any or all of the others." In this region the natural regeneration of ponderosa pine offers two contrasting expectations for the frequency of the necessary coincidence of these requirements.

The Black Hills represents a rare success story in the conversion of the original old-growth forests to increasingly well-stocked and manageable second-growth forests (Boldt and Van Deusen, 1974). This despite the totally unregulated exploitation prior to the establishment of the Forest Reserve in 1897, a disastrous beetle epidemic from 1895 to 1909, and frequent fires. Natural reproduction is easy because good to excellent seed crops occur every 2 to 5 years (average about 3); a favorable rainfall pattern exists in that the spring and summer receive most of the annual rainfall (May and June are the wettest months); and the average soil is a fairly rich, friable loam or silt loam. All of the high-forest methods have been practiced in the Black Hills with satisfactory regeneration of the stands. However, the uniform two-cut shelterwood with about 40 square feet of basal area per acre in the seed cut is the present generally recommended method. The past history of various partial cuts, however, has produced stands with a good understory of pine regeneration (Fig. 7-6). Competition from ground cover, rodents, and grazing damage are common problems in planting the limited area in poorly or nonstocked conditions. Site preparation, poisoning of rodents, and fencing against livestock are corrective measures. A rigorous climate, short growing season, limited rainfall, and generally shallow soils impose restraints on growth. But the relative ease of successful natural reproduction assures a fully utilized growth capacity with a low investment for a profitable timber economy.

The first forest experiment station in the U.S. was established in 1908 at Fort Valley, Arizona (near Flagstaff) to research ponderosa pine regeneration and growth because, unlike the Black Hills, much of the surrounding forest was open and parklike with no regeneration (Pearson, 1910). Regeneration has occurred on occasion in other areas in the past whether the seed-tree, shelterwood, or group-selection methods had been used. Pearson's research probed the many factors influencing successful establishment and tended to attribute regeneration failure to the excessive grazing pressures until the success of the

Figure 7-6.   Mature timber ready for a final cut on an area seed-cut over 40 years ago. The understory of young trees has come in since cutting and are late being released. Present management calls for release when seedlings are 3 feet high. Black Hills Nat. For. S.D. (U.S. For. Serv.).

1919 seedling crop. The coincidence of a bumper seed crop in the fall of 1918, an exceptional 3.54 inches of rain in May 1919, germination in June, a scanty ground cover from long years of severe overgrazing, and early rains in 1920 resulted in the Southwest's ubiquitous 1919 ponderosa pine age class. Stand densities in the 1919 groups are similar to the stand treated in the Taylor Woods. Yet exclosures set out earlier to measure the impact of grazing on ground cover failed to regenerate in 1919 because of the grass competition. No repeat of the 1919 wave of reproduction has occurred for lack of timely site preparation because the grazing pressure has been markedly reduced and, until 1966, timber management has required sowing grass in cutover areas to reduce the erosion potential even where erosion was a minor factor (Larson and Schubert, 1969; Stewart and Beebe, 1974). Schubert has found the shelterwood method, that leaves about 40 square feet of basal area per acre in the seed cut, and the group-selection method in conjunction with timely site preparation can provide natural regeneration in years following a good cone crop if the summer rains occur in late June or early July. Good seed years occur every 3 or 4 years with partial crops in off years. Mice, squirrels, and insects destroy almost all seeds in off years and the number of seeds per cone is low in an off year compared to numbers in a good year. A favorable rain pattern has a probability of every 3 to 5 years so natural regeneration is difficult to predict yet seedling numbers increase slowly if ground cover competition is low (Heidmann *et al.*, 1977). For the usual rain pattern in Arizona following a good seed year, moisture is plentiful in early May but the temperature is too low to permit germination. The May and June drought prevents germination when the temperature is right so germination occurs with the beginning of the summer rains. If the rains come in early July, then some of the seedlings develop sufficient root penetration to survive the fall drought period of several weeks and the frost heaving of early winter and spring (Larson, 1963). If the rains come in late July or in August, the seeds germinate but the seedlings die during the fall drought or succumb to frost heaving (Heidmann, 1976).

The large areas in poorly or nonstocked condition and the uncertainty of natural regeneration on recently cut areas have stimulated interest in planting (Schubert *et al.*, 1970; Hall, 1971; Sprackling, 1977). Planting success, as usual, varies with the quality of the stock (including seed source) (Schubert and Pitcher, 1973), planting skill, site preparation, availability of moisture to the seedling, and protection from rodents and grazing.

In the Southern Rocky Mountains spring (May and June) is usually wet in ponderosa pine forests bordering on the Great Plains in contrast to the droughty spring in Arizona, Utah, southwest Colorado, and parts of New Mexico. With the more favorable rain pattern, natural regeneration hinges more on the uncertainty of adequate seed supply since the other requirements for good regeneration are controllable.

Ponderosa pine is an intolerant species yet successful reproduction requires a certain amount of shade where moisture is a limiting factor in establishment. Thus, while the clearcutting and seed-tree methods can be used successfully for regenerating stands in the Black Hills, climatic conditions are too severe for their use over most of the region.

In site preparation for natural regeneration logging slash is piled or mechanically bunched along main roads and firebreaks are burned. Otherwise the slash is undisturbed except as lopping and scattering will improve chances of seedling establishment by its added protection from grazing animals and by its amelioration of the microsite. Unless unduly numerous, snags are retained for their contribution in maintaining the population of raptor and other birds (Scott, 1978).

The groupwise uneven-aged form generally found in the region's old-growth ponderosa pine stands have on the whole been maintained by past harvesting practices though large areas of even-aged and two-storied stands have been created especially in the Black Hills. These stands are in dire need of intensive forest management, especially on the more productive sites, if production is to be maximized and if the needs represented by the other uses of the forest are to be satisfied (Schubert, 1976; Myers, 1974). Thinnings (Gaines and Kotok, 1954) and improvement cuts are probably the most needed treatments for correcting the excessive densities and growth impedance of badly formed, slow growing or diseased trees overtopping better trees.

Since most of the region's timber is on public lands and since timber harvesting on public lands is done under contract by private operators, the kind of silvicultural results depends upon the quality of the stand prescription and its execution under the supervision of the sales administrator. Jones (1974) has made the following statement that expresses very well the ultimate responsibility for some past unsatisfactory performances. "Poor silviculture may result from a poor silvicultural prescription, poor marking, or a contract that is weak in some important respect. It may also grow out of poor timber sale administration."

What the sales administrator could demand in way of logging, skidding, loading, and hauling methods in an era of low stumpage prices and narrow profit margins was restricted. Today, the high stumpage values and the dearth of quality timber provide a leverage for obtaining the kind of logging performance that meets the silvicultural needs of a particular stand.

Susceptibility to Damage. Logging damage is a major cause of man-made mortality and environmental deterioration. The damage begins with road and landing construction and continues with destruction of regeneration, scarring of residual trees, compaction of soil, stream-channel damage, and creation of erosion hazards. Excessive logging damage is not necessarily an immutable part of a logging chance because large volumes have been removed even from partially cut areas with a tolerable amount of damage. Damage can be reduced in many ways (Schubert, 1974; Barrett et al., 1976).

Damaging agents, in addition to man, are many and the importance of any one depends frequently on the stage of development and location of a stand though some agents are a continual threat. Fire is the most common destructive agent especially in young stands. In older stands, the direct losses from fire are likely to escape notice except in severe burns.

However, indirect losses from windthrow, cat-faced trunks and heart rot are primarily a consequence of fire damage. Lightning is a major cause of mortality among the overmature trees in northern Arizona (Pearson, 1950) but has not been recognized as serious in other localities. Windthrow is a constant threat in old-growth stands with a history of fires and in partially cut groups or stands where growth conditions or soil conditions reduce the wind firmness of a typically windfirm species.

Insects of many kinds attack ponderosa pine and are endemic in the region. There are pine seed moths, cone beetles, tip moths, and scales which affect reproduction and growth but their impacts are seldom serious though tip moths have been disastrous in plantations (Lessard and Jennings, 1976; Stevens and Jennings, 1977). Bark beetles cause great losses in an epidemic and are a constant source of attrition in old growth under endemic conditions. The western pine beetle causes the greatest losses while the *Ips* and the red turpentine beetles tend to be scavengers. Diseases are important causes of loss. Red rot is common over the whole region and accounts for most of the cull in old-growth stands. In young growth the incidence of infection can be reduced by pruning.

Fomes and *Armillaria* root rots are more spotty in their distribution but build up in stumps from logging or thinning to where they infect and kill young growth (Roth *et al.*, 1977). Root rots make older trees more susceptible to windthrow. Dwarf mistletoe, where it occurs, is a major cause of mortality and unlike beetle losses is a major threat to young stands (Hawksworth, 1961; 1977). Dwarf mistletoe is patchy in occurrence. Limb rust is a killer of older trees and is particularly prevalent in Arizona and Utah. There are many other diseases some serious like gall rust and damping off (for germinants) while others like needle cast result in growth losses and little mortality.

Animal damage causes serious losses especially in the regeneration period. The losses begin with the depletion of the seed supply by mice, chipmunks, and squirrels and can become devastating in plantations with gophers, sheep, cattle, and big game. A stand past the sapling stage is susceptible to porcupine damage and porcupines have a preference for the larger, faster growing trees in a young stand.

Interior Douglas-fir Type Group (Mixed Conifer Type)

Place in Ecological Succession. Douglas-fir in this type group is generally regarded as the *glauca* variety. As indicated earlier, the Douglas-fir zone has more moisture than the ponderosa pine zone and is warmer than the spruce-fir zone. The environment during the growing season is milder because the increased precipitation combined with the lower evapotranspiration ratio reduces the moisture stresses that so frequently determine the success or failure of seedling establishment. As a consequence, with an environment favorable to species from zones above and below it, stands in the Douglas-fir zone tend to be a mixture of species. The composition varies with the number of species in a particular geographic area and their silvical character. Mixed stands are quite prevalent and have a rich assortment of species in the Southwest and southern Colorado (Jones, 1974). Farther north in northern Utah and southern Idaho, Douglas-fir tends to form pure stands for lack of associated species.

In the southern part of the region, mixed conifer stands may have varying proportions of ponderosa pine, Douglas-fir, corkbark fir, southwestern white pine,[4] blue spruce, white fir, aspen, and Engelmann spruce. The composition depends upon elevation, aspect, and the past history of an area especially as it relates to fire. Where fires had been common, there is a predominance of the more fire-resistant ponderosa pine and Douglas-fir. Since ponderosa pine acts as a pioneer species in the Douglas-fir zone, it frequently dominates and names the forest cover type. Engelmann spruce with corkbark fir in the southern part of region replaced by subalpine fir in the northern part of the region are in mixture with Douglas-fir at the higher elevations and north slopes while ponderosa pine is associated at the lower elevations and warmer slopes. Aspen is

---

[4]Southwestern white pine seems to create a problem for taxonomists with a name depending on who is quoted: *Pinus flexilis* var. *reflexa* or *Pinus strobiformis*.

part of composition over the whole region except the lower drier parts of the Douglas-fir zone. White fir and southwestern white pine are associates of Douglas-fir with southwestern white pine tending to be the pine member of a mixture on cooler moisture slopes while white fir is a regular associate. In the northern part of the region, lodgepole pine is an upper elevational component of mixed stands.

Fire exclusion or control has changed the structure and composition of the ponderosa pine cover type (Cooper, 1960) because fires ran through some stands as frequently as every eight years before the region was settled by white man. Fire exclusion has changed structure by removing a natural thinning agent and perhaps in a more significant function in revamping composition by removing a cleaning- or stand-improvement agent. Early fires established ponderosa pine on Douglas-fir sites and subsequent fires prevented Douglas-fir from reoccupying an area. At present such stands may have a variety of understories composed of Douglas-fir and any of the other more tolerant species depending on seed sources. The dominance of Douglas-fir may be challenged by Engelmann spruce if an area has escaped fire for a long enough period at the moister higher elevations. Silviculturally, the problem is the replacement of a highly valuable species with others of lesser value and an evaluation of the means available to reverse the obvious successional trend.

Present fuel buildup is so great that a prescribed burn likely would kill everything. Crown fires were rare before 1900, but now a prescribed burn in mild weather will crown in places (Lindermuth, 1960). However, the use of prescribed burns designed to meet the objectives on areas with homogeneous conditions may well have a place in management decisions.

Growth Rates and Rotation Age or Size.   The volume of the average stand varies within the region from 8,500 board feet per acre with a maximum of 35,000 in the northwest to 15,000 and a maximum of 60,000 in the southeast (Krauch, 1956). Site-index curves for Douglas-fir in New Mexico (Edminster and Jump, 1976) supplement the only other site-index curves developed for the northern and central Rocky Mountains (Brickell, 1968).

A series of partially cut plots were installed in New Mexico, where the average volume per acre was 26,000 board feet in trees over 12 inches d.b.h. and the composition was 61 percent Douglas-fir, 23 percent white fir, and 14 percent ponderosa pine and limber pine (Krauch, 1956), a greater percentage of the white fir (86 percent) than of the Douglas-fir (48 percent) was removed, leaving an average residual stand of 10,600 board feet. The annual gross increment over 20 years was 203 board feet per acre, while the net increment was 168 board feet. In spite of the discrimination against it in the cut, white fir contributed disproportionately to the growth rate, first, because it grew faster than Douglas-fir and, secondly, because it contributed most of the ingrowth on account of the preponderance of white fir in the smaller size classes. The mean-annual increment was not proportional to residual volumes because of the discrepancy in size classes making up the residual volumes on the various plots. Reserve stands with 3,700 and 15,600 board feet per acre gave net growths of 163 and 206 board feet per acre and gross growths of 164 and 283 board feet, respectively. Growth was reduced and mortality increased where the residual trees were in the older age classes. Mortality is high in virgin forests.

The diameter-age relation in a virgin stand was determined to be as follows: 12 inches, 130 years; 18 inches, 150 years; 24 inches, 174 years; and 30 inches, 201 years (Krauch, 1956). It is reported that trees over 140 years may be poor bark beetle risks.

Cultural Practices.   A seed supply is prerequisite to regeneration and the various species are quite different in the amount and frequency of seed production. Ponderosa pine has lighter crops and less frequent good crops than at lower elevations. Some of the planting problems may be tied to seed provenance when the more abundant seed at lower elevations provides the ponderosa pine seedlings planted close to the upper edge of the species altitudinal range. Blue spruce has moderate to heavy cone crops in most years. Douglas-fir and Engelmann spruce have reasonably good seed crops every 2 to 3 years in the Southwest but Douglas-fir seed production is more irregular in the northern part of the region with good crops only every 4 to 5 years. Corkbark fir and white fir seed production lacks the regularity of Engelmann spruce but they do better than ponderosa pine. Southwestern white pine produces seed on a par with ponderosa pine but the seed is unique in being practically wingless. Its distribution seems to depend upon rodents and birds caching the seed at some distance from the tree.

With a seed supply, the amount and kind of site preparation and the specific growing conditions that are needed for reproduction depend upon the stand structure and its composition. Stand structures can be variable with one, two, three or more stories and with low or high densities. Composition can be even more variable because any of the associated species may be in the dominant story with or without one species dominant enough to name the type while each of the understories may have a different composition. The relative tolerance of the species, the density and species of the overstory, and seed bed conditions under the canopy explain the variations. The tolerances of the associated species over the region have been given as subalpine fir $\geq$ Engelmann spruce $\geq$ corkbark fir $>$ white fir $>$ Douglas-fir $\geq$ blue spruce $>$ southwestern white pine $>$ ponderosa pine $\geq$ lodgepole pine $\geq$ aspen.

Single-stored stands may be: young stands created by logging or beetle-killing of older age classes or planting, former two- or three-storied stands where the lower stories have been eliminated by fire or grazing, or aspen stands where seed source of more tolerant species is missing and before the canopy begins to break up. The need for some seedling protection until they are established (in spite of the better moisture regime) tend to reduce any reliance on the clearcutting or seed-tree methods. The shelterwood method provides a favorable environment for the regeneration of any of the conifer species and the regeneration of aspen will be discussed later. A shelterwood method with dwarf mistletoe in the residual trees is still frequently feasible if the removal cut is done promptly after the seedlings are established.

There are times and places where clearcutting may be necessary, in which case the need for protection for the first few years is still essential for adequate stocking. On north and east slopes natural regeneration can be had more easily than on moderate south slopes while on steep south and west slopes only the most fortuitous weather can bring it about. Numerous examples show the frequent futility of planting such a site. Nature has regenerated exposed areas by creating favorable microsites, but the table-top-clean cutover areas with all slash windrowed and burned is not nature's way. Figure 7-7 illustrates nature's success while Fig. 7-8 illustrates the self-defeating ecologically unsound approach to regeneration of the cutover area. However, careful partial cutting in similar stands to Fig. 7-8 demonstrates the potential of retaining the advanced reproduction and poles (Fig. 7-9). Nature's clearcut with its abundant regeneration resulting from a good seedbed and lowered rodent population (Fig. 7-7) later presents difficult problems in management. In contrast, a clearcut stand, that had had little advanced growth, would be less jack-strawed and a broadcast prescribed burn could provide a seedbed and protection for regeneration. If planting is desirable, the area could not be machine planted (most planting stock needs a protected environment for a couple of years as well as grazing protection), but hand planting would permit the choice of planting spots in spite of considerable surface debris.

Figure 7-7.   Dense Engelmann spruce regeneration that came up in the shade of jack-strawed blowdowns after a fire. Apache Nat. For. Arizona (U.S. For. Serv.).

Figure 7-8. Clearcut with the slash burned and seeded to grass before it was spot seeded to ponderosa pine and southwestern white pine with little survival. Burro Creek, Apache Nat. For, Arizona (U.S. For. Serv.).

Figure 7-9. A commercial clearcutting in the same mixed conifer type as Fig. 7-8 six years after slash was handpiled and burned. Seedlings had also established since logging. Burro Creek, Apache Nat. For., Arizona (U.S. For. Serv.).

On a shaded site with gravelly loam soil, Engelmann spruce develops roots 2 to 4 inches long the first year with corkbark fir and Douglas-fir doing only a little better while southwestern white pine has a root penetration in the first year of 5 to 9 inches or what Engelmann spruce may reach in 6 or 7 years (Jones, 1971). In the same study, one-year seedlings in a clearcut area had root penetrations by ponderosa pine of 5 to 7 inches, southwestern white pine 5 to 9 inches, white fir 5 to 8 inches, and Douglas-fir 2 to 5 inches while corkbark fir and Engelmann spruce had no seedlings to measure. In a small opening the root penetrations were much the same but species vigor changed with no ponderosa pine, few vigorous Douglas-firs or white firs and many vigorous Engelmann spruce and corkbark fir. Older seedlings in the clearcut area grew well with ponderosa pine's average height at any age > Douglas-fir > Engelmann spruce > southwestern white pine but Douglas-fir had the tallest individual trees. In the small opening all species were 5 inches tall after 5 to 6 years.

Windthrow poses a problem in opening up closed stands. A uniform shelterwood applied over a stand could spell disaster in an area subject to high winds or having shallow rooted trees due to species, soil depth, wet soils, or clay soils. Progressive strip shelterwood or even progressive clearcut-strip shelterwood provides wind protection as well as good regeneration potential.

Seed-bed condition at the time of seed fall is the key to success of natural regeneration. Site preparation should be done when a seed crop is predictable within the time a prepared site maintains seed-bed and growing conditions favorable for seedling establishment. Seeds need covering for germination. In addition to the high root competition of grass when an area has a well-established ground cover of grass and forbs, this condition results in higher populations of destructive agents like mice, pocket gophers, and grazing animals along with the reportedly allelopathic impact of some grasses on seed viability.

Two-storied unmanaged stands usually reflect the progress of succession as where fire prevention permits Douglas-fir to establish under an old ponderosa pine stand, where conifers move into an aspen stand, or where Engelmann spruce and subalpine fir invade a lodgepole pine stand. In each case, the stand prescription for treatment depends upon the decision as to whether the understory meets management objectives. If Douglas-fir advanced regeneration is considered a low-cost desirable alternative to the risk of losing control of the site or to the costs of site preparation and ponderosa pine establishment, then the overstory is removed (a liberation or improvement cut depending on age of the understory). Such a decision is based on the understory surviving the logging operation, a poor sales administrative job means a nonstocked or understocked Douglas-fir stand (on a steep south-facing slope a type conversion to grass). Where the Douglas-fir is undesirable then a shelterwood cut favoring ponderosa pine is made that removes any overstory Douglas-fir, rips up as much of the understory Douglas fir as possible with the logging, and does a prescribed burn to eliminate the rest of the Douglas-fir and reduce the slash hazard. Such a drastic decision would be unlikely today unless the understory was seriously infected with dwarf mistletoe. In a managed stand, the understory is probably predominantly of the desired species as the result of a shelterwood seed cut, so the removal cut is made to release the understory.

Three-or-more-storied stands are candidates for uneven-aged management. Old-growth stands whether mixed or predominantly Douglas-fir are usually uneven-aged. Other storied stands have developed as a consequence of the broad range in tolerance among the associated species. Ponderosa pine may have an understory of Douglas-fir, and, as the stand matures, white fir is able to establish where seedling Douglas-firs are unable to compete, thus creating a three-storied stand. Even with openings large enough for Douglas-fir to regenerate if under pine, Douglas-fir does not establish under Douglas-fir while white fir can. At higher elevations, southwestern white pine, Douglas-fir, corkbark fir, and Engelmann spruce tend to mix in multistoried form especially if logging opens up a two-storied stand. Aspen is ubiquitous at the middle and higher elevations and may serve as a nurse crop (See Fig. 7-13) for any of the associated species. The aspen may be gradually replaced by the overtopping conifers. However, even in old-growth uneven-aged stands there are residual old aspen and some suckers retain a competitive growth rate in openings.

The problems of handling multistoried stands are primarily associated with windthrow, mistletoe, and a higher percentage of poor-quality or cull trees. Windthrow hazard requires a gradual reduction in density rather than a heavy partial cut. The presence of dwarf mistletoe may affect the choice of trees removed. Since each species of dwarf mistletoe has a particular host, there is a high probability that in a mixed stand some of the species are free of their parasites and the stand composition can be manipulated accordingly. The Douglas-fir mistletoe is the most prevalent and the most serious problem in stand management. In stands being brought under management, improvement and sanitation cuts provide most of the material removed. However, conditions in most old-growth stands are such that if all the trees that should be removed in an improvement cut were taken, it would be a clearcutting. This means that improvements in composition and quality should be done gradually. There are combinations of circumstances that might realistically require clearcutting, but there are no circumstances so pressing that the clearcutting cannot be done in a fashion to preserve a forest presence and to retain a semblance of aesthetic quality.

Susceptibility to Damage.   Fire is the spectacular agent of destruction and it is particularly destructive in stands of the thin-barked species like Englemann spruce, subalpine and corkbark firs, and lodgepole pine. Any young-growth stand is susceptible to fire. Fire can be a tool but in the mixed conifer type, other than in site preparation with various slash disposal means, the weather is on the average too unfavorable for burning. When the weather favors burning, it is too dangerous to burn.

Insects cause serious losses with the insects peculiar to Douglas-fir causing the most damage: Douglas fir bark beetle, western spruce budworm and tussock moth. The tussock moth may damage white fir, corkbark fir, and blue spruce.

Diseases cause the highest losses with no spectacular signs. Decay is a dominant cause of cull in all old growth but its significances will decline with the conversion of the forests to young growth. The really serious disease is dwarf mistletoe. Ponderosa pine, Douglas-fir, blue spruce, Engelmann spruce, white fir, subalpine fir, and southwestern white pine are hosts for different species of dwarf mistletoe though the dwarf mistletoe of the spruces is mostly limited to Arizona. In old growth Douglas-fir, dwarf mistletoe is region-wide and a serious present and future danger. In areas logged over and burned the young stands may be free of the disease (Alexander and Hawksworth, 1975).

Lodgepole Pine Type Group

Lodgepole pine has a greater area and volume in the region (Table 7-1) than does Douglas-fir. However, most of the research on its silviculture and management has been done in the northern Rocky Mountains so the main treatment of the species is presented in Chapter 8. In the Middle and Southern Rocky Mountain Region, particularly in Wyoming and Colorado, there are large areas of pure lodgepole pine without any of the more tolerant associated species. The lack of tolerant tree competition in those areas that have escaped fire for long periods has resulted in the development of uneven-aged stands so characteristic of a climax forest. Since lodgepole pine forms an edaphic climax in certain environments (around wet sites within the ponderosa pine zone in Oregon), it may well be that it forms a climax in this region.

Throughout most of its range lodgepole pine management tends to rely on the abundance of serotinous cones, that have been produced over a period of years, to act as a reservoir of seed for regenerating a stand. Since serotinous cones must be exposed to 140 °F to open, the usual recommendation is to clearcut and bring the cones close to the ground where the ground temperature is adequate to open them. The excessive amount of seed gives rise often to very dense stands (Fig. 7-10) while better spacing takes advantage of lodgepole pines growth potential (Fig. 7-11). The effect of density on average stand diameter is illustrated by Fig. 7-12. It shows the average stand diameter decreases rapidly with increasing numbers of trees up to 2,000 stems per acre then the slope of the curve decreases but probably not as much as in Fig. 7-12. Diameter growth of the largest trees in a stand is much less influenced by number of trees per acre.

Lodgepole pine, however, may have a low percentage of serotine in some places. Without serotine, the silviculture of lodgepole pine reverts to the normal concern for seed supply from the current crop of cones opening on the tree and distributed by wind. Regeneration may be difficult in localities characterized by late spring and summer drought when snow remains on the east and north aspects, to which the species is restricted, until the end of May or

Figure 7-10. Typical dense stand of lodgepole pine that has come in after a forest fire. Trunks of burned trees still remain on the ground. Medicine Bow Nat. For., Wyoming (U.S. For. Serv.).

Figure 7-11. Uncut lodgepole pine in King Creek drainage at about 9,000-feet elevation. Fraser Exp. Forest., Colorado (U.S. For. Serv.).

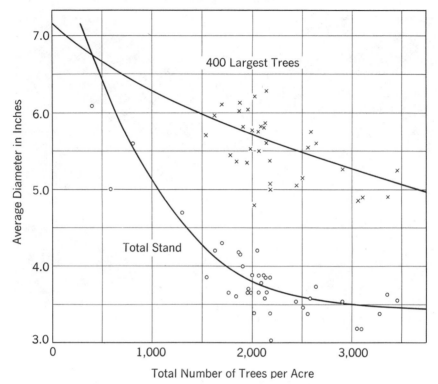

Figure 7-12.   The average stand diameter and the average stand diameter of the 400 largest trees per acre, for the same stands, in relation to the number of trees per acre. Data drawn from plots in a 47-year-old stand, Cache District, Wasatch Nat. For., Utah (Daniel and Barnes, 1958).

later. Seeds from the previous year's crop (lodgepole pine produces some cones almost every year) germinate in late June or early July when high evaporative stresses and soil temperatures are expected in exposed sites. Even though lodgepole pine is more intolerant than ponderosa pine, microsite protection must be developed under open conditions because it is a delicate germinant. When a stand with serotinous cones is clearcut, considerable care is exercised that the slash is well scattered over the area to spread the seed and to provide some microsite protection needed for seedling survival. For the same reason, nonserotinous lodgepole pine should be cut in narrow clearcut strips for adequate seeding from the side. Site preparation should leave a fairly even covering of slash especially for those areas of the clearcut beyond the protection of a south and west margin of trees. Site preparation is essential to provide a mineral soil without grass competition. The finer the soil texture the more necessary is the presence of a protective slash. Delayed site preparation allows a buildup of pocket gophers which are very destructive of seedling or planting stock.

In the Uinta Mountains, Colorado and Wyoming, summer showers in combination with coarse- to medium-textured soils makes regeneration with a one-shot seed source (provided by serotinous cones) reasonably certain with the microsite protection of the slash. An exposure as severe as one resulting from clearcutting rarely happens in nature. The assumption that lodgepole pine is adapted to clearcutting because it depends on a forest fire to perpetuate itself fails to recognize the difference between a clearcutting and a fire-killed forest. A fire-killed forest has a lot of standing shade, seed released on an ash-covered soil before grass or forbs invade the area, and a reduced rodent population. Lodgepole pine has a small seed (94,000 per pound) and a rapid rate of growth in full sunlight once established. The same fire eliminates the danger of dwarf mistletoe infection which exists where trees on the margin of an opening provide the seed.

Aspen Type Group

In western United States aspen is a component of many of the forest cover types but rarely covers extensive areas as the predominant species except in Colorado and Utah. Like lodgepole pine, it is intolerant and the same question arises as to the cause of the extensive pure stands including many with the uneven-aged structure associated with climax vegetation. Whether aspen dominates a site because past fires have eliminated the competition of all the more tolerant tree species or whether the climate and soil conditions preclude the establishment of other trees from seed while aspen survives because of its clonal growth habit has not been resolved to everyone's satisfaction.

In the West, aspen has little market for the technical forest products such as pulp, timber, firewood, or charcoal. However, in the region, the aspen might rank the most valuable of the forest cover types on a per acre basis if it were possible to sum the contributions of each type in terms of all values produced, namely, timber, water, forage, wildlife, aesthetics, and recreation.

Aspen is variable in morphology and behavior and this is particularly noticeable in the West because aspen occurs in clones which accentuates the genetical contrasts. The attempts to organize the variability to form taxonomic groupings have been unsuccessful as the total variation may occur within a limited area (Barnes, 1969).

Place in Ecological Succession.   Aspen has a broad altitudinal range. It is a common associate in the Douglas-fir and Engelmann spruce zones even occurring with ponderosa pine where a summer rain pattern in present. The winter temperatures get much colder for aspen areas from southern New Mexico to Wyoming. Of more importance is the decrease of the April to June mean monthly average of daily high temperatures from south to north because it indicates a shorter growing season since the July and August temperatures are quite similar in the south and north. The longer growing season in the south may account for the relatively larger average size of the aspen in the southwest.

Aspen can be a prominent part of the forest vegetation in areas with a precipitation below 16 inches to over 40 inches. In the western part of the region the winter fraction of the total precipitation increases and summer precipitation decreases from south to north while in the eastern part the spring precipitation increases from south to north with May and June dry in New Mexico and wet in the mountains of eastern Wyoming (DeByle, in press).

Soils derived from a wide range of parent materials support aspen growth but the soils with the best growth are derived from basaltic rocks, limestones, and calcareous shales. A wide range of soil textures are possible with the medium-textured loams and sandy loams being the most frequent. The profile of the soil under an aspen stand is fairly characteristic with a 0 horizon that is very thin or patchy from the rapid breakdown of the aspen leaves and dead ground cover and an A_1 horizon that contains a high percentage of incorporated organic matter. Aspen leaves may contribute a ton of dry matter per acre per year and the understory vegetation another ton and their fast decomposition means a rapid turnover of nutrients in a stand (Jones and Trujillo, 1975).

In spite of aspen being a very intolerant species and growing within the range of a number of much more tolerant species, it occurs in pure stands over some large areas. The reasons for this situation were mentioned previously. It is probably climax in many areas with high isolation and droughty soils where conifer seedlings can not establish while aspen suckers can draw on water resources tapped by the parent roots. Under most circumstances, the presence of aspen serves as a nurse crop for the establishment of conifers (Fig. 7-13). A common phenomenon is the extension of a narrow margin of aspen into a meadow from the margin of a conifer type and the progressive invasion of the aspen by conifers.

Reproduction.   Reproduction of western aspen is generally limited to suckering. Western aspen produce seed but spring or summer droughts usually kill off any seedlings that might germinate. The present western aspen distribution is considered to date from a period of a more favorable climate for seedling establishment; that is, postglacial times of 8,000 to 10,000 years ago. The rare occurrence of seed regeneration in the West has resulted in large clones of 25 to 200 acres (Kemperman and Barnes, 1976). In the Lake States, where seedling establishment is common, the clones tend to be small.

Suckers develop on aspen roots that are usually within 2 inches of the surface. The roots tend to undulate in their growth and suckers arise singly or in clusters at the high points along these lateral roots. In fact some of the lateral roots maintain a uniform diameter (about 0.25 inches) without branching for long distances just below the soil surface and give rise to suckers (Baker, 1925). Roots of some clones may have as many as 50 shoot primordia or potential suckers per linear inch of root (Schier, 1972). Under an overstory of aspen few suckers develop and those that do survive grow very poorly even if released. Control over suckering is attributed to apical dominance where the flow of auxins from the crown to the roots suppresses bud development. In spite of the tremendous potential to produce suckers that the root system of a clearcut

Figure 7-13.   Dense aspen with Engelmann spruce invading the stand and with a good herbaceous ground cover. Carson Nat. For., New Mexico (U.S. For. Serv.).

aspen stand has only a small percentage of that potential actually develops into suckers. The suckers which emerge the earliest begin to produce auxins which suppress further development of primordia in the vicinity. The buds or primordia with the greatest chance of emerging quickly are those on the portions of a root that are closest to the surface. It frequently happens that several suckers emerge almost simultaneously from a particular high point on a root which produces the common clumping of suckers. Suckering requires that the root on which a bud is developing have sufficient carbohydrate reserves to provide the energy needed by the bud to grow to the surface and to grow the leaves necessary to make the sucker self-sufficient. Thus, a bud developing below a certain depth may not have the available energy reserves to reach the surface or auxins from suckers starting closer to the surface on the same root inhibit further growth.

Baker (1925) reports the average number of suckers per acre on three clearcut areas in Utah that were cut the previous fall as being 54,360 the first year after cutting, 39,280 the second year, 28,340 the third year, and 23,110 by the fourth year. When an area is clearcut in the spring, a substantial number of suckers are produced in the same year with the bulk of the suckers coming up the following year. Where intense fires have burned over an area, the suckers are fewer and come from deeper roots and the numbers may increase over a period of several years.

Dense stands of aspen suckers have a continuous rapid reduction in numbers as Baker's data indicate. In spite of the genetic uniformity of a clone, the individual suckers do not have an even start because they emerge at different times. Thus, in a clump one sucker frequently dominates the group and the others are suppressed. Part of the success of rapid natural thinning is due to the vigorous indeterminate growth of young aspen. The rapid expansion of the crowns of the most dominant suckers further suppress the tardy starters and slower growers. When older stands have losses in tree numbers, the determinate growth of the branches slows crown closure and the stand begins to open up. Once this starts, stand deterioration is rapid.

Suckers have the advantage over stump sprouts because the sucker usually develops its own root system much like a seedling. Also the minor attachment of the sucker to the parent tree reduces the risk of direct infection of rot-producing fungi. Aspen rarely forms root grafts anywhere in its range, but the western aspen's habit of maintaining a large number of root connections among suckers of the same parent reduces the predictability of the consequences of cutting or poisoning one tree (Tew *et al.*, 1969).

Growth Rates.   Aspen in the Rocky Mountains is a much longer-lived species than in the Lake States. Stands up to 200 years old have been found. Initial height growth of the suckers seems reasonably the same irrespective of site quality. Thus, dominant suckers reach about 10 feet in 6 to 8 years, but further growth depends largely on site quality (Jones and Trujillo, 1975). Height growth in aspen is accumulated rapidly on the best sites but levels off at 120 years. Conifers grow slower than aspen but their growth does not slow down so early. Conifers will finally overtop aspen.

Colorado and the Southwest have a better growth potential than Utah. In Utah, Baker's site I has a height of 77 feet at 80 years (total age) and 83 feet at 150 years. Jones site-index curves (Jones, 1967) indicate a height of 90 feet at 80 years (age at d.b.h.) on his best site and 115 feet at 150 years. The difference may represent the effect of summer rains in the Southwest as compared to droughty summers in Utah.

Diameter growth is also rapid initially compared to conifers then it slows down and the conifers maintain their rate of growth (Baker, 1925). Aspen diameter growth does not have the same relation to site quality that height growth has and aspen stand density seems to have much less effect on the diameter of the dominants than conifer stand density. Diameter growth is not necessarily tied to height growth as some stands have thick boles and others have slender boles at similar ages: dominants on one study area were over 24 inches d.b.h. at 137 years and 84 feet high while on another area no dominant was larger than 20 inches d.b.h. at 148 years and 110 feet high (DeByle, in press).

The only attempt at yield-table construction for aspen (Baker, 1925) is based on data from a limited area in central Utah. At 120 years, the yield table on a per acre basis shows that site 1 (average height of dominants 82 feet) has 177 square feet of basal area with 5,350 cubic feet and 15,400 board feet. In contrast, a 0.1-acre plot in Arizona, selected as having maximum stocking for aspen (Schlaegel, 1975) (site index 78: height at 80 years at d.b.h.), had 411 square feet of basal area per acre (not counting the understory of conifers with an additional 115 square feet) and 115,500 board feet gross per acre (International ¼ inch rule). Age of the plot was 162 years and the average height of dominant trees about 109 feet with the tallest trees 121 feet.

Rotation Age or Size.   Rotation age for aspen in the region depends on site quality and the incidence of decay. The incidence of decay and the rate of deterioration vary with site quality and with the genetic variation among clones. Culmination of the mean-annual increment for production in tons of cellulose, cubic feet of bole wood or board feet with a minimum diameter of 12 inches occurs at very different ages. In the Rocky Mountains, the market for aspen is primarily for sawlogs. Thus, site qualities incapable of producing an aspen sawlog at an age before decay reduces a tree to a cull call for a different management objective than aspen logs. Baker gives the pathological rotation[5] age for aspen as: for site 1, 120 years with an average stand diameter (ASD) of 11.2 inches; for site 2, 110 years with an ASD of 8.9 inches; for site 3, 100 years with an ASD of 7.1 inches; and for site 4, 80 years with an ASD of 5.3 inches. The average stand diameter is strongly influenced by the number of small trees but sites 3 and 4 are unlikely to have any merchantable trees before decay is dominant. At 80 or 90 years decay becomes significant but stands on the best sites are merchantable though there are a lot of small trees. On the best sites, the rate of ingrowth of the smaller trees to merchantable diameters surpasses the rate of cull production up to an age of 110 or more.

Sites suitable for timber production may be more valuable in an alternate use. Also an alternative use may serve as the management objective for sites that are incapable of producing merchantable stands or where a market for aspen sawlogs does not exist. A short rotation may be used to provide browse for big game or to maintain the increased water production that follows clearcutting. Aesthetic values may warrant the minimum management necessary to prevent stand deterioration. The tendency of conifers to take over aspen sites may be encouraged or the area planted to speed this development.

Cultural Practices.   The reproduction of an aspen stand has the simplest silvicultural solution of any forest cover type, that is, clearcut for assured reproduction. Whether the reproduction results in an established stand depends on how the clearcutting is done and how the area is treated after the clearcutting. If only the merchantable material is cut leaving the unmerchantable trees, then the reproduction that occurs is likely to be sparse because of the inhibiting effect of the residual stand. Growth of individual stems is likely to be poor because of the competition with older trees. Adequately stocked stands re-

[5]The pathological rotation is the point where the rates of growth and cull production are the same.

duced to about 10 percent of the original basal area will regenerate adequately and the suckers will develop normally. The removal of the residual stand can be done by felling or pushing over the trees, herbicide treatment, or burning. Burning is an economic method unless the fire escapes into adjacent coniferous timber. However, it is difficult to burn an aspen stand hot enough to kill the trees for lack of a uniformly distributed fuel supply to carry the fire under moderate burning conditions.

Aspen stands under heavy grazing pressure may deteriorate. Attrition occurs in several ways as a stand matures and the overstory begins to open up: elk, on overpopulated winter ranges, gnaw the bark and kill the trees by girdling or making an entrance for disease; sheep, deer, elk, and cattle show a preference for young aspen suckers; and the site disturbance caused by grazing animals assists the invasion of conifers which displace the aspen. As the stand opens up, it would regenerate to aspen except that the suckers are eliminated by the grazing animals. Roots lose the power to continue to produce more suckers as their store of carbohydrate becomes depleted. Loss of aspen results in ground cover changes to species that can resist the grazing pressure. Since an aspen stand tends to slow snow melt, the runoff peaks are raised when the aspen is gone (DeByle, in press). Regeneration by clearcutting will succeed only when the area cut is so large as to preclude the grazing population from doing more than a thinning of the suckers. Small clearcut areas are a focal point for concentrated grazing. This explains the failure to regenerate many areas where cutting or fires otherwise created the right conditions for reproduction. Two clearcut plots established in 1934 show the effect of grazing. One was surrounded by a deer-proof fence and the other by a sheep- and cattle-tight fence (Mueggler and Bartos, 1977). Figure 7-14 shows the two plots in 1975 with the deer-proof plot fully stocked with aspen and the cattle exclosure devoid of aspen.

Thinnings.   Thinning recommendations are based on the research experience of the Lake States and assume that thinnings will only be done on sites capable of growing sawtimber (DeByle, in press). If a one-time noncommercial thinning is planned, then it should be applied when the suckers are about 25 feet tall (12 to 18 years old for western aspen) to a spacing of 8 × 8 feet. Commercial thinning is not recommended in western aspen because the damage done to the residual trees would introduce the number one killing disease—sootybark canker.

Planting.   Aspen planting is rare in the West. However, it likely will become more common as greater emphasis is placed on aspen as a fuel-break species, as a nurse crop on devastated spruce-fir sites, as a cover for strip-mine spoil banks, and as a means of reestablishing aspen stands where poor management has prevented natural regeneration (DeByle, in press). Provenance of the planting material is critical but material from the same habitat type can be recommended. Genetic considerations, insofar as they can be judged from the phenotype, should be considered in selecting clones for propagation.

Figure 7-14.   Grindstone Flat exclosures showing the dense stand of aspen within the deer-proof fence and the lack of aspen within the cattle and sheep exclosure. The two plots were clearcut in 1934. Beaver Mountain, Fishlake Nat. For., Utah (U.S. For. Serv.).

There are four sources of planting stock: seed, root cuttings, greenwood cuttings, and wildling transplants. When available, seed can be used to produce nursery seedlings. Root cuttings are short segments of roots which are planted about one inch below the surface of the soil. Results have been poor, even where suckers have developed very few have rooted. Greenwood cuttings are a relatively new and successful Danish method of propagating aspen vegetatively. Selected root cuttings are given favorable conditions for suckering; when the suckers are a few inches long with a pair of leaves, they are cut from the root cutting and placed in a rooting media where they root and grow to plantable size (Schier, 1978).

Susceptibility to Damage.   Damaging agents are many for western aspen with the most serious being the diseases. There is considerable clonal variability in susceptibility to damaging agents (DeByle, in press). Trunk cankers are a major mortality factor and the most important killers of aspen in the west. In the order of their virulence, the common cankers are sootybark, *Hypoxylon*, black, and *Cytospora*. Infections are usually associated with wounds whether from insects, weather, falling snags, elk, or humans.

Butt and trunk rots are primarily responsible for the high percentage of cull in merchantable sized aspen. The amount of rot increases with age and decreasing site quality. The most important fungus in aspen decay is *Phellinus tremulae.* Rot-inducing fungi gain entrance through wounds caused by insects, fire scars, and damage as in campgrounds and through dead branches and infected roots.

Leaf diseases do not seem to be important in the region but local outbreaks of a leaf-spot disease *(Marssonina populi)* has caused severe damage in Utah when heavy infections occurred in two successive years.

The western tent caterpillar is a defoliator that does conspicuous damage to aspen which is its preferred host in the region. A series of years with complete defoliation will kill some clones and do serious damage to others. A number of wood borers are associated with aspen of which the poplar borer is one of the most important and it may be associated with particular habitat types. The aspen ambrosia beetle attacks weakened aspen and it may be a carrier of black canker.

Frosts damage new growth in the growing season but even the most severely damaged trees recover.

Wind damage is primarily windthrow and the presence of root rot is associated with serious losses. The excessive opening up of a stand may result in windthrow or breakage.

Lightning-struck trees die at once (Hinds and Krebill, 1975).

Sun scald is a common occurrence where a stand is partially cut or along road right of ways and it is a cause of canker infection.

Snow damage may on occasion be excessive.

Engelmann Spruce—Subalpine Fir Type Group

Spruce-fir type has the second largest area of any of the commercial timber types in the region and contains the largest volume in cubic feet and board feet. Spruce-fir, Douglas-fir, and ponderosa pine have about 78 percent of their commercial area in sawtimber. Access has been the restraining factor in the exploitation of the type as well as the lack of a pulpwood market. Shipping spruce to the Lake States after World War II, when the utilization of the enormous volumes of beetle killed timber challenged foresters, proved uneconomic.

Place in Ecological Succession.   The Engelmann spruce zone usually extends to timber line except as whitebark pine forms the timberline species within the limits of its range. Above 10,000 feet, Engelmann spruce and subalpine fir have little competition and beyond 11,000 feet, Engelmann spruce usually forms relatively pure stands. At lower elevations, the species mix with lodgepole pine and aspen and finally form elements of the mixed conifer type. The lower boundary of the type drops in elevation toward the north and reaches 7,500 feet in northern Utah. There are inversions of the normal order of the zones as Engelmann spruce and subalpine fir follow the cool moist areas of streams and steep northern slopes to lower elevations.

Rainfall usually exceeds 25 inches per year and its distribution depends upon the location of the stand within the region. Again, it is not the total that is so significant as it is its effectiveness, that is, a low potential evapotranspiration/precipitation ratio (Holdridge *et al.*, 1971) or high effective moisture.

On a clearcut 3.7-acre study area at 10,600 feet on the Fraser Experimental Forest, the mean maximum (June to October) air temperature at 4.5 feet in a weather shelter over a five year period was 66 °F on a 10 percent north slope and 68 °F on a 10 percent south slope. The bare unshaded granitic soil's average maximum temperature on the north slope was 109 °F compared to 131°F for an unshaded litter surface while on the south slope the respective temperatures were 124 °F and over 140 °F. Shaded average maximum soil temperatures for the two sites were, respectively, 88 °F and 110 °F (Noble and Alexander, 1977). When it is realized that the temperatures are average maximums with many days exceeding them and that lethal soil-surface temperatures begin at 130 °F, the necessity for shade and a mineral soil surface for delicate spruce seedlings and almost as susceptible subalpine fir seedlings, is obvious if natural regeneration is desired. The average rainfall during summer period was 8.0 inches on the north slope and 9.8 inches on the south slope with 20 to 25 storms per season. The two areas are 3.5 miles apart. On the College Forest, Logan, Utah at 8,400 feet elevation, the absolute maximum temperature has been below 80 °F but the summer evapotranspiration/precipitation ratio is much higher because the rainfall is low with many summers experiencing two-month periods without rain.

Engelmann spruce and subalpine fir establish on a wide variety of soils from gravelly sandy loams to silt loams derived from granitic, basaltic, or sandstone parent materials. Successful regeneration on coarse-textured soils need frequent rains to maintain the moisture supply which explains the successful regeneration of narrow clearcut strips in Colorado and the lack of good regeneration except on very protected sites, even on silty loam soils, where summer rains are infrequent as in many parts of Utah.

Engelmann spruce and subalpine fir form a climax in which the dominant species depends on such factors as the age of the stand or its origin. Engelmann spruce is a long-lived species with trees commonly over 300 years in undisturbed stands. Subalpine fir is a relatively short-lived tree because of its susceptibility to root rot though some trees reach 250 years or more. In an old stand the spruce is dominant though subalpine fir may be dominant in the younger age classes.

Stands are commonly uneven-aged but enormous areas can be even-aged. The even-aged condition may be prevalent in localities where catastrophies are frequent and climatic conditions are favorable to natural regeneration. Fires produce even-aged stands with a high proportion of Engelmann spruce because the seedbed conditions are favorable due to the exposed mineral soil and shade of the down or standing trees and because the seed of the spruce flies so much better then the fir seed. Overmature stands decimated by bark beetles are converted to relatively even-aged condition because the small diameter trees in the understory survive (Schmid and Hinds, 1974). Subalpine fir is usually dominant in the understory because Engelmann spruce can rarely establish under itself except on rotten logs and bare soil while subalpine fir does so. The forest floor under Engelmann spruce has a lethal effect on overwintering Engelmann spruce seed (Daniel and Glatzel, 1966) and other conifer seeds including subalpine fir (Daniel and Schmidt, 1972). The cause of the loss of viability is the presence of the fungus *Geniculodendron pyriforme* (Salt, 1974) which has been isolated in seeds of various spruce species and spreads between seeds in favorable forest litter at temperatures too low for other fungi to develop strongly.

Lodgepole pine and/or aspen are frequent associates of Engelmann spruce and subalpine fir and replace the spruce and fir after fires. If the area burned has not been too large, the tolerant species establish under the intolerants and finally replace them.

Grass invades burns very quickly but it is suppressed by the trees where regeneration occurs concurrently. If tree regeneration fails or is destroyed by a second fire or animal damage, then the area converts to a grass cover. Reforestation of grass areas requires thorough site preparation and planting. Trees invade meadows along the margins where the shade of the tree margin reduces the vigor of the grasses which allows seedlings to establish. Frequently, as mentioned earlier, aspen invades the margins of a meadow with suckers and acts as a nurse crop for the conifer seedlings. A continuation of this slow invasion eventually displaces the grass and the meadow becomes forested.

Growth Rates.   Inasmuch as the spruce-fir forests are primarily old growth, there has been very little in the way of growth studies done in them. The results of a reinventory in 1957 of 61 permanent sample plots established in 1950 are given in Table 7-4 (List, 1959).

If only 3 board feet per cubic foot is allowed for aspen then gross growth averages 268 board feet per acre but mortality drops the net growth to 116 board feet per acre. The high mortality in subalpine fir and aspen are responsible for the low net growth. While the average stocking in the area where the plots are located is about 12,600 board feet per acre, the average is low because of the many open areas and low stocking of some stands. Four ½-acre plots selected as representative of maximum spruce-fir density for an evapotranspiration study (Hart and Eaton, 1971) had an average basal area of 295 square feet and 48,000 board feet per acre with trees varying in age between 200 and 275 years.

Growth-prediction plots were established in undisturbed even-aged stands of spruce-fir in Colorado and Wyoming (Alexander *et al.*, 1975) and the data were used in a revision of the field and computer procedures for managed-stand yield tables (Myers, 1971). The results indicate that the yields including commercial thinnings for a two-cut shelterwood method would vary from 40,900 board feet

TABLE 7-4

Periodic Annual Board-Foot (Scribner Rule) Growth Per Acre (Aspen in Cubic Feet)
Based on 1950 and 1957 Inventories[1]

Growth	Engelmann Spruce and Douglas-fir	Subalpine Fir	Lodgepole Pine	Total	Aspen
Board feet in 1950	5,393	4,833	434	10,660	371.6
Board feet in 1957	6,110	4,790	502	11,402	395.5
Gross Growth	113	121	10	244	8.1
Mortality	11	127	0	138	4.7
Net Growth	102	–6	10	106	3.4

[1]Volumes for trees 12 inches d.b.h. and larger.

for a growing stock level of 80 that was held at 80 square feet for the rotation to 52,200 board feet for a growing stock level of 120 that was held at 120 square feet for the rotation or a mean-annual increment of 273 to 348 board feet per acre per year. The tables assume that 30 years is sufficient to grow a stand to 3.5 inches average stand diameter. At rotation age of 150 years the average stand diameter would vary between 27.2 and 32.5 inches depending on the growing stock level that was selected and that the stand could sustain. However, in the western part of the region, it takes 40 to 50 years for a sapling to reach 3.5 inches d.b.h. when growing in the open. On average sites, it takes about 100 years to add the next 20 or more inches after the 3.5 inch diameter is reached if the tree is released from competition.

Cultural Practices.   Natural regeneration requirements have been simply summarized for spruce-fir (actually for all species) by Roe and Schmidt (1964) as forming a reproduction triangle with the sides of the equilateral triangle being (1) seed supply (including all the factors which influence it), (2) seedbed (including all the site conditions influencing a seed's chances of becoming a seedling), and (3) growing conditions (including damaging agents, competition, and climatic vagaries). The triangle illustrates very well that planting provides answers to the problems of seed supply and seedbed which places the whole burden of regeneration success on having proper growing conditions.

Seed supply depends upon location within the region with frequent good crops along the Wasatch Mountains of Utah (five very good, six good, seven fair, three poor, and two blank years in a 23-year record, 1947–1969). On the Colorado Plateaus, the White River Plateau had very good crops every 5 to 7 years while for the Uncompaghre Plateau the interval was every 2 to 4 years. Just west of the Continental Divide, Fraser Experimental Forest had only a moderate seed supply (one very good, two good, three fair, and four poor in 10 years) (Alexander, 1969). Engelmann spruce has light seed (135,000 seeds per pound) with a big wing, so it has the ability to fly up to 10 chains or more (Squillace, 1954). However, half the seed falls usually within about two chains of the seed source especially in anything but a bumper crop year. Engelmann spruce seed is dispersed in considerable quantities over clearcut strips up to 12 chains wide in years with good or better seed crops so seedling establishment seems to be limited more by environment than by seed supply (Ronco, 1970). Subalpine fir has fewer good seed years than Engelmann spruce in this region in contrast to their seeding habits in the Northern Rockies.

Seedbed conditions influence the effectiveness of the seed supply. A receptive seedbed, such as a freshly exposed mineral soil with adequate dead shade, reduces greatly the number of seeds per established seedling and extends the effective seeding distance. Any lengthening of the interval between site preparation and a good seed year followed by a couple of years of favorable rainfall, increases the ratio of seeds to seedlings which reduces the effective seeding distance. The seedbed loses its receptiveness for seed as rain, wind, and sun harden the surface and fill up the cracks and crevices where a seed may lodge. Northern aspects have a greater effective seeding distance than southern aspects partly because winds are predominantly west and southwest and partly because the environment is more favorable. An undisturbed 0 horizon produced under spruce is an unfavorable seedbed for spruce and only slightly better for subalpine fir and when exposed to direct insolation its low heat conductivity causes a rapid buildup to lethal temperatures.

Growing conditions determine whether the newly emerged seedling survives to become an established seedling. Under a partial overstory, a seedling may survive for years before dying while in the open if a seedling survives for five years, it is mostly likely well established. First year mortality in the spruce-fir type is the expected thing. It is not how many will survive but whether any will survive. The expectations are greater in areas with frequent summer rains. The key is moisture because Engelmann spruce has a slow-developing root that reaches 3 to 4 inches in length the first year in a coarse-textured soil (Noble, 1973) and 2 to 3 inches or less in a clay loam soil. Timely rains are necessary for survival in the first year and even a protected microsite gives a new seedling only a little longer waiting period. Succeeding years must also be favorable especially the second year as the roots must penetrate to 8 to 12 inches for a seedling to be considered established.

Engelmann spruce and subalpine fir stands have the same structural patterns as discussed for Douglas-fir and the mixed conifer types, that is, single-storied, two-storied, and three- or multistoried structures. Inasmuch as spruce-fir is a climax type in the region, uneven-aged stands predominate except as catastrophies give rise to dense fairly even-aged stands. These may be dense enough to prevent an understory from developing until they begin to break up when overmature or when partially logged. Where single-storied stands have to be opened up for natural reproduction, windthrow hazard is a serious constraint. Root rot, wet, or shallow soils, and topography that funnels the wind into a cut area contribute to the hazard. On deep well-drained soils, Engelmann spruce is reasonably wind firm. Progressive strip shelterwood should be used to establish the seedlings especially on south and west slopes. The size of a seedling considered established depends on local competitive factors. The strips should be backed into the wind and each strip's width times length should be an adequate area for an economic logging operation. The width may range from 2 to 5 chains depending on potential wind damage. Since no regeneration need be sacrificed a thorough exposure of mineral soil can be made to favor the spruce. On northern slopes, progressive strip clearcutting (two to three chains wide) may be useful but its use depends on the rate of incursion of grass, gophers, and animal damage. Grass is a problem because of the long period before a spruce seedling can compete with it successfully. In clearcutting, sufficient large slash should be left to impede animals and discourage ground cover without neglecting the creation of adequate mineral soil exposure.

Two-storied stands offer a better chance for retaining a forested condition after removing the overstory than does a single-storied stand because of the time factor in seedling establishment. Removal of the overstory is like the final cut of the shelterwood method. To be successful the understory needs to survive the logging operation. Early horse logging shows were very successful in retaining advanced reproduction as up to 50 percent survived (Alexander, 1957). Tractor logging has also been successful in protecting the advanced reproduction, but it takes close supervision and more importantly the reduction of the overstory by felling and skidding in several stages. Where the probability of the understory surviving is low, then logging should follow the single-storied procedure, that is, the shelterwood method. However, while any residual advanced growth will enhance the chances of new seedling establishment, the need for a careful removal of the final cut is just postponed and if the regeneration can not survive the area should not be cut. Planting, especially on exposed sites, has proved ill advised on many occasions.

Uneven-aged stands generally have a groupwise structure or can be harvested using the group-selection method. Continuous protection of the site is the distinctive characteristic of the selection method, so the size and shape of the groups need to be designed to ensure site protection. A circular or square area of only ½ acre on a south slope (165 feet in diameter or 148 feet on a side) would leave a large fraction unprotected. Group selection reduces logging damage and by a light improvement cut in surrounding groups postlogging mortality can be reduced. The amount of improvement cutting in surrounding groups depends on the degree of wind hazard and the amount of damage done in the removal. A group can often be located where a second group with a good understory can have the overstory removed through the clearcut group with little damage to that understory. With appropriate sized groups; seed supply is plentiful, a good seedbed can be created easily, and good growing conditions maintained. A study that used four 8-acre plots and removed 60 percent of the stand (with heavy windthrow as a consequence), was made on the Fraser Experimental Forest using a control, alternate strip clearcutting, group selection and single-tree selection methods. It showed group selection with the most regeneration and the greatest improvement in composition (Love, 1960).

The above procedures for regenerating variously structured stands depends on their being located where natural regeneration through a favorable conjunction of good seed years with adequate rains can be expected and where growing conditions will permit the seedlings continued growth. There are many localities where long summer droughts, rapid invasion of grass or quick buildup of gophers, deer, or domestic animal populations make successful natural regeneration unlikely. For even-aged stands on difficult sites progressive narrow clearcut strips (i.e., shelterwood) should be planted with every effort being made to retain any advanced regeneration. In uneven-aged stands, the clearcut groups should be planted. Planting should follow immediately after logging.

Advanced reproduction is a gift that should be protected by careful control of the logging operation. The warped and twisted understory that is mostly subalpine fir recovers rapidly once released, but its greatest asset is retaining control of the site while acting as a nurse crop for the establishment of spruce. A more rapid transition to quality growth can be had by planting the openings to spruce. A well-planted, high-quality, 3-0 spruce seedling in such a situation will shorten the rotation age by at least 10 years in the western portion of the region. Planted seedlings need protection until they are thoroughly acclimatized and until the roots have developed sufficiently to support an exposed crown. The high mortality of plantations may result from high light intensity (Ronco, 1970) or high evapotranspiration stress from high ground temperatures and ground-level winds. Whatever the reason the answer is protection of advanced regeneration, by logging slash for shade or for elevating the wind level, or by the edge effect of a stand margin.

Susceptibility to Damage. Old-growth Engelmann spruce-subalpine fir stands are susceptible to spruce beetle attack about in proportion to the degree that spruce dominates the composition of the overstory. A study of four infestations suggests that the characteristics of a potential outbreak stand are (1) the higher the percentage of spruce the greater the potential, (2) basal area of 150 to 200 square feet per acre concentrated in large-diameter spruce, (3) single- or two-storied stands, and (4) an average rate of diameter growth of 0.04 inch or less per 10 years (Schmid and Hinds, 1974).

Salvaging the beetle-killed trees can maintain the forest cover and increase the amount of spruce regeneration or it can disrupt the area and set regeneration back by many years through careless logging. Restricted salvage permits maintenance of the forest while clearcutting and mechanical skidding favors a conversion to a dense herbaceous ground cover.

Areas of recently beetle-killed timber have an increase in forage for deer and elk. The availableness of the forage depends on how soon the site is dominated by trees or how soon the windthrow loss (1.5 percent per year) renders the forage inaccessible. Sheep and cattle damage to the leaders of seedlings is more prevalent than damage by deer and elk. Livestock damage is particularly destructive in recent plantations and grazing should be restricted. Rabbits prefer subalpine fir and do little damage to spruce and a tree needs to be above snow depth before the leader is out of reach.

Pinyon-Juniper Type Group

The pinyon-juniper type has been important in the early settlement of the region as a source of fuel, edible nuts, and fence posts but these values have been largely displaced (Johnson and Innis, 1966). In the recent past this type has been viewed negatively with most efforts designed to eliminate it for increased forage or water conservation. Eradication has been difficult and the cost/benefit ratio has been too often negative for both forage production and increasing stream flow. In fact, its eradication has been shown to have an insignificant effect on stream flow (Dortignac, 1960; Gifford, 1973). Chaining[6] by the Bureau of Land Management on their lands went from a peak of 80,000 acres in 1967 to fewer than 5,000 acres in 1972 (Aro, 1975). However, the use of herbicides may provide a positive cost/benefit ratio for increased forage production (Evans et al., 1975). At present it is a neglected resource except as it is an important winter range for game animals and a low-carrying-capacity range for sheep and cattle grazing.

The pinyon-juniper zone lies below the ponderosa pine zone and has an average elevational range of 5,000 to 7,500 feet with the zone descending in places to 3,200 feet and upward to 10,000 feet. Junipers have a broader distribution than the pines and extend to a lower elevation. Pinyon-juniper covers the most extensive area of any tree cover type in the region with an area between 40 to 50 million acres. Three species of pine and six species of juniper are found in the type group. However, *Pinus edulis* and *P. monophylla* comprise the bulk of the pines and *Juniperus osteosperma* and *J. monosperma* comprise the bulk of the junipers (Lanner, 1975).

Precipitation for the type as a whole varies between 10 and 18 inches. The lower boundary of the type was used as a guide to establish the 10-inch line in mapping the rainfall isohyetal lines of Utah. The type develops on a wide range of soils derived from sandstones, basalts, and limestone.

Under a stand, the soil classification depends upon the local rainfall pattern. It may range from an Aridisol in the dry arid areas to a Mollisol in the moister areas with a good ground cover or even to a Vertisol on the flat lava surfaces of the Mogollon Rim. The soil is usually coarse textured or if high in clay then it contains a large fraction of coarse particles on rock fragments. Trees establish on sites with very shallow soils and survive by root penetration into the rock crevasses.

The root systems of the various species have widespread laterals. One juniper examined had a 24-inch stem diameter and possessed an 80-foot-diameter

---

[6]Chaining is pulling over the trees in a narrow swath (100 feet) of a pinyon-juniper stand using two tractors connected by a heavy anchor chain.

root system, as well as deep penetrating roots which followed the cracks in the rocks (Woodbury, 1947).

Place in Ecological Succession. A large but debatable portion of the present area of the type has been established through the invasion of former grasslands. Overgrazing is believed to have weakened the grass to where the trees, sagebrush, and other shrubs could invade and take over the site. Historical records and soil profiles confirm the spread of the type from the steep rocky slopes, where it is undoubtedly climax, to the deeper, richer soils of gentle topography.

Growth Rates. The average diameter growth at 50 years for three species was 0.68 inch per 10 years (Howell, 1941). Pinyon pine took 100 years to grow 12 feet in height and 240 years to reach 31 feet; juniper does not exceed this rate (Chapman and Behre, 1918). Utah juniper on its best site in open stands has a height of 8.4 feet in 21 years (Miller, 1921). Volume and height growth vary widely, depending upon whether the measurements are made at the upper elevational limit of the type on good sites with high rainfall or at the lower limit where the poor sites with low rainfall produce many-stemmed, short, and scraggly trees.

The average yield of unmanaged stands was 11.4 standard cords per acre, with a range of 0.8 to 24.8 cords. The presence of pinyon pine in the composition improved yield, as the juniper type averaged 9.7 cords per acre (Howell, 1941), or 7.5 cords (Herman, 1953). A mixed stand in Utah had an average yield of 4.5 cords (Johnson, 1965).

Cultural Practices. The stands are usually uneven-aged (Fig. 7-15) unless the area was cutover for charcoal and firewood or chained though rapid invasion creates relatively even-aged stands too. A closed stand is a rare condition associated with rich sites where the pinyon pine grows to 50 feet or more in height. Densities vary from scattered trees to 60 to 70 percent crown cover with grasses or shrubs in the understory and openings (Fig. 7–15). Seed production in pinyon pines begins when the tree is 3- to 4-feet tall (25-years-old) and may have 20 bushels of cones per acre at maturity. The seeds are quite large (*P. edulis* 1,900 per pound and *P. monophylla* 1,110 USDA For. Serv., 1974) and edible with large quantities harvested by man, birds, and rodents. Seed crops are frequent for *P. monophylla* (about every 2 years) but much less frequent for *P. edulis* (about 2 to 5 years but closer to 5). Commercially collected seeds have a high germination capacity (above 80 percent) but germination capacity and germinative energy fluctuate widely with the temperature regimen.

Junipers produce seed at an early age (10 to 20 years). *J. monosperma* is dioecious and takes only one year to mature its seeds (18,300 per pound) with good crops every 2 to 5 years, while *J. osteosperma* is primarily monoecious and takes 2 years to mature its seeds (4,950 per pound) with good crops about every

Figure 7-15.   Pinyon-juniper stand showing *Juniperus osteosperma* on the left and *Pinus edulis* in the center and right. The sparse grass cover is characteristic where heavily grazed (Book Cliffs, east of Price, Utah). On the Mesa Verde Plateau with National Park protection grass is the prominent ground cover with good density and growth.

2 years. Juniper seeds have a pulpy cone attractive to birds and rodents, and the seeds have an impervious seed coat; so the birds, rabbits, and even mice act as distribution agents. Juniper seeds do not readily germinate and in nature may germinate over a period of years.

The pinyon pines and junipers are intolerant but as seedlings they survive in moderate shade. In fact, establishment takes place only within the protective confines of a sagebrush or other shrub except as it may occur within the margins of the tree crown. As a rule, the seedling develops adjacent to the shrub's main stem. Whether this happens because the grazing cattle and sheep would destroy any unprotected germinants or more probably under such an arid environment because the moisture regimen adjacent to the stem is more favorable to survival is uncertain.

Susceptibility to Damage. Fire is a constant danger because of the dry conditions and the flammability of the trees because their crowns are so close to the ground. When there is sufficient ground cover to carry the fire from tree to tree, the whole stand is frequently killed. Prehistorically, frequent fires may have confined the type to the steeper rocky slopes.

Severe drought extending over a period of years result in widespread losses. The pinyon pines are more susceptible to drought than the junipers so mixed stands have been reduced to pure juniper.

Heart rot (*Fomes juniperinus*) renders most of the overmature stands unmerchantable. Witches-broom and stem diseases (*Gymnosporangium* spp.) cause heavy losses and serious deformities in junipers. Mistletoe is a serious problem and it is a conspicuous threat to the stands along the south rim of the Grand Canyon of the Colorado River.

Pinyon pines are reasonably resistant to diseases though heart rots (*Fomes* spp.) frequently destroy the value of overmature trees. Insects affecting pinyon pine have not developed into epidemic proportions of the bark beetles in other conifers. Pinyon needle scale and pinyon sawfly are defoliators that with repeated defolitation can kill or weaken trees to where they are susceptible to *Ips* attacks.

BIBLIOGRAPHY

Alexander, M. E., and F. G. Hawksworth. 1975. Wildland fires and dwarf mistletoes: a literature review of ecology and prescribed burning. *USDA For. Ser. Gen. Tech. Rep. RM-14.* 12 pp.

Alexander, R. R. 1957. Damage to advanced reproduction in clearcutting spruce-fir. *U.S. For. Serv., Rocky Mt. For. and Range Exp. Stn. Res. Note 27.* 3 pp.

Alexander, R. R. 1969. Seedfall and establishment of Engelmann spruce in clearcut openings: a case history. *USDA For. Serv. Res. Pap. RM-53.* 8 pp.

Alexander, R. R., W. D. Shepperd, and C. B. Edminster. 1975. Yield tables for managed even-aged stands of spruce-fir in the central Rocky Mountains. *USDA For. Serv. Res. Pap. RM-134.* 20 pp.

Aro, R. S. 1975. Pinyon-juniper woodland manipulation with mechanical methods. In: *The Pinyon-Juniper Ecosystem: A Symposium.* pp. 67–75. Utah State Univ., Coll. Natural Resour., Logan.

Baker, F. S. 1925. Aspen in the central Rocky Mountains. *USDA Bull. No. 1291.* 47 pp.

Baker, F. S., and C. F. Korstian. 1931. Suitability of brushlands in the Intermountain region for the growth of natural or planted western yellow pine forests. *USDA Tech. Bull. 256.* 83 pp.

Baker, F. S. 1934. *Theory and practices of silviculture.* McGraw-Hill. New York. 502 pp.

Barnes, B. V. 1969. Natural variation and delineation of clones of *Populus tremuloides* and *P. grandidentata* in northern lower Michigan. *Silvae Genet.* 18:132–142.

Barrett, J. W., S. S. Tornbom, and R. W. Sassaman. 1976. Logging to save ponderosa pine regeneration: a case study. *USDA For. Serv. Res. Note PNW-273. 13 pp.*

Bates, C. G. 1923. Physiological requirements of Rocky Mountains trees. *J. Agr. Res.* 24:97–164.

Bates, C. G. 1924. Forest types of the central Rocky Mountains as affected by climate and soil. *USDA Bull. 1233.* 152 pp.

Berndt, H. W., and R. D. Gibbons. 1958. Root distribution of some native trees and understory plants growing on three sites within ponderosa pine watershed in Colorado. *U.S. For. Serv., Rocky Mt. For. and Range Exp. Stn. Pap. 37.* 14 pp.

Boldt, C. E., and J. L. Van Deusen. 1974. Silviculture of ponderosa pine in the Black Hills: the status of our knowledge. *USDA For. Serv. Res. Pap. RM-124.* 45 pp.

Brickell, J. E. 1968. A method for constructing site index curves from measurements of tree age and height—its application to inland Douglas-fir. *USDA For. Serv. Res. Pap. INT-47.* 23 pp.

Bruce, D. 1942. Maturity selection. *The Timberman* 43:20–26, 32.

Chapman, H. H., and C. E. Behre, 1918. Growth and management of pinon in New Mexico. *J. For.* 16:215–217.

Clements, F. E. 1910. The life history of lodgepole burn forests. *U.S. For. Serv. Bull.* 79. 56 pp.

Cooper, C. F. 1960. Changes in vegetation, structure, and growth of southwestern pine forests since white settlement. *Ecol. Monogr.* 30:129–164.

Daniel, T. W. 1942. The comparative transpiration rates of several western conifers under controlled conditions. Ph.D. dissertation, Univ. Calif. Berkeley. 190 pp.

Daniel, T. W., and G. H. Barnes. 1958. Thinning a young stand of lodgepole pine. In *Proc. Soc. Amer. For. Ann. Mtg.,* pp. 159–163.

Daniel, T. W. and G. Glatzel. 1966. Duff. A lethal seedbed for overwintering Engelmann spruce seeds. In: *Proc. Sixth World For. Cong.,* Madrid. pp. 1420–1424.

Daniel, T. W., and J. Schmidt. 1972. Lethal and non-lethal effects of the organic horizons of forested soils on the germination of seeds from several associated conifer species of the Rocky Mountains. *Can. J. For. Res.* 2:179–184.

Daubenmire, R. F. 1943. Vegetational zonation in the Rocky Mountains. *Bot. Rev.* 9:325–393.

Daubenmire, R. F., and J. B. Daubenmire. 1968. Forest vegetation of eastern Washington and northern Idaho. *Wash. Agr. Exp. Stn. Tech. Bull. 60.* Pullman. 104 pp.

DeByle, N. V. (ed.). (In press.) Aspen: ecology and management in the western United States. *USDA For. Serv., Rocky Mt. For. and Range Exp. Stn. Res. Pap.*

Dortignac, E. J. 1960. Water yield from pinyon-juniper woodland. In *Symp. Water Yield in Relation to Environment in the Southwestern United States.* SW and Rocky Mt. Div. of AAAS, Desert and Arid Zones Res. Comm. (Alpine, Texas). Unpublished.

Dunning, D. 1928. A tree classification for the selection forests of the Sierra Nevada. *J. Agr. Res.* 36:755–771.

Edminster, C. B., and L. H. Jump. 1976. Site index curves for Douglas-fir in New Mexico. *USDA For. Serv. Res. Note RM-326.* 3 pp.

Egan, J. E. 1954. Silvicultural foundations for national forest cutting practice in the ponderosa pine stands of the Southwest. *J. For.* 52:756–766.

Ensign, E. T. 1888. Forest conditions in the Rocky Mountains. *USDA For. Div. Bull.* 2. pp. 41–153.

Evans, R. A., R. E. Eckert, Jr., and J. A. Young. 1975. The role of herbicides in management of pinyon-juniper woodlands. In *Symp. The Pinyon-Juniper Ecosystem.* pp. 83–89. Utah State Univ., Coll. Natural Resour., Logan.

Fenneman, N. M. 1931. *Physiography of Western United States.* McGraw-Hill Book Co., New York. 534 pp.

Fowells, H. A., and B. M. Kirk. 1945. Availability of soil moisture to ponderosa pine. *J. For.* 43:601–604.

Gaines, E. M., and E. S. Kotok. 1954. Thinning ponderosa pine in the southwest. *U.S. For. Serv. Rocky Mt. For. and Range Exp. Stn. Pap. 17.* 20 pp.

Gifford, G. F. 1973. Runoff and sediment yields from runoff plots on chained pinyon-juniper sites in Utah. *J. Range Manage.* 26:440–443.

Hall, D. O. 1971. Ponderosa pine planting techniques, survival, and height growth in the Idaho batholith. *USDA For. Serv. Res. Pap. INT-104.* 28 pp.

Hart, G. E., and F. D. Eaton. 1971. Comparison of actual and potential evapotranspiration in a subalpine stand of spruce and fir. Utah State Univ., Dept. For. Sci. 3rd Forest Meteorology Symp. Syracuse, N.Y. 8 pp. mineographed, unpublished.

Hawksworth, F. G. 1961. Dwarf mistletoe of ponderosa pine in the Southwest. *USDA Tech. Bull. 1246.* 112 pp.

Hawksworth, F. G. 1977. The 6-class dwarf mistletoe rating system. *USDA For. Serv. Gen. Tech. Rep. RM-48.* 7 pp.

Heidmann, L. J. 1976. Frost heaving of tree seedlings: a literature review of causes and possible control.*USDA For. Serv. Gen. Tech. Rep. RM-21.* 10 pp.

Heidmann, L. J., F. R. Larson, and W. J. Rietveld. 1977. Evaluation of ponderosa pine reforestation techniques in central Arizona. *USDA For. Serv. Res. Pap. RM-190.* 10 pp.

Herman, F. R. 1953. A growth record of Utah juniper in Arizona. *J. For.* 51:200–201.

Hinds, T. E., and R. G. Krebill. 1975. Wounds and canker diseases on western aspen. *USDA For. Serv. For. Pest Leaf.* 152. 9 pp.

Holdridge, L. R., W. C. Grenke, W. H. Hatheway, T. Liang, and J. A. Tosi, Jr. 1971. *Forest environments in tropical life zones–a pilot study.* Pergamon, New York. 747 pp.

Hornibrook, E. M. 1939. A modified tree classification for use in growth studies and timber marking in Black Hills ponderosa pine. *J. For.* 39:483–488.

Howell, J. Jr. 1941. Pinon and juniper woodlands in the Southwest. *J. For.* 39:542–545.

Johnson, W. H. 1965. Economic analysis of charcoal production from the pinyon-juniper type. *Utah State Univ. Agr. Exp. Stn. Rep.,* Logan.

Johnson, W. H., and D. R. Innis. 1966. A bibliography of the pinyon-juniper woodland type in the southwestern United States. *Utah State Univ. Agr. Exp. Stn., Mimeo Series 501,* Logan.

Jones, J. R. 1967. Aspen site index in the Rocky Mountains. *J. For.* 65:820–821.

Jones. J. R. 1971. Mixed conifer seedling growth in eastern Arizona. *USDA For. Serv. Res. Pap. RM-77.* 19 pp.

Jones, J. R. 1974. Silviculture of southwestern mixed conifers and aspen. *USDA For. Serv. Res. Pap. RM-122.* 44 pp.

Jones, J. R., and D. P. Trujillo. 1975. Development of some young aspen stands in Arizona. *USDA For. Serv. Res. Pap. RM-151.* 11 pp.

Keen, F. P. 1936. Relative susceptibility of ponderosa pine to bark-beetle attack. *J. For.* 34:919–927.

Keen, F. P. 1950. The influence of insects on ponderosa pine silviculture. *J. For.* 48:186–188.

Kemperman, J. A., and B. V. Barnes. 1976. Clone size in American aspens. *Can. J. Bot.* 54:2603–2607.

Krauch, H. 1936. Some factors influencing Douglas-fir reproduction in the Southwest. *J. For.* 34:601–608.

Krauch, H. 1956. Management of Douglas-fir timberland in the Southwest. *U.S. For. Ser. Rocky Mt. For. and Range Exp. Stn: Pap.* 40. 59 pp.

Lanner, R. M. 1975. Piñon pines and junipers of the southwestern woodlands. In *Symp. The Pinyon-Juniper Ecosystem.* pp. 1–17. Utah State Univ., Coll. Natural Resour. Logan.

Larson, M. M. 1963. Initial root development of ponderosa pine seedlings as related to germination date and size of seed. *For. Sci.* 9:456–460.

Larson, M. M., and G. H. Schubert. 1969. Root competition between ponderosa pine seedlings and grass. *USDA For. Serv. Res. Pap. RM-54.* 12 pp.

Lessard, G., and D. T. Jennings. 1976. Southwestern pine tip moth damage to ponderosa pine reproduction. *USDA For. Serv. Res.. Pap. RM-168.* 8 pp.

Lindermuth, A. W. Jr. 1960. A survey of effects of intensive burning on fuels and timber stands of ponderosa pine in Arizona. *USDA For. Ser. Rocky Mt. For. and Range Exp. Stn. Pap. 54.* 22 pp.

List, P. 1959. Growth prediction in spruce-fir on the Utah State University forest. M.S. thesis, Utah State Univ., Logan. 53 pp.

Love, L. D. 1960. The Fraser Experimental Forest—its work and aims. *USDA For. Serv. Rocky Mt. For. and Range Exp. Stn. Pap. 8* (revised).

Merriam, C. H. 1898. Life zones and crop zones of the U.S. *U.S. Bureau Biol. Sur. Bull. 10.* 79 pp.

Meyer, W. H. 1938 and 1961. Yield of even-aged stands of ponderosa pine. *USDA Tech. Bull. 630.* 60 pp.

Miller, F. H. 1921. Reclamation of grasslands by Utah juniper on the Tusayan Nat. For., Arizona. *J. For.* 19:647−651.

Minor, C. O. 1964. Site index curves for young-growth ponderosa pine in northern Arizona. *USDA For. Serv. Res. Note RM-37.* 8 pp.

Mogren, E. W. 1956. A site index classification for ponderosa pine in northern Colorado. *Colo. A. and M. Coll. Res. Note 5,* Fort Collins. 2 pp.

Mueggler, W. F., and D. L. Bartos. 1977. Grindstone Flat and Big Flat Exclosures—a 41-year record of changes in clearcut aspen communities. *USDA For. Serv. Res. Pap. INT-195.* 16 pp.

Munger, T. T., A. J. F. Branstrom, and E. L. Kolbe. 1936. Maturity selection system applied to ponderosa pine. *West Coast Lumberman* 63:33, 44.

Myers, C. A. 1971. Field and computer procedures for managed stand yield tables. *USDA For. Serv. Res. Pap. RM-79.* 24 pp.

Myers, C. A. 1974. Multipurpose silviculture in ponderosa pine stands of the Montane Zone of central Colorado. *USDA For. Serv. Res. Pap. RM-132.* 15 pp.

Noble, D. L. 1973. Engelmann spruce seedling roots reach depth of 3 to 4 inches their first season. *USDA For. Serv. Res. Note RM-241.* 3 pp.

Noble, D. L., and R. R. Alexander. 1977. Environmental factors affecting natural regeneration of Engelmann spruce in the central Rocky Mountains. *For. Sci.* 23:420−429.

Pearson, G. A. 1910. Reproduction of western yellow pine in the Southwest. *U.S. For. Serv. Circular 174.* 16 pp.

Pearson, G. A. 1931. Forest types in the Southwest as determined by climate and soil. *USDA Tech. Bull. 247.* 144 pp.

Pearson, G. A. 1934. Grass, pine seedlings and grazing. *J. For.* 32:545−555.

Pearson, G. A. 1940. Shade effects in ponderosa pine. *J. For.* 38:778−780.

Pearson, G. A. 1942. Improvement selection cutting in ponderosa pine (with comments by Bruce, Munger, Randall and Carter). *J. For.* 40:753−766.

Pearson, G. A. 1943. The facts behind improvement selection. *J. For.* 41:740−752.

Pearson, G. A. 1950. Management of ponderosa pine in the Southwest. *U.S. For. Serv. Agr. Monogr. 6.* 218 pp.

Roe, A. L., and W. C. Schmidt. 1964. Factors affecting natural regeneration of spruce in the Intermountain region. *USDA For. Serv. Int. For. and Range Exp. Stn., Mimeo. Rep.* 68 pp.

Ronco, F. 1970. Engelmann spruce seed dispersal and seedling establishment in clearcut forest openings in Colorado—a progress report. *USDA For. Serv. Res. Note RM-168.* 8 pp.

Roth, L. F., C. G. Shaw III, and L. Rolph. 1977. Marking ponderosa pine to combine commercial thinning and control of *Armillaria* root rot. *J. For.* 75:644‖647.

Rydberg, P. A. 1913. Phytogeographical notes on Rocky Mountain Region. *I. Alpihe Region. Bull. Torrey Bot. Club* 40:677−687.

Salman, K. A., and J. W. Bongberg. 1942. Logging high-risk trees to control insects in the pine stands of northeastern California. *J. For.* 40:533−539.

Salt, G. A. 1974. Etiology and morphology of *Geniculodendron pyriforme*, Gen. and Sp. nova—a pathogen of conifer seeds. *Trans. Brit. Mycol. Soc.* 63:339—351.

Schier, G. A. 1972. Apical dominance in multishoot cultures from aspen roots. *For. Sci.* 18:147—149.

Schier, G. A. 1978. Vegetative propagation of Rocky Mountain aspen. *USDA For. Serv. Gen. Tech. Rep. INT-44.* 13 pp.

Schlaegel, B. E. 1975. Estimating aspen volume and weight of individual trees, diameter classes or entire stands. *USDA For. Serv. Gen. Tech. Rep. NC-20.* 16 pp.

Schmid, J. M., and T. E. Hinds. 1974. Development of spruce-fir stands following spruce beetle outbreaks. *USDA For. Serv. Res. Pap. RM-131.* 16 pp.

Schubert, G. H. 1974. Silviculture of southwestern ponderosa pine: the status of our knowledge. *USDA For. Serv. Res. Pap. RM-123.* 71 pp.

Schubert, G. H. 1976. Silvicultural practices for intensified forest management. In: *Trees—the Renewable Resource.* p. 37—54. Proc. Rocky Mt. For. Ind. Conf., Tucson.

Schubert, G. H., L. J. Heidmann, and M. M. Larson, 1970. Artificial reforestation practices for the Southwest. *USDA Agric. Hdb. 370.* 25 pp.

Schubert, G. H., and J. A. Pitcher. 1973. A provisional tree seed-zone and cone-crop rating system for Arizona and New Mexico. *USDA For. Serv. Res. Paper RM-105.* 8 pp.

Scott, V. E. 1978. Characteristics of ponderosa pine snags used by cavity-nesting birds in Arizona. *J. For.* 76:26—28.

Sprackling, J. A. 1977. Early field survival of bare-root, container-grown, and potted ponderosa pine seedlings in south-central Nebraska. *USDA For. Serv. Res. Note RM-335.* 2 pp.

Squillace, A. E. 1954. Engelmann spruce seed dispersal into a clearcut area. *USDA For. Serv. Int. For. and Range Exp. Stn. Res. Note 11.* 4 pp.

Stevens, R. E., and D. T. Jennings. 1977. Western pine-shoot borer: a threat to intensive management of ponderosa pine in the Rocky Mountain area and Southwest. *USDA For. Serv. Gen. Tech. Rep. RM-45.* 8 pp.

Stewart, R. E., and T. Beebe. 1974. Survival of ponderosa pine seedlings following control of competing grasses. In: *Proc. West. Soc. Weed Sci. 27: 55—58.* Hawaii.

Stuart, E. Jr., and J. Roeser Jr. 1944. Effect of thinning in the Black Hills. *J. For.* 42:279—280.

Tew, R. K., N. V. DeByle, and J. D. Schultz. 1969. Intraclonal root connections among quaking aspen trees. *Ecology* 50:920—921.

Thomson, W. G. 1940. A growth rate classification of southwestern ponderosa pine. *J. For.* 38:547—553.

USDA Forest Service. 1974. Seeds of woody plants in the United States. *USDA For. Serv. Agric. Hdb. 450.* 883 pp.

USDA Forest Service. 1978. Forest statistics of the United States, 1977. *Review Draft.* 133 pp.

U.S. Geol. Surv. 1966. *National atlas of the United States of America.* Atlas sheet 61. Arlington, Va. 335 pp.

U.S. Weather Bureau. 1957. Climatic summary of the United States. Reprinted series 11. *U.S. Dept. of Commerce.*

Weaver, H. 1951. Observed effects of prescribed burning on perennial grasses in the ponderosa pine forests. *J. For.* 49:267—271.

Wiedman, R. H. 1939. Evidences of racial influences in a 25-year test of ponderosa pine. *J. Agr. Res.* 59:855—887.

Woodbury, A. M. 1947. Distribution of pigmy conifers in Utah and northeastern Arizona. *Ecology* 28:113—126.

8

The Northern Rocky Mountain Region

David L. Adams

LOCATION

The Northern Rocky Mountain Region includes the states of Idaho and Montana and the northeastern corner of Washington (Fig. 7-1). This area is essentially the northern province of the Rocky Mountain system.

FOREST STATISTICS

Area

Thirty-five percent of Idaho is classified as forest land, while 25 percent of Montana falls into this category. However, the forests of Idaho and western Montana present the largest unbroken area of forest land in the United States. In this area, over 80 percent of the land is forested.

Eastern Montana, by contrast, is short-grass prairie, with only scattered open stands of ponderosa pine and juniper. Southern Idaho, principally the Snake River Plains, has a cover of sagebrush and grass, with scattered woodlands of singleleaf pinyon, junipers, aspen, lodgepole pine, and Douglas-fir (*glauca* variety). Trees occur above the sagebrush where topography and increasing elevation provide the minimal site conditions for tree growth.

Of more than 44 million total acres of forest land in Idaho and Montana, approximately 30 million are classed as commercial and 14 million as noncommercial. The latter class includes high rocky lands bearing light-timber stands as well as productive land which has been reserved for nontimber use. Large tracts of federal forest land in Idaho and Montana are now managed as wilderness, and additional roadless areas are being studied for possible wilderness classification. Although much of the forest land included within wilderness and

TABLE 8-1

Forest Land Classification and Net Sawtimber Volume

State	Total Land Area (Thousand Acres)	Total Forest Land Area (Thousand Acres)	Commercial (Thousand Acres)	Productive but Reserved (Thousand Acres)	Unproductive (Thousand Acres)			Sawtimber Volume (MM Cubic Feet)
					Total	Reserved	Unreserved	
Idaho	52,913.1	21,726.6	13,540.6	2,848.3	5,337.7	611.2	4,726.5	26,642.7
Montana	93,175.2	22,559.3	14,359.4	2,710.5	5,489.4	1,374.6	4,114.8	19,240.7
Total	146,088.3	44,285.9	27,900.0	5,558.8	10,827.1	1,985.8	8,841.3	45,883.4

Source: USDA For. Serv., 1978

national parks is relatively unproductive, over 5.7 million acres of commercial forest land have been reserved for nontimber use.

Character of Forest Land Ownership

National forests, containing 64 percent of the commercial forest lands, are the dominant ownership. The Bureau of Land Management, Bureau of Indian Affairs, and other holdings add to the Federal total. State lands comprise almost 5 percent of the commercial forest area, while county and municipal ownership is minor. Forest industries control only 7 percent and small private woodlots account for 19 percent of the commercial forest land base. Thus only 1 acre in 4 is privately owned.

Forest Inventory

Almost all of the sawtimber volume of 45,883.4 million cubic feet is softwood (Table 8-2). Sixty seven percent of the commercial forest area is in sawtimber, 20 percent in poletimber stands, 10 percent in seedling to sapling size, and about 3 percent is nonstocked area. Two-thirds of the sawtimber volume of the entire Rocky Mountains is found in Idaho and Montana. Nationally, these states rank fifth and sixth in sawtimber, respectively, exceeded only by the three Pacific Coast states and Alaska (USDA For. Serv., 1973).

Growth exceeds cut for the region in terms of both total growing stock and sawtimber. For example, total growth amounted to 1,154 million cubic feet in 1977 which was considerably greater than the comparable removal figure of 630 million cubic feet. Removals from the live sawtimber inventory (trees exceeding 9.0 inches d.b.h.) on commercial forest land were 3.625 billion board feet as contrasted with annual growth of 4.357 billion board feet (USDA For. Serv., 1978).

TABLE 8-2

Percent of Net Sawtimber Volume on Commercial Forest Land by Species

Species	percent
Douglas-fir	30.2
True firs (mainly grand fir)	15.6
Lodgepole pine	13.1
Ponderosa pine	11.3
Engelmann spruce	8.5
Western larch	7.5
Western white pine	4.4
Western redcedar	4.4
Western hemlock	2.9
Other softwood species	1.3
Hardwood (mainly cottonwood and aspen)	0.7

Source: USDA For. Serv., 1978

THE PHYSICAL ENVIRONMENT

Physiography

Virtually all the forested area in the region is mountainous. Terrain is typically rugged and steep, with little level land.

From the west, the rolling Palouse grassland of the Columbia Basin province (Fig. 7-1) forms the basal plain at about 2,500 feet and extends fingerlike into the Camas Prairie, an elevated plateau around Craigmont, Idaho. The Snake River Plains of southern Idaho, which are relatively flat and dominated by sagebrush, break into rough grassland and then into timber, with the transition to mountainous topography to the north, east, and south.

In south-central Montana, many of the more important rivers—the Madison, Gallatin, Yellowstone, Jefferson, and Missouri—have broad, grassy, valley floors well suited for farm and cattle development. West of the Continental Divide, drainage is through the Snake, Salmon, Clearwater, St. Joe, Spokane, Pend Oreille, Clark Fork, Bitterroot, Flathead, and Kootenai rivers, all of which ultimately reach the Columbia. Although these rivers are characterized by narrow, canyonlike valleys, wider sections subject to agricultural development add much to the diversity of the economy. Hells Canyon of the Snake River is the deepest gorge in North America, with an average depth of over a mile. The steep canyon of the Salmon River was known by Indians as the "river of no return." The broken topography makes road design and location very difficult. No other region in the country has such continuous mountain terrain and such a diverse, rugged area.

Four large lakes—Coeur d'Alene, Priest, and Pend Oreille in Idaho, and Flathead in Montana—are renowned for their beauty. Flathead is the largest natural lake within one state in the United States. In the higher mountain areas, lakes formed by glacial erosion are abundant.

Elevation at Lewiston, Idaho, near the confluence of the Clearwater and Snake rivers is 738 feet, the low point in the region. The highest peaks, Mount Borah in Idaho and Granite Mountain in Montana exceed 12,000 feet. Numerous peaks are in the 10,000-foot class, but most of the area is below 6,000 feet. The best forest development is found generally between 2,000 and 6,000 feet.

Geology and Soils

Parent materials are principally of granite, basalt, schist, quartzite, argillite, rhyolite, and metamorphosed sedimentaries. A light to heavy cover of loess and volcanic ash along the western fringes contributes a beneficial influence in soil development. Most soils are loamy, but those developed from granite have a tendency to coarseness. The soils are typically Entisols and Alfisols, light brown to brown, with a generally thick surface layer of forest litter, and a weakly developed ashy-gray podzolic layer (U.S. Dept. Agr., 1938; U.S. Dept. Agr., 1975). They are usually of granular or single-grained floury structure. Subsoils commonly are yellowish-brown to light grayish-brown, becoming more compact and gray with depth. Soil profiles are weakly developed in steeper areas of excessive drainage. Soil pH ranges from 4.5 to 6.5.

At higher elevations soils are generally thin, coarse and rocky. Soil formation here is slow because of the short growing season and steep, rocky slopes, which in turn make soil accumulation very slow. Organic matter and nitrogen content of soils typically increase with elevation, due to lower temperature and the short season during which decomposing organisms are active. Organic matter also increases at low elevations in forested grasslands.

Across the northern part of the region and elsewhere at higher elevations, the soil forming process has been greatly influenced by glaciation. Active glaciers are still present, especially in the Glacier Park area of western Montana; many high mountain areas are bared rock, where the soils were abraded by glacial action.

Valleys in areas of continental and local glaciation are filled with glacial till. The coarse, well-drained soils developed on the glacial tills tend to be droughty because of their low water retention.

Climate and Weather

The Rocky Mountains exert a major influence on the region's climate. Prevailing westerly winds along well-developed storm tracks extend the coastal climate inland to the western slopes of the northern Rockies; thus, the climate here is milder than would be expected at this latitude. Winter precipitation, summer drought, and moderate annual range of temperatures are characteristic. As a result of this climate, Pacific coastal species such as western redcedar, western hemlock, and grand fir are common, particularly at lower to mid-elevations in the northwestern part of the region.

Precipitation, and hence vegetation patterns are strongly influenced by elevational changes and proximity to the major mountain ranges; the Bitterroot Divide and the Continental Divide are particularly important. The transition from grassland to timber on the western slopes normally occurs where precipitation reaches about 15 inches annually, the minimum amount required to support tree growth in this region. There is a gradual increase in precipitation with rising elevation, and the western crests of the Bitterroot Range receive as much as 70 inches. The rain-shadow effect of these mountain ranges creates an abrupt change in climate and vegetation on the eastern slopes.

Precipitation varies from 20 to 40 inches annually over much of the commercial forest area; however, the extensive sagebrush areas to the south may receive only about 10 inches while the Great Plains grasslands and Palouse Prairies bordering on the east and west receive 13 to 20 inches.

For the region as a whole, January is the wettest month (Baldwin, 1973). There is an irregular monthly decrease in precipitation until July and August when there may be little or no rainfall. Autumn rains usually start in September.

Average annual snowfall in the forests will vary from 16 to 230 inches. Over much of the commercial forest range, snowfall accumulates to depths of 40 to 70 inches each winter. In some subalpine habitats, depth and persistence of snow cover limit tree growth and occurrence.

The frost-free period begins in May, or in June at higher elevations or in frost pockets. The first killing frost comes in September, or in August in higher mountain areas, where frosts can be anticipated every month of the year. Most of the forest area will have a frost-free period ranging from 70 to 120 days; at lower elevations it may extend to 160 days.

West of the Continental Divide summer days are usually bright and clear, while a majority of winter days are cloudy. The east side is generally clear throughout the year, because the prevailing westerlies top the divide and descend to the basal plains as warming and drying (subsidence) winds. This situation often gives rise to the Chinook wind.

West of the divide, temperatures are generally mild for this latitude because of the ameliorating coastal influence. Summer-day temperatures of 80 °F to 90 °F are usual, and nights are cool. Maximum temperatures rarely reach 100 °F in the timbered areas. Mean-annual temperatures are in the range of 44 °F to 47 °F, whereas July temperatures average 58 °F to 68 °F. Minimum temperatures infrequently reach −40 °F.

East of the divide, extremes of temperature are greater—winters are colder and summers hotter. In the forests, summer temperatures rarely become uncomfortably hot due to low relative humidity; nights are generally cool.

Dry lightning storms are a significant hazard in the region, causing 70 percent of the forest fires. Summer rains in the area are sporadic and often intense. Thunderstorms with damaging precipitation rates are more likely to occur on the east side of the Bitterroot Mountains than elsewhere in the region. Stream runoff peaks in late spring, with rapid snow melt from mountain watersheds. Streams flow bank full, and floods may occur along larger streams when snowmelt coincides with extra heavy spring rains. Damaging floods have also resulted from heavy winter rains falling on a snowpack. Where gradients are steep, stream channels are often scoured at these times.

Winds are most violent in February and March, occasionally causing serious windfall losses. For example, the heavy blow-down of Engelmann spruce in 1949 gave rise to a critical spruce bark beetle epidemic, and the need for a spruce salvage program. The Beaverhead, Flathead, and Kootenai national forests suffered 200 million board feet of blow-down during the 1948−1950 period, when winds up to 100 miles per hour occurred (U.S. Dept. Agr., 1952).

Occasional east winds may exert an extremely drying influence and in fire season lead to critical burning conditions. Relative humidities of 25 percent or less are common in summer; extremes of 5 to 10 percent may occur. Such conditions promote high transpiration rates and depletion of much needed soil moisture. Cold-air drainage in narrow mountain valleys usually leads to dew formation during the night in areas where cold air pools. This microclimatic influence can be highly important in reducing transpiration stress and aiding seedling survival in flatter areas. However, the same conditions often cause frost-related regeneration problems.

THE MAJOR FOREST TYPE GROUPS

The Society of American Foresters (1954) reports 16 different forest cover types in the region, while the U.S. Forest Service survey has classified the commercial forest into eight different types: Douglas-fir, ponderosa pine, white pine, western larch, lodgepole pine, spruce-fir, hardwoods, and coniferous woodland.

Forest cover types are commonly used to describe existing stand composition. However, the use of habitat types as a forest land stratification system can be used to predict the capabilities of the site and better predict the results of vegetative manipulations. A habitat type is the aggregation of units of land capable of producing similar plant communities at climax (Daubenmire and Daubenmire, 1968). Habitat types, as commonly used in the northern Rocky Mountains, are named after the climax community (termed an association). The first part of the name is based upon the climax tree species and the second part of the name after the dominant and characteristic understory species in the climax community (e.g., *Pseudotsuga menziesii/Physocarpus malvaceus*). All habitat types having the same dominant tree species at climax form a series.

Habitat types are widely used throughout the northern Rocky Mountain area as an aid in making land management decisions. As noted in Chapter 7 this technique is also used in the Middle and Southern Rocky Mountain Region. The use of habitat types is predicated upon the concept that wise land-use planning must be constrained by the inherent capability of the land to produce resources, and that land capability can be assessed through this system of site classification. Although the use of habitat types is stressed here, it should be recognized that this is but one aid in making land management decisions. Just as important are land types which also consider geology, soils, and physiography.

Daubenmire (1966) recognized the environmental gradient in explaining the relative ecological position and extent of occurrence of tree species. The distribution and ecological roles of inland northwest tree species relative to habitat types are shown in Figs. 8-1 and 8-2. In Fig. 8-1, species are arranged to show the usual order in which they are encountered as elevation increases. The horizontal bars designate lower and upper limits of each species relative to the climatic gradient. That portion of a species amplitude in which it can maintain a self-reproducing population with forest competition (i.e., climax) is indicated by the stippled area. Thus, western hemlock is always climax, western larch always seral, and grand fir is climax at its lower, warmer, drier limits but seral in stands where western redcedar or western hemlock are climax. Projection of these relationships to the horizontal axis delineates forest zones (or series in habitat-type classification). Associates of any species can be determined by following a vertical line up and down from any position on a species amplitude bar.

The role of seral, fire-type species is well indicated in Fig. 8-2. Western white pine, western larch, and lodgepole pine are seral through a range of habitats but climax in none of them in northern Idaho or western Montana (the

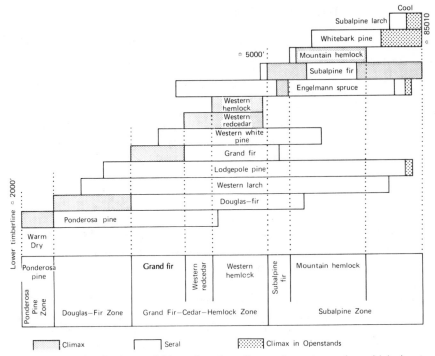

Figure 8-1. Amplitudes and hierarchy of coniferous trees in northern Idaho/eastern Washington along a climatic gradient. (Revised from Daubenmire, 1966; Johnson, 1979.)

ecological role of a species may be different in another geographic region; e.g., lodgepole pine is considered to be climax on some habitats in south-central Idaho) (Steele *et al.*, 1975).

Initially the habitat-type method of ecosystem classification was developed for northern Idaho and eastern Washington by Daubenmire (1952). To date, because of the environmental diversity, a large number of habitat types have been recognized in the northern Rockies. Daubenmire and Daubenmire (1968) described 22 for northern Idaho and eastern Washington. Using a more precise classification system, Pfister *et al.* (1977) listed 64 forest habitat types for Montana, and Steele *et al.* (1975) noted 46 types for central and eastern Idaho. Parallel rangeland habitat types are available for Montana (Mueggler and Handl, 1974), northern Idaho and eastern Washington (Daubenmire, 1970), and typing of sagebrush grass communities of southern Idaho is nearing completion (Hironaka, 1977).

HISTORY OF FOREST USE

Agriculture

After the Civil War, agricultural settlement grew rapidly in the fertile grassland areas and open timbered foothills. Farmland extension in recent years has been slow, but gradually the deep loessal soils on level to rolling lands are being

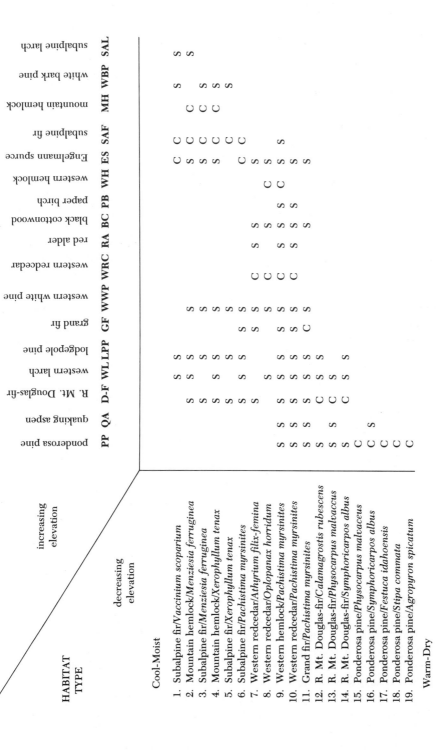

TREE SPECIES

Figure 8-2. Successional status of overstory trees in closed stands related to habitat types in northern Idaho and adjacent Washington. Climax trees are designated by "C"; seral trees by "S"; Elevational relationships are generalized and locally are strongly affected by aspect and slope position. (Revised from Daubenmire and Daubenmire 1968; Johnson, 1979.)

349

cleared for agriculture reducing the forest area. Encouraged by subsidy and support prices, owners have cleared some land which proved marginal for agricultural purposes and too steep to cultivate on a long-time basis. Occasional tracts of cleared land are reverting to forest. Limitations to agricultural expansion are imposed by land productivity, frost problems, and accessibility. Only localized areas offer opportunity for agricultural use of forest lands.

Grazing

The livestock industry had a vital influence on the history of western development. Most of the western ranges became overgrazed during the livestock boom of the 1880s. Although much of this region, especially the higher country, was once grazed by sheep, the number of sheep now grazed on the national forests of northeastern Washington, northern Idaho, and western Montana has decreased dramatically. Drought and severe winters combined with overgrazing nearly wrecked the livestock industry on several occasions (U.S. Govt. Print. Off., 1936). Improved management in recent years has stabilized this important industry. About 3 million cattle and sheep now use the forest ranges of the region seasonally. As dense stands provide little or no forage, only half of the forest area is grazed. Cutover areas provide an important source of forage until tree development reduces understory growth.

Logging

Logging in the region began with the construction of the first sawmill in the Bitterroot Valley of western Montana in the late 1840s.

Annual lumber production exceeded 450 million board feet shortly after 1900 and by 1910 increased to over 1 billion board feet. From 1925 until 1945, the cut hit a peak of 1.5 billion board feet annually, but the depression of the middle 1930s sharply reduced production (Steer, 1948). Currently, more than 2 billion board feet are being produced each year.

Forests in this region were still pretty much in their virgin state at the turn of the century (Hutchison and Winters, 1941). Logging for local use by small mills resulted in selective cutting of better trees. Western white pine provided the only lumber that could pay the freight for shipment outside the region and leave a margin of profit. Active demand for white pine, especially between 1910 and 1925, brought about extensive clearcutting and scarcity of readily available stumpage of this premium species. After 1925, the cut of white pine declined because production could not be sustained at such high levels.

The other conifers, the so-called mixed species, at first had relatively low market value and, as a rule, could not be cut and shipped profitably to outside markets. Recently, demands have brought about sharp increases in stumpage and lumber prices of these trees. The expanded cut since World War II has been based largely on species other than white pine, and the problem of "inferior species" has been minimized.

From skidding with oxen and horses in the early days, yarding techniques utilizing crawler tractors, rubber-tired skidders, helicopters, balloons, and a variety of cable systems have evolved. Flumes and river driving were used extensively in the past; the last full-log river drive in the U.S. took place on the Clearwater River in 1970.

During the heyday of white pine logging, rail transportation was used extensively. Old railroad grades now form roadbeds of paved logging roads. Although a few companies still transport large volumes of logs from woods to mill by rail, the truck has come to be the backbone of log transportation. Most logging is done in summer and fall, but winter operations are not unusual. Skidding on the snow is often desirable to reduce soil disturbance and damage to regeneration.

Fire

Forests in this region are among the most flammable in the United States, posing critical protection problems. The great Idaho fire of 1910, one of the most destructive in history, combined with other fires in the region that year, burned over 3.5 million acres (Jemison, 1950). Nearly 9 billion board feet of timber were destroyed. In places, the fire burned so hot that little organic material remained.

While regeneration of trees is usually prompt after a single burn, brush fields commonly follow a second or double burn on the same area. Over 60 years is often required for trees to replace the brush that follows the burn. Millions of acre-years of potential growth have been lost due to nonstocking following fires. Major fire years—1919, 1926, 1929, 1931, 1934, and 1967—brought about heavy losses, but the trend of burned acreage has been steeply downward since about 1940. Accessibility due to expanding road systems, lookouts, air patrols, mechanized equipment, smokejumpers, better knowledge, and improved organization have, over the years, reduced losses to a point where fires no longer pose a critical threat to forest management. However, the potential for serious fires still exists.

Wildfire historically has played a major role in shaping the character of forests in the Northern Rocky Mountains, creating large acreages in young age classes and favoring even-aged stands of seral species. Prior to 1940 only precipitation had a greater impact (Wellner, 1970b). The reduction in area burned in recent years is a major cause for the trend toward increasing composition of climax species in the forests. In terms of forest cover types, climax forests are limited in extent, while seral species, favored by fire-caused disruption of forest succession, are widespread. Most western larch, lodgepole pine, and western white pine are a direct result of past fires.

Animals

Early reports indicate that big game was sparse in the dense timber stands of the region. For example, the Lewis and Clark Expedition in 1805 noted that deer and elk were present, but rare as they crossed the Bitterroot Mountains.

Much of the time the men were without game and, to survive, were forced to kill their horses for food (Hosmer, 1917).

In that same area, large fires in 1910, 1919, and 1934 set the stage for a great build-up in elk herds (Leege, 1968). Huge brush fields of scouler willow, redstem ceanothus, serviceberry, Rocky Mountain maple, and other shrubs became established following the fires, providing the browse and cover needed by these animals. After 20 to 30 years, much of the browse grew beyond animal reach, with young trees overtopping and suppressing the brush, leading to the decline of big-game numbers. A program of prescribed burning to reestablish and recondition brush fields has been implemented as part of an effort to maintain elk herds.

Insects and Diseases

Insects and diseases have played an important role in shaping the present forests and in dictating the direction of management. The Northern Rocky Mountains are probably plagued by a greater variety of pests than any other forest region in the United States. Huge outbreaks of the mountain pine beetle, the Engelmann spruce bark beetle, and western pine beetle, among others, have destroyed billions of board feet of timber over millions of acres.

Many outbreaks of defoliators such as the Douglas-fir tussock moth, the western spruce budworm, and the larch casebearer have occurred over the short history of forestry in the region and are still an important factor today. Defoliation of trees over large areas by the spruce budworm and other insects eliminates age classes of timber, vastly increases fire hazard, and reduces recreational values (Johnson and Denton, 1975).

Diseases also greatly impact the forests and the direction of silviculture. It has been estimated that the annual impact of dwarf mistletoe alone on Douglas-fir, western larch, and lodgepole pine exceeds 258 million cubic feet (USDA For. Serv., 1969). Another disease with great economic impact has been white pine blister rust. Several wood rots cause tremendous losses. Trees weakened by diseases such as the Indian paint fungus are very susceptible to wind breakage as well as to insect and other disease problems.

The high incidence of insect and disease problems coupled with poor accessibility in many areas has led to a management heavily oriented toward salvage of damaged and infested stands. A more subtle, but very important effect of insects and diseases is to favor tolerant species and hasten forests toward climax conditions, which may or may not be consistent with management objectives (Wellner, 1978).

The Forests Today

Old-growth forests still predominate over much of the Northern Rocky Mountain Region. Roads are being pushed into many stands for the first time, while other areas have been previously entered on two or three occasions for removal of the best individuals. The latter situation has resulted in forests comprised largely of overmature trees of less desirable species, defective trees, or trees which were too small to attract attention when the stands were first logged. A great deal of the forestry effort is therefore oriented toward conversion of old-growth and high-graded stands. As more of the area comes under management and as the silvicultural knowledge improves, present insect and disease problems will be reduced or made more manageable, and managers will be able to focus attention toward other aspects of intensive resource management.

There is already a trend toward good forestry practices. The larger industrial operators are committed to sustained-yield forestry and are rapidly utilizing available silvicultural knowledge to increase production from their lands. A long-range cooperative effort in tree improvement involving some 20 companies and state and federal agencies is an example of the increased interest in intensive timber culture. Recent development and application of such silvicultural tools as the Stand Prognosis Model (see pg. 360) and a system of habitat typing (see pg. 347) have led to more thorough preparation of sound silvicultural prescriptions. Further, in 1972 Region 1 of the Forest Service inaugurated a noteworthy program to train and certify silviculturists. This program, titled Continuing Education in Forest Ecology and Silviculture (CEFES), includes three 4-week sessions of college-level instruction at three participating schools of forestry and specified field work. To date, more than 190 persons, including some from outside the Forest Service, have successfully completed the programs.

SILVICULTURE OF THE MAJOR TYPE GROUPS

Western White Pine Type Group

(Including the western redcedar and western hemlock types.) The western white pine cover type is essentially analogous to the Daubenmires' (1968) *Tsuga heterophylla/Pachistima myrsinites, Thuja plicata/Pachistima myrsinites,* and the northern parts of the *Abies grandis/Pachistima myrsinites* habitat types (Fig. 8-2). These habitat types are the most productive in the interior west and are characterized by a broad representation of tree species. Western redcedar, western hemlock, grand fir, western larch, Douglas-fir, ponderosa pine, lodgepole pine, subalpine fir, and Engelmann spruce are commonly found in association with western white pine. At the intermediate altitudes (2,000 to 5,500 feet) where the *Tsuga heterophylla* series occurs, soil drought, common at lower altitudes, is a limiting factor only during extremely dry years. Inadequate heat, which appears to be limiting at higher altitudes, does not impose a limitation on tree development in this rich forest belt (Daubenmire and Daubenmire, 1968).

Western white pine grows abundantly in Idaho from the Clearwater River northward and in adjacent northeastern Washington, as well as in scattered areas of Montana west of the Continental Divide. Soils are variable, but all must be able to supply the abundant moisture needed by white pine. Most white pine sites have some available soil moisture throughout the growing season except during periods of extreme drought. Surface drying, so prominent a characteristic in the arid summer period, will typically leave some available soil moisture at the 8- to 10-inch soil depth. (Fig. 8-3).

Figure 8-3.   Old-growth western white pine stand on lands of Potlatch Corp. in northern Idaho (K. D. Swan, U.S. For. Serv.).

Place in Ecological Succession.   Western white pine is a seral species (Fig. 8-2), and its abundance in the Northern Rocky Mountain Region is largely due to fire history. Stands are typically even-aged (Haig *et al.*, 1941). At times, the white pine may form almost pure stands, but characteristically it occurs in mixtures with the species noted previously. With sufficient light, white pine will outgrow all competing species except larch and lodgepole pine, both of which hold an early height-growth advantage. By age 50 white pine will surpass lodgepole pine in height and at maturity equal the larch.

On protected sites, white pine regeneration will do best on open areas, but on exposed sites, partial shade is beneficial. This shade protects seedlings against excessive insolation and high soil-surface temperatures. Drought is especially severe during late summer on south- and west-facing slopes. Survival of seedlings is dependent upon deep initial root penetration (Haig *et al.*, 1941) to maintain contact with available soil moisture. White pine, Douglas-fir, western larch, and grand fir are all benefited by vigorous root-system growth of seedlings located in full sunlight. Western redcedar and western hemlock seedlings with shallow root systems suffer heavy mortality on exposed sites due to early drying of the surface soil layer.

On shaded, cool, and relatively moist sites, root penetration of pine is poor. Numerous seedlings die in late summer due to surface drying. Even though soil moisture may be ample at greater depths, it is not reached by the shallow roots. Larsen (1929, 1930), Huberman (1935), Haig et al. (1941), Deitschman and

Figure 8-4.   Old-growth western redcedar (K.D. Swan, U.S. For. Serv.).

Pfister (1973), Boyd (1969), and others have stressed the seral nature of western white pine and the climax character of the cedar, hemlock, and grand fir associations (Fig. 8-4).

Growth Rates.   The western white pine type comprises some of the most productive forests in North America. On good sites (site index 60 at 50 years), fully stocked natural stands will produce mean-annual increments of 100 to 150 cubic feet per acre based on a 120-year rotation (Haig, 1932). Periodic annual increment in the pole stage may exceed 200 cubic feet per acre. Excellent stands of mature white pine may yield 20,000 cubic feet per acre. Basal areas in well stocked second-growth stands of 250 to 300 square feet per acre are common, and as much as 400 square feet per acre is not unusual in mature and overmature stands.

Rotation Age or Size.   Western white pine is characteristically a straight, tall, slender, narrow-crowned tree, on occasion producing twelve logs (16.3 feet) to a tree. Maximum diameters are in the 48- to 60-inch range, although larger trees have been cut. Board-foot growth in natural stands on good sites culminates at about 120 years; however, some stands have grown well to about 160 years. Although individual trees may exceed 400 years in age, stands over 200 years old are usually on the downgrade and contain much decay and mortality.

Economic factors will probably act to reduce the rotation for sawtimber to less than 80 years, but longer rotations can best capture the site potentials with the species indigenous to the white pine type. Trees in this type characteristically get off to a slow start, but once they are established they do well for a long period, with culmination of cubic foot mean-annual increment in natural stands at about 100 years. Intensive intermediate culture may lengthen silvicultural rotations by maintaining stand vigor and growth. Practices such as thinning and fertilization can bring about earlier merchantability, hence shorter rotations, but such financial or technical rotations will be at the expense of potential site production.

The rotation age for grand fir, an important component of this type, is often governed by the incidence of the Indian paint fungus. Although older stands frequently contain high proportions of rot, fast-growing second-growth grand fir can be carried to ages of 80 to 90 years in a relatively sound condition.

Much of the rot prevalent in old-growth western hemlock and western redcedar also can be avoided by managing for rotations of less than 100 years. Western larch, western white pine, and Douglas-fir can be grown to ages in excess of 120 years without significant rot occurrence; however, throughout the western white pine type root-rot "centers" can be locally damaging to most of the commercial species.

Cultural Practices.   In recent years emphasis in the white pine type has changed from silviculture aimed at developing stands with a high proportion of white pine, to management oriented toward maintenance of species diversity. The severe impact of white pine blister rust, as well as the incidence of pole blight and bark beetles, have encouraged foresters to spread the risks of insect and disease susceptibility among the several commercially desirable species that occur in the type. The uncertainty of the comparative future values also favors the use of species mixtures in regeneration planning.

Prompt natural regeneration is normally achieved on favorable sites under any of the even-aged silvicultural systems when an adequate seed source is reserved (Haig et al., 1941; Boyd, 1969). Boyd's case histories of regeneration in the western white pine type illustrate how the choice of system can alter the density and species composition. Particularly on the more mesic sites (western hemlock−pachistima habitat type), adequate diverse natural regeneration can be expected within 5 to 10 years after the regeneration cut. Although hemlock is normally the most abundant species in the newly regenerated stands in this habitat type, it is more likely to remain dominant under some shade—as when a shelterwood stand is not removed early in the regeneration process. More species variety is likely to be retained in the subsequent stand under conditions of full sunlight.

Advance regeneration of shade tolerant species is commonly present under merchantable-size timber in this type and can provide important stocking for the next rotation. If the advance regeneration can adjust to the environment created by removing the overstory it can shorten the rotation and reduce the need for site preparation and/or planting. However, not all advance regeneration is able to adjust. Grand fir advance regeneration is most prevalent in the white pine type. This species releases best on cedar and hemlock climax habitat types but does not do well after release on grand fir habitat types (Ferguson and Adams, 1979). Other factors including the degree of prerelease suppression, the amount of logging damage, and tree age can be used to predict how advance grand fir regeneration will perform following release. Release of advance western redcedar regeneration has not met with a great deal of success. This species frequently exhibits good initial response to overstory removal only to decline after about 5 years. This phenomenon has been attributed to the root rot Armillaria mellea by some researchers, but additional study is under way to identify the problem and to describe the stand and site conditions conducive to successful release. Residual overstory density and the length of time until it is removed are critical factors influencing reproduction development (Deitschman and Pfister, 1973). Even a light amount of shading soon inhibits growth of intolerant species such as western larch, Douglas-fir, and western white pine. Heavy shading will eventually result in losses to even the tolerant grand fir so that the species diversity may be reduced to western hemlock and western redcedar.

The regeneration period on drier white pine sites, such as the grand fir/pachistima habitat type, may exceed 20 years (Boyd, 1969). On the sites that Boyd studied, grand fir was the most abundant species regenerated, with large components of western white pine and Douglas-fir. As would be expected on a grand fir/pachistima habitat type, grand fir tended to dominate stands regenerated under selection cutting, while shelterwood and clearcutting resulted in greater species variety.

If prompt tree regeneration is not achieved, many white pine sites will be rapidly occupied by shrubs, prolonging the reproduction period. For example, records of succession following logging on hemlock/pachistima and grand fir/pachistima sites in northern Idaho show rapid development of tall shrub communities (over 1 meter tall) following logging and burning (Wittinger et al., 1977). On hemlock/pachistima sites the tall shrub union reached its peak in botanical composition (over 60 percent) within 3 to 5 years following logging. Even within a given habitat type there is much variation in the tendency for shrub development; south slopes may develop shrub cover rather quickly, while many flats and north slopes may stay relatively open and receptive to regeneration for longer periods. Much of the lower vegetation which invades harvested sites is attractive habitat for gophers and other rodents (page 361).

Damaging frosts can be expected on many sites within the white pine region throughout the growing season. For example, low temperatures in June have reached 25 °F on lowland meadow sites in northern Idaho. Young grand fir, Douglas-fir, and Englemann spruce seedlings were heavily damaged, while western white pine, lodgepole pine, and ponderosa pine were apparently not affected (Larson, 1977). Air-drainage patterns that stagnate cold air must be considered in planning for harvest and regeneration activities. Clearcuts should be avoided in frost pockets; however partial cuttings such as the shelterwood method help to ameliorate the effects of low growing-season temperatures. Planting of less frost-susceptible species such as lodgepole and ponderosa pines on frost problem areas may also be necessary.

Lodgepole pine, which has not been favored in past management, has much potential, particularly on sites with regeneration problems. It can frequently be established in areas subject to frost damage and on other adverse sites. Lodgepole is second only to western larch in rapid initial growth but it must be managed on a short rotation due to mountain pine beetle and root rot problems. Vigor must be maintained in the stand to obtain desirable growth rates, but if kept open so that crowns and growth are maintained, it can exhibit very respectable production on white pine sites.

Use of the habitat type classification helps match species to site. For example, western white pine cannot be expected to survive on a site identified as Douglas-fir/ninebark habitat type, whereas a grand fir/pachistima habitat type is a wetter, cooler site on which white pine, grand fir, and several other species are likely to regenerate and grow successfully (Fig. 8-1). Numerous studies have demonstrated that habitat types can also be useful in understanding other relationships such as potential for wildlife forage production, susceptibility to dwarf mistletoe and to certain insect infestations, likelihood of regeneration competition, and soil moisture depletion rates (Pfister et al., 1971). Specific management guidelines have been developed based upon these relationships.

Mechanical site preparation or broadcast burning followed by planting is a common regeneration procedure in overmature and defective stands. Also, since blister rust resistant white pine seed and planting stock are now available, clearcutting and planting are being used to restore white pine as a manageable species. (The nature of the blister rust problem is discussed on page 362.) White pine in plantations appears to have markedly superior growth when compared with natural stands (Boyd and Deitschman, 1964)—an additional factor leading toward more plantation establishment.

Although natural regeneration is sometimes hard to attain on dry, south-facing slopes, the problem of overstocking often results from natural regeneration on the more mesic sites. In densely regenerated stands, early cleanings coupled with precommercial thinnings are often desirable for selecting the best species combinations and distributions (Deitschman and Pfister, 1973).

Numerous studies have emphasized the importance that judicious thinnings can play in the development of stands in the western white pine type. Foiles (1972) reported on responses to various kinds of commercial thinnings in an 87-year-old stand dominated by white pine and grand fir. He concluded that the choice between thinning methods should depend on the primary objective of the thinning. Light crown thinning, reducing the basal area from 237 to 192 square feet per acre, best satisfied the goal of harvesting mortality while maintaining near maximum volume production. Moderate crown thinning which removed about 80 square feet per acre gave the best diameter-growth response in the residual trees. Foiles suggested the application of a selection thinning in mixed stands in which the dominant western white pines are infected with blister rust. This action would allow harvest of the white pines while merchantable, thereby releasing other species in the subdominant crown level for better growth. This study also illustrated the differences in response to thinning among the species involved. The more tolerant trees retained relatively full crowns and therefore more quickly utilized the increased growing space created by the thinnings.

In an earlier study, Foiles (1955) found that thinnings from below were also effective in stimulating diameter growth on the remaining trees. Light and moderate low thinnings resulted in the greatest net cubic-foot volume, while heavy thinnings were suggested as more useful for increasing board-foot volume growth.

Although fertilization is not a widespread practice in this type, the application of nitrogen has been shown to produce significant responses, particularly when applied in combination with thinning. Studies of Douglas-fir and grand fir indicated that growth increases of 30 percent or more can be expected over a wide variety of stand conditions (Scanlin et al., 1976).

Stand development and growth are difficult to predict. On many sites several of the 10 coniferous species which are native to the type occur together. This species diversity combined with mixtures of age and size classes, the growth impact of pests such as the larch casebearer and white pine blister rust, and site variations caused by slope, aspect, altitude, soil type, precipitation, and other stand and site variables, make the use of managed-stand yield tables impractical as a means of forecasting stand development.

A stand-prognosis model developed by scientists of the USDA Forest Service, Intermountain Forest and Range Experiment Station is a workable alternative to more traditional yield-table forecasting methods (Stage, 1973). This set of computer programs combines quantitative silvicultural knowledge with past growth data from a sampled stand to make a prognosis of the course of development that the forest stand is expected to follow under alternative management prescriptions. This model is designed to provide output to help answer a wide variety of management questions. These range from predicting the success of establishment of natural regeneration following harvest cutting, to describing the expected stand development under alternative thinning and/or fertilization schedules or under the influence of an insect epidemic.

Silvicultural prescriptions for stands throughout the region must consider not only the requisites for culture of timber but also the likely effects of silvicultural practices on the related resources. This concept is most commonly attributed to the multiple-use management of public forest lands. However, small private and industrial forests are subject to close public scrutiny and a certain amount of control, as through Idaho's Forest Practices Law. This law, in addition to insuring prompt regeneration of forest lands following harvest, is strongly oriented to encourage forestry practices which minimize degradation of water quality.

As in other forested regions, removal of vegetation through timber-harvesting activities has a pronounced effect on snow accumulation and melt. However, the problems of management throughout most of the northern Rocky Mountains differ from those in regions of the west where timber growth is not so heavy and where water is in short supply. Instead of being primarily concerned with increasing water yields from snow pack, the overriding watershed management question in this region is how to safely dispose of the increased water yields that accompany timber harvesting (Satterlund and Haupt, 1972). Management guidelines are based largely on the concept of accentuating natural diversity, thereby helping to desynchronize the peak flows from tributaries within a major watershed. Computer models of snowpack accumulation and melt which integrate the effects of vegetative cover, climate, and topography aid in designing timber harvesting systems (USDA For. Serv., 1974).

Silvicultural practices, particularly harvest activities and the attendant road development, also affect wildlife populations and habitats. The relationships between logging and big game have recently been of particular concern. The harvest systems employed, as well as the methods of skidding and slash disposal, directly influence such wildlife factors as forage, cover, the interspersion of type edges, and water (Denney, 1976). A study of forb and shrub production in the western white pine type of northern Idaho indicated that clearcuts which were broadcast burned produced five times more available and palatable twigs for big game than other silvicultural methods (Irwin, 1976). Leege (1969) earlier reported that clearcutting operations in some areas of northern Idaho have opened up timber stands, forming brush fields which provide the winter food supply for deer and elk. These clearcuttings in some areas have allowed elk populations to hold their own or increase. Fires resulted in huge brushfields of willow, red-stem ceanothus, and other shrubs, encouraging a build-up of elk herds. Clearcutting, along with controlled burning of some brushfields, may help to provide needed food supplies. However, the size, shape, and arrangement of clearcuts in relation to adjacent unlogged areas must be carefully considered in planning for timber harvests to maximize benefits to big game. Wildlife habitat coordination guidelines such as those for elk in northern Idaho (USDA For. Serv., 1977b) provide managers with a basis for predicting animal response to habitat changes and disturbance factors. The percent cover that must be retained to produce various levels of elk use by habitat types, and the effects of roads, method of slash disposal, season of logging, grazing, of domestic livestock, and other factors are programmed for use in forest land-use planning.

Even though timber harvest may increase forage for big game in some areas, there are also negative impacts. Disturbance caused by the logging process may alter wildlife habits, logging debris may restrict movement, and access through logging roads may increase hunting pressure. These are just a few of the inter-related factors which must be considered in evaluating silvicultural alternatives.

Susceptibility to Damage. Management of forests of the western white pine type group is complicated by species susceptibility to many damaging agents. A great deal of the stand management in the area has revolved about insect and disease considerations, with increased emphasis on silvicultural control. Because of its relative value and regional importance, particular attention has been focused on western white pine.

White pine may be regarded as a reasonably windfirm tree. Haig et al. (1941) cite losses of seed trees averaging 5 to 10 percent over a 10- to 20-year period. Occasionally losses may be much more severe due to extreme winds or to lack of windfirmness in intermediate and codominant trees left in the residual stand after partial cutting.

The thin bark of western white pine renders it susceptible to damage by fire. Basal fire scars on white pine are common, and serve as avenues of entrance for wood-rotting fungi. Insects, especially bark beetles, are attracted to trees scarred or killed by fires.

Pocket gophers, porcupines, snowshoe hares, and other rodents are common pests throughout the white pine type (Stoszek, 1977). Pocket gophers are particularly damaging in plantations where they prune roots, girdle, and clip seedling stems. Conifer seedlings form part of the winter diet of snowshoe hares. Seedling stems may be readily clipped off; repeated clipping stunts and deforms tree growth. Hares prefer a brushy habitat, so removal of protective brush cover will reduce habitat suitability and consequently lessen their impact. Chemical repellants applied to seedlings before outplanting have also been effective.

Although big game and domestic livestock damage young trees by browsing, trampling, antler rubbing, compacting the soil, and pulling out recently planted seedlings, the degree of impact is not known and very little is being done to avoid this source of injury.

White pine blister rust has been a major factor influencing management of western white pine. This disease was first discovered in the inland northwest in 1927. Western white pine is much more susceptible to blister rust than eastern white pine. Young trees (seedlings, saplings, and poles) are most critically affected. Mature timber may be infected and killed, too, but this often takes many years, so that sawtimber trees may be salvaged before they die. Early efforts to stop the disease were centered around eradicating a necessary alternate host (*Ribes* spp.) for the blister rust fungus, and in using various chemical stem treatments, but these techniques were largely unsuccessful.

Rust-free trees in heavily infected natural stands have provided the basis for a long-term program to develop western white pine planting stock which is genetically resistant to white pine blister rust. Experimentation beginning in 1950 established that in these rust-free trees, rust resistance was under strong genetic control, and that resistance was transmissable to seed-propagated offspring (Bingham *et al.*, 1953).

The U.S. Forest Service has undertaken a rust-resistance breeding program which has resulted in production of significant quantities of seed from seed orchards. Additional seed orchards have been established, and it is expected that all needs for resistant planting stock will soon be satisfied. Resistance to the blister rust in the F_2 generation is about 66 percent in the nursery situation; field resistance is even greater.

Another approach toward taking advantage of the natural resistance present in white pine stands has been suggested (Hoff and McDonald, 1977). In stands with high mortality, judicious selection of leave trees for regeneration by the seed-tree or shelterwood methods should result in about 20 percent resistant progeny. This is enough to provide adequate stocking of resistant seedlings.

The presence of root and stem rots weighs heavily in the formulation of management plans. Extreme defect in hemlock and grand fir is caused by the Indian paint fungus. Overmature trees generally are culled due to this disease, but smaller, suppressed trees may also be badly infected. Certain stands of these species contain very little defect, but others will have few trees free of rot. Decay caused by laminated root rot, which frequently extends into the main stem, has resulted in extensive losses in western redcedar, particularly in the moist cedar growing regions of the Clearwater and St. Joe River drainages in northern Idaho (Livingston *et al.*, 1977). Decay is most common in old-growth timber, but recent reports of decay in cedar poles is cause for concern. Another root rot, the shoestring fungus, infects all Northern Rocky Mountain species and, as elsewhere, is a particular problem on droughty sites and on sites with fluctuating water table (Stoszek, 1977). This fungus is known to be associated with weakened trees, so measures which keep the stand continuously vigorous help to alleviate shoestring damage.

Phellinus decay in cedar is often accompanied by damage caused by other fungi, particularly the brown cubical pocket rot, the major rot of cedar in the Northern Rocky Mountains. No effective control is available for this fungus.

Laminated root rot is also an important disease of grand fir, Douglas-fir and western larch, where salvage and conversion to less susceptible species, mainly western redcedar and western hemlock, is the only useful control. Mottled root disease, caused by a complex of several fungi, is commonly present in stems exhibiting *Phellinus* symptoms, and is commonly associated with bark beetle activity (Partridge *et al.*, 1978).

Old-growth grand fir and hemlock stands infected with Indian paint fungus are usually highly defective, with cull often running over 50 percent. Since this decay is related to stand vigor and density and fast-growing trees tend to remain sound, short rotations and thinnings can be used for control.

The western spruce budworm is the inland northwest's most common and destructive defoliating insect (Partridge *et al.*, 1978). A current infestation in Montana and northern Idaho covers over 4 million acres (USDA For. Serv., 1977b).

Many outbreaks of this conifer-feeding species have been reported over the past 50 years in stands of Rocky Mountain Douglas-fir, true firs, Englemann spruce, and western larch. Visible defoliation caused by western spruce budworm has been reported somewhere in the Northern Rocky Mountains every year since 1922.

The tussock moth has caused periodic defoliation of Douglas-fir, grand fir, and subalpine fir. The most recent infestation from 1972 to 1974 affected nearly 100,000 acres in Idaho and Montana. Although most attacked trees survived in this area, the weakened trees are more susceptible to damage from bark beetles, diseases, and drought. Grand fir is the preferred host, and overdense, mature stands on low-productivity sites, upper slopes, and ridge tops are subject to substantially higher defoliation than are young stands (Stoszek *et al.*, 1977; Heller and Miller, 1977).

Western white pine is attacked by several insects, with the mountain pine beetle causing the most damage. Although young, vigorous trees are fairly resistant, mature and overmature white pine stands often sustain heavy losses to this bark beetle (Wellner, 1965).

Grand fir is impacted by localized but often severe infestations of the fir engraver. This bark beetle which attacks most true firs in the west, reached outbreak proportions in Idaho in the early 1960s causing heavy tree mortality. Damage due to the fir engraver is still very extensive. Since chemical control methods appear limited under forest conditions, increased emphasis is being focused on cultural methods which will remove trees predisposed to attack, and maintain stand vigor and resistance through regulation of density and composition (Schenk *et al.*, 1976).

Although tree-growth loss and mortality are frequently attributed to a single causal factor, investigations have established strong relationships between such agents as bark beetles and root rots (Partridge and Miller, 1972). Drought, competition, logging injury, animal damage, root rot, or loss of vigor in old age may predispose trees or stands to additional damage by various agents. Epidemic outbreaks of insects, rapid spread of diseases, and abnormal rodent damage are usually related to one or more stand or site conditions. It may, therefore, be inaccurate in many cases to ascribe losses to a single cause. Furthermore, silvicultural prescriptions are often complicated by the various damaging agents and the needs of the several species, as when thinnings performed with the aim of maintaining tree vigor and reducing the susceptibility to insects favors the spread of root diseases.

Douglas-fir Type Group

(Including the Douglas-fir/larch type.) Rocky Mountain Douglas-fir is typically found higher in elevation and on more moist soils than ponderosa pine. It occurs in extensive pure stands, often even-aged, in central Idaho and in western Montana as a broad belt between ponderosa pine and spruce-fir zones. In the lower portion of the spruce-fir zone, Douglas-fir occurs as a fire type. Thus, the Douglas-fir type occupies the same relative position in the Northern as in the Middle and Southern Rocky Mountains. The Rocky Mountain Douglas-fir type is by far the most predominant in the Northern Rocky Mountains, occupying over 9 million acres or about one-third of the region's commercial forest land and accounting for over 30 percent of the standing volume (USDA For. Serv., 1978).

Western larch, a frequent associate of Douglas-fir in the northern part of the region, is likewise a valuable commercial species. Western larch is the predominant tree species on some 2.7 million acres of commercial forest land and is also a component in most of the other forest types in the Northern Rocky Mountains Region west of the Continental Divide. The annual volume cut of larch exceeds all species except Douglas-fir (Schmidt et al., 1976). Douglas-fir and western larch are marketed together as construction grade lumber and both are also major pole species. (Fig. 8-5).

Western larch and Douglas-fir occur together as a characteristic cover type of the northern Rockies. This is especially true in northwestern Montana and northern Idaho, an area with a history of devastating fires, where Douglas-fir—larch stands dominate large areas. Variations range from pure larch to the common Douglas-fir—larch mixture. Typical associates include lodgepole pine, western white pine, subalpine fir, and ponderosa pine. Grand fir is a common associate of Douglas-fir in northern Idaho.

Place in Ecological Succession.   Douglas-fir is climax on three of Daubenmires' (1968) eastern Washington and northern Idaho habitat types (the *Pseudotsuga menziesii* series; Fig. 8-1 and 8-2). The *Pseudotsuga* series is the forest belt occurring generally above the pure forests of ponderosa pine where

Figure 8-5.   Western larch overstory with Douglas-fir predominating in the reproduction (K. D. Swan, U.S. For. Serv.)

moisture becomes adequate for Douglas-fir seedlings to survive. With moisture levels permitting successful establishment, growth, and development of grand fir seedlings, the *Pseudotsuga* climax belt transgresses into the grand fir zone. With sufficient moisture, grand fir has greater competitive ability than does the Douglas-fir. Douglas-fir occurs as a seral species on several habitat types in the more moist *Tsuga heterophylla* and *Abies lasiocarpa* series. Its wide range of adaptability is also evident in central Idaho and Montana where it occurs as a major seral species on a large number of habitat types in addition to those where it is climax (Steele *et al.*, 1975; Pfister *et al.*, 1977). *Pseudotsuga* habitat types cover a much broader environmental gradient in Montana than is found in northern Idaho, ranging from relatively dry savanna-like situations to dry-cold sites which have understories similar to those found in some of the *Abies lasiocarpa* habitat types.

Western larch, the most shade-intolerant species of the region, occurs only as a seral species. At the lower, warmer and drier end of its range, larch is found in association with ponderosa pine and Douglas-fir on habitat types in the *Pseudotsuga menziesii* series. On the more moist sites, characteristic of the *Tsuga heterophylla* series, it is found with grand fir, white pine, western red-cedar and western hemlock. On the cool, moist, habitat types in the *Abies lasiocarpa* series, larch is associated with Engelmann spruce, subalpine fir, mountain hemlock, and whitebark pine (Schmidt *et al.*, 1976). Western red-cedar, western hemlock, and grand fir are more shade tolerant than the Douglas-fir. However, Douglas-fir is more tolerant than western larch and lodgepole pine. Larch is more long-lived and exhibits greater resistance to fire than the Douglas-fir.

Thus, Douglas-fir is both a climax and seral species—replacing ponderosa, lodgepole, and western larch, but being replaced in turn on suitable sites by cedar-hemlock, spruce-fir, and grand fir. Larch would lose out to Douglas-fir in the absence of fire, but with burning or logging disturbances that leave a bare-soil seedbed, western larch will reproduce readily and outgrow Douglas-fir.

Growth Rates. Quality of Douglas-fir is usually IV or V (site indexes from 80 to 120 feet at a base age of 100 years) when compared with the growth of this species in the Pacific Northwest (McArdle and Meyer, 1930). On poor sites growth may be very slow, and trees may not reach sawlog size before old age and decadence overtake them. On more favorable sites, however, Douglas-fir has excellent growth potential, and under management should continue as a leading timber species in the region. Pfister *et al.* (1977) estimated ranges of yield capabilities of habitat types where Douglas-fir is climax from about 20 to over 100 cubic feet per acre per year. However, the yield capabilities of some of the wetter habitat types where Douglas-fir is seral are much greater (over 140 cubic feet per acre per year), and as Roe (1951) indicated, its growth will generally compare favorably with that of associated species. The better, more merchantable stands of mature Douglas-fir will commonly yield from 3,000 to 6,500 cubic feet per acre.

Douglas-fir growing on the loose granitic soils of central Idaho is usually of poor quality. Sweep is common in these stands, and trees over 20 inches d.b.h. tend to develop ring shake and pitch seams. In contrast, residual soils derived from basalt support quality stands with better growth rates.

Larch has the capacity while young to grow more rapidly in height than any of its associates. It achieves dominance early, and this must be maintained for good growth and vigor. During early life diameter growth is also rapid, but in old age slows down to less than 1 inch in 20 to 30 years. Partial cutting in mature and overmature larch stands (over 100 years age) usually fails to stimulate growth (Roe, 1948). However, cultural practices can improve and prolong growth of individual trees if applied before significant reduction in crown lengths and tree vigor takes place (Schmidt et al., 1976). Total western larch volume, based on a 120-year rotation varies from about 3,000 cubic feet per acre on very poor sites to over 13,000 cubic feet per acre on the best sites.

Rotation Age or Size.   LeBarron (1948a) suggested a rotation of 120 to 140 years for Douglas-fir and larch on average sites. This rotation is based on biological considerations. In dense mixed stands, Douglas-fir tends to die out at about 120 years. Loss in vigor due to competition for light is believed to predispose Douglas-fir to root rots and bark beetle infestations. Under intensive management, with thinnings and improvement cutting applied, it should be possible to produce sawtimber crops in 60 to 80 years.

Cultural Practices.   Early spacing-control measures are essential in larch and Douglas-fir forests to maintain stand vigor and to concentrate growth on trees with greatest potential. This is particularly important if larch is to be favored. Once serious crown reduction occurs, as often experienced in heavily-stocked larch stands, the ability of the potential crop trees to respond to later release is greatly reduced. Thirty to 40 percent crown length is needed to maintain good tree vigor (Schmidt et al., 1976).

Douglas-fir, more shade tolerant than western larch, is better able to withstand early shading, and young trees of good vigor respond well to release by thinning or partial cutting (Roe, 1950). Mixed Douglas-fir—larch stands typically contain a significant component of other conifers, such as lodgepole pine, Engelmann spruce, subalpine fir, ponderosa pine, western hemlock, and western redcedar. Early cultural work is most effective in developing the stand composition best suited for the management objectives.

Stands of vigorous Douglas-fir can be successfully regenerated by any of the even-age methods. On climax habitats, even the selection method can be used. Roe (1955) stressed seedbed preparation and seed supply as basic for regeneration of larch in larch-fir mixtures. Douglas-fir appears to be less sensitive to seedbed conditions than western larch; in fact, some studies have indicated a greater percent stocking of litter-covered plots than plots with exposed mineral soil (Ryker, 1975; Hatch and Lotan, 1969). But, where a mineral seedbed is prepared and a seed source is present, larch tends to dominate its associated species (Schmidt et al., 1976). Although mechanical scarification can be successfully used to expose mineral soil for regeneration, prescribed burning is also a viable alternative on favorable topography in the larch-fir type (Boyd and Deitschman, 1969; Schmidt et al., 1976). The relatively thick bark helps to protect mature western larch and Douglas-fir trees from heat damage, so burning can be used in either seed-tree or shelterwood systems.

Both Douglas-fir and larch are commonly infected by dwarf mistletoe. Clearcutting provides the best alternative for elimination of the mistletoe from the new stand (Kimmey and Graham, 1960). The presence of this plant parasite frequently precludes use of other regeneration methods. Factors including harvest costs and the lower cost of site preparation also favor application of clearcutting. The clearcutting or seed-tree methods, however, are not applicable for regeneration of larch–Douglas-fir stands on highly exposed sites due to excessive surface-soil temperature or on sites without cold-air drainage (Stoszek, 1977). The presence of subalpine fir is usually a good indicator of frost-prone areas that will cause difficulty.

The seed-tree method provides essentially the same environmental conditions as clearcutting, but has the advantages of more-uniform seed dispersal and greater control over species composition. On exposed sites and where aesthetic or frost-damage preventative considerations may preclude the clearcutting or seed-tree methods, strip-shelterwood cuttings along the contours may be appropriate. This method has the flexibility of adjusting the density of the residual stand to fit management needs. A two-stage shelterwood cut is most applicable to this type; early removal of the residual overstory is necessary if larch is to be maintained as a strong component, or if there is need to prevent infection by dwarf mistletoe.

Shearer (1974) reported on studies which demonstrated that clearcutting followed by broadcast burning on north- and east-facing slopes usually leaves the cutover receptive to natural regeneration if sufficient seed is produced. On hot, dry, and steep south- and west-facing slopes, shelterwood or small patch clearcuts provide greater assurance of regeneration success by leaving a greater seed source and more site protection. However, south and west aspects are often difficult to regenerate no matter what is done, and it is on these slopes that competition from tall shrubs is most prevalent.

As was pointed out earlier, both Rocky Mountain Douglas-fir and western larch grow in widely diverse environments, necessitating individual-stand prescriptions tailored to site conditions and management objectives. For example, on the drier-habitat types, Douglas-fir seedlings require shading, while on more moist sites the seedlings grow successfully in the open. In many places, particularly frost-prone areas in southern Idaho and southwestern Montana, lodgepole pine serves as a nurse crop to Douglas-fir. Mortality of lodgepole caused by bark beetles releases the Douglas-fir understory so, over time, Douglas-fir becomes dominant.[1]

Both fall and spring planting has been successful for larch and Douglas-fir, but larch is particularly sensitive to early fall and late spring planting largely because of its physiological status (Sinclair and Boyd, 1973). Douglas-fir is commonly planted as 2-0 stock and western larch as 1-0.

Mixed stands are preferable to pure plantations in Douglas-fir–larch forests. A combination of shade intolerant and semitolerant species not only increases utilization of the site but also provides insurance against forest-pest outbreaks. The particular mixture of species to be interplanted is dictated by site

[1]Personal communication with Charles Wellner, USDA For. Serv.

characteristics—on drier sites ponderosa pine is better suited to grow with larch and Douglas-fir, whereas on wetter sites lodgepole pine, Engelmann spruce, western white pine, or grand fir might be considered as desirable associated species. On frost-prone sites, however, pines will out-compete the frost susceptible larch (Stoszek, 1977). In southeastern Idaho and southwestern Montana there is a belt where neither ponderosa pine nor western larch grows; here lodgepole pine is the major associate of Douglas-fir.

Early ground cover plant community successional stages following disturbances by logging and fire provide important browse for elk and deer. Big-game habitat may be enhanced through proper timing and location of timber-harvest activities to create a favorable distribution of foraging areas proximal to the needed hiding and thermal cover.

Although forage for domestic livestock is not generally abundant in dense Douglas-fir—larch stands, the more open stands and openings created by timber harvest provide grazing opportunities. Exclusion of livestock during the initial tree-regeneration period is desirable to avoid grazing and trampling damage, but moderate grazing of clearcut and shelterwood areas is often a compatible use once the seedlings are well established. Where the Douglas-fir type occurs in stringers and north slopes intermixed with shrublands and grasslands, such as in the southern part of the region, it provides valuable cover for both domestic livestock and big game.

Susceptibility to Damage. Douglas-fir and western larch are generally regarded as windfirm species. Losses to windfall, however, occur in subdominant trees left after cutting. Young trees of both species are quite susceptible to fire damage, but the thick basal bark on older trees provides a degree of protection from surface fires, with western larch being the most fire resistant species in the Northern Rocky Mountains. Bark beetles, defoliators, needle diseases, dwarf mistletoe, root rots and wood decays are all important causes of tree mortality, growth loss, and timber degrade in this type.

The Douglas-fir beetle is the most important insect pest of Douglas-fir in Idaho and Montana. Serious outbreaks continue to cause heavy mortality in several widely scattered areas throughout the northern Rocky Mountains (Livingston et al., 1977). Another insect of concern in the management of Douglas-fir is the Douglas-fir tussock moth.

Douglas-fir is also one of the major western spruce budworm hosts. A current outbreak of this defoliator, which also infests true firs, spruce, and larch covers approximately 5.4 million acres in Washington, Oregon, Idaho, and Montana (Livingston et al., 1977). Defoliation by the budworm reduces radial and height increment, and often results in top kill and tree mortality. Even light budworm populations can cause serious losses in seed production and heavy infestations have resulted in total seed crop failure (USDA For. Serv., 1977b). Although specific silvicultural controls have not been developed, budworm populations and damage can be lowered by reduction of the true fir component, cutting and burning in Douglas-fir—ponderosa pine stands to favor ponderosa pine regeneration, and maintaining stands of thrifty, fast-growing trees (Williams, *et al.*, 1971; Williams and Shea, 1971). Thinning has the potential for reducing budworm damage to western larch since the more vigorous trees with large-diameter shoots are severed less often than those with small-diameter shoots. An additional thinning effect is that vigorous trees are better able to recuperate rapidly following budworm damage (Schmidt and Fellin, 1973; Schmidt *et al.*, 1976).

The larch casebearer has become the most serious insect enemy of western larch since its discovery in Idaho in 1957. By 1972 this defoliator had infested more than half of the western larch type (Denton, 1972). In addition to mortality, vigor loss and serious diameter-growth suppression have occurred. Tunnock and others (1969) reported up to 94 percent reduction in radial growth in a 4- to 5-year period. Larch can soon lose its dominance in mixed stands as a result of defoliation-caused growth losses. This can have long-term management implications since larch can maintain itself in mixed stands only as long as it holds a dominant position in the crown canopy (Schmidt *et al.*, 1976). Direct control of the casebearer with aerial sprays is possible on a local basis but biological controls probably hold the most promising hope for a long-term solution to the problem. Most of the biological control efforts have centered around the introduction of *Agathis pumila* a host-specific European parasite of larch casebearer. Some of the native parasites and predators are also effective.

Dwarf mistletoe is probably the most serious disease of western larch and Douglas-fir, with severe infections reducing growth by one-half in young trees. Mistletoe also predisposes larch to insects and fungal infections, reduces seed vitality, and causes direct mortality (USDA For. Serv., 1965). Where the seed-tree or shelterwood methods are used to regenerate infected stands it is important to remove the residual overstory as soon as regeneration is established since the plant parasite may infect the seedlings as well.

Laminated root rot and shoestring root rot are probably the most serious pathogens of Douglas-fir (U.S. Dept. Agr., 1975). Root rots cause mortality in trees of all ages and the only control measure available is to salvage infected trees and encourage establishment of less susceptible species in the root rot centers. Thinning in infected stands may favor spread of the disease (Partridge et al., 1978).

Heartwood decays, such as that caused by red ring rot, account for losses of much merchantable volume; however, managing young-growth stands on rotations of less than 100 years should reduce the damage.

Lodgepole Pine Type Group

Lodgepole pine ranks third as a cover type behind the Douglas-fir and ponderosa pine types in the West. Eighty percent of the acreage is found in four Rocky Mountain States (Wikstrom, 1957). Montana and Idaho have the greatest acreage with 4.7 and 3.1 million acres, respectively, followed by Wyoming and Colorado with 1.9 million each.

Lodgepole pine is a pioneer species whose occurrence in the region is mainly related to fire history. It can be found in a great variety of topographic, edaphic, and climatic conditions, but grows especially well on gentle slopes and in basins (Tackle, 1965). Its broad adaptability is evidenced by its presence in habitat types ranging from the relatively warm and dry Douglas-fir zone (series) to the upper portions of the cool-moist subalpine fir zone (Fig. 8-1). Within the region lodgepole pine expresses a remarkable amount of variation. At low elevations in northern Idaho, it tends to be open-coned, has black, deeply fissured bark, and is relatively short-lived (80 to 100 years). At high elevations in eastern Montana and southern Idaho it bears primarily serotinous cones, has a yellow-orange bark, and is relatively long-lived (200 to 400 years) (Lotan, 1976). Although exceptions are not uncommon, cones are generally serotinous, an important factor in the establishment of vast even-aged, pure and often very dense stands. In addition to its typical occurrence in pure even-aged stands, lodgepole is commonly found in association with the other northern Rocky Mountain conifers, and in two-, three-, or multiaged stands. (Fig. 8-6).

Place in Ecological Succession. Lodgepole pine is usually seral throughout much of the region, being replaced by more tolerant species in the absence of fire or other disturbance. However, under certain topographic and edaphic circumstances it is able to persist through many generations with little or no evidence of replacement by other conifers. Before the time of well-organized fire control, fires starting in late July or August sometimes burned until extinguished by September rains. These fires, burning in undeveloped country with only natural weather controls, covered vast areas. The result was extensive pure stands of lodgepole pine whose serotinous cones and early seed-producing habits gave it a large advantage over other tree species in repopulating the burns. Fire will kill the relatively thin-barked lodgepole pine easily, but when this happens, the pine is likely to replace itself through release of the seed supply bound up in the cones (Boe, 1948).

Climax stands of lodgepole pine appear primarily on gentle terrain, particularly in broad valleys at upper elevations (Steele et al., 1975; Pfister et al., 1977). On slopes above the valleys, pine is frequently replaced by Douglas-fir, Engelmann spruce, and subalpine fir. Lodgepole pine's adaptability to frost pockets and fluctuating water tables undoubtedly contributes to its success in maintaining itself on some sites.

Growth Rates. Because the tree occurs over a wide range of sites, growth can be expected to vary considerably. Generally, however, it makes rapid early growth which can be prolonged with spacing control. Thrifty stands can produce over 40 cubic feet per acre per year, but in the absence of management lower yields are more common.

High densities of reproduction, especially on poor sites, lead to so-called "dog hair" stands. Such stands, because of poor crown differentiation, often

Figure 8-6.   Dense stand of lodgepole pine typical of many that have regenerated following wildfires (K. D. Swan, U.S. For. Serv.)

stagnate and never grow to commercial size. Heavy thinnings at an early age are needed to obtain satisfactory growth (Adams, 1969; Tackle, 1954). It has been estimated that medium-site Montana stands which produce only 6,000 board feet per acre in natural stands can yield 23,000 board feet per acre in 120 years by thinning and maintaining stand vigor (Wikstrom and Wellner, 1961). This indicates the excellent timber production possibility that might be realized from more intensive silviculture.

Rotation Age or Size. Medium-site (about site index 50 at 50 years) Montana stands reach a culmination in cubic-foot increment between 70 and 90 years, and in board-foot at about age 130 (Tackle, 1965). Bark beetle problems more prevalent in older, less vigorous stands will probably encourage the use of relatively short rotations in the future.

Where lodgepole pine occurs in mixtures with western white pine, western larch, Douglas-fir, and grand fir, it is seldom able to exist for much longer than 100 years. These species, growing to larger sizes, usually suppress the lodgepole and limit its size and longevity. However, some of the largest individual lodgepole stems are found on these better sites.

Maintenance of adequate spacing through thinnings can bring average stem diameters to merchantable size in rotations of 60 to 80 years. Average diameters at 120 years on good sites may reach 17 inches (Wikstrom and Wellner, 1961).

Cultural Practices. Where timber production is a major management objective, clearcutting is the most practical method of regenerating mature and overmature lodgepole pine stands (Alexander, 1972). The species germinates best in full sunlight and on mineral soil or disturbed duff. Another very important factor governing the choice of regeneration method is the high incidence of dwarf mistletoe in many mature stands. This widespread disease causes considerable growth loss and mortality, and the infections develop more rapidly in the overstory of partially cut stands. Since reproduction that develops under an infected overstory is subject to infection, the mistletoe is best controlled by separating new and old stands. Partial cutting systems may increase blowdown problems since lodgepole pine is generally considered susceptible to windfall. The degree of serotiny in a given stand plays an important role in prescribing for regeneration cuttings. Regeneration methods such as shelterwood or seed-tree cuts depend primarily on seed from cones which open at maturity. Regeneration of large clearcut areas is more dependent on seed from cone-bearing slash; thus, stocking levels will vary considerably with cone-habit and slash treatment. Where cones are serotinous, large quantities of seed are generally available for release following harvest. Although a broadcast burn may help to melt the resin that binds the scales together, there is usually enough solar heat near the soil surface to release the seeds from closed cones.

Watershed, wildlife habitat, recreation, and aesthetic considerations may, in some cases, preclude or reduce the use of clearcutting in this type. Guidelines for partial cutting of old-growth lodgepole pine stands in the central Rocky Mountains prepared by Alexander (1972) are generally applicable in the north. Recommended cutting practices vary depending on management objectives, but all must be tempered by such factors as stand condition, windfall, insect and disease susceptibility, and the risk of potential fire damage. Such management prescriptions may involve combinations of small clearcuts, partial cutting treatments, and no cutting on some areas.

Natural regeneration is usually quite successful following clearcutting and site preparation, but planting is sometimes necessary on large clearcuts in areas with nonserotinous cones, and on areas where site preparation has destroyed too much of the seed crop. Naturally regenerated lodgepole pine stands are characteristically dense; thinning is the cultural practice most needed to develop stands of high value and quality. Studies indicate, however, that once stagnation has set in it may be difficult to overcome (Tackle, 1965). Very early thinning may be necessary to achieve adequate release. In older stands growth response is highly correlated with crown size, vigor, and the amount of release (Taylor, 1937). Beyond the juvenile stage, lodgepole pine does not build crown rapidly after release; close attention to crown size is therefore an important aspect in marking for thinning.

As is frequently the case in many forest types, the market for small logs governs the amount of thinning that can be done. The increased use of small-log mills, the demand for roundwood in the pulp industry, and local markets for posts, corral poles, and mine timbers help to make thinning of lodgepole pine stands economically feasible. Eighty to 100 square feet of basal area per acre should be left after thinning to fully occupy the site (LeBarron, 1952). Where Engelmann spruce and Douglas-fir are associated with lodgepole, the usual recommendation is to give preference to the former species. Opportunity should be taken to mark for removal all trees with stem gall rust cankers, as well as trees badly infected by dwarf mistletoe (LeBarron, 1948b).

Susceptibility to Damage.   Residual trees in partially cut stands are subject to blowdown, and practical limitations in the degree and location of cutting should be made in order to avoid such losses. Open stands of intermediate and co-dominant trees are most susceptible to windthrow, but this tendency varies with soil conditions, stand density, and degree of exposure caused by topography.

Many stands are infected with dwarf mistletoe reducing growth of infected trees by an estimated one-third (Gill, 1957). This parasite also increases mortality and reduces quality and seed production. As indicated in the discussion of regeneration, clearcutting is frequently prescribed in order to avoid spreading the infection from one generation to the next. All infected trees should be cut and any infected reproduction should be destroyed in order to assure complete freedom from the disease in the area. Pruning of infected branches may be locally helpful, but is probably of very limited value in operational mistletoe control. Since the spread of mistletoe seed from infected crowns proceeds slowly into openings, clearcut blocks of 40 to 75 acres can serve as a means of control (LeBarron, 1952). Partial cutting and thinning increase damage to residual trees since the parasite develops most rapidly in vigorous hosts (Alexander, 1972; Tackle, 1965). Where partial cutting cannot be avoided, the degree of infection on individual trees can be quantified through use of a six-class dwarf mistletoe rating system (Hawksworth, 1977). This decision-making tool aids in establishing stand-management priorities, in estimating growth loss and mortality, in helping to detect suitable seed trees, and in quantifying infection hazard of overstory trees to understory stands.

In addition to dwarf mistletoe, several heart and root rot fungi and stem rusts cause growth loss, mortality and cull in lodgepole pine. Among the most damaging is the western gall rust which kills seedlings and saplings and individual branches of larger trees. Trees with galls on the main stem also have a high windbreak risk (Partridge et al., 1978). Since multiple galls on branches indicate a genetically susceptible individual, the removal of these trees in thinnings and other stand improvement cuttings should help to develop a more resistant stand.

The mountain pine beetle is the most important insect attacking lodgepole pine. Always endemic, it becomes epidemic periodically with several major outbreaks reported in the Northern Rocky Mountains since the early 1900s (Crookston et al., 1977). Among the more significant was an infestation of the Big Hole Basin region during the late 1920s and 1930s resulting in mortality of 74 percent of the trees 6 inches and larger at breast height over a large area of varying topography and stand conditions. It is evident, however, that certain stand, climatic, and site conditions are particularly conducive to development of epidemic beetle populations.

The intensive research effort aimed at silvicultural control of the mountain pine beetle in lodgepole pine forests is a good example of the necessary linkage of stand management and pest management activities. In fact, for all tree species in the region, pest management considerations must be an integral part of stand-management planning. Knowledge of the beetle, its host, and the conditions necessary to produce epidemic beetle populations have been used to develop stand risk classification systems as well as to direct preventative and suppressive stand-management treatments.

Risk-classification schemes are helpful in identifying potential trouble spots and in setting priorities for preventative or suppressive activities, since it is impractical to propose treatments for all lodgepole pine stands. Various classifications have been developed based on different aspects of beetle-host-site interactions. For example, an historical infestation map (Crookston et al., 1977) can direct managers to areas of large or repeated beetle epidemics of the past. A British Columbia system (Safranyik et al., 1974) identifies climatic regions conducive to beetle survival; another prepared for use in the Rocky Mountains (Amman et al., 1977) assigns numerical risk factors to stands according to elevation, latitude, average age, and average d.b.h. Mahoney (1977) related indexes of stand vigor to resistance to beetle infestation, and Schenk et al. (1980) used measures of average stand competitive stress and of host availability as independent variables in an equation which predicts the level of beetle-caused mortality. Such systems are valuable not only in the identification of susceptible stands, but also for guiding the management of lodgepole pine stands in order to maintain conditions unfavorable to mountain pine beetle populations and favorable to tree growth (Mahoney, 1978).

Other bark beetles, defoliators and shoot and bud insects cause damage, sometimes locally severe, throughout the region, but none has been so persistently troublesome in lodgepole pine as the mountain pine beetle. As changes in management intensity bring about more investment in plantation culture new pest problems are likely to surface. The western pine-shoot borer, stunting height growth of lodgepole pine and ponderosa pine serves as a good example. This native moth, long considered unimportant, has caused an estimated 25 percent reduction in volume yield in eastern Oregon pine plantations (Stoszek, 1973). The impact of its widespread occurrence in the Northern Rocky Mountain Region has not been assessed.

Ponderosa Pine Type Group

This type is covered in detail in Chapter 7. The following discussion will concentrate on management aspects specific to the Northern Rocky Mountain Region. As a commercial forest type ponderosa pine occupies about 5.5 million acres in the region. It is present as a noncommercial type on an additional 2 million acres (Wellner, 1970a). Throughout most of the Northern Rocky Mountains this species occupies the first forest zone above the grasslands (Fig. 8-7). The most extensive areas of ponderosa pine in this region are found on south slopes in Idaho below the Salmon River. In northern Idaho and western Montana it is found on drier sites in smaller bodies intermingled with other forest types (Weidman, 1936).

Place in Ecological Succession. Ponderosa pine stands first appear as outliers in protected spots or on rocky sites and in pure open stands on the drier sites, increasing in density as moisture conditions improve. At higher elevations, with increasing precipitation, Douglas-fir, lodgepole pine, grand fir and other species become associated in mixture. In warmer, drier, lower-elevation zones (Fig. 8-1) ponderosa pine is the climax coniferous species. It becomes seral farther up the moisture-temperature gradient, where it achieves its best development.

Wildfire has been the major factor in maintaining ponderosa pine over much of the acreage where it now grows (Wright, 1978). It also has created a predominance of even-aged or two-storied stands in the Northern Rocky Mountains instead of the uneven-aged forests found in many other parts of the West. Ponderosa pine is generally uneven-aged only where it is the climax species. However, frequent fires where Douglas-fir is climax have caused uneven-aged ponderosa pine stands.

Growth Rates. Growth rates for ponderosa pine in the region vary from less than commercial to maximum annual potentials exceeding 2,000 board feet per acre (Lynch, 1953).

Cultural Practices. Natural regeneration of ponderosa pine following harvest is irregular on most sites in the northern Rockies, particularly in western

Figure 8-7. Ponderosa pine in central Idaho (U.S. For. Serv.).

Montana and in central Idaho. Distinct "waves" of regeneration in the past are related to coincidence of a good seed crop and an initial growing season with higher than usual moisture and cool temperatures (Foiles and Curtis, 1973). The interval between such coincidence may be as long as 20 years (Foiles and Curtis, 1965). When natural regeneration is used, care must be taken to time the site preparation to coincide with seed production, to protect seed crops from squirrels, and to reduce rodent populations. In a study of natural ponderosa pine regeneration in western Montana, Shearer and Schmidt (1970) found that small forest animals consumed 24 of 25 pine seeds that matured. Red squirrels harvested 66 percent of the mature cones, and deer mice, chipmunks, and birds accounted for an additional 30 percent of the dispersed seeds. Protection of the seed crop from animal depredation is vital to the regeneration process.

Because of irregularity in natural ponderosa pine regeneration, clearcutting followed immediately by mechanical site preparation and planting is sometimes preferred. However, all of the high-forest methods have been successfully applied in the type; partial-cutting methods are probably most widely used.

The ready accessibility in the valley floors and in the foothills has placed ponderosa pine forests in a truly multiple-use role. In the early days of settlement, ponderosa pine was the natural choice of species to be utilized because of its superior lumber quality and accessibility (Lynch, 1953). Silvicultural practices in the type have been greatly affected by multiple-use constraints and varying landowner management goals. Owners of small ponderosa pine woodlots frequently desire a more or less constant income from their lands, and tend toward selection management. Even under natural conditions, ponderosa pine forests come closer to selection forests than any other forest type, because of past fire history. They are, therefore, more amenable to systems that cut only a portion of the stand. Group selection and shelterwood systems are commonly used throughout the region, and the seed-tree method—combined with broadcast burning to prepare the site—has been used successfully in northwestern Montana.

When regeneration is not promptly obtained, competing vegetation rapidly invades ponderosa pine sites where site preparation has not been practiced. Heavy mechanical scarification appears to be the most effective site-preparation technique (Shearer and Schmidt, 1970); however, care must be taken to avoid soil compaction and damage to residual trees. Where brush competition is a problem, mechanical site preparation is preferred over burning because brush species regenerate readily from subterranean organs and dormant seeds in the soil (Foiles and Curtis, 1973).

Much public attention has been drawn to the use of terracing as a site-preparation measure in southern Idaho and in the Bitterroot Valley of Montana (Worf et al., 1970). This method has resulted in a high level of planting stock survival but is considered aesthetically displeasing due to its unnatural appearance. Although substantial evidence is lacking, soil displacement through terracing and similar measures has the potential for long-term reduction of site productivity. Another regeneration problem common to ponderosa pine plantation establishment is the damage caused by pocket gophers. Canopy openings created by harvest or wildfire, and the successional vegetation that follows, improve gopher habitat (Barnes, 1973). Gopher densities are frequently high when the newly established seedlings are young and most vulnerable to root pruning, stem girdling, and clipping by gophers. Losses of 30 percent in two or three years in ponderosa pine plantations have been reported (Dingle, 1956). Although direct control through trapping and poisoning are the techniques most frequently employed; removal of forage to make the area less suitable for gopher occupation probably has the greatest potential for long-lasting control (Barnes, 1973).

The choice of species to be regenerated as well as the choice of regeneration method is strongly influenced by insect and disease problems. For example, advanced ponderosa pine reproduction in mature forests may be retained to form the new stand. However, dwarf mistletoe is prevalent in much of the region where ponderosa pine is the climax species; partial-cutting methods transfer the infection from one generation to the next. In stands where advanced regeneration is heavily infected it is usually best to destroy the advanced growth and rely upon regeneration following the harvest. The fact that management goals of many landowners dictate partial-cutting methods poses a real problem.

On habitat types (Daubenmire and Daubenmire, 1968) where ponderosa pine is in a seral position a somewhat different set of problems exists. For example, Douglas-fir, western larch, and lodgepole pine are common associates on Douglas-fir types. Dwarf mistletoe infections on these habitat types are severe on the associated species but do not attack ponderosa pine (Foiles and Curtis, 1973). Other pest problems on these sites include the western spruce budworm, common on Douglas-fir, and the larch casebearer, which defoliates western larch. Bark beetles cause mortality in lodgepole pine, ponderosa pine, and Douglas-fir. The presence or probability of a particular disease or insect pest may dictate the tree species to be encouraged, and hence, the regeneration method. The differing silvical requirements of the associated species allow species-composition manipulation through careful selection and application of regeneration methods.

In planning for any cutting practice which creates logging slash, one must recognize the potential problems. In addition to the obvious fire hazard, logging debris may provide an environment in which bark beetle populations may expand. Much of this problem can be avoided by carefully timing logging and slash disposal relative to the insect life cycle.

Ponderosa pine does best with an abundance of growing space. Extremely dense stands may stagnate and never achieve commercial development, a situation most likely to be found on the lower-quality sites. As described in Chapter 7 height growth of ponderosa pine is not affected materially by stand density throughout much of its range. However, in the northern Rockies height growth is significantly reduced by dense stocking on poor sites. This has necessitated the development of site-index curves adjusted for various degrees of stocking (Lynch, 1953). However, lateral shading during the sapling and pole stages is needed to promote natural pruning of lower branches.

Thinning is an important practice for increasing diameter growth of crop trees and maintaining stand vigor. Although heavy cuts appear to be most effective in increasing individual-tree growth, total per-acre production may suffer. From thinning tests in eastern Washington and northern Idaho, Foiles (1970) reported 50 percent faster individual-tree growth after moderate thinnings (removal of 30 percent of the basal area) and 100 percent faster growth after heavy commercial thinnings. The heavy thinning, in which larger trees were removed, resulted in annual growth of only 161 board feet per acre as compared with 338 board feet for the uncut controls. However, thinnings in 34-year-old ponderosa pine plantations on the University of Idaho Experimental Forest in northern Idaho to maintain adequate growing space resulted in maintenance of per-acre production coupled with a 400 percent increase in average diameter growth (Hanley and Adams, 1976).

Genetic improvement (Wang and Patee, 1976), irrigation, and fertilization (Mosher, 1960) have also increased ponderosa pine growth in the region.

Spruce-Fir Type Group

The spruce-fir type group, composed of Englemann spruce and subalpine fir, occupies the uppermost of the major forest zones, usually above 5,000 feet in the Northern Rocky Mountains where cool moist conditions generally prevail

(Fig. 8-1). Spruce is more abundant than fir, as a rule, and achieves better development. The type extends generally through an altitudinal range of about 2,000 feet. However, the total altitudinal range is somewhat greater, because these species are found in protected valleys and ravines below the spruce-fir zone. In the northern part of the region, spruce-fir is a very productive type at lower elevations. Engelmann spruce will occur below the limits of subalpine fir and is often a major component of stands in *Abies grandis, Thuja plicata* and *Tsuga heterophylla* habitat types (Pfister *et al.*, 1977) (Fig. 8-8). Mountain hemlock may be an important associate, locally; alpine larch, which inhabits the higher-elevation areas, is a rare component of the type. Whitebark pine and limber pine form small groups or open stands along windswept slopes and ridges.

Frequently there will be groupwise arrangements of the different species, broken by bare or rocky areas and meadow openings. Much of the spruce is mature and overmature, reflecting a marked deficiency of pole and sapling age classes. Although duff and litter accumulation is not great in most northern Rocky Mountain forests, depth in spruce-fir stands is generally greater than in other types. Pfister *et al.* (1977) listed average duff depth in *Abies lasiocarpa* habitat types of up to 7.5 centimeters. Mosses and lichens are often abundant on the forest floor. A rich herbaceous flora is found where forest stands are not too dense. Toward the upper limits of growth, trees are dwarfed and stunted and the herbaceous flora becomes less diverse and abundant. Timberline is usually found at about 6,500 feet in northern Idaho and Montana and at about 10,000 feet in the southern part of the Northern Rocky Mountain Region.

Place in Ecological Succession.   The ecological niche occupied by the spruce-fir type is easier to classify than some of the other Northern Rocky Mountain types, because the composition is much less variable. Spruce and fir dominate the zone, and except in the lower parts, there are few or no forest tree competitors. Daubenmire and Daubenmire (1968) recognize an *Abies lasiocarpa* habitat-type series which comprises most of the range of habitat types featuring the combination of spruce and fir. Spruce is considered seral throughout the *Abies lasiocarpa* series in northern Idaho and in south-central Idaho where there is much high-altitude terrain supporting the spruce-fir combination. A separate *Picea* series has been described in the Montana habitat-typing system by Pfister *et al.* (1977) and Steele *et al.* (1975) recognize a limited area of *Picea* climax in southern Idaho. On moderately moist and cool sites between the *Pseudotsuga* series and the *Abies lasiocarpa* series Engelmann spruce assumes a climax role. This niche is occupied by climax grand fir farther to the west, excluding spruce from climax status. However, the more moderate maritime climate required for grand fir is replaced by a more continental climate in Montana, excluding grand fir and providing a climax niche for Engelmann spruce. When fires occur in the spruce-fir type, lodgepole pine, Douglas-fir, and white pine may form nearly pure, temporary stands. On sites with greater moisture and moderate temperatures, these seral stands are

Figure 8-8.   Engelmann spruce—subalpine fir stand in western Montana (U.S. For. Serv.).

rapidly replaced by the climax spruce-fir type. Fire protection and mountain pine beetle depredations help to speed the process. On drier, more exposed sites with greater temperature fluctuations, seral stands of lodgepole pine may persist for hundreds of years without repeated fires. Recurring fires on moist sites also can retard succession and maintain the seral stand (Pfister *et al.*, 1977). On some sites, old burns will often remain barren or bushy for a long period of time. There are more difficulties in reestablishing forest cover here than in other forest types.

Subalpine fir appears to regenerate more satisfactorily on heavy duff and moss than does spruce, which is more successful on mineral soil or decayed wood. Locally, the mountain hemlock is climax along with the spruce-fir but is of limited distribution. It is often found as overmature islands or small stands. This must be due to mountain hemlock's longevity and greater size, and more specific microsite requirements for reproduction; subalpine fir reproduces more readily on most sites where the two species occur together.

Growth Rates.   There is little information on growth and yield in the spruce-fir type of the Northern Rocky Mountains, but growth appears to vary from very good to poor. Spruce makes the best growth and develops to the largest size. In places where soil and moisture are favorable, generally at lower altitudes, spruce stands have annual growth capabilities of up to 130 cubic feet per acre per year (Pfister *et al.*, 1977) and will ultimately yield 6,000 to 8,000 cubic feet per acre. Individual overmature specimens of Engelmann spruce, 200 to 300 years of age, may have diameters of 36 to 48 inches and produce several clear logs. Timber from high elevations is limby and rough, with extremely slow growth and regeneration. Timberline habitat types are usually considered noncommercial forest land.

Cultural Practices.   Cultural practices as described for the spruce-fir type in Chapter 7 are generally applicable in the Northern Rocky Mountains. As in the central and southern Rockies, alternatives for management are greatly reduced in areas where overmature stands predominate. Much of the spruce-fir zone has been remote and inaccessible due to its location at high elevations. Only limited cutting in this type was done prior to a spruce bark beetle epidemic which began with a hugh blowdown in 1949. The salvage program initiated to control this epidemic and to utilize the dead timber was the first large-scale experience in spruce-fir type operations. Due to better accessibility, the productive spruce-fir belt across northern Montana, northern Idaho, and northeastern Washington features a better age-class distribution than is typical of the type.

Cuttings made during the salvage program were most frequently patch, block, or strip clearcutting, with dozer piling and burning of slash. Good reproduction of spruce generally has been obtained in openings with mineral-soil seedbeds and an adjacent seed supply. Spruce seed may be disseminated in adequate quantities as far as 660 feet from a well-stocked seed source (Roe and DeJarnette, 1965; Roe, 1967). A receptive seedbed is an equally important factor in determining regeneration success in terms of both seedling numbers and composition. Subalpine fir reproduces more successfully on duff than does Engelmann spruce, so site-preparation treatments may strongly influence the ratio of spruce to subalpine fir reproduction. In a northern Idaho study of site preparation after clearcutting, subalpine fir was the most abundant and widely distributed species on control areas where no site preparation was done (Boyd and Deitschman, 1969). Scarification increased the ratio of spruce to subalpine fir, producing 5 to 12 times more spruce seedlings per acre than subalpine fir.

While openings are soon invaded by grasses in the central and southern Rockies (see Chapter 7), shrubs are much more prevalent in the Northern Rocky Mountains and create difficult competition problems in certain habitat types.

Although clearcutting is frequently recommended for harvesting overmature stands, reproduction of spruce is frequently difficult because of the environmental extremes associated with these high-elevation sites. On many sites in the spruce-fir type, clearcutting may allow excessive reradiation at night, and also form an impoundment for air drainage. These factors can combine to promote severe frost conditions even during summer months. Although spruce and fir tolerate and even require cool growing conditions, they are only moderately tolerant to heavy frost. Consequently, regeneration success on these clearcuts may require a nurse crop of highly frost-resistant lodgepole pine to return the site to production, and to moderate the environment and promote other regeneration. The shelterwood method may be more favorable for promoting spruce and fir reproduction.

Although Engelmann spruce can be regenerated satisfactorily with the shelterwood method, the risk of blowdown always is present after any partial cutting in this type. As after clearcutting, seedbed preparation is helpful; however, broadcast burning is not recommended in partial cuttings since the thin-barked spruce trees are easily damaged by fire. Selection methods are recommended for obtaining reproduction where uneven-aged structure is present. Given room to grow, Engelmann spruce trees are likely to continue adding significant diameter growth up to an age of 300 years (LeBarron and Jemison, 1953). In northern Idaho thrifty 180-year-old spruce were still growing at the rate of two inches per decade 25 years after a heavy thinning. Commercial thinnings aid in maintaining good growth as well as in providing an opportunity to salvage subalpine fir stems while they are still sound.

Spruce-fir forests are important as a source of water in the Northern Rocky Mountains, necessitating careful land management to maintain water quality and to enhance the availability of water for use in power production, irrigation, and for domestic and industrial purposes.

Erosive soils and steep topography are common in many areas of the spruce-fir zone. These characteristics, coupled with relatively high precipitation, increase the difficulty of management. Vegetative recovery after disturbance is slow, particularly at the higher elevations (Pfister et al., 1977), so recreational use as well as grazing of domestic livestock must be carefully controlled. Use of these sensitive areas as summer range by elk, deer, bears, and other big game adds still another dimension to the land management picture.

A considerable amount of the wilderness and back-country acreage of the Northern Rocky Mountains is land of the spruce-fir type. Although silviculture in the traditional sense is not practiced in classified wilderness, the distribution and control of human use, the detection and control of insect pests, and the use of wildfires to effect changes are forms of vegetation and soils management integral to the overall maintenance of the forest ecosystem.

Susceptibility to Damage. The spruce-fir type is subjected to winds more severe than those which occur at lower elevations. With shallow and often near-saturated soils, the superficially rooted spruce is vulnerable to strong winds. During November 1949, high winds in the region blew down millions of feet of spruce timber and set the stage for the spruce bark beetle epidemic which followed. The situation was aggravated by the fact that most of the timber was overripe, and more susceptible to windthrow than vigorous young timber would be. In making selection or partial cuttings, one must recognize the danger and try to leave stands in a windfirm condition.

Fire danger is generally low at the higher elevations because cool, moist conditions and the short growing season limit the period of fire danger. Yet, severe fires occur within the zone.

The spruce gall aphid, easily detected due to the unsightly cone-like galls, is widespread throughout many spruce-fir stands. Although the marketability of Christmas trees may be seriously reduced by infestations, the impact on forest trees is unimportant (Partridge et al., 1978). The western spruce budworm is the most serious defoliator of the true firs, as well as Douglas-fir. The Douglas-fir tussock moth also has caused defoliation damage to the firs in this type. The Engelmann spruce beetle, which caused so much damage in the past, is still the most serious problem of mature spruce stands. Whitebark and lodgepole pines, frequently important species in the spruce-fir complex, are heavily damaged by mountain pine beetle; dwarf mistletoe is a major factor governing management of lodgepole pine stands in the spruce-fir type. The primary disease problem in the true firs is the Indian paint fungus. Cull in some old-growth stands is over 50 percent, but this decay is related to stand vigor, age, and density, so short rotations and thinnings are major considerations in planning for control. Growth rates are reduced by yellow witches broom which may also predispose infested trees to other agents (Livingston et al., 1977).

BIBLIOGRAPHY

Adams, D. L. 1969. Stocking levels for lodgepole pine. Ph.D. dissertation, Colo. State Univ., Ft. Collins, Colo. 164 pp.

Alexander, R. R. 1972. Partial cutting practices in old-growth lodgepole pine. *USDA For. Serv. Res. Pap. RM-92.* 18 pp.

Amman, G. D., M. D. McGregor, D. B. Cahill, and W. H. Klein. 1977. Guidelines for reducing losses of lodgepole pine to the mountain pine beetle in unmanaged stands in the Rocky Mountains. *USDA For. Serv. Tech. Rep. INT-36.* 19 pp.

Baldwin, J.L. 1973. Climates of the United States. *USDC–NOAA.* 47 pp.

Barnes, V. G. 1973. Pocket gophers and reforestation in the Pacific Northwest: a problem analysis. *U.S. Fish and Wildl. Serv. Special Sci. Rep. Wildlife No. 155.* 18 pp.

Bingham, R. T., A. E. Squillace, and J. W. Duffield. 1953. Breeding blister rust resistant western white pine. *J. For.* 51:163–168.

Boe, K. N. 1948. Natural regeneration of lodgepole pine on seedbeds created by clearcutting and slash disposal. USDA For. Serv., *No. Rocky Mtn. For. and Range Exp. Stn. Res. Note 99.* 1 p.

Boyd, R. J., and G. H. Deitschman. 1964. Development of young western white pine plantations. *USDA For. Serv. Res. Note INT-18.* 6 pp.

Boyd, R. J. and G. H. Deitschman. 1969. Site preparation aids natural regeneration in western larch–Engelmann spruce strip clearcuttings. *USDA For. Serv. Res. Pap. INT-64* 10 pp.

Boyd, R. J. 1969. Some case histories of natural regeneration in the western white pine type. *USDA For. Serv. Res. Pap. INT-63.* 24 pp.

Buchanan, T. S. 1948. *Poria weirii.*, its behavior and occurrence on species other than cedars. *Northwest Sci.* 22:7–12.

Crookston, N. L., R. W. Stark, and D. L. Adams. 1977. Outbreaks of mountain pine beetle in lodgepole pine forests—1945 to 1975. *Univ. of Idaho. For. Wildl. and Range Exp. Stn. Bull. No.* 22. Moscow. 7 pp.

Daubenmire, R. F. 1952. Forest vegetation of northern Idaho and adjacent Washington and its bearing on concepts of vegetation classification. *Ecol. Monogr.* 22:301–330.

Daubenmire, R. 1966. Vegetation: identification of typal communities. *Science* 151:291–298.

Daubenmire, R. 1970. Steppe vegetation of Washington. *Wash. Agric. Exp. Stn. Tech. Bull.* 62. Pullman 131 pp.

Daubenmire, R., and J. B. Daubenmire. 1968. Forest vegetation of eastern Washington and northern Idaho. *Wash. Agric. Exp. Stn. Tech. Bull.* 60. Pullman. 104 pp.

Deitschman, G. H., and R. D. Pfister. 1973. Growth of released and unreleased young stands in the western white pine type. *USDA For. Serv. Res. Pap. INT-132.* 14 pp.

Denney, R. N. 1976. Relationships of logging to big game. (Mimeo.)

Denton, R. E., and S. Tunnock. 1968. Low-volume application of malathion by helicopter for controlling larch casebearer. *J. Econ. Entomol.* 61(2):582–583.

Denton, R. E. 1972. Establishment of *Agathis pumila* (Ratz.) for control of larch casebearer and notes on native parasitism and predation in Idaho. *USDA For. Serv. Res. Note INT-164.* 5 pp.

Dingle, R. W. 1956. Pocket gophers as a cause of mortality in eastern Washington pine plantations. *J. For.* 54:832–835.

Ferguson, D. E. and D. L. Adams. 1979. Guidelines for releasing advance grand fir from overstory competition. *Univ. of Idaho, For., Wildl. Range Exp. Stn. Note, No. 35.* . Moscow. 3 pp.

Foiles, M. W. 1955. Thinning from below in a 60-year-old western white pine stand. *USDA For. Serv. Res. Note 19, No. Rocky Mtn. For and Range Exp. Stn.* 5 pp.

Foiles, M. W. 1970. Commercial thinning to produce ponderosa pine sawlogs in the Inland Empire. *USDA For. Serv. Res. Pap. INT-72.* 10 pp.

Foiles, M. W. 1972. Responses in a western white pine stand to commercial thinning methods. *USDA For. Serv., Res. Note INT-159.* 8 pp.

Foiles, M. W., and J. D. Curtis. 1965. Natural establishment of ponderosa pine in central Idaho. *USDA For. Serv. Res. Note INT-35.* 4 pp.

Foiles, M. W., and J. D. Curtis. 1973. Regeneration of ponderosa pine in the northern Rocky Mountain-Intermountain region. *USDA For. Serv. Res. Pap. INT-145.* 44pp.

Gill, L. S. 1957. Dwarf mistletoe of lodgepole pine. *USDA For. Serv. For. Pest Leaflet 18.* 7 pp.

Graham, D. P. 1958. Results of some silvicultural tests in pole blight diseased white pine stands. *J. For.* 56:284–287.

Haig, I. T., K. P. Davis, and R. H. Weidman. 1941. Natural regeneration in the western white pine type. *USDA Tech Bull. No.* 767. 99 pp.

Haig, I. T. 1932. Second-growth yield, stand and volume tables for the western white pine type. *USDA Tech Bull. No.* 323. 67 pp.

Hanley, D. P., and D. L. Adams. 1976. Thinning increases growth in young ponderosa pine plantations of the Palouse range. *Univ. of Idaho, For., Wildl. and Range Exp. Stn., Note No.* 26. Moscow. 4 pp.

Hatch, C. R., and J. E. Lotan. 1969. Natural regeneration of Douglas-fir in central Montana. *USDA For. Serv. Res. Note INT-85.* 4 pp.

Hawksworth, F. G. 1977. The 6-class dwarf mistletoe rating system. *USDA For. Serv., Gen. Tech. Rep. RM-48.* 7 pp.

Heller, R. C., and W. A. Miller. 1977. Color infrared photos define site conditions favorable for Douglas-fir tussock moth outbreaks. pp. 43–50 In: Proc. 6th Bienn. Workshop aerial color photography in the plant sciences and related fields. *Colo. State Univ.*, Ft. Collins. 10 pp.

Hironaka, M. 1977. Second year's report, habitat-type classification for grasslands and shrublands of southern Idaho. *Coll. For., Wildl. and Range Sci., Univ. of Idaho*, Moscow. 38 pp.

Hoff, R. J., and G. I. McDonald. 1977. Selecting western white pine leave-trees. *USDA For. Serv., Res. Note INT-218.* 2 pp.

Hosmer, J. K. 1917. *History of the expedition of captains Lewis and Clark.* Vols. 1 and 2. A. C. McClurg and Co., Chicago. 1083 pp.

Huberman, M. A. 1935. The role of western white pine succession in northern Idaho. *Ecology* 16:37–151.

Hutchison, S. B., and R. K. Winters. 1941. Northern Idaho's forest problem. *USDA For. Serv., N. Rocky Mtn. For. and Range Exp. Stn. For. Sur. Release 19.* 24 pp.

Irwin, L. L. 1976. Effects of intensive silviculture on big game forage sources in northern Idaho. pp. 135–142. In: *Elk-Logging-Roads Symp. Univ. of Idaho, For., Wildl. and Range Exp. Stn.*, Moscow.

Jemison, G. M. 1950. Forty years of forest research in the Northern Rocky Mountain Region. In: *Fortieth Annu. Rep. USDA For. Serv., No. Rocky Mtn. For. and Range Exp. Stn.* 62 pp.

Johnson, F. D. 1979. Idaho forest habitat types training manual. *Univ. of Idaho, Forest. Wildl. and Range Exp. Stn.* Moscow. 44 pp.

Johnson, P. C., and R. E. Denton. 1975. Outbreaks of the western spruce budworm in the American northern Rocky Mountain area from 1922 through 1971. *USDA For. Serv., Gen. Tech. Rep. INT-20.* 144 pp.

Kimmey, J. W., and D. P. Graham. 1960. Dwarf mistletoes of the Intermountain and Northern Rocky Mountain regions and suggestions for control. *USDA For. Serv., Res. Pap. INT-60.* 19 pp.

Larsen, J. A. 1929. Fires and forest succession in the Bitterroot Mountains of northern Idaho. *Ecology* 11:67–76.

Larsen, J. A. 1930. Forest types of the northern Rocky Mountains and their climatic controls. *Ecology* 11:631–672.

Larson, M. J. 1977. Regeneration of meadow-associated forest stands in central north Idaho. Ph.D. dissertation. Univ. of Idaho, Coll. For., Wildl. and Range Sci., Moscow. 106 pp.

Leaphart, C. D. 1958. Pole blight—how it may influence western white pine management in light of current knowledge. *J. For.* 56:746–751.

LeBarron, R. K. 1948a. Review of published information on the larch-Douglas-fir type. *USDA For. Serv., No. Rocky Mtn. Forest and Range Exp. Stn. Pap. 15.* 15 pp.

LeBarron, R. K. 1948b. Cutting lodgepole pine in the northern Rocky mountains. pp. 339–403. In: Proc. Soc. Am. For. Ann. Mtg.

LeBarron, R. K. 1952. Silvicultural practices for lodgepole pine in Montana. *USDA For. Serv., No. Rocky Mtn. For. and Range Exp. Stn. Pap. 33.* 19 pp.

LeBarron, R. K. and G. M. Jemison. 1953. Ecology and silviculture of the Engelmann spruce-alpine fir type. *J. For.* 51:349–355.

Leege, T. A. 1968. Prescribed burning for elk in northern Idaho. *Ann. Proc. Tall Timbers Fire Ecology Conf. No. 8.* Tallahassee, Fla.

Leege, T. A. 1969. Burning seral brush range for big game in northern Idaho. *Trans. North Amer. Wildl. Conf.* 34:429–438.

Livingston, R. L., J. Schwandt, D. Almas, and D. Beckman. 1977. Forest insect and disease conditions in Idaho, 1976. *Idaho Dept. Lands, Rep.* 77-1.

Lotan, J. E. 1976. Cone serotiny—fire relationships in lodgepole pine. *Proc. Montana Tall Timbers Fire Ecology Conf. and Fire and Land Manage. Symp., No. 14.* 1974:267−278.

Lynch, D. W. 1953. Growth of young ponderosa pine stands in the Inland Empire. *USDA For. Serv. Res. Pap. INT-36.* 16 pp.

Mahoney, R. L. 1977. Classifying lodgepole pine stands as resistant or susceptible to mountain pine beetle. M.S. thesis, Univ. of Idaho, Moscow. 28 p.

Mahoney, R. L. 1978. Lodgepole pine/mountain pine beetle risk classification methods and their application. pp. 106−113 In: Theory and practice of mountain pine beetle management in lodgepole pine forests. *Symp. Proc. Wash. State Univ.* Pullman, April 25−27, Univ. of Idaho, For., Wildl. and Range Exp. Stn., Moscow.

McArdle, R. E., and W. H. Meyer. 1930. The yield of Douglas-fir in the Pacific Northwest. *USDA Tech. Bull. No. 201.* 64 pp.

Mosher, M. M. 1960. Preliminary report of irrigation and fertilization of ponderosa pine. *Wash. State Univ. Agric. Exp. Stn. Circ. 365.* Pullman 5 pp.

Mueggler, W. F., and W. P. Handl. 1974. Mountain grassland and shrubland habitat types of western Montana. *USDA For. Serv. Interim Rep. Intermtn. For. and Range Exp. Stn. and Region I.* 89 pp.

Partridge, A. D., and D. L. Miller. 1972. Bark beetles and root rots related in Idaho conifers. *Plant Dis. Rep.* 56(6):498−500.

Partridge, A. D., E. R. Canfield, and D. L. Kulhavy. 1978. Keys to major disease, insect and related problems of forests in northern Idaho. *Rev. ed. Univ. of Idaho For., Wildl. and Range Exp. Stn.,* Moscow. 100 pp.

Pfister, R. D., J. Schmautz, D. On, and C. Brown. 1971. Management implications by habitat types. Mimeo. *USDA For. Serv.* Region I habitat type training session. 30 pp.

Pfister, R. D., B. L. Kovalchik, S. F. Arno, and R. C. Presby. 1977. Forest habitat types of Montana. *USDA For. Serv. Gen. Tech. Rep. INT-34.* 174 pp.

Roe, A. L. 1948. Thirty-nine years growth in a cut-over larch stand. *USDA For. Serv. No. Rocky Mtn. For. and Range Exp. Stn. Res. Note 70.* 6 pp.

Roe, A. L. 1950. Response of western larch and Douglas-fir to logging release in western Montana. *Northwest Sci.* 24:99−104.

Roe, A. L. 1951. Growth tables for cut-over larch−Douglas-fir stands in the upper Columbia Basin. *USDA For. Serv. No. Rocky Mtn. Forest and Range Exp. Stn. Pap. 30.* 24 pp.

Roe, A. L. 1955. Cutting practices in Montana larch−Douglas-fir. *Northwest Sci.* 29(1):23−34.

Roe, A. L. and G. M. DeJarnette. 1965. Results of regeneration cutting in a spruce-subalpine fir stand. *USDA For. Serv. Res. Pap. INT-17.* 14 pp.

Roe, A. L. 1967. Seed dispersal in a bumper spruce seed year. *USDA For. Serv. Res. Pap. INT-39.* 10 pp.

Ryker, R. A. 1975. A survey of factors affecting regeneration of Rocky Mountain Douglas-fir. *USDA For. Serv. Res. Pap. INT-147.* 19 pp.

Safranyik, L., D. M. Shrimpton, and H. S. Whitney. 1974. Management of lodgepole pine to reduce losses from the mountain pine beetle. *Can. For. Serv., Pac. For. Res. Cent. For. Tech. Rep. 1.* 24 pp.

Satterlund, D. R., and H. F. Haupt. 1972. Vegetation management to control snow accumulation and melt in the northern Rocky Mountains. pp. 200−205. In: *Proc. Nat. Symp. Watersheds in Transition.*

Scanlin, D. P., H. Loewenstein, and F. H. Pitkin. 1976. Two-year response of north Idaho stands of Douglas-fir and grand fir to urea fertilizer and thinning. *University of Idaho, For., Wildl. and Range Exp. Stn., Bull. No. 18,* Moscow. 17 pp.

Schenk, J. A., R. L. Mahoney, J. A. Moore, and D. L. Adams. 1976. Understory plants as indicators of grand fir mortality due to the fir engraver. *J. Entomol. Soc. Brit. Columbia, 73, Dec. 31, 1976.*

Schenk, J. A., R. L. Mahoney, J. A. Moore, and D. L. Adams. 1980. A model for hazard rating lodgepole pine stands for mortality by mountain pine beetle. *For. Ecol. Mgmt.* 3:000–000.

Schmidt, S. C., and D. G. Fellin. 1973. Western spruce budworm damage affects form and height growth of western larch. *Can. J. For. Res.* 3:17–26.

Schmidt, W. C., R. C. Sherrer, and A. L. Roe. 1976. Ecology and silviculture of western larch forests. *USDA For. Serv., Tech. Bull. No. 1520,* 96 pp.

Shearer, R. C. 1974. Early establishment of conifers following prescribed broadcast burning in western larch/Douglas-fir forests. In *Proc. Montana Tall Timbers Fire Ecology Conf. and Fire and Land Manage. Symp.,* No. 14:481–500.

Shearer, R. C., and W. C. Schmidt. 1970. Natural regeneration in ponderosa pine forests of western Montana. *USDA For. Serv. Res. Pap. INT-86.* 19 pp.

Sinclair, C., and R. J. Boyd. 1973. Survival comparisons of three fall and spring plantings of four coniferous species in northern Idaho. *USDA For. Serv. Res. Pap. INT-139.* 20 pp.

Society of American Foresters. 1954. Forest cover types of North America (exclusive of Mexico). *Soc. Am. For.* Washington, D.C. 67 pp.

Stage, A. R. 1973. Prognosis model for stand development. *USDA For. Serv. Res. Pap. INT-137.* 32 pp.

Steele, R., R. D. Pfister, R. A. Ryker, and J. A. Kittams. 1975. Forest habitat types of central Idaho. *USDA For. Serv. INT Review Draft.* 191 pp.

Steer, H. B. 1948. Lumber production in the United States 1799–1946. *USDA Misc. Publ. No. 669.* 233 pp.

Stoszek, K. J. 1973. Damage to ponderosa pine plantations by the western pine-shoot borer. *J. For.* 71:701–705.

Stoszek, K. J. 1977. Protection concerns in plantation establishment. In *Proc. Tree Planting in the Inland Northwest.* Wash. State Univ. Pullman. 21 pp.

Stoszek, K. J., H. L. Osborne, P. G. Mika, and J. A. Moore. 1977. The relationships of site and stand attributes and management practices to Douglas-fir tussock moth epidemics. *Final Rep. Coll. For., Wildl. and Range Sci., Univ. of Idaho,* Moscow. 49 pp.

Tackle, D. 1954. Lodgepole pine management in the intermountain region—a problem analysis. *USDA For. Serv., Misc. Pub. 2. Intermtn. For. and Range Exp. Stn.* 53 pp.

Tackle, D. 1965. Lodgepole pine. In Silvics of forest trees of the United States. pp. 373–383. *USDA For. Serv., Agric. Hdbk. No. 271..*

Taylor, R. F. 1937. A tree classification for lodgepole pine in Colorado and Wyoming. *J. For.* 35:868–875.

Terrell, T. T. 1956. Engelmann spruce beetle infestation in the northern Rocky Mountain Region, 1955. *USDA For. Serv. Intermtn. Forest and Range Exp. Stn.* 7 pp. (mimeo)

Tunnock, S., R. E. Denton, C. E. Carlson, and W. W. Janssen. 1969. Larch casebearer and other factors involved with deterioration of western larch stands in northern Idaho. *USDA For. Serv. Res. Pap. INT-68.* 10 pp.

U.S. Dept. Agriculture. 1938. *Soils and men, yearbook of agriculture, 1938.* U.S. Govt. Print. Off., Washington, D.C. 1232 pp.

U.S. Dept. Agriculture. 1952. *Insects, yearbook of agriculture, 1952.* U.S. Govt. Print. Off., Washington, D.C. 780 pp.

U.S. Dept. Agriculture. 1975. Soil taxonomy. *Agric. Handbook No. 436.* U.S. Govt. Print. Off., Washington, D.C. 745 pp.

USDA Forest Service. 1965. Silvics of forest trees of the United States. *Agric. Hdbk. No. 271.* 762 pp.

USDA Forest Service. 1969. Program analysis for research and development on western dwarf mistletoes. 36 pp.

USDA Forest Service. 1973. The outlook for timber in the United States. *USDA For. Serv., For. Resour. Rep. No. 20.* 367 pp.

USDA Forest Service. 1974. Forest hydrology. Hydrologic effects of vegetation manipulation, Part II. 224 pp.

USDA Forest Service. 1975. Forest insect and disease conditions in the intermountain states during 1975. Forest insect and disease control. *USDA For. Serv., Intermtn. Region.*

USDA Forest Service. 1977a. Elk habitat coordinating requirements for northern Idaho. *USDA For. Serv. No. Region.* 46 pp.

USDA Forest Service. 1977b. Draft environmental statement, western spruce budworm management plan. *USDA For. Serv. Northern Region.* 325 pp.

USDA Forest Service. 1978. Forest statistics in the United States. 1977. Washington. D.C. 133 pp.

U.S. Government Printing Office. 1936. The western range. *Senate Doc. 199, 74th Congr. 2nd sess.*

Wang, C. W., and R. K. Patee. 1976. Regional variation of ponderosa pine, the five-year result. *Univ. of Idaho, For., Wildl. and Range Exp. Stn. Bull. No. 10,* Moscow. 8pp.

Washburn, R. I., R. L. Livingston, and G. P. Markin. 1977. An aerial test of orthene against the larch casebearer. *USDA For. Serv. Res. Note INT-226.* 6 pp.

Weidman, R. H. 1936. Timber growing and logging practice in ponderosa pine in the Northwest. *USDA Tech. Bull. 511,* 91 pp.

Wellner, C. A. 1965. Western white pine. pp. 478–487 In: Silvics of forest trees of the United States. *USDA For. Serv., Agric. Hdbk. No. 271.*

Wellner, C. A. 1970a. Regeneration problems of ponderosa pine in the northern Rocky Mountains. In: Regeneration of Ponderosa Pine—Symp. Proc. School of For. Oregon State Univ. Corvallis. 1969. 7 pp.

Wellner, C. A. 1970b. Fire history in the northern Rocky Mountains; the role of fire in the intermountain west. pp. 42–63 In: *Intermountain Fire Res. Council Symp. Proc.*

Wellner, C. A. 1978. Forest-management considerations, effects of past events. pp. 185–189. In: M. H. Brooks, Stark, R. W., and Campbell, R. W. (eds.), The Douglas-fir tussock moth: a synthesis. *USDA For. Serv. Sci. Ed. Agency Tech. Bull. 1585.* 331 pp.

Wikstrom, J. H. 1957. Lodgepole pine—a lumber species. *USDA For. Serv. Res. Pap. 46.* 15 pp.

Wikstrom, J. H., and C. A. Wellner. 1961. The opportunity to thin and prune in the northern Rocky Mountain and intermountain regions. *USDA For. Serv., Res. Pap. 61.*

Williams, C. B., Jr., and P. J. Shea. 1971. Insecticides. In: Toward integrated control. Proc. 3rd Annu. Northwestern Forest Insect Work Conf. New Haven, Conn., Feb. 17–19, 1970. *USDA For. Serv. Res. Pap. NE-194.* 129 pp.

Williams, C. B., Jr., P. J. Shea, and G. S. Walton. 1971. Population density of western spruce budworm as related to stand characteristics in the Bitterroot National Forest. *USDA For. Serv. Res. Pap. PSW-72.* 8 pp.

Wittinger, W. T., W. L. Pengelly, L. L. Irwin, and J. M. Peek. 1977. A 20-year record of shrub succession in logged areas in the cedar-hemlock zone of northern Idaho. *Northwest Sci.* 51(3):161–171.

Worf, W. A., R. H. Cron, S. C. Trotter, O. L. Copeland, S. B. Hutchison, and C. A. Wellner. 1970. Management practices on the Bitterroot National Forest. *USDA For. Serv. Northern Region and Intermtn. For. and Range Exp. Stn.* 100 pp.

Wright, H. A. 1978. The effect of fire on vegetation in ponderosa pine forests. *Texas Tech. Univ. Range and Wildl. Infor. Ser. No. 2.* 21 pp.

9

The California Region

John A. Helms

LOCATION

The California region is unique due to the combination of distinctive species, a Mediterranean climate characterized by hot, dry summers, and the extent and variety of multiple uses of the forests.

The silviculture of California forests is not only characterized by distinctive ecological and silvical features of site and species, it is also highly influenced by societal considerations. California ranks within the first three states in terms of national timber production, producing 5.3 billion board feet in 1976. Yet the importance of forestry in the state is dwarfed by the magnitude of agriculture and industry. Also, because California is the most populous state in the nation, forests play a critical role in both the production of water and in providing recreational opportunities. As a result, ecological, managerial, and societal constraints have resulted in distinctive silvicultural approaches which reflect not only purely technical considerations of soils and species characteristics, but also taxes, forest practice legislation, local county ordinances, and public policy.

Forests extend across the full width of the state in northern California and then extend southward on both sides of the immense central valley formed by the Sacramento and San Joaquin River drainages (Fig. 9-1). To the west, the commercial forests occur in the northern coast range and become more sporadic with distance into southern California. To the east, extensive forests occur in the Sierra Nevada. In southern California, commercial forests give way to chaparral and woodland which continue, with isolated small areas of forest, to the Mexican border.

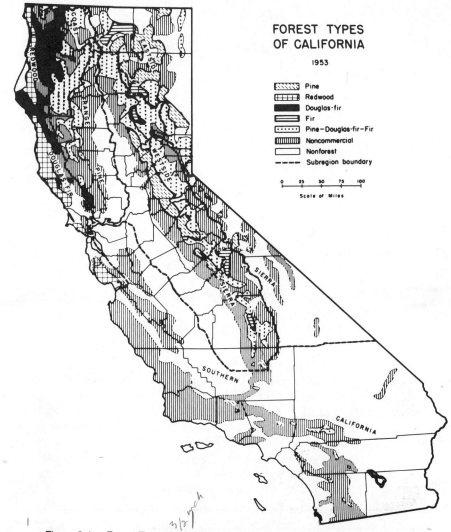

FOREST TYPES
OF CALIFORNIA

1953

Pine	
Redwood	
Douglas-fir	
Fir	
Pine-Douglas-fir-Fir	
Noncommercial	
Nonforest	
Subregion boundary	

0   25   50   75   100

Scale of Miles

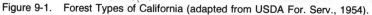

Figure 9-1.   Forest Types of California (adapted from USDA For. Serv., 1954).

FOREST STATISTICS[1]

Area

California is second only to Alaska in terms of total forest land area. Forest land constitutes 40 percent of the area of the state, 40 million acres out of the total 100 million acres (Table 9-1). Of this forest area there are about 17.9

[1]Much of the information in this section was provided by Charles L. Bolsinger, Forest Resources Evalaution Unit, USDA For. Serv., Pacific Northwest Forest and Range Experiment Station, Portland, Oregon.

TABLE 9-1

Area of Major Vegetation Types in California, 1975

Land Use or Vegetation Type	Area (Million Acres)	Percent
Productive forest	17.944	17.9
Unproductive forest	22.216	22.2
Coastal sagebrush	2.300	2.3
Inland sagebrush	3.800	3.8
Desert	23.900	23.9
Grassland	12.000	12.0
Riparian, marsh, tidelands	0.700	0.7
Barren	1.800	1.8
Agriculture	11.000	11.0
Urban, industrial, roads, and other	4.390	4.4
Total	100.050	100.0

Source: Charles L. Bolsinger, Forest Resources Evaluation Unit, USDA For. Serv., Pacific Northwest Forest and Range Experiment Station, Portland, Oregon.

million acres of land manageable for timber production, with a growth potential of at least 20 cubic feet of wood per acre per year. Not all this area is available for commercial operations, since some 1.4 million acres, or 8 percent, of this productive land is in parks, wilderness, and other reservations where timber is generally not harvested. This reserve contains 7 percent of the redwood type, 7 percent of the Douglas-fir, 11 percent of the true fir, 8 percent of the ponderosa pine type, and most of the giant sequoia. The remaining 16.3 million acres are classified as commercial forest land. However, this land base may continue to shrink due to further withdrawals and restrictions on use. Since 1953, the total commercial forest area in California has decreased by about one million acres because of grazing development, roads, construction of reservoirs and power lines, urban expansion, and park and wilderness dedication.

Character of Forest Land Ownership

The breakdown of commercial forest land by ownership is shown in Table 9-2.

The U.S. Forest Service administers 17 national forests in California containing 50.1 percent of the commercial forest land in the state. Because of the multiple-use management objectives, and because of restrictions on timber harvesting due to roadside areas, steep ground, streamside areas, and visual considerations, about 90 percent of all timber produced from the national forests comes from approximately 62 percent of the area. The national forests are characterized as being of generally lower site quality than other ownerships

TABLE 9-2

Area (in Thousands of Acres) of Commercial Forest Land by Forest Type, Based on Plurality of Stocking, and Ownership, California, 1975

Forest Type	National Forest	Other Public	Forest Industry	Other Private Timber Growers	Farmer and Miscellaneous Private	All Ownerships
Douglas-fir	1,542	90	400[a]	198	501	2,731
Ponderosa and Jeffrey pines[b]	3,098	46	368	232	587	4,331
Lodgepole pine	189	—	10	33	29	261
True firs[c]	2,575	29	524	386	237	3,751
Incense-cedar	d	28[e]	199	266	158	651
Redwood	21[f]	20[g]	308[h]	10[h]	291[h]	650
Hardwoods	426	222	588	151	1,452	2,839
Nonstocked	317	34	111	72	224	758
North Coast areas logged since inventory	—	30	180	—	117	327
Total	8,168	499	2,688	1,348	3,596	16,299

Source: Charles L. Bolsinger, Forest Resources Evaluation Unit, USDA For. Serv., Pacific Northwest Forest and Range Experiment Station, Portland, Oregon.

[a] Includes small amounts of western hemlock and Sitka spruce in Del Norte and Humboldt Counties.
[b] Includes sugar, Coulter, knobcone, Monterey, and Bishop pines; and incense-cedar in national forests.
[c] Includes white, grand, California and Shasta red firs, western white pine, and mountain hemlock stands intermingled with true fir stands in high mountain forests.
[d] Combined with ponderosa and Jeffrey pines.
[e] Includes small amounts of western red and Port-Orford-cedars in Del Norte and Humboldt Counties.
[f] Includes 16,000 acres of coast redwood in coastal areas and 5,000 acres of giant sequoia in the Sierra Nevada Mountains.
[g] Includes 18,000 acres of coast redwood and 2,000 acres of giant sequoia.
[h] Coast redwood.

with 17 percent of national forest lands classified in the highest two productivity classes (Table 9-3). Another characteristic is that because of early heavy cutting on private lands, the national forests now contain two-thirds of the state's remaining old-growth forests.

Total land area in the Other Public category is 3 percent of the state's total commercial forest land. About 48 percent of this area is administered by the Bureau of Land Management that generally includes lands that are steep and of relatively low site quality. Other owners include the Bureau of Indian Affairs, the state, counties, municipalities, and the Department of Defense.

Forest industry holdings include 16.5 percent of the state's commercial forest land and one-third of the land that is in private ownership. These owners operate wood-using plants. Industry has, on the average, the highest site-quality lands with 49 percent of its holdings in productivity classes 1 and 2 (Table 9-3). Industry has a softwood inventory that is 10 percent of the state's total and has the highest proportion of the state's young-growth stands.

Forest lands in the Other Private Timber Growers category are owned by companies that grow timber for sale and do not have their own wood-processing plants. This category contains 8.3 percent of the commercial forest land in California.

About 10 percent of the commercial forest land is owned by farmers and ranchers and an additional 12 percent by miscellaneous noncorporate owners including individuals, banks, churches, and real estate companies. This large proportion of land is generally intermediate in site quality between that owned by industry and by the public. A substantial inventory exists in this category (Table 9-3). However, because of the large numbers of owners with diverse interests and management objectives, considerable uncertainty prevails regarding projected levels of timber supply from this category.

Forest Inventory

The total inventory of growing stock (over 5 inches d.b.h.) on commercial forest land is 49,667 million cubic feet and the net volume of sawtimber (over 11 inches d.b.h.) is estimated to be 235,650 million board feet Scribner rule (Table 9-4).

Softwood growing stock totals 45,974 million cubic feet on 13.46 million acres. The proportion of this inventory by ownership is shown in Table 9-4. This table shows that 61 percent of the inventory is administered by the U.S. Forest Service. Other public ownership administers 2 percent, industry 16 percent and other private and miscellaneous 21 percent. Of particular interest is the high proportion of the growing stock held in the farmer and miscellaneous category (13.6 percent) since this group currently does not contribute significantly to timber supply.

The breakdown of softwood growing stock by species and size class is shown in Table 9-5. The species comprising the highest proportion of the volume are the true firs—California white fir and California red fir—and Douglas-fir, each with about 28 percent of the growing stock. Ponderosa pine and Jeffrey pine

TABLE 9-3

Area (in Thousands of Acres) of Commercial Forest Land by Site Class (Biological Potential Without Management) and Ownership Class, California, 1975

Site Class (Biological Potential)[a]	National Forest	Other Public	Forest Industry	Miscellaneous Private Large Holdings Managed for Timber	Other Miscellaneous Private and Farmer	All Ownerships
165 cubic feet or more	533	44	686	100	501	1,864
120 to 164 cubic feet	824	72	633	151	721	2,401
85 to 119 cubic feet	1,918	99	502	255	792	3,566
50 to 84 cubic feet	3,576	199	542	436	1,033	5,786
20 to 49 cubic feet	1,317	85	325	406	504	2,637
All classes	8,168	499	2,688	1,348	3,551[b]	16,254

Source: Charles L. Bolsinger, Forest Resources Evaluation Unit, USDA For. Serv., Pacific Northwest Forest and Range Experiment Station, Portland, Oregon.

[a] See definition of biological potential, page 401.

[b] Excludes 6,000 acres in Central Coast and 39,000 acres in southern California for which information is not available.

TABLE 9-4

Net Volume of Growing Stock and Sawtimber on Commercial Forest Land by Ownership and Softwoods and Hardwoods, California, 1975

| | Growing Stock (Million Cubic Feet) | | | Sawtimber | | | | | |
| | | | | Million Board Feet (Scribner Rule) | | | Million Board Feet (International ¼-Inch Rule) | | |
Ownership	Softwoods	Hardwoods	Total	Softwoods	Hardwoods	Total	Softwoods[a]	Hardwoods[b]	Total
National Forest	28,072	1,134	29,206	142,883	2,814	145,697	157,958	2,955	160,913
Other Public	1,108	283	1,391	5,668	560	6,228	6,356	572	6,928
Forest Industry	7,457	679	8,136	35,940	1,181	37,121	40,883	1,206	42,089
Other Private Timber Growers	3,068	121	3,189	15,091	177	15,268	c	c	c
Farmer and Miscellaneous Private	6,269	1,476	7,745	28,246	3,090	31,336	50,397	3,342	53,739
All ownerships	45,974	3,693	49,667	227,828	7,822	235,650	255,594	8,075	263,669

Source: Charles L. Bolsinger, Forest Resources Evaluation Unit, USDA For. Serv., Pacific Northwest Forest and Range Experiment Station, Portland, Oregon.

[a] Includes trees 9.0 inches d.b.h. and larger.
[b] Includes trees 11.0 inches d.b.h. and larger.
[c] Included with farmer and miscellaneous private.

TABLE 9-5

Net Volume (in Millions of Cubic Feet) of Growing Stock on Commercial Forest Land by Species and by Diameter Class, All Ownerships, California, 1975

Species	Diameter Class (Inches)										All Classes
	5.0 to 6.9	7.0 to 8.9	9.0 to 10.9	11.0 to 12.9	13.0 to 14.9	15.0 to 16.9	17.0 to 18.9	19.0 to 20.9	21.0 to 28.9	29.0 and Larger	
Softwoods											
Douglas-fir	202	335	374	437	500	595	582	588	2,285	6,888	12,786
Ponderosa and Jeffrey pines	149	237	334	386	515	486	498	541	2,318	3,660	9,124
True firs	258	415	556	641	705	721	782	745	3,012	4,969	12,804
Hemlock	3	2	8	6	9	6	11	7	39	38	129
Sugar pine	21	49	52	66	68	84	105	115	629	2,166	3,355
White pine	2	4	5	9	10	11	16	14	70	90	231
Redwood	28	56	90	132	172	243	254	274	953	2,100	4,302
Sitka spruce	—	—	4	—	—	4	5	8	19	8	48
Engelmann and other spruces	—	—	1	1	1	—	—	1	2	1	7
Redcedar	a	1	—	—	—	—	—	2	4	11	18
Incense-cedar	70	103	106	110	138	129	122	127	411	688	2,004
Lodgepole pine	24	49	63	76	72	82	66	74	220	144	870
Other softwoods	12	8	20	21	23	25	14	14	53	107	297
Total	769	1,259	1,613	1,885	2,213	2,386	2,455	2,510	10,015	20,870	45,975

Hardwoods

Cottonwood and aspen	a	2	4	3	4	3	3	a	1	1	21
Red alder	3	8	8	6	7	9	6	5	7	5	64
Oak[b]	132	199	201	175	166	142	125	108	362	186	1,796
Other hardwoods[c]	111	190	189	192	172	185	147	124	321	181	1,812
Total	246	399	402	376	349	339	281	237	691	373	3,693
Total all species	1,015	1,658	2,015	2,260	2,562	2,725	2,736	2,748	10,706	21,243	49,668

Source: Charles L. Bolsinger, Forest Resources Evaluation Unit, USDA For. Serv., Pacific Northwest Forest and Range Experiment Station, Portland, Oregon.

a Less than 500,000 cubic feet.

b About 60 percent is California black oak; 40 percent consists of California white oak, Oregon white oak, California live oak, canyon live oak, and interior live oak.

c About 60 percent is tanoak; 30 percent is madrone; 10 percent consists mainly of big leaf maple and California laurel.

together constitute 20 percent of the total; with coast redwood and sugar pine, being the next most abundant with 9.4 percent and 7.3 percent respectively.

Hardwood growing stock totals 3,693 million cubic feet on about 2,839,000 acres of commercial forest (Tables·9-2 and 9-5). Most of this growing stock is in California black oak, tanoak, Pacific madrone, and red alder. Fifty-two percent of the hardwood inventory is in sizes greater than 15 inches (Table 9-5). This proportion is much higher than the national average. Total acreage of hardwood forest including noncommercial lands is approximately 15 million acres. Most commercial hardwood land (77 percent) is in private ownership (Table 9-2). Due primarily to past logging and burning àctivities, especially on private land, a considerable area on the north coast is now classified as hardwood that originally was conifer forest with some hardwood in the understory. Although these hardwoods now constitute the dominant cover, they are relatively small in size and the commercial timber volume on these lands is still composed of existing larger conifer trees (Oswald, 1972).

Annual net growth of growing stock and sawtimber (including the small proportion of hardwood growth) is 802 million cubic feet (Table 9-6). This is equivalent to an average of 49 cubic feet per acre per year on all commerical forest lands. This low current performance is due to a combination of both under- and overstocked areas, a legacy of cutover lands, and a high proportion (68 percent) of sawtimber classified as old growth, which is relatively slow growing (Oswald and Hornibrook, 1966). Annual harvest totals 79 million cubic feet indicating that, on the average, harvest volume is equivalent to growth. Considerable variability occurs, however, and harvest exceeds growth on those lands where old growth is being removed to make way for more rapidly growing

TABLE 9-6

Net Annual Growth of Growing Stock and Sawtimber on Commercial Forest Land in California, 1975

Ownership	Growth of Growing Stock (Million Cubic Feet per Year)	Growth of Sawtimber (Million Board-Feet per Year, Scribner Rule)
National Forests	379.7	1,660.0
Other Public	21.9	90.1
Forest Industry	162.5	748.3
Other Private Timber Growers	56.5	245.9
Farmer and Miscellaneous Private	181.0	835.0
All ownerships	801.6	3,579.3

Source: Charles L. Bolsinger, Forest Resources Evaluation Unit, USDA For. Serv., Pacific Northwest Forest and Range Experiment Station, Portland, Oregon.

young growth. Growth exceeds harvest on lands where harvesting level is low. The high proportion of inventory on national forest lands and the distribution of current harvest among various landownerships indicate the critical importance of public policy on future supplies, forest practices, and silviculture.

Potential productivity of California's commercial forest land is high. It is estimated that fully stocked natural stands (i.e., without management) might produce 97 cubic feet per acre per year compared with the average national potential of 75. Using this definition of "biological potential," Bolsinger[2] has shown that commercial forests in California represent 3 percent of the national total but constitute 13 percent of the lands capable of producing greater than 165 cubic feet per acre per year.

Native California hardwoods have a high capacity for growth and have the highest net growth rate (2.3 percent) of all timber species relative to the size of the inventory base (Wall, 1978). This is no doubt due to the generally smaller size of hardwood trees and the fact that many of them are growing from sprouts.

THE PHYSICAL ENVIRONMENT

Physiography

California is characterized by a Central Valley, some 400 miles long, formed by the Sacramento and San Joaquin river systems which join and flow into San Francisco Bay. The mountains that surround this valley include the Cascade and Sierra Nevada Mountains to the east, the Coast Range to the west, the Klamath Mountains in the north, the Transverse and Peninsular Mountains of Southern California, and the Modoc Plateau in the northeast.

East of the Central Valley, the dominant mountain range is the Sierra Nevada, an enormous tilted fault block. In early tertiary times this area was a low plain. Subsequent uplifting and erosion has created the Sierra Nevada of today which is characterized by massive granitic outcroppings. In the north, the fault block is less steeply tilted, is lower in elevation, and comprises the Cascade Range which is characterized by extensive lava flows.

The forests of the Sierra Nevada may be grouped into three major zones. The lower montane forests occur from 1,000 to 6,000 feet in the north and from 4,000 to 7,000 in the south. Characteristic species are ponderosa pine, Digger pine, and MacNab cypress on the more xeric sites, and California white fir and mixed conifer species on the more mesic sites. The upper montane forests, varying from 6,000 to 9,000 feet in elevation depending upon latitude, consist primarily of California red fir, Jeffrey pine, and lodgepole pine. The subalpine forests occur from 8,000 to 10,000 feet in the north and from 9,500 to 12,000 feet in the south. These forests are characterized by the presence of mountain hemlock, western white pine, whitebark pine, foxtail pine, and limber pine (Rundel et al., 1977).

[2]Information provided by Charles L. Bolsinger, Forest Resources Evaluation Unit, USDA For. Serv., Pacific Northwest Foest and Range Experiment Station, Portland, Oregon.

The Coast Range parallels the Pacific Ocean from the Oregon border to about Santa Cruz. It consists of long ridges, formed by folding and faulting, which generally reach only 2,000 to 4,000 feet with a few exceeding 6,000 feet in elevation. These mountains support productive and diverse forests which include grand fir, Port-Orford-cedar, Sitka spruce, Douglas-fir, coast redwood, western redcedar, western hemlock, and Sargent cypress (Griffin and Critchfield, 1972; Axelrod, 1977).

The Klamath Mountains, reaching elevations between 6,000 and 8,000 feet, form a transition area between typical Northwest- and California-centered species. Consequently these mountains contain a distinctive and highly diverse mix of tree and shrub species. There are also some endemic and relict populations occurring in scattered stands (Sawyer and Thornburgh, 1977). Dominant conifers present include Douglas-fir, ponderosa pine, sugar pine, California white and red fir, and mountain hemlock. Interesting relict species with larger ranges elsewhere include Pacific silver fir, Alaska-cedar, subalpine fir, Engelmann spruce, and foxtail pine, while Brewer spruce is endemic.

The boundary between "northern" and "southern" California is usually taken to be just south of the Tehachapi Mountains at a latitude of about 35° N. In southern California the climate becomes drier; on the coast the vegetation becomes dominated by woodland, whereas to the east are the Mojave and Colorado deserts. The southern California mountains have substantial areas of conifer and oak forest. At lower elevation there are extensive areas of woodland and chaparral which have a very high fire danger. At mid-elevations there are open pine stands consisting mainly of Coulter, Digger, ponderosa, and Jeffrey pines; and singleleaf pinyon. Other species include bristlecone fir, bigcone Douglas-fir, oaks, cypresses, and western juniper. At higher elevations common species include California white fir, incense-cedar, lodgepole, sugar, and limber pines, and with junipers on exposed ridges.

Northeastern California is characterized by the Modoc Plateau which lies east of Mt. Lassen (about latitude 40° N) and extends northward to the Oregon border. This Plateau, which lies at 3,000 to 4,000 feet in elevation, consists of a thick accumulation of lava flows and tuff beds which have developed a topography of occasional lakes, marshes, and sluggish rivers among rough irregular patterns of dry hills. Mean annual rainfall is 12 to 25 inches depending on elevation, and vegetaion therefore consists of mosaics of forest, woodland, and shrubland depending largely on precipitation and soil type. The poorer sites carry scattered *Juniperus* species, Jeffrey pine, and incense-cedar. With increasing elevation and precipitation, ponderosa pine, oak, California white and red fir become more prevalent.

Geology and Soils

The geomorphic provinces and major rock types of California are shown in Fig. 9-2. These may be briefly described as follows:

1. Granitic: the southerly two-thirds of the Sierra Nevada.
2. Volcanic: mainly of Tertiary and Quaternary origin, or as recent as a few

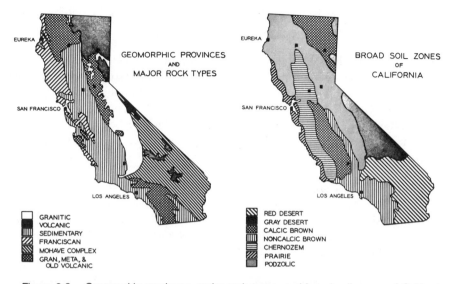

GEOMORPHIC PROVINCES
AND
MAJOR ROCK TYPES

BROAD SOIL ZONES
OF
CALIFORNIA

GRANITIC
VOLCANIC
SEDIMENTARY
FRANCISCAN
MOHAVE COMPLEX
GRAN., META., &
   OLD VOLCANIC

RED DESERT
GRAY DESERT
CALCIC BROWN
NONCALCIC BROWN
CHERNOZEM
PRAIRIE
PODZOLIC

Figure 9-2. Geomorphic provinces, major rock types, and broad soil zones of California (from Univ. Calif., 1960).

thousand years ago in parts of the Cascades. They also occur as basaltic lava flows in the northeastern Modoc Plateau, and as isolated masses east of the Sierra Nevada and throughout the Mojave Desert.

3. Sedimentary: Cretaceous, Tertiary, and Quaternary deposits often of considerable thickness. Unconsolidated gravels underlie the Central Valley. The South Coast Range is made up of raised and folded sedimentary beds. These also occur in the Southern California Coastal Plain and Colorado Desert.

4. Franciscan: A complex mixture of sedimentary, basic, and ultra-basic rocks of Jurassic and Cretaceous origin. This province contains sandstone, chert, limestone, lava, intrusive basalt, and serpentinized peridotite. It occurs in the North Coast and parts of the South Coast Ranges.

5. Mojave Complex: Undifferentiated mixture of alluvial, sedimentary, metamorphic, granitic, and volcanic rocks of all ages including some pre-Cambrian. Occurs east of the Sierra Nevada and Southern California Mountains.

6. Granitic, metamorphic, and old volcanic: Paleozoic and older with some formed as late as the Cretaceous. Occurs in the Klamath Mountains, northern Sierra, Southern California Mountains, and in isolated masses in the South Coast Range.

Currently, about 70 percent of the possible number of forest soils have been surveyed resulting in the description of 168 forest-soil series (Colwell, 1979). From the standpoint of forest management, the most important properties of these soils are those that influence productivity and erodability.

The important soil factors influencing growth of conifers in California are depth and texture, permeability, chemical characteristics, and drainage and runoff (Storie and Wieslander, 1948). The best sites on the Coast Range are on deep loam to clay loam soils at elevations of 100 to 3,000 feet (Colwell, 1979). These soils, which are derived from sedimentary rocks (Hugo soil series), or from schist (Josephine series), are extensive in distribution, and carry high-quality Douglas-fir, coast redwood, and associated species. In the Sierra Nevada and Cascade Ranges, the best mixed-conifer forests are on deep-loam, clay-loam, and some clay soils where average rainfall is more than 40 inches (Colwell, 1979). The principal soil series are Cohassett (from basalts and andesites), Aiken (from basic volcanics), and Holland (from granites, rhyolites, and diorites) which are reddish-brown, deep, well-drained soils. Some low-site-quality areas within the mixed-conifer type which carry shrubs, Jeffrey pine, incense-cedar, and Digger pine are characterized by soils derived from weathered serpentine and peridotite intrusions which are high in magnesium and often low in both potassium and calcium. A typical soil of the high elevation true-fir type is the Corbett series which is an excessively drained gray-brown, deep, immature, coarse-textured soil developed in place from granites and granodiorites.

The potential erodability of soils is important in California because the forests commonly occur on steep slopes. Potential erodability has important implications on choice of timber harvesting practices and response of soils to road construction and site preparation. Soils with highest potential for surface erosion in the Sierra Nevada and Cascade mountains are coarse-textured and derived from either acid igneous or from soft or weakly consolidated rocks. Coarse-textured soils from tuff and ash deposits are also highly erodable. On steep slopes of the Coast Range, high probability of mass slumping and landslides exist when soils such as the Atwell series become saturated with water. This is particularly so when the slopes are modified by road construction or timber harvesting.

Climate and Weather

The typical California climate is zonally sub-tropical (33 to 42° N latitude) combining the features of both arid and humid climates. Generally, summers are hot and dry, and winters are cool and moist. One-third of the state is classified as arid. However, there is a remarkable variety of climates within California that vary latitudinally and also with elevation. This can be deduced from Fig. 9-3 which illustrates patterns of precipitation and both January and July mean temperatures.

The prevailing climates can be associated with the broad forest types that they support. Baker (1944) describes these in considerable detail and they may be grouped into four broad types:

1. The Pacific Coast climate which characterizes the Klamath Mountains in southwestern Oregon, the Coast Ranges of California, and the coastal area. This climate supports the productive redwood and Douglas-fir forests. It

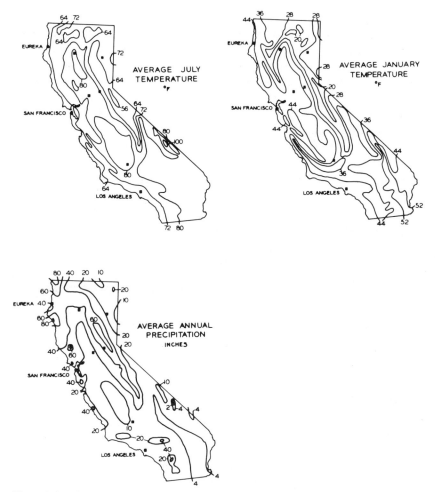

Figure 9-3.   Average temperatures in January and July, and average annual precipitation in California (from Univ. Calif., 1960).

can be characterized by coastal summer fogs and cool oceanic air which often results in lower temperatures at elevations less than 3,000 feet and consequently somewhat higher mean temperatures at higher elevations. Winter rains range from over 100 inches on the northwest coast to less than 20 in east-facing rain shadows. Temperature is moderate but conditions become drier and warmer with increasing distance from the ocean. The growing season (mean temperature greater than 5.5 °C) varies from 90 days at 10,000 feet to 365 days at elevations lower than 1,500 feet. In the Klamath Mountains, the frostless season varies from 30 days at 8,000 feet to 270 days inland at sea level.

2.   The western slope of the Sierra Nevada carries woodland and ponderosa pine at low elevation, mixed conifer at mid-elevation, and true fir at high

elevation. This broad climatic region is characterized by hot, dry summers, especially at low elevation. Winter precipitation varies from about 30 to 70 inches with lesser amounts occurring in the southern Sierra and at lower elevations. In the northern part of this climatic region, the growing season varies from 90 days at 10,000 feet to 365 days at elevations lower than 1,500 feet. The frostless season varies from 30 days at 8,000 feet to 270 days inland at sea level. On the west slopes of the southern Sierra, the growing season varies from 135 days at 10,000 feet to 365 days at elevations lower than 1,800 feet. The frostless season varies from 30 days at 10,000 feet to 255 days inland at sea level.

3.   Northeastern California, with its east-side ponderosa pine forests at typical elevations of 4,000 feet, has summer temperatures similar to those on the west slope of the Sierra Nevada. However, mean winter temperatures are several degrees lower. The growing season is 200 days and the frostless period is 120 days.

4.   Southern California is characterized by oak woodlands, chaparral, and forests in the mountains which have a remarkably warm climate compared with that in the southern Sierra. Mean July temperatures range from 18 to 27 °C. Precipitation varies from 10 inches at sea level to 49 inches at 8,000 feet. The growing season is from 180 days at 10,000 feet to 365 days at elevations lower than 4,000 feet. The frostless season varies from 90 days at 10,000 feet to 365 days at sea level.

This variation in climate and soils associated with latitude and elevation produces distinctive vegetation which can be illustrated in three east-west transects across the state (Fig. 9-4 and Table 9-7).

The "typical" California climate of warm, dry summers without precipitation and cool, wet winters has considerable silvicultural significance, particularly with respect to regeneration. Because seedlings must survive the summer with the water that is stored in the soil after precipitation ends in April or May, it is most important that the potentially rapid growth of competing shrubs and grasses is controlled through good site preparation. This is particularly true at elevations above 3,000 to 4,000 feet where there is a period of only a few weeks in the spring between snow melt and the development of dry surface-soil conditions. The greatest cause of mortality in most areas, except perhaps the north coast, is the development of evaporative stress within the plant. Silviculturists therefore need to recognize this severe climatic constraint and its variation with slope and aspect when prescribing reproduction cuttings, site preparation, and methods of regeneration.

MAJOR FOREST TYPE GROUPS

Six type groups have been designated for the region: redwood, mixed conifer, true fir, ponderosa pine, California oak woodland, and California chaparral. The first three will be given principal coverage in this chapter.

TABLE 9-7

Vegetation Associations Along Three East-West Transects in California (Limited to Dominant Species that Show High Constancy Throughout the Type, and to Species of Particular Interest)

1. Alpine Fell-Fields
Carex helleri
Festuca brachyphylla
Poa rupicola
Luzula spicata
Oxyria digyna
Draba densifolia

2. Creosote Bush Scrub
Larrea divaricata
Franseria dumosa
Prosopis juliflora var. *glandulosa*

3. Closed-Cone Pine Forest
Pinus radiata
P. muricata
P. contorta

4. Chaparral
Adenostoma fasciculatum
Rhamnus crocea
Quercus dumosa
Ceanothus spp.
Arctostaphylos spp.
Pickeringia montana

5. Coastal Prairie
Festuca idahoensis
Danthonia californica
Calamagrostis nutkaensis ssp. *holciformis*

6. Coastal Sage Scrub
Artemisia californica
Salvia mellifera
Eriogonum fasciculatum

7. Coastal Strand
Artemisia pycnocephala
Franseria chamissonis
Lupinus arboreus
L. chamissonis
Abronia maritima
Atriplex leucophylla
Haplopappus ericoides
Mesembryanthemum nodiflorum

8. Douglas-fir Forest
Pseudotsuga menziesii
Lithocarpus densiflorus
Arbutus menziesii
Castanopsis chrysophylla

9. Foothill Woodland
Pinus sabiniana
Quercus douglasii
Aesculus californica
Ceanothus cuneatus

TABLE 9-7 (cont.)

Vegetation Associations Along Three East-West Transects in California (Limited to Dominant Species that Show High Constancy Throughout the Type, and to Species of Particular Interest)

10. Valley Grassland
Originally with various bunchgrasses such
as *Stipa pulchra*, *S. cernua*, *Poa scabrella*,
Aristida divaricata; now largely replaced by
annual species of *Bromus*, *Festuca*, *Avena*,
etc.

11. Joshua Tree Woodland
Yucca brevifolia and var. *jaegeriana*
Juniperus californica
   or *J. osteosperma* (*J. utahensis*)
Salazaria mexicana
Lycium andersonii

12. Lodgepole Forest
Pinus contorta
Tsuga mertensiana
Artemisia rothrockii

13. Mixed Evergreen Forest
Lithocarpus densiflorus
Arbutus menziesii
Castanopsis chrysophylla
Umbellularia californica
Acer macrophyllum
Quercus kelloggii
Pseudotsuga menziesii

14. North Coastal Coniferous Forest
Thuja plicata
Tsuga heterophylla
Picea sitchensis
Pseudotsuga menziesii
Abies grandis
Chamaecyparis lawsoniana

15. Northern Juniper Woodland
Juniperus occidentalus
Pinus jeffreyi
P. monophylla
Artemisia tridentata

16. Northern Oak Woodland
Quercus garryana
Q. kelloggii
Arctostaphylos manzanita

17. Northern Coastal Scrub
Baccharis pilularis
Mimulus aurantiacus
Rubus vitifolius

18. Pinon-Juniper Woodland
Juniperus californica
   or *J. osteosperma* (*J. utahensis*)
Purshia glandulosa

19. Red Fir Forest
Abies magnifica
Pinus monticola
Ceanothus cordulatus

20. Redwood Forest
Sequoia sempervirens
Lithocarpus densiflorus
Vaccinium ovatum
Oxalis oregona
Polystichum munitum

21. Subalpine Forest (northern)
Pinus albicaulis
P. contorta
Tsuga mertensiana
Pinus balfouriana[a]
P. flexilis[a]

22. Subalpine Forest (southern)
Pinus contorta
P. monticola
P. jeffreyi
Castanopsis sempervirens

25. Mixed Conifer Forest
Pinus ponderosa
P. lambertiana
Libocedrus decurrens
Abies concolor
Pseudotsuga menziesii
Quercus kelloggii
Sequoiadendron giganteum[a]

23. Southern Oak Woodland
Quercus agrifolia
Q. engelmannii
Juglans californica

24. Sagebrush Scrub
Artemisia tridentata
Chrysothamnus nauseosus ssp.
   speciosus and *mohavensis*

Source: Adapted from University California, 1960; and Munz and Keck, 1959.
[a] Occurs in Monterey-Yosemite transect only.

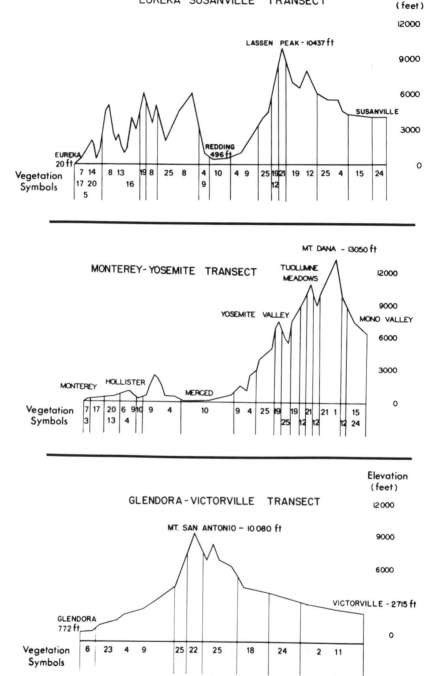

Figure 9-4. Three east-west transects across northern, central, and southern California showing the relationship between elevation and vegetation. Symbols for vegetation correspond to those in Table 9-7 (adapted from Univ. of Calif., 1960).

410

Ponderosa pine is given major treatment in Chapter 7. Although of minor commercial significance the last two groups are important in forest land management in the region.

HISTORY OF FOREST USE

The extent and character of California's commercial forest, and the silvicultural approaches that have developed, have been markedly influenced by the history of land use and the development of the state over the past century. The factors that have been particularly important in shaping California silviculture are the following:

1. Steep topography, high erosion hazard, and large trees, particularly on the north coast, have combined to present considerable technical difficulties in timber harvesting.

2. Extensive logging, particularly on private lands, has resulted in substantial areas that are currently understocked or converted to a dominant cover of hardwood. The most important species historically have been ponderosa pine and sugar pine in the Sierra Nevada. In the 1940s, logging emphasis shifted to northern California where the principal species harvested changed to Douglas-fir. Current forestry activities are in a transition from old-growth harvesting to young-growth management. Harvesting the overstory of intolerant old-growth has resulted in young-growth stands that commonly have a higher proportion of the more tolerant true firs, incense-cedar, and hardwoods than existed in the uncut stands. This change in stand composition has been aided by the absence, until recently, of any program of prescribed burning and artificial regeneration.

3. California forests have been subject to a continuing sequence of natural calamities resulting from insects, disease, weather, and fire.

4. Concerns with timber supply and conservation, and increases in stumpage values have contributed to making forest managers much more concerned with silvicultural questions of growing trees rather than simply harvesting them. This has ushered in an era of more sophisticated management involving the employment of a larger number of professional foresters.

5. The rapid buildup of population in the state has greatly increased both the demand for wood products and general concerns for the environment. However, despite the fact that the timber industry in California is the second largest in the nation, it is relatively small in comparison to the economic worth of agriculture and other industries in the state. Consequently, the political and business climate for forestry may not be as favorable as in some other regions.

6. The diverse needs of a large population for varied amenities from forest land have resulted in considerable withdrawals of acreage for wilderness,

parks, and other uses. Although this may, in the broad view, be desirable, the net result is a lowering of the base acreage from which the demand for timber can be met.

7. Over the past decade, a marked increase in public regulation of forest practices has resulted in more restrictive state forest practice rules and county ordinances with their requirements for environmental impact statements and standards of minimum acceptable practices.

These factors have generated incentives and pressures that have combined to increase the importance of silviculture in California forestry. One tangible outcome has been the U.S. Forest Service's program of certifying silviculturists. This has led to the development of silvicultural prescriptions which define the integration of treatments aimed at achieving specific management objectives, while recognizing ecological, managerial, and societal constraints.

SILVICULTURE OF THE MAJOR TYPE GROUPS

Redwood Type Group

The redwood type group extends as an almost continuous coastal belt 400 miles long and 5 to 35 miles wide. It ranges from the southwest corner of Oregon to southern Santa Cruz County in California with stringers occurring as far south as southern Monterey County (Roy, 1980; Bolsinger,[3]). Redwoods occur on about 1,600,000 acres with 114,000 acres in parks. About 650,000 acres of redwood forest land are classified as commercial (Bolsinger,[3]). About 34,000 acres of commercial redwood forest are in public ownership; 318,000 acres are owned by private timber-growing organizations; and 291,000 acres are owned by farmers and miscellaneous private owners (Table 9-2).

Place in Ecological Succession   The coast redwood forests are unique. They grow most vigorously in a cool, coastal belt where there is no large seasonal variation in temperatures because of summer fogs and winter and spring rain. They do not, however, tolerate strong winds or ocean salt. For silvicultural purposes the type can be separated into two distinct parts. First, the alluvial flats which support the magnificent pure stands of very tall redwoods at extremely high levels of basal area. These stands, most of which are now in parks, contain the world's tallest tree (367 feet) and produce accumulations of wood unequaled in any other place. The second kind of redwood forest is that which grows on the steep hillsides, commonly mixed with Douglas-fir, Sitka spruce, grand fir, western hemlock, western redcedar, and Port-Orford-cedar. These stands give way to Douglas-fir, hardwoods and finally to grassland-oak

[3]Information provided by Charles L. Bolsinger, Forest Resources Evaluation Unit, USDA Forest Service, Pacific Northwest Forest and Range Experiment Station, Portland, Oregon.

woodland mosaics as elevation and dryness increase eastward from the coast (Boe, 1973; Zinke, 1977).

Succession on alluvial flats starts following fire, logging, windthrow, or siltation after flooding. Swordfern, bracken fern, redwood sprouts, redwood seedlings, and numerous species of herbs constitute the initial vegetative community. *Baccharis* and *Rubus* species may also be present and, as succession develops, California laurel, grand fir, and other conifers become associated. As the stand develops, the rapidly growing redwood sprouts dominate and their capacity for developing high densities when young-growth shades out most other species except for the very tolerant. Most existing stands on the alluvial flats are about 800 years old although redwood may grow vigorously for 2,000 years.

A characteristic of the alluvial flats is the periodic flooding which deposits layers of silt throughout the stand. This silt layer assists in the maintenance of pure stands by killing understory vegetation and other conifers by burying their root systems. Redwood is not killed by siltation and in fact benefits from it because the species has the remarkable capacity to grow rootlets vertically into the newly deposited silt layer and also to send out a new root system from the stem. Each flooding and silting therefore gives rise to a new root system and the burying of the stem at ground level results in the trees lacking the obvious buttswell that is common to other large trees.

On the hillsides where redwood occurs with a mixture of other conifers and hardwoods, succession begins after disturbance with sprouts of tanoak, redwood, and Pacific madrone plus seedlings of Douglas-fir and ephemeral herbaceous species such as fireweed. Sprouting hardwoods often dominate the site initially but after 70 to 80 years the hardwoods are overtopped by redwood and Douglas-fir (Zinke, 1977).

Growth Rates.   Growth on redwood sites is rapid, as is shown by the site index curves in Fig. 9-5 and by the yields shown in Table 9-8. Basal area in unmanaged stands reaches 1,000 square feet per acre and yield tables indicate that net volume production on the highest sites (site index 240) at a stocking level of 400 square feet per acre can reach the phenomenal rate of 1,400 cubic feet per acre per year at the age of 10 years (Lindquist and Palley, 1967). At age 100 years, on the highest sites, stands at basal area levels of 400 and 900 square feet per acre still have net 10-year periodic annual increments of 354 and 656 cubic feet per acre per year, respectively.

Cultural Practices.   Redwoods have been extensively harvested since the mid 1800s both for wood products and in order to convert the rich lands to agriculture. Because of redwood's sprouting capacity, much of the logged and burned land, and abandoned pasture and crop lands now carry excellent stands of young-growth redwood. Redwood lumber, especially from old-growth, is highly prized for exterior siding, sills, garden furniture, and decking because of

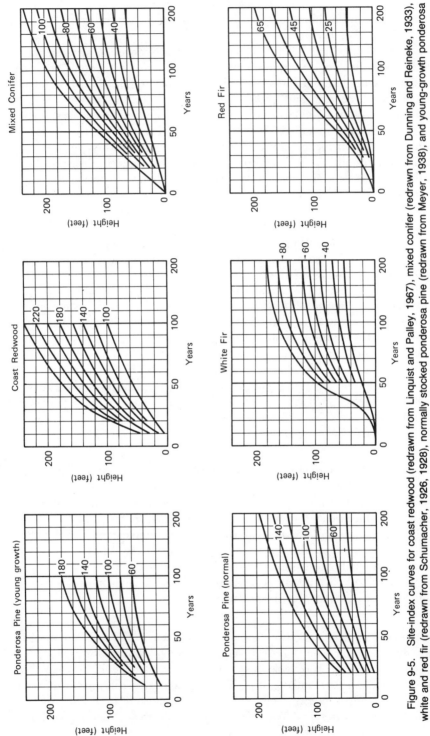

Figure 9-5. Site-index curves for coast redwood (redrawn from Linquist and Palley, 1967), mixed conifer (redrawn from Dunning and Reineke, 1933), white and red fir (redrawn from Schumacher, 1926, 1928), normally stocked ponderosa pine (redrawn from Meyer, 1938), and young-growth ponderosa pine (redrawn from Arvanitas et al., 1964).

TABLE 9-8

Yields of Young-Growth Coast Redwood (Cubic Feet per Acre) of Trees Larger than
4.5 Inches d.b.h. to a 4-Inch Top

Age (Years)	Site Index at 100 Years							
	100	120	140	160	180	200	220	240
20	200	450	1,000	2,270	3,990	5,910	7,860	9,940
30	500	1,050	2,500	4,400	7,040	10,000	13,000	16,200
40	1,000	2,300	4,500	7,250	10,550	14,250	18,000	22,000
50	2,100	3,800	6,800	10,100	14,060	18,500	23,000	27,800
60	3,600	5,820	9,220	12,960	17,450	22,480	27,580	33,020
70	5,200	8,000	11,750	15,880	20,820	26,380	32,000	38,000
80	6,900	10,140	14,190	18,640	23,990	29,980	36,060	42,540
90	8,800	12,260	16,580	21,340	27,050	33,450	39,940	46,860
100	10,600	14,280	18,880	23,940	30,010	36,820	43,720	51,080

Source: Lindquist and Palley, 1963.

its resistance to decay. Somewhat surprisingly, lumber from young-growth is commanding exceptionally high prices for use in those same products.

HARVESTING. Most of the harvesting of redwood has been in old-growth stands. This has been a formidable engineering task because of the immense size of the trees (over 6 feet d.b.h. and 200 feet in height is common), the steepness of the slopes, and the fact that "beds" of mounded soil must be provided to reduce stem breakage on felling. The commonly used approach has been clearcutting because in some areas selective cutting of these tall trees at high stocking levels resulted in severe windthrow of residual trees and in epicormic branching. Clearcutting, particularly in redwood stands carrying enormous volumes per acre (20,000 to 400,000 cubic feet per acre), often resulted in an appearance of gross devastation. Despite the technical correctness of the method from the standpoints of harvesting and obtaining prompt regeneration, the public outcry against the practice encouraged managers to limit the size of clearcut blocks and to use the selection method if possible. This method, however, creates future problems in hillside stands that have an understory of tanoak and Pacific madrone because the treatment tends to release the understory. This has been shown to be the case in hillside stands that were partially logged in the early 1900s and now have an abundance of hardwoods. In using the selection method, undesirable species must be controlled. If herbicides cannot be used for this purpose, control will be both expensive and difficult. The situation would change if the smaller diameter hardwoods could be economically utilized.

Control of soil disturbance and surface runoff is of major concern on the steep and unstable hillsides. Soils in this area have a natural tendency to slump when saturated with water, and in these high-rainfall areas it is important that silvicultural treatments do not compound this problem by inappropriate road construction, skidding, and site preparation practices.

REGENERATION.   Natural regeneration of redwood from seed is limited because of three factors. First, the quantity of seed produced is variable among trees and stands; with some trees failing to produce any seed at all unless considerable disturbance occurs at their base (Muelder and Hansen, 1961a). Second, redwood seed has characteristically low viability (less than 10 percent). Third, on undisturbed sites, redwood germinants are especially susceptible to death from root rot and damping-off fungi that are present in the litter (Muelder and Hansen, 1961b). No redwood reproduction is found in these undisturbed stands. However, freshly deposited silt from flooding on alluvial flats provides a medium that is relatively free from soil pathogens, permitting successful establishment of natural redwood regneration.

The amount of redwood being planted is increasing, particularly using stock grown in containers. When planting redwood, it must be remembered that trees are being established which will reproduce themselves vegetatively by sprouting for many generations. Consequently, particular care must be exercised in selecting seed from the most desirable, locally adapted genotypes. Because planted redwoods constitute the center of a future clump, initial spacing is likely to be at least 16 to 20 feet with other conifers planted between if higher initial stocking is desired. Important new approaches to planting with superior stock include the use of rooted cuttings and plants developed from tissue culture. These approaches are not yet operational but are at an advanced stage of experimentation.

Regeneration in the redwood type is generally assured because most harvested redwoods sprout from both stumps and roots. To ensure that stump sprouts have a straight base and are windfirm, it is preferable to keep stump height as low as possible. After harvest the stump becomes surrounded with a large number of sprouts which intially grow 10 to 15 feet in height in the first three years, after which growth slows down. Experiments in thinning 4- to 5-year-old sprouts on old-growth redwood stumps have shown that 5 years after heavy thinning, sprout diameter nearly doubled (Boe, 1974). As the sprouts develop, mortality is rapid, causing a marked reduction in number. The remaining sprouts continue to grow rapidly for several decades but by age 50 to 60 years, on good sites, young Douglas-fir which regenerated from seed immediately after harvest, commonly has equivalent height. Since costs are high, there is a trend to planting rather than seeding.

INTERMEDIATE TREATMENTS.   One of the treatments of most concern is precommercial thinning. Extensive areas on the coast which were regenerated by a combination of sprouting, natural seeding, and aerial seeding are overstocked. So, interest in the costs and benefits of precommercial thinning is increasing.

Commercial thinning in young-growth stands is increasing as light cable harvesting equipment becomes available. Because of stump and root sprouting, young-growth redwood trees characteristically occur in clumps. Thus in tree marking, the silviculturist is actually managing clumps rather than individual trees.

SILVICULTURAL SYSTEMS

Alluvial Flats: Pure redwood stands with little or no woody shrubs in the understory can be managed under even- or uneven-aged systems. Clearcutting would be the logical even-aged system to use because of the relative ease of slash disposal and prompt regeneration from stump sprouts. Some difficulty may be experienced in controlling stocking as distribution of redwood regeneration will be determined by the distribution of the cut redwood stumps. Also, regulating stocking may involve interplanting and precommercial thinning. The effects of commercial thinning even-aged redwood stands are still not well known. If a light, low thinning is done, sprouting is less abundant and less vigorous and probably would not develop as a significant understory. However, a thinning which opens up the canopy generally results in vigorous sprouting which should then develop as a younger-age class. Successive thinnings from above would then be likely to result in a change to an uneven-aged structure.

Neither the seed-tree nor the shelterwood system is advisable due to the unpredictability of seed crops, low viability, and because shelter is not needed to enhance sprout development.

Uneven-aged stands of redwood can be developed by both single-tree and group-selection systems. The tolerance and sprouting characteristics of redwood make selection systems a good choice, particularly in visually-sensitive areas.

Hillside Stands: On hillsides where redwood is mixed with associated conifers, hardwoods, and woody shrubs, the system chosen can still be either even- or uneven-aged. Clearcutting permits easier site preparation, slash disposal, and control of species composition and stocking. Seed-tree and shelterwood systems can be used to facilitate regeneration of species other than redwood, but site preparation and slash disposal are more difficult to accomplish without damaging residual trees. Also, precommercial thinning will probably be necessary in these naturally regenerated stands.

Uneven-aged systems of single-tree and group selection can be employed but site preparation, slash disposal, fire hazard reduction, control of species composition, and harvesting are more difficult.

Silvicultural systems, however, are not selected entirely on the basis of biological or managerial considerations. Social concerns are equally important. An example is the development of county ordinances in the highly populated San Franciso peninsula. These ordinances have been designed to restrict forest practices to a greater degree than the State Forest Practices Act in recognition of the urbanized nature of the forests and associated conservation values. Restrictions on the management of redwood stands include minimum stocking standards, a prohibition of clearcutting, a minimum diameter of 12 inches below which trees may not be thinned, and limitations on harvesting to 60 percent of the standing volume over 18 inches d.b.h. These regulations, therefore, preclude precommercial thinning as a treatment to improve stand quality, and oblige the manager to adopt the selection system of management. In the well-stocked, 50-year-old redwood stands that occur in this area, silviculturally sound prescriptions leading to the management of uneven-aged stands currently include: the maintenance of basal area between 275 and 375 square feet per acre, residual growing stock levels of 5,800 cubic feet per acre, and maximum tree size at time of harvest of about 32 inches d.b.h. With this prescription, expected yields are about 330 cubic feet per acre.

Susceptibility to Damage   Coast redwood is relatively free from insect and disease pests. Of the few that do some damage are the heart rots *Poria sequoiae* and *P. albipellucida* which appear to enter the stem through fire scars, and the redwood bark beetle which attacks weakened, felled, or fire-scorched trees.

Mixed-Conifer Type Group

This type, formerly described as the ponderosa pine−sugar pine−fir type (Soc. Am. For. 1954) and now the Sierra Nevada Mixed-Conifer Type (Soc. Am. For. 1980), occurs principally on east-facing slopes of the Coast Range and west-facing slopes of the Sierra Nevada at elevations from 3,000 to 6,000 feet (Fig. 9-6). It occupies about 13.6 million acres making it the largest single vegetation type in California (Barbour and Major, 1977). About 7.8 million acres of the type are classified as commercial forest.

Place in Ecological Succession.   The type consists of California white fir, ponderosa and sugar pine, incense-cedar, California black oak, and Douglas-fir in variable mixtures or in small groups of single species (Tappeiner, 1980). Hardwood associates are Pacific madrone, tanoak, golden chinkapin and Pacific dogwood. Mixed-conifer forests occur as a distinct and major type between the Pacific ponderosa pine type at lower elevations and the true-fir forests at higher elevations. The proportion of species in the type varies with ponderosa pine and incense-cedar predominating at lower elevation and on warmer, south-facing slopes, and with California white fir predominating at higher elevation and on cooler, north-facing slopes. Douglas-fir and California black oak generally occur at mid-elevation throughout the type. Sugar pine is most common on more mesic, higher-quality sites. Jeffrey pine is often an associate at upper elevations and also occurs on serpentine soils. California red fir may occur in the mixture at extreme upper elevations and in cold-air drainages (Tappeiner, 1980). An occasional associate is giant sequoia which occurs to a very limited extent in 75 small groves, most of which are reserved from harvesting.

Figure 9-6.   Mixed-conifer type group (P. M. McDonald, USDA For. Serv., Pacific Southwest Exp. Stn.).

The mixed-conifer forest has played an important role in California forestry since the gold rush period of the 1850s. The most utilized species were ponderosa pine and sugar pine which were extracted by oxen, "donkey" engines, and flumes. One of these flumes was about 50 miles long and served five sawmills, all owned by the same company. Later, these methods were replaced by railroad, steam tractors, and then by caterpillar tractors, and the species exploited were broadened to include Douglas-fir, incense-cedar, and California white fir. A century of selective cutting, combined with a fire-exclusion policy, has resulted in a mixed-conifer forest with a much higher proportion of California white fir and incense-cedar than existed in the original stands. Fortunately, industry is utilizing these previously undesirable species and, currently, the value of young-growth sawtimber is tending to be similar for all species.

Shade tolerance of the species overlaps with ponderosa pine and California black oak being most intolerant, sugar pine and Douglas-fir intermediate, and California white fir most tolerant. Incense-cedar is difficult to classify and has a wide range of shade tolerance. Succession within the mixed-conifer type varies with original stand composition, associated species, and type of disturbance, particularly fire and insects (Rundel et al., 1977; Tappeiner, 1980). Fire and logging have commonly begun a successional sequence starting with

Ceanothus, Arctostaphylos, and *Prunus* species. These shrub species rapidly dominate the site and persist for several decades until tolerant white fir and other conifers break through the shrub canopy. Once the conifers form an overstory, the shrubs lose vigor and form a minor component of the understory. Ponderosa pine, sugar pine, and to some extent Douglas-fir will only become a significant part of the new stand if seeds of those species fall into the area within one to two years after disturbance.

Two ground-cover species are of particular importance in influencing the success of natural conifer establishment. These are squaw carpet and bear-clover. Both species have deep root systems and rapidly deplete the soil of available moisture during the summer. Conifer seedlings cannot become established in competition with bear-clover whereas squaw carpet seems to favor survival of conifer seedlings by maintaining an apparently more favorable microclimate immediately above the mats (Tappeiner and Helms, 1971).

Growth Rates.   Site productivity and yield can be estimated by using site index curves that have been developed for unmanaged stands on the west slope of the Sierra Nevada (Fig. 9-5 and Table 9-9). Desired stocking at a given age will vary depending on whether the stand in question has a higher proportion of intolerant pine or tolerant fir. Guidelines have been developed by the U.S.

TABLE 9-9

Yields of Unmanaged Mixed Conifer (Cubic Feet per Acre) Including Trees 2 Inches d.b.h. and Over

Age	Site Index at 100 years									
(years)	25	30	40	50	60	70	80	90	100	110
30	930	1,060	1,420	1,800	2,200	2,650	3,200	3,770	4,380	4,850
40	1,590	1,800	2,410	3,090	3,770	4,550	5,500	6,500	7,450	8,450
50	2,260	2,590	3,480	4,440	5,420	6,560	7,940	9,300	10,700	12,000
60	2,950	3,350	4,510	5,790	7,020	8,550	10,300	12,100	13,900	15,500
70	3,500	4,000	5,350	6,850	8,450	10,200	12,200	14,300	16,500	18,400
80	4,000	4,540	6,100	7,800	9,520	11,500	13,800	16,200	18,600	20,900
90	4,420	5,000	6,750	8,600	10,500	12,700	15,200	17,800	20,700	23,100
100	4,830	5,500	7,400	9,450	11,500	13,900	16,600	19,500	22,600	25,200
110	5,200	5,950	8,000	10,200	12,300	14,900	17,900	21,000	24,250	27,200
120	5,600	6,390	8,550	10,800	13,200	16,000	19,100	22,500	26,000	29,000
130	5,900	6,700	9,050	11,500	14,000	16,900	20,300	24,000	27,500	30,700
140	6,220	7,070	9,550	12,100	14,750	17,750	21,400	25,200	29,000	32,400
150	6,550	7,430	10,000	12,700	15,450	18,550	22,400	26,400	30,400	34,000

Source: Dunning and Reineke, 1933.

Forest Service (Table 9-10), based on the growth of natural unmanaged stands, which show the maximum and desired levels of stocking. Table 9-10 shows the extent to which stocking increases with the proportion of true fir in the mixed-conifer stand. It also permits comparisons to be made among other forest types in the Sierra Nevada. Plantations and precommercially thinned stands will undoubtedly require a lower stocking than those illustrated in Table 9-10. In general, it is expected that today's young-growth stands on better sites will be managed to maintain stocking levels of about 150 to 300 square feet of basal area per acre, residual stocking levels of about 4,000 cubic feet per acre, with the expectation of producing about 150 to 200 cubic feet per acre per year.

Cultural Practices. Silvicultural prescriptions must be based on the existing characteristics of specific groups of vegetation. It is not possible to identify a single best approach to the silviculture of this type because of the great diversity in stand structure, composition, and management objectives. The mixed-conifer forest has extreme variability in stocking, varying from openings to dense groups of trees that have basal areas of about 350 square feet per acre or more. Within these groups, live crown ratios are commonly less than 30 percent. Because of this great variability in stocking, stands are generally slow-growing relative to their potential.

HARVESTING.   Typically, private timber companies with extensive lands are currently practicing a type of uneven-aged management. Their harvest cuttings are generally relatively light with emphasis on removing decadent trees and overmature old growth. Regeneration is either assured by the presence of advanced growth, or is obtained by natural seeding or planting. The U.S. Forest Service has a general policy of even-aged management in its "standard forest zone" and in the mixed-conifer forest their harvests usually utilize (1) small clearcuttings 15 to 35 acres in size; (2) sanitation harvests to remove residual old growth or diseased, suppressed, or poor-formed young growth; or (3) overstory removal where the harvesting of overmature timber in a two-or-more-storied stand releases the understory of immature trees which becomes the next crop. At this initial stage of management, stands are commonly dense and beyond the age when rapid response to release might be expected.

Salvage cutting has been important in mixed-conifer forests to harvest mortality (1.2 billion board feet annually) from overmaturity, insects, and disease. An extreme situation occurred in 1976–1977 where, after the major drought, the volume of mortality over a 2½-year period was estimated to be about 8.6 billion board feet. The salvage of this enormous volume constitutes a major problem and some of it will probably be lost due to difficulties of access, the economics of logging, and low volumes per acre.

REGENERATION.   In overstocked stands that are selectively harvested, no additional regeneration is immediately desired. Clearcutting of small groups of even-aged overmature trees is usually followed by planting. The most common species planted is ponderosa pine, partly because of its historical importance,

TABLE 9-10

Maximum and Desired Basal Area Stocking by Stand Age and Working Group

Basal Area (Square Feet)

Age	Red Fir		Ponderosa Pine		Subalpine		Mixed Conifer[a]			
							Pines		Fir	
	Desired	Maximum	Desired	Maximum	Desired	Maximum	Desired	Maximum	Desired	Maximum
50	130	250	150	226	100	185	160	230	190	265
60	165	290	155	228	125	215	180	248	230	319
70	190	325	160	228	140	240	195	264	265	360
80	210	355	165	228	155	250	205	277	285	387
90	235	380	170	228	170	265	210	288	300	394
100	260	400	175	228	180	285	215	298	300	397
110	275	425	175	228	180	300	215	305	300	400
120	290	440	175	228	180	310	215	312	300	400
130	305	460	175	228	180	320	215	319	300	400

140	320	470	175	228	180	325	215	324	300	400
150	330	480	175	228	180	325	215	329	300	400
160	335	485	180	228	180	325	215	333	300	400
170	335	490	180	228	185	325	210	336	290	400
180	335	495	180	228	185	325	210	338	280	400
190	335	500	180	228	185	325	210	339	280	400
200	340	505	180	228	185	325	210	340	280	400
210	340	505	175	228	185	325	210	340	280	400
220	340	510	175	228	185	325	210	340	280	400
230	340	510	175	228	185	325	210	340	280	400
240	345	510	170	228	185	325	210	340	280	400
250	345	515	170	228	185	325	210	340	280	400

Source: Data from: USDA, 1973, Timber Management Plan, Period 1973–1982.
a The desirable and maximum stocking levels rise with the amount of white fir in a stand. The pine and fir columns represent the limits for stands of nearly pure pines (ponderosa and sugar) vs stands of nearly pure white fir. Growth and yield projections were based on pine stocking levels. A preponderance of pines would be expected under intensive management because of their apparent successional nature in the mixed-conifer type.

and partly because it has high survival on exposed sites. Douglas-fir and sugar pine planting has also been successful on mesic sites. On small areas, single-species plantations will not remain pure but will become mixed with mostly California white fir and incense-cedar by seeding-in from the sides. Some planting is also being done with white fir but survival of this species currently varies between 40 to 80 percent.

A major regeneration concern is the restocking of areas burned by wildfires which are frequent in the mixed-conifer type. These areas are usually planted with ponderosa pine. Planting of burned areas, plus the conversion of old brush fields, has resulted in over 500,000 acres of ponderosa pine plantations in California, most of which are in the mixed-conifer and ponderosa pine types.

The most important consideration in planning for regeneration in the mixed-conifer forest is recognition of the annual summer drought in prescribing site preparation. The most common cause of seedling mortality is lack of available soil moisture. Silvicultural prescriptions, therefore, should recognize exposed areas where special attention must be paid to considerations of water relations and shade. Soil moisture availability is enhanced by removing competing vegetation, and this treatment generally results in satisfactory survival although it increases evaporative stress on regeneration.

The methods chosen for reproduction cutting will have considerable influence on resulting regeneration. In general, the more shade and cover left after harvest, the higher the proportion of California white fir and incense-cedar in the mix of regeneration. For the principal species of conifers, shrubs, and hardwoods, seedling height growth increases as the intensity of cutting method increases from single-tree selection to clearcutting (McDonald, 1976). The importance of choice of method of slash disposal will also have an effect on regeneration by influencing the kind and degree of shrub competition. For example, areas which have been mechanically windrowed have resulted in a cover dominated by sprouting manzanita, whereas adjacent areas which were broadcast burned have become densely covered mainly with Ceanothus due to the differential effect of fire in stimulating the germination of their seeds. Studies in the Sierra Nevada have shown that the duff and soil under virgin, largely overmature stands have almost 3 million viable seeds per acre of shrubs, grass and assorted dicotyledonous plants (Quick, 1956; Gordon, 1980). Because the mature stands sampled were up to 300 years of age, it can be seen that shrub seeds can remain viable in the soil and duff for exceedingly long periods of time. Even though shrubs may not currently occur in a stand, site preparation treatments, particularly those using fire, can stimulate their seed germination and lead to development of a considerable shrub cover.

An extensive analysis of natural regeneration by Fowells and Stark (1965) has shown that cutworms and drought are the most important causes of first-year mortality (Table 9-11). Losses from drought on south slopes were 50 percent on uncut areas, but only 23 percent on clearcut areas due primarily to higher available soil moisture. After eight years, total height of ponderosa pine averaged 50 inches on clearcut south slopes but only 5 inches in the partially cut

TABLE 9-11

Percent of First-Year Seedlings Killed, by Species and by Cause of Mortality,
Stanislaus-Tuolumne Experimental Forest, 1935–1942

Species	Cause of Mortality						
	Frost	Rodent	Insect	Fungi	Heat	Drought	Miscellaneous
Ponderosa pine	1.3	7.3	29.4	1.6	0.5	27.8	4.8
Sugar pine	8.0	5.1	9.9	0.2	0.0	28.8	5.1
White fir	9.9	8.3	30.7	4.0	0.0	25.1	10.8
Incense-cedar	2.4	4.8	52.0	3.1	0.0	19.8	6.2

Source: Fowells and Stark, 1965.

north slope. On uncut areas, growth of pine seedlings was negligible and survival of both incense-cedar and California white fir was too poor to provide an estimate of height growth. Despite the typical 4-month summer drought in the Sierra Nevada, it can be concluded that soil moisture is nearly always available to seedlings, provided that competition from other plants is minimized. Natural regeneration, therefore, is an appropriate silvicultural option, especially if seedfall coincides with site preparation or if competition from hardwoods and shrubs can be reduced by a combination of shade and site preparation. However, removal of the overstory is essential to enable adequate height growth of all species once the seedlings are established.

INTERMEDIATE TREATMENTS. Plantations of ponderosa pine in California often grow well. However, in those instances where a cover of aggressive shrub species develops, extreme competition for soil moisture during the dry summer months can lead to virtual stagnation in height growth. Silvicultural prescriptions must therefore include follow-up release treatments to ensure satisfactory stand development. This is particularly true on old burns, or after site preparation by broadcast burning, where fire has stimulated a dense cover of shrubs from stored seeds. Release should be planned for at the time of regeneration and is usually needed at least once to ensure satisfactory plantation establishment.

Intermediate cuttings can be made in young even-aged groups which are 50 to 100 years of age. This practice is not common in stands at the lower end of this age range because older-aged stands predominate. The primary objectives of intermediate cuttings are to harvest potential mortality and to control species composition. Reentries are recommended at about 10-year intervals.

Historically, fire has played an important role in the mixed-conifer type. Many small fires with a 4- to 20-year frequency, kept the forest open and helped maintain a mosaic of vegetation. With fire exclusion, California white fir and incense-cedar were encouraged, canopies tended to close, shrubs and herbs declined, and intense fires were encouraged due to buildup of fuels. In unmanaged stands 60 to 100 years of age, mean fuel weight of down material varies considerably but is commonly between 25 to 150 tons per acre depending upon elevation and species mix. This fuel loading is significantly increased by slash produced after harvesting. Prescribed burning is receiving increased attention due to its beneficial effects of reducing fire hazard, in site preparation for both planting and natural regeneration, and in providing better food and habitat for herbivores. There is also some evidence that prescribed burning may assist in controlling dwarf mistletoe and insects such as the cone midge. Prescribed fire must be used with considerable care because young stands less than about 20 years of age are susceptible to damage. In young stands, thin bark and foliage reaching to the ground provides a "fuel ladder" for fire to extend into the tree crowns. Thrifty sugar pine and California white fir stands up to about 80 years of age can be severely degraded if fire damage causes infection points for stem decay. The effects of prescribed fire, however, are usually controlled by selecting between spring and fall burns, and by carefully prescribing the weather and fuel moisture conditions for the burn.

Tree-improvement programs are in progress in California, sponsored primarily by the U.S. Forest Service (Kitzmiller, 1976) with additional programs developed by cooperative agreements between the State Department of Forestry and private industry. Major effort is being placed on Douglas-fir and ponderosa pine with lesser effort on other species. Considerable work has been done in attempting to breed sugar pine that has resistance to white pine blister rust which became established in California in 1930. The rust is of considerable importance in the northern, moister part of the state. Research has identified a type of resistance controlled by a single dominant gene. Breeding programs are being developed to exploit this resistance as well as to developing a broader genetic base of resistance controlled by polygenes (Kinloch, 1976).

SILVICULTURAL SYSTEMS.   The mixed-conifer forest is a highly productive type and its diversity and complexity make it especially attractive for multiple use. The structure of mixed-conifer forests is essentially uneven-aged but the stands commonly consist of small even-aged groups. Occasionally, relatively even-aged stands occur. Management can therefore tend to enhance the even- or uneven-aged nature of stands depending on management objectives and silvicultural practices. Probably all silvicultural systems are applicable to the mixed-conifer type. In fact, on any one forest it is likely that a variety of systems will be utilized in different locations depending upon topography, aspect, site, current stand condition, and management goals.

Within uneven-aged harvesting methods it is apparent that individual-tree selection often creates conditions unfavorable to natural regeneration as even the tolerant fir has difficulty in becoming established. Group selection should be used, with the size of the group being between one to two times the height of the residual stand depending upon whether a higher proportion of tolerant or intolerant species is desired to be regenerated. Frequently, on high-quality sites, noncommercial Pacific madrone, tanoak or shrub species may become established after group or single-tree selection cutting. On such sites it will be difficult to maintain stocking of commercial species without labor-intensive practices such as hand-weeding, or spot-spraying or injecting with herbicide. Another problem in maintaining uneven-aged stands is that it is very difficult to control the accumulation of fuels and to use prescribed burning without damaging reproduction.

Clearcutting in mixed-conifer forests can be followed by planting of single species or mixtures, and if the clearcut blocks are small, considerable seeding-in will occur from adjoining stands. The even-aged condition can be maintained by intermediate treatments, or uneven-agedness can be developed permitting natural conifer seedlings to become established among the planted stock. Clearcutting has the advantage that it enables a more feasible control of competing shrubs and hardwoods, and facilitates reduction of fuels from slash compared with other silvicultural systems.

Susceptibility to Damage. Forest pests in the mixed-conifer forest include insects, diseases, animals, and weeds. The important insect and disease pests that cause damage to ponderosa pine and true-fir trees are discussed in those sections of this chapter that deal with these vegetation types. Blister rust has been mentioned earlier in this chapter. Principal insect pests of Douglas-fir in California include the western spruce budworm which is an important defoliator, the Douglas-fir beetle, which attacks weakened trees and, when epidemic, can kill apparently healthy trees on extensive areas, the fir engraver beetle which attacks thin-barked young trees, tops of older trees, and fresh slash from logging, windthrow and snow breakage, and the fir flatheaded borer. Several diseases are prevalent which will either kill or weaken the trees thus pre-disposing them to insect attack. Important diseases on Douglas-fir include dwarf mistletoe, the root diseases *Fomes annosus*, black stain fungus, and shoestring fungus, the heart-rot fungus red ring rot, and red-brown butt rot. Incense-cedar is attacked by cedar bark beetles and by *Fomes annosus*, shoestring fungus, true mistletoe, and pocket dry rot. In addition to these pests, trees in mixed-conifer forests are subject to other insects and diseases that attack cones, seeds, and seedlings.

Silvicultural practices aimed at maintaining vigorous stands can reduce considerably the potential impact of insect pests. Stands should be thinned to prevent overstocking, and Dunning's tree class or Keen's risk-rating systems (Daniel *et al.*, 1979) are used to identify high-risk trees which should be removed.

Animal pests vary from depradations on seeds by birds, chipmunks and squirrels, to bark-stripping, girdling and cutting by small rodents, pocket gophers, porcupines, bears, and deer. The impact of animals is particularly important to reproduction. Gophers are of particular importance, especially in the true firs, as they can destroy plantations of 1- to 10-feet-tall trees.

True-Fir Type Group

The true-fir forests were previously described as part of the pine-Douglas-fir type; now, because of their increased importance they are described as a separate type. They occur primarily at high elevation in the Sierra Nevada and also in the northwestern portion of the Coast Range. At lower elevations near 5,500 feet, the true-fir forest grades into the mixed-conifer type and thus has a preponderance of California white fir. At higher elevation, from 6,500 to 8,000 feet, the type has an increased proportion of California and Shasta red fir, which grows in characteristically dense, even-aged stands. Associated species at high elevation include members of the California mixed subalpine forest type (Soc. Am. For. 1980). The area of true-fir forest classified as commercial is 3,751,000 acres or about 23 percent of the total commercial forest area in California (Table 9-2). In the early 1960s, the true-fir forests had almost no economic value. They had obvious value as watersheds and for recreation, but their wood was not considered desirable. As a result of the recent recognition of commercial importance of the firs, little experience has been obtained in developing true-fir management systems.

Place in Ecological Succession. The true-fir forests are regarded as climax. Daniel *et al.* (1979) rank white fir as tolerant and red fir as intermediate in tolerance. Typically, wildfires have begun successional development by creating brushfields which overtop and suppress the growth of California white fir reproduction for several decades. The long-term viability of seeds of pioneer wood and herbaceous species was discussed in connection with the mixed-conifer type. Characteristic woody shrubs include mountain whitethorn, greenleaf manzanita, roundleaf snowberry, snowbrush, Sierra gooseberry, Sierra chinkapin, pinemat manzanita, and sticky currant. Associated conifers at lower elevations include those of the mixed-conifer forest. Successional development leading to California red fir is slower because of the shorter growing season at higher elevation and the inherently slow fir seedling growth rate.

At higher elevations, red fir associates are Jeffrey and western white pine, with lodgepole pine occurring locally in areas with a high water table or near streams and meadows. Mountain hemlock, whitebark pine, limber pine and subalpine fir become associated at the upper elevations. True-fir stands are commonly pure and even-aged with California white fir characteristically being able to persist, and eventually grow through dense shrub understories. Natural openings are common and are filled with lupine and other forbs which are prime habitat for endemic populations of gophers. Stands of California red fir are typically so dense as to preclude the development of an understory. When overmature, these stands become quite defective due to lack of vigor and damage from insects, disease, and storms. As overmature California red fir stands break up, groups of red fir reproduction (0.1 to 0.5 acre) may occur in the openings. Although California red and white fir stands may mix intimately, there is no known occurrence of hybridization.

Growth Rates. Growth and yield of true-fir forests are truly impressive. Site index curves for normally stocked stands of California white and red fir are shown in Fig. 9-5. A comparison of these curves shows that early height growth of white fir is quite slow, probably because many white fir stands grew slowly through a dense cover of shrubs or in an understory. Height development of both species in managed plantations will undoubtedly be superior to that from unmanaged stands. Yield for unmanaged stands of white and red fir can be compared in Tables 9-12(a) and 9-12(b). These tables indicate that, at the same age and site, red fir can produce twice as much volume per acre as white fir (3,190 cubic feet per acre for red fir compared with 1,360 cubic feet per acre for white fir at age 150 years on site index 60).

Cultural Practices

HARVESTING. Mature true-fir forests often have a basal area of 500 square feet per acre. Stands of this size and density are most easily harvested by some form of clearcutting. This not only facilitates felling and slash disposal but also enhances snow accumulation and water yield. Clearcutting also results in less windthrow than does partial cutting and is desirable where dwarf mistletoe is prevalent in the mature stand. If strip clearcutting is used, the strips should be oriented perpendicular to prevailing winds and limited to 150 to 200 feet in width. Where blocks are prescribed, these should not exceed 200 to 250 feet in diameter (Gordon, 1970). Shelterwoods leaving 10, 20, and 30 windfirm trees per acre with good site preparation have resulted in 6,000 to 25,000 seedlings per acre six years after harvest. The higher number of sheltering trees per acre may not necessarily result in a higher number of established seedlings. However, a large seedling number would not generally be desirable as it could result in slower seedling growth and increased need for precommercial thinning. As noted earlier, where natural openings have occurred in mature true-fir stands, it is common to find abundant regeneration. This indicates that selection cutting, particularly by groups, should be a successful harvesting method leading to natural regeneration, providing adequate site preparation is done.

REGENERATION. White fir produces seed every 1 to 4 years with a heavy crop every 3 to 9 years. Good red fir seed crops occur every 2 to 3 years. Seeding is also prolific with up to 600,000 sound seeds falling per acre in a good year. This abundance of seed facilitates the prompt establishment of dense, even-aged stands following disturbance or site preparation, providing the area does not become dominated first by shrubs. It is commonly regarded that natural regeneration is readily attained in the true-fir type, providing site preparation coincides with a good seed crop. Recent work has shown, however, that the abundance of established seedlings in shelterwood cuttings appears to be independent of the extent of the seed crop in surrounding stands.[4] The size

[4]R. J. Laacke, USDA Forest Service, Pacific Southwest Forest and Range Experiment Station, personal correspondence.

TABLE 9-12

Yields in Cubic Feet per Acre

(a) White Fir, 4 Inches d.b.h. and Over

Age (Years)	Site Index at 50 Years						
	30	40	50	60	70	80	90
50	2,150	2,700	3,800	5,300	6,700	8,100	9,000
60	3,000	3,800	5,300	7,400	9,400	11,400	12,600
70	3,600	4,500	6,400	9,000	11,400	13,700	15,200
80	4,000	5,000	7,100	10,000	12,700	15,200	16,900
90	4,300	5,500	7,700	10,800	13,700	16,600	18,400
100	4,600	5,800	8,200	11,500	14,600	17,600	19,600
110	4,800	6,100	8,600	12,000	15,400	18,500	20,500
120	5,000	6,350	8,900	12,500	15,900	19,200	21,300
130	5,150	6,550	9,200	12,950	16,400	19,800	22,000
140	5,300	6,700	9,400	13,300	16,800	20,300	22,600
150	5,450	6,900	9,650	13,600	17,200	20,800	23,100

(b) Red Fir, 8 Inches d.b.h. and Over

Age (Years)	Site Index at 50 Years				
	20	30	40	50	60
50	1,800	2,450	3,200	4,050	5,000
60	2,450	3,400	4,350	5,600	6,950
70	3,200	4,400	5,700	7,200	9,000
80	4,050	5,550	7,200	9,050	11,400
90	4,950	6,800	8,800	11,100	13,850
100	5,950	8,150	10,550	13,400	16,700
110	7,200	9,800	12,700	16,100	20,100
120	8,450	11,650	15,100	19,150	23,900
130	9,650	13,200	17,150	21,700	27,200
140	10,600	14,550	18,950	23,950	30,000
150	11,350	15,600	20,100	25,500	31,900

Source: White fir—Schumacher, 1926; Red fir—Schumacher, 1928.

of the .opening should not be greater than one to two times the height of the dominant trees because of potentially inadequate seed distribution and the development of adverse microclimatic conditions. With larger, more exposed openings, and if seed is not immediately available, the site may be rapidly taken over by woody shrubs and herbaceous plants.

Silvicultural considerations relating to natural regeneration of true firs are complex. Germinating conifer seeds need some shade in order for the seedlings to become established, but subsequently need full exposure for maximum growth and development. Too much exposure causes early mortality due to excessive heat. Gordon (1970) has shown for example that conifer seedlings are often killed at temperatures of 55 °C and that surface soil temperatures in true-fir forest clearcuts commonly exceed 65 °C on mineral soil surfaces and under 1 cm. of litter. In order to enhance regeneration, harvesting should coincide with a good seed crop. However, as this is not usually possible, final site preparation can be delayed until a good seed crop is present. This permits the seed to fall on bare mineral soil and for the conifer seedlings to become established before the development of competition from woody shrubs and herbs. A high degree of success in natural regeneration can, however, result in the need for subsequent precommercial thinning. If a shrub cover develops, true fir can be established under it, and eventually grow to shade it out, but stand establishment is delayed 30 years or more.

Survival of planted stock varies from 40 to 80 percent but is commonly at the low end of this range. Despite this, increased planting is being done: (1) because of advantages in prompt stand establishment, (2) because adequate trees for seed and shelter may not be available, (3) to give control over spacing, or (4) to permit the use of improved stock. Success in planting true firs is increasing as nursery practices such as fumigation to control root diseases, date of lifting, and control of low temperature during storage are refined. Date of planting is also crucial. Planting just after snow melt when the soil is too cool for root growth and water uptake results in poor survival. Currently, comparisons are being made of survival and growth of bare-root stock with container-grown stock. Results to date are inconclusive. It will probably be desirable to have both types of seedlings available for outplanting in particular locations. The most important consideration in seedling production is that seedlings should have a high root-growth capacity to ensure rapid establishment after outplanting.

Height growth of red and white fir seedlings is intially slow compared with that of ponderosa, Jeffrey, and lodgepole pines, and often with competing woody shrubs. After about four years, growth rates become equivalent to those of the pines, providing the firs are given adequate sunlight. Lodgepole pine, which commonly occurs in California red fir stands, also initially outgrows the fir, but the firs will eventually overtop the pine.

INTERMEDIATE TREATMENTS. Due to dense initial stocking, true-fir stands typically require precommercial thinning. This can become a desirable commercial Christmas tree operation if regeneration is of sufficient quality and access is adequate. Because lateral branches turn up after the main stem is harvested, several rotations of Christmas trees can be grown from each stump.

Many less-dense stands at lower elevation have an understory of advance regeneration. A common silvicultural question is whether the removal of the overstory will result in the advance growth growing at an acceptable rate after overstory removal. Advance growth that is growing as little as 1 to 2 inches in height per year and at 70 to 100 rings per radial inch is unlikely to respond to release. However, if the understory height growth is in excess of 6 inches per year, postrelease height growth can exceed 12 inches per year and diameter growth can reach 2 to 4 rings per inch (Gordon, 1973). Commercial thinning of young true-fir stands is currently not an operational practice because most harvesting is in old-growth stands.

Snow damage can be extensive in young true-fir stands, but both species have an amazing capacity to straighten up during the following growing season. Because of the variability of this damage and possible mortality, precommercial thinning treatments should be conservative.

At high elevation, the commonly cold, dry conditions cause young unmanaged stands to accumulate large amounts of undecomposed litter and slash resulting from natural mortality. Slow rates of decomposition of this accumulated material result in a significant tie-up of potentially available nutrients. Under even-aged management, prescribed fire may be a useful tool to release these nutrients and to control any understory vegetation, providing this can be done without damaging the thin-barked trees.

SILVICULTURAL SYSTEMS. True-fir forests are typically even-aged and pure. Young stands can be managed to maintain this condition or, if desired, can be grown to create an uneven-aged structure. There are two difficulties with uneven-aged stands. First, young trees will be continually infected with dwarf mistletoe. On good sites, however, height growth rates are commonly sufficient for the trees to outgrow the mistletoe. Second, uneven-aged systems lead to problems of slash disposal and reduction of fire hazard.

Shelterwood systems, either with uniform tree spacing or by group, can be used with more shelter provided on steep, south-facing slopes than on flat ground or on north-facing slopes. Once regeneration is established, it is important that the overstory be removed in order to ensure adequate seedling growth. Harvesting the overstory and disposal of its slash is difficult and more costly due to the presence of established regeneration.

Selection systems may also be prescribed to develop and maintain uneven-aged true-fir stands. The choice between single-tree and group systems depends on management objectives and also on the degree to which shelter or exposure is needed for seedling establishment and subsequent development. It should be expected therefore that choice of silvicultural system on any one forest will change with differences in such sites factors as aspect, slope, soil depth, and competing vegetation.

Susceptibility to Damage. Insect damage to old-growth unmanaged stands commonly exceeds that from all other causes. Fir engraver beetle is a major killer of trees from pole-size to mature, especially those weakened by drought or the *annosus* root-rot. The fir engraver also breeds in slash and maximum risk of population buildup results from woods operations that take place in March through September. A frequent associate of engraver beetles is the round-headed fir borer. Other destructive insects include the flatheaded fir borer which attacks injured, mistletoe-infected, dying, and fire-killed trees, sawflies, western spruce budworm, Douglas-fir tussock moth, and white fir needleminer which are important defoliators. Lesser damage is caused by fir pole beetles which attack slash and weakened saplings and poles. On lodgepole pine, an important insect that attacks terminal shoots, especially on young trees, is the white pine weevil.

The most important disease on both California red and white fir is dwarf mistletoe, especially in old stands of red fir (Gordon and Roy, 1973). In young stands, dwarf mistletoe has not been known to occur on saplings less than 3 feet tall. Shoestring fungus and *Fomes* are common root rots, and Indian paint fungus and red ring rot are common trunk rots of both species. Wind damage is more prevalent, especially in California red fir, than in conifers growing at lower elevation. This is due to exposure to strong winds, the steep, exposed nature of the mountainous areas where true firs occur, shallow soils, and to the prevalence of stem and root rots. Because damage from insects and disease occurs in decadent, overstocked stands, it is thought that potential pest impacts can be reduced by maintaining stocking at sufficiently low levels to maintain health and vigor.

Ponderosa Pine Type Group

Ponderosa pine is discussed most fully in the Middle and Southern Rocky Mountain Region chapter. Here, attention is given to its role in forests of the California Region because of its characteristically more rapid growth rates.

Within California, ponderosa pine occurs in four forest cover types recognized by the Society of American Foresters (Soc. Am. For., 1980):

1. Pacific Ponderosa Pine. This forms the lowest elevation true coniferous forest in the Sierra Nevada, southern Cascades, and Klamath Mountains. This type consists of nearly pure ponderosa pine where, by definition, basal area stocking exceeds 80 percent of the total. It occurs in a general elevation range of about 1,000 to 3,000 feet, increasing from north to south. At lower elevations it grades into mostly oak forests, Digger pine, or woodlands.

2. Pacific Ponderosa Pine—Douglas-fir. This type borders the Pacific Ponderosa Pine type at higher elevation. It occurs most commonly in the Klamath Mountains of southwestern Oregon and northern California and occupies the eastern slopes of the Coast Range southward to Napa County. It has an elevation range of between 1,500 to 4,000 feet and, similar to the Pacific Ponderosa Pine type, it commonly occurs in disjunct areas because of separation by other vegetation. A distinctive characteristic of this type is the absence of California white fir.

3. Sierra Nevada Mixed-Conifer. This type is discussed as a separate section within this chapter. It contains a considerable proportion of ponderosa pine, especially at lower elevations within its range. The type is distinguished from the Pacific Ponderosa Pine—Douglas-fir type by containing more than 20 percent white fir.

4. Interior Ponderosa Pine. This type consists of slower-growing ponderosa pine that occurs in the lower rainfall areas on the east-facing slopes of the Sierra Nevada and on the Modoc Plateau in northeastern California. These pine stands are relatively pure and even-aged.

Ponderosa pine occurring in the first three types mentioned above is commonly referred to as "west-side pine" (Fig. 9-7) and its growth characteristics are markedly superior to the "east-side pine" of the Interior Ponderosa Pine type. To simplify discussion, a broad comparison will be made between "west-side" and "east side" pine in California.

West-side Ponderosa Pine

PLACE IN ECOLOGICAL SUCCESSION.   Ponderosa pine in this area commonly occurs in pure stands or with small amounts of conifer and hardwood associates that are found more abundantly in the Sierra Nevada Mixed-Conifer type. A characteristic ground cover is bear-clover, which often grows densely and, because of its deep root system and capacity for sprouting, constitutes an aggressive competitor for pine regeneration.

The Pacific Ponderosa Pine type can be considered as being transitional to

Figure 9-7.   Ponderosa pine type group "Westside" (P. M. McDonald, USDA For. Serv., Pacific Southwest Exp. Stn.)

the Sierra Nevada Mixed-Conifer type. It is found on the better sites with the poorer sites commonly having a cover of oaks and chaparral. On these better sites, ponderosa pine is climax. The Pacific Ponderosa Pine—Douglas-fir type can be considered transitional to the Pacific Mixed-Evergreen type, made up of Douglas-fir, tanoak, and Pacific madrone, prevalent in the Klamath Mountains. Here, successional climax is more likely to be Douglas-fir rather than ponderosa pine. However, the successional patterns are complex due to the great diversity of soils, slopes, and aspects within the Klamath Mountains area. This complexity, compounded by disturbances due to harvesting, pests, storms and fires, provides a diversity of situations that is favorable to the continued presence of both ponderosa pine and Douglas-fir.

Being the conifer forest closest to population centers in the valleys, west-side pine was heavily utilized by the pioneers and for the construction of cities and towns that grew up in the valleys and foothills. Because this type merges with the oak woodland and chaparral types, its range has diminished during the past 150 years due to early logging and fires which were used to clear vegetation for gold prospecting and to create livestock feed. Today, urban development is occurring in this type.

GROWTH RATES. Because of generally good site quality, growth of west-side ponderosa pine is excellent and exceeds that from anywhere else in the species' natural range. Diameter growth rate of 3 to 4 rings per radial inch and annual height growth of 36 inches are common on extensive areas of high site quality. On sites of average quality, annual growth is more commonly 6 to 8 rings per inch and 24 inches in height. Fig. 9-5 presents site-quality curves and Table 9-13 provides normal yields for unmanaged ponderosa pine. More recently, tables have been prepared showing the growth performance of unthinned ponderosa pine plantations in terms of site index, age, and spacing (Oliver and Powers, 1978). As shown in Table 9-14, mean annual increment at age 50 years is 291 to 303 cubic feet per acre per year depending on site quality.

Interesting data have been obtained by Oliver (1979a) from extensive levels-of-growing-stock studies in ponderosa pine plantations planted in 1950 at 4,000 foot elevation. Rainfall is 60 inches annually and site index is 140 feet at 100 years (Meyer, 1938). Stand characteristics and growth after thinning are shown in Table 9-15 for the two extreme levels of stocking.

Table 9-15 shows the marked effect of thinning on increasing diameter and height growth, but reducing by up to one-half the basal area and volume growth rates on a stand basis. It is important to consider, however, that although volume production is greatest on the most densely stocked plot, maximum-value production may occur on a less densely stocked area where total volume is less but individual trees are larger.

In managing ponderosa pine it is important to ensure that initial growth is acceptable. In an analysis of ten plantations that varied in age from 16 to 50 years, Oliver and Powers (1971) showed that site quality had a profound effect on the time taken to reach breast height. Predominant trees took an average of

TABLE 9-13

Yields for Unmanaged Ponderosa Pine (Cubic Feet per Acre) of Trees 11.6 Inches d.b.h. and Over

Age (Years)	Site Index—at 100 Years												
	40	50	60	70	80	90	100	110	120	130	140	150	160
20								40	120	280	530	1,060	1,880
30						60	200	470	970	1,860	2,750	3,760	4,910
40				30	120	340	820	1,740	2,770	3,990	5,230	6,580	7,950
50			30	150	410	970	2,060	3,230	4,600	6,170	7,670	9,260	10,780
60		30	120	400	990	2,040	3,280	4,710	6,320	8,080	9,830	11,520	13,140
70		90	310	870	1,870	3,090	4,440	6,110	7,910	9,730	11,590	13,380	15,080
80	50	220	710	1,650	2,720	4,110	5,540	7,310	9,210	11,100	13,030	14,880	16,640
90	110	470	1,310	2,400	3,520	5,010	6,520	8,310	10,280	12,230	14,200	16,110	17,940
100	240	870	1,960	3,100	4,270	5,790	7,310	9,130	11,140	13,140	15,160	17,430	19,020
110	460	1,370	2,560	3,710	4,890	6,420	7,950	9,780	11,800	13,900			
120	780	1,820	3,060	4,220	5,410	6,950	8,490	10,330	12,360	14,540			
130	1,140	2,210	3,460	4,640	5,850	7,400	8,950	10,800	12,840	15,070			
140	1,450	2,550	3,810	5,000	6,230	7,780	9,340	11,200	13,250	15,500			
150	1,720	2,840	4,110	5,320	6,560	8,120	9,680	11,550	13,600	15,850			
160	1,950	3,080	4,360	5,600	6,840	8,420	9,990	11,850	13,950	16,200			
170	2,160	3,300	4,590	5,840	7,090	8,680	10,270	12,150	14,250	16,550			
180	2,360	3,510	4,810	6,060	7,320	8,920	10,500	12,400	14,550	16,900			
190	2,550	3,710	5,020	6,270	7,530	9,140	10,750	12,650	14,850	17,250			
200	2,730	3,900	5,220	6,470	7,730	9,340	10,950	12,850	15,100	17,600			

Source: Meyer, 1938.

TABLE 9-14

Growth of Unthinned Ponderosa Pine Plantations at Age 50 Years at Site Index 80 and 120; Spacing = 12 × 12 Feet

Dimension	Site Index 80 (50 Years)[a]	Site Index 120 (50 Years)[a]
Diameter (inches)	15	17
Height (feet)	71	88
Basal Area (square feet per acre)	291	303
Net Volume (cubic feet per acre)	7472	8768

Source: Oliver and Powers, 1978.

[a] Site index from Powels and Oliver, 1978.

TABLE 9-15

Growth of Thinned Ponderosa Pine Plantation, Elliot Ranch

Dimension	GSL 40[a]	GSL 160[a]
Stand Characteristics 5 Years After Thinning at Age 20 Years		
Stems per acre	75	492
DBH (inches)	12	8
Height (feet)	54	41
Live Crown (percent)	66	56
Basal Area (square feet per acre)	62	189
Volume (cubic feet per acre)	1193	3315
Mean Periodic Annual Increment For 5-year Period After Thinning		
Diameter (inches)	0.5	0.2
Height (feet)	2.5	1.7
Basal Area (square feet per acre)	4.7	9.0
Gross Volume (cubic feet per acre)	116	255

Source: Oliver, 1979a.

[a] GSL is the growing stock level in square feet per acre which the stand is expected to reach when average diameter is 10 inches (see Myers, 1967).

11.4 years to reach breast height on the poorest sites measured (site index 30 feet at 50 years), 6.6 years on site index 80, and 4.4 years on site index 120. In a similar study by the U.S. Forest Service on the Stanislaus National Forest, the average time taken for the best 100 trees from four plantations on sites II and III to reach breast height was four and a half years. These same trees reached 16.3 feet in 10 years.

CULTURAL PRACTICES.   Because this type merges with the mixed-conifer type at its upper elevations, and because many of the associated shrub and tree species of these two types are similar, the silvicultural systems, site preparation, planting, release techniques, and fuels management, as well as associated diseases and insects are essentially common to both types. All these considerations are discussed previously in connection with the Mixed-Conifer Type Group.

The silvicultural techniques used in west-side pine must recognize its relative intolerance to shade; consequently clearcutting, seed-tree, and group selection are appropriate reproduction methods. When regeneration is by planting, site preparation must adequately control hardwoods and competition from bear-clover. Survival of 80 to 90 percent is common using 1-0 bare-root stock. Planting density is generally 300 to 500 seedlings per acre.

Data from levels-of-growing-stock studies indicate that desired basal area for plantations at 25 to 40 years of age should be between 80 to 150 square feet per acre.

ROTATION AGE OR SIZE.   Estimates of rotation length vary. Using culmination of mean-annual increment, the U.S. Forest Service anticipates rotations of 80 to 100 years. Using economic criteria, shorter rotations of 40 to 60 years are recommended for ponderosa pine on good sites (Teeguarden, 1968).

SUSCEPTIBILITY TO DAMAGE.   Higher volume production may be obtained at higher levels of stocking than those suggested earlier, but the lesser growth of individual trees may increase the susceptibility of the stand to attacks by diseases and insects, and to snow breakage. Pure ponderosa pine stands, especially when unmanaged, are probably more susceptible to damage from insects and disease than pines growing mixed with other species. Of particular importance are the western pine beetle, mountain pine beetle, and red turpentine beetle which, in addition to attacking ponderosa pine, attack Jeffrey, sugar, and lodgepole pines. Also of importance is the California fivespined *ips* which breeds most prolifically in logs and slash from spring harvesting operations, and the pine reproduction weevil which can be destructive in ponderosa and Jeffrey pine plantations.

Diseases of particular concern in pine stands are the root rot *Fomes*, and the root and butt rots of the shoestring fungus, blackstain fungus, and red-brown butt rot. These fungi can kill trees outright or predispose them to attack by insects such as the western pine beetle. A needle disease which can become serious in pine is the *Elytroderma* blight.

Insect and disease problems are especially prevalent in natural, unmanaged young-growth stands that are 50 to 70 years old and that have a basal area on high site-quality land of greater than about 200 square feet per acre. To enhance wood value production and to lessen susceptibility to pests, it appears desirable to maintain vigorously-growing stands at stocking levels well below this point, particularly on poorer sites. The major animal pest is porcupine which feeds on the inner bark, causing extensive damage in some areas by girdling the tops of trees. Control of porcupine may be done through poisoning or shooting. The natural predator of the porcupine, the fisher, has been largely eliminated because of its valuable fur.

East-side Ponderosa Pine

PLACE IN ECOLOGICAL SUCCESSION.   This type occurs on about 3.5 million acres throughout the northeast of California and extends southward in a narrow band along the east slope of the Sierra Nevada. Precipitation is low, between 10 and 25 inches, soils are shallow and stony, elevation is 3,000 to 5,000 feet, and topography consists of gently rolling hills. The forests commonly occur as relatively small even-aged groups up to 5 or 10 acres in size. Ponderosa pine and Jeffrey pine are common, together with some incense-cedar, frequent openings of grass, snowbrush ceanothus and greenleaf manzanita. Successional development in this type is towards ponderosa and Jeffrey pines.

Large-scale timber harvesting began in the northeast in the early 1900s. Annual production has varied greatly but lumber production has been the chief industry of the area. Early high grading simply took the best trees and the effects of logging and fires have resulted in stands of varying quality. In later years, attempts have been made to manage the forests on a sustained-yield basis. The problems confronting early attempts at management included the periodic outbreaks of bark beetles which caused extensive damage in the overstocked, unmanaged stands; determination of annual growth and allowable cut; and how to create a balanced series of age-classes. One of the most notable outputs from U.S. Forest Service research in east-side ponderosa pine was the concept of Unit Area Control, or management by small homogeneous groups or condition classes (Hallin, 1959). Other important contributions from studies in the east-side pine type include the risk-rating systems predicting susceptibility of trees to bark beetle attack that were developed by Keen (1936) and Salman and Bongberg (1942).

GROWTH RATES.   Because of low rainfall and poor soils, site index at age 100 years varies from 60 to 80 (Meyer site classes IV and V) and growth is slow. Volume production of east-side pine is about one-half that of west-side pine. Data from Oliver and Powers (1978) show that at age 50 years, 12 × 12-foot spaced plantations on site index 40 (base age 50 years) have a mean height of 36 feet, a mean diameter of 9.7 inches, a basal area of 132 square feet per acre, and a total net volume per acre of 1,595 cubic feet.

In an earlier publication, Oliver (1972) reports growth after thinning in plots of both natural stands and plantations of east-side pine. Basal area after thinning ranged from 13 to 149 square feet per acre. Over this range, mean-annual diameter growth, over a period of between 5 to 16 years after thinning, range from 0.46 inch per year for the plot at 13 square feet per acre to 0.08 inch per year for the plot at 148 square feet. Basal area growth of the 43 largest trees per acre ranged from 2.1 to 0.6 square feet per acre per year, and height growth ranged from 1.4 to 0.3 feet per year over the same range in basal area stocking. Volume growth increased with increase in basal area up to 75 cubic feet per acre per year at 80 square feet per acre. At this stocking level, which Oliver suggests might be optimal for the stands studied, annual diameter growth is 0.16 inch and annual height growth is 0.7 foot. In a later study of growth over a 15-year period after thinning, based entirely on plantation-grown ponderosa and Jeffrey pine in northeastern California, Oliver (1979b) found that optimum basal area for volume production (in both cubic and board foot measures) to be 110 square feet per acre. Volume production at this level of basal area was 97 cubic feet per acre per year. Individual tree vigor is better in plantations because of initial stocking control and trees usually reach a given size at a younger age. Thus plantations might be expected to carry greater stocking than natural stands.

CULTURAL PRACTICES.   Because the east-side pine stands occur in even-aged groups, regeneration cutting is most logically by clearcutting. Then because of the infrequency of seed grops, and the unreliability of establishment due to summer drought, regeneration is best achieved by planting. Partial harvests are done mainly to reduce loss to insects.

Site preparation must anticipate competition from woody shrubs and, because of low precipitation, precommercial thinning and intermediate treatments should be done to achieve maximum stocking levels in young-growth stands of about 80 to 110 square feet per acre by age 50 to 70 years.

Inventories of natural, unmanaged stands indicated average standing volumes of about 3,100 cubic feet per acre. U.S. Forest Service management plans recommended a rotation of 140 years. In this time period, dominants in natural stands may average 21 inches d.b.h. Under management it is expected that dominants would attain 24 inches d.b.h. within the 140-year rotation. Cutting cycles are recommended as 20 years with the average harvest per acre being 480 cubic feet. At the end of the rotation the final crop may consist of 31 to 49 dominants averaging 24 inches d.b.h. (Hallin, 1959). More recently, concerns have been expressed regarding the economic feasibility of such long rotations.

California Oak Woodland Type Group

Place in Ecological Succession.   This vegetation type is extremely complex. In general, it consists of a highly variable density of trees, mostly oaks, in association with grasses, chaparral, and a rather common conifer—Digger pine. The hardwood trees include blue oak, interior live oak, Oregon white oak, canyon live oak, coast live oak, valley oak, and sometimes California black oak, California laurel, Pacific madrone, and California buckeye. The chaparral includes numerous species from such genera as *Arctostaphylos*, *Ceanothus*, *Rhamnus*, and *Rhus (Toxicodendron)*. The grasses and associated herbaceous vegetation are mostly annuals (Fig. 9-8).

Wieslander and Gleason (1954) found the California oak woodland to include about 1.5 million acres of woodland and about 7.5 million acres of woodland-grass. In the woodland, trees dominate along with various mixtures of chaparral species or oaks and chaparral. Where the chaparral is well represented, this category is often referred to as woodland-chaparral. The woodland-grass category is typically rather open with scattered trees in a continuous cover of grass. Most of the oaks are common to both categories, although valley oak is more closely associated with the woodland-grass grouping.

Figure 9-8. Oak woodland. (P. M. McDonald, USDA For. Serv., Pacific Southwest Exp. Stn.)

The combination of evergreen and deciduous oak canopy with grassy ground cover distinguish the California oak woodland type from those types adjacent to it. Occasionally, grassland occurs with shrub vegetation, however, the true grassland type emerges at lower elevation. At higher elevations, the type merges in complex fashion into the montane forest, which can consist of both conifers or hardwoods. Griffin (1977) noted that the combination of indicator woodland oaks, as well as their density, can only be arbitrarily separated from interior forms of the mixed-hardwood forest.

Ecologically, the arborescent species which make up the California oak woodland are broadleafed sclerophylls and deciduous trees. Like the chaparral, the oaks are deep rooted and well adapted to a harsh environment, and can withstand high water stress. Poorer soils and hotter slopes support fewer trees at wider spacings than do better soils on cooler slopes. Likewise, more trees grow at the bottom of a long continuous slope than at the top. The better, deeper soils at the bottom retain more moisture longer in the year (Griffin, 1973).

Characteristically, the California oak woodland is recognized as a climax, but it is more likely to be a polyclimax—either oak or chaparral can become dominant where there is no disturbance. Cooper (1922) noted that chaparral species increased in places where disturbance was curtailed for a long time. Disturbance such as from fires favors an increase in the proportion of live oaks because these species are more prolific sprouters than deciduous oaks.

The upper elevational boundary of the oak woodland borders a forest where ponderosa pine often predominates. Past fires, followed by their exclusion, plus the harvesting and insect activity in pines, drought, and grazing all contribute to a continual changing of the woodland forest boundaries.

Cultural Practices   Historically, the woodland oaks have been regarded as being of limited value. They have simply been felled to increase pasturage, to convert to agricultural land, or for fuelwood. Some felling has been done to increase water yield but studies by Pitt et al. (1978) have shown that, although water yields may increase by nearly 60 percent, this practice also increases the likelihood of soil slippage, erosion, and sedimentation. No serious attempts have been made to manage oak for wood products. Over the past decade, however, increasing use has been made of valley oak for high-grade lumber, pallet stock, and fuelwood. The potential value of some of the oaks for wood products is, however, becoming increasingly clear. A wide variety of products is possible incuding lumber, pallets, furniture, toy blanks, parquet flooring, and wine cooperage.

California Chaparral Type Group

The word "chaparral" originates from the Spanish language and has come to denote thickets of scrub oak as well as dense brushfields in general. Typically, California chaparral is part of a worldwide type of vegetation called broad sclerophyll: "broad" simply meaning broad leaves, and "sclerophyll" pertaining to thick hard stiff flat leaves containing special tissue for minimizing water loss.

This type group occupies areas having the generalized Mediterranean climate of hot dry summers and cool wet winters. Broad sclerophylls can be of the prostrate, shrub, or arborescent life forms. The shrubby life form usually predominates, probably in response to the harsh environment consisting of summer drought, low nutrient availability, steep slopes, skeletal soils, and frequent fires.

In California, the chaparral type extends over about 8.5 million acres, and ranges from the Oregon state line to the Mexican border. East to west, chaparral is found along the bluffs near the ocean to the semi-desert or desert margins.

The adaptability of the many chaparral species to their harsh environment is due to such characteristics as:

1.   A deep and extensive root system (Lewis and Burgy, 1964, Helmers et al., 1955) with extensive development in the upper foot of soil and horizontal extent of roots greater than the vertical projection of the crown (Miller and Ng, 1977).

2.   The capacity to withstand severe moisture stress (Waring, 1969) and to minimize water loss by having a thick cuticular tissue on leaves and twigs (Cooper, 1922).

3.   The capacity to fix nitrogen as in *Ceanothus* and other genera (Delwiche et al., 1965).

4. The capacity of seeds to germinate only after severe disturbance such as fire or logging when vegetative competition has been reduced greatly.

5. The capacity to sprout quickly and vigorously from root crowns.

6. The capacity of some plants to produce frequent and heavy seed crops especially in the spring following a wet year (Keeley, 1977).

7. Some species produce toxic metabolites which inhibit development of potentially competing plants (allelopathy).

Because of the frequency of fire, most chaparral appears to be in some phase of secondary succession. Chaparral may persist in a nearly pure state on the same area for many generations and this may be due to the occurrence of fires. There are types of chaparral, however, such as the shrub form of California black oak where fire is probably not needed for their maintenance.

Management and use of the chaparral falls far short of its potential because of lack of knowledge and economic limitations. To date, most management has consisted either of protection from burning, or of conversion to grass or trees in wildland and urban settings. Reducing fire hazard is of critical concern and much work has been done in constructing fuel breaks and in reducing the size of the continuous stands of brush. The most important use of chaparral is in maintaining soil stability and in controlling surface runoff on the commonly steep slopes.

Increased use can be made of shrubs for highway beautification and site rehabilitation (Dehgan et al., 1977). In particular, chaparral could be managed to include more open space for grass. This would provide a greater diversity of habitat and food for wildlife, would reduce fire hazard, and would generally be regarded as more aesthetically pleasing.

BIBLIOGRAPHY

Axelrod, D. I. 1977. Outline history of California vegetation. In M. G. Barbour and J. Major (eds.). *Terrestrial vegetation of California.* pp. 130–193. John Wiley and Sons, New York.

Arvanitas, L. G., J. Lindquist, and M. Palley. 1964. Site index curves for even-aged young-growth ponderosa pine of the west-side Sierra Nevada. *Univ. Calif. Agr. Exp. Stn. Calif. For and For. Prod. No. 35.* Berkeley. 8 pp.

Baker, F. S. 1944. Mountain climates of the western United States. *Ecol. Monogr.* 14(2):223–254.

Barbour, M. G. and J. Major. 1977. *Terrestrial vegetation of California.* John Wiley and Sons, New York. 1002 pp.

Boe, K. N. 1973. Redwood. *In:* Silvicultural system for the major forest types of the United States. *USDA For. Serv. Agr. Hdb. No. 445.* pp. 23–30.

Boe, K. N. 1974. Thinning promotes growth of sprouts on old-growth redwood stumps. *USDA. For. Serv. Res. Note PSW-290.* 5 pp.

Colwell, W. L. Jr. 1979. Forest soils of California. In R. J. Laacke (ed). California Forest Soils. pp. 69–88. Univ. Calif. Div. Agr. Sci. Berkeley.

Cooper, W. S. 1922. The broad-sclerophyll vegetation of California. An ecological study of the chaparral and its related communities. *Carnegie Inst. of Wash. Publ. 319.* pp. 1–124.

Daniel, T. W., J. A. Helms, and F. S. Baker, 1979. *Principles of silviculture*. McGraw-Hill, New York. 500 pp.

Dehgan, D., J. M. Tucker, and B. S. Takher. 1977. *Propagation and culture of new species of drought-tolerant plants for highways*. Univ. Calif., Davis. 154 pp.

Delwiche, C. C., P. J. Zinke, and C. M. Johnson. 1965. Nitrogen fixation by Ceanothus. *Plant Physiol.* 40:1045—1047.

Dunning, D. and L. H. Reineke. 1933. Preliminary yield tables for second-growth stands in the California pine region. *USDA For. Serv. Tech. Bull. 354*. 24 pp.

Fowells, H. A. and N. B. Stark. 1965. Natural regeneration in relation to environment in the mixed conifer type of California. *USDA For. Serv. Res. Pap. PSW-24*. 14 pp.

Gordon, D. T. 1970. Natural regeneration of white and red fir: influence of several factors. *USDA For. Serv. Res. Pap. PSW-58*. 32 pp.

Gordon, D. T. 1973. Released advanced reproduction of white and red fir: Growth, damage, mortality. *USDA For. Serv. Res. Pap. PSW-95*. 12 pp.

Gordon, D. T. 1980. Red fir. In: S.A.F. Forest cover types of North America. Revised Edition. Soc. Am. For. Washington, D.C. (in press).

Gordon, D. T., and D. F. Roy. 1973. Red fir-white fir. In: Silvicultural systems for the major forest types of the United States. *USDA For. Serv. Agr. Hdb. No. 445*. 114 pp.

Griffin, J. R. 1973. Xylem sap tension in three woodland oaks of central California. *Ecology* 54:152—159.

Griffin, J. R. 1977. Oak woodland. In M. G. Barbour and J. Major (eds.). *Terrestrial vegetation of California*. John Wiley and Sons, New York, pp. 384—415.

Griffin, J. R. and W. B. Critchfield, 1972. The distribution of forest trees in California. *USDA For. Serv. Res. Pap. PSW-82*. 114 pp.

Hallin, W. E. 1959. The application of Unit Area Control in the management of Ponderosa-Jeffrey pine at Blacks Mountain Experimental Forest. *USDA For. Serv. Tech. Bull. 1191*. 96 pp.

Helmers, H., J. S. Horton, G. Juhren, and J. O'Keefe. 1955. Root systems of some chaparral plants in southern California. *Ecology* 36:667—678.

Keeley, J. E. 1977. Seed production, seed populations in soil, and seedling production after fire for two congeneric pairs of sprouting and nonsprouting chaparral shrubs. *Ecology* 58:820—829.

Keen, F. P. 1936. Relative susceptibility of ponderosa pine to bark beetle attack. *J. For.* 34:919-927.

Kinloch, B. 1976. Breeding for white pine blister rust resistance in sugar pine: an operational plan for Region Five. In Kitzmiller, J. H. (ed.) *Tree Improvement Master Plan for the California Region*. USDA For. Serv., San Francisco, 123 pp.

Kitzmiller, J. H. 1976. Tree Improvement Master Plan for the California Region. *USDA For. Serv.*, San Francisco. 123 pp.

Lewis, D. C. and R. H. Burgy. 1964. The relationship between oak tree roots and ground water in fractured rock as determined by tritium tracing. *J. Geophys. Res.* 69:2579—2588.

Lindquist, J. L., and M. N. Palley. 1963. Empirical yield tables for young-growth redwood. *Univ. Calif. Agr. Exp. Stn. Bull. 776*. Berkeley, 47 pp.

Lindquist, J. L., and M. N. Palley. 1967. Prediction of stand growth of young redwood. *Univ. Calif. Agr. Exp. Stn. Bull. 831*. Berkeley, 64 pp.

McDonald, P. M. 1976. Forest regeneration and seedling growth from five cutting methods in north central California. *USDA For. Serv. Res. Pap. PSW-115*. 10 pp.

Meyer, W. H. 1938. Yield of even-aged stands of ponderosa pine. *USDA For. Serv. Tech. Bull. 630*. 59 pp.

Miller, P. C., and E. Ng. 1977. Root-shoot biomass ratios in shrubs in southern California and central Chile. *Madrono* 24:215—223.

Muelder, D. W. and J. H. Hansen. 1961a. Observations on cone bearing of *Sequoia sempervirens*. *Univ. Calif. Agr. Exp. Stn. Calif. For. and For. Prod. No. 26*. Berkeley, 6 pp.

Muelder, D. W. and J. H. Hansen. 1961b. Biotic factors in natural regeneration of *Sequoia sempervirens*. *Int. Union For. Res. Org. 13th Congr*. Vienna.

Munz, P. A., and D. D. Keck. 1959. A California flora. *Univ. Calif. Press*, Berkeley. 1681 pp.

Myers, C. A. 1967. Growing stock levels in even-aged ponderosa pine. *USDA For. Serv. Res. Pap. RM-33*. 8 pp.

Oliver, W. W. 1972. Growth after thinning ponderosa and Jeffrey pine pole stands in northeastern California. *USDA For. Serv. Res. Pap. PSW-85*. 8 pp.

Oliver, W. W. 1979a. Growth of planted ponderosa pine thinned to different stocking levels on a productive site. *USDA For. Serv. Res. Pap*. (in press).

Oliver, W. W. 1979b. Fifteen-year growth patterns after thinning a ponderosa—Jeffrey pine plantation in northeastern California. *USDA For. Serv. Res. Pap*. (in press).

Oliver, W. W., and R. F. Powers. 1971. Early height growth of ponderosa pine forecasts dominance in plantations. *USDA For. Serv. Res. Note PSW-250*. 4 pp.

Oliver, W. W., and R. F. Powers. 1978. Growth models for ponderosa pine. I. Yield of unthinned plantations in northern California. *USDA For. Serv. Res. Pap. PSW-133*. 21 pp.

Oswald, D. D. 1972. Timber Resources of Mendocino and Sonoma Counties, California. *USDA For. Serv. Res. Bull. PNW-40*. 76 pp.

Oswald, D. D., and E. M. Hornibrook. 1966. Commercial forest area and timber volume in California, 1963. *USDA For. Serv. Res. Bull. PSW-4*. 16 pp.

Pitt, M. D., Robert H. Burgy, and H. F. Heady. 1978. Influences of brush conversion and weather patterns on runoff from a northern California watershed. *J. Range Mgt*. 31(1):23−27.

Powers, R. F., and W. W. Oliver. 1978. Site classification of ponderosa pine stands under stocking control in California. *USDA For. Serv. Res. Pap. PSW-128* 9 pp.

Quick, C. R. 1956. Viable seeds from the duff and soil of sugar pine forests. *For. Sci*. 2(1):36−42.

Roy, D. F. *1980. Redwood. In S.A.F. Forest cover types of North America*. Revised Edition. Soc. Am. For. Washington, D.C. (in press).

Rundel, P. W., D. J. Parsons, and D. T. Gordon. 1977. Montane and subalpine vegetation of the Sierra Nevada and Cascade Ranges. In: M. G. Barbour and J. Major (eds.). *Terrestrial vegetation of California*. pp 559−599. John Wiley and Sons, New York.

Salman, K. A., and J. W. Bongberg. 1942. Logging high-risk trees to control insects in the pine stands of northeastern California. *J. For*. 40: 533−539.

Saywer, J. O., and D. A. Thornburgh. 1977. Montane and subalpine vegetation of the Klamath Mountains. In M. G. Barbour and J. Major (eds.). *Terrestrial vegetation of California*. pp 699−732. John Wiley and Sons, New York.

Schumacher, F. X. 1926. Yield, stand, and volume tables for white fir in the California pine region. *Univ. Calif. Bull*. 407. Berkeley. 26 pp.

Schumacher, F. X. 1928. Yield, stand, and volume tables for red fir in California. *Univ. Calif. Bull*. 456. Berkeley. 29 pp.

Soc. Am. Foresters. 1954. *Forest cover types of North America*. Soc. Am. For., Washington, D.C. 67 pp.

Soc. Am. Foresters, 1980. *Forest cover types of North America*. Revised Edition. Soc. Am. Foresters, Washington, D.C. (In press).

Storie, R. E., and A.E. Wieslander. 1948. Rating soils for timber sites. Proc. Soil Sci. Soc. Am. 13: 499−509.

Tappeiner, J. C. 1980. Sierra Nevada Mixed Conifer. In *Forest cover types of North America*. Revised Edition. Soc. Am. Foresters, Washington, D.C. (In press).

Tappeiner, J. C., and J. A. Helms. 1971. Natural regeneration of Douglas-fir and white fir on exposed sites in the Sierra Nevada of California. *Am. Midl. Nat.* 86(2):358–370.

Teeguarden, D. E. 1968. Economics of replacing young-growth ponderosa pine stands. . a case study. *USDA For. Serv. Res. Pap. PSW-47.* 16 pp.

USDA For. Serv. 1954. Forest statistics for California. *USDA For. Serv. Calif. For. and Range Expt. Stn. For. Serv. Release 25.* 66 pp.

USDA For. Serv. 1973. Stanislaus National Forest Timber Management, Sonora, CA. 48 pp.

Univ. Calif. 1960. Forest and wildlands in California. An introductory outline. *Univ. Calif. Agr. Ext. Serv. Unpubl.* 32 pp.

Wall, B. R. 1978. Timber resources of the Sacramento area, California, 1972. *USDA For. Serv. Res. Bull. PNW-73.* 62 pp.

Waring, R. H. 1969. Forest plants of the eastern Siskiyous: Their environmental and vegetational distribution. *Northwest Sci.* 43(1):1–16.

Wieslander, A. E., and C. H. Gleason. 1954. Major brushland areas of the Coast Ranges and Sierra Cascade foothills in California. *USDA For. Serv. Calif. For. and Range Exp. Stn. Misc. Pap. 15.* 9 pp.

Zinke, P. J. 1977. The redwood forest and associated north coast forest. In M. G. Barbour and J. Major (eds.). *Terrestrial vegetation of California.* pp 679–698. John Wiley and Sons, New York.

10

The Pacific Northwest Region

David R. M. Scott

LOCATION

Although the entire states of Washington and Oregon comprise the Pacific Northwest Region, the emphasis in this chapter will be on the forests west of the Cascade crest (Figs. 10-1 and 10-2). This is because the forests east of the Cascade Mountains are very similar to those of the Rocky Mountains. In southwestern Oregon, the forests are analogous to those of northern California and so will be dealt with only briefly here.

FOREST STATISTICS

Area

Table 10-1 shows several important facts. Western Oregon and western Washington are 80 percent forested and of this, 90 percent in Oregon and 77 percent in Washington is commercial forest land. Nine percent of the productive forest land in western Washington is reserved or deferred. In eastern Oregon, 35 percent of the land area is forested and about 72 percent of this is commercial; in eastern Washington, 40 percent is forested with 77 percent commercial. In other words, while the total land area of the Pacific Northwest east of the Cascade Mountains is almost twice that on the west side, eastside commercial forest land area is only about 80 percent of that on the west side; and, as subsequent sections show, the average productivity is much less.

Character of Forest Land Ownership

Table 10-2 summarizes commercial forest land ownership. Private land comprises 59 percent in western Washington (39 percent industrial forestry) and 45 percent in western Oregon (27 percent owned by forest industry). There is

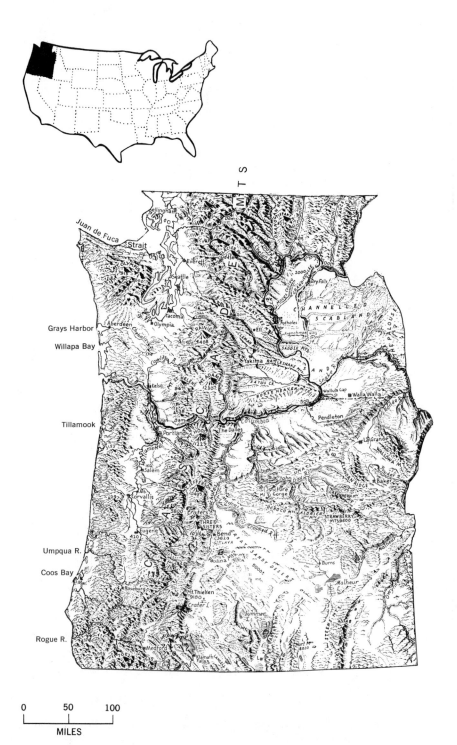

Figure 10-1. The Pacific Northwest Region.

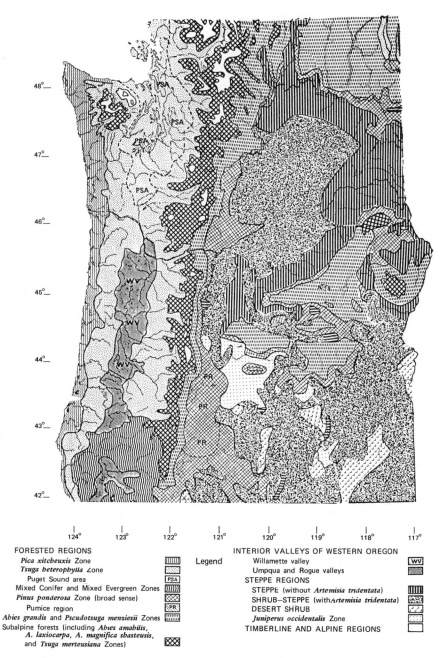

 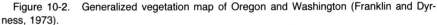
Figure 10-2.   Generalized vegetation map of Oregon and Washington (Franklin and Dyrness, 1973).

449

TABLE 10-1

Land Area of the Pacific Northwest by State, Subregion, and Major Land Classes 1977 (Thousand Acres)

Land Use	Oregon		Washington	
	Western	Eastern	Western	Eastern
Forest land				
Commercial	13,875.0	10,560.0	9,788.0	8,134.0
Productive reserved	303.0	413.0	1,024.0	720.0
Productive deferred	109.0	175.0	150.0	168.0
Other forest	1,080.0	3,508.0	1,645.0	1,552.0
Total—forest	15,367.0	14,656.0	12,607.0	10,574.0
Nonforest land				
Range	2,009.0	20,313.7	894.4	7,236.2
Other	1,791.0	7,421.3	2,341.6	8,951.8
Total—nonforest	3,800.0	27,735.0	3,236.0	16,188.0
Total land area	19,167.0	42,391.0	15,843.0	26,762.0

Source: USDA For. Serv., 1978.

much less private ownership east of the Cascades: in Washington, 36 percent with only 9 percent in forest industry, and in Oregon, 27 percent private and 15 percent in industrial ownership.

Public land in western Oregon is primarily administered by the U.S. Forest Service (33 percent) and Bureau of Land Management (14 percent); in eastern Oregon, almost exclusively by the U.S. Forest Service (67 percent). In Washington there is less national forest land (22 percent west and 36 percent east of the Cascades), almost no Bureau of Land Management acreage, and far more state (14 percent west and 9 percent east) and Indian land (16 percent east of the Cascades).

To summarize, there is a higher proportion of public land—particularly federal—in Oregon and of private land in Washington; also there is more industrial, state, and Indian ownership in Washington.

Forest Inventory

The cubic volumes inventory is shown in Table 10-3. It is apparent that western Oregon and Washington have almost three times (on 25 percent more commercial forest area) the growing stock found east of the Cascades, and that Douglas-fir and hemlock are by far the most important species. East of the mountains, Douglas-fir, the pines, and true firs are most important. Hardwoods are relatively unimportant throughout the Pacific Northwest.

TABLE 10-2

Area of Commercial Timberland in the Pacific Northwest by State, Subregion, and Ownership, 1977 (Thousand Acres)

Ownership	Oregon		Washington	
	Western	Eastern	Western	Eastern
Public				
Federal				
National forest	4,586.0	7,046.0	2,200.0	2,967.0
Bureau of Land				
Management	1,996.0	182.0	2.0	45.0
Other	1.0	5.0	68.0	100.0
Total federal	6,583.0	7,233.0	2,270.0	3,112.0
Indian	—	377.0	187.0	1,359.0
State	790.0	68.0	1,358.0	726.0
County and municipal	135.0	4.0	176.0	6.0
Total public	7,508.0	7,682.0	3,991.0	5,203.0
Private				
Forest industry	3,716.0	1,627.0	3,581.0	738.0
Farm	1,385.0	1,024.0	434.0	1,383.0
Other	1,266.0	227.0	1,782.0	810.0
Total private	6,367.0	2,878.0	5,797.0	2,931.0
Total commercial	13,875.0	10,560.0	9,788.0	8,134.0

Source: USDA For. Serv., 1978.

Nonstocked area comprises about 5 percent of the total commercial forest land throughout the region (USDA For. Serv., 1978).

Oregon has the largest annual cut of any state. Washington ranks second in some references. In annual growth, Washington is third and Oregon fourth. West of the Cascades almost 60 percent of the commercial land is in the highest (120+) site class, a far higher proportion than in any other section of the United States (USDA For. Serv., 1978).

Due to the amount of old growth remaining (40 percent of the softwood volume west of the Cascades is over 29 inches in diameter), cut exceeds growth by 50 percent in Oregon and by 20 percent in Washington. This is primarily a function of west-side conditions. Mortality is over one-third of growth in Oregon and one-fourth of growth in Washington (USDA For. Serv., 1978).

In brief, timber volumes in the Pacific Northwest are large, there are still substantial amounts of old growth, growth potential is high, annual cut and mortality are very large, and Douglas-fir and hemlock are the most important species.

TABLE 10-3

Growing Stock on Commercial Timberland in the Pacific Northwest by State, Subregion, and Species, 1977 (Million Cubic Feet)

Species	Oregon		Washington	
	Western	Eastern	Western	Eastern
Softwoods				
Douglas-fir	35,818.0	3,262.0	15,303.0	5,690.0
Ponderosa and Jeffrey pine	640.0	8,257.0	32.0	3,704.0
True firs	4,149.0	4,464.0	5,736.0	2,576.0
Western hemlock	7,453.0	570.0	15,689.0	553.0
Sugar pine	696.0	65.0	—	—
Western white pine	440.0	98.0	107.0	243.0
Redwood	91.0	—	—	—
Sitka spruce	881.0	—	585.0	—
Englemann and other spruces	65.0	565.0	31.0	612.0
Western larch	26.0	904.0	10.0	1,628.0
Western redcedar	1,223.0	7.0	3,335.0	230.0
Incense-cedar	549.0	99.0	—	—
Lodgepole pine	253.0	3,835.0	137.0	1,415.0
Other conifers	313.0	6.0	117.0	67.0
Total softwoods	52,597.0	22,132.0	41,082.0	16,718.0
Hardwoods				
Cottonwood and aspen	33.0	19.0	190.0	110.0
Red alder	2,801.0	2.0	4,189.0	5.0
Oak	524.0	3.0	—	—
Other hardwoods	1,838.0	1.0	1,153.0	56.0
Total hardwoods	5,196.0	25.0	5,532.0	171.0
Total all species	57,793.0	22,157.0	46,614.0	16,889.0

Source: USDA For. Serv., 1978.

THE PHYSICAL ENVIRONMENT

Physiography

The following summary is derived from Franklin and Dyrness (1973), Atwood (1940), and the Forest Soils Committee (1957). A total of 15 physiographic provinces may be distinguished in the Pacific Northwest. These may be grouped in the west into two north-south chains of relatively young, rugged mountains with an intervening trough and in the east, into a lava plateau with "islands" of mountains.

The western of the two mountain chains is close to the Pacific coast and includes, starting from the north, the Olympic Mountains, which occupy much of the Olympic Peninsula and form a peneplain with a number of monadnocks extending 2,000 to 3,000 feet above the general mountaintop level to an altitude of about 8,000 feet. South of the Olympics lie the Coast Ranges, which rise to approximately 4,000 feet. All of the coastal mountains from the Olympics south are bordered to the west by a narrow coastal plain which shows many clearly defined terraces, indicative of recent uplift.

The northern portion of the Puget Sound-Willamette Valley lowland is dominated by the complex coastline of Puget Sound. While the land beneath it may have sunk appreciably, Puget Sound is not a simple preglacial river valley, but rather is a more complicated system of embayments formed by the advance and retreat of the Vashon glacier. Glaciation extended southward to the vicinity of the present-day location of the Nisqually River, and in this locality, from sea level to an elevation of about 1,000 feet. A number of present-day rivers flow from the Cascades into the Sound, forming alluvial valleys that contain the best soils of the region. South from Puget Sound to the Columbia River lies a 100-mile stretch of lowland that is covered by the outwash from the last glaciation, except in places where the underlying Tertiary rock comes to the surface.

The Willamette Valley is the southern geographical equivalent of Puget Sound, but is composed of a flood plain covered with young alluvial material over Tertiary bedrock, which is exposed in places.

The Cascade Mountains parallel the Puget Sound-Willamette Valley lowland. The northern Cascades province is approximately 100 miles wide and is joined on the east by the Okanogan Highlands to an extension of the Rocky Mountains and on the south, to the southern Washington Cascades. These two provinces reach an elevation of 8,000 feet, with a number of higher volcanic peaks standing out at altitudes of 9,600 to 14,400 feet. Glaciers are common at the higher elevations. Streams have dissected these mountains into many deep valleys with steep sides.

South of the Columbia River in Oregon the Cascades are divided into two physiographic provinces: (1) the Western Cascades, a low-lying hill region which gradually rises from the Willamette Valley to an elevation of about 4,000 feet, forming most of the Cascade Range in Oregon; and (2) the High Cascades, composed of a number of volcanic peaks similar to those in Washington. These peaks are composed of cinder piles, interbedded with lava flows.

In southwestern Oregon the Coast Ranges and the parallel Cascades come together in a physiographic province referred to as the Klamath Mountains. This area is comprised of deeply dissected mountains, much older than the Coast Ranges to the north and rising to 6,000 feet.

One of the most extensive lava plateaus in the world, the Columbia and Snake River Plateau, lies in eastern Washington and Oregon. Generally this is an area of rolling topography, deeply dissected by water-formed canyons and containing an "island" of mountains—the Blue Mountains of northeastern Oregon. Most of this area is drained by the Columbia River, except for a portion directly east of the Cascades in southern Oregon, where the great Sandy Desert is without external drainage.

Geology and Soils

Although the geology of the Pacific Northwest is complicated, McKee (1972) provides an excellent description.

Bedrock varies greatly in age. The oldest, represented by the Applegate Group in the Siskiyous, is of Triassic origin, but most appears to date from Tertiary time.

Surficial geology indicates that the mountains of the region are composed of metamorphic acid intrusives, basic igneous extrusives, and sedimentary rock, while the glaciated Puget Sound lowlands are largely till in the northern parts and outwash material in the south, with alluvial soils in the river valleys. The Willamette Valley is composed of old-valley fill and recent alluvium. In certain areas marine shale and coastal-sediment parent material dominate.

The Columbia Basin is underlain by Tertiary basalt. The overlying fluvial, lacustrian, aeolian, and glacial sediments form terraces and other features (Highsmith, 1957). The plains of eastern Oregon are similar to the Columbia Basin geologically, and the Blue Mountains are an intrusion of the northern Rocky Mountains similar to the mountains in northeastern Washington.

Because of a diverse climate, parent material, glacial history, and vegetation, the Pacific Northwest contains a variety of great soil groups. Eight of the ten orders in the new soil taxonomy are substantially represented in the region. Inceptisols are the most extensive with Alfisols and Ultisols also being important orders. Entisols, Mollisols, Spodosols, and Histosols are present to a lesser extent.

While podzolization is the dominant soil-forming process in the Puget Sound area, it is not intensive in the mild moist climate. Inceptisols have formed on the younger glacial landscapes and Alfisols and Ultisols are found on older surfaces. Inceptisols usually exhibit thin A_1 horizons and thin or discontinuous A_2 horizons. The B horizons are thick but not strongly developed. At higher elevations cooler and wetter climates promote more intensive soil formation and Spodosols (podzols) are found, showing the typical eluvial A_2 horizon and illuvial spodic B horizon. Throughout the Cascades of Oregon and Washington soils influenced by volcanic ash (Andepts) are found and there is an extensive area of such soils on the east side of the Cascades in southern Oregon.

The stream beds and flood plains in the northwest, as in other parts of the region, contain alluvial soils (Entisols) which have little profile development except for a thin A_1 horizon. In alluvial areas of high water tables Aquents and Aquolls are found. Mountainous terrain or other steep topography commonly has shallow, poorly developed Entisols (lithosols).

Along the Pacific coast and in southwestern Oregon, except at high altitudes, older landscapes and a warmer climate give rise to Ultisols—that is, well-developed soils which usually have thin, unincorporated, organic layers, an A_1 horizon, and a B horizon that may be subdivided on a textural basis. These Humults are high in organic matter.

East of the Cascades, where a more severe and arid climate prevails, the forested areas occur on Alfisols (brown forest and grey-wooded soils), except for certain high elevation sites where Spodosols have developed. As rainfall decreases and the forests become more sparse, the Alfisols grade into soils of higher base status and thicker A₁ horizons (Mollisols). These Mollisols, with extended dry periods (Xerolls), cover extensive desert areas in interior Washington and Oregon. Areas with low organic-matter incorporation and low rainfall, such as desert sites, are represented by Aridisols.

Climate and Weather

Franklin and Dyrness (1973) provide a thorough synthesis of U.S. Weather Bureau data for the Pacific Northwest.

The combination of seasonal climate controls, proximity to the Pacific Ocean, and physiographic features provide the Pacific Northwest with remarkable climatic variation. The ocean is a major influence on the climate, serving as a source of moisture and as a control of temperature extremes. Air masses moving east from the ocean extend its effects over the entire region, although with diminishing magnitude as distances increase and physiographic barriers intervene.

During the summer an atmospheric high-pressure zone known as the "Pacific High" is located just off the Pacific Northwest coast. This zone tends to prevent cyclonic disturbances from approaching the region and directs them northward to Alaska. This weather phenomenon, together with dry, northwest winds coming from the Pacific High, gives the area relatively dry summers. In winter, the high-pressure zone moves southward and allows the "Aleutian Low" to come into position off the coast, permitting a succession of cyclonic storms to sweep over the area. This regional pattern produces the relatively mild, wet winter and dry summer climate which is considered the trademark of the Pacific Northwest.

Not so generally appreciated are the major climatic variations produced by the two parallel, north-south mountain chains, the Olympic-Coast Range chain and the Cascades. As the moisture-laden air masses move inward, they are forced upward and are cooled, losing much of their moisture on the west-facing, windward slopes. The east-facing, lee slopes receive much less precipitation and rainshadows in certain areas produce semidesert conditions even on the east side of the Olympic Peninsula and in the San Juan Islands. This orographic influence, together with the variation in temperature and length of growing season inherent to increased altitude, provides distinct climatic zones in the Pacific Northwest. Highsmith (1957) divides these into four types; the marine coast, the protected western lowlands, the Cascade Mountain area, and the modified interior. Each type has physiographic connotations that allow for easy delineations.

Needless to say, the marine coastal climate is dominated by proximity to the ocean. Summers are relatively dry, with only 8 percent of the annual, total precipitation of 60 to 80 inches falling during this period. Temperatures are moderate during the summer (August, the hottest month, averages 55 to 59°F), but there is only about 50 percent sunlight, due to fog. Winter climate on the coast is mild (January averages 40 °F) but very windy, raw, and cloudy, with rain from 17 to 20 days each month. The frost-free period is long—over 250 days. The slopes of the coastal mountains are progressively wetter and cooler with increasing altitude and more of the precipitation is in the form of snow. However, the climate remains mild and moist and provides excellent conditions for forest growth.

The protected western lowlands comprise the Puget Sound-Willamette Valley trough and have the typical dry, sunny summers and mild, wet winters characterizing the region. Annual precipitation is generally under 42 inches. July temperatures average between 60 and 70 °F. Occasional hot, dry east winds lower humidity and may create serious forest fire danger during July and August, which are practically rainless. The first fall frost usually occurs between October 15 and November 15 and the last spring frost between March 15 and April 1. Winter is mild, with January temperatures averaging about 39 °F, and with frequent, light precipitation. Many winters pass without appreciable snowfall, although occasional heavy snows have been recorded.

The Cascade Mountain zone has the same relationship to the western lowlands that the coastal mountains have to the Coastal Plain. Summers are relatively short, dry, and sunny, while winters are characterized by abundant precipitation and, due to the altitude, enormous depths of snow. Snow at the 5,500-foot elevation reaches 200 to 600 inches annually and may remain on the ground through July.

The modified interior climate east of the Cascades has very little precipitation except on isolated mountain masses, generally less than 20 inches annually, with certain locations receiving as little as 5 to 7 inches. Summer precipitation is very low, but in contrast to the area west of the Cascades, winter precipitation is also quite modest. However, there may be more extension of rainfall into spring. December, the wettest month, has only 1 to 2 inches of precipitation. Winters tend to be colder and sunnier with increasing distance from the Cascades. Summers are sunny and warm with occasional convectional showers providing early season moisture. July temperatures average 70 to 74 °F. Due to the clear weather, warm days are usually followed by cool nights. Increased precipitation and lower temperatures are associated with increased elevation in the Okanogan and Blue Mountains.

THE MAJOR FOREST TYPE GROUPS

A very substantial amount of research has been directed, for more than half a century, to describing and classifying the complex and strongly zoned vegetation of the Pacific Northwest or portions thereof. Fortunately, for both foresters and other plant ecologists, this wealth of information from all sources (published and unpublished) was synthesized into a single, thorough, scholarly publication in 1973 by Franklin and Dyrness of the U.S. Forest Service. For more detail, the reader is directed to this publication and the very complete bibliography found therein. The following descriptions are drawn in large measure from this comprehensive work, as is Fig. 10-2, which shows the geographic distribution of the vegetation zones.

The zonal concept of Daubenmire (1968) is used by Franklin and Dyrness (1973) as a basis for classification. This concept describes a zone as an area in which one plant association is the climax where soil or topography are not sufficiently limiting to alter the overall effect of macroclimate, that is, the climatic climax. Such a zone is usually, although not always by Franklin and Dyrness, named for the dominant or characteristic climax species. The brief description of the forest ecology of the Pacific Northwest which follows is considered within this zonal context.

The *Tsuga heterophylla* zone might be considered the benchmark of the region west of the crest of the Cascade Mountains, since it is the largest in geographical area and most important in productivity. Much of this zone was, and is, occupied by subclimax forests dominated by coastal Douglas-fir, generating the common term "Douglas-fir region" for all of western Oregon and western Washington. Although climatic climax stands are rare, stands that have been undisturbed for several centuries are common and successional trends apparent. It is evident that western hemlock is the typical climax species on mesic sites. Western redcedar is the principal climax species on wet sites. On very dry sites coastal Douglas-fir plays the climax role. Grand fir occurs sporadically in a tolerant role but under conditions which, frankly, are not understood. Big-leaf maple is the only hardwood tree that occurs in other than seral stands and then rarely. Pacific silver fir is found at upper elevations in the *Tsuga heterophylla* zone, particularly in the northern Cascades and in the Olympics, and occasionally is present at surprisingly low elevations. Pacific yew occurs sparingly in the understory nearly everywhere.

The composition of subclimax stands is quite varied depending on the nature of the previous stand, the type(s) and frequency of disturbances, and the edaphic and climatic environment. Before the influence of modern man, it appears that catastrophic fire, at one-century or longer intervals, was common, resulting in the replacement of Douglas-fir stands by Douglas-fir regeneration in the snag or dying tree areas. Red alder, the other presently ubiquitous seral species, was largely confined to areas of more frequent disturbance, that is, stream beds, by virtue of its shorter life span. With the advent of logging followed by slash burning, the natural cycle of Douglas-fir following Douglas-fir was disrupted and its seed source reduced. As a result, red alder, by virtue of its abundant, light seed and immunity from fire and logging, became a much more prominent component of many young stands.

Western white pine, ponderosa pine, lodgepole pine, Oregon white oak, and even grass-dominated prairies can be present around Puget Sound on dry sites associated with deep glacial outwash and the rainshadow of the Olympic Mountains. At the southern limits of the *Tsuga heterophylla* zone in Oregon incense-cedar, sugar pine, and ponderosa pine may be found. Black cottonwood is found along streambeds, as is Oregon ash. Bigleaf maple is common.

Pacific madrone occupies certain very dry sites. Sitka spruce occurs near the coast, adjacent to the *Picea sitchensis* zone, and in the heads of some valleys in the north half of the Washington Cascades. Port-Orford-cedar is an important species in a limited area of the southern Oregon Coastal Range.

The use of understory species to indicate productivity potential has long been recognized in the *Tsuga* zone and has been recently used in the delineation of plant associations (*sensu* Daubenmire) in certain areas. While the exact details vary with site, species such as ocean spray, Pacific rhododendron, and salal characterize the drier, less productive areas; Oregon grape and vine maple somewhat more mesic ones; and swordfern and Oregon oxalis the most favorable and productive locations. Generally there is a tendency to increasing dryness from north to south in the *Tsuga* zone, which is reflected in the understory species array over a local gradient of soil moisture.

A narrow strip along the Pacific Coast is designated the *Picea sitchensis* zone (Fig. 10-2), although, as Franklin and Dyrness (1973) and others have pointed out, it could be considered a variant of the *Tsuga heterophylla* zone due to the presence of Sitka spruce in seral stages. Its position between the ocean and the Coastal Mountains makes for a very wet, mild climate and frequent fog eases moisture stress even in the relatively rain-free summer season. Forest composition and successional patterns are somewhat similar to those described in wetter and more productive portions of the *Tsuga* zone, except that Sitka spruce plays a larger role and Douglas-fir a much less important one, being primarily confined to drier sites.

The most common natural disturbance is blowdown, which often results in abundant hemlock reproduction, either previously established or subsequently seeded. Sitka spruce and red alder reproduction are favored by mineral soil exposure, which may occur as a result of windthrow mounds, stream flooding, and combinations of logging and slash burning. One of the more striking features of the zone, despite its tremendous individual tree growth and overall forest productivity, is the prevalence of dense, relatively long-lived shrub communities in early successional stages. These communities of salmonberry, elderberry, salal, vine maple, and huckleberry may develop after fire or logging or beneath an initial tree canopy of the relatively short-lived red alder. They may remain for decades.

The general tendency is for the understory tree reproduction of all mature conifer forests to be dominated by western hemlock reproduction.

Shore pine stands are found on sand dunes immediately adjacent to the coast and red alder, shore pine, western white pine and western redcedar in swamps.

Contained within the southern portion of the *Tsuga* zone in Oregon is the interior valley or *Pinus-Quercus-Pseudotsuga* zone (Fig. 10-2). Because this zone lies in the rainshadow of the Coast Range and the Siskiyou Mountains, it is the driest and warmest area west of the Cascades in Oregon and Washington. The Willamette, Rogue, and Umpqua valleys were covered largely by grassland and oak savannas in the middle 1800s and therefore were among the first areas settled for agricultural purposes. Apparently this original grassland condition was caused and sustained by fires set by Indians. Succession in the absence of fire apparently has a general trend of grass → oak → conifer.

On driest and warmest sites ponderosa pine is important, while Douglas-fir and grand fir may be the climax species in more mesic circumstances. South of the *Tsuga* zone and above the interior valley zone in southwestern Oregon on the west slope of the Cascades and in the Siskiyou Mountains is an extremely complex forest containing elements from west and east of the Cascades, as well as from California. This area (Fig. 10-2) is described by Franklin and Dyrness (1973) as comprising the mixed evergreen or *Pseudotsuga-sclerophyll* zone in the western Siskiyous and the mixed conifers or *Pinus-Pseudotsuga-Libocedrus-Abies* zone in the eastern Siskiyous and southwestern Cascades. In the former, Douglas-fir and tanoak are the principal climax species while ponderosa, Jeffrey, sugar, and knobcomb pine and incense and Port-Orford-cedar are important seral species. In the latter, white or grand fir are the major climax species, although Douglas-fir or incense-cedar may play this role on warm, dry sites, and western hemlock on the more northern and cooler and wetter areas. Ponderosa, sugar and white pine, Douglas-fir, and incense-cedar are important seral species. Similar forested areas are described in more detail in the California chapter.

The *Abies amabilis* zone occurs above the *Tsuga* zone on the west slopes of the Cascades from the Canadian border to about 43° North latitude in Oregon and in the Olympic Mountains. It also occurs sporadically in the northern Coast Range in Oregon and on the east slopes of the Cascades in Washington. This zone's elevational limitations range from 2,000 to 4,000 feet in northern Washington and 3,000 to 4,500 feet in Oregon. At its southern extremity in Oregon (south of 43° or 44° N latitude) it is replaced by the *Abies concolor* and *Abies magnifica shastensis* zones. Tree composition varies but generally the major climax species is Pacific silver fir, with western hemlock playing a lesser role at low elevations. Hemlock, Douglas-fir, noble fir, and white pine are typical seral species although other elements of the lower *Tsuga heterophylla* zone and higher *Tsuga mertensiana* zone are not uncommon. *Vaccinium* spp. are typical of the shrub layer, although Oregon grape and salal are found on drier sites and a rich variety of herbs and devil's club on wetter areas.

The *Abies amabilis* zone is characterized by a cooler and wetter climate than the *Tsuga heterophylla* zone. Perhaps most significant ecologically is the fact that there is much more snow, which accumulates to depths of 3 to 10 feet. This is considered to be the reason for the interesting and unusual ecological role change of western hemlock, the climax species of the lower, more mesic *Tsuga* zone and subclimax in the more severe, higher *Abies* zone. The overwinter accumulation of debris in the snow pack and its greater duration beneath a canopy favor the sturdier Pacific silver fir seedlings over the more fragile hemlock seedlings. As a result, hemlock reproduction is found on the forest floor beneath a canopy low in the *Abies* zone, on fallen logs only at somewhat higher elevations (presumably because such logs emerge earlier from the snowpack), and finally only where there is no canopy, which has the effect of eliminating

the debris in the snowpack and lessening its duration. However, if the snowpack is over 10 feet in depth, its duration alone makes hemlock reproduction
uncertain (Scott *et al.*, 1976). Alder-dominated communities are common,
maintained by frequent snow avalanching.

The highest forested zone on the west slopes of the Cascades and in the
Olympic and Klamath Mountains is the *Tsuga mertensiana* zone, which extends
from 4,000 to 5,500 feet in northern Washington and from 5,500 to over 6,000
feet in southern Oregon. Mountain hemlock is the general climax species,
although subalpine fir is common on drier sites and Pacific silver fir is very
important in Washington and northern Oregon. Lodgepole pine, subalpine fir,
and even mountain hemlock can all play a pioneer role. The lower portion of
this zone is closed forest and the upper part is composed of tree clumps interspersed with shrubby or herbaceous subalpine plant communities. The trees
frequently extend upward farthest where snow depth and duration is least, for
example, on narrow, windswept ridges.

Above the limit of trees is the alpine zone, dominated by ericaceous species
in lower parts and herbaceous species in the upper elevations. This condition is
not widespread in the Pacific Northwest. Above and interspersed with the
alpine zone are limited areas of perpetual snow and ice (Fig. 10-2).

East of the Cascade Mountains in Oregon and Washington treeless steppe
(grassland) and shrub-steppe (sagebrush) vegetation is native to the hottest and
most arid portions (Fig. 10-2). Franklin and Dyrness (1973) group the forested
areas into seven zones in order of increasing elevation and hence generally
cooler and wetter climate. These are the *Juniperus occidentalis, Pinus ponderosa, Pinus contorta, Pseudotsuga menziesii* (plus *Libocedrus decurrens*),
Abies grandis (plus *Abies concolor*), *Tsuga heterophylla* (plus *Thuja plicata*),
and the *Abies lasiocarpa* zones. Of these, only the *Pinus contorta* zone is not a
true climatic climax, but is caused by extensive deposits of volcanic ash in south
central Oregon. Franklin and Dyrness (1973) are careful to point out, however,
that this elevational sequence varies substantially within the region. All of these
eastern zones are dealt with in detail in other chapters and while the Pacific
Northwest specifics may vary somewhat, they will not be described further.
They occur on the east slope of the Cascades in Oregon and Washington, in the
Blue Mountains, and the Okanogan Highlands (Fig. 10-2).

It is difficult to summarize the many combinations of tree species in the
Pacific Northwest into type groups that have an ecological basis and at the same
time provide a framework for explaining the thrust of silvicultural practice.

For example, in the *Tsuga heterophylla* zone the intolerant tree species
might be ecologically categorized as the Douglas-fir-red alder type group,
after the two most common species; the tolerant species could be characterized
as the western hemlock-western redcedar type group for the same reason.
However, silviculture in this part of the region is almost entirely directed to the
management of coastal Douglas-fir.

Similarly, in the *Picea sitchensis* zone the seral stands are composed of varying combinations of red alder, spruce, Douglas-fir, hemlock, and cedar and the

climax stands are again the western hemlock-western redcedar type group. However, in this zone, silviculture is usually directed to the management of western hemlock and Sitka spruce and to a more limited extent, of Douglas-fir.

With this type of reasoning in mind and in order to discuss the silvical characteristics of the major species and the resulting, appropriate silvicultural practices where this information is most suitable and applicable, and to minimize repetition, the major forest type groups suggested by the USDA Forest Service (1973) to outline silvicultural systems will be followed. For the Pacific Northwest these are (1) the western hemlock-Sitka spruce type group to cover silviculture in the *Picea sitchensis* zone; (2) coastal Douglas-fir for the *Tsuga heterophylla* zone; (3) true fir-mountain hemlock for the *Abies amabalis* and *Tsuga mertensiana* zones primarily; (4) the mixed conifers of southwestern Oregon type group for the complex of several zones in this part of the region; (5) the northwest ponderosa pine type group for the *Pinus ponderosa* and *Pinus contorta* zones at low elevations east of the Cascades; and (6) the mixed-pine-fir type group for all of the other forested zones east of the Cascades in the Pacific Northwest. The first three will be dealt with in more detail than the last three, which are fully described in other chapters. They will be considered only insofar as silvicultural practice in the Pacific Northwest is unique.

HISTORY OF FOREST USE

After the overland expeditions to the Pacific Northwest by Mackenzie in 1793 and by Lewis and Clark in 1805, English and American fur trading companies established posts in the region, and between the 1830s and 1850s thousands of settlers arrived. In the latter part of the century westward movement of population took place. This migration was further stimulated by the completion of the first direct, transcontinental railway link in 1883.

West of the Cascade Mountains initial settlement was restricted to waterways because these were the only accessible areas in the dense forests. The Willamette Valley was the only large area of land suitable for agriculture without extensive clearing. Other river valleys were cleared by logging and converted to agricultural lands. Most sites other than the better alluvial soils proved submarginal for agriculture.

In eastern Oregon and Washington agricultural development started before the middle of the 19th century on unforested steppe and steppe-shrub vegetation and after 1850 assumed major proportions. Adjacent forested lands were used extensively for grazing of both sheep and cattle, especially during the summer season (Meinig, 1968; Oliphant, 1968).

Logging started in the early 1800s with the installation of a sawmill near Vancouver, Washington, by the Hudson Bay Company. Initially, harvesting of trees was confined to areas that were within skidding distance of mills (or water) by teams of oxen or horses; but this was not necessarily a very limiting factor since there were literally thousands of miles of shoreline on Puget Sound and the coastal rivers of Oregon and Washington. The California gold rush created a very substantial demand for wood in the middle of the 19th century and consequently an increase in timber harvesting and lumber production in the Pacific Northwest (Steen, 1969).

With the advent of the steam donkey, power skidding was introduced in the 1890s. The first donkeys were simply vertical, steam-driven spools around which a few turns of cable were made, but rapid improvement resulted in the introduction of multiple-drum systems. At the same time, with the completion of the transcontinental railways in the 1880s, logging railroads developed from the original small, upright-boiler locomotives on wooden rails to specialized and highly efficient equipment. The transcontinental railways also brought a supply of highly skilled civil engineers, whose expertise became available to the logging industry.[1] These developments allowed the logging operations to move away from the immediate vicinity of water, which had provided the earlier means of transportation, to any area where suitable railway grades could be established.

Although logging trucks and tractors were tried in the 1920s, their use was not widespread until the 1930s. However, because of the greater flexibility possible with trucks and caterpillar tractors, these had almost entirely replaced railroads by the end of World War II. Specialized off-highway trucks were developed to carry large loads and continuous-track hauling units were used alone or in combination with cable-skidding machinery. These equipment changes allowed expansion of logging operations into areas where topography and/or size had precluded railroad logging.

The two decades from 1950 to 1970 included a discovery that cable skidding was preferable to continuous track skidders on many soils and on steep topography, as well as the development of rubber-tired skidders for frequent, partial cuts in small dimensioned stands. In addition, self-loading trucks came into use and many main logging roads were hard-topped. The 1970s have seen the introduction of mechanical shears for felling; low-pressure, wide, rubber-tracked skidders; balloon and helicopter logging; and light cable equipment capable of lateral yarding in partial cuts. Currently two major concerns are logging without significant impact on water regimes and improving the energy efficiency of logging techniques.

Forest use west of the Cascades started on areas accessible to water, progressed inland, and onto more extreme topography, as logging equipment improved and demand increased. Virgin timber is still being cut on the higher slopes of the Olympics and western slopes of the Cascades but the age classes of the second forest follow the original, regional pattern of harvesting. Clearcutting has been and still is almost universal, frequently followed by burning the logging slash.

East of the Cascades, forest utilization also started at lower elevations as the farmers and ranchers required wood, progressing upward as a wood-using in-

---

[1]Personal communication—Doyle Burke.

dustry developed. However, harvesting was most frequently a partial cut of currently merchantable stems in a complex forest mosaic of species, age, and size.

SILVICULTURE OF THE MAJOR TYPE GROUPS

Western Hemlock–Sitka Spruce Type Group

Place in Ecological Succession.   Although western hemlock dominates this type group, there are various admixtures of other species, depending on location, site, and disturbance patterns. Sitka spruce is a component when there was sufficient mineral soil at the time of stand establishment. Western redcedar is found on upland sites but is more important in wetter areas. Douglas-fir occurs on the drier sites, particularly if there is a history of fire. Lesser amounts of grand fir and Pacific silver fir are present in the Washington part of the type group. In southern Oregon redwood, Port-Orford-cedar and Oregon myrtle are frequently present. Shore (lodgepole) pine is found on the dunes immediately adjacent to the coast and in swamps, as is western white pine. Red alder is very common and abundant on areas where recent disturbance has provided a mineral-soil seedbed, as well as in swamps.

Stand structure is usually even-aged, the older stands originating after blowdown or, much less frequently, fire. The younger stands are established after clearcutting, followed sometimes by fire. If the stands are sufficiently mature, tree reproduction, primarily western hemlock, but also western redcedar and Sitka spruce, will be established, especially on fallen logs and where the overstory canopy has started to open. Nontree understory species are listed in the previous section describing major forest types. It is rare, at least in modern times, to find areas where disturbance has been absent for sufficiently long periods of time for classical all-age structure to develop.

This type group includes as major species western hemlock and western redcedar, which are considered to be the principal, tolerant, climax species in both the *Picea sitchensis* and the *Tsuga heterophylla* zones, and Sitka spruce, a long-lived and relatively tolerant species. Of the other, less well-represented species, grand fir and Pacific silver fir are very tolerant and all others more or less intolerant, although the exact successional status of Port-Orford-cedar and Oregon myrtle is debatable (Franklin and Dyrness, 1973).

It could be argued that the type group is climax by virtue of the fact that its most important member, western hemlock, is the archetypal climax species west of the crest of the Cascades, below the area of influence of the true firs (about $2,500 \pm 500$ feet, depending on local circumstances). However, it must also be recognized that the dominant component of most stands, old or young, natural or man influenced, originated following a disturbance and, while in most areas the forest composition is floristically dominated by western hemlock, it is not all-aged, but rather even-aged, or if old enough, two or three aged.

Since many of the tree species in the type group are more important in other forest types of the Pacific Northwest or other regions, only western hemlock, western redcedar, and Sitka spruce will be considered in detail. Grand fir and Port-Orford-cedar will be treated more briefly. The ecological descriptions that follow are derived from Fowells (1965) and Minore (1979).

Western hemlock is very tolerant, a prolific seeder after 20 or 25 years and commonly bears annual seed crops, although heavy crops occur only every 3 or 4 years. Due to the tolerance of hemlock, seed bearing is not so restricted to open-growth or dominant trees, as with other, less tolerant species. Hemlock seed dissemination is excellent and has been classed as better than any other conifer in the Pacific Northwest. Germination takes place on any seedbed that is sufficiently moist. Under such conditions, even decaying wood offers excellent conditions for hemlock germination. Seedlings are quite shallow rooted and thus are at a disadvantage on sites subject to drought during the growing season. Initial height growth is relatively slow and, even at more mature stages, height development is not so rapid as Douglas-fir, red alder, most pines, nor Sitka spruce. Western hemlock does not tolerate so much continual root flooding as redcedar, and is considered to be susceptible to windthrow, due to its shallow roots. Fire usually causes severe damage because of hemlock's thin bark.

Western redcedar is also classed as very tolerant and is an excellent seed producer, ranking second only to western hemlock among the principal conifers in the region. However, dissemination of seed is not very efficient and cannot be compared to hemlock nor Douglas-fir. Vegetative reproduction develops from adventitious buds when living parts of redcedar trees come in contact with the ground, particularly on wet sites. Redcedar seed germinates well regardless of type of seedbed, but mortality of seedlings from disease, drought, and heat injury is very high.

Although height growth is slow compared to other species, redcedar is long lived and eventually reaches large size. It apparently tolerates wet conditions better than most of its associates, but grows slowly if flooding is extreme. It is very susceptible to fire injury, more so than any other conifer in the region, and is quite shallow rooted.

The range of Sitka spruce is restricted to areas of very humid climate along the coast and in the heads of certain west-facing valleys in the northern half of the Washington Cascades. It is classed as tolerant, long lived, and has fast juvenile height growth. Sitka spruce, starting at age 20, is a frequent seed producer but is not so prolific as western hemlock. Seed dissemination is good. Although germination can occur on a variety of seedbeds, it is best on mineral soil in partial shade. Sitka spruce shows greatest growth advantage over associated species on the better sites.

Grand fir is classed as tolerant and is a moderate seed producer after 20 years of age. Seed dissemination is not outstanding but appears adequate for distances of about 200 feet. Germination of seed is low, but apparently occurs equally on all types of seedbeds. Seedlings develop a taproot rapidly, are quite resistant to drought or heat injury, and so sustain less mortality than some associated species. Juvenile height growth is rapid, approaching that of Douglas-fir.

Port-Orford-cedar is considered tolerant, producing some seed every year, with heavy seed crops every four or five years, although seed quality is poor and dissemination modest at best. It is capable of moderate height growth but slows appreciably if overtopped. The species is long lived, shallow rooted and very susceptible to fire.

Growth Rates. It is universally agreed that potential yields in the hemlock-spruce type group are among the highest in the world for coniferous forests, but beyond this there is much debate.

The original data of Meyer (1937) for mixed hemlock-spruce unmanaged stands has been refined for pure hemlock stands by Barnes (1962) and others, most recently Wiley (1978). Maximum, net, mean-annual increments on best sites (120 foot height at 50 years) and highest densities of more than 365 cubic feet (to a 4-inch inside bark) at age 70 were found by Wiley (1978), who also postulated mean gross yields of almost 425 cubic feet annually on the same site and rotation. Of course, these data represent the most productive site and stocking conditions, but average conditions also give impressive yields.

Less is known about unmanaged yields of the other major species in the type group since they rarely occur in pure stands; therefore, there has been neither the opportunity nor the incentive to develop reliable yield tables. Needless to say, there are tremendous accumulations of biomass in old-growth stands of all species, but since these data bear little relationship to current or future silvicultural practice or yield potential, they will not be included.

Information about managed yields in the hemlock-spruce type group is still in its infancy in the Pacific Northwest (Bruce and Hoyer, 1976), but there is a substantial amount of data from Europe, where the major species have been grown in managed plantations for long periods of time and represent in many locations the most productive species. However, highest European site indices are usually substantially lower than those found on best sites in the Pacific Northwest. Despite the obvious dangers in comparing yields from such widely separate and different environments, some interesting and thought-provoking points emerge from these European data. The work of Bradley *et al.* (1966) in Britain serves as an example, although similar information is also available from several countries of mainland Europe.

The highest site index of western hemlock in the British managed yield tables approximates 100 feet at 50 years and on this site, maximum mean-annual increment (to a 3-inch top outside bark) culminates at 55 years at 330 cubic feet. The initial stand spacing was about 6 × 6 feet and thinning started at 15 years. This was repeated every 5 years, reducing the stand to a density of 133 stems per acre at 55 years. Almost exactly 50 percent of total production was removed in the thinnings.

In the Pacific Northwest, Wiley (1978) gives a mean-annual increment in unmanaged stands of hemlock of the same site index and age (and maximum density) of 296 cubic feet (to a 4-inch top inside bark), although in these unmanaged stands growth does not culminate until age 80 at 310 cubic feet. The comparison, while not precise, is sufficiently close to suggest that other comparisons are possible.

Aldhous and Low (1974) found by numerous paired plot comparisons in managed British plantations that western hemlock usually had better yields than Douglas-fir, as did western redcedar and grand fir, particularly on more productive sites. The authors warn, however, that most comparisons are based on relatively young plantations, 20 to 40 years old, and that more time is needed to reach final judgments. In these comparisons, grand fir also surpassed Sitka spruce on better sites.

One of the most interesting current debates in the Pacific Northwest concerns the relative yields of western hemlock and Douglas-fir. This is possibly due to past (and present!) chauvinism about Douglas-fir and the consequent planting of this species in both hemlock-spruce coastal forest type and the true fir-hemlock high-elevation forest type. Evidence is now emerging that hemlock may have the superior site index on certain areas (Steinbrenner, 1976); that at equal site indices, hemlock has very superior unmanaged yields (Wiley, 1976); and that on some locations, even when Douglas-fir has superior site index, hemlock has higher, unmanaged, maximum mean-annual increment (Handley, 1976). However, comparable spacing trials, admittedly of short duration and few in number, indicate superior dimension development of Douglas-fir at all spacings (Smith, 1976); so the evidence is mixed and as yet somewhat inconclusive.

Rotation Age.   The rotations referred to above are based on maximum, average, annual yields which culminate at 50 to 65 years in managed stands, and at over 80 years in unmanaged stands. There is every evidence that operational rotations for wood production will be substantially less than these, due to both economic and pathological considerations.

Cultural Practices

REPRODUCTION METHODS.   As pointed out by many observers in the past and recently summarized by Franklin (1976), Williamson (1976), and Ruth and Harris (1973), it is ecologically possible to use almost any of the classical silvicultural systems, with the exception of the seed-tree method, to establish abundant reproduction in the hemlock-spruce type group. The seed-tree method is prohibited by lack of windfirmness. In fact, as Williamson (1976) states, an embarrassing abundance of reproduction, particularly hemlock, frequently results from any cut ranging from a heavy shelterwood involving the removal of about 30 percent of the basal area to complete clearcutting. Advanced reproduction is frequently present in older stands, particularly under holes in the canopy, and a selection system appears feasible, if desired. This same advanced reproduction, if not destroyed by the harvest cut or subsequent site treatment, responds to release very well and may dominate subsequently established seedlings (Williamson, 1976). In such cases, what are thought of as seed cuts in shelterwoods or clearcuts in more usual practice in reality should be regarded as removal cuts in naturally occuring (or at least unmanaged for) shelterwood systems.

Hemlock reproduction appears to establish itself well on almost any seedbed in the coastal area and Sitka spruce and cedar are found on many seedbeds, too, but appear to be more favored by reductions of organic material. Reproduction of the latter two species also appears to be more adversely affected by an overstory than that of hemlock (Fowells, 1965).

Despite the apparent flexibility of reproduction options, in practice, clearcutting, with or without reliance on advanced regeneration, is almost universally used in operational silviculture. Partial cuts are unnecessary to obtain satisfactory reproduction and, in previously unmanaged stands, are not windfirm. Franklin (1976) points out that there is also the possibility that, with partial cuts in stands with a firmly established subordinate vegetation, there may be a real danger of such species outcompeting tree reproduction and creating brush-dominated systems. Additionally, if dwarf mistletoe has infected the hemlock, it is necessary to eliminate the overwood as well as any infected, advanced reproduction to eliminate this parasite from the new stand.

While natural reproduction is usually abundant after cutting, it is necessary to regenerate artificallly areas where brushfields have developed. It has also been common practice in the past to plant spruce or Douglas-fir to add a greater mixture of these species to the overwhelming natural hemlock reproduction (Ruth and Harris, 1973).

Cleary et al. (1978) provide an extremely thorough, in-depth synthesis of current knowledge about regeneration techniques in the Pacific Northwest, from seed collection to cleaning operations in established reproduction stands. The reader is directed to this publication for a complete bibliography and detailed discussion.

Despite the tolerance of the principal desired species in the hemlock-spruce forest type, it is essential to provide for appropriate control of competing vegetation. Newton (1976) indicates that direct seeding requires most site preparation, since it is essential to have a moist germinating bed, protection from direct sun, and absence of broadleaf vegetation whose debris crushes the young hemlock seedlings. This is best accomplished by flattening slash, light mechanical scarification, sometimes by burning, and perhaps the use of herbicides. Planting small seedlings requires much the same type of site preparation, but large seedlings require only chemical methods. Needless to say, the effort involved in these manipulations varies greatly, depending on the nature of the competing species, the amount of residual logging slash, the topography, and the soil characteristics. Specifics range from no treatment at all to sophisticated combinations of mechanical, chemical, and burning techniques. Gratkowski (1975) gives an excellent review of herbicide applications in silvicultural practice in the Pacific Northwest.

Growing and planting bare-root western hemlock seedlings successfully has been a problem in the past and the development of container-grown seedlings was widely heralded as a solution in the late 1960s and early 1970s. However, recent improvement in bare-root seedling production techniques (Cowles, 1976) have led many foresters to favor large bare-root stock in the coastal hemlock-spruce forest, if planting is needed, because the rapid development of competing species makes the smaller, container-grown stock less feasible (Newton, 1976; Long, 1976). Nevertheless, others still favor container stock (Arnott, 1976).

INTERMEDIATE OPERATIONS. Cleanings have been alluded to in the preceding section. Newton (1976) suggests that, while the removal of overstory competition is important, hemlock, at least, grows to advantage with medium density, equal-sized competition. Gratkowski (1975) provides specific details of the type of herbicide and timing of application for releasing hemlock and spruce from common competing species. These include red alder, bigleaf and vine maple, salmonberry, willow, cherry, and elderberry.

Thinning in hemlock has been investigated for almost two decades (Malmberg, 1966; Walkup, 1976; Bruce and Hoyer, 1976) and recently, early density control or precommercial thinning has been increasingly used in operational silviculture in the hemlock-spruce forest type group (Waterman, 1976). However, most thinning research in the Pacific Northwest has dealt specifically with Douglas-fir. The concepts are generally applicable to the hemlock-spruce type and will be considered in detail in following sections.

While thinning generally reduces total gross volume growth per acre, early thinning in precommercial sizes provides a gain in the development rate of the remaining trees, and later thinning in commercial dimensions recovers mortality that would otherwise be lost. Generally, precommercial thinning should be done as early as possible, but in hemlock this concept should be applied with caution, since more reproduction may be established after the thinning. If the remaining members of the thinned stand are not sufficiently advanced to maintain dominance, the effort will be wasted. Spacing should be appropriate to the dimension desired at the next cut, whether it be another thinning or the final harvest. Since hemlock is not thought to develop dimension as rapidly as Douglas-fir (although this may be debated on some sites), density left after precommercial thinning is generally greater than in the case of Douglas-fir (Waterman, 1976).

Thinning later in the rotation (commercial thinning) has not been operationally applied to any extent in the hemlock-spruce forest type group in the Pacific Northwest for several reasons; lack of markets, concern about damage to the residual stand, scarcity of precommercially thinned stands of sufficient age or appropriate natural stocking, and lack of knowledge of techniques and results. However, managed-stand yield tables, using research plot data from all sources, are presently being prepared (Bruce and Hoyer, 1976) and some limited examples of repeated thinning are available (Walkup, 1976). Of course, European managed yield tables can be useful approximations, if used cautiously (Bradley et al. 1966; Aldhous and Low, 1974).

Current operational planning contemplates an initial spacing at about age 15 or a bit younger. If no further thinning is planned, density will be about 300 to 400 trees per acre and final harvest at about age 40. If a commercial thinning is planned at about age 25, initial density will be greater, perhaps 600 to 800 stems per acre; the commercial thinning will reduce this to 300 or less, followed by final harvest at age 40. Atkinson (1976) provides an interesting economic analysis of these general regimes, contrasted with an unmanaged stand.

FERTILIZATION.   Fertilizing with nitrogen has been investigated for almost 30 years and is widely used in current operational silviculture in the Pacific Northwest, but results in the hemlock-spruce coastal forest type are disappointing in both unthinned and thinned stands (Institute of Forest Resources, 1979). Reasons are unknown and under investigation but currently, fertilization is not part of operational silviculture in this forest type.

TREE IMPROVEMENT.   Piesch (1976) and Duffield (in press) synthesize the status of tree improvement in the hemlock-spruce forest type. Briefly, the program is in its infancy; research was started only about 1968 (in Canada) and currently a number of cooperatives and individual private and public agencies are involved in selection for seed production or breeding purposes, but are not near any operational program. The important species, hemlock and spruce, exhibit ample genetic variation for improvement efforts. These are primarily concerned with increasing productivity.

PURPOSES OTHER THAN WOOD PRODUCTION.   There is little or no operational silviculture aimed at values other than wood production in the hemlock-spruce forest type group, aside from some consideration in parks and campgrounds. Here efforts are made to reduce hazard trees, maintain naturalness, and provide diversity.[2] However, according to Brown,[3] guidelines for wildlife habitat are currently being developed, based on the concepts used by Thomas (1979) for areas east of the Cascades. Public agencies, both federal and state, have set aside a number of outstanding examples of natural stands in the hemlock-spruce forest type for research purposes; here the silviculture is aimed at protection (Franklin et al., 1972).

Harr (1976) summarizes a number of research findings concerning the effects of forest manipulation on stream flow and concludes that, while road building and clearcutting have a local, onsite effect of increasing annual yields and summer low flows, the overall effect on a large watershed is extremely small, unless over 12 percent is seriously impacted.

Bacon and Twombly (1978) make a number of suggestions about silvicultural practice for landscape management in the hemlock-spruce forest type and while these specifically apply to southeast Alaska, they are equally valid in areas of steep terrain in Oregon and Washington. These include starting the cut at the

[2]Personal communication—John Pinkerton.
[3]Personal communication—Reade Brown.

tops of slopes and progressing downward; logging in narrow, partially concealed corridors; conforming to natural landform features; and, if possible, partial cutting. This last is infrequently feasible in mature hemlock, but may be possible in certain Sitka spruce river bottom stands.

Susceptibility to Damage. There is much evidence of windthrow as a primary cause of disturbance and destruction in the hemlock-spruce forest type. The combination of shallow-rooted species, heavy rainfall, and high coastal winds produces both annual and catastrophic, periodic losses. Perhaps less notorious but of equal concern to the silviculturist is the mounting evidence that wind pruning of foliage may be very important in causing a sharp reduction in productivity of the coastal forests at ages of less than 100 years (Grier, 1976).

Western hemlock is extremely susceptible to disease (Driver, 1976), but probably only three parasites will present significant problems during intensive silvicultural practice. *Fomes annosus* is probably the most serious and limiting factor, since hemlock is so easily wounded. This disease is extremely successful on any cut surface, spreading through roots to adjacent, untouched stems. Cutting of high stumps (3 feet) in precommercial thinning or the immediate application of borax or zinc chloride to stumps and injuries in older stands appears to help control this very important root and butt rot (Morrison and Wallis, 1976). However, it is still possible that the prevalence of *Fomes annosus* will limit both the rotation length and the number of cultural entries feasible in western hemlock. The teapot fungus may be a serious cause of mortality to seedlings on soil that has been treated by burning (Driver, 1976). The solution is to delay planting for several years following fire. Dwarf mistletoe has been referred to in previous sections. Control is very possible if infected, individual stems of hemlock, particularly of superior stature, are eliminated in either reproduction or intermediate operations. Sitka spruce has no serious diseases in young, managed stands, nor does western redcedar.

The blackheaded budworm and the western hemlock looper, both defoliators, are the only two serious insect pests on hemlock (Shepard, 1976). The Sitka spruce weevil, the same species as the white pine weevil, causes stem deformation in young spruce and the spruce aphid has at times caused severe mortality. Western redcedar has few insect enemies (Fowells, 1965).

Evans (1976) has summarized what is known about the impact of animals on trees in the hemlock-spruce forest type. While numerous birds and animals destroy seed or cotelydonous seedlings and bear damage trees in pole and small sawtimber sizes, it is generally recognized that animal damage to young conifer plantations is by far the most serious impact and that all tree species may be affected. The animals include mice, rabbits, hares, mountain beaver, deer, and elk. Control varies, depending on the animal. There is currently no poison registered for control of nongame animals, so alteration of environment, physical protective devices, trapping, and repellants are used. Physical protection, repellants, and special hunting regulations are the principal means of alleviating game species damage.

Coastal Douglas-fir Type Group

Place in Ecological Succession.   West of the Cascade Mountains, more or less pure stands of Douglas-fir are considered to be the benchmark forest communities of the Pacific Northwest, but in reality there are a number of variations. The original old-growth forests, whose origin was primarily periodic, catastrophic fire, frequently had understory components of western hemlock and western redcedar. If the original disturbance was sufficiently removed or moderate, these same, more tolerant species were represented in the overstory as well. Although these forests are now largely eliminated by logging, the younger stands, which originated most often following fire in the logging slash, are still characterized by a preponderance of Douglas-fir. However, they may range from pure stands of this species to pure red alder. A component of hemlock and cedar is also common, particularly in the northern parts of the Pacific Northwest. (For ecological details, see preceding sections of this chapter.)

The coastal Douglas-fir forest type is commonly considered to be subclimax and this is certainly true except on certain very dry, sterile sites.

On very xeric soils Douglas-fir may be the major tree species of the climax stand. Western hemlock, the usual climax, is ill-adapted to such environments and does not invade in an aggressive fashion. Such sites are susceptible to frequent fire, which also discriminates against the tolerant species and favors Douglas-fir. Occasionally Douglas-fir will develop small, even-aged groups, much like the stand structure of ponderosa pine east of the Cascades and in contrast to the even-aged Douglas-fir stands universally found on more mesic sites on the west side of the Cascade crest.

The major species are listed as medium to very intolerant by Fowells (1965) and/or Minore (1979) and, under usual circumstances, require a disturbance for successful establishment. An example of this is illustrated in Figs. 10-3 and 10-4. These show an area in the foothills of the Cascades immediately after a fire and approximately 30 years later, when a well-stocked stand of Douglas-fir has developed. Such conditions do not always prevail. Repeated fire, or combinations of fire and logging often will eliminate the seed-bearing trees so thoroughly that the vegetative cover is dominated by brush species. This situation occurs most frequently on good sites where subordinate species grow well and are usually present to take advantage of any opening in the tree canopy.

The species composition of tree reproduction following disturbance is an interesting and complex ecological phenomenon. The competitive relationship between Douglas-fir and red alder during immature stages is an example.

Douglas-fir is a species of medium tolerance, long life, large size, and moderately rapid juvenile height growth. It does not sprout, but after 25 years of age bears good seed crops every 5 to 7 years. The seed disseminates well to about six tree lengths; occasionally, under very favorable conditions, it may travel much farther—up to one-half mile.

Red alder is considered a very intolerant tree. It is relatively short lived and

Figure 10-3.   Scene immediately following an extensive fire in 1926 in the foothills of the Cascades. Mount Rainier is in the background.

Figure 10-4.   The same view shown in Fig. 10-3, but 33 years later. Note the snags still standing in the vigorous young stands of Douglas-fir and the patch clearcuts in the unburned foothills in the background.

small sized when compared to associated conifers, but has very rapid juvenile height growth. Sprouting takes place freely from very small stumps, but this trait disappears with age. Seed crops occur annually after the alder is about 10 years old. Heavy seed crops are produced on a cycle of approximately 4 years and even light crops produce abundant numbers of alder seed, which disseminate over great distances. Alder has the ability to fix atmospheric nitrogen through mycorrhizal associations.

If seedlings of both species are established in mixture, the composition of the resulting mature stand may vary with site quality and density of reproduction. The rapid initial growth of alder may result in heights of 15 feet at 5 years or 40 feet at 10 years on good sites. Such growth far surpasses Douglas-fir heights because fir grows relatively slowly for the first 5 years and does not equal alder in height until 20 or 25 years old. The better the site quality, the more pronounced is the initial height advantage of alder. If seedling stocking is sufficiently dense to allow alder to overtop and suppress Douglas-fir for a number of years, the resulting mature stand will be predominantly alder. On the other hand, if seedling spacing is wide enough to allow Douglas-fir to remain unsuppressed by alder until it passes the alder in height, the fir will overtop the alder and form a pure stand. Alder rarely maintains a closed canopy beyond 60 to 80 years, even on excellent sites, and individual trees over 100 years old are rare.

On medium-quality sites, alder has less height advantage over Douglas-fir and the two species compete more equally. Alder on medium sites seldom reaches large size, nor does it completely eliminate Douglas-fir, as it may on good sites. On the poorest, dry sites, alder rarely attains tree size, is a competitor of Douglas-fir seedlings only, and is eliminated when the tree canopy closes.

Western white pine is superior to Douglas-fir on poor sites. On good sites, the growth of these two species with very similar silvical characteristics would appear the same, although there is no concrete information comparing yields in the coastal region of the Pacific Northwest. White pine usually occurs as scattered individual stems or small groups, although Allen (1959) refers to one area in which white pine dominates a stand and contributes more than 50 percent of the total volume. Individual stem development of white pine and Douglas-fir, however, is equal on better sites and white pine is superior on very poor sites (Small, 1965). While there is evidence from pollen analysis that white pine was once a more important species in the Pacific Northwest (Hansen, 1947), white pine blister rust presently prevents serious consideration of this species in management. However, in addition to superior growth on poor site, white pine shows evidence of being relatively immune to diseases that seriously affect young Douglas-fir, notably yellow ring rot (Hadfield and Johnson, 1977). For this reason, it may be an excellent species on ring-rot infected sites if rust-resistant strains can be developed.

Lodgepole may also be present on excessively drained, sterile soils, but appears to have no advantage in growth over Douglas-fir on such sites. Since lodgepole pine is quite intolerant, it is usually overtopped and eliminated by fir except on the very poorest soils, where it may form a physiographic climax.

Black cottonwood is a very intolerant species, a prolific seeder and sprouter, relatively long lived, and capable of excellent growth in appropriate environments. This species needs a moist seedbed for successful germination and complete freedom from overhead competition for seedling survival. In addition, cottonwood requires the most productive areas to develop its spectacular growth potential. Such sites, where not cleared for agricultural purposes, usually support the most luxuriant vegetation of the region. As a result, they are rarely available for successful cottonwood invasion, even immediately after disturbance, because of the rapid revegetation of other species. Since all requirements for successful establishment and growth of cottonwood are commonly met on new alluvial deposits, it is on such areas that cottonwood stands are found. Once established on good sites ahead of competing vegetation, cottonwood makes excellent height growth and gives high yields. Many good cottonwood areas are flooded annually for short periods during the season when growth is dormant.

In bogs and swamps, where there are long, continuous periods of flooding and where the water is stagnant, Douglas-fir grows very poorly if at all and even alder is greatly reduced in vigor. In such locations, strangely enough, western white pine and lodgepole pine, two species well suited to very dry sites (as previously described) are abundant. Although they do not grow at optimum rates in swamps, these two species are apparently able to survive the continuous root flooding better than others of the type group. As a result, they often are the first trees to invade such sites and in later successional stages, occur in mixture with western redcedar. In some cases, lodgepole pine is the sole tree species on stagnant bogs, forming a physiographic climax.

Growth Rates.   Although it is generally recognized that the coastal Douglas-fir forest type, like the hemlock-spruce forest type, is among the most productive, natural, coniferous forests of the world, there is still no really firm information about yields under intensive management for an entire rotation in the Pacific Northwest; nor is there likely to be any substantial amount of such data for a decade or two. It is therefore necessary to rely either on estimates based on unmanaged yields or upon managed yields where Douglas-fir has been planted as an exotic, or finally, upon models derived from stand information available after short-term treatment.

Mean-annual net increments at age 50 vary from over 50 to more than 200 cubic feet per year in unmanaged stands, depending on site quality (McArdle *et al.*, 1961). Estimates of gross yield increase these values by 15 to 20 percent (Staebler, 1955) or 45 to 85 percent (Curtis, 1967), depending upon mensurational techniques and assumptions.

Bruce (1969) has compared these unmanaged gross yields with managed yields of the same site indices in Europe and New Zealand. Generally it appears that managed stands are more productive than the unmanaged gross estimates and that the difference becomes greater as site quality increases. While much of the evidence is tenuous, it is not unreasonable to suggest that in managed stands of Douglas-fir, the poorer sites may well produce approximately 100 cubic feet per acre of mean-annual increment and the very best may well exceed 400 cubic feet annually at appropriate rotations (40 to 70 years). Dimension development of 4 to 6 rings to the inch at breast height can be obtained with density control for such rotations on all sites, although perhaps at some sacrifice of yield, particularly on less productive sites.

Reukema and Bruce (1977) and Bruce *et al.* (1977) provide a simulation model of yield and the effect of thinning. A more refined model of managed stand yields will soon be available.[4]

Alder yields have been summarized recently by Chambers (1974). Unmanaged stands vary between 81 and 190 cubic feet mean-annual increment at age 60. Debell *et al.* (1978) suggest that average yields of about 300 cubic feet per acre are possible in managed stands at rotations of about 10 years on the best sites.

Black cottonwood is capable of excellent yields. Smith and Blom (1970) report yields in excess of 475 cubic feet mean-annual increment at 15 years, with dimensions of 12 inches d.b.h. and heights of 79 feet.

Rotation Age. Potential rotation lengths vary a great deal, depending on the specific objectives of management. Red alder for energy or pulpwood and Douglas-fir for Christmas trees may well be grown on rotations of a decade or less. For maximum yield, Douglas-fir should probably be grown on rotations of 40 to 60 years, depending on site, but these may be shortened for economic reasons. On the other hand, certain public agencies are still contemplating rotations approximating 100 years or more, when a variety of social considerations enter their management plan. The most common rotations currently being used for Douglas-fir are from 40 to 80 years by both private and public agencies. Red alder and black cottonwood rotations are shorter.

Cultural Practices

REPRODUCTION METHODS. Even-aged management is appropriate on most sites to the ecological requirements of Douglas-fir and the other species in the type group. Clearcutting has been and is widely considered to be the appropriate reproduction method, although unintentional seed-tree and more recently, shelterwood techniques are also successful (Williamson, 1973). Not so widely appreciated is the fact that on certain sterile and dry sites Douglas-fir may be the climax species and, at least theoretically, could be reproduced by the group selection method.

In the past, the old-growth forest was clearcut except for a period during the 1930s (Munger, 1930, 1933, 1939), when selection methods were tried on inappropriate sites and therefore proved unsuccessful. Clearcutting, usually accompanied by burning of the logging slash, most often resulted in tree reproduction, but species composition and speed of seedling establishment frequently left something to be desired. If fire occurred again in a short period of time, stocking of tree species might be reduced to unacceptable levels. On south-facing slopes tree reproduction frequently failed. In both circumstances nontree species became dominant.

Currently the most common silvicultural practice is clearcutting, followed by

---

[4]Personal communication—Robert O. Curtis.

appropriate site preparation, and planting. However, the details of this overall procedure vary with site, stand condition, and management constraints of the particular public or private agency. Cleary *et al.* (1978) provide an exceptionally thorough synthesis of information about reproduction methods in the Pacific Northwest and should be referred to for detail and a complete bibliography.

When utilization is high and subordinate vegetation minimal, no site preparation may be required. At the other extreme, if amounts of residual material are large, the competing vegetation luxuriant, and the danger of animal damage or disease high, it may be necessary to combine mechanical scarification, burning, and chemical treatment to provide adequate planting conditions. Of course, steepness of terrain and soil characteristics limit the use of certain equipment. Costs vary substantially and these, as well as availability of equipment and skilled personnel, obviously play an important role in the final selection of site preparation methods. Specific non-economic recommendations may be found in Cleary *et al.* (1978).

Following site preparation, the decision as to planting, direct seeding, or reliance on natural reproduction must be made. In the coastal Douglas-fir forest type, reliance on natural regeneration is currently the exception because too frequently it is so erratic and slow that it will not meet either the management objectives of most agencies nor the legal requirements for reforestation in Washington and Oregon.

Although red alder is rarely the object of management, natural reseeding may be relied upon because of its prolific seed production and excellent dispersion.

Direct seeding was regarded with some enthusiasm in the 1950s and 1960s, due to the development of predator-repelling coatings, but it has steadily declined in use since then. Despite the appeal of relatively low cost, results have not been sufficiently reliable to satisfy management objectives. Site preparation must be more thorough to assure mineral soil seedbeds and minimal vegetative competition; even then losses from seed or seedling predators, heat, and frost injury to cotelydenous seedlings make results uncertain. In addition, direct seeding under the best conditions requires much more seed than planting and suitable provenances of seed may be limited.

However, if appropriate seed is available, direct seeding is still being carried out when seedlings are not available, when planting is too difficult on rocky sites, or when the combination of available planting crews and the length of planting season makes planting impossible on all areas that require reforestation. Seeding is usually done in November and January at rates of about one pound per acre.

Planting is currently regarded as the standard method of establishing reproduction in the coastal Douglas-fir forest type. Seedlings are usually 2-0 or 2-1. Great strides have been made in developing better quality stock through reduction of density in the nursery beds, root undercutting and wrenching regimes, and appropriate fertilizing and irrigation. Techniques of handling and storing seedlings from nursery bed to planting have also been greatly refined in recent years.

In the late 1960s and 1970s, when it was thought that container-grown seedlings would solve most planting problems, particularly on difficult sites, substantial investments were made in container facilities. The advantages lay in quicker, more flexible production schedules; less planting shock; better planting by unskilled or careless crews; lengthening of the planting season; and better seedlings of some species, particularly hemlock and the true firs, which were difficult to produce and plant with conventional bare-root techniques. The initial wave of enthusiasm, however, was quickly tempered by high costs, difficulties with root binding and frost heaving, and most especially in Douglas-fir, by small size, which predisposed the container-grown seedlings to greater damage from competing vegetation and predators. While the use of container seedlings will undoubtedly continue for some species and sites, and refinement of growing regimes and containers will eliminate some of the problems, operational silviculturists currently favor well-developed, bare-root stock in the coastal Douglas-fir forest type.

Black cottonwood is usually planted with cuttings, which can be taken from mature trees, but most commonly are "whips" or natural seedlings, often 6 to 8 feet tall, which are cut and planted. Red alder seedlings have been raised experimentally in both nursery beds and containers and wildlings have been transplanted (Kenady, 1978). There is only modest operational planting of cottonwood and practically none of red alder.

Planting densities vary from about 650 to 400 or less per acre. The higher densities are planted when mortality is anticipated, on more productive sites, and if "precommercial" thinning is planned to select for quality and spacing at an early age.

Control of competing vegetation, or cleaning, is an integral part of establishing reproduction. Not only is the direct competition of undesired species severe in the excellent growing conditions of the Douglas-fir forest type, but also the habitat for predator animals created by the presence of such species is often critical. Undesired vegetation, depending on circumstance, includes everything from grass to tree species and is usually chemically controlled. An excellent summary of specific techniques is provided by Gratkowski (1975), but due to current government regulations on herbicide use and new chemical developments, these should be regarded as ephemeral.

There is ample evidence, though, of the importance of cleaning on both successful reproduction and on the growth and yield of established seedlings of both tolerant and intolerant species in the Pacific Northwest. Most silvicultural prescriptions routinely include this operation, either preplanned because of past experience in similar circumstances or applied as need develops.

While clearcutting is the most common reproduction method in the Douglas-fir forest type, Isaac (1943) initiated a growing awareness of the possibilities of the shelterwood method. However, there has been little operational use of this system until recently. Currently Hughes (1979) reports that on national forests in Oregon and Washington there are more than 400,000 acres of planned shelterwood cuts and the final removal cut has been made on more than 30,000 acres of this total. Most of these have been carried out in the last seven to eight years. Additionally, there are more than 1,200,000 acres of unintentional shelterwood with satisfactory, established regeneration in need of removal cutting. It is unclear how much of this acreage is in the coastal Douglas-fir forest type, but a substantial portion is, particularly on severe sites in the southern parts of the region. It should be emphasized that these figures apply only to uniform shelterwood and make no mention of the very considerable edge effect, which is really a strip shelterwood environment, found on the periphery of clearcut areas.

Shelterwood has been found to have a very favorable effect on both survival and growth of coastal Douglas-fir reproduction on extreme sites, such as south-facing slopes, in the hotter, drier parts of the region. It may protect against frost damage in certain topographic situations, or prevent a high water table from rising until the reproduction is sufficiently advanced to control the water level by its own transpirational use. In addition to these sites, where shelterwood may be a necessity to successful reproduction, there are other sites where shelterwood cutting provides a surer method of obtaining natural regeneration than clearcutting. However, it is not superior to clearcutting and planting in terms of reproduction results, although out-of-pocket costs may be less. Shelterwood is also used along streams to retain a constant forest cover. Finally, and of increasing importance, are areas where shelterwood represents an aesthetic alternative to clearcutting, even though needed for no other purpose.

The disadvantages of the uniform shelterwood system are its greater harvesting expense, restrictions on or higher cost of site preparation, and possible damage to regeneration inflicted by the removal cut. It is also unfeasible if the overwood may infect the reproduction with disease or parasites. Some of these problems may be remedied with careful execution or the substitution of strip or group shelterwood. For example, in uniform shelterwood, site preparation by burning has been successfully carried out on coastal Douglas-fir; careful planning of skidding roads and directional felling, combined with young and small reproduction, can minimize damage during the removal cut. Another imaginative and unique technique involves leaving the protective overwood of smaller, unmerchantable trees or species, underplanting, and then simply killing the overwood in place and allowing it to fall gradually.

When shelterwood is used for aesthetic purposes, it is sometimes not realized that once the removal cut is made, the reproduction is indistinguishable from that established by clearcutting. Therefore, size and arrangement of such shelterwoods should be properly designed.

It is also apparent that shelterwood cuttings, or at least the seed cuts, have sometimes been used to provide required wood production without incurring the stigma of clearcutting, but with little thought to the problems of completing of the system.

Uniform shelterwoods should be used with caution in previously unmanaged, old stands, particularly where canopies are still intact, because there is substantial chance of serious windthrow damage following the seed cutting. On the other hand, if the canopy is already opened up by virtue of age or poor site, it may well be quite windfirm. In this case, all that may be necessary is site preparation to remove the undesired understory and prepare a seedbed or planting site. In managed stands of rotation age in the future, the shelterwood system will be more easily applied where desired, since the trees will be smaller and more windfirm.

INTERMEDIATE OPERATIONS. Despite the fact that managed stand data based on entire rotations are not available in the Pacific Northwest, even for coastal Douglas-fir, there has been a great deal of research on thinning and much operational application. Early (or "precommercial") thinning is now almost universally considered to be an integral part of operational silviculture. Thinning in stands of currently saleable dimension is common, although there is some debate about its economic feasibility in previously unmanaged stands. Silvicultural prescriptions now usually include an early, nonmerchantable thinning, at least, and then subsequent merchantable thinnings, depending on management objectives, site quality, and terrain. Where slopes of more than 30 percent are not considered feasible for thinning with currently-used rubber-tired skidders, light cable devices are being developed which operate on narrow roads and can skid at right angles to the main line. These may revolutionize thinning practices on steep slopes.

Present knowledge of the effects of thinning on yield in coastal Douglas-fir is found in Worthington (1961, 1966); Worthington and Staebler (1961); Reukema (1970, 1972, 1975); Reukema and Pienaar (1973); Wiley and Murray (1974); Hoyer (1975); and Reukema and Bruce (1977). In the following synthesis, specifics apply to coastal Douglas-fir but concepts apply generally to the Pacific Northwest forest types.

Contrary to common opinion, thinning reduces total yield in stands where normal crown differentiation is taking place. This excludes stands that are so dense and on such poor sites that stagnation occurs. On medium sites (site index III), total utilizable volume can be increased 15 percent by early (pre-commercial) thinning and 15 percent by thinning at later (commercial) stages. Gains from early thinning are greater than this on less productive sites, and those from later thinning are greater on more productive sites. Board-foot increases are higher following early thinnings than later ones. There is less advantage from later thinning as merchantable standards decrease, while early thinning gains increase as merchantable standards become less. Early-thinning gains are greater with shorter rotations, while late-thinning advantages increase with longer rotations. If the average diameter of a thinned stand is compared with an equal number of the largest trees per acre in an unthinned stand, the difference is surprisingly small.

Early thinning should be done when the stand is 10 to 15 years old and 10 to 20 feet tall. This timing produces maximum effect on improved height growth, along with selection of superior stems, and will minimize damage to the residual stand. Beyond this stage, these effects will be decreased.

On low-quality sites, early thinning prevents stagnation and results in a lasting improvement in height growth (or site index). Thinning shock, a temporary reduction in height growth, is common if first thinning is delayed beyond about 20 years, particularly on less productive sites.

Early thinning should also be for spacing appropriate to the size that the trees will grow by the next harvest, be it another thinning or final harvest cut. Generally 250 to 400 trees per acre are recommended. Four hundred trees per acre results in an average diameter of 8 inches when the next thinning will be necessary. Lower densities result in somewhat lower total yields but greater board-foot values.

Maximizing production in a stand that has not previously been commercially thinned involves thinning when mortality reaches merchantable size. Later thinning is very important in stands which have been thinned earlier but not reduced to rotation densities. This is because crown differentiation has been narrowed by the early thinning and stagnation possibilities increased.

The interval between successive thinnings should increase with advancing age and decreasing site quality. A logical progression is from initial crown thinnings to later low thinnings. Exact thinning-regime plans vary substantially. The more intensive ones contemplate an initial density adjustment when the reproduction is about 10 feet tall, with a spacing of 10 feet or closer. This is followed by commercial thinning starting at age 15 to 20 depending on dimension, and subsequent thinning at 4- to 10-year intervals to rotations of 40 to 60 years. At the other extreme, on sites that are considered to be commercially unthinnable because of terrain or poor productivity, some agencies plan an initial, early thinning, if necessary, and to allow the stand to develop to rotation age with no further treatment.

Drew and Flewelling (1979) have prepared what appears to be a very useful technique of stand density management in Douglas-fir stands. Tree size and density are related to crown closure, imminent competition-mortality, and maximum size-density relationships. It allows the silviculturist to examine the tradeoff between maximizing tree size or stand yield.

There is little experience with thinning regimes in the other principal species in the forest type.

FERTILIZATION. As mentioned above, research into fertilizer effects on forest growth has been underway for three decades in the Pacific Northwest and a very substantial operational application to Douglas-fir stands has been common for more than a decade. The most recent research information is summarized in Institute of Forest Resources (1979) from a regionwide network of almost 1,500 plots established since 1969. An application of 200 pounds of nitrogen per acre results in a growth increase of 17 percent in unthinned stands and 25 percent in thinned stands. Four hundred pounds per acre raises these figures to 20 percent in unthinned and 28 percent in thinned stands. In unthinned stands there is also significantly greater response as site quality decreases. An economic analysis shows that, based on rate of return, highest priority goes to older, previously thinned stands on site quality II and III, where "real" rates of interest are about 14 percent.

With such results, it is no wonder that nitrogen fertilization is an extremely attractive, intermediate operation in the coastal Douglas-fir forest type. Operational applications vary from starting immediately after precommercial thinning at about age 12 and applying 200 pounds per acre every 5 years until rotation age is reached, to a short-term payoff by fertilizing only within 10 years of the final harvest cut.

The use of red alder, either in alternate rotations, or mixed during a single rotation with Douglas-fir to provide a nitrogen amendment is an intriguing silvicultural alternative to direct fertilizer application. Available data certainly point to substantial yield increase in mixed stands (Miller and Murray, 1978). If such mixtures are attempted, it is necessary to maintain a careful control and the alder should be established at a later date than the Douglas-fir (Stubblefield and Oliver, 1978). The economic feasibility of such silvicultural practice is largely dependent on the price of nitrogen fertilizer (Atkinson and Hamilton, 1978).

TREE IMPROVEMENT.   Silen (1978) synthesizes present knowledge concerning the genetics of Douglas-fir and Duffield (in print) summarizes the status of tree improvement in the coastal Douglas-fir forest type. The most conspicuous features are seed orchards and seed-production areas. These were first established in the middle 1950s and there has been a considerable loss from graft incompatibility. As a result, the program has shifted to the designation of large numbers of roadside, cone-bearing trees for operational seed collection and concurrent progeny testing in carefully designed experiments. In 1979 there were 16 cooperative programs in Douglas-fir tree improvement, each involving two to eight agencies, and a number of breeding units or seed zones. More than 20,000 trees have been selected and testing involves 700,000 seedlings at 173 sites. In other words, initial tree improvement in Douglas-fir has been started on a major scale in Washington and Oregon but aside from progress in technique, there are currently few operationally applicable results.

PURPOSES OTHER THAN WOOD PRODUCTION.   The effect of cutting practices on water yields is similar to that reported for the hemlock-spruce forest type. Harvesting of timber *per se* has only local effects on water yield regimes and does not appear to affect large drainages (Harr, 1976). The roads associated with logging, however, may have an effect on water quality and there are laws in both Oregon and Washington dealing with the specifics of road building and logging practice, aimed at controlling such impact. Operationally, except for restrictions on herbicides, slash burning, and, in some instances, limiting human access, there is little change in conventional silvicultural practice on areas managed primarily as watersheds.[5]

National forest lands have been categorized for visual sensitivity throughout the Pacific Northwest. Bacon and Twombley (1978) suggest ways in which coastal Douglas-fir may be managed to enhance landscape values. These guidelines principally involve the use of smaller cutting units, partial cutting, and

[5]Personal communication—Joseph Monaghan.

moving toward the viewer from the initial entries, all applied to a specific condition.

Guidelines for silvicultural enhancement of wildlife habitat are currently being developed[6] following the principles established by Thomas (1979). These are discussed in following sections of the chapter.

There are numerous recreational areas and parks throughout the coastal Douglas-fir forest type where the silviculture is primarily directed to preserving safety, naturalness, and aesthetic quality.

Forest areas that have been roaded are heavily used in the Pacific Northwest for motorized dispersed recreation away from organized camping sites. Currently, silvicultural guidelines are being developed to enhance dispersed recreational values. These will follow the recreational opportunity spectrum principles developed by Clarke and Stankey (1979) in which accessibility, other resource use, on-site characteristics, privacy, human impact, and regimentation are influenced by appropriate silvicultural practice.

A number of research natural areas have been established in the coastal Douglas-fir forest type to preserve typical cover types (Franklin et al., 1972). Here silviculture is directed to protection of the *status quo*.

Susceptibility to Damage. While the coastal Douglas-fir forest type does not suffer the endemic wind damage found in the hemlock-spruce coastal forest, it is subject to periodic catastrophic damage when water-soaked soil and abnormal wind storms combine. Unmanaged and older stands appear to be most affected.

Laminated root rot has the dubious distinction of being, together with animal damage, the most biologically limiting factor in intensive silvicultural practice of coastal Douglas-fir. Hadfield and Johnson (1977) summarize current knowledge of possible silvicultural treatments under a variety of conditions. In essence, it is necessary to eliminate host species, dead or alive, from infected sites for long periods of time, perhaps a half century. Resistant or immune species include redcedar, ponderosa pine, incense-cedar, red alder, and cottonwood. Intermediately susceptible species include western white pine, Sitka spruce, and western hemlock. Mechanical removal of infected stumps and large roots of susceptible species, together with substitution of resistant or intermediately resistant species, appears to be the only feasible silvicultural treatment.

Another pathogen that may prove very important is the teapot fungus which has been considered important on seedlings only for a few years after slash burning; therefore, it might be controlled by delayed reproduction establishment. Morgan et al. (1974), however, report that it may be associated with mortality in older stands following ground fire.

Disease in young red alder and black cottonwood does not appear to be silviculturally significant, although with advancing age, these species are subject to attacks from a number of fungi.

[6]Personal communication—Reade Brown.

There is little problem with insects in the coastal Douglas-fir forest type. The Douglas-fir beetle has caused damage in old-growth Douglas-fir on dry sites, but in managed, young stands, will probably be relatively unimportant. Defoliators, such as the tent caterpillar, attack red alder and cottonwood, but at present this is of little economic consequence.

Animal damage from game and nongame species in the Douglas-fir forest type is similar to that described for the hemlock-spruce forest type, except that it is more severe and important, ranking with laminated root rot as a silvicultural problem. Possible solutions are similar to those discussed in previous sections of the chapter.

True Fir-Mountain Hemlock Type Group

Place in Ecological Succession. The typical stand is a mature mixture of several species, the overstory having been established by a catastrophy, usually fire, but sometimes wind, and the understory structured according to the age and intactness of the overstory. Species composition varies with latitude, altitude, and aspect, or any other feature that affects climate. The major species are Douglas-fir, western white pine, and noble fir, which are relatively intolerant; western hemlock, Pacific silver fir, mountain hemlock, subalpine fir, Englemann spruce, and Shasta red fir, which are more tolerant. Major variations include the absence of noble fir from the North Cascades and the Olympic Mountains, Shasta red fir replaces it in southern Oregon. Also Douglas-fir is reduced as an intolerant species and western hemlock as a tolerant species, with increasing elevation and hence snowpack. This is most evident with higher north latitude and on the west slope of the Olympics.

The type group includes intolerant and tolerant species, but regardless of composition, most stands have a disturbance origin. Except for noble fir, mountain hemlock, and Pacific silver fir, the silvical characteristics of the important species have been detailed elsewhere in this chapter or in the California or Rocky Mountain chapters.

The following is drawn from Fowells (1965) and Minore (1979). Noble fir is classed as intolerant. It bears very light seed crops annually after 20 to 30 years, with good crops occurring infrequently. Seed dissemination is medium, similar to that of Douglas-fir. Germination percentage is quite low, but occurs on any seedbed that is sufficiently moist. Although noble fir seedlings grow slowly at first and apparently develop no efficient taproot, they subsequently grow as rapidly as any of the associated species. Noble fir often holds a dominant position in mixed stands. It is considered a long-lived species, perhaps more so than any of the true firs.

Pacific silver fir is tolerant. Seed production starts at 20 years with good crops at 2- or 3-year intervals. Dissemination is only moderate because the seed is relatively large. Germination is low but occurs on any sufficiently moist medium. Pacific silver fir exhibits an ability to respond to release after many years of suppression beneath a canopy. Indeed, such shaded conditions appear necessary to survival on relatively warm dry sites, although seedling growth under these conditions is not so good as in the open. Pacific silver fir is relatively long lived and grows to large size.

Mountain hemlock is considered tolerant but perhaps less so than western hemlock and Pacific silver fir. It begins bearing seed at age 20, has some seed every year, with very heavy crops every few years. It germinates readily on any sufficiently moist seedbed. The seedlings are able to survive wet, cold soils very well and recover from damage created by snow movement and from periods of suppression. Mountain hemlock may reproduce by layering.

Growth Rates. There is little precise information about growth rates in the true-fir—mountain hemlock forest type group. Large volumes of sawtimber have been measured and individual tree dimensions are impressive on some of the better stands several centuries old (Fowells, 1965). However, because extensive harvesting in the forest type has occurred recently and species composition is so varied, not even unmanaged yield tables have been published.

It is generally believed that growth rates compare to the lower values found in the coastal Douglas-fir or hemlock-spruce forest type groups. Site-index and height-growth curves have been developed for noble fir (Herman *et al.*, 1978) and Douglas-fir (Curtis *et al.*, 1974) in these high-elevation forests. However, site-index-curve form of common species such as Douglas-fir or western hemlock may be different from that at lower elevations (Curtis *et al.*, 1974), thus making use of the yield tables developed for the latter tenuous in the true fir-mountain hemlock type.

There are some data to indicate that individual stem dimension development of Pacific silver fir is superior to that of western hemlock only at high elevations and on poor site.[7] Murray (1973) compared site indices of noble fir and Pacific silver fir with those of Douglas-fir on a number of sites on the upper Cascade slopes in western Washington and concluded that Douglas-fir was superior to Pacific silver fir at all locations. Noble fir, on the other hand, was equal to Douglas-fir if the Douglas-fir 50-year index was less than 90 and elevation greater than 2,700 feet. At lower elevations and higher Douglas-fir site index, Douglas-fir was superior.

Bradley *et al.* (1966) include managed yield tables for noble fir in Britain. Best sites show a height of 83 feet at 50 years and a maximum mean-annual increment (at 60 years) of 305 cubic feet per acre. Best Douglas-fir yields in Britain exceed this by at least 10 percent but at similar site index (82 feet at 50 years), Douglas-fir has only a mean-annual increment of 178 cubic feet at 60 years. This indicates that caution should be exercised in equating site index and yield in comparing species.

Rotation Age. There is no published information about rotation lengths. There is, of course, the general principle that rotations of maximum mean

[7]Personal communication—John Grant.

increments or given size are longer on less productive sites, so it might be logical to assume longer rotations than currently proposed for more productive zones.

Cultural Practices

REPRODUCTION METHODS.   The almost universal harvesting method in the true fir-mountain hemlock forest type group has been clearcutting, with and without site preparation, usually in the form of burning, then planting. In many ways, these practices have been simply a continuation of those used at lower elevations and not necessarily well-thought-out silvicultural prescriptions. Results have been very erratic and regeneration inadequacies have been common. Franklin and Herman (1973) provide a general synthesis of these problems and suggest alternate silvicultural systems. In many older stands reproduction is established beneath the overstory and, if not destroyed by the logging and/or subsequent site preparation, may provide adequate stocking. This silvicultural method should be regarded as a shelterwood rather than a clearcut. However, response to release may be slow if the advanced reproduction is old and small, and species composition may not be desirable. For example, Wagner[8] found that at 3,700 feet in the central Washington Cascades, only Pacific silver fir was represented significantly in the advanced regeneration under a predominantly hemlock overstory but that hemlock reproduction was preponderantly established in the clearcut after logging. Post-logging regeneration was usually superior in size to surviving, advanced regeneration of the same species 15 years after the logging.

Sullivan (1978) found a close correlation between habitat types and regeneration characteristics in the true fir-mountain hemlock zone in Oregon. On more mesic habitat types clearcutting resulted in adequate regeneration of noble fir and Douglas-fir; on other more severe environments, shelterwood conditions seemed necessary; and on still others, post-logging regeneration was so difficult to obtain that harvesting of any kind was a questionable practice unless advanced regeneration was present and could be preserved. Site preparation, particularly burning, appeared to be a doubtful practice in most habitat types.

There appears to be little question that a uniform shelterwood environment of some type is favorable to many species, except where it may have adverse effects, as noted in previous sections, by prolonging the duration of the snowpack and crushing seedlings with winter-storm-produced debris. The shelterwood effect is probably related to amelioration of temperature extremes and moisture stress. The costs and difficulties of logging and the doubtful windfirmness of partial cuts in mature old growth suggest strip shelterwood as a suitable alternative. So-called "small patch" clearcuts, probably group shelterwoods, are also gaining favor, although there may be frost-pocket dangers if these are sited incorrectly.

[8]Personal communication—Robert Wagner.

Site preparation by slash burning should also be used with care since too often it has resulted in vegetation failures, particularly on south-facing slopes. It destroys any residual, advanced regeneration and frequently creates such harsh microclimatic conditions that neither natural regeneration nor planted seedlings survive at acceptable rates. In this case, brush fields may develop. If possible, site preparation should be restricted to that created by log skidding during the harvesting operation and even this should be carefully planned to minimize disturbance.

Planting failures have possibly been more common in the true fir-mountain hemlock forest than in the lower zones due to harsh environments, limited and late planting seasons, difficult planting sites, and the intractability of some of the species, particularly western hemlock, to bare-root nursery production. Recent evidence suggests that container-grown seedlings offer real promise in solving most of these problems (Cleary *et al.*, 1978). Supplementing natural regeneration with planting is currently a common practice.

INTERMEDIATE OPERATIONS.   There is little information about or experience with thinning in the true fir-mountain hemlock type group since the forests are largely either old growth or too young and small for anything other than a first density adjustment. A common silvicultural prescription on high-elevation, low-productivity sites is to thin precommercially to final crop density and then to do a final harvest cut.

FERTILIZATION.   Fertilizing western hemlock in the Cascades has produced a significant response in younger, thinned stands (Institute of Forest Resources, 1979). Increases of 25 percent in periodic mean increment over a 4-year period have been obtained. However, unthinned stands or older stands show very erratic response to fertilization.

Reproduction of Pacific silver fir exhibits a substantial height increase in response to nitrogen fertilizer (Gallagher, 1964). At least one agency operationally fertilizes such stands.

PURPOSES OTHER THAN WOOD PRODUCTION.   The true fir-mountain hemlock forest type is extremely high in water, wildlife, recreational, and aesthetic values relative to wood production potential—probably much more so than the lower-elevation forest types. However, the status of silviculture directed toward these values is similar to that described in previous sections for the hemlock-spruce and Douglas-fir forest types in that there is considerable interest and planning, but as yet little or no operational application.

There is one difference. The national parks of the Pacific Northwest contain more area in this forest type than any other. The U.S. National Park Service silvicultural practices directed to the preservation of naturalness or rehabilitation of impacted areas are therefore primarily in the true fir-hemlock type west of the crest of the Cascades.

Susceptibility to Damage.   All the damage possibilities that are detailed in other sections relate to the same species in the true fir-mountain hemlock forest type. Additionally, the balsam wooly aphid causes severe damage to Pacific silver fir and subalpine fir but not noble fir; and western white pine is significantly damaged by white pine blister rust (Fowells, 1965). Fire and windthrow have been the most widespread historical disturbances.

Mixed Conifers of Southwestern Oregon

Place in Ecological Succession. The mixed conifers occupy the same ecological position as the pine-Douglas-fir-true fir type described in the California chapter. They comprise a varied mixture of tolerant and intolerant species including ponderosa pine, sugar pine, Douglas-fir, western hemlock, Sitka spruce, Port-Orford-cedar, incense-cedar, grand fir, white fir, Jeffrey pine, knobcomb pine, California black oak, canyon live oak, Oregon white oak, and tanoak.

Cultural Practices. Minore (1973) suggests that clearcutting is generally unsuccessful in the drier interior and that shelterwood is more successful. A recently developed practice consists of leaving a shelterwood of unmerchantable species, preparing the site mechanically, and planting Douglas-fir. After the reproduction is safely established the overstory is killed in place and allowed to fall slowly and naturally. As a result, there is no damage to reproduction.

Nearer the coast, the environment is less extreme and clearcutting followed by chemical site preparation and planting may be appropriate. Animal damage is severe and must be controlled.

Mixed Pine–Fir of Eastern Oregon and Washington

Place in Ecological Succession. The principal species are both intolerant—ponderosa pine, lodgepole pine, and western larch—and relatively tolerant—interior Douglas-fir and grand fir. The forest type is most similar to the Douglas-fir-larch type but also includes at higher elevations a mountain hemlock-subalpine fir forest type. These types are described in the Rocky Mountain chapters. The historical stands were subjected to frequent, low-intensity fire which forced the fire-resistant species into a more or less clumpwise arrangement—that is, ponderosa pine, western larch and, to a certain extent, Douglas-fir. With modern fire protection, probably more or less effective for the past 50 years, the tolerant species, Douglas-fir and grand fir (or white fir in south central Oregon), became more abundant. In other words, the forest type contains both pioneer and climax species, was originally a fire-climax type, but in modern times has shifted more to a climatic-climax composition.

Cultural Practices

WOOD PRODUCTION. Historically, cutting practice in the mixed conifer type has been a single-tree selection based on size and species. Large trees were selected in the mosaic of stands, ponderosa pine, western larch, and interior Douglas-fir being the favored species. This practice, together with the fire-exclusion mentioned in the previous section, resulted in a shift in floristic composition toward the more tolerant species and a denser composition toward the more tolerant species and a denser canopy.

Seidel (1973) outlines the silvicultural possibilities that conform to the ecological requirements of the several species, ranging from clearcutting for the more intolerant to shelterwood for the tolerant.

However, current operational practice is most frequently geared to even-aged management and consists of removing all merchantable timber in a first cut. If the remaining unmerchantable stand warrants the operation, it is then thinned out to a 15- to 20-foot spacing and will be reentered at about 20-year intervals, the final cut being a shelterwood reproduction cut. If the nonmer-chantable stand is inadequate, mechanical site preparation and planting of 2-0 bare-root ponderosa pine are carried out. This latter is somewhat contradictory because there is a general feeling that Douglas-fir is superior to ponderosa pine in dimension, yield, and wood quality as a managed species. This is contrary to the regard in which old-growth ponderosa pine was held relative to other species. However, planting of species other than ponderosa or lodgepole pine has been very unsuccessful.

In the Blue Mountains and the east slope of the Cascades, Seidel (1979) found that regeneration established after clearcutting in upper-slope, mixed-conifer forests was better with higher elevation, northerly aspects, greater slope, and increased severity of burning. Regeneration was adversely affected by the amount of competing grass. Advanced reproduction was important in high-elevation mountain hemlock when there was no burning (Seidel, 1979).

PURPOSES OTHER THAN WOOD PRODUCTION.   There has been more fact-finding about silvicultural applications to wilderness, wildlife, range, and water values in the mixed-conifer forest type than in any other type in the Pacific Northwest, although this has not been followed by wide-scale operational application to date. An exception is the present program of prescribed burning to restore certain national park lands to the ecological status they were in before being influenced by modern fire prevention. Also a very few areas are being managed for wildlife values.

Thomas (1979) describes in some detail the silvicultural practices necessary in the Blue Mountains to favor either featured wildlife species or to manage for species richness. In either case these revolve around (1) scheduling of stand treatments; (2) arrangement of stands in time and space; (3) stand condition; (4) size of treated area; and (5) land type. Examples are given of the wood production sacrifices necessary for adjustments made in these factors to increase wildlife habitat values.

Hall (1975) provides a specific example of the silvicultural methods necessary to combine range and forest values in the mixed-conifer—pinegrass community in the Blue Mountains. These include reducing tree density, shifting species composition from true fir towards ponderosa pine, clearcutting in patches, and seeding orchard grass to replace the native pinegrass. These practices will reduce wood production but will increase forage for range stock.

Helvey *et al.* (undated) reported little effect of timber harvesting on water yield, with the exception of greater snow accumulation in certain areas, on four small watersheds in the Blue Mountains.

Northwestern Ponderosa Pine Forest Type Group

Place in Ecological Succession. The type is similar to those described in the California and Rocky Mountain chapters but has a major variant in the lodgepole pine stands that form a physiographic climax on the pumice soils of south central Oregon. Other species may include Douglas-fir, grand fir, white fir, and western larch in minor quantities. The type is both pioneer and climax at lower elevations and subclimax to the mixed-pine–fir type at higher and more mesic sites on the east slope of the Cascades and in the Blue and Okanogan Mountains.

Cultural Practices. Barrett (1973) gives details of possible silvicultural systems. Clearcutting and planting are feasible where the physical environment is not too extreme but shelterwood may be necessary on very hot, dry sites. In the latter case, if the overstory is infected by dwarf mistletoe the overstory must be removed before the reproduction is attacked.

Operational silviculture by private agencies is much the same as that described for the mixed-pine–fir type. Merchantable trees are harvested and if there is a suitable small residual stand, it is thinned to an 18- or 20-foot spacing. Otherwise the area is planted with 2-0 bare-root seedlings, lodgepole pine on flats where there is danger of frost or where there is a high water table, and ponderosa pine everywhere else.

Lodgepole pine stands on pumice soils are clearcut, the slash windrowed and burned, and the entire site disked and then planted with 2-0 bare-root seedlings.

High standards of quality control and handling of the seedlings are necessary to ensure satisfactory survival rates.

BIBLIOGRAPHY

Aldhous, R. R., and A. J. Low. 1974. The potential of western hemlock, western redcedar, grand fir and noble fir in Britain. *Forestry Commission Bull. 49.* Her Majesty's Stationery Office, London, England.

Allen, J. W. 1959. White pine in western Washington. *J. For.* 57:573–576.

Arnott, J. T. 1976. Survival and growth of western hemlock in British Columbia. In *Proc.—Western Hemlock Mgmt. Conf. Univ. Wash.*, Coll. For. Resour., Seattle, pp. 196–200.

Atkinson, W. A. 1976. Some aspects of the economics of western hemlock management. *In: Proc.—Western Hemlock Mgmt. Conf. Univ. of Wash. Coll. For. Resour.*, Seattle. pp. 306–315.

Atkinson, W. A., and Hamilton, W. I. 1978. The value of red alder as a source of nitrogen in Douglas-fir/alder mixed stands. In Proc. Symp. Utilization and Management of Alder. *USDA For. Serv. Gen. Tech. Rep. PNW-70.* pp. 337–351.

Atwood, W. W. 1940. *The physiographic provinces of North America.* Ginn & Co., Boston. 536 pp.

Bacon W. R., and A. D. Twombly. 1978. National forest landscape management. Volume 2, Chapter Timber. Draft. *USDA For. Serv.* 295 pp.

Barnes, G. H. 1962. Yield of even-aged stands of western hemlock. *USDA Tech. Bull. 1273.* Washington, D.C.

Barrett, J. W. 1973. Northwestern ponderosa pine. *In* Silvicultural systems for the major forest types of the United States. *USDA For. Serv. Agri. Hdb. 445.* pp. 17–19.

Bradley, R. T., J. M. Christie, and D. R. Johnston. 1966. Forest management tables. *Forestry Commission Booklet 16.* Her Majesty's Stationery Office, London, England. 218 pp.

Bruce, D. 1969. Potential production in thinned Douglas-fir plantations. *USDA For. Serv. Res. Pap. PNW-87.* 22 pp.

Bruce, D., and G. Hoyer, 1976. Status report. Development of regional managed-stand yield tables for western hemlock from pooled data. In: *Proc.—Western Hemlock Mgmt. Conf.* Univ. of Wash., Coll. For. Resour., Seattle. 220 pp.

Bruce, D., D. J. DeMars, and D. L. Reukema. 1977. Douglas-fir managed yield simulator— DFIT—user's guide. *USDA For. Serv. Gen. Tech. Rep. PNW-57.* 26 pp.

Chambers, C. J. 1974. Empirical yield tables for predominantly alder stands in western Washington. *Wash. State Dept. Nat. Resour. DNR Report 31.* Olympia. 70 pp.

Clarke, R., and G. H. Stankey. 1979. *The recreation opportunity spectrum, a framework for recreation planning, management, and research.* Unpubl. manuscript. 60 pp.

Cleary, B. D., R. D. Greaves, and R. K. Hermann. 1978. Regenerating Oregon's forests. A guide for the regeneration forester. *Oregon State Univ. Ext. Serv.* Corvallis. 286 pp.

Cowles, D. P. 1976. Bareroot production of western hemlock seedlings. In *Proc.—Western Hemlock Mgmt. Conf.* Univ. Wash. Coll. For. Resour., Seattle, pp. 170–172.

Curtis, R.O. 1967. A method of estimation of gross yield of Douglas-fir. *For. Sci. Monog. 13.* 24 pp.

Curtis, R. O., F. R. Herman, and D. J. Demars. 1974. Height growth and site index for Douglas-fir in high elevation forests of Oregon-Washington Cascades. *For. Sci.* 20:307–315.

Daubenmire, R. 1968. *Plant communities.* Harper and Row. New York. 300 pp.

Debell, D. S., R. F. Strand, and D. L. Reukema. 1978. Short-rotation production of red alder: some options for future forest management. In Proc. Symp. Utilization and management of alder. *USDA For. Serv. Gen. Tech. Rep. PNW-70.* pp. 231–244.

Drew, T. J., and J. W. Flewelling. 1979. Stand density management: an alternative approach and its application to Douglas-fir plantations. *For. Sci.* 25(3):518–532.

Driver, C. H. 1976. Disease impact concerns in the intensive culture of western hemlock. In: *Proc.—Western Hemlock Mgmt. Conf.* Univ. Wash., Coll. For. Resour., Seattle, pp. 126–127.

Duffield, J. W. in press. Better trees for Northwest forests. *West, For. Conserv. Assoc.* Portland.

Evans J. 1976. Wildlife damage and western hemlock management in the Pacific Northwest. In *Proc.—Western Hemlock Mgmt. Conf.* Univ. of Wash., Coll. For. Resour., Seattle, pp. 148–154.

Forest Soils Com. of the Douglas-fir Region. 1957. *An introduction to the forest soils of the Douglas-fir region of the Pacific Northwest.* Univ. Wash., Seattle.

Fowells, H. A. 1965. Silvics of forest trees of the United States. *USDA For. Serv. Agr. Hdb. 271.* 762 pp.

Franklin, J. F. 1976. Effects of uneven-aged management on species composition. *Uneven-aged silviculture and management in the western United States.* In *Proc. In-Service Workshop, Redding, California, October 19–21, 1976.* USDA For. Serv. Tbr. Mgmt. Res., Washington, D.C. pp. 64–70.

Franklin, J. F., F. C. Hall, C. T. Dyrness, and C. Maser. 1972. Federal research natural areas in Oregon and Washington. A Guidebook for scientists and educators. *USDA For. Serv. Pacific NW For. and Range Exp. Stn.,* Portland.

Franklin, J. F., and Herman, F. R. 1973. True fir-mountain hemlock. In Silvicultural systems for the major forest types of the United States. *USDA For. Serv. Agr. Hdbk. 445.* pp. 13–15.

Franklin, J. F., and C. T. Dyrness. 1973. Natural vegetation of Oregon and Washington. *USDA For. Serv. Gen. Tech. Rep. PNW-8.* 417 pp.

Gallagher, L. U. 1964. A study of the effects of fertilization with nitrogen and potassium on the growth and nutrition of *Abies amabalis* with associated greenhouse trials. Masters thesis, Univ. Wash., Seattle.

Gratkowski, H. 1975. Silvicultural use of herbicides in Pacific Northwest Forests. *USDA For. Serv. Gen. Tech. Rep. PNW-37,* 44 p.

Grier, C. C. 1976. Biomass, productivity, and nitrogen-phosphorus cycles in hemlock-spruce stands of the central Oregon coast. In *Proc.—Western Hemlock Mgmt. Conf.* Univ. Wash., Coll. For. Resour., Seattle, pp. 71–81.

Hadfield, J. S., and D. W. Johnson. 1977. Laminated root rot. A guide for reducing and preventing losses in Oregon and Washington forests. *USDA For. Serv. Pacific NW Reg.*

Hall, F. C. 1975. *Range management as a counterpart of forest management.* Mimeo. Wash. State Univ. Pullman.

Handley, D. L. 1976. The yield potential of western hemlock. In *Proc.—Western Hemlock Mgmt. Conf.* Univ. of Wash., Coll. For. Resour., Seattle. pp. 221–227.

Hansen, H. P. 1947. Postglacial forest succession, climate, and chronology in the Pacific Northwest. *Trans. Am. Phil. Soc., N.S.* 37(1):1–133.

Harr, R. D. 1976. Forest practices and streamflow in western Oregon. *USDA For. Serv. Gen. Tech. Rep. PNW-49.* 18 p.

Helvey, J. D., C. Johnson, A. R. Tiedemann, W. B. Fowler, and G. O. Klock, (undated) Climatic and hydrologic characteristics of four small watersheds in the Blue Mountains and some impacts of forest management on these characteristics. *USDA For. Serv.* 2 pp.

Herman, F. R., R. O. Curtis, and D. J. Demars. 1978. Height growth and site index estimates for noble fir in high-elevation forests of the Oregon-Washington Cascades. *USDA For. Serv. Res. Note PNW-243.*

Highsmith, R. M., Jr. 1957 *Atlas of the Pacific Northwest resources and development.* 2d ed. Oregon State Coll. Corvallis. 140 pp.

Hoyer, G. E. 1975. Attaining intensive management goals by precommercial thinning at age 15. A Special Dept. Natural Resour. Intern. Rep. *For. Land Mgmt. Div. Contrib. No. 186.* Olympia. 9 pp.

Hughes, J. 1979. Shelterwood cutting in region 6. Task force report. *USDA For. Serv. Pacific NW Region.* 55 pp.

Institute of Forest Resour. 1979. Regional forest nutrition research project. Biennial Report 1976–78. *Contribution No. 37.* Univ. Wash., Coll. For. Resour., Seattle. 46 pp.

Isaac, L. A. 1943. *Reproductive habits of Douglas-fir.* Charles Lathrop Pack Forestry Foundation, Washington, D.C. 107 pp.

Kenady, R. M. 1978. Regeneration of red alder. In Proc. Symp. Utilization and Management of Alder. *USDA For. Serv. Gen. Tech. Rep. PNW-70.* pp. 183–191.

Long, A. J. 1976. Regeneration performance of western hemlock in Washington and Oregon. In *Proc.—Western Hemlock Mgmt. Conf.* Univ. Wash. Coll. For. Resour., Seattle. pp. 201–205.

McArdle, R. E., W. H. Meyer, and D. Bruce. 1961. The yield of Douglas-fir in the Pacific Northwest. *USDA For. Serv. Tech. Bull.* 201. Washington, D.C. 74 p.

Malmberg, D. B. 1966. Early thinning trials in western hemlock (*Tsuga heterophylla* (Raf.) Sarg.) related to stand structure and product development. Ph. D. dissertation, Univ. Wash., Seattle.

McKee, B. 1972. *Cascadia. The geologic evolution of the Pacific Northwest.* McGraw-Hill Book Co., New York. 394 pp.

Meinig, D. W. 1968. *The great Columbia plain. A historical geography, 1805–1910.* Univ. Wash. Press, Seattle and London. 576 pp.

Meyer, W. H. 1937. Yield of even-aged stands of Sitka spruce and western hemlock. *U.S. Dept. Agr. Tech. Bull. 544.* 86 pp.

Miller, R. E., and M. D. Murray. 1978. The effects of red alder on growth of Douglas-fir. In Proc. Symp. Utilization and Management of Alder. *USDA For. Serv. Gen. Tech. Rept. PNW-70.* pp. 283–306.

Minore, D. 1973. Mixed conifers of southwestern Oregon. In Silvicultural systems for the major forest types of the United States. *USDA For. Serv. Agr. Hdbk. 445.* pp. 10–12.

Minore, D. 1979. Comparative autecological characteristics of northwestern tree species—a literature review. *USDA For. Serv. Gen. Tech. Rep. PNW-87.* 72 pp.

Morgan, P. D., E. K. Wallin, and C. H. Driver. 1974. Occurrence of *rhizina* root rot in an old-growth conifer stand in the Pacific Northwest. *Plant Disease Reporter,* 38(6) 3 pp.

Morrison, D. J., and G. W. Wallis. 1976. Disease following thinning in western hemlock stands. In *Proc.—Western Hemlock Mgmt. Conf.* Univ. Wash., Coll. For. Resour., Seattle, pp. 137–141.

Munger, T. T. 1930. Ecological aspects of the transition from old forests to new. *Sci.* 72:327–332.

Munger, T. T. 1933. Practical application of silviculture to overmature stands now existing on the Pacific coast. In *Proc. Pacific Sci. Cong.* 5:4023–4030.

Munger, T. T. 1939. The silviculture of tree selection cutting in the Douglas-fir region. *Univ. Wash. For. Club Quart.* 12(2):5–13.

Murray, M. D. 1973. True firs or Douglas-fir for timber production on upper slopes in western Washington? Master's thesis, Univ. Idaho, Moscow. 58 pp.

Newton, M. 1976. Site preparation requirements for western hemlock. In *Proc.—Western Hemlock Mgmt. Conf.* Univ. Wash., Coll. For. Resour. pp. 191–195.

Oliphant, J. O. 1968. *On the cattle ranges of the Oregon country.* Univ. Wash. Press, Seattle & London. 372 pp.

Piesch, R. F. 1976. Tree improvement in western hemlock. In: *Proc.—Western Hemlock Mgmt. Conf.* Univ. Wash., Coll. For. Resour., Seattle. pp. 155–165.

Reukema, D. L. 1970. Forty-year development of Douglas-fir stands planted at various spacings. *USDA For. Serv. Res. Pap. PNW-100.* 21 pp.

Reukema, D. L. 1972. Twenty-one year development of Douglas-fir stands repeatedly thinned at varying intervals. *USDA For. Serv. Res. Pap. PNW-141.* 23 pp.

Reukema, D. L. 1975. Guidelines for precommercial thinning of Douglas-fir. *USDA For. Serv. Gen. Tech. Rep. PNW-30.* 10 pp.

Reukema, D. L., and L. V. Pienaar. 1973. Yields with and without repeated commercial thinnings in a high-site-quality Douglas-fir stand. *USDA For. Serv. Res. Pap. PNW-155.* 15 pp.

Reukema, D., and D. Bruce. 1977. Effects of thinning on yield of Douglas-fir: concepts and some estimates obtained by simulation. *USDA For. Serv. Gen. Tech. Rep. PNW-58.* 36 pp.

Ruth, R. H., and A. S. Harris. 1973. Western hemlock-Sitka spruce. In Silvicultural systems for the major forest types of the United States. *USDA For. Serv. Agr. Hdbk. 445.* pp. 5–7.

Scott, D. R. M., J. N. Long, and J. Kotar. 1976. Comparative ecological behavior of western hemlock in the Washington Cascades. In *Proc.-Western Hemlock Mgmt. Conf.* Univ. of Wash., Coll. For. Resour., Seattle. pp. 26–33.

Seidel, K. W. 1973. Mixed pine-fir of eastern Oregon and Washington. In Silviclutural systems for the major forest types of the United States. *USDA For. Serv. Agr. Hdbk. 445.* pp. 15–17.

Seidel, K. W. 1979. Regeneration in mixed conifer clearcuts in the Cascade Range and the Blue Mountains of eastern Oregon. *USDA For. Serv. Res. Pap. PNW-248.* 24 pp.

Shepherd, R. F. 1976. Major insect pests of western hemlock. In *Proc.—Western Hemlock Mgmt. Conf.* Univ. Wash., Coll. For. Resour., Seattle. pp. 142–147.

Silen, R. R. 1978. Genetics of Douglas-fir. *USDA For. Serv. Res. Pap. WO-35.* 34 pp.

Small, C. 1965. Growth comparisons of Douglas-fir and western white pine. Master's thesis, Univ. Wash., Seattle.

Smith, J. H. G. 1976. Spacing trials in plantations. In *Proc.—Western Hemlock Mgmt. Conf.* Univ. Wash., Coll. For. Resour., Seattle. pp. 210–219.

Smith J. H. G., and G. Blom. 1970. Poplar spacing trials show way to gains in wood yield. *Can. For. Ind.*, July 1970. pp. 40–41.

Staebler, G. R. 1955. Extending the Douglas-fir yield tables to include mortality. In Proc. *Soc. Am. Foresters* pp. 55–59.

Steen, H. K. 1969. Forestry in Washington to 1925. Ph. D. dissertation, Univ. Wash., Seattle. 296 pp.

Steinbrenner, E. C. 1976. Soil-site relationships and comparative yields of western hemlock and Douglas-fir. In: *Proc.—Western Hemlock Mgmt. Conf.* Univ. Wash., Coll. For. Resour., Seattle. pp. 236–238.

Stubblefield, G. , and C. D. Oliver. 1978. Silvicultural implications of the reconstruction of mixed alder/conifer stands. In Proc. Symp. Utilization and Management of Alder. *USDA For. Serv. Gen. Tech. Rept. PNW-70.* pp. 307–320.

Sullivan, M. J. 1978. Regeneration of tree seedlings after clearcutting on some upper-slope habitat types in the Oregon Cascade Range. *USDA For. Serv. Res. Pap. PNW-245.* 17 pp.

Thomas, J. W. 1979. Wildlife habitats in managed forests—the Blue Mountains of Oregon and Washington. *USDA For. Serv. Agr. Hdbk. 553.* 512 pp.

USDA For. Serv. 1973. Silvicultural systems for the major forest types of the United States. *Agri. Hdbk. 445.* 114 pp.

USDA For. Serv. 1978. *Forest statistics of the U.S. 1977.* USDA For. Serv., Washington. D.C. 133 pp.

Walkup, R. H. 1976. Stocking control, growth, and yield following precommercial thinning of western hemlock. A case study report on CT-7. In *Proc.—Western Hemlock Mgmt. Conf.* Univ. Wash., Coll. For. Resour., Seattle. pp. 206–209.

Waterman, S. J. 1976. Stocking control in the Douglas-fir region. In *Proc.—Western Hemlock Mgmt. Conf.* Univ. of Wash., Coll. For. Resour., Seattle. pp. 239–243.

Wiley, K. N. 1976. Site index and yield of western hemlock. In *Proc.—Western Hemlock Mgmt. Conf.* Univ. Wash., Coll. For. Resour., Seattle. pp. 228–235.

Wiley, K. N. 1978. Net and gross yields for natural stands of western hemlock in the Pacific Northwest. *Weyerhauser For. Pap. 19.* Centralia, Wash. 124 pp.

Wiley, K. N., and M. D. Murray. 1974. Ten year growth and yield of Douglas-fir following stocking control. *Weyerhaeuser For. Pap. 14.* Centralia, Wash. 88 p.

Williamson, R. L. 1973. Coastal Douglas-fir. In Silvicultural systems for the major forest types of the United States. *USDA For. Serv. Agr. Hdbk. 445.* pp. 8–10.

Williamson, R. L. 1976. Natural regeneration of western hemlock. In *Proc.—Western Hemlock Mgmt. Conf.* Univ. Wash., Coll. For. Resour., Seattle. pp. 166–169.

Worthington, N. P. 1961. Some observations on yield and early thinning in a Douglas-fir plantation. *J. For.* 59:331–334.

Worthington, N. P. 1966. Response to thinning 60-year-old Douglas-fir. *USDA For. Serv. Res. Note PNW-35.* 3 pp.

Worthington, N. P., and G. R. Staebler. 1961. Commercial thinning of Douglas-fir in the Pacific Northwest. *USDA Tech. Bull. 1230.* Washington, D.C. 124 pp.

11

The Alaska Region

David R.M. Scott

LOCATION

The region comprises the state of Alaska, a narrow strip along the upper northwest coast of Canada and the entire northwestern tip of the North American continent. Alaska is by far the largest of the 50 states, consisting of a total of 363 billion acres and covering a range from about 55° to 73° N latitude and 130° to 180° W longitude plus a few degrees east (Fig. 11-1).

FOREST STATISTICS

Several important points about the forests of Alaska are shown in Tables 11-1, 11-2, and 11-3:

Area

While it is generally recognized that commercial forest land (that capable of producing annually at least 20 cubic feet of wood per acre) comprises only a small fraction—little more than 1 percent—of interior Alaska, it is not well known that coastal Alaska, a region commonly thought of as covered by dense old-growth forests, is less than 40 percent forested and little more than one-half of this is considered to be of commercial quality (Table 11-1).

Character of Forest Land Ownership

The predominance of public ownership of commercial forest land is evident in Table 11-2, showing the U.S. Forest Service with major responsibility in coastal Alaska and the Bureau of Land Management and the state of Alaska in the interior. It should be pointed out that at the time of publication this ownership pattern is still fluid. Native land claims, state selection of lands, and exact management objectives of remaining federal lands have not been finalized in many areas.

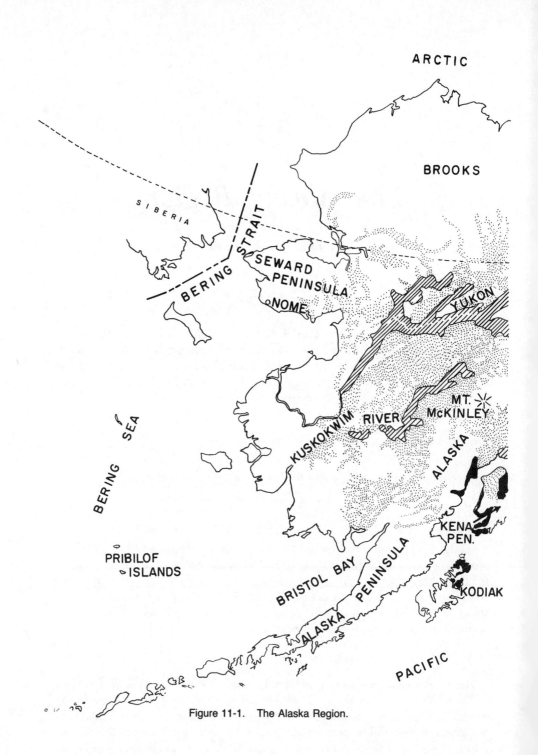

Figure 11-1.　The Alaska Region.

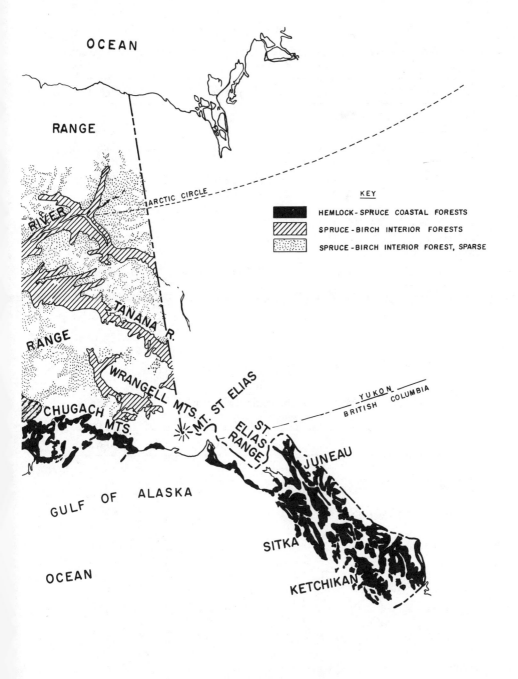

OCEAN

RANGE

RIVER

ARCTIC CIRCLE

TANANA R.

RANGE

WRANGELL MTS.

CHUGACH MTS.

MT. ST ELIAS

ST. ELIAS RANGE

JUNEAU

YUKON
BRITISH COLUMBIA

GULF OF ALASKA

SITKA

KETCHIKAN

OCEAN

KEY

HEMLOCK-SPRUCE COASTAL FORESTS

SPRUCE-BIRCH INTERIOR FORESTS

SPRUCE-BIRCH INTERIOR FOREST, SPARSE

50   0   50   100   150   200
SCALE

TABLE 11-1

Land Area of Alaska (in Thousands of Acres) by Subregion and Major Classes of Land

Land Use	Interior Alaska	Coastal Alaska
Forest land		
Commercial	4,109.9	7,040.2
Productive, reserved	—	193.3
Productive, deferred	—	318.8
Other forest	101,694.1	5,788.6
Total	105,804.0	13,340.9
Nonforest land		
Range land	214,921.1	16,550.6
Other land	8,864.9	3,034.6
Total land area	329,590.0	32,926.0

Source: USDA For. Serv., 1978.

TABLE 11-2

Area of Commercial Timberland (in Thousands of Acres) in Alaska by Subregion and Ownership, 1977

Ownership	Interior Alaska	Coastal Alaska
Public		
Federal		
National forest	—	6,528.7
Bureau of Land Management	1,584.6	77.7
Other	121.8	4.0
Total federal	1,706.4	6,610.4
Indian	84.6	22.0
State	2,005.9	322.4
County and municipal	109.6	—
Total public	3,906.5	6,954.8
Private		
Forest industry	—	0.2
Other	203.4	85.2
Total private	203.4	85.4
Total, all ownerships	4,109.9	7,040.2

Source: USDA For. Serv., 1978.

TABLE 11-3

Growing Stock (in Millions of Cubic Feet) on Commercial Timberland in Alaska by
Subregion and Species

Species	Interior Alaska	Coastal Alaska
Softwoods		
True firs	—	150.7
Western hemlock	—	25,459.7
Sitka spruce	—	8,835.1
Other spruce	2,431.0	—
Western redcedar	—	1,619.3
Lodgepole pine	—	47.7
Other	—	2,076.4
Total softwoods	2,431.0	38,188.9
Hardwoods		
Cottonwood and aspen	822.3	260.1
Red alder	—	124.5
Other	1,245.9	—
Total hardwoods	2,068.2	384.6
Total—all species	4,499.2	38,573.5

Source: USDA For. Serv., 1978.

Forest Inventory

The growing-stock inventory shown in Table 11-3 indicates the overwhelming preponderance of the coastal softwood species, primarily western hemlock and secondarily Sitka spruce. By comparison, the amounts of interior spruce and the hardwoods in both interior and coastal subregions are modest indeed.

By way of contrast, it is estimated that the current net growth on commercial forest land in the interior is approximately four times that on the coast (USDA For. Serv., 1978), presumably because the coastal forests are predominantly overmature old growth or very recent cutover lands. This, of course, bears no relationship to potential productivity under managed conditions, as may be seen in subsequent sections.

THE PHYSICAL ENVIRONMENT

Physiography

Atwood (1940) and Wahrhaftig (1965) describe the physiography of Alaska in detail and form the basis for the following very abbreviated synthesis.

There are four major physiographic regions in Alaska: the Pacific Mountain system, the Intermountain Plateaus, the Rocky Mountain system, and the Interior Plains or Arctic Coastal system (Fig. 11-1). The reader will immediately recognize that this classification is analogous to the general physiography of the western United States from the Pacific Ocean to the Great Plains.

The Pacific Mountain system comprises two parallel areas south to north in southeastern Alaska and then swinging westward. The more western and southerly of these is a continuation of the Coast Range and the Olympic Mountains to the south. It includes the Island Range of southeastern Alaska, the Fairweather Range, the St. Elias Range, and the Kenai-Chugach Mountains to Kodiak Island. The eastern and northerly areas are a continuation of the Cascade Mountains and include the coastal ranges of southern Alaska, the Alaska Range, the Aleutian Range, and the Aleutian Islands. Mount McKinley, the tallest mountain in North America, is part of this system.

The Inland Passage, Cooper River Lowlands, Cook Inlet-Susitna Lowlands, and Shelikof Strait, which form the trough between these mountain ranges, are continuations of the Willamette Valley-Puget Sound trough in the Pacific Northwest.

The Intermountain Plateaus, north of the Pacific Mountain system, comprise the majority of interior Alaska and consist of wide valleys, dissected uplands, and lowland basins covered by alluvial deposits. The principal river systems are the Yukon, Koyukuk, Porcupine, Tanana, and Kuskokwim.

The Rocky Mountain system is represented by the Brooks Range, which extends from the Canadian border to the Arctic Ocean at elevations of about 8,500 feet in the east to 2,800 feet in the west.

North of the Brooks Range is the Arctic Coastal Plain, narrow at its eastern end but widening to 250 miles in the west.

Geology and Soils

Brooks (1906) gives the first comprehensive account of the geology of Alaska. The 1974 report of the Joint Federal-State Land Use Planning Commission (JFSLUPC) updates and summarizes these findings as follows; The Alaska Range and Coast Mountains are composed of limestones and shales intruded by masses of granitic rocks. The Kenai and Chugach Mountains are sedimentary with ultramorphic intrusions. The lowlands between the two mountain areas are underlaid by thick beds of clostic or fragmented older rocks.

Glaciation was not intensive north of the Alaska Range (Brooks, 1906; Lutz, 1959a, 1959b) but outwash material did collect in interior Alaska beyond the extent of the ice. South of the Alaska Range surficial geology is dominated by glaciation.

While permafrost is sporadic south of the Alaska Range, northward it is common, although discontinuous, to the limits of tree growth. From this line north it is almost universal (Lutz and Caporaso, 1958).

The central plateaus consist of gneisses and metamorphic sediments. The Brooks Range is composed of folded and faulted limestone, its foothills forming the Arctic Coastal Plain, all underlaid by thick sediments.

Podzolization is the principal soil-forming process south of the Alaska Range (Godman and Gregory, 1953; Stephens *et al.*, 1970; Harris *et al.*, 1974), caused by the organic accumulations on the soil surface, the abundant precipitation, and generally cool climate.

The soils beneath the more productive coastal forests are well drained and usually rather coarse-textured (JFSLUPC, 1973). However, on poorly drained sites, Histosols develop with very thick organic layers, little mineral soil development, and a dramatic decrease in productivity. One of the more interesting and universal causes of such poorly drained sites is the excess of precipitation over evapotranspiration. It is estimated that poorly drained peat soils occupy both depressions and slopes over about 30 percent of the coastal forest (JFSLUPC, 1973).

Lutz (1953, 1956, 1959b), JFSLUPC (1973), and Bailey (1976) provide descriptions of the soils of interior Alaska. Podzolization is still the dominant soil-forming process on well-drained, forested, upland sites, although the intensity is lessened with increased latitude, possibly due to lack of precipitation. Spodosols and Inceptisols are developed on these sites. On river-bottom alluvial deposits there are Inceptisols and Entisols. Histosols are found on wet areas where there is a heavy, surface organic layer.

Most soils are shallow and quite young. The low soil temperatures inhibit soil development since neither chemical nor biological weathering can progress rapidly. Low soil temperatures also slow the growth of higher plants, probably due to unfavorable root environment. Shortness of growing season may also be an ecological factor.

Interior Alaska soils contain little clay and the upper layers appear to be of loessial origin. Fertility levels are low in most cases.

An interesting feature of local relief is attributed to the permafrost (Lutz, 1959a). In small mountain valleys drained by streams which do not have flood plains, north-facing slopes are commonly steeper than south-facing slopes. This may be the result of more active physical and chemical weathering of the unfrozen south-facing slopes and more downhill movement of soil and rocks. The silt mantle is also much thicker on the south-facing areas.

Climate and Weather

Searby (1968) and Watson, Branton, and Newman (1971) offer comprehensive descriptions of Alaskan climate. Four major zones may be differentiated: maritime, transitional, continental, and Arctic.

The maritime zone includes southeastern Alaska, the coastal area of the Gulf of Alaska, the southern part of the Alaskan Peninsula, and the Aleutian Islands. It is a northern extension of the coastal climate described in Chapters 9 and 10 and is characterized by relatively cool summers, mild winters, and high precipitation. This is largely due to the Aleutian low-pressure systems which allow Pacific storms to move inland, bearing with them a steady flow of moisture-laden, relatively warm air masses. Annual precipitation in southeastern Alaska varies from 25 to 225 inches, occurring within 220 to 230 days. Heavy snowfall occurs at higher elevations (above 2,500 feet) and results in dramatic vegetative changes, ice fields, and glaciers. This precipitation level, however, is substantially reduced on the Kenai Peninsula and on the southern side of the Alaska Range. Mean annual temperature in the maritime zone is 7 °C, with a small seasonal variation of 4 °C, due to the warming influence of the Alaska Current in the winter and the prevalence of cloudy weather at all seasons—275 days in southeastern Alaska. Water content of snowfall is quite high, approximately a one to four ratio. The growing season is 220 days long.

The continental zone extends southward from the crest of the Brooks Range across interior Alaska to the transitional zone, which comprises the north side of the Alaskan Peninsula, its west coast, and the western offshore islands. Temperatures in the continental zone show great seasonal variation (38 °C) and precipitation is much lower than that of the coastal zone, ranging from about 20 inches at the mouth of the Yukon River to less than 8 inches at Fort Yukon in the northeastern interior. Precipitation during the growing season—about 90 days—accounts for half of the total.

Lutz (1959a) pointed out that temperature and precipitation in interior Alaska are well balanced to promote plant growth. An increase in one climatic factor without a compensating increase in the other would lead to less favorable conditions: more precipitation alone would result in prolonged snow cover, while higher temperature alone would thaw the permafrost, allow better drainage, and encourage semidesert conditions.

The transitional zone, as its name implies, is midway between coastal and continental zones in temperature and precipitation regimes.

The Arctic climatic zone lies north of the crest of the Brooks Range. It is more extreme in temperature and drier than the continental climate, has a shorter frost-free growing season—about 60 days—and is unforested.

THE MAJOR FOREST TYPE GROUPS

The forests of southeastern Alaska are described by Hutchison (1967) and Harris and Farr (1974). Timberline varies from 3,000 feet above sea level in the south to less than 2,000 feet in the north, but stands of commercial quality rarely occur over about 1,500 feet. The forests may be considered variants of the coastal hemlock-spruce forests of the Pacific Northwest (Chapter 10).

Although there are many similarities to more southerly forests with the same species designation, there is the usual difference which is found in most northern vegetation type extensions: certain species that are important in more southern locations are entirely absent or play only minor ecological roles. Sitka spruce and western hemlock are major species. Red alder occurs as far north as Yakutat Bay on stream bottoms, along beaches, and on landslide areas. Black cottonwood, a tree of the lowlands, is found as far north as Cook Inlet. Lodgepole pine grows on open-muskeg areas throughout southeastern Alaska. Western redcedar, however, is found only as far north as Frederick Sound and other lowland coastal species of the Pacific Northwest are lacking in southeastern Alaska.

There is an interesting altitudinal contraction of the sequence of life zones found farther south. Mountain hemlock, subalpine fir, and Alaska cedar, which occur in the upper *Abies amabalis* zone and in the *Tsuga mertensiana* zone in Washington, are also found in southeastern Alaska, although other tree species present between the coastal forest and the *Abies amabalis* zone in the Pacific Northwest are absent in Alaska. Subalpine fir is found only in the extreme southern tip of southeastern Alaska, but mountain hemlock and Alaska cedar, which occur primarily at higher elevations in the southern part, grow at sea level and mix with Sitka spruce and western hemlock in the northern part of southeastern Alaska. Pacific silver fir has a very local distribution in the southern part of the panhandle.

The forests of interior Alaska were first described ecologically by Lutz (1953, 1956, 1959a, 1959b) and more recently by Zasada and Viereck, together with a number of co-workers. These forests are the extreme northwestern extension of the transcontinental boreal forest of Canada, which also occurs in the northern portions of the Lake States and New England (see Chapters 2 and 3).

There are five major species: white spruce, black spruce, paper birch (both Alaska and Kenai), quaking aspen, and balsam poplar. Of lesser importance and extent are black cottonwood and tamarack or eastern larch. In general terms, the spruces tend to be the climax species and the others subclimax, but successional patterns are quite varied depending on the nature of the physical environment, disturbance patterns, and change (Fig. 11-2).

The Joint Federal-State Land Use Planning Commission (1973) provides a convenient framework for ecological description by delineating three broad forest types: the bottomland spruce-hardwood forest, the upland spruce-hardwood forest, and the lowland spruce-hardwood forest.

The bottomland spruce-hardwood forest occupies the flood plains and lower south-facing slopes of the major rivers: the Yukon, Tanana, Kuskakwim and Susitna. Flooding is a common disturbance, which adds nutrients, prevents heavy surface organic accumulations, and slows permafrost development (Neiland and Viereck, 1977). Successional stages include a pioneer willow-alder thicket followed by balsam poplar and/or black cottonwood with understories of alder, willow, rose, and viburnum. At about 100 years these hardwood stands are replaced by white spruce and the understory shrubs by feather mosses. If organic layers on the soil surface develop from lack of disturbance, permafrost may come nearer the surface and black spruce and sphagnum moss become conspicuous members of the community. These forests, at least in cottonwood or balsam poplar and white spruce stages, are the most productive in interior Alaska.

The upland spruce-hardwood forest occupies the interior slopes and hills up to about 3,000 feet in elevation at the eastern border of Alaska and 1,000 feet in the lower Yukon River valley and on the Seward Peninsula. Fire is almost the single and universal form of disturbance. Species such as fireweed and willow

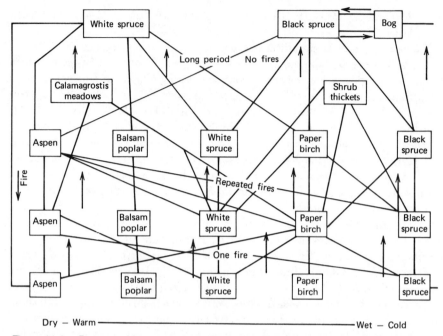

Figure 11-2.   Patterns of forest succession following fire in interior Alaska (Viereck, 1973).

are almost immediately followed by suckering aspen and sprouting birch, if the fire intensity was not too great. Hotter or more frequent fires which destroy the underground vegetative sources necessitate invasion by seed. Aspen tends to dominate on south-facing slopes and birch on the others. The hardwoods are replaced by white spruce, the rate depending on seed supply and seedbed conditions. Shrubs give way to mosses and as permafrost rises, black spruce may well become dominant. Black spruce is also favored by certain fire regimes due to semiserotinous cones, so that it often becomes established immediately following fires. On north-facing slopes with shallow soil over permafrost black spruce succeeds the birch-dominated pioneer stage.

The spruce-hardwood forest in the uplands is usually much less productive than in the bottomlands—in fact, most is currently considered noncommercial (Neiland and Viereck, 1977).

The lowland spruce-hardwood forest occurs on some of the poorly drained basins and floodplain terraces. Permafrost is close to the surface and organic layers are thick. Subordinate vegetation is dominated by sphagnum and feather mosses and lichens. Fire occurs more frequently than in any other forest (Viereck, 1973) but because of wetness (standing water at times), does not seriously affect the organic layers. The fire crowns in the serotinous black spruce and as a result, black spruce follows black spruce. If fire does not occur, the black spruce canopy may open into a woodland of thick sphagnum and scattered trees: spruce, tamarack, and birch. Needless to say, productivity is extremely low.

For the purpose of silvicultural discussions that follow two type groups are designated for the interior forests. These are the spruce type group (Interior Alaska) and the hardwood type group (Interior Alaska).

The coastal and interior forests of Alaska mix in a few locations such as the Kenai Peninsula, where there is a cross between white and Sitka spruce (*Picea lutzii*).

HISTORY OF FOREST USE

The Indians of southeastern Alaska made little impression on the forests. They used western redcedar, Sitka spruce, black cottonwood, and Alaska cedar for canoes, houses, household and personal items, and ceremonial masks and totems but their livelihood was derived almost entirely from the sea. The forests were relatively fireproof and immense. Except in the immediate vicinities of villages, there was no impact (Harris and Farr, 1974).

Russian colonization of Alaska resulted in the first sawmill in 1833 at Sitka and some further modest use of the forests for building houses and ships. In 1867 the United States purchased Alaska from Russia. Despite the fact that there was no government sale of timber for the next 30 years, there was an illegal expansion of timber cutting both for domestic and export purposes. Harris and Farr (1974) state that by 1889 11 sawmills were in operation in southeastern Alaska. In 1900 purchase of government timber by bid was permitted; in 1902 the Alexander Archipelago Forest Reserve was formed; and the Tongass National Forest was established in 1907. Exploitation of the forests increased, particularly during the two World Wars, when high-quality Sitka spruce was required for aircraft construction. Almost all logging, however, was confined to areas that were within cable-skidding distance of salt water.

In 1954 the first pulp mill was completed near Ketchikan and in 1960 another was established at Sitka. An export market for cants commenced in the late 1950s. These developments tremendously accelerated the previously limited use of southeastern Alaskan forests. However, despite this history of activity, 90 percent of the commercial forest land remained in sawtimber in 1977 (USDA For. Serv., 1978).

Strangely enough, man—both aboriginal and modern—has made much more impact on the forests of interior Alaska than on those of the coast. This is not through direct use of wood products, which has been almost infintesimally small by a sparse population in an immense landscape, but by deliberate or accidental starting of fires (Lutz, 1953, 1956, 1959b; Viereck, 1973). The Indians used fire for hunting, berrying, combatting insects, signaling, and other purposes. With the advent of white man, the frequency of man-caused fires was increased, not only due to a widespread belief that the forests were semiworthless and limitless, but also that fire produced a better game habitat, made prospecting easier, reduced insects, and provided dead wood for fuel.

Fire is undoubtedly most significant in establishing the vegetation patterns in interior Alaska (Viereck, 1973; Zasada, 1971). Natural fires are common but man-caused fires may well have been even more important in the past.

Aside from fire, the use of the interior forest by man for shelter and fuel has been almost entirely limited to areas around settlements and camping sites.

The Forests Today

Data supplied by the USDA Forest Service (1978) indicate that the commercial coastal forests of Alaska are still more than 90 percent in old growth; for this reason, the cut is more than four times the annual growth. However, natural mortality is more than one and one half times the cut. About one half of 1 percent of the commercial forest area is nonstocked.

In the interior, due to fire, the size and age distribution of the timber on commercial forest land is quite different. About 45 percent of the area is sawtimber, more than 1 percent is nonstocked, and the remainder is in young stands. As a result, annual growth is four times greater than on the coast, but the cut is less than 5 percent of growth and mortality is 2 and one half times the cut (10 percent of growth).

SILVICULTURE OF THE MAJOR TYPE GROUPS

Western Hemlock—Sitka Spruce Type Group (Coastal Alaska)

Place in Ecological Succession. Harris and Farr (1974) provide excellent syntheses of the forest ecology and silviculture in southeastern Alaska. For more detail and complete bibliographies the reader should refer to this publication.

The typical site comprises an uneven-aged stand dominated by hemlock with varying mixtures of Sitka spruce, primarily in the overstory. Depending on latitude, elevation, site, age, and originating disturbance, there may be a component of western redcedar, Alaska-yellow-cedar, subalpine fir, or mountain hemlock. A major variation occurs west of the Kenai Peninsula, where Sitka spruce is the only species. Subordinate vegetation includes a number of mosses, several *Vaccinium* species, devil's club, and salal.

The hemlock—Sitka spruce type group is the climax type for southeastern Alaska. It either succeeds Sitka spruce and/or red alder, which are established on mineral soil, or may itself regenerate following moderate disturbances. In the latter case, the hemlock—Sitka spruce assumes an even-aged stand structure that eventually develops into an uneven-aged condition if the disturbance is not soon repeated. In the process, the proportion of Sitka spruce in the type group is usually reduced because spruce is less tolerant than hemlock. The circumstances that permit hemlock and Sitka spruce to be major species in both subclimax and climax stands are similar to those outlined for the coastal subzone of the Pacific Northwest and are explained in detail in Chapter 10.

While rated as very tolerant and the equal of western hemlock in this characteristic throughout most of its range, western redcedar is apparently much less
tolerant than the hemlocks in the southern tip of southeastern Alaska. This is
undoubtedly due to the fact that redcedar is at the northern extremity of its
range. To establish reproduction successfully, it must have warmer conditions
than are found beneath a heavy overstory canopy in Alaska.

The silvical characteristics of Alaska-cedar have been summarized by Andersen (1959). It is relatively slow growing and long lived, but is less tolerant than
hemlock. Alaska-cedar competes to best advantage with hemlock on sites too
wet for best hemlock growth.

Mountain hemlock is also moderate in growth but is perhaps almost as tolerant as western hemlock (Dahms, 1959). Seed production, dissemination, and
germination are very similar to those of western hemlock.

The silvical characteristics of the other species in the type group are similar
to those given in Chapter 10.

Growth Rates.   Harris and Farr (1974) summarize the yield studies that
have been made in the type group. Site index at 100 years averages only two
thirds (106 feet) of the average in Oregon and Washington (156 feet) and generally declines with increasing latitude.

Although there are variations, normal, unmanaged yields for similar site
indices are comparable with those of the Pacific Northwest. However, there is
some evidence of more and smaller trees per acre in Alaska and a falloff of
height growth between 50 and 100 years, compared to more southerly locations.

Maximum mean-annual increment for unmanaged stands of average site
quality is about 130 cubic feet per acre. This might be increased by cultural
practice to about 200 cubic feet (Harris and Farr, 1974).

Rotation Age or Size.   For maximum production, rotations might approximate 75 years if intensive silvicultural practice were undertaken. Current U.S.
Forest Service policy suggests this on the better sites, with precommercial
thinning. On poorer sites (less than site index 100) and with no early density
control, rotations will be longer.

Cultural Practices.   The ecological characteristics of the hemlock—Sitka
spruce type in southeastern Alaska are similar to those described in Chapter 10,
allowing wide potential for various methods of reproduction cutting. However,
clearcutting with natural regeneration has been, for all practical purposes, the
only method used in coastal Alaska for many reasons: lack of windfirmness in
the old-growth forests, difficult terrain, desirability of reducing road costs,
dangers of erosion or mass wasting caused by road building, incidence of mistletoe in hemlock, the favorable effect of higher solar radiation on organic
matter decomposition, generally successful natural regeneration, including a
higher proportion of Sitka spruce, and economics (Harris and Farr, 1974).

In recent years concern has been expressed about clearcutting for aesthetic, wildlife, and environmental reasons. Currently much more consideration is being given to the size, shape, and distribution of clearcut units, as well as to the possibilities of shelterwood and selection systems in particularly sensitive areas, such as roadsides, sites of high recreational value, and streamsides.

After cutting, there is no slash disposal, site preparation, nor artificial regeneration.[1] Six hundred trees per acre is thought ideal and current policy is to consider artificial regeneration necessary if there are fewer than 125. The sites where unsatisfactory stocking is most probable are the stream-terrace areas with alluvial soils of the Tonwek or Tuxekan series (Harris, 1967). Site quality is excellent and competition from shrubs and alder makes rapid establishment of natural conifer reproduction after logging very unlikely.

Aerial seeding and planting have had only limited, experimental or pilot-plant scale application in Alaska (Harris and Farr, 1974). Aerial seeding has been shown to increase stocking; planting has been done only with hemlock and spruce wildlings.

There is little arable land area available in southeastern Alaska for a bare-root nursery and seedlings raised in more southern latitudes have difficulty adjusting dormancy patterns to the northern photoperiods. Currently, the U.S. Forest Service is developing a facility in this area to produce Sitka spruce container seedlings initially, then hemlock and cedar. It is anticipated that scalping will be necessary, followed by chemical release, at least on the better river-bottom sites, although both 2,4-D and 2,4,5-T are banned.

Until 1975, thinning in coastal Alaska was limited to older stands or to a few trials that generally were too conservative (Harris and Farr, 1974). In that year a program of density control was initiated in 10- to 15-year-old stands which is scheduled to reach a 10,000-acre-per-year level by 1985. This is about two thirds of the area that is annually planned for reproduction cutting. Spacing will vary from 600 to 300 per acre, depending on site and anticipating subsequent thinning regimes, which on some sites will be at about 20-year intervals.

Fertilizing with urea was tried experimentally in southeastern Alaska in the late 1960s and the results were sufficiently encouraging to support pilot-plant applications on several thousand acres (Harris and Farr, 1974). Sitka spruce reproduction was particularly responsive. However, there is currently no operational fertilization.

Susceptibility to Damage. The black-headed budworm and the hemlock sawfly have caused periodic (10- to 30-year), widespread defoliation in western hemlock and the budworm also attacks Sitka spruce. Other insects, such as spruce budworm, hemlock looper, and Sitka spruce beetle, are present but cause little damage.

Western dwarf mistletoe is the most serious disease in unmanaged western

[1]This section is derived from a personal interview in 1977 with David Johnson, Regional Silviculturist, USDA For. Serv., Juneau, unless otherwise noted.

hemlock but can be controlled in reproduction by clearfelling and removal of any infected advanced reproduction. Root and stem rots in old growth include *Fomes pinicola* on Sitka spruce, *Armillaria mellea* and *Fomes annosus* on western hemlock, and *Poria albipellucidia* and *P. weirii* most important on western redcedar. The impact may well be lessened as the old growth is cut, but *Poria* and *Fomes* have remained significant in managed young stands in the Pacific Northwest.

The forests of coastal Alaska appear to be relatively immune to both natural and man-caused fire compared to most forested regions. Few fires over 10 acres have been recorded since 1900 (Harris and Farr, 1974), an extraordinary circumstance in an area so large and inaccessible. There is evidence of a few large fires at 100-year intervals in the past.

Wind damage, however, is very important in these forests. Both hemlock and Sitka spruce are shallow rooted and old-growth stands affected by root and stem rot are particularly susceptible to windthrow and stem breakage. Loss occurs every year and periodically catastrophic storms cause tremendous damage. Age-class patterns reflect the windfall effects.

An unusual damage in southeastern Alaska is fluting or vertical grooving on the stem. It results in loss of yield and seems to be specific in particular locations. Cause is unknown (Harris and Farr, 1974).

Swanston (1974) suggests that mass wasting in southeastern Alaska is caused by steep slopes, heavy rain, young shallow soils, and soil runoff. It can occur on fully forested areas but is certainly intensified by logging, as currently practiced. It is suggested that substituting balloon or skyline logging for highlead logging systems may help, but some areas may have to be left unlogged or partial-cutting methods used, in order to maintain a constant forest cover. It is estimated that there are 3,800 large-scale landslides on the Tongass National Forest (Harris and Farr, 1974).

Spruce Type Group (Interior Alaska)

Place in Ecological Succession.   A typical site, either bottomland or upland, on commercial forest land consists of a stand of white spruce, possibly with some mixture of black spruce and balsam poplar on the bottomlands and black spruce and aspen on the south-facing uplands. The latter is replaced by birch or other upland aspects (Lutz, 1956; Zasada, 1976; Zasada *et al.*, 1977; Neiland and Viereck, 1977). The understory is typically composed of willows, alders, and mosses, together with some grasses and forbs.

Variations occur where drainage is poor or if permafrost comes closer to the surface. Under these circumstances, black spruce becomes more important.

The spruce type is regarded as the climax type of interior Alaska. However, there is some question as to whether white spruce will not be replaced by black spruce ultimately, if there is a very long period of no disturbance with the resulting development of shallow permafrost (Lutz, 1956; Viereck, 1970).

Because of the frequency of disturbance, spruce does not occur in pure stands over extensive areas. Rather, the landscape is a mosaic of conditions, including areas of shrubs or grass, hardwood stands, mixed stands, and spruce stands. The boundaries of these types are set by the pattern of past fires.

White spruce stands usually occupy those areas that have been subjected to least disturbance, although spruce may reproduce following fire if there is a suitable seed source. In such circumstances, an even-aged stand is established. Uneven-aged spruce stands originate through the gradual establishment of spruce reproduction beneath an existing tree canopy.

White spruce is tolerant and does not produce seed at early ages nor very frequently. Seed dispersal is not so good as that of the intolerant hardwood associates. Although germination often occurs on organic material, it appears best on mineral soil.

White spruce is very susceptible to fire damage, due to thin bark, low-hanging live crown and surficial rooting habit. Fuel, both needle litter and scales of cones cut by squirrels, accumulates in spruce stands and, as a result, fires are hot and very damaging. Lichen growth on spruce also spreads fires to the crowns.

Heights of mature white spruce in interior Alaska range from 85 to 100 feet and diameters up to 24 inches. Permafrost must be at least 24 to 36 inches below the soil surface for spruce to grow well.

Black spruce is tolerant and produces seed at earlier ages and more regularly than white spruce. A single crop is released gradually over a period of several years; as a result, there is nearly always a supply of seed in cones on the trees. Black spruce stands are as susceptible to fire damage on upland sites as white spruce, but due to the semiserotinous cones, black spruce is provided with an invaluable means of reproduction following fires. The relationship between black spruce regeneration and fire was discussed in Chapter 3. Germination of its seed occurs on raw-humus seedbeds but is better on mineral soil. Reproduction by layering is also common.

Black spruce is uniquely adapted to growth on wet sites and as a result is the permanent type on areas where drainage is poor (slopes of less than 10 percent), or where the permafrost is within 2 feet of the surface. However, the growth on poorly drained sites is not impressive. Heights of 45 feet and diameters of 8 or 9 inches are maximum and stands on such areas are considered noncommercial.

Black spruce may invade upland sites following fire when there is a seed source on adjoining unburned, wet sites. On these better situations its growth is more comparable with that of white spruce.

Growth Rates and Rotation Ages or Size. Farr (1967) presents the best available data for the growth of white spruce in interior Alaska. Site index at 100 years varies from 41 to 106 feet. On the best sites (index 100), annual unmanaged yields (to a 4-inch top) of about 50 cubic feet per acre occur at age 60. Every 10-foot decrease in site index results in about a 10-cubic-foot decrease of mean-annual increment and an increase in the length of rotation required to reach the maximum. At site index 60 a maximum mean-annual increment of about 18 cubic feet is reached at age 110.

With thinning to recover mortality and control density, it may be possible to increase these unmanaged yields by 50 percent.

Cultural Practice.   Zasada *et al.* (1977) point out that prior to 1970 there was only custodial or exploitive use of interior Alaskan forests. In other words, there is little on-the-ground evidence, experimental or operational, of alternatives for cultural practice. Added to this is the general transcontinental experience in the boreal forest that white spruce is a difficult species to reproduce, increasingly so from east to west. The environmental conditions for spruce reproduction in interior Alaska may very well be the most difficult of all because of site degradation related to cold soils, the presence of permafrost, and the rapid development of moss-organic layers (Viereck, 1970).

Zasada (1972, 1973a) suggests that clearcutting and shelterwood methods combined with appropriate seedbed preparation, either mechanical or fire, to create a mineral soil or a mixed mineral-organic soil seedbed, would simulate the natural establishment of spruce following fire. However, because natural seed crops occur so infrequently, a direct seeding or planting is probably necessary. In addition, control of competing vegetation may be very important, due to slow initial height growth of spruce seedlings.

Zasada *et al.* (1977) report that patch scalping increased seedling density and that seedling size was somewhat greater in small clearcuts (almost group shelterwoods) than in uniform shelterwood conditions.

Five years after treatment in a 70-year-old spruce stand, thinning more than doubled individual-tree basal-area increment, fertilizing with nitrogen increased it by 50 percent, and thinning and fertilizing together produced more than a threefold response (Van Cleve and Zasada, 1976).

Viereck (1973) indicates that conditions immediately after fire in the willow shrub stage provide four to five times as much browse for moose as do closed black spruce stands. However, the lichens upon which caribou graze (they also utilize grass, sedge, and shrubs) are most abundant in 50- to 100-year-old stands, are very susceptible to fire, and slow to reinvade.

Susceptibility to Damage.   It is apparent that, while only sketchy information is available, substantial amounts of damage occur to the spruce forests of interior Alaska due to various root and stem pathogens (JFSLUPC, 1974; Zasada *et al.*, 1977). For example, it is estimated that decay is present in the merchantable stems of 37 percent of white spruce.

The most destructive insect is the spruce bark beetle, which destroys large numbers of trees over extensive areas.

The susceptibility of spruce to fire and the prevalence of this damage has been covered in previous sections.

Hardwood Type Group (Interior Alaska)

Place in Ecological Succession. There are four species of hardwoods in interior Alaska: balsam poplar, black cottonwood, quaking aspen, and paper birch. While they occur in mixture with each other and with white and black spruce, they tend to occupy distinct physiographic positions. Older stands characteristically have an understory of spruce (Lutz, 1956; Neiland and Viereck, 1977).

Balsam poplar and black cottonwood occur on bottomland alluvial soils subject to both flooding and fire. Typical understory species consist of alders, willows, wild rose, and viburnum.

Quaking aspen occurs on the warmest south-facing, upland slopes. Understory species are twinflower, fireweed, buffalo berry, willows, bedstraw, and lousewort.

Paper birch stands tend to be on the cooler upland aspects, particularly those facing east and west, and also north. Understory is composed of shrubs, alder, rose, gooseberry, willows, and viburnum.

The hardwoods are all intolerant and are generally regarded as subclimax to the spruces in interior Alaska.

Black cottonwood seeds and sprouts well, appears to require the moist, mineral seedbed and excellent soil of recent alluvial deposits and grows very rapidly. On the best sites in interior Alaska it may attain a height of 120 feet and a diameter of 30 inches in 100 years (Neiland and Viereck, 1977).

The following discussion of the silvical characteristics and behavior of the other species is largely from Lutz (1953, 1956, 1959a).

Balsam poplar produces abundant seed that is disseminated widely by wind, and sprouts by root suckers. At maturity, due to its thick bark, it is the most fire-resistant tree in interior Alaska. It grows to diameters of more than 4 feet and heights of 100 feet and occurs in pure stands on new alluvium as a pioneer stage of primary succession. Poplar may be followed by white spruce unless periodic flooding occurs, when the poplar becomes a physiographic climax. Occasionally it invades upland sites following fire which destroys the seed source of other species. Permafrost, if present under balsam poplar, is at depths of at least 3 to 6 feet. Following repeated severe fires, poplar, like birch and aspen, may be replaced by a plant community dominated by subordinate vegetation.

Quaking aspen is also a tremendous seed producer. It sprouts in great numbers, but in the form of root suckers rather than from the stump. Heights of 70 feet and diameters of 12 inches are maximum in interior Alaska. The invasion of white spruce beneath aspen stands is similar to that under birch stands. Fire can be very damaging to aspen stands, but the abundance of root suckers following fire may result in even higher numbers of aspen in the succeeding stands. Quaking aspen is a good indicator of site because it is less tolerant of cold, poorly drained areas than any other tree in interior Alaska and permafrost must be at least 48 inches from the surface for good aspen growth. This species sometimes forms a physiographic climax on hot, steep, south-facing slopes where the soil is dry due to excessive drainage, but on such sites, stands are usually very open and show poor growth.

Paper birch (either Alaska or Kenai, which are barely distinguishable under field conditions) is an abundant seed producer after 10 years of age and sprouts prolifically from root collars when young. The dissemination of birch seed by wind is excellent. Birch usually develops as a pure type, and occasionally aspen, or rarely balsam poplar, occurs in the main canopy. After birch is 80 years old, white spruce reproduction invades beneath the stand, and at 100 to 120 years of age the birch declines in vigor and does not maintain a full canopy. Heights at maturity are about 80 feet and diameters are 18 to 20 inches. Permafrost, if found at all under a birch stand, is usually at least 36 to 48 inches from the surface.

Young birch is thin barked and easily killed by fire. While the bark of mature trees is thicker, the outer layer peels from the stem and is readily ignited. However, there is a limited amount of fuel on the forest floor beneath birch, due to relatively rapid decay of litter, so that surface fires are not so serious as in conifer stands. Birch will be completely destroyed if burned repeatedly and the area will revert to a fireweed-grass or shrub community.

Growth Rates and Rotation Age or Size.   Viereck and Foote (1970) suggest that the bottomland hardwoods, that is, black cottonwood and balsam poplar, are the most productive stands in interior Alaska, reaching unmanaged maximum mean increments almost twice those of the best spruce or about 100 cubic feet per acre annually.

Gregory and Haack (1965) give data that suggest that aspen on the best sites may attain a maximum mean-annual increment of about 55 cubic feet at age 65 and birch about 25 to 28 cubic feet at rotation in excess of 80 years. Average yields are much less in all species.

Cultural Practices.   Zasada (1973b) summarizes the opinions of numerous observers in suggesting that clearcutting is possibly the only reproduction method that will be successful with all four hardwood species. Sprouting and/or rootsuckering abilities will often assume vegetative reproduction but frequent seeding and good seed dispersal also result in seedling reproduction, if mineral soil is available.

Van Cleve (1973) has shown substantial height and diameter response to fertilization in aspen.

Susceptibility to Damage.   A number of defoliating and seed and cone insects affect the hardwoods of interior Alaska but little detail is known. In 1974 and 1975 the spearheaded black moth defoliated millions of acres of birch (Werner, 1977). The aspen tortix was epidemic over large areas in the 1960s (Beckwith, 1968).

Snowshoe hares and moose may have an impact on hardwood during young stages.

Susceptibilities to fire have been considered in previous sections.

BIBLIOGRAPHY

Andersen, H. E. 1955. Alder control on cutover areas. *USDA For. Serv., Alaska For. Res. Center Tech. Note 25.* 1 p.

Anderson, H. E. 1959. Silvical characteristics of Alaska-cedar. *USDA For. Serv., Alaska For. Res. Center Stn. Pap. 11.* 10 pp.

Atwood, W. W. 1940. *The physiographic provinces of North America.* Ginn & Co., Boston, 535 pp.

Bailey, R. G. 1976. Description of the ecoregions of the United States. *USDA For. Serv., Intermtn. Reg.* Ogden.

Beckwith, R. C. 1968. The large aspen tortrix, *Choristoneura conflictana* (Wlkr.), in interior Alaska. *USDA For. Serv. Res. Note PNW-81,* 10 pp.

Brooks, A. E. 1906. The geography and geology of Alaska. *U. S. Geol. Survey Prof. Paper 45.* 327 pp.

Dahms, W. G. 1959. Silvical characteristics of mountain hemlock. *USDA For. Serv. Silvical Ser. 11.* 8 pp.

Farr, W. A. 1967. Growth and yield of well-stocked white spruce stands in Alaska. *USDA For. Serv. Res. Paper PNW-53,* 30 pp.

Godman, R. M., and R. A. Gregory. 1953. Physical soil characteristics related to site quality in climax stands of southeast Alaska. *USDA For. Serv. Alaska For. Res. Center Tech. Note 17.* 1 p.

Gregory, R. A., and P. M. Haack. 1965. Growth and yield of well-stocked aspen and birch stands in Alaska. *USDA For. Serv. Res. Paper NOR-2.*

Harris, A. S. 1967. Natural reforestation on a mile-square clearcut in southeast Alaska. *USDA For. Serv. Res. Pap. PNW-52,* 16 pp.

Harris, A. S. and W. A. Farr, 1974. The forest ecosystem of southeast Alaska. 7. Forest ecology and timber management. *USDA For. Serv. Gen. Tech. Rep. PNW-25.* 109 p.

Harris, A. S., O. K. Hutchison, W. R. Meehan, D. H. Swanston, A. E. Helmers, J. C. Hendee, and T. M. Collins. 1974. The forest ecosystem of southeast Alaska. 1. The setting. *USDA For. Serv. Gen. Tech. Rep. PNW-12.* 40 pp.

Hutchison, O. K. 1967. Alaska's forest resource. *USDA For. Serv. Res. Bull. PNW-19.* 74 pp.

Joint Federal-State Land Use Planning Commission for Alaska. 1973. *Major ecosystems of Alaska (map).* Anchorage: JFSLUPC.

Joint Federal-State Land Use Planning Commission for Alaska. 1974. *Alaska regional profiles, Vol. IV Southeast region. Vol. VI Yukon region.* Univ. Alaska Arctic Environ. Info. and Data Center, Anchorage.

Lutz, H. J. 1953. The effects of forest fires on the vegetation of interior Alaska. *USDA For. Serv. Alaska For. Res. Center Stn. Pap. 1.* 33 pp.

Lutz, H. J. 1956. The ecological effects of forest fires in Alaska. *USDA Tech. Bull. 1133,* 121 pp.

Lutz, H. J. 1959a. *Ecology of the forests of interior Alaska.* Walker-Ames Lectures, Univ. Washington, Seattle. Unpublished manuscript.

Lutz, H. J. 1959b. Aboriginal man and white man as historical causes of fires in the boreal forest, with particular reference to Alaska. *Yale Univ., Sch. For. Bull. 65.* New Haven, 49 pp.

Lutz, H. J. and A. P. Caporaso. 1958. Indicators of forest land classes in air-photo interpretation of the Alaska interior. *USDA For. Serv. Alaska For. Res. Center Stn. Pap. 10.* 31 pp.

Neiland, B. J., and L. A. Viereck. 1977. Forest types and ecosystems. In *Proc. Symp. North American Forest Lands at Latitudes North of 60 Degrees*, Univ. Alaska, Fairbanks, pp. 109–136.

Searby, H. W. 1968. Climate of Alaska. *Climatography of the United States 60-49. Climates of the States, Alaska*. U. S. Dept. Comm. Environ. Sci. Serv. Adm., Environ. Data Serv. 15 pp.

Stephens, F. R., C. R. Gass, and R. F. Billings. 1970. The muskegs of southeast Alaska and their diminished extent. *Northwest Sci.* 44(2):123–130.

Swanston, D. N. 1974. The forest ecosystem of southeast Alaska. 5. Soil mass movement. *USDA For. Serv. Gen. Tech. Rep. PNW-17*. 22 pp.

USDA For. Serv. 1978. Forest statistics of the U. S. 1977. *USDA For. Serv. (draft)* 133 pp.

Van Cleve, K. 1973. Short term growth response to fertilization in young quaking aspen. *J. For.* 71:758–759.

Van Cleve, K. and J. C. Zasada. 1976. Response of 70-year-old white spruce to thinning and fertilization in interior Alaska. *Can. J. For. Res.* 6:145–152.

Viereck, L. A. 1970. Forest succession and soil development adjacent to the Chena River in interior Alaska. *Arctic and Alp. Res.* 2:1–26.

Viereck, K. 1973. Wildlife in the Taiga of Alaska. *J. Quat. Res.* 3:465–495.

Viereck, K. and M. J. Foote, 1970. The status of *Populus balsamifera* and *P. trichocarpa* in Alaska. *Can. Field-Naturalist.* 84:169–173.

Wahrhaftig, N. F. N. 1965. Physiographic divisions of Alaska. *U. S. Geol. Survey, Prof. Pap.* 482. 52 pp.

Watson, C. E., G. I. Branton, and J. E. Newman. 1971. Climatic characteristics of selected Alaskan locations. *Univ. Alaska Inst. Agr. Sci. Tech. Bull.* 2. 56 pp.

Werner, R. A. 1977. Biology and behavior of the spear-marked black moth, *Rheumaptera hastata*, in interior Alaska. *Ann. Entomol. Soc. Am.* 70:328–335.

Zasada, J. C. 1971. Natural regeneration of interior Alaska forests—seed, seedbed, and vegetative reproduction considerations. In *Proc. Symp. Fire in the Northern Environment*, College (Fairbanks), Alaska.

Zasada, J. C. 1972. Guidelines for obtaining natural regeneration of white spruce in Alaska. *USDA. For. Serv. Pacific NW For. and Range Expt. Stn.* 16 pp.

Zasada, J. C. 1973a. Interior Alaska white spruce. *USDA For. Serv. Agr. Hdb.* 445:20–21.

Zasada, J. C. 1973b. Interior Alaska hardwoods. *USDA For. Serv. Agr. Hdb.* 445:21–22.

Zasada, J. C. 1976. Alaska's interior forests—ecological and silvicultural considerations. *J. For.* 74:333–337.

Zasada, J. C., K. Van Cleve, R. A. Werner, J. A. McQueen, and E. Nyland. 1977. Forest biology and management in high-latitude North American forests. In *Proc. Symp. North American Forest Lands at Latitudes North of 60 Degrees*, Univ. Alaska, Fairbanks. pp. 137–195.

I
Appendix

Common and Scientific Names
of Trees Mentioned in the Text

Common Name	Scientific Name[1]
Alaska-cedar	*Chamaecyparis nootkatensis* (D. Don) Spach
Alder, red	*Alnus rubra* Bong.
Ash	
black	*Fraxinus nigra* Marsh.
green (red)	*F. pennsylvanica* Marsh.
pumpkin	*F. profunda* (Bush) Bush
white	*F. americana* L.
Aspen	
bigtooth	*Populus grandidentata* Michx.
quaking (trembling)	*P. tremuloides* Michx.
Baldcypress	*Taxodium distichum* (L.) Rich.
Basswood, American (white)	*Tilia americana* L.
Beech, American	*Fagus grandifolia* Ehrh.
Birch	
Alaska paper	*Betula papyrifera* var. *neoalaskana* (Sarg.) Raup
gray	*B. populifolia* Marsh.
Kenai (paper)	*B. papyrifera* var. *kenaica* (W.H. Evans) Henry
paper	*B. papyrifera* Marsh.
river	*B. nigra* L.
sweet (black)	*B. lenta* L.
yellow	*B. alleghaniensis* Britton
Blackgum (black tupelo)	*Nyssa sylvatica* Marsh.

[1]Scientific names from Little, E. L., Jr., 1979. Check list of United States trees (native and naturalized). USDA Agr. Hdbk. 541. 375 pp.

Boxelder	*Acer negundo* L.
Buckeye	
California	*Aesculus californica* (Spach) Nutt.
yellow	*A. octandra* Marsh.
Butternut	*Juglans cinerea* L.
Buttonbush, common	*Cephalanthus occidentalis* L.
California laurel (Oregon myrtle)	*Umbellularia californica* (Hook. & Arn.) Nutt.
Cherry	
black	*Prunus serotina* Ehrh.
pin	*P. pensylvanica* L.f.
Chestnut, American	*Castanea dentata* (Marsh.) Borkh.
Chinkapin, giant (golden)	*Castanopsis chrysophylla* (Dougl.) A. DC.
Cottonwood	
black	*Populus trichocarpa* Torr. & Gray
eastern	*P. deltoides* Bartr. ex Marsh.
narrowleaf	*P. angustifolia* James
swamp	*P. heterophylla* L.
Cucumbertree	*Magnolia acuminata* L.
Cypress	
MacNab	*Cupressus macnabiana* A. Murr.
Sargent	*C. sargentii* Jeps.
Dogwood	
flowering	*Cornus florida* L.
Pacific	*C. nutallii* Audubon
roughleaf	*C. drummondii* C.A. Mayer
Douglas-fir	
(coastal form)	*Pseudotsuga menziesii* (Mirb.) Franco var. *menziesii*
(Rocky Mountain form)	*P. menziesii* var. *glauca* (Beissn.) Franco
bigcone	*P. macrocarpa* (Vasey) Mayr
Elm	
American	*Ulmus americana* L.
cedar	*U. crassifolia* Nutt.
winged	*U. alata* Michx.
Fir	
balsam	*Abies balsamea* (L.) Mill.
bristlecone	*A. bracteata* D. Don ex Poiteau
California red (Shasta red)	*A. magnifica* A. Murr.
California white	*A. concolor* var. *lowiana* (Gord.) Lemm.
corkbark	*A. lasiocarpa* var. *arizonica* (Merriam) Lemm.
Fraser	*A. fraseri* (Pursh) Poir.
grand	*A. grandis* (Dougl. ex D. Don) Lindl.
noble	*A. procera* Rehd.
Pacific silver	*A. amabilis* (Dougl.) Forbes
subalpine	*A. lasiocarpa* (Hook.) Nutt.
white	*A. concolor* (Gord. & Glend.) Lindl. ex Hildebr.

Hackberry	*Celtis occidentalis* L.
Hawthorn	*Crataegus* spp.
Hemlock	
eastern	*Tsuga canadensis* (L.) Carr.
mountain	*T. mertensiana* (Bong.) Carr.
western	*T. heterophylla* (Raf.) Sarg.
Hickory	
bitternut	*Carya cordiformis* (Wangenh.) K. Koch
mockernut	*C. tomentosa* (Poir.) Nutt.
pignut	*C. glabra* (Mill.) Sweet
shagbark	*C. ovata* (Mill.) K. Koch
water	*C. aquatica* (Michx. f.) Nutt.
Holly	*Ilex* spp.
Honeylocust	*Gleditsia triacanthos* L.
Hophornbeam, eastern (ironwood)	*Ostrya virginiana* (Mill.) K. Koch
Hornbeam, American (blue beech)	*Carpinus caroliniana* Walt.
Incense-cedar	*Libocedrus decurrens* Torr.
Juniper	
one-seed	*Juniperus monosperma* (Engelm.) Sarg.
Utah	*J. osteosperma* (Torr.) Little
western	*J. occidentalis* Hook.
Larch	
subalpine	*Larix lyalii* Parl.
western	*L. occidentalis* Nutt.
Locust, black	*Robinia pseudoacacia* L.
Madrone, Pacific	*Arbutus menziesii* Pursh
Magnolia	
Fraser	*Magnolia fraseri* Walt.
southern	*M. grandiflora* L.
Maple	
bigleaf	*Acer macrophyllum* Pursh
black	*A. nigrum* Michx. f.
red	*A. rubrum* L.
silver	*A. saccharinum* L.
striped	*A. pensylvanicum* L.
sugar	*A. saccharum* Marsh.
vine	*A. circinatum* Pursh
Mulberry	*Morus* spp.
Oak	
bear	*Quercus ilicifolia* Wangenh.
black	*Q. velutina* Lam.
blackjack	*Q. marilandica* Muenchh.
blue	*Q. douglasii* Hook. & Arn.
bluejack	*Q. incana* Bartr.
burr	*Q. macrocarpa* Michx.
California black	*Q. kelloggii* Newb.
canyon live	*Q. chrysolepis* Liebm.

cherrybark	*Q. falcata* var. *pagodifolia* Ell.
chestnut	*Q. prinus* L.
chinkapin	*Q. muehlenbergii* Engelm.
coast live	*Q. agrifolia* Née
delta post	*Q. stellata* var. *missippiensis* (Ashe) Little
interior live	*Q. wislizeni* A. DC.
laurel	*Q. laurifolia* Michx.
northern pin	*Q. ellipsoidalis* E. J. Hill
northern red	*Q. rubra* L.
Nuttall	*Q. nuttallii* Palmer
Oregon white	*Q. garryana* Dougl. ex Hook.
overcup	*Q. lyrata* Walt.
pin	*Q. palustris* Muenchh.
post	*Q. stellata* Wangenh.
scarlet	*Q. coccinea* Muenchh.
Shumard	*Q. shumardii* Buckl.
southern red	*Q. falcata* Michx.
swamp chestnut	*Q. michauxii* Nutt.
swamp white	*Q. bicolor* Willd.
turkey	*Q. laevis* Walt.
valley	*Q. lobata* Née
water	*Q. nigra* L.
white	*Q. alba* L.
willow	*Q. phellos* L.
Pawpaw	*Asimina triloba* (L.) Dunal
Pecan	*Carya illinoensis* (Wangenh.) K. Koch
Persimmon, common	*Diospyros virginiana* L.
Pine	
Coulter	*Pinus coulteri* D. Don
Digger	*P. sabiniana* Dougl.
eastern white	*P. strobus* L.
foxtail	*P. balfouriana* Grev. & Balf.
jack	*P. banksiana* Lamb.
Jeffrey	*P. jeffreyi* Grev. & Balf.
knobcone	*P. attenuata* Lemm.
limber	*P. flexilis* James
loblolly	*P. taeda* L.
lodgepole (shore)	*P. contorta* Dougl. ex Loud.
longleaf	*P. palustris* Mill.
pitch	*P. rigida* Mill.
pinyon	*P. edulis* Engelm.
pond	*P. serotina* Michx.
ponderosa	*P. ponderosa* Dougl. ex Laws.
red	*P. resinosa* Ait.
sand	*P. clausa* (Chapm. ex Engelm.) Vasey ex Sarg.
shortleaf	*P. echinata* Mill.
singleleaf pinyon	*P. monophylla* Torr. & Frem.
slash	*P. elliottii* Engelm.
spruce	*P. glabra* Walt.
sugar	*P. lambertiana* Dougl.

Table Mountain	*P. pungens* Lamb.
Virginia	*P. virginiana* Mill.
western white	*P. monticola* Dougl. ex D. Don
whitebark	*P. albicaulis* Engelm.
Planertree	*Planera aquatica* Gmel.
Pondcypress	*Taxodium distichum* var. *nutans* (Ait.) Sweet
Poplar, balsam	*Populus balsamifera* L.
Port-Orford-cedar	*Chamaecyparis lawsoniana* (A. Murr.) Parl.
Privet	*Ligustrum* spp.
Redcedar	
eastern	*Juniperus virginiana* L.
western	*Thuja plicata* Donn ex D. Don
Redbay	*Persea borbonia* (L.) Spreng.
Redbud, eastern	*Cercis canadensis* L.
Redwood	*Sequoia sempervirens* (D. Don) Endl.
Sassafras	*Sassafras albidum* (Nutt.) Nees
Sequoia, giant	*Sequoiadendron giganteum* (Lindl.) Buchholz
Serviceberry	*Amelanchier* spp.
Silverbell, Carolina	*Halesia carolina* L.
Sourwood	*Oxydendrum arboreum* (L.) DC.
Spruce	
black	*Picea mariana* (Mill.) B.S.P.
blue	*P. pungens* Engelm.
Brewer	*P. brewerana* Wats.
Engelmann	*P. engelmannii* Parry ex Engelm.
red	*P. rubens* Sarg.
Sitka	*P. sitchensis* (Bong.) Carr.
white	*P. glauca* (Moench) Voss
Sugarberry	*Celtis laevigata* Willd.
Sweetbay	*Magnolia virginiana* L.
Sweetgum	*Liquidambar styraciflua* L.
Sycamore, American (plane tree)	*Platanus occidentalis* L.
Tamarack	*Larix laricina* (Du Roi) K. Koch
Tanoak	*Lithocarpus densiflorus* (Hook. & Arn.) Rehd.
Tupelo	
swamp (blackgum)	*Nyssa sylvatica* var. *biflora* (Walt.) Sarg.
water	*N. aquatica* L.
Walnut, black	*Juglans nigra* L.
White-cedar	
Atlantic	*Chamaecyparis thyoides* (L.) B.S.P.
northern	*Thuja occidentalis* L.
Willow, black	*Salix nigra* Marsh.
Yellow-poplar	*Liriodendron tulipifera* L.
Yellowwood	*Cladrastis kentukea* (Dum.-Cours.) Rudd
Yew, Pacific	*Taxus brevifolia* Nutt.

II
Appendix

Common and Scientific Names
of Insects Mentioned in the Text

Common Name	Scientific Name[1]
Aphid	
balsam woolly	*Adelges piceae* Ratz.
eastern spruce gall	*A. abietis* L.
Ant, Texas leaf-cutting	*Atta texana* Buckley
Beetle	
black turpentine	*Dendroctonus terebrans* Oliv
cedar bark	*Phloeosinus punctatus* LeConte
Columbian timber	*Corthylus columbianus* Hopk.
cottonwood leaf	*Chrysomela scripta* F.
Douglas-fir	*Dendroctonus pseudotsugae* Hopkins
fir engraver	*Scolytus ventralis* LeConte
fir pole (Douglas-fir pole)	*Pseudohylesinus nebulosus* LeConte
mountain pine (Black Hills)	*Dendroctonus ponderosae* Hopkins, (= monticolae Hopkins)
pine engraver	*Ips pini* Say
red turpentine	*Dendroctonus valens* LeConte
redwood bark	*Phloeosinus sequoiae* Hopkins
southern pine	*Dendroctonus frontalis* Zimm.
spruce (Engelmann spruce-bark)	*D. rufipennis* Kirby (= *borealis* Hopkins = *engelmanni* Hopkins = *obesus* Mannerheim)
western pine	*D. brevicomis* LeConte (= *barberi* Hopkins)
Beetles	
cone	*Conophthorus* spp.
engraver	*Ips* spp.

[1]Scientific names based on: Baker, W. L. 1972. Eastern forest insects. USDA For. Serv. Misc. Publ. 1175. 642 pp. and Furniss, R. L., and V. M. Carolin, 1977. Western forest insects. USDA For. Serv. Misc. Publ. 1339. 654 pp.

Borer

bronze birch	*Agrilus anxius* Gory
cottonwood twig	*Gypsonoma haimbachiana* Kft.
fir flatheaded	*Melanophila drummondi* Kirby
red oak	*Enaphalodes rufulus* Hald.
roundheaded fir	*Tetropium abietis* Fall
sugar maple	*Glycobius speciosus* Say
turpentine	*Buprestis apricans* Hbst.
western pineshoot	*Eucosma sonomana* Kearfott
white oak (oak timberworm)	*Arrhenodes minutus* Drury

Borers, clear wing   *Paranthrene* spp.

Budworm

jack pine	*Choristoneura pinus* Freeman
Modoc	*C. viridis* Freeman
spruce	*C. fumiferana* Clemens
western blackheaded	*Acleris gloverana* Walsingham
western spruce	*Choristoneura occidentalis* Freeman

Carpenterworms   *Cossula* spp.
                                  Prionoxystus spp.

Casebearer, larch   *Coleophora laricella* Hbn.

Caterpillar

forest tent	*Malacosoma disstria* Hubner
variable oak leaf	*Heterocampa manteo* Dbldy.
western tent	*Malacosoma californicum* Packard

Cynipids, gallforming   *Callirhytis* spp.

Looper

cypress	*Anacamptodes pergracilis* Hulst
western hemlock	*Lambdina fiscellaria lugubrosa* Hulst

Moth

Douglas-fir tussock	*Orgyia pseudotsugata* McDunnough
gypsy	*Porthetria dispar* L.
	(*lymantria dispar*)
Nantucket tip	*Rhyocionia frustrana* Comstock
spearheaded black	*Rheumaptera hastata* L.

Moths, pine seed   *Laspeyresia* spp.

Needleminer, white fir   *Epinotia meritana* Heinrich

Sawfly

balsam fir	*Neodiprion abietis* Harris
hemlock	*N. tsugae* Middleton
pinon	*N. edulicolus* Ross
conifer	*N.* spp.

Sawyer

southern pine	*Monochamus titillator* F.
spotted pine (pine sawyer beetle)	*M. maculosus* Halderman (= *clamator* LeConte)
white-spotted (pine sawyer beetle)	*M. scutellatus* Say

Scale
  beech   *Cryptococcus fagi* Baer.
  pinon   *Matsucoccus acalyptus* Herbert
Spittlebug, Saratoga   *Aphrophora saratogensis* Fitch
Tortrix, aspen   *Choristoneura conflictana* Walker
Walkingstick   *Diapheromera fermorata* Say
Weevil
  pales   *Hylobius pales* Herbst.
  pine reproduction   *Cylindrocopturus eatoni* Buchanan
  pitch-eating   *Pachylobius picivorus* Germ.
  white pine (Sitka spruce)   *Pissodes strobi* Peck
Weevils, nut   *Curculionidae spp.*

III
Appendix

Common and Scientific Names of Organisms Associated with Diseases Mentioned in the Text

Common Name	Scientific Name[1]
Blight, chestnut	*Endothia parasitica* (Murr.) P.
Brown-spot needle blight	*Scirrhia acicola* (Dearn.) Sigg.
Canker,	
cytospora	*Valsa sordida* Nits.
nectria	*Nectria* spp.
pitch	*Fusarium lateritium pini* Hepting
hypoxylon	*Hypoxylon mammatum* (Wahl.) Mill.
hypoxylon	*H. pruinatum* (Klotzsch.) Cke.
sooty-bark (black)	*Cenangium singulare* Rehm.
sterile conk	*Poria obliqua* (Pers. ex Fr.) Karst.
Dieback, birch	*Nectria galligena* Bres.
Disease	
beech bark	*N. coccinea* var. *faginata* Loh., Wats. & Ay.
Dutch elm	*Ceratocystis ulmi* (Buism.) C. Mor.
leaf-spot	*Marssonina populi* (Lib.) Magn.
little-leaf	*Phytophthora cinnamomi* Rands
Elytroderma blight	*Elytroderma deformans* (Weir) Dark.
Fungus	
blackstain	*Verticicladiella wageneri* Kend.
false tinder	*Fomes igniarius* (L. ex Fr.) Kickx.
false tinder	*Phellinus (Fomes) tremulae* (Bond.) Bond. & Boriss

[1]Scientific names based on Hepting, G. H. 1971. Diseases of forest and shade trees of the United States. USDA For. Serv. Agr. Hdbk. 386. 658 pp.

Indian paint	*Echinodontium tinctorium* E. & E.
teapot	*Rhizina undulata* Fr.
Mistletoe, dwarf	*Arceuthobium* spp.
Needle case	*Davisomycella medusa* (Dear.) Dark.
Needle cast	*Lophodermella (Hypodermella) cerina* (Dark.) Dark.
Phloem necrosis	*Morsus ulmi* (virus)
Rot	
brown-cubical	*Daedalea juniperina* Murr.
brown-cubical	*Fomes subroseus* Weir
brown-pocket	*Stereum taxodii* Lentz & McKay
butt	*Ustilina vulgaris* Tul.
cinnamon-brown	*Poria albipellucida* Baxt. *P. rivulosa* (B. & C.) Cke.
heart (butt)	*Fomes connatus* (Weinm. ex Fr.) Gill
heart	*F. juniperinus* (Schrenk) Sac. & Syd.
heart	*F. pinicola* (Swartz ex Fr.) Cke.
heart	*Phellinus (Fomes) tremulae* (Bond.) Bond. & Boriss
laminated-root (blackstain fungus)	*Poria (Phellinus) weirii* (Murr.) Murr.
pecky	*Polyporus amarus*
red	*P. anceps* Pk.
red-brown-butt (butt)	*P. schweinitzii* Fr.
red-heart	*Stereum sanguinolentum* Alb. & Schw. ex Fr.
redwood-brown-cubical	*Poria sequoiae* Bonar
red-ring (red heart)	*Fomes pini* (Thore ex Fr.) Karst
root	*F. annosus* (Fr.) Cke.
shoe-string root and butt	*Armillaria mellea* (Vahl. ex Fr.) Quel.
trunk	*Polyporus glomoratus* Pk.
Rust	
cedar apple	*Gymnosporangium juniperi virginianae* Schw.
Comandra blister	*Cronartium comandrae* Pk.
cone	*C. strobilinum* Hedge.
eastern gall	*C. quercuum* (Berk.) Miy.
fusiform	*C. fusiforme* Hedg. & Hunt
limb	*Peridermium filamentosum* Peck
Melampsora	*Melampsora medusae* Thum.
sweetfern	*Cronartium comptoniae* Arth.
western-gall	*Peridermium harknessii* J. P. Moore (*Cronartium coleosporioides*) (Diet. & Holw.) Arth.)
white pine blister	*Cronartium ribicola* Fisch.
yellow witches' broom	*Chrysomyxa arctostaphyli* Diet.
Wilt, oak	*Ceratocystis fagacearum* (Bretz) Hunt

Index